B

COLLINS

CANADIAN

THESAURUS

HarperCollinsPublishersLtd

This book is based on the
Collins Ringbinder Thesaurus,
published by
HarperCollins Publishers
PO Box, Glasgow G4 0NB.

NOTE

Entered words that we have reason to believe constitute trademarks have been designated as such. However, neither the presence nor absence of such designation should be regarded as affecting the legal status of any trademark.

Printed and bound in Canada

INTRODUCTION

The Collins Ringbinder Thesaurus is a practical word-finding aid, designed to help the student who wants to find a better word to replace one that is not quite right in its context.

The name 'thesaurus' comes from a Greek word meaning treasure, treasury, or storehouse, and the Thesaurus is so named because it is a treasury or storehouse of words. Its purpose is to provide lists of words which mean the same, or almost the same, as the word which the user of the book has in mind, so that an alternative can be chosen.

There are many reasons why an alternative word might be wanted. It may be that the original word is felt to be inappropriate in some way – perhaps it is too formal or too colloquial, perhaps it is not quite precise in conveying the intended meaning, or somehow does not suit the tone of the piece of writing. Perhaps it is a perfectly suitable word in its context, but one that has already been used – the desire to avoid repetition is a frequent reason for consulting a thesaurus. Sometimes a word that is known to exist just will not come to mind; on such occasions the elusive word can be discovered by looking up an equivalent term in the Thesaurus. For these, and many other purposes which the user will soon discover, the Thesaurus is an invaluable help to anyone interested in improving their command of the English language.

The Collins Ringbinder Thesaurus is arranged, like a dictionary, in a single alphabetical listing of main-entry words. If the main-entry word has more than one meaning, synonyms for the different meanings are found at the one entry. The full range of alternatives is thus available at a glance.

The criterion for selecting the 9250 main-entry words has been that the word in question is likely to be looked up as an entry in its own right. If the source word in question does not occur as a main entry (say, *mélange*) synonyms may still be found by trying a simpler word of the same general meaning (say, *jumble* or *hotchpotch*). Terms denoting specific things often have no synonyms (*begonia*, *oxygen*, *ankle*, for example). Such items are not included unless they have alternative names or give rise to a figurative use. *Retina*, for example, is not a headword; but *eye* is entered with both literal and figurative senses, while *ear* is given figurative senses only.

The Collins Ringbinder Thesaurus is an invaluable help to the student concerned to improve his or her command of the English language. Whatever the task – whether writing an essay, compiling a report, or preparing a piece of oral English – the owner of this book will never be at a loss for the right word to use.

EXPLANATORY NOTES

1. Under each main entry word, the synonyms are arranged alphabetically. When a word has distinctly separate meanings, separate numbered lists are given for the different senses.

2. Where it is desirable to distinguish between different parts of speech, labels have been added as follows: *n.* (noun), *v.* (verb), *adj.* (adjective), *adv.* (adverb), *pron.* (pronoun), *conj.* (conjunction), *prep.* (preposition), *interj.* (interjection). See entries for *living, local.*

3. Usually the synonyms for a particular part of speech are grouped together. Thus, in the entry *catch* synonyms for all the verb senses are given first, followed by synonyms for all the noun senses. Sometimes, however, noun and verb functions are very closely associated in specific meanings, and where this is the case the synonyms are grouped by meanings.

4. When a headword has more than one meaning *and* can function as more than one part of speech, a new part-of-speech function is shown by a large swung dash (~), as in the entry for *glance* or *grasp.*

5. Much-used phrases appear as main entries; for instance, *act for* comes after *act.* Expressions such as *en route* or *off and on* are also given as main entries within the alphabetical listing. Short idiomatic phrases are entered under their key word and are to be found either at the end of the entry or immediately following the sense with which they are associated. Thus, the phrase *familiar with* appears as sense 2 of the entry *familiar,* since the synonyms in sense 1 most closely approximate to the meaning of the phrase.

6. Plural forms that have a distinctly separate meaning, such as *provisions,* are entered at their own alphabetical position, while those with a less distinct difference, such as *scraps,* are given as a separate sense under the singular form, e.g. *scrap* . . . 3. *Plural* . . .

7. A label in brackets applies only to the synonym preceding it while one which is not bracketed relates to the whole of that particular sense. Labels have been abbreviated when a readily understandable shortened form exists, such as *Sl.* (Slang), *Inf.* (Informal), and *Fig.* (Figurative).

A

abandon *v.* 1. desert, forsake, jilt, leave, leave behind 2. evacuate, quit, vacate, withdraw from ~*n.* 3. careless freedom, dash, recklessness, unrestraint, wantonness, wild impulse, wildness

abandonment dereliction, desertion, forsaking, jilting, leaving

abbey cloister, convent, friary, monastery, nunnery, priory

abdicate abandon, abjure, abnegate, cede, forgo, give up, quit, relinquish, renounce, resign, retire, surrender, vacate, waive, yield

abduct carry off, kidnap, make off with, run away with, run off with, seize, snatch (*Sl.*)

abhor abominate, detest, hate, loathe, shrink from, shudder at

abhorrent abominable, detestable, disgusting, distasteful, hated, hateful, horrible, horrid, loathsome, odious, offensive, repulsive

abide 1. accept, bear, brook, endure, put up with, stand, submit to, suffer, tolerate 2. continue, endure, last, persist, remain, survive

abide by 1. agree to, conform to, follow, obey, observe, submit to 2. carry out, discharge, fulfil, hold to, keep to, stand by

ability aptitude, capability, capacity, competence, competency, expertise, expertness, facility, faculty, flair, force, gift, knack, power, proficiency, skill, talent

abject 1. base, cringing, despicable, dishonourable, fawning, grovelling, ignominious, low, mean, servile, slavish, submissive, vile, worthless 2. deplorable, forlorn, hopeless, miserable, outcast, pitiable, wretched

ablaze 1. afire, alight, blazing, burning, fiery, flaming, ignited, lighted, on fire 2. brilliant, flashing, gleaming, glowing, illuminated, incandescent, luminous, radiant, sparkling

able accomplished, adept, adequate, capable, clever, competent, effective, efficient, experienced, expert, fit, fitted, gifted, masterly, powerful, practised, proficient, qualified, skilful, skilled, strong, talented

able-bodied firm, fit, hale, hardy, healthy, hearty, lusty, powerful, robust, sound, staunch, stout, strapping, strong, sturdy, vigorous

abnormal atypical, curious, deviant, eccentric, exceptional, extraordinary, irregular, odd, peculiar, queer, singular, strange, uncommon, untypical, unusual, weird

abnormality bizarreness, deformity, deviation, eccentricity, exception, flaw, irregularity, oddity, peculiarity, singularity, strangeness, uncommonness, unexpectedness, unnaturalness, unusualness, weirdness

abolish annul, blot out, cancel, destroy, do away with, eliminate, end, eradicate, expunge, extinguish, extirpate, invalidate, nullify, obliterate, overthrow, overturn, put an end to, quash, rescind, revoke, stamp out, subvert, suppress, terminate, void, wipe out

abolition cancellation, destruction, elimination, end, ending, eradication, extermination, extinction, extirpation, obliteration, overthrow, overturning, revocation, stamping out, subversion, suppression, termination, wiping out

abominable base, contemptible, despicable, detestable, disgusting, execrable, foul, hateful, heinous, hellish, horrible, horrid, loathsome, obnoxious, odious, repellent, repugnant, repulsive, revolting, terrible, vile

abominate abhor, detest, hate, loathe, shudder at

abomination antipathy, aversion, detestation, disgust, distaste, hate, hatred, repugnance, revulsion

abound be plentiful, crowd, flourish, increase, luxuriate, overflow, proliferate, swarm, swell, teem, thrive

abounding abundant, bountiful, copious, full, lavish, luxuriant, overflowing, plenteous, plentiful, profuse, prolific, rich, teeming

about *prep.* 1. as regards, concerned with, concerning, dealing with, on, re, referring to, regarding, relative to 2. adjacent, beside, circa (*used with dates*), close to, near, nearby 3. around, encircling, on all sides, round, surrounding 4. all over, over, through, throughout ~*adv.* 5. almost, approaching, approximately, around, close to, more or less, nearing, nearly, roughly

above 1. *prep.* beyond, exceeding, higher than, on top of, over, upon 2. *adj.* aforementioned, aforesaid, earlier

abrade erase, erode, file, grind, rub off, scour, scrape away, scrape out, wear away, wear down, wear off

abrasive annoying, biting, caustic, cutting, galling, grating, hurtful, irritating, nasty, rough, sharp, unpleasant

abreast *au fait*, conversant, familiar, informed, in touch, knowledgeable

abridge abbreviate, compress, condense, contract, curtail, cut, cut down, diminish, epitomize, lessen, précis, reduce, shorten, summarize, trim

abroad beyond the sea, in foreign lands, out of the country, overseas

abrupt 1. blunt, brisk, brusque, curt, direct, gruff, impolite, rough, rude, short, terse, uncivil, ungracious 2. precipitous, sharp, sheer, steep, sudden

absence 1. absenteeism, truancy 2. default, defect, deficiency, lack, need, omission, privation, want

absent 1. away, elsewhere, gone, lacking, missing, not present, out, truant, unavailable, wanting 2. absent-minded, abstracted, daydreaming, distracted, dreamy, empty, faraway, heedless, inattentive, musing, oblivious, preoccupied, unaware, unconscious, unheeding, unthinking, vacant, vague

absent-minded abstracted, bemused, distracted, dreaming, dreamy, engrossed, faraway, forgetful, heedless, oblivious, preoccupied, unaware, unthinking

absolute 1. complete, downright, entire, out-and-out, outright, perfect, pure, sheer, thorough, total, unqualified, utter 2. categorical, certain, decided, definite, exact, genuine, positive, precise, sure, unequivocal 3. autocratic, despotic, dictatorial, full, sovereign, supreme, unbounded, unconditional, unlimited, unqualified, unquestionable, unrestrained, unrestricted

absolutely 1. completely, entirely, fully, perfectly, purely, thoroughly, totally, utterly, wholly 2. categorically, certainly, decidedly, decisively, definitely, exactly, genuinely, infallibly, positively, precisely, surely, truly 3. autocratically, despotically, dictatorially, fully, supremely, unconditionally, unrestrainedly

absolution deliverance, discharge, forgiveness, freeing, indulgence, liberation, mercy, pardon, release, remission, setting free

absolutist arbiter, authoritarian, autocrat, despot, dictator, totalitarian, tyrant

absolve acquit, clear, deliver, discharge, excuse, exonerate, forgive, free, let off, loose, pardon, release, remit, set free

absorb 1. consume, devour, digest, drink in, exhaust, imbibe, receive, soak up, suck up, take in 2. captivate, engage, engross, fascinate, fill, fill up, fix, hold, immerse, occupy, preoccupy, rivet

absorbed 1. captivated, engaged, engrossed, fascinated, fixed, held, immersed, involved, lost, occupied, preoccupied, rapt, riveted, wrapped up 2. consumed, devoured, digested, exhausted, imbibed, received

absorbing arresting, captivating, engrossing, fascinating, gripping, interesting, intriguing, preoccupying, riveting, spellbinding

abstain avoid, cease, desist, forbear, forgo, give up, keep from, refrain, refuse, renounce, shun, stop, withhold

abstention abstaining, abstinence, avoidance, forbearance, refraining, refusal, self-control, self-denial

abstinence abstemiousness, forbearance, moderation, self-denial, self-restraint, soberness, sobriety, temperance

abstinent abstaining, abstemious, continent, forbearing, moderate, sober, temperate

abstract *adj.* 1. abstruse, complex, conceptual, deep, general, occult, philosophical, profound, separate, subtle, theoretical, unpractical, unrealistic ~*n.* 2. digest, epitome, essence, outline, précis, recapitulation, résumé, summary, synopsis ~*v.* 3. abridge, condense, digest, epitomize, outline, précis, shorten, summarize 4. detach, extract, isolate, remove, separate, steal, take away, withdraw

abstraction 1. absent-mindedness, inattention, preoccupation, remoteness 2. concept, generality, idea, notion, theorem, theory, thought

abstruse abstract, complex, dark, deep, mysterious, obscure, perplexing, profound, recondite, vague

absurd crazy, farcical, foolish, idiotic, illogical, irrational, laughable, ludicrous, nonsensical, preposterous, ridiculous, senseless, silly, stupid

absurdity craziness, folly, foolishness, idiocy, incongruity, irrationality, joke, ludicrousness, nonsense, senselessness, silliness, stupidity

abundance 1. affluence, bounty, fullness, plenteousness, plenty, profusion 2. affluence, fortune, opulence, riches, wealth

abundant ample, bountiful, copious, exuberant, filled, full, lavish, luxuriant, overflowing, plenteous, plentiful, profuse, rich, teeming

abuse *v.* 1. damage, exploit, harm, hurt, ill-treat, injure, maltreat, mar, misapply, misuse, oppress, spoil, wrong 2. curse, defame, disparage, insult, libel, malign, revile, scold, slander, smear, swear at, traduce, upbraid, vilify, vituperate ~*n.* 3. damage, exploitation, harm, hurt, ill-treatment, imposition, maltreatment, misapplication, misuse, oppression, spoiling, wrong 4. blame, calumniation, castigation, censure, cursing, defamation, disparagement, insults, invective, libel, reproach, revilement, scolding, slander, swearing, tirade, traducement, upbraiding, vilification, vituperation

abusive 1. censorious, disparaging, insulting, libellous, maligning, offensive, opprobrious, reproachful, reviling, rude, scathing, scolding, slanderous, traducing, upbraiding, vilifying, vituperative 2. brutal, cruel, destructive, harmful, hurtful, injurious, rough

abyss abysm, chasm, gulf, pit, void

academic *adj.* 1. bookish, erudite, highbrow, learned, lettered, literary, scholarly, scholastic, school, studious 2. conjectural, impractical, notional, speculative, theoretical ~*n.* 3. academician, don, fellow, lecturer, master, professor, pupil, scholar, scholastic, schoolman, student, tutor

accede 1. accept, acquiesce, admit, agree, assent, comply, concede, concur, consent, endorse, grant, yield 2. assume, attain, come to, enter upon, inherit, succeed, succeed to (*as heir*)

accelerate expedite, forward, further, hasten, hurry, pick up speed, precipitate, quicken, speed, speed up, spur

acceleration expedition, hastening, hurrying, quickening, speeding up, spurring, stimulation

accent *n.* 1. beat, emphasis, force, rhythm, stress 2. inflection, intonation, modulation, pronunciation, tone ~*v.* 3. accentuate, stress, underline, underscore

accept 1. obtain, receive, secure, take 2. accede, acknowledge, acquiesce, admit, adopt, affirm, agree to, approve, believe, concur with, consent to, cooperate with, recognize, swallow (*Inf.*) **3.** defer to, put up with, stand, submit to, suffer, take, yield to **4.** acknowledge, admit, assume, take on, undertake

acceptable 1. agreeable, gratifying, pleasant, pleasing, welcome **2.** adequate, admissible, all right, fair, moderate, passable, satisfactory, so-so (*Inf.*), tolerable

acceptance 1. obtaining, receipt, securing, taking **2.** accession, acknowledgment, acquiescence, admission, adoption, affirmation, agreement, approbation, approval, assent, belief, compliance, concession, concurrence, consent, cooperation, permission, recognition, stamp *or* seal of approval **3.** deference, standing, submission **4.** acknowledgment, admission, assumption, undertaking

accepted acceptable, acknowledged, admitted, agreed, agreed upon, approved, authorized, common, confirmed, conventional, customary, established, normal, recognized, regular, time-honoured, traditional, usual

access admission, admittance, course, door, entrance, entrée, entry, key, path, road

accessibility 1. approachability, nearness, obtainability, possibility, readiness **2.** approachability, cordiality, friendliness, informality **3.** exposedness, openness, susceptibility

accessible 1. achievable, at hand, attainable, available, handy, near, nearby, obtainable, on hand, possible, reachable, ready **2.** affable, approachable, available, conversable, cordial, friendly, informal **3.** exposed, liable, open, subject, susceptible, vulnerable, wide-open

accessory 1. abettor, accomplice, assistant, associate (*in crime*), colleague, confederate, helper, partner **2.** addition, adjunct, adornment, aid, appendage, attachment, component, convenience, decoration, extension, extra, frill, help, supplement

accident 1. calamity, casualty, chance, collision, crash, disaster, misadventure, mischance, misfortune, mishap, pile-up **2.** chance, fate, fortune, hazard, luck

accidental casual, chance, fortuitous, haphazard, incidental, random, uncertain, unexpected, unforeseen, unintended, unintentional, unplanned, unpremeditated, unwitting

accidentally by accident, by chance, by mistake, fortuitously, haphazardly, inadvertently, incidentally, randomly, undesignedly, unintentionally

acclaim 1. *v.* applaud, approve, celebrate, cheer, clap, commend, exalt, extol, hail, honour, laud, praise, salute, welcome **2.** *n.* acclamation, applause, approbation, approval, celebration, commendation, exaltation, honour, plaudits, praise, welcome

acclimatization adaptation, adjustment, naturalization

acclimatize accommodate, accustom, adapt, adjust, become seasoned to, get used to, inure, naturalize

accommodate 1. billet, board, cater for, harbour, house, lodge, put up, quarter, shelter **2.** aid, assist, furnish, help, oblige, provide, serve, supply **3.** comply, compose, conform, fit, harmonize, modify, reconcile, settle

accommodating complaisant, considerate, cooperative, friendly, helpful, hospitable, kind, obliging, polite, unselfish, willing

accommodation board, digs (*Inf.*), harbouring, house, housing, lodging(s), quartering, quarters, shelter, sheltering

accompany attend, conduct, convoy, escort, go with, usher

accompanying added, additional, attached, attendant, connected, fellow, joint, related, supplementary

accomplice accessory, ally, assistant, associate, collaborator, colleague, confederate, helper, henchman, partner

accomplish achieve, attain, bring off (*Inf.*), carry out, complete, conclude, do, effect, execute, finish, fulfil, manage, perform, produce, realize

accomplished adept, cultivated, expert, gifted, masterly, polished, practised, proficient, skilful, skilled, talented

accomplishment 1. achievement, bringing about, carrying out, completion, conclusion, doing, effecting, execution, finishing, fulfilment, performance, production, realization **2.** achievement, act, attainment, coup, deed, exploit, feat, stroke, triumph **3.** ability, achievement, art, attainment, proficiency, skill, talent

accordingly as a result, consequently, ergo, hence, in consequence, so, therefore, thus

according to 1. as believed by, as maintained by, as stated by, in the light of, on the authority of **2.** after, after the manner of, in accordance with, in conformity with, in harmony with, in keeping with, in line with, in step with, in the manner of

account *n.* **1.** chronicle, description, history, narration, narrative, recital, record, relation, report, statement, story, tale, version **2.** *Commerce* balance, bill, book, books, charge, inventory, invoice, ledger, reckoning, register, score, statement, tally **3.** basis, cause, consideration, ground, grounds, interest, motive, reason, regard, sake ~*v.* **4.** assess, believe, calculate, consider, count, deem, esteem, estimate, hold, judge, rate, reckon, regard, think, value

accountability answerability, liability, responsibility

accountable amenable, answerable, charged with, liable, obliged, responsible

account for clarify, clear up, elucidate, explain, illuminate, justify, rationalize

accredit authorize, certify, commission, depute, empower, endorse, entrust, guarantee, license, recognize, sanction, vouch for

accredited appointed, authorized, certified, commissioned, endorsed, guaranteed, licensed, official, recognized, sanctioned, vouched for

accumulate accrue, amass, build up, collect, gather, grow, hoard, increase, pile up, stockpile, store

accumulation aggregation, build-up, collection, gathering, heap, hoard, increase, mass, pile, stack, stock, stockpile, store

accuracy carefulness, correctness, exactitude, faithfulness, faultlessness, niceness, nicety, precision, strictness, truth, truthfulness, veracity

accurate close, correct, exact, faithful, faultless, just, meticulous, nice, precise, proper, regular, right, scrupulous, strict, true, truthful, unerring

accurately correctly, exactly, faithfully, faultlessly, justly, meticulously, nicely, precisely, properly, regularly, rightly, scrupulously, strictly, truly, truthfully, unerringly

accursed bedevilled, bewitched, condemned, cursed, damned, doomed, hopeless, ill-fated, ill-omened, luckless, ruined, undone, unfortunate, wretched

accusation allegation, attribution, charge, complaint, imputation, incrimination, indictment, recrimination

accuse blame, censure, charge, impute, incriminate, indict, recriminate, tax

accustom acclimatize, adapt, familiarize, habituate, inure, season, train

accustomed 1. acclimatized, adapted, familiar, given to, habituated, in the habit of, inured, seasoned, trained, used **2.** common, conventional, customary, established, everyday, expected, habitual, normal, ordinary, regular, routine, set

ace adept, champion, dab hand (*Inf.*), expert, genius, master, star, virtuoso, winner, wizard

ache *v.* hurt, pain, smart, suffer, throb, twinge

achieve accomplish, attain, bring about, carry out, complete, do, earn, effect, execute, finish, fulfil, gain, get, obtain, perform, procure, reach, win

achievement accomplishment, attainment, completion, execution, fulfilment, performance, production, realization

acid acrid, biting, pungent, sharp, sour, tart

acidity acridity, bitterness, pungency, sharpness, sourness, tartness

acknowledge 1. accept, acquiesce, admit, allow, concede, confess, declare, grant, own, profess, recognize, yield **2.** answer, notice, react to, recognize, reply to, respond to, return

acknowledged accepted, admitted, answered, conceded, declared, professed, recognized, returned

acknowledgment 1. acceptance, acquiescence, admission, allowing, confession, yielding **2.** answer, appreciation, credit, gratitude, reaction, recognition, reply, response, return, thanks

acquaint announce, apprise, disclose, divulge, enlighten, inform, let (someone) know, notify, reveal, tell

acquaintance associate, colleague, contact

acquainted apprised of, *au fait*, aware of, cognizant of, conscious of, conversant with, familiar with, informed of, in on, privy to, versed in

acquiesce accept, agree, assent, bow to, comply, concur, conform, consent, give in, go along with, submit, yield

acquiescence acceptance, agreement, assent, compliance, concurrence, conformity, consent, giving in, submission, yielding

acquire amass, attain, buy, collect, earn, gain, gather, get, obtain, pick up, procure, realize, receive, secure, win

acquisition buy, gain, possession, prize, property, purchase

acquisitive avaricious, avid, greedy, predatory, rapacious

acquit absolve, clear, deliver, discharge, exculpate, exonerate, free, fulfil, liberate, release, relieve, vindicate

acquittal absolution, clearance, discharge, exculpation, exoneration, liberation, release, relief, vindication

acrimonious astringent, bitter, caustic, censorious, cutting, irascible, mordant, petulant, pungent, rancorous, sarcastic, severe, sharp, spiteful, tart, testy, trenchant

acrimony asperity, astringency, bitterness, ill will, mordancy, peevishness, rancour, sarcasm, spleen, tartness, virulence

act *n.* **1.** action, blow, deed, doing, execution, exertion, exploit, feat, operation, performance, step, stroke, undertaking **2.** bill, decree, edict, enactment, law, measure, ordinance, resolution, statute **3.** performance, routine, show, sketch, turn ~*v.* **4.** acquit, bear, behave, carry, carry out, comport, conduct, do, enact, execute, exert, function, go about, make, move, operate, perform, react, serve, strike, take effect, undertake, work **5.** affect, counterfeit, feign, imitate, perform, pose, posture, pretend, put on, seem **6.** act out, characterize, enact, impersonate, mime, mimic, perform, personate, personify, play, play *or* take the part of, portray, represent

act for deputize for, fill in for, replace, represent, serve, stand in for, substitute for, take the place of

acting *adj.* **1.** interim, *pro tem*, provisional, substitute, surrogate, temporary ~*n.* **2.** dramatics, impersonation, performance, performing, portrayal, portraying **3.** dissimulation, feigning, imitating, imitation, imposture, play-acting, posing, posturing, pretence, pretending, seeming, shamming

action 1. accomplishment, achievement, act, deed, feat, move, operation, performance, step, stroke, undertaking **2.** activity, energy, force, liveliness, spirit, vigour, vim, vitality **3.** battle, combat, conflict, fighting, warfare **4.** case, cause, lawsuit, litigation, proceeding, prosecution, suit

actions bearing, behaviour, comportment, conduct, demeanour, deportment, manners, ways

active 1. acting, astir, at work, doing, functioning, in action, in force, in operation, live, moving, operative, running, working **2.** bustling, busy, engaged, full, involved, occupied, on the go (*Inf.*), on the move **3.** alert, animated, diligent, energetic, industrious, lively, nimble, on the go (*Inf.*), quick, spirited, sprightly, spry, vibrant, vigorous, vital, vivacious

activity 1. action, animation, bustle, exertion, hurly-burly, hustle, labour, life, liveliness, motion, movement, stir, work **2.** hobby, interest, job, labour, occupation, pastime, project, pursuit, scheme, task, undertaking, venture, work

actor actress, dramatic artist, leading man, performer, play-actor, player, Thespian, tragedian, trouper

actress actor, dramatic artist, leading lady, performer, play-actor, player, starlet, Thespian, trouper

actual 1. absolute, categorical, certain, definite, factual, indisputable, indubitable, physical, positive, real, substantial, tangible, undeniable, unquestionable **2.** current, existent, extant, live, living, present, present-day, prevailing

actually as a matter of fact, de facto, essentially, indeed, in fact, in reality, in truth, literally, really, truly

acute 1. clever, discerning, discriminating, incisive, intuitive, keen, observant, perceptive, perspicacious, sharp, smart, subtle **2.** needle-shaped, pointed, sharp, sharpened

acuteness cleverness, discernment, discrimination, intuitiveness, keenness, perception, perceptiveness, perspicacity, sharpness, smartness, subtlety

adamant determined, firm, fixed, immovable, inexorable, inflexible, insistent, intransigent, obdurate, resolute, rigid, set, stiff, stubborn, unbending, uncompromising, unrelenting, unshakable, unyielding

adapt accommodate, adjust, alter, apply, change, comply, conform, fit, habituate, make, match, modify, prepare, qualify, remodel, shape, suit, tailor

adaptability changeability, compliancy, flexibility, malleability, pliancy, resilience, versatility

adaptable adjustable, compliant, easy-going, flexible, malleable, modifiable, plastic, pliant, resilient, versatile

adaptation adjustment, alteration, change, conversion, modification, refitting, shift, transformation, variation, version

add 1. amplify, append, attach, augment, enlarge by, include, increase by, supplement **2.** add up, compute, count up, reckon, sum up, total, tot up

addendum addition, adjunct, affix, appendage, appendix, attachment, augmentation, extension, postscript, supplement

addict dope-fiend (*Sl.*), junkie (*Sl.*), user (*Inf.*)

addicted dedicated, dependent, devoted, hooked (*Sl.*), obsessed, prone

addiction craving, dependence, habit, obsession

addition 1. adding, adjoining, affixing, amplification, attachment, augmentation, enlargement, extension, inclusion **2.** addendum, adjunct, appendage, appendix, extension, extra, gain, increase, increment, supplement

additional added, extra, fresh, further, more, new, other, spare, supplementary

address *n.* **1.** abode, domicile, dwelling, home, house, location, lodging, place, residence **2.** direction, inscription, superscription **3.** discourse, disquisition, dissertation, harangue, lecture, oration, sermon, speech, talk ~*v.* **4.** apostrophize, greet, hail, invoke, salute, speak to, talk to **5.** discourse, give a speech, give a talk, harangue, lecture, orate, sermonize, speak, talk

add up add, compute, count up, reckon, sum up, total, tot up

adept able, accomplished, adroit, dexterous, expert, practised, proficient, skilful, skilled, versed

adequacy competence, fairness, satisfactoriness, sufficiency, tolerability

adequate capable, competent, enough, fair, passable, satisfactory, sufficient, suitable, tolerable

adhere attach, cement, cling, fasten, fix, glue, glue on, hold fast, paste, stick, stick fast

adherent admirer, advocate, devotee, disciple, fan, follower, hanger-on, partisan, supporter, upholder, votary

adhesive 1. *adj.* clinging, gummy, holding, sticking, sticky, tacky, tenacious **2.** *n.* glue, gum, paste

adieu farewell, goodbye, parting, valediction

adjacent adjoining, alongside, beside, bordering, close, near, neighbouring, next door, touching

adjoining adjacent, bordering, connecting, contiguous, joined, joining, near, neighbouring, next door, touching

adjourn defer, delay, discontinue, interrupt, postpone, prorogue, put off, recess, stay, suspend

adjournment deferment, delay, discontinuation, interruption, recess, stay, suspension

adjudicate adjudge, arbitrate, decide, determine, judge, referee, settle, umpire

adjudication arbitration, decision, determination, finding, judgment, pronouncement, ruling, settlement, verdict

adjust adapt, alter, arrange, compose, dispose, fit, fix, harmonize, make conform, measure, modify, order, reconcile, redress, regulate, remodel, set, settle, suit

adjustable flexible, malleable, modifiable, movable, tractable

adjustment adaptation, alteration, arrangement, arranging, fitting, fixing, modification, ordering, rectification, redress, regulation, remodelling, setting, tuning

ad-lib *v.* extemporize, improvise, make up, speak extemporaneously, speak impromptu, speak off the cuff

administer conduct, control, direct, govern, manage, oversee, run, superintend, supervise

administration 1. conduct, control, direction, execution, government, management, overseeing, performance, provision, running, superintendence, supervision **2.** executive, governing body, government, management, ministry, term of office

administrative executive, governmental, management, managerial, organizational, regulatory, supervisory

admirable commendable, estimable, excellent, exquisite, fine, laudable, meritorious, praiseworthy, rare, superior, valuable, wonderful, worthy

admiration adoration, affection, amazement, appreciation, approval, astonishment, delight, esteem, pleasure, praise, regard, respect, surprise, wonder

admire adore, appreciate, approve, esteem, idolize, look up to, praise, prize, respect, think highly of, value, worship

admirer 1. beau, boyfriend, lover, suitor, sweetheart, wooer **2.** devotee, disciple, enthusiast, fan, follower, partisan, supporter, worshipper

admissible acceptable, allowable, allowed, passable, permissible, permitted, tolerable, tolerated

admission 1. access, entrance, entrée, entry, initiation, introduction **2.** acknowledgment, allowance, avowal, concession, confession, declaration, disclosure, divulgence, profession, revelation

admit 1. allow, allow to enter, give access, initiate, introduce, let in, receive, take in **2.** acknowledge, affirm, avow, concede, confess, declare, disclose, divulge, profess, reveal **3.** agree, allow, grant, let, permit, recognize

adolescence 1. boyhood, girlhood, minority, teens, youth **2.** boyishness, childishness, girlishness, immaturity, youthfulness

adolescent 1. *adj.* boyish, girlish, growing, immature, juvenile, puerile, teenage, young, youthful **2.** *n.* juvenile, minor, teenager, youngster, youth

adopt 1. accept, appropriate, approve, assume, choose, embrace, endorse, espouse, follow, maintain, ratify, select, support, take on, take over, take up **2.** foster, take in

adoption 1. acceptance, approbation, appropriation, approval, assumption, choice, embracing, endorsement, espousal, ratification, support, taking on, taking over, taking up **2.** adopting, fosterage, fostering, taking in

adore admire, cherish, dote on, esteem, exalt, glorify, honour, idolize, love, revere, reverence, venerate, worship

adorn beautify, deck, decorate, embellish, enhance, enrich, garnish, grace, ornament, trim

adornment decoration, embellishment, frill, frippery, ornament, trimming

adrift afloat, drifting, unanchored, unmoored

adulation blandishment, fawning, fulsome praise, servile flattery, sycophancy, worship

adult 1. *adj.* full grown, fully developed, fully grown, grown-up, mature, of age, ripe **2.** *n.* grown *or* grown-up person (man *or* woman), grown-up

advance *v.* **1.** accelerate, bring forward, bring up, come forward, elevate, go ahead, go forward, go on, hasten, move onward, move up, press on, proceed, progress, promote, send forward, send up, speed, upgrade **2.** adduce, allege, cite, offer, present, proffer, put forward, submit, suggest **3.** lend, pay beforehand, raise (*price*), supply on credit ~*n.* **4.** advancement, amelioration, betterment, breakthrough, furtherance, gain, growth, improvement, progress, promotion, step **5.** appreciation, credit, deposit, down payment, increase (*in price*), loan, prepayment, retainer, rise (*in price*) **6. advances** approach, approaches, moves, overtures, proposals, proposition ~*adj.* **7.** beforehand, early, foremost, forward, in front, leading, prior

advanced avant-garde, extreme, forward, higher, late, leading, precocious, progressive

advancement advance, amelioration, betterment, gain, growth, improvement, preferment, progress, promotion, rise

advantage aid, ascendancy, asset, assistance, avail, benefit, blessing, boon, convenience, edge, gain, good, help, interest, lead, profit, service, start, superiority, sway, upper hand, use, utility, welfare

advantageous 1. dominant, favourable, superior **2.** beneficial, convenient, helpful, profitable, useful, valuable, worthwhile

adventure chance, contingency, enterprise, experience, exploit, hazard, incident, occurrence, risk, speculation, undertaking, venture

adventurer daredevil, hero, heroine, swashbuckler, traveller, venturer, wanderer

adventurous adventuresome, audacious, bold, dangerous, daredevil, daring, enterprising, foolhardy, hazardous, headstrong, intrepid, rash, reckless, risky

adverse conflicting, contrary, detrimental, disadvantageous, hostile, inexpedient, inopportune, negative, opposing, opposite, reluctant, repugnant, unfavourable, unfortunate, unfriendly, unlucky, unpropitious, unwilling

adversity affliction, bad luck, calamity, disaster, distress, hardship, hard times, ill-fortune, ill-luck, misery, misfortune, mishap, reverse, sorrow, suffering, trial, trouble, woe

advertise advise, announce, declare, display, inform, make known, notify, praise, proclaim, promote, promulgate, publicize, publish, puff, tout

advertisement ad (*Inf.*), advert (*Inf.*), announcement, bill, blurb, circular, commercial, display, notice, placard, poster, promotion, publicity, puff

advice admonition, caution, counsel, guidance, help, injunction, opinion, recommendation, suggestion, view

advisable apt, desirable, expedient, fit, fitting, judicious, politic, profitable, proper, prudent, seemly, sensible, sound, suitable, wise

advise admonish, caution, commend, counsel, enjoin, recommend, suggest, urge

adviser aide, authority, coach, confidant, consultant, counsel, counsellor, guide, helper, lawyer, mentor, right-hand man, solicitor, teacher, tutor

advisory advising, consultative, counselling, helping, recommending

advocate **1.** *v.* advise, argue for, campaign for, champion, defend, encourage, favour, plead for, press for, promote, propose, recommend, speak for, support, uphold, urge **2.** *n.* backer, campaigner, champion, counsellor, defender, promoter, proposer, speaker, spokesman, supporter, upholder

affable amiable, benevolent, benign, civil, congenial, cordial, courteous, friendly, genial, good-humoured, good-natured, kindly, mild, obliging, pleasant, sociable, urbane

affair **1.** activity, business, circumstance, concern, episode, event, happening, incident, interest, matter, occurrence, proceeding, project, question, subject, transaction, undertaking **2.** amour, intrigue, liaison, relationship, romance

affect **1.** act on, alter, bear upon, change, concern, influence, interest, involve, modify, regard, relate to, sway, transform **2.** assume, contrive, feign, imitate, pretend, sham, simulate

affectation appearance, artificiality, façade, false display, insincerity, mannerism, pose, pretence, pretentiousness, sham, show, simulation

affected artificial, assumed, conceited, contrived, counterfeit, feigned, insincere, mannered, precious, pretended, pretentious, put-on, sham, simulated, stiff, studied, unnatural

affecting moving, pitiable, pitiful, poignant, sad, saddening, touching

affection attachment, care, desire, feeling, fondness, friendliness, good will, inclination, kindness, liking, love, tenderness, warmth

affectionate attached, caring, devoted, doting, fond, friendly, kind, loving, tender, warm, warm-hearted

affinity analogy, closeness, compatibility, connection, correspondence, kinship, likeness, relation, relationship, resemblance, similarity

affirm assert, attest, aver, avouch, avow, certify, confirm, declare, maintain, state, swear, testify

affirmation assertion, averment, avouchment, avowal, confirmation, declaration, oath, pronouncement, ratification, statement, testimony

affirmative agreeing, approving, assenting, concurring, confirming, consenting, positive

afflict burden, distress, grieve, harass, hurt, oppress, pain, plague, trouble, try, wound

affluence abundance, fortune, opulence, plenty, profusion, prosperity, riches, wealth

affluent moneyed, opulent, prosperous, rich, wealthy, well-off, well-to-do

afford bear, spare, stand, sustain

afraid alarmed, anxious, apprehensive, cowardly, faint-hearted, fearful, frightened, intimidated, nervous, scared, timid, timorous

afresh again, anew, newly, once again, once more, over again

after afterwards, behind, below, following, later, subsequently, succeeding, thereafter

again **1.** afresh, anew, another time, once more **2.** also, besides, furthermore, in addition, moreover, on the contrary, on the other hand

against **1.** counter, hostile to, in contrast to, in defiance of, in opposition to, in the face of, opposed to, opposing, resisting, versus **2.** abutting, close up to, facing, fronting, in contact with, on, opposite to, touching, upon

age *n.* **1.** date, day(s), duration, epoch, era, generation, lifetime, period, span, time **2.** advancing years, decline (*of life*), majority, maturity, old age, senescence, senility, seniority ~*v.* **3.** decline, deteriorate, grow old, mature, mellow, ripen

aged age-old, ancient, antiquated, antique, elderly, getting on, grey, hoary, old, senescent, superannuated

agency bureau, business, department, office, organization

agent **1.** advocate, deputy, emissary, envoy, factor, go-between, negotiator, rep (*Inf.*), representative, substitute, surrogate **2.** agency, cause, force, instrument, means, power, vehicle

aggravate **1.** exacerbate, exaggerate, heighten, increase, inflame, intensify, magnify, make worse, worsen **2.** *Inf.* annoy, exasperate, get on one's nerves (*Inf.*), irk, irritate, needle (*Inf.*), nettle, pester, provoke, tease, vex

aggression assault, attack, encroachment, injury, invasion, offence, offensive, onslaught, raid

aggressive belligerent, destructive, hostile, offensive, pugnacious, quarrelsome

aghast amazed, appalled, astonished, astounded, awestruck, confounded, horrified, horror-struck, shocked, startled, stunned

agile active, acute, alert, brisk, clever, lithe, lively, nimble, quick, sharp, sprightly, spry, supple, swift

agitate **1.** beat, convulse, disturb, rock, rouse, shake, stir, toss **2.** alarm, arouse, confuse, disquiet, distract, disturb, excite, ferment, fluster, incite, inflame, perturb, rouse, trouble, upset, work up, worry

agitation **1.** convulsion, disturbance, rocking, shake, shaking, stir, stirring, tossing, turbulence **2.** alarm, arousal, clamour, commotion, confusion, discomposure, disquiet, distraction, disturbance, excitement, ferment, flurry, fluster, incitement, outcry, stimulation, trouble, tumult, turmoil, upset, worry

agitator demagogue, firebrand, inciter, rabble-rouser, revolutionary, troublemaker

agog avid, curious, eager, enthralled, enthusiastic, excited, expectant, impatient, in suspense, keen

agony affliction, anguish, distress, misery, pain, pangs, suffering, throes, torment, torture, woe

agree **1.** accede, acquiesce, admit, allow, assent, be of the same mind, comply, concede, concur, consent, engage, grant, permit, see eye to eye, settle **2.** accord, answer, chime, coincide, conform, correspond, fit, get on (together), harmonize, match, square, suit, tally

agreeable **1.** acceptable, delightful, enjoyable, gratifying, pleasant, pleasing, pleasurable, satisfying, to one's liking, to one's taste **2.** acquiescent, amenable, approving, complying, concurring, consenting, in accord, responsive, sympathetic, well-disposed, willing

agreement **1.** accord, accordance, compatibility, compliance, concert, concord, concurrence, conformity, congruity, consistency, correspondence, harmony, similarity, union **2.** arrangement, bargain, compact, contract, covenant, deal (*Inf.*), pact, settlement, treaty, understanding

agriculture culture, farming, husbandry, tillage

aground ashore, beached, foundered, grounded, high and dry, on the rocks, stranded, stuck

ahead along, at an advantage, at the head, before, forwards, in advance, in front, in the foreground, in the lead, leading, on, onwards, winning

aid *v.* **1.** abet, assist, befriend, encourage, favour, help, promote, relieve, second, serve, subsidize, succour, support, sustain ~*n.* **2.** assistance, benefit, encouragement, favour, help, relief, service, succour, support **3.** aide, aide-de-camp, assistant, helper, second, supporter

aim **1.** *v.* aspire, attempt, design, direct, endeavour, intend, level, mean, plan, point, propose, purpose, resolve, seek, set one's sights on, sight, strive, take aim (at), train, try, want, wish **2.** *n.* ambition, aspiration, course, design, desire, direction, end, goal, intent, intention, mark, object, objective, plan, purpose, scheme, target, wish

aimless chance, erratic, haphazard, pointless, purposeless, random, stray, undirected, unguided, unpredictable, wayward

air *n.* **1.** atmosphere, heavens, sky **2.** blast, breath, breeze, draught, puff, waft, whiff, wind, zephyr **3.** ambience, appearance, atmosphere, aura, bearing, character, demeanour, effect, feeling, flavour, impression, look, manner, mood, quality, style, tone **4.** circulation, display, dissemination, exposure, expression, publicity, utterance, vent, ventilation **5.** aria, lay, melody, song, tune ~*v.* **6.** aerate, expose, freshen, ventilate **7.** circulate, communicate, declare, disclose, display, disseminate, divulge, exhibit, expose, express, give vent to, make known, make public, proclaim, publicize, reveal, tell, utter, ventilate, voice

airiness **1.** breeziness, freshness, lightness, openness, windiness **2.** ethereality, insubstantiality, lightness, weightlessness **3.** animation, blitheness, breeziness, buoyancy, gaiety, happiness, high spirits, jauntiness, light-heartedness

airing **1.** aeration, drying, freshening, ventilation **2.** excursion, jaunt, outing, promenade, stroll, walk **3.** circulation, display, dissemination, exposure, expression, publicity, utterance, vent, ventilation

airless breathless, close, heavy, muggy, oppressive, stale, stifling, stuffy, suffocating, sultry, unventilated

airs affectation, affectedness, haughtiness, hauteur, pretensions, superciliousness

airy **1.** blowy, breezy, draughty, fresh, gusty, light, lofty, open, spacious, uncluttered, well-ventilated, windy **2.** aerial, delicate, ethereal, fanciful, flimsy, illusory, imaginary, immaterial, incorporeal, insubstantial, light, vaporous **3.** animated, blithe, buoyant, cheerful, cheery, debonair, gay, happy, high-spirited, jaunty, light, light-hearted, lively, merry, nonchalant

alarm *v.* **1.** distress, frighten, panic, scare, startle, terrify, unnerve **2.** alert, arouse, signal, warn ~*n.* **3.** anxiety, dismay, distress, fear, fright, panic, scare, terror, unease **4.** alarm-bell, alert, bell, danger signal, distress signal, siren, warning

alarming dismaying, distressing, disturbing, frightening, scaring, shocking, startling, terrifying

alcoholic *n.* boozer (*Inf.*), dipsomaniac, drunk, drunkard, hard drinker, inebriate, soak (*Inf.*), sot, sponge (*Inf.*), toper, wino (*Inf.*)

alert **1.** *adj.* agile, attentive, brisk, careful, heedful, lively, nimble, observant, on guard, on the ball (*Inf.*), perceptive, quick, ready, spirited, sprightly, vigilant, wary, watchful, wide-awake **2.** *n.* alarm, signal, siren, warning **3.** *v.* alarm, forewarn, inform, notify, signal, warn

alias **1.** *adv.* also called, also known as, otherwise, otherwise known as **2.** *n.* assumed name, *nom de guerre*, *nom de plume*, pen name, pseudonym, stage name

alibi defence, explanation, plea

alien 1. *adj.* adverse, exotic, foreign, inappropriate, incompatible, not native, opposed, outlandish, remote, repugnant, separated, strange, unfamiliar 2. *n.* foreigner, outsider, stranger

alight[1] *v.* come down, descend, disembark, dismount, get down, get off, land, light, perch, settle, touch down

alight[2] *adj.* ablaze, aflame, blazing, burning, fiery, flaming, flaring, lighted, lit, on fire

alike analogous, corresponding, equal, equivalent, even, identical, parallel, similar, the same, uniform

alive 1. animate, breathing, having life, living, subsisting 2. active, existent, existing, extant, functioning, in existence, in force, operative 3. active, alert, animated, awake, brisk, cheerful, eager, energetic, full of life, lively, quick, spirited, sprightly, spry, vigorous, vital, vivacious

all *adj.* 1. every bit of, the complete, the entire, the sum of, the total of, the whole of 2. each, each and every, every, every one of, every single 3. complete, entire, full, greatest, perfect, total, utter ~*n.* 4. aggregate, entirety, everything, sum, sum total, total, total amount, totality, whole ~*adv.* 5. altogether, completely, entirely, fully, totally, utterly, wholly

allergic affected by, sensitive, susceptible

alley alleyway, backstreet, lane, passage, passageway, pathway, walk

alliance affinity, agreement, association, coalition, combination, confederation, federation, league, marriage, pact, treaty, union

allied affiliated, associated, bound, combined, confederate, connected, in league, joined, kindred, married, related, unified, united, wed

allot allocate, apportion, assign, budget, designate, earmark, set aside, share out

allotment 1. allocation, grant, lot, measure, portion, quota, ration, share, stint 2. kitchen garden, patch, plot, tract

all-out complete, determined, full, full-scale, maximum, optimum, resolute, supreme, total, undivided, unlimited, unstinted, utmost

allow 1. acknowledge, acquiesce, admit, concede, confess, grant, own 2. approve, authorize, endure, let, permit, sanction, stand, suffer, tolerate

allowance 1. allocation, amount, grant, lot, measure, pension, portion, quota, ration, share, stint, stipend, subsidy 2. admission, concession, sanction, sufferance, toleration 3. concession, deduction, discount, rebate, reduction

allow for arrange for, consider, foresee, make allowances for, plan for, provide for, take into account

all right *adj.* 1. acceptable, adequate, fair, O.K. (*Inf.*), passable, satisfactory ~*adv.* 2. acceptably, adequately, O.K. (*Inf.*), satisfactorily

allusion glance, hint, indirect reference, innuendo, intimation, mention, suggestion

ally accessory, accomplice, associate, collaborator, colleague, confederate, friend, helper, partner

almighty absolute, all-powerful, omnipotent, supreme

almost about, all but, approximately, as good as, close to, just about, nearly, not quite, practically, virtually

alone abandoned, apart, deserted, desolate, detached, forsaken, isolated, lonely, lonesome, only, separate, single, sole, solitary, unaccompanied, unaided, unassisted, unattended, uncombined, unescorted

aloud audibly, clearly, distinctly, intelligibly, out loud, plainly

already as of now, at present, before now, by now, by that time, by then, by this time, even now, previously

also additionally, along with, and, as well, as well as, besides, further, furthermore, in addition, including, into the bargain, moreover, on top of that, plus, to boot, too

alter adapt, adjust, amend, change, convert, modify, recast, reform, remodel, reshape, revise, shift, transform, turn, vary

alteration amendment, change, difference, diversification, metamorphosis, modification, revision, shift, transformation, variance, variation

alternate 1. *v.* act reciprocally, follow in turn, interchange, intersperse, oscillate, rotate, substitute, take turns, vary 2. *adj.* alternating, every other, every second

alternative *n.* choice, option, other (*of two*), preference, recourse, selection, substitute

alternatively if not, instead, on the other hand, or, otherwise

although albeit, despite the fact that, even if, even supposing, even though, notwithstanding, though, while

altogether 1. absolutely, completely, fully, perfectly, quite, thoroughly, totally, utterly, wholly 2. all in all, all things considered, as a whole, collectively, generally, in general, *in toto*, on the whole 3. all told, in all, taken together

always consistently, continually, ever, evermore, every time, forever, *in perpetuum*, invariably, perpetually, repeatedly, unceasingly, without exception

amass accumulate, aggregate, assemble, collect, compile, garner, gather, heap up, hoard, pile up, rake up, scrape together

amateur dabbler, dilettante, layman, nonprofessional

amaze alarm, astonish, astound, bewilder, bowl over (*Inf.*), daze, shock, stagger, startle, stun, stupefy, surprise

amazement astonishment, bewilderment, confusion, marvel, perplexity, shock, surprise, wonder

ambassador agent, consul, deputy, diplomat, emissary, envoy, legate, minister, plenipotentiary, representative

ambiguous doubtful, dubious, equivocal, inconclusive, indefinite, indeterminate, obscure, puzzling, uncertain, unclear, vague

ambition 1. aspiration, desire, drive, eagerness, enterprise, longing, striving, yearning, zeal 2. aim, aspiration, desire, dream, end, goal, hope, intent, objective, purpose, wish

ambitious aspiring, avid, desirous, driving, eager, enterprising, hopeful, intent, purposeful, striving, zealous

ambush *n.* cover, hiding, hiding place, lying in wait, retreat, shelter, trap

amenable acquiescent, agreeable, open, persuadable, responsive, susceptible, tractable

amend alter, ameliorate, better, change, correct, enhance, fix, improve, mend, modify, rectify, reform, remedy, repair, revise

amendment 1. alteration, amelioration, change, correction, improvement, modification, reform, remedy, repair, revision 2. addendum, addition, adjunct, alteration, attachment, clarification

amenity advantage, comfort, convenience, facility, service

amiable affable, agreeable, benign, charming, cheerful, engaging, friendly, genial, kind, kindly, lovable, obliging, pleasant, pleasing, sociable, winsome

amid amidst, among, amongst, in the middle of, in the midst of, in the thick of, surrounded by

ammunition armaments, explosives, munitions, powder, rounds, shot and shell

among, amongst 1. amid, in association with, in the middle of, in the midst of, midst, with 2. between, to each of 3. in the company of, in the group of, in the number of, out of 4. by all of, by the joint action of, by the whole of, mutually, with one another

amount 1. expanse, extent, magnitude, mass, measure, number, quantity, supply, volume 2. addition, aggregate, extent, sum total, total, whole

amount to add up to, aggregate, become, come to, develop into, equal, grow, mean, purport, total

ample abounding, abundant, big, bountiful, broad, capacious, commodious, copious, expansive, extensive, full, generous, great, large, lavish, liberal, plenteous, plentiful, plenty, profuse, rich, roomy, spacious, substantial, wide

amuse beguile, charm, cheer, divert, enliven, entertain, occupy, please, recreate, regale

amusement 1. cheer, delight, diversion, enjoyment, entertainment, fun, gratification, interest, laughter, merriment, mirth, pleasure, recreation, sport 2. distraction, diversion, entertainment, game, hobby, joke, lark, pastime, prank, recreation, sport

amusing charming, cheerful, comical, delightful, diverting, droll, enjoyable, entertaining, funny, humorous, interesting, jocular, laughable, lively, merry, pleasant, pleasing, witty

analyse 1. estimate, evaluate, examine, investigate, judge, test 2. break down, consider, dissect, dissolve, divide, resolve, separate, study

analysis 1. breakdown, dissection, dissolution, division, enquiry, examination, investigation, scrutiny, separation, sifting, test 2. estimation, evaluation, opinion, study

analytic, analytical diagnostic, discrete, dissecting, inquiring, investigative, logical, organized, problem-solving, questioning, rational, searching, studious, systematic, testing

anarchist insurgent, nihilist, rebel, revolutionary, terrorist

anatomy dissection, division, enquiry, examination, investigation, study

ancestor forebear, forefather, precursor, progenitor

ancient aged, antediluvian, antiquated, antique, archaic, early, hoary, old, olden, old-fashioned, out-of-date, superannuated, timeworn

and along with, also, as well as, furthermore, in addition to, including, moreover, plus, together with

anecdote reminiscence, short story, sketch, story, tale, yarn

angel 1. archangel, cherub, divine messenger, guardian spirit, seraph 2. darling, dear, dream, gem, ideal, jewel, paragon, saint

angelic celestial, cherubic, ethereal, heavenly, seraphic

anger 1. *n.* annoyance, displeasure, exasperation, fury, ill humour, ill temper, indignation, ire, irritability, irritation, outrage, passion, pique, rage, resentment, spleen, temper, vexation, wrath 2. *v.* affront, annoy, displease, enrage, exasperate, excite, gall, incense, infuriate, irritate, madden, nettle, offend, outrage, pique, provoke, rile, vex

angle *n.* 1. bend, corner, crook, crotch, cusp, edge, elbow, intersection, knee, nook, point 2. approach, aspect, outlook, perspective, point of view, position, side, slant, standpoint, viewpoint ~*v.* 3. cast, fish

angry annoyed, choleric, displeased, enraged, exasperated, furious, heated, hot, ill-tempered, incensed, indignant, infuriated, irascible, irate, ireful, irritable, irritated, nettled, outraged, passionate, piqued, provoked, raging, resentful, wrathful

animal 1. *n.* beast, brute, creature 2. *adj.* bestial, bodily, brutish, carnal, fleshly, gross, physical, sensual

animate activate, embolden, encourage, enliven, excite, fire, impel, incite, inspire, invigorate, kindle, move, quicken, revive, rouse, spark, spur, stimulate, stir, urge

animosity animus, antagonism, antipathy, bad blood, bitterness, enmity, hate, hatred, hostility, ill will, malice, rancour, resentment

annals accounts, archives, chronicles, history, journals, memorials, records, registers

annihilate abolish, destroy, eradicate, exterminate, extinguish, obliterate, wipe out

announce advertise, broadcast,

declare, disclose, give out, intimate, make known, proclaim, promulgate, publish, report, reveal, tell

announcement advertisement, broadcast, bulletin, communiqué, declaration, disclosure, intimation, proclamation, publication, report, statement

annoy anger, bedevil, bore, bother, displease, disturb, exasperate, harass, harry, irk, irritate, madden, molest, needle (*Inf.*), nettle, pester, plague, provoke, rile, ruffle, tease, trouble, vex

annoyance anger, bother, displeasure, disturbance, exasperation, irritation, nuisance, provocation, trouble, vexation

annoying bothersome, displeasing, disturbing, exasperating, galling, harassing, irksome, irritating, maddening, troublesome, vexatious

annual once a year, yearlong, yearly

annually by the year, each year, every year, once a year, per annum, per year, year after year, yearly

anomalous abnormal, eccentric, exceptional, incongruous, inconsistent, irregular, odd, peculiar, rare, unusual

anomaly abnormality, departure, eccentricity, exception, incongruity, inconsistency, irregularity, oddity, peculiarity, rarity

anonymous incognito, nameless, unacknowledged, unidentified, unknown, unnamed, unsigned

answer 1. *n.* acknowledgment, defence, explanation, reaction, refutation, rejoinder, reply, report, response, retort, return, riposte 2. *v.* acknowledge, explain, react, rejoin, reply, resolve, respond, retort, return, solve

answerable accountable, chargeable, liable, responsible, subject, to blame

answer for be accountable for, be answerable for, be liable for, be responsible for, be to blame for

antagonism antipathy, conflict, contention, discord, dissension, friction, hostility, rivalry

antagonist adversary, competitor, contender, enemy, foe, opponent, opposer, rival

antagonize alienate, anger, annoy, disaffect, estrange, insult, irritate, offend, repel

anthem canticle, chant, chorale, hymn, psalm

anticipate 1. await, count upon, expect, forecast, foresee, foretell, hope for, look for, predict 2. antedate, forestall, intercept, prevent

anticipation awaiting, expectancy, expectation, foresight, foretaste, forethought, hope, premonition

anticlimax bathos, disappointment, letdown

antipathy antagonism, aversion, bad blood, disgust, dislike, distaste, enmity, hatred, hostility, ill will, loathing, rancour, repugnance

antique *adj.* 1. aged, ancient, elderly, old 2. archaic, obsolete, old-fashioned, outdated ~*n.* 3. bygone, heirloom, object of virtu, relic

antiquity 1. age, ancientness, elderliness, old age, oldness 2. ancient times, distant past, olden days

antiseptic 1. *adj.* aseptic, clean, hygienic, pure, sanitary, sterile, unpolluted 2. *n.* bactericide, disinfectant, germicide, purifier

antisocial alienated, misanthropic, reserved, retiring, unfriendly, unsociable, withdrawn

anxiety apprehension, care, concern, disquiet, distress, misgiving, nervousness, restlessness, solicitude, suspense, tension, unease, uneasiness, worry

anxious apprehensive, careful, concerned, distressed, disturbed, fearful, fretful, in suspense, nervous, restless, solicitous, tense, troubled, uneasy, watchful, worried

apart 1. afar, alone, aside, away, cut off, distant, distinct, divorced, excluded, independent, isolated, separate, singly, to itself, to oneself, to one side 2. asunder, in bits, in pieces, into parts, to bits, to pieces 3. **apart from** aside from, besides, but, except for, excluding, not counting, other than, save

apartment accommodation, compartment, quarters, room, rooms, suite

apathetic cool, emotionless, impassive, insensible, passive, stoic, stoical, torpid, unconcerned, unemotional, unfeeling, uninterested, unmoved, unresponsive

apathy coolness, impassivity, indifference, insensibility, listlessness, passiveness, passivity, stoicism, torpor, unconcern, unfeelingness, unresponsiveness

apiece each, for each, from each, individually, respectively, separately, severally, to each

aplomb balance, calmness, composure, coolness, equanimity, poise, self-assurance, self-confidence, stability

apologetic contrite, penitent, sorry

apologize ask forgiveness, beg pardon, express regret, say sorry

apology confession, defence, excuse, extenuation, vindication

appal alarm, astound, daunt, dismay, harrow, horrify, outrage, petrify, scare, shock, terrify, unnerve

appalling alarming, astounding, awful, daunting, dire, dreadful, fearful, frightful, ghastly, grim, harrowing, hideous, horrible, horrid, horrifying, intimidating, petrifying, scaring, shocking, terrible, terrifying

apparatus appliance, device, equipment, gear, implements, machine, machinery, materials, means, mechanism, outfit, tackle, tools, utensils

apparent clear, conspicuous, discernible, distinct, evident, indubitable, manifest, marked, obvious, open, overt, patent, plain, understandable, unmistakable, visible

apparently it appears that, it seems that, on the face of it, ostensibly, outwardly, seemingly, superficially

apparition 1. appearance, manifestation, presence, vision 2. chimera, ghost, phantom, spectre, spirit, spook (*Inf.*), visitant, wraith

appeal *n.* 1. entreaty, invocation, petition, plea, prayer, request, suit, supplication 2. allure, attraction, beauty, charm, fascination, interestingness, pleasingness ~*v.* 3. adjure, apply, ask, beg, beseech, call, call upon, entreat, implore, petition, plead, pray, refer, request, solicit, sue, supplicate 4. allure, attract, charm, engage, entice, fascinate, interest, invite, please, tempt

appear 1. arise, arrive, attend, be present, come forth, come into sight, come out, come to light, develop, emerge, issue, loom, materialize, occur, surface, turn out, turn up 2. look (like *or* as if), occur, seem, strike one as 3. be apparent, be clear, be evident, be obvious, be plain 4. be created, be developed, be invented, be published, come into being, come out 5. act, enter, perform, play, play a part, take part

appearance 1. advent, arrival, debut, emergence, introduction, presence 2. air, aspect, bearing, demeanour, expression, face, figure, form, image, look, looks, manner 3. front, guise, image, impression, outward show, pretence

appendix addition, adjunct, postscript, supplement

appetite craving, demand, desire, hunger, liking, longing, passion, relish, stomach, taste, zeal, zest

appetizing delicious, inviting, mouthwatering, palatable, savoury

applaud approve, cheer, clap, commend, eulogize, extol, laud, praise

applause acclamation, approval, cheering, cheers, handclapping, laudation, ovation, plaudit, praise

appliance apparatus, device, gadget, implement, instrument, machine, mechanism, tool

applicable apposite, appropriate, apt, fit, fitting, germane, pertinent, relevant, suitable, useful

applicant candidate, inquirer, petitioner, suitor, suppliant

application 1. function, pertinence, practice, purpose, relevance, use, value 2. appeal, claim, inquiry, petition, request, requisition, suit 3. assiduity, attentiveness, commitment, dedication, diligence, effort, hard work, industry, perseverance, study

apply 1. bring into play, bring to bear, carry out, employ, engage, execute, exercise, practise, put to use, use, utilize 2. appertain, be applicable, be appropriate, bear upon, be fitting, be relevant, fit, pertain, refer, relate, suit 3. anoint, bring into contact with, cover with, lay on, paint, place, put on, smear, spread on, touch to 4. claim, inquire, make application, petition, put in, request, requisition, solicit, sue 5. be diligent, be industrious, commit, concentrate, dedicate, devote, direct, give, pay attention, persevere, study, try, work hard

appoint 1. allot, arrange, assign, choose, decide, designate, determine, establish, fix, set, settle 2. assign, choose, commission, delegate, elect, install, name, nominate, select

appointed 1. allotted, arranged, assigned, chosen, decided, designated, determined, established, fixed, set, settled 2. assigned, chosen, commissioned, delegated, elected, installed, named, nominated, selected

appointment 1. arrangement, assignation, consultation, date, engagement, interview, meeting, rendezvous, session, tryst (*Archaic*) 2. assignment, job, office, place, position, post, situation

apportion allocate, allot, assign, deal, dispense, distribute, divide, dole out, measure out, mete out, share

apportionment allocation, allotment, assignment, dealing out, distribution, division

apposite appertaining, applicable, appropriate, apropos, apt, befitting, germane, pertinent, proper, relevant, suitable, suited, to the point, to the purpose

appreciate 1. be appreciative, be grateful for, be indebted, be obliged, be thankful for, give thanks for 2. acknowledge, be alive to, know, perceive, realize, recognize, take account of, understand 3. esteem, like, prize, rate highly, regard, relish, respect, savour, treasure, value 4. gain, grow, improve, increase, inflate, rise

appreciation 1. acknowledgment, gratefulness, gratitude, indebtedness, obligation, thanks 2. admiration, assessment, awareness, cognizance, enjoyment, esteem, knowledge, liking, perception, realization, recognition, regard, relish, respect, sensitivity, sympathy, valuation 3. gain, growth, improvement, increase, rise 4. notice, praise, review, tribute

appreciative 1. beholden, grateful, indebted, obliged, thankful 2. admiring, aware, cognizant, conscious, enthusiastic, mindful, perceptive, pleased, respectful, responsive, sensitive, sympathetic, understanding

apprehend 1. arrest, capture, catch, pinch (*Inf.*), run in (*Sl.*), seize, take, take prisoner 2. appreciate, comprehend, conceive, grasp, know, perceive, realize, recognize, think, understand

apprehension 1. alarm, anxiety, concern, disquiet, doubt, dread, fear, foreboding, misgiving, mistrust, unease, uneasiness, worry 2. arrest, capture, seizure 3. awareness, comprehension, grasp, intellect, intelligence, ken, knowledge, perception 4. belief, concept, conception, conjecture, idea, impression, notion, opinion, sentiment, thought, view

apprehensive afraid, alarmed, anxious, concerned, fearful, foreboding, mistrustful, uneasy, worried

apprentice beginner, learner, novice, pupil, student

approach *v.* 1. advance, catch up, come close, come near, come to, draw near, gain on, meet, move towards, near, push forward, reach 2. appeal to, apply to, make advances to, make a proposal to, make overtures to, sound out 3. approximate, be comparable to, be like, come close to, come near to, compare with, resemble ~*n.* 4. access, advance, advent, arrival, avenue, coming, drawing near, entrance, nearing, passage, road, way 5. approximation, likeness, semblance 6. *Often plural* advance, appeal, application, invitation, offer, overture, proposal, proposition 7. attitude, course, manner, means, method, mode, procedure, style, technique, way

appropriate *adj.* 1. apposite, apropos, apt, becoming, befitting, belonging, congruous, correct, felicitous, fit, fitting, opportune, pertinent, proper, relevant, right, seemly, suitable, to the point, to the purpose, well-suited, well-timed ~*v.* 2. annex, arrogate, assume, commandeer, confiscate, expropriate, impound, seize, take, take over, take possession of, usurp 3. embezzle, filch, misappropriate, pilfer, pocket, steal

approval 1. acquiescence, agreement, assent, authorization, blessing, compliance, confirmation, consent, countenance, endorsement, leave, licence, mandate, O.K. (*Inf.*), permission, sanction, the go-ahead (*Inf.*), the green light (*Inf.*) 2. acclaim, admiration, applause, appreciation, approbation, commendation, esteem, favour, good opinion, liking, praise, regard, respect

approve 1. acclaim, admire, applaud, appreciate, be pleased with, commend, esteem, favour, have a good opinion of, like, praise, regard highly, respect, think highly of 2. accede to, accept, advocate, agree to, allow, assent to, authorize, bless, concur in, confirm, consent to, countenance, endorse, give the go-ahead (*Inf.*), give the green light (*Inf.*), go along with, mandate, O.K. (*Inf.*), pass, permit, ratify, recommend, uphold

approximate *adj.* 1. close, near 2. estimated, inexact, loose, rough ~*v.* 3. approach, border on, come close, come near, resemble, touch, verge on

approximately about, almost, around, circa (*used with dates*), close to, generally, just about, loosely, more or less, nearly, not far off, relatively, roughly

approximation conjecture, estimate, estimation, guess, guesswork, rough calculation, rough idea

apron pinafore, pinny (*Inf.*)

apt 1. applicable, apposite, appropriate, befitting, correct, fit, fitting, germane, pertinent, proper, relevant, seemly, suitable, to the point, to the purpose 2. disposed, given, inclined, liable, likely, of a mind, prone, ready 3. astute, bright, clever, expert, gifted, ingenious, intelligent, prompt, quick, sharp, skilful, smart, talented, teachable

arable fertile, fruitful, ploughable, productive, tillable

arbiter adjudicator, arbitrator, judge, referee, umpire

arbitrary capricious, erratic, fanciful, inconsistent, optional, personal, random, subjective, unreasonable, whimsical, wilful

arbitrate adjudge, adjudicate, decide, determine, judge, referee, settle, umpire

arbitration adjudication, decision, judgment, settlement

arbitrator adjudicator, arbiter, judge, referee, umpire

arc arch, bend, bow, crescent, curve, half-moon

arch[1] archway, curve, dome, span, vault

arch[2] 1. accomplished, chief, consummate, expert, finished, first, foremost, greatest, highest, leading, main, major, master, pre-eminent, primary, principal, top 2. artful, frolicsome, knowing, mischievous, pert, playful, roguish, saucy, sly, waggish, wily

archetype classic, form, ideal, model, original, pattern, prototype, standard

architect designer, master builder, planner

architecture building, construction, design, planning

archives annals, chronicles, documents, papers, records, registers, rolls

arctic 1. far-northern, polar 2. cold, freezing, frosty, frozen, gelid, glacial, icy

ardent avid, eager, enthusiastic, fervent, fiery, hot, impassioned, intense, keen, passionate, spirited, vehement, warm, zealous

ardour avidity, eagerness, enthusiasm, feeling, fervour, fire, heat, intensity, keenness, passion, spirit, vehemence, warmth, zeal

arduous burdensome, difficult, exhausting, fatiguing, hard, harsh, heavy, onerous, painful, punishing, rigorous, severe, steep, strenuous, taxing, tiring, tough, troublesome

area 1. district, locality, neighbourhood, patch, plot, realm, region, sector, sphere, stretch, territory, tract, zone 2. part, portion, section, sector 3. sunken space, yard

arena 1. amphitheatre, field, ground, park (*Inf.*), ring, stadium, stage 2. battleground, domain, field, lists, province, realm, scene, scope, sphere, territory, theatre

argue 1. altercate, bandy words, bicker, disagree, dispute, fall out (*Inf.*), feud, fight, have an argument, quarrel, squabble, wrangle 2. assert, claim, contend, controvert, debate, discuss, dispute, expostulate, hold, maintain, plead, question, reason, remonstrate 3. demonstrate, evince, exhibit, imply, indicate, point to, show, suggest

argument 1. altercation, barney (*Inf.*), clash, controversy, difference of opinion, disagreement, dispute, feud, fight, quarrel, row, squabble, wrangle 2. assertion, claim, contention, debate, discussion, dispute, plea, pleading, remonstrance, remonstration 3. case, defence, dialectic, ground(s), logic, polemic, reason, reasoning

argumentative belligerent, combative, contrary, opinionated, quarrelsome

arid barren, desert, dried up, dry, parched, sterile, waterless

arise 1. appear, begin, come to light, commence, crop up (*Inf.*), emanate, emerge, ensue, follow, happen, issue, occur, originate, proceed, result, set in, spring, start, stem 2. ascend, climb, lift, mount, move upward, rise, soar, tower

aristocracy elite, gentry, *haut monde*, nobility, noblesse (*Literary*), patricians, peerage, upper class

aristocrat grandee, lady, lord, noble, nobleman, patrician, peer

aristocratic blue-blooded, elite, gentlemanly, highborn, lordly, noble, patrician, titled, upper-class, well-born

arm[1] *n.* 1. appendage, limb, upper limb 2. bough, branch, department, division, extension, offshoot, section, sector 3. authority, command, force, might, potency, power, strength, sway

arm[2] *v.* 1. *Esp. with weapons* array, deck out, equip, furnish, issue with, outfit, provide, rig, supply 2. mobilize, muster forces, prepare for war, take up arms

armada fleet, flotilla, navy, squadron

armaments arms, guns, munitions, ordnance, weapons

armed arrayed, equipped, fitted out, fortified, furnished, guarded, in arms, prepared, primed, provided, ready, strengthened, supplied, under arms

arms 1. armaments, firearms, guns, ordnance, weaponry, weapons 2. blazonry, crest, escutcheon, heraldry, insignia

army 1. armed force, land forces, legions, military, soldiers, soldiery, troops 2. *Fig.* array, horde, host, multitude, pack, swarm, throng, vast number

aroma bouquet, fragrance, odour, perfume, redolence, savour, scent, smell

aromatic balmy, fragrant, perfumed, pungent, redolent, savoury, spicy

around *prep.* 1. about, encircling, enclosing, on all sides of, surrounding 2. about, approximately, circa (*used with dates*), roughly ~*adv.* 3. about, all over, everywhere, here and there, in all directions, on all sides, throughout, to and fro 4. at hand, close, close at hand, close by, near, nearby, nigh (*Archaic or dialect*)

arouse agitate, awaken, call forth, enliven, excite, foster, goad, incite, inflame, instigate, kindle, move, provoke, quicken, rouse, sharpen, spark, spur, stimulate, stir up, summon up, waken, wake up, warm, whet, whip up

arrange 1. array, class, dispose, file, form, group, line up, marshal, order, organize, position, range, rank, set out, sort 2. adjust, agree to, come to terms, compromise, construct, contrive, determine, devise, plan, prepare, schedule, settle 3. adapt, instrument, orchestrate, score

arrangement 1. array, classification, design, display, disposition, form, line-up, order, organization, rank, setup (*Inf.*), structure, system 2. adaptation, instrumentation, interpretation, orchestration, score, version

array arrangement, collection, display, disposition, exhibition, formation, line-up, marshalling, muster, order, parade, show, supply

arrest 1. *v.* apprehend, capture, catch, detain, lay hold of, run in (*Sl.*), seize, take, take into custody, take prisoner 2. *n.* apprehension, capture, cop (*Sl.*), detention, seizure

arrival advent, appearance, entrance, occurrence, taking place

arrive appear, befall, come, enter, get to, happen, occur, reach, show up (*Inf.*), take place, turn up

arrogance bluster, conceit, hauteur, insolence, loftiness, lordliness, pomposity, pompousness, presumption, pretentiousness, pride, scornfulness, superciliousness, swagger

arrogant assuming, blustering, conceited, contemptuous, disdainful, haughty, high-handed, imperious, insolent, lordly, overbearing, pompous, presumptuous, pretentious, proud, scornful, supercilious

arrow 1. bolt, dart, flight, quarrel, reed (*Archaic*), shaft (*Archaic*) 2. indicator, pointer

arsenal ammunition dump, armoury, arms depot, magazine, ordnance depot, stock, stockpile, store, storehouse, supply

art adroitness, aptitude, artistry, craft, craftsmanship, dexterity, expertise, facility, ingenuity, knack, knowledge, mastery, method, profession, skill, trade, virtuosity

artful adept, adroit, clever, crafty, cunning, deceitful, designing, dexterous, ingenious, intriguing, masterly, politic, proficient, resourceful, sharp, shrewd, skilful, sly, smart, subtle, tricky, wily

article 1. commodity, item, object, piece, substance, thing, unit 2. composition, discourse, essay, feature, item, paper, piece, story, treatise

articulate 1. *adj.* clear, coherent, comprehensible, eloquent, expressive, fluent, intelligible, lucid, meaningful, vocal 2. *v.* enunciate, express, pronounce, say, speak, state, talk, utter, voice

artificial 1. man-made, manufactured, plastic, synthetic 2. bogus, counterfeit, ersatz, fake, imitation, mock, sham, simulated, specious, spurious

artisan artificer, craftsman, mechanic, skilled workman, technician

artistic aesthetic, beautiful, creative, cultivated, cultured, decorative, elegant, exquisite, graceful, imaginative, refined, sensitive, stylish

as *conj.* 1. at the time that, during the time that, just as, when, while **2.** in the manner that, in the way that, like **3.** that which, what **4.** because, considering that, seeing that, since **5.** in the same manner with, in the same way that, like **6.** for instance, like, such as ~*prep.* **7.** being, in the character of, in the role of, under the name of **8. as for** as regards, in reference to, on the subject of, with reference to, with regard to, with respect to **9. as it were** in a manner of speaking, in a way, so to say, so to speak

ascend climb, float up, fly up, go up, lift off, mount, move up, rise, scale, slope upwards, soar, take off, tower

ascent 1. climb, climbing, mounting, rise, rising, scaling, upward movement **2.** gradient, incline, ramp, rise, upward slope

ascertain confirm, determine, discover, establish, find out, fix, identify, learn, make certain, settle, verify

ascribe assign, attribute, charge, credit, impute, put down, refer, set down

ashamed bashful, blushing, crestfallen, discomfited, distressed, embarrassed, guilty, humiliated, mortified, prudish, reluctant, remorseful, shamefaced, sheepish, shy, sorry

ashore aground, landwards, on dry land, on land, on the beach, on the shore, shorewards, to the shore

aside alone, alongside, apart, away, beside, in reserve, on one side, out of mind, privately, separately, to one side, to the side

ask 1. inquire, interrogate, query, question, quiz **2.** appeal, apply, beg, beseech, claim, crave, demand, entreat, implore, petition, plead, pray, request, seek, solicit, sue, supplicate **3.** bid, invite, summon

asleep dead to the world (*Inf.*), dormant, dozing, sleeping, slumbering

aspect 1. air, appearance, attitude, bearing, condition, countenance, demeanour, expression, look, manner **2.** angle, facet, feature, side

aspiration aim, ambition, dream, endeavour, goal, hope, longing, object, objective, wish, yearning

aspire aim, crave, desire, dream, hanker, hope, long, pursue, seek, wish

aspiring *adj.* ambitious, eager, hopeful, wishful, would-be

ass 1. donkey **2.** blockhead, dolt, dope (*Sl.*), dunce, fool, halfwit, idiot, jackass, nincompoop, nitwit, numskull, simpleton

assassin executioner, hatchet man (*Sl.*), hit man (*Sl.*), killer, murderer

assassinate eliminate (*Sl.*), hit (*U.S. sl.*), kill, liquidate, murder, slay

assault 1. *n.* aggression, attack, charge, invasion, offensive, storm, storming, strike **2.** *v.* attack, charge, invade, lay into, set about, set upon, storm

assemble 1. accumulate, amass, bring together, call together, collect, come together, congregate, convene, convoke, flock, forgather, gather, marshal, meet, muster, rally, summon **2.** connect, construct, erect, fabricate, fit together, join, make, piece together, set up

assembly 1. accumulation, aggregation, body, collection, company, conference, congregation, council, crowd, diet, flock, gathering, group, mass, meeting, rally, throng **2.** construction, erection, fabrication, manufacture

assent 1. *v.* accede, accept, acquiesce, agree, allow, approve, comply, concur, consent, grant, permit **2.** *n.* acceptance, accord, acquiescence, agreement, approval, consent, permission, sanction

assert affirm, allege, avow, contend, declare, maintain, profess, state, swear

assess 1. compute, determine, estimate, evaluate, fix, gauge, judge, rate, value, weigh **2.** fix, impose, levy, rate, tax, value

assessment 1. determination, estimate, judgment, rating, valuation **2.** charge, demand, duty, evaluation, impost, levy, rate, rating, tax, taxation, toll

asset 1. advantage, aid, benefit, blessing, boon, help, resource, service **2.** *Plural* capital, estate, funds, goods, holdings, means, money, possessions, property, reserves, resources, valuables, wealth

assign 1. appoint, choose, name, nominate, select **2.** allocate, allot, consign, give, grant

assignment appointment, charge, commission, duty, job, mission, position, post, responsibility, task

assist aid, back, boost, collaborate, cooperate, expedite, facilitate, further, help, reinforce, second, serve, succour, support, sustain, work for, work with

assistance aid, backing, boost, collaboration, cooperation, furtherance, help, helping hand, reinforcement, relief, service, succour, support

assistant accessory, accomplice, aide, ally, associate, auxiliary, backer, collaborator, colleague, helper, helpmate, henchman, partner

associate 1. *v.* affiliate, ally, combine, connect, couple, join, league, link, mix, pair, relate, unite, yoke **2.** *n.* ally, colleague, companion, comrade, co-worker, follower, friend, mate, partner

association 1. alliance, band, clique, club, company, confederacy, confederation, cooperative, corporation, federation, fraternity, group, league, partnership, society, syndicate, union **2.** blend, bond, combination, concomitance, connection, correlation, identification, mixture, pairing, relation, tie, union

assorted different, diverse, diversified, heterogeneous, mixed, motley, sundry, varied, various

assortment array, choice, collection, diversity, hotchpotch, jumble, medley, *mélange*, miscellany, mishmash, mixture, selection, variety

assume 1. accept, believe, expect, fancy, imagine, presuppose, suppose, surmise, suspect, take for granted, think **2.** affect, feign, imitate, impersonate, mimic, put on, sham, simulate **3.** accept, enter upon, put on, set about, shoulder, take on, take over, take responsibility for, take up, undertake

assumed affected, bogus, counterfeit, fake, false, feigned, fictitious, imitation, made-up, sham, simulated, spurious

assumption belief, conjecture, inference, premise, premiss, presumption, surmise

assurance 1. affirmation, declaration, guarantee, oath, pledge, promise, vow, word, word of honour **2.** aggressiveness, assuredness, boldness, certainty, confidence, conviction, coolness, courage, faith, firmness, nerve, poise, self-confidence, sureness

assure 1. convince, embolden, encourage, hearten, persuade, reassure, soothe **2.** guarantee, pledge, promise, swear, vow **3.** make certain, make sure, seal, secure

astonish amaze, astound, bewilder, confound, daze, stagger, stupefy, surprise

astonishing amazing, astounding, bewildering, breathtaking, staggering, stupefying, surprising

astonishment amazement, awe, bewilderment, stupefaction, surprise, wonder

astute adroit, artful, bright, calculating, canny, clever, crafty, cunning, intelligent, keen, knowing, perceptive, sagacious, sharp, shrewd, sly, subtle, wily

asylum harbour, haven, refuge, retreat, safety, sanctuary, shelter

atheism disbelief, godlessness, irreligion, paganism, scepticism, unbelief

atheist disbeliever, pagan, sceptic, unbeliever

athlete competitor, contender, contestant, games player, runner, sportsman

athletic 1. *adj.* able-bodied, active, energetic, fit, muscular, powerful, robust, strapping, strong, sturdy, vigorous **2.** *pl. n.* contests, exercises, gymnastics, races, sports

atmosphere 1. air, heavens, sky **2.** air, aura, character, climate, feel, feeling, flavour, mood, quality, spirit, surroundings, tone

atom fragment, grain, iota, jot, mite, molecule, morsel, particle, scrap, shred, speck, spot, tittle, trace, whit

atrocious barbaric, brutal, cruel, fiendish, infamous, infernal, inhuman, monstrous, ruthless, savage, vicious, wicked

atrocity abomination, barbarity, brutality, crime, cruelty, enormity, evil, horror, outrage, villainy

attach add, adhere, bind, connect, couple, fasten, fix, join, link, secure, stick, tie, unite

attached affectionate towards, devoted, fond of, possessive

attachment bond, clamp, connection, connector, coupling, fastening, joint, junction, link, tie

attack *n.* **1.** assault, charge, foray, incursion, inroad, invasion, offensive, onset, onslaught, raid, rush, strike **2.** abuse, censure, criticism, denigration **3.** access, bout, convulsion, fit, paroxysm, seizure, spasm, spell, stroke ~*v.* **4.** assault, charge, fall upon, invade, raid, rush, set about, set upon, storm **5.** abuse, blame, censure, criticize, impugn, malign, revile, vilify

attain accomplish, achieve, arrive at, bring off, complete, earn, fulfil, gain, get, grasp, reach, realize, secure, win

attempt 1. *n.* attack, bid, crack (*Inf.*), endeavour, go, shot (*Inf.*), try, undertaking, venture **2.** *v.* endeavour, essay, experiment, seek, strive, tackle, take on, try, undertake, venture

attend 1. appear, be at, be here, be present, be there, frequent, go to, haunt, show oneself, show up (*Inf.*), turn up, visit **2.** hear, heed, listen, look on, mark, mind, note, notice, observe, pay attention, pay heed, regard, watch **3.** *With* **to** apply oneself to, concentrate on, devote oneself to, look after, see to, tale care of **4.** accompany, escort, guard, squire, usher

attendance audience, crowd, gate, house, number present, turnout

attendant aide, assistant, auxiliary, companion, escort, flunky, follower, guard, guide, helper, servant, steward, usher, waiter

attention 1. concentration, consideration, heed, mind, scrutiny, thinking, thought, thoughtfulness **2.** consideration, notice, recognition, regard **3.** care, concern, looking after, ministration, treatment

attentive alert, careful, concentrating, heedful, mindful, observant, regardful, studious, watchful

attic garret, loft

attitude 1. approach, frame of mind, mood, opinion, outlook, position, posture, stance, standing, view **2.** air, aspect, bearing, carriage, condition, demeanour, manner, pose, position, posture, stance

attract allure, charm, decoy, draw, enchant, endear, engage, entice, incline, interest, invite, lure, tempt

attraction allure, charm, draw, enticement, fascination, interest, lure, magnetism

attractive agreeable, appealing, beautiful, captivating, charming, engaging, fair, fetching, good-looking, gorgeous, handsome, interesting, inviting, lovely, magnetic, pleasing, pretty, seductive, tempting

attribute 1. *v.* apply, assign, blame, charge, lay at the door of, refer **2.** *n.* aspect, characteristic, facet, feature, indication, mark, note, point, property, quality, quirk, sign, symbol, trait, virtue

audacious adventurous, bold, brave, courageous, daredevil, daring, fearless, intrepid, rash, reckless, risky

audacity 1. adventurousness, boldness, bravery, courage, daring, nerve, rashness, recklessness **2.** cheek, defiance, effrontery, impertinence, impudence, insolence, nerve

audible clear, discernible, distinct

audience 1. congregation, crowd, gathering, house, listeners, viewers 2. consultation, hearing, interview, reception

auspicious bright, encouraging, favourable, fortunate, happy, hopeful, lucky, propitious, rosy

austere 1. cold, forbidding, grave, grim, hard, serious, severe, solemn, stern, stiff 2. abstemious, abstinent, puritanical, sober, solemn, Spartan

austerity 1. coldness, harshness, inflexibility, rigour, solemnity, sternness 2. economy, rigidity, self-denial

authentic actual, authoritative, faithful, genuine, real, reliable, true, valid

authenticity actuality, genuineness, truth, truthfulness, validity

author composer, creator, father, founder, inventor, maker, mover, originator, parent, planner, producer, writer

authoritarian autocratic, despotic, dictatorial, disciplinarian, doctrinaire, domineering, harsh, imperious, rigid, severe, strict, tyrannical

authority 1. charge, command, control, domination, dominion, force, government, influence, might, power, prerogative, right, rule, strength, supremacy, sway, weight 2. authorization, licence, permission, permit, sanction, warrant 3. arbiter, expert, master, professional, scholar, specialist, textbook

authorize 1. empower, enable, entitle, give authority 2. allow, approve, confirm, countenance, give leave, license, permit, ratify, sanction, warrant

autocracy absolution, despotism, dictatorship, tyranny

automatic 1. mechanical, push-button, robot, self-activating, self-propelling, self-regulating 2. habitual, mechanical, perfunctory, routine, unconscious

autonomous free, independent, self-governing, sovereign

auxiliary accessory, aiding, ancillary, assisting, helping, reserve, secondary, subsidiary, substitute, supplementary

available accessible, applicable, at hand, free, handy, obtainable, on hand, on tap, ready, to hand, vacant

avalanche 1. landslide, landslip, snow-slide, snow-slip 2. barrage, deluge, flood, inundation, torrent

avaricious close-fisted, covetous, grasping, greedy, mean, miserly, parsimonious, penurious, stingy

avenge punish, repay, requite, retaliate, revenge, take satisfaction for, take vengeance

avenue access, approach, boulevard, channel, course, drive, entrance, entry, pass, path, road, route, street, way

average *n.* 1. mean, medium, midpoint, norm, normal, par, rule, run, standard *~adj.* 2. fair, general, indifferent, mediocre, middling, moderate, normal, not bad, ordinary, regular, so-so (*Inf.*), standard, tolerable, typical 3. intermediate, mean, median, medium, middle

averse disinclined, hostile, ill-disposed, loath, opposed, reluctant, unfavourable, unwilling

aviator aeronaut, airman, flier, pilot

avid ardent, devoted, eager, enthusiastic, fanatical, fervent, intense, keen, passionate, zealous

avoid avert, bypass, circumvent, dodge, elude, escape, evade, keep away from, prevent, shirk, shun, sidestep, steer clear of

await 1. anticipate, expect, look for, stay for, wait for 2. attend, be in readiness for, be in store for, be ready for, wait for

awake alert, alive, aroused, attentive, aware, conscious, not sleeping, observant, on guard, on the alert, on the lookout, vigilant, wakeful, waking, watchful, wide-awake

awaken activate, alert, arouse, awake, call forth, excite, incite, kindle, provoke, revive, rouse, stimulate, stir up, wake

awakening *n.* activation, arousal, awaking, revival, rousing, stimulation, stirring up, waking, waking up

award *v.* 1. accord, allot, apportion, assign, bestow, confer, decree, endow, gift, give, grant, render *~n.* 2. adjudication, bestowal, conferment, decision, decree, gift, order, presentation 3. decoration, gift, grant, prize, trophy, verdict

aware alive to, apprised, attentive, cognizant, conscious, conversant, familiar, knowing, mindful, sensible, wise (*Inf.*)

awareness appreciation, attention, consciousness, familiarity, knowledge, mindfulness, perception, realization, recognition, understanding

away *adv.* 1. abroad, elsewhere, from here, from home, hence, off 2. apart, at a distance, far, remote 3. aside, out of the way, to one side *~adj.* 4. abroad, elsewhere, gone, not here, not present, not there, out

awesome alarming, amazing, astonishing, awe-inspiring, awful, breathtaking, daunting, dreadful, fearful, fearsome, formidable, frightening, horrible, horrifying, imposing, impressive, intimidating, magnificent, majestic, overwhelming, redoubtable, shocking, solemn, stunning, stupefying, terrible, terrifying, wonderful, wondrous

awful alarming, appalling, deplorable, dire, distressing, dreadful, fearful, frightful, ghastly, gruesome, hideous, horrible, nasty, shocking, terrible, ugly, unpleasant

awfully badly, disgracefully, disreputably, dreadfully, unforgivably, unpleasantly, wickedly, woefully, wretchedly

awkward 1. artless, blundering, bungling, clownish, clumsy, coarse, gauche, gawky, graceless, ham-fisted, inelegant, inept, inexpert, lumbering, maladroit, oafish, rude, stiff, uncoordinated, uncouth, ungainly, ungraceful, unpolished, unrefined, unskilful, unskilled 2. cumbersome, difficult, inconvenient, troublesome, unhandy, unmanageable, unwieldy 3. annoying, difficult, disobliging, exasperating, intractable, irritable, perverse, prickly, stubborn, touchy, troublesome, trying, unhelpful

awkwardness 1. clumsiness, coarseness, gaucheness, gaucherie, gawkiness, gracelessness, inelegance, ineptness, inexpertness, maladroitness, oafishness, rudeness, stiffness, uncoordination, uncouthness, ungainliness 2. cumbersomeness, difficulty, inconvenience, troublesomeness, unwieldiness 3. delicacy, embarrassment, inconvenience 4. difficulty, disobligingness, stubbornness, touchiness, unhelpfulness

axe *n.* 1. chopper, hatchet 2. **the axe** *Inf.* cancellation, cutback, discharge, dismissal, termination, the boot (*Sl.*), the chop (*Sl.*), the sack (*Inf.*), wind-up *~v.* 3. chop, cut down, fell, hew

axiom adage, aphorism, dictum, fundamental, maxim, postulate, precept, principle, truism

axiomatic 1. accepted, assumed, fundamental, given, granted, manifest, self-evident, understood, unquestioned 2. aphoristic, pithy, terse

axis axle, centre line, pivot, shaft, spindle

axle axis, pin, pivot, rod, shaft, spindle

B

baby 1. *n.* babe, bairn (*Scot.*), child, infant, newborn child 2. *adj.* diminutive, dwarf, little, midget, mini, miniature, minute, pygmy, small, tiny, wee 3. *v.* coddle, cosset, humour, indulge, mollycoddle, overindulge, pamper, pet, spoil, spoon-feed

babyish baby, infantile, juvenile, namby-pamby, puerile, silly, soft (*Inf.*), spoiled

back *v.* 1. abet, advocate, assist, champion, countenance, encourage, endorse, favour, finance, sanction, second, side with, sponsor, subsidize, support, sustain, underwrite 2. backtrack, go back, regress, retire, retreat, reverse, turn tail, withdraw *~n.* 3. backside, end, far end, hind part, hindquarters, posterior, rear, reverse, stern, tail end *~adj.* 4. end, hind, hindmost, posterior, rear, tail

backbone 1. *Medical* spinal column, spine, vertebrae, vertebral column 2. courage, determination, firmness, fortitude, grit, hardihood, mettle, moral fibre, nerve, pluck, resolution, resolve, steadfastness, strength of character, tenacity, toughness, will, willpower 3. basis, foundation, mainstay, support

backer advocate, angel (*Inf.*), benefactor, patron, promoter, second, sponsor, subscriber, supporter, underwriter, well-wisher

backfire boomerang, disappoint, fail, flop, miscarry, rebound, recoil

background breeding, circumstances, credentials, culture, education, environment, experience, history, qualifications, tradition, upbringing

backing accompaniment, advocacy, aid, assistance, encouragement, endorsement, funds, grant, moral support, patronage, sponsorship, subsidy, support

backlash backfire, boomerang, counteraction, reaction, recoil, repercussion, resentment, response, retaliation

backlog excess, hoard, reserve, reserves, resources, stock, supply

back out abandon, cancel, chicken out (*Inf.*), give up, go back on, recant, renege, resign, retreat, withdraw

backslider recidivist, turncoat

back up aid, assist, bolster, confirm, corroborate, reinforce, stand by, support

backward *adj.* 1. bashful, diffident, hesitating, late, reluctant, shy, sluggish, unwilling 2. behind, behindhand, dense, dull, retarded, slow, stupid, subnormal, undeveloped *~adv.* 3. aback, behind, in reverse, rearward

bacteria bacilli, germs, microorganisms

bad 1. defective, deficient, faulty, imperfect, inadequate, incorrect, inferior, poor, substandard, unsatisfactory 2. damaging, dangerous, detrimental, harmful, hurtful, injurious, ruinous, unhealthy 3. base, corrupt, criminal, delinquent, evil, immoral, mean, sinful, vile, villainous, wicked, wrong 4. naughty, unruly 5. decayed, mouldy, off, putrid, rancid, rotten, sour, spoiled 6. ailing, diseased, ill, sick, unwell 7. adverse, discouraged, discouraging, distressing, gloomy, grim, melancholy, troubled, unfortunate, unpleasant

badge brand, device, emblem, mark, sign, token

badger bully, chivvy, goad, harass, harry, hound, importune, nag, pester, plague, torment

badinage banter, chaff, drollery, mockery, persiflage, pleasantry, raillery, repartee, teasing, waggery, wordplay

badly 1. carelessly, defectively, faultily, imperfectly, inadequately, incorrectly, ineptly, poorly, shoddily, wrong, wrongly 2. unfortunately, unsuccessfully 3. criminally, evilly, immorally, improperly, naughtily, shamefully, unethically, wickedly

bag *v.* acquire, capture, catch, gain, get, kill, land, shoot, take, trap

baggage bags, belongings, equipment, gear, luggage, suitcases, things

baggy billowing, bulging, droopy, floppy, ill-fitting, loose, oversize, roomy, sagging, seated, slack

bail[1] *n.* bond, guarantee, guaranty, pledge, security, surety, warranty

bail[2], **bale** *v.* dip, drain off, ladle, scoop

bait 1. *n.* allurement, attraction, bribe, decoy, enticement, inducement, lure, snare, temptation 2. *v.* irritate, needle (*Inf.*), persecute, provoke, tease, torment

baked arid, dry, parched, scorched

balance *v.* 1. level, match,

poise, stabilize, steady **2.** adjust, compensate for, counteract, counterbalance, equalize, equate, make up for, neutralize, offset ~*n.* **3.** correspondence, equilibrium, equipoise, equity, equivalence, evenness, parity, symmetry **4.** composure, equanimity, poise, stability, steadiness **5.** difference, remainder, residue, rest, surplus

balcony **1.** terrace, veranda **2.** gallery, gods, upper circle

bald **1.** baldheaded, depilated, hairless **2.** uncovered

balk **1.** demur, evade, flinch, hesitate, jib, recoil, refuse, resist, shirk **2.** baffle, bar, check, defeat, hinder, obstruct, prevent, thwart

ball globe, orb, pellet, sphere, spheroid

ballast balance, equilibrium, sandbag, stabilizer, weight

ballot election, poll, polling, vote, voting

ballyhoo babble, commotion, fuss, hubbub, hue and cry, hullabaloo, noise, racket, to-do

ban **1.** *v.* banish, debar, disallow, exclude, forbid, outlaw, prohibit, proscribe, restrict, suppress **2.** *n.* boycott, censorship, embargo, prohibition, proscription, restriction, suppression, taboo

banal commonplace, everyday, hackneyed, humdrum, old hat, ordinary, pedestrian, platitudinous, stale, stereotyped, stock, threadbare, tired, trite, vapid

band[1] bandage, belt, bond, chain, cord, fetter, ribbon, shackle, strap, strip, tie

band[2] **1.** assembly, association, body, clique, club, company, coterie, crew (*Inf.*), gang, horde, party, society, troop **2.** ensemble, group, orchestra

bandage **1.** *n.* compress, dressing, gauze, plaster **2.** *v.* bind, cover, dress, swathe

bandit brigand, crook, desperado, freebooter, gangster, gunman, hijacker, marauder, outlaw, pirate, robber, thief

bang *n.* **1.** boom, burst, clang, clap, clash, detonation, explosion, peal, pop, report, shot, slam, thud, thump **2.** blow, box, bump, cuff, hit, knock, punch, smack, stroke, wallop (*Inf.*), whack ~*v.* **3.** bash (*Inf.*), beat, bump, clatter, crash, hammer, knock, pound, rap, slam, strike, thump

banish deport, drive away, eject, evict, exclude, exile, expel, ostracize, outlaw, shut out, transport

banishment deportation, exile, proscription

banisters balusters, balustrade, handrail, rail, railing

bank[1] **1.** *n.* depository, fund, hoard, repository, reserve, savings, stock, store, storehouse **2.** *v.* deal with, deposit, keep, save

bank[2] *n.* **1.** embankment, heap, mass, mound, pile, ridge **2.** brink, edge, margin, shore, side ~*v.* **3.** amass, heap, mass, mound, pile, stack **4.** camber, cant, incline, pitch, slant, slope, tilt, tip

bank[3] *n.* array, file, group, line, rank, row, sequence, series, succession, tier, train

bankrupt broke (*Inf.*), destitute, exhausted, failed, impoverished, insolvent, lacking, ruined, spent

banner burgee, colours, ensign, flag, pennant, standard, streamer

banquet dinner, feast, meal, repast, revel, treat

baptism **1.** christening **2.** beginning, debut, dedication, initiation, introduction

bar *n.* **1.** batten, crosspiece, paling, pole, rail, rod, shaft, stake, stick **2.** deterrent, hindrance, impediment, obstacle, rail, railing, stop **3.** canteen, counter, inn, lounge, pub (*Inf.*), public house, saloon, tavern **4.** bench, court, courtroom, dock, law court **5.** *Law* barristers, counsel, court, tribunal ~*v.* **6.** barricade, bolt, fasten, latch, lock, secure **7.** ban, exclude, forbid, hinder, keep out, obstruct, prevent, prohibit, restrain

barbarian *n.* **1.** hooligan, lout, ruffian, savage, vandal **2.** bigot, boor, ignoramus, illiterate, lowbrow, philistine

barbaric primitive, rude, uncivilized, wild

barbarism coarseness, crudity, savagery, uncivilizedness

bare **1.** denuded, exposed, naked, nude, peeled, shorn, stripped, unclad, unclothed, uncovered, undressed **2.** barren, blank, empty, lacking, mean, open, poor, scanty, scarce, unfurnished, vacant, void, wanting

barely almost, hardly, just, only just, scarcely

bargain *n.* **1.** agreement, business, compact, contract, negotiation, pact, pledge, promise, stipulation, transaction, treaty, understanding **2.** (cheap) purchase, discount, giveaway, good buy, good deal, good value, reduction, snip (*Inf.*) ~*v.* **3.** agree, contract, covenant, promise, stipulate, transact **4.** barter, buy, deal, haggle, sell, trade, traffic

barge canal boat, flatboat, lighter

bark[1] *n.* casing, cortex (*Anat., bot.*), covering, crust, husk, rind, skin

bark[2] *n./v.* bay, growl, howl, snarl, woof, yap, yelp

barmy *Also* **balmy** crazy, daft, foolish, idiotic, insane, loony (*Sl.*), nuts (*Sl.*), nutty (*Sl.*), odd, silly, stupid

barrage battery, bombardment, gunfire, salvo, shelling, volley

barren **1.** childless, infecund, infertile, sterile, unprolific **2.** arid, desert, desolate, dry, empty, unfruitful, unproductive, waste

barrier **1.** bar, barricade, blockade, boundary, ditch, fence, obstacle, obstruction, railing, rampart, stop, wall **2.** difficulty, drawback, hindrance, impediment, limitation, obstacle, restriction, stumbling block

barter bargain, exchange, haggle, sell, swap, trade, traffic

base *n.* **1.** bed, bottom, foot, foundation, groundwork, pedestal, rest, stand, support **2.** basis, core, essence, essential, fundamental, heart, key, origin, principal, root, source **3.** camp, centre, headquarters, home, post, settlement, starting point, station ~*v.* **4.** build, construct, depend, derive, establish, found, ground, hinge, locate, station

baseless groundless, unfounded, unjustified, unsubstantiated, unsupported

bashful blushing, coy, diffident, nervous, reserved, retiring, self-conscious, sheepish, shrinking, shy, timid, timorous

basic central, essential, fundamental, indispensable, intrinsic, key, necessary, primary, underlying, vital

basics brass tacks (*Inf.*), core, essentials, facts, hard facts, nitty-gritty (*Sl.*), practicalities, principles, rudiments

basis base, bottom, footing, foundation, ground, groundwork, support

bass deep, deep-toned, grave, low, low-pitched, resonant, sonorous

bastard **1.** *n.* illegitimate (child), love child, natural child **2.** *adj.* counterfeit, false, illegitimate, imperfect, impure, irregular, misbegotten, sham, spurious

bastion bulwark, citadel, defence, fortress, prop, rock, stronghold, support

bat bang, hit, rap, smack, strike, swat, thump, wallop (*Inf.*), whack

batch accumulation, amount, collection, crowd, group, lot, pack, set

bath **1.** *n.* ablution, douche, shower, soak, tub, wash **2.** *v.* bathe, clean, scrub down, soak, soap, sponge, tub, wash

bathe **1.** *v.* cleanse, immerse, moisten, rinse, soak, steep, wash, wet **2.** *n.* dip, swim

baton club, mace, rod, staff, stick, truncheon, wand

batten[1] board up, cover up, fasten down, fix, nail down, secure

batten[2] fatten, flourish, gain, grow, increase, prosper, thrive, wax

batter **1.** assault, beat, belabour, break, buffet, lash, pelt, pound, smash, smite, thrash **2.** bruise, crush, deface, demolish, destroy, disfigure, hurt, injure, mar, maul, ruin, shatter, shiver

battery assault, attack, beating, mayhem, onslaught, physical violence, thumping

battle action, attack, combat, encounter, engagement, fight, fray, hostilities, skirmish, war, warfare

batty barmy (*Sl.*), bats (*Sl.*), bonkers (*Sl.*), cracked (*Sl.*), crackers (*Sl.*), crazy, dotty (*Sl.*), eccentric, insane, loony (*Sl.*), mad, nuts (*Sl.*), nutty (*Sl.*), odd, peculiar, potty (*Inf.*), touched

bay[1] cove, gulf, inlet, sound

bay[2] alcove, niche, nook, opening, recess

bay[3] bark, bell, clamour, cry, growl, howl, yelp

bazaar **1.** exchange, market, marketplace, mart **2.** bring-and-buy, fair, fête

be **1.** be alive, breathe, exist, inhabit, live **2.** abide, continue, endure, last, obtain, persist, prevail, remain, stand, stay, survive

beach coast, sands, seashore, seaside, shingle, shore, strand, water's edge

beacon beam, bonfire, flare, lighthouse, sign, signal, watchtower

bead blob, bubble, dot, drop, droplet, globule, pill

beak **1.** bill, neb (*Archaic or dialect*), nib **2.** nose, proboscis, snout **3.** *Naut.* bow, prow, ram, rostrum, stem

beam *n.* **1.** girder, joist, plank, rafter, spar, support, timber **2.** gleam, glimmer, glint, glow, radiation, ray, shaft, streak, stream ~*v.* **3.** glare, gleam, glitter, glow, radiate, shine, transmit **4.** grin, laugh, smile

bear **1.** bring, carry, convey, move, take, tote, transport **2.** allow, endure, permit, put up with (*Inf.*), stomach, suffer, tolerate, undergo **3.** beget, breed, bring forth, generate, give birth to, produce, yield

bearable endurable, supportable, sustainable, tolerable

bearer carrier, conveyor, messenger, porter, runner, servant

bearing **1.** air, aspect, attitude, behaviour, carriage, demeanour, deportment, manner, mien, posture **2.** *Naut.* course, direction, point of compass **3.** connection, import, pertinence, relation, relevance

bear out confirm, endorse, justify, prove, support, uphold, vindicate

bear with be patient, make allowances, tolerate, wait

beast **1.** animal, brute, creature **2.** barbarian, brute, fiend, monster, ogre, sadist, savage, swine

beastly **1.** barbarous, bestial, brutal, brutish, coarse, cruel, depraved, inhuman, monstrous, sadistic, savage **2.** awful, foul, mean, nasty, unpleasant

beat *v.* **1.** bang, batter, break, buffet, cane, cudgel, drub, flog, hit, knock, lash, maul, pound, punch, strike, thrash, whip **2.** conquer, defeat, excel, outdo, outrun, overcome, subdue, surpass, vanquish ~*n.* **3.** blow, hit, lash, punch, slap, strike, swing, thump **4.** flutter, palpitation, pulsation, pulse, throb **5.** accent, cadence, measure, metre, rhythm, stress, time **6.** circuit, course, path, rounds, route, way

beaten **1.** cowed, defeated, disheartened, frustrated, overcome, overwhelmed, thwarted, vanquished **2.** blended, foamy, frothy, mixed, stirred, whipped, whisked

beautiful appealing, attractive, charming, comely, delightful, exquisite, fair, fine, good-looking, gorgeous, graceful, handsome, lovely, pleasing, radiant, stunning (*Inf.*)

beautify adorn, bedeck, deck, decorate, embellish, enhance, garnish, grace

beauty **1.** attractiveness, bloom, charm, elegance, fairness, glamour, grace, handsomeness, loveliness, pulchritude, seemliness **2.** belle, charmer, cracker (*Sl.*), good-looker, stunner (*Inf.*), Venus

becalmed settled, still, stranded

because as, by reason of, in that, on account of, owing to, since, thanks to

beckon bid, gesticulate, gesture, motion, nod, signal, summon, wave at

become **1.** alter to, be transformed into, change into, evolve into, grow into, mature into, ripen into **2.** embellish, enhance, fit, flatter, grace, harmonize, ornament, set off, suit

becoming attractive, comely, flattering, graceful, neat, pretty, tasteful

bed **1.** bedstead, berth, bunk, cot, couch, divan, pallet **2.** area, border, garden, patch, plot, row, strip

bedclothes bedding, bed linen, blankets, coverlets, covers, eiderdowns, pillowcases, pillows, quilts, sheets

bedeck adorn, array, decorate, embellish, festoon, ornament, trim

bedevil afflict, annoy, distress, fret, frustrate, harass, irk, irritate, pester, plague, torment, trouble, vex, worry

bedridden confined, incapacitated, laid up (*Inf.*)

bedrock bed, bottom, foundation, rock bottom, substratum

beef *Inf.* brawn, flesh, heftiness, muscle, physique, robustness, sinew, strength

befitting appropriate, becoming, fit, fitting, right, seemly, suitable

before **1.** *adv.* ahead, earlier, formerly, in advance, in front, previously, sooner **2.** *prep.* earlier than, in advance of, in front of, in the presence of, prior to

beforehand before now, earlier, in advance, previously, sooner

befriend advise, aid, assist, back, benefit, favour, help, patronize, side with, stand by, succour, support, sustain, uphold, welcome

beg **1.** beseech, crave, desire, entreat, implore, importune, petition, plead, pray, request, solicit, supplicate **2.** cadge, call for alms, sponge on

beggar cadger, mendicant, scrounger (*Inf.*), sponger (*Inf.*), supplicant, tramp, vagrant

begin commence, embark on, initiate, instigate, institute, prepare, set about, set on foot, start

beginner amateur, apprentice, fledgling, freshman, greenhorn (*Inf.*), initiate, learner, neophyte, novice, recruit, starter, student, tenderfoot, trainee, tyro

beginning birth, commencement, inauguration, inception, initiation, onset, opening, origin, outset, preface, prelude, rise, rudiments, source, start, starting point

begrudge be jealous, envy, grudge, resent

behave **1.** act, function, operate, perform, run, work **2.** act correctly, conduct oneself properly, mind one's manners

behaviour **1.** actions, bearing, carriage, conduct, demeanour, deportment, manner, manners, ways **2.** action, operation, performance

behind *prep.* **1.** after, at the back of, at the rear of, following, later than **2.** at the bottom of, causing, initiating, instigating, responsible for **3.** backing, for, in agreement, on the side of, supporting *~adv.* **4.** after, afterwards, following, in the wake (of), next, subsequently **5.** behindhand, in arrears, in debt, overdue

behold consider, contemplate, discern, eye, look at, observe, regard, scan, view, watch, witness

being **1.** actuality, existence, life, living, reality **2.** entity, essence, nature, soul, spirit, substance **3.** animal, beast, body, creature, human being, individual, living thing, mortal, thing

belated delayed, late, overdue, tardy

beleaguered beset, besieged, bothered, harassed, nagged, persecuted, plagued, put upon, set upon, vexed

belief **1.** admission, assurance, confidence, conviction, credit, feeling, impression, judgment, notion, opinion, persuasion, reliance, theory, trust, view **2.** credence, credo, creed, doctrine, dogma, faith, ideology, principles, tenet

believe **1.** accept, be certain of, be convinced of, count on, credit, depend on, have faith in, hold, place confidence in, swear by, trust **2.** assume, consider, gather, guess, imagine, judge, postulate, presume, reckon, speculate, suppose, think

believer adherent, convert, devotee, disciple, follower, proselyte, supporter

bellow bawl, call, clamour, cry, howl, roar, scream, shout, shriek, yell

belong **1.** *With* **to** be at the disposal of, be held by, be owned by **2.** *With* **to** be allied to, be a member of, be associated with, be included in **3.** attach to, be connected with, be part of, fit, go with

belongings effects, gear, goods, personal property, possessions, things

beloved adored, cherished, darling, dear, dearest, loved, precious, sweet

below **1.** *adv.* beneath, down, lower, under, underneath **2.** *prep.* inferior, lesser, lesser than, subject, subordinate, unworthy of

belt band, girdle, girth, sash, waistband

bemused bewildered, confused, dazed, fuddled, muddled, perplexed, stunned, stupefied, tipsy

bench **1.** form, pew, seat, settle **2.** counter, table, workbench, worktable **3.** court, courtroom, judge, judges, judiciary, magistrate, magistrates

bend **1.** *v.* bow, buckle, contort, curve, diverge, flex, incline, lean, stoop, swerve, turn, twist, veer, warp **2.** *n.* angle, arc, bow, corner, crook, curve, hook, loop, turn, twist

beneath **1.** *adv.* below, in a lower place, underneath **2.** *prep.* below, inferior to, less than, lower than, unbefitting, underneath, unworthy of

beneficial advantageous, favourable, healthful, helpful, useful, valuable, wholesome

benefit **1.** *n.* advantage, aid, asset, blessing, boon, favour, gain, good, help, interest, profit, use **2.** *v.* advance, aid, assist, avail, better, enhance, further, improve, profit, promote, serve

bent *adj.* **1.** angled, arched, bowed, crooked, curved, hunched, twisted **2.** *With* **on** determined, inclined, insistent, resolved, set *~n.* **3.** ability, aptitude, flair, forte, inclination, penchant, proclivity, propensity, talent

bequest dower, endowment, estate, gift, heritage, inheritance, legacy, settlement, trust

bereavement death, deprivation, loss

berserk crazy, frenzied, insane, mad, manic, rabid, raging, violent, wild

berth *n.* **1.** bed, billet, bunk **2.** anchorage, dock, harbour, haven, pier, port, quay, wharf

beseech ask, beg, crave, entreat, implore, importune, petition, plead, pray, solicit, sue, supplicate

beside abreast of, adjacent to, alongside, at the side of, close to, near, nearby, neighbouring, next door to, next to, overlooking

besides *adv.* also, as well, further, furthermore, in addition, moreover, otherwise, too, what's more

besiege beleaguer, beset, blockade, encircle, encompass, hedge in, hem in, lay siege to, shut in, surround

besotted **1.** befuddled, drunk, intoxicated, stupefied **2.** doting, hypnotized, infatuated, smitten, spellbound

best *adj.* **1.** chief, finest, first, first-class, first-rate, foremost, highest, leading, outstanding, perfect, pre-eminent, superlative, supreme, unsurpassed **2.** apt, correct, most desirable, most fitting, right **3.** greatest, largest, most *~adv.* **4.** advantageously, excellently, most fortunately **5.** extremely, greatly, most deeply, most fully, most highly *~n.* **6.** choice, cream, elite, finest, first, flower, pick, prime, top

bestial animal, beastly, brutal, brutish, carnal, depraved, gross, inhuman, low, savage, sensual, sordid, vile

bestow accord, allot, award, commit, confer, donate, entrust, give, grant, impart, lavish, present

bet **1.** *n.* ante, gamble, hazard, pledge, risk, speculation, stake, venture, wager **2.** *v.* chance, gamble, hazard, pledge, risk, speculate, stake, venture, wager

betray **1.** be disloyal, break with, double-cross (*Inf.*), inform on *or* against, sell out (*Inf.*) **2.** disclose, divulge, evince, expose, give away, lay bare, let slip, reveal, show, tell, tell on, uncover, unmask **3.** abandon, desert, forsake, jilt, walk out on

betrayal **1.** disloyalty, double-cross (*Inf.*), double-dealing, duplicity, falseness, perfidy, sell-out (*Inf.*), treachery, treason, trickery **2.** disclosure, revelation, telling

better *adj.* **1.** bigger, excelling, finer, fitter, greater, higher quality, larger, preferable, superior, surpassing, worthier **2.** cured, fitter, healthier, improving, more healthy, on the mend (*Inf.*), progressing, recovering, stronger, well **3.** bigger, greater, larger, longer *~adv.* **4.** in a more excellent manner, in a superior way, to a greater degree

between amidst, among, halfway, in the middle of, mid

beverage draught, drink, liquid, liquor, refreshment

bevy covey, flight, flock

bewail cry over, deplore, grieve for, lament, moan, mourn, regret, repent, rue, wail

beware avoid, be careful (cautious, wary), guard against, heed, look out, mind, shun, steer clear of, take heed, watch out

bewilder bemuse, confound, confuse, daze, mix up, mystify, perplex, puzzle

bewildered confused, dizzy, giddy, mystified, perplexed, puzzled, startled, surprised, taken aback, uncertain

bewitch allure, beguile, charm, enchant, entrance, fascinate, spellbind

bewitched charmed, enchanted, entranced, spellbound

beyond above, apart from, at a distance, away from, before, farther, out of range, out of reach, over, past, remote

bias favouritism, inclination, leaning, narrow-mindedness, one-sidedness, partiality, prejudice, proneness, propensity, tendency, turn, unfairness

biased distorted, one-sided, partial, prejudiced, slanted, swayed, twisted, warped, weighted

bicker argue, disagree, dispute, fight, quarrel, squabble

bid *v.* **1.** offer, proffer, propose, submit, tender **2.** call, greet, say, tell, wish **3.** ask, call, charge, command, desire, direct, enjoin, instruct, invite, require, solicit, summon, tell *~n.* **4.** offer, price, proposal, proposition, sum, tender **5.** attempt, effort, try, venture

bidding behest, call, charge, command, demand, invitation, order, request, summons

big **1.** bulky, burly, colossal, enormous, extensive, gigantic, great, huge, hulking, immense, large, mammoth, massive, prodigious, sizable, spacious, substantial, vast, voluminous **2.** eminent, important, leading, main, powerful, principal, prominent, serious, significant, valuable, weighty **3.** generous, gracious, heroic, magnanimous, noble, princely **4.** arrogant, boastful, bragging, conceited, haughty, inflated, pompous, pretentious, proud

bill[1] *n.* **1.** account, charges, invoice, reckoning, score, statement, tally **2.** advertisement, broadsheet, circular, handbill, handout, leaflet, notice, placard, playbill, poster **3.** measure, projected law, proposal *~v.* **4.** charge, debit, figure, invoice

bill[2] beak, mandible

billet **1.** *n.* accommodation, barracks, lodging, quarters **2.** *v.* accommodate, berth, quarter, station

billow *n.* **1.** breaker, surge, swell, tide, wave **2.** cloud, deluge, flood, rush, surge, wave *~v.* **3.** balloon, puff up, rise up, roll, surge, swell

bind *v.* **1.** attach, fasten, glue, hitch, lash, paste, rope, secure, stick, strap, tie, tie up **2.** compel, constrain, force, necessitate, oblige **3.** confine, detain, hamper, hinder, restrain, restrict **4.** bandage, dress, wrap **5.** border, edge, finish, hem, trim

binding *adj.* compulsory, indissoluble, irrevocable, mandatory, obligatory, unalterable

birth 1. childbirth, delivery, nativity, parturition **2.** beginning, emergence, genesis, origin, rise, source **3.** ancestry, background, blood, breeding, descent, genealogy, line, lineage, nobility, pedigree, race, stock, strain

bisect cut in half, cut in two, divide in two, halve

bit[1] chip, crumb, fragment, grain, iota, jot, mite, morsel, part, piece, scrap, slice, speck, tittle, whit

bit[2] brake, check, curb, restraint, snaffle

bite *v.* **1.** chew, clamp, crunch, crush, cut, gnaw, grip, hold, nibble, nip, pierce, pinch, rend, seize, snap, tear, wound ~*n.* **2.** itch, nip, pinch, prick, sting, tooth marks, wound **3.** food, light meal, morsel, mouthful, piece, snack **4.** edge, piquancy, spice

bitter 1. acid, acrid, astringent, sharp, sour, tart, unsweetened, vinegary **2.** hostile, morose, rancorous, resentful, sore, sour, sullen

bitterness 1. acerbity, acidity, sharpness, sourness, tartness **2.** grudge, hostility, pique, rancour, resentment

bizarre curious, eccentric, extraordinary, fantastic, freakish, grotesque, ludicrous, odd, off-beat, outlandish, outré, peculiar, queer, strange, unusual, weird

black *adj.* **1.** dark, dusky, ebony, inky, jet, murky, sable, starless, swarthy **2.** *Fig.* depressing, dismal, distressing, doleful, foreboding, funereal, gloomy, hopeless, lugubrious, mournful, ominous, sad, sombre **3.** bad, evil, iniquitous, nefarious, villainous, wicked ~*v.* **4.** ban, bar, blacklist, boycott

blacken 1. befoul, cloud, darken, make black, smudge, soil **2.** calumniate, decry, defame, defile, denigrate, dishonour, malign, slander, smear, smirch, stain, sully, taint, tarnish, traduce, vilify

blackguard bounder (*Brit. inf.*), miscreant, rascal, rogue, scoundrel, swine, villain, wretch

blacklist *v.* ban, bar, boycott, debar, exclude, expel, ostracize, preclude, proscribe, reject, snub, vote against

black magic necromancy, sorcery, voodoo, witchcraft, wizardry

blackmail *n.* bribe, exaction, extortion, hush money (*Sl.*), intimidation, protection (*Inf.*), ransom

blackness darkness, duskiness, gloom, murkiness

blackout *n.* **1.** coma, faint, oblivion, swoon, unconsciousness **2.** power cut, power failure

black sheep disgrace, ne'er-do-well, outcast, prodigal, renegade, reprobate, wastrel

blame *n.* **1.** culpability, fault, guilt, incrimination, liability, onus, responsibility **2.** accusation, censure, charge, complaint, condemnation, criticism, recrimination, reproach, reproof ~*v.* **3.** accuse, admonish, censure, charge, chide, condemn, criticize, disapprove, find fault with, hold responsible, reprehend, reproach, reprove, tax, upbraid

blameless above suspicion, clean, faultless, guiltless, innocent, in the clear, irreproachable, perfect, stainless, unblemished, upright, virtuous

bland 1. boring, dull, flat, humdrum, insipid, tasteless, tedious, vapid, weak **2.** affable, amiable, congenial, courteous, friendly, gentle, gracious, smooth, suave, urbane

blank *adj.* **1.** bare, clean, clear, empty, plain, spotless, unfilled, unmarked, void, white **2.** at a loss, bewildered, confounded, confused, nonplussed, uncomprehending ~*n.* **3.** emptiness, empty space, gap, nothingness, space, vacancy, vacuum, void

blanket *n.* **1.** cover, coverlet, rug **2.** carpet, cloak, coat, coating, covering, envelope, film, layer, mantle, sheet, wrapper, wrapping ~*v.* **3.** cloak, cloud, coat, conceal, cover, hide, mask, obscure

blare blast, boom, clang, honk, hoot, peal, resound, roar, trumpet

blaspheme curse, damn, desecrate, execrate, profane, swear

blasphemous godless, impious, profane, sacrilegious, ungodly

blasphemy cursing, desecration, execration, impiety, impiousness, profaneness, profanity, sacrilege, swearing

blast *n./v.* **1.** blare, blow, clang, honk, peal, scream, toot, wail ~*n.* **2.** bang, blow-up, burst, crash, explosion, outburst, salvo, volley ~*v.* **3.** blow up, break up, burst, demolish, destroy, explode, ruin, shatter

blatant brazen, conspicuous, flagrant, glaring, naked, obvious, ostentatious, outright, overt, prominent, sheer

blaze *n.* **1.** bonfire, conflagration, fire, flame, flames **2.** beam, brilliance, flare, flash, glare, gleam, glitter, glow, light, radiance ~*v.* **3.** beam, burn, fire, flame, flare, flash, glare, gleam, glow, shine **4.** boil, explode, flare up, fume, seethe

bleak 1. bare, barren, chilly, cold, desolate, exposed, gaunt, open, raw, windswept, windy **2.** cheerless, depressing, dismal, dreary, gloomy, grim, hopeless, joyless, sombre, unpromising

bleed 1. exude, flow, gush, lose blood, ooze, run, seep, shed blood, spurt, trickle, weep **2.** drain, draw *or* take blood, exhaust, extort, extract, fleece, milk, reduce, sap

blemish *n.* blot, blotch, blur, defect, disfigurement, disgrace, dishonour, fault, flaw, imperfection, mark, smudge, speck, spot, stain, taint

blend *v.* **1.** coalesce, combine, compound, fuse, intermix, merge, mingle, mix, unite **2.** complement, fit, go well, go with, harmonize, suit ~*n.* **3.** alloy, amalgam, composite, compound, concoction, fusion, mix, mixture, synthesis, union

bless 1. consecrate, dedicate, exalt, extol, glorify, hallow, magnify, ordain, praise, sanctify, thank **2.** bestow, endow, favour, give, grace, grant, provide

blessed 1. adored, beatified, divine, hallowed, holy, revered, sacred, sanctified **2.** endowed, favoured, fortunate, granted, lucky

blessing 1. benediction, benison, consecration, dedication, grace, invocation, thanksgiving **2.** approval, backing, consent, favour, leave, permission, regard, sanction, support **3.** advantage, benefit, boon, bounty, favour, gain, gift, godsend, good fortune, help, kindness, profit, service, windfall

blight *n.* **1.** canker, decay, disease, fungus, infestation, mildew, pest, rot ~*v.* **2.** blast, destroy, injure, nip in the bud, ruin, shrivel, wither **3.** annihilate, crush, dash, disappoint, frustrate, mar, nullify, ruin, spoil, wreck

blind *adj.* **1.** eyeless, sightless, unseeing, unsighted, visionless **2.** *Fig.* careless, heedless, ignorant, inattentive, inconsiderate, indifferent, insensitive, neglectful, oblivious, prejudiced, thoughtless, unaware of, unconscious of, uncritical, undiscerning, unmindful of, unobservant, unreasoning **3.** hasty, impetuous, irrational, mindless, rash, reckless, senseless, unthinking, violent, wild ~*n.* **4.** camouflage, cloak, cover, façade, feint, front, mask, screen, smoke screen

blindly aimlessly, at random, confusedly, frantically, indiscriminately, instinctively, madly, purposelessly, wildly

bliss beatitude, blessedness, ecstasy, euphoria, happiness, heaven, joy, paradise, rapture

blissful delighted, ecstatic, elated, enchanted, euphoric, happy, joyful, rapturous

blister abscess, boil, canker, carbuncle, cyst, pimple, sore, swelling, ulcer

blithe buoyant, carefree, cheerful, cheery, debonair, gay, happy, jaunty, light-hearted, merry, mirthful, sprightly, sunny, vivacious

blizzard blast, gale, snowstorm, squall, storm, tempest

block *n.* **1.** bar, brick, cake, chunk, cube, hunk, ingot, lump, mass, piece, square **2.** bar, barrier, blockage, hindrance, impediment, jam, obstacle, obstruction, stoppage ~*v.* **3.** choke, clog, close, obstruct, plug, stop up **4.** bar, check, deter, halt, hinder, impede, obstruct, stop

blockade barrier, closure, hindrance, impediment, obstacle, obstruction, restriction, siege, stoppage

blood 1. gore, lifeblood, vital fluid **2.** ancestry, birth, descent, extraction, family, kindred, kinship, lineage, relations

bloodshed blood bath, butchery, carnage, gore, killing, massacre, murder, slaughter

bloodthirsty brutal, cruel, ferocious, inhuman, ruthless, savage, vicious, warlike

bloody 1. bleeding, blood-soaked, bloodstained, raw **2.** cruel, ferocious, fierce, savage

bloom *n.* **1.** blossom, blossoming, bud, flower **2.** *Fig.* beauty, flush, freshness, glow, health, heyday, lustre, perfection, prime, radiance, rosiness ~*v.* **3.** blossom, blow, bud, burgeon, open, sprout

blossom *n.* **1.** bloom, bud, flower, flowers ~*v.* **2.** bloom, burgeon, flower **3.** *Fig.* bloom, develop, flourish, grow, mature, progress, prosper, thrive

blot *n.* **1.** mark, patch, smear, smudge, speck, splodge, spot **2.** blemish, blur, defect, disgrace, fault, flaw, spot, stain, taint

blow[1] *v.* **1.** blast, breathe, exhale, fan, pant, puff, waft **2.** flow, rush, stream, whirl **3.** bear, buffet, drive, fling, flutter, sweep, waft **4.** pipe, play, sound, trumpet, vibrate ~*n.* **5.** blast, draught, flurry, gale, gust, puff, strong breeze, tempest, wind

blow[2] *n.* **1.** bang, buffet, knock, punch, rap, smack, stroke, thump, wallop (*Inf.*), whack **2.** *Fig.* bombshell, calamity, catastrophe, disappointment, disaster, jolt, misfortune, reverse, setback, shock, upset

blow up 1. distend, enlarge, expand, fill, inflate, swell **2.** blast, bomb, burst, detonate, explode, go off, rupture, shatter **3.** enlarge, enlarge on, exaggerate, heighten, magnify, overstate

blue 1. azure, cobalt, navy, sapphire, ultramarine **2.** *Fig.* dejected, depressed, despondent, dismal, downcast, downhearted, fed up, gloomy, glum, low, melancholy, sad, unhappy

blueprint design, draft, layout, outline, pattern, pilot scheme, plan, project, prototype, scheme, sketch

bluff 1. *v.* deceive, delude, fake, feign, humbug, lie, mislead, pretend, sham **2.** *n.* bluster, boast, deceit, deception, fake, feint, fraud, humbug, idle boast, lie, mere show, pretence, sham, show, subterfuge

blunder 1. *n.* error, fault, mistake, oversight, slip **2.** *v.* botch, bungle, err

blunt 1. dull, rounded, unsharpened **2.** *Fig.* bluff, brusque, forthright, frank, impolite, outspoken, plain-spoken, rude, tactless, trenchant, uncivil

blur *v.* **1.** befog, cloud, darken, dim, fog, make hazy, mask, obscure, soften **2.** blot, smear, smudge, spot, stain ~*n.* **3.** blear, confusion, dimness, fog, haze, indistinctness, obscurity

blush colour, crimson, flush, redden, turn red

bluster 1. *v.* boast, brag, bulldoze, bully, domineer, hector, rant, roar, storm, swagger, swell, vaunt **2.** *n.* bombast, bragging, bravado, crowing, swagger

board *n.* **1.** panel, plank, slat, timber **2.** daily meals, food, meals, provisions **3.** committee, conclave, council, directorate, directors, panel, trustees ~*v.* **4.** embark, embus, enplane, enter, entrain, mount **5.** accommodate, feed, house, lodge, put up, quarter, room

boast *v.* 1. bluster, brag, crow, exaggerate, puff, strut, swagger, talk big (*Sl.*), vaunt 2. be proud of, exhibit, flatter oneself, possess, show off ~*n.* 3. avowal, brag, swank (*Inf.*), vaunt 4. gem, joy, pride, pride and joy, source of pride, treasure

boastful cocky, conceited, crowing, egotistical, puffed-up, swaggering, swollen-headed, vainglorious

body 1. build, figure, form, frame, physique, shape, torso, trunk 2. cadaver, carcass, corpse, dead body, remains 3. bulk, essence, main part, mass, material, matter, substance 4. association, band, collection, company, congress, corporation, society 5. crowd, horde, majority, mass, mob, multitude, throng

bog fen, marsh, mire, morass, peat bog, quagmire, slough, swamp

bogey 1. apparition, bogeyman, goblin, hobgoblin, imp, spectre, spirit, spook (*Inf.*), sprite 2. bugbear, nightmare

bogus artificial, counterfeit, dummy, fake, false, forged, fraudulent, imitation, sham, spurious

bohemian avant-garde, eccentric, exotic, left bank, nonconformist, offbeat, unconventional, unorthodox

boil agitate, bubble, churn, effervesce, fizz, foam, froth, seethe

boisterous bouncy, clamorous, impetuous, loud, noisy, riotous, rollicking, rowdy, rumbustious, unrestrained, unruly, uproarious, vociferous, wild

bold 1. adventurous, audacious, brave, courageous, daring, dauntless, enterprising, fearless, gallant, heroic, intrepid, valiant 2. bright, colourful, conspicuous, eye-catching, flashy, lively, loud, prominent, spirited, striking, strong, vivid

bolt *n.* 1. bar, catch, latch, lock 2. peg, pin, rivet, rod 3. spring, sprint 4. arrow, dart, missile, projectile, shaft, thunderbolt ~*v.* 5. bar, fasten, latch, lock, secure 6. cram, devour, gobble, gorge, gulp, guzzle, stuff, wolf 7. abscond, bound, dash, escape, flee, fly, hurtle, jump, leap, run, rush, spring, sprint

bomb 1. *n.* bombshell, charge, device, explosive, grenade, mine, missile, projectile, rocket, shell, torpedo 2. *v.* attack, blow up, bombard, destroy, shell, strafe, torpedo

bona fide authentic, genuine, lawful, legal, legitimate, real, true

bond *n.* 1. band, binding, chain, cord, fastening, fetter, link, shackle, tie 2. affinity, attachment, connection, link, relation, tie, union 3. compact, contract, covenant, guarantee, obligation, pledge, promise, word ~*v.* 4. bind, connect, fasten, fix together, fuse, glue, gum, paste

bonus benefit, bounty, commission, dividend, extra, gift, gratuity, hand-out, prize, reward

book *n.* 1. manual, publication, roll, textbook, tome, tract, volume, work 2. album, diary, jotter, notebook, pad ~*v.* 3. arrange for, bill, charter, engage, line up, make reservations, organize, reserve, schedule

boom *v.* 1. bang, blast, crash, explode, resound, reverberate, roar, roll, rumble, thunder 2. develop, expand, flourish, gain, grow, increase, intensify, prosper, spurt, succeed, swell, thrive ~*n.* 3. bang, blast, burst, clap, crash, explosion, roar, rumble, thunder 4. advance, development, expansion, gain, growth, improvement, increase, spurt, upsurge

boon advantage, benefaction, benefit, blessing, favour, gift, grant, present, windfall

boost *n.* 1. help, improvement, praise, promotion 2. heave, hoist, lift, push, raise, shove, thrust 3. addition, expansion, improvement, increase, increment, jump, rise ~*v.* 4. advance, advertise, assist, encourage, foster, further, improve, inspire, plug (*Inf.*), praise, promote, support, sustain 5. elevate, heave, hoist, lift, push, raise, shove, thrust

boot *v. Inf.* dismiss, eject, expel, kick out, oust, sack (*Inf.*), throw out

border 1. bound, boundary, bounds, brim, brink, confine, confines, edge, hem, limit, limits, lip, margin, rim, skirt, verge 2. borderline, boundary, frontier, line, march

borderline doubtful, indecisive, indefinite, indeterminate, inexact, marginal, unclassifiable

bore[1] 1. *v.* drill, mine, penetrate, pierce, sink, tunnel 2. *n.* borehole, calibre, drill hole, hole, shaft, tunnel

bore[2] 1. *v.* be tedious, bother, exhaust, fatigue, pall on, tire, trouble, vex, wear out, weary, worry 2. *n.* bother, drag (*Sl.*), dull person, nuisance, pain (*Inf.*), pest, tiresome person

boredom apathy, dullness, ennui, flatness, monotony, sameness, tedium, tediousness, weariness

boring dead, dull, flat, humdrum, insipid, monotonous, routine, stale, tedious, tiresome, tiring, unexciting, uninteresting, unvaried, wearisome

borrow 1. take on loan, use temporarily 2. acquire, adopt, appropriate, copy, imitate, obtain, pilfer, pirate, simulate, steal, take, use, usurp

bosom *n.* 1. breast, bust, chest 2. affections, emotions, feelings, heart, sentiments, spirit ~*adj.* 3. boon, cherished, close, intimate, very dear

boss[1] chief, director, employer, executive, foreman, gaffer (*Inf.*), governor (*Inf.*), head, leader, manager, master, overseer, owner, supervisor

boss[2] knob, nub, nubble, point, protuberance, stud, tip

botch *v.* blunder, bungle, cobble, fumble, mar, mend, mess, muff, patch, spoil

bother 1. *v.* alarm, annoy, concern, dismay, distress, disturb, harass, inconvenience, irritate, molest, nag, pester, plague, put out, trouble, upset, vex, worry 2. *n.* annoyance, bustle, difficulty, flurry, fuss, inconvenience, irritation, nuisance, pest, problem, strain, trouble, vexation, worry

bottom *n.* 1. base, basis, bed, deepest part, depths, floor, foot, foundation, groundwork, lowest part, pedestal, support 2. lower side, sole, underneath, underside ~*adj.* 3. base, basement, basic, fundamental, ground, last, lowest, undermost

bounce *v.* 1. bound, bump, jump, leap, rebound, recoil, ricochet, spring, thump ~*n.* 2. bound, elasticity, give, rebound, recoil, resilience, spring, springiness 3. animation, dynamism, energy, go (*Inf.*), life, liveliness, pep, vigour, vitality, vivacity, zip (*Inf.*)

bound[1] *adj.* 1. cased, fastened, fixed, secured, tied, tied up 2. certain, destined, doomed, fated, sure 3. compelled, constrained, forced, obligated, obliged, pledged, required

bound[2] *v./n.* bounce, caper, frisk, gambol, hurdle, jump, leap, pounce, prance, skip, spring, vault

bound[3] *n. Usually plural* border, boundary, confine, edge, extremity, fringe, limit, line, march, margin, rim, verge

boundary barrier, border, borderline, bounds, brink, confines, edge, extremity, fringe, frontier, limits, margin, precinct

boundless endless, immense, incalculable, inexhaustible, infinite, measureless, unbounded, unconfined, unending, unlimited, untold, vast

bountiful 1. abundant, ample, copious, lavish, plenteous, plentiful, prolific 2. beneficent, generous, liberal, munificent, openhanded, princely, unstinting

bout competition, contest, encounter, engagement, fight, match, set-to

bow *v.* 1. bend, droop, genuflect, incline, make obeisance, nod, stoop 2. accept, comply, concede, defer, give in, relent, submit, surrender, yield ~*n.* 3. bending, bob, genuflexion, inclination, nod, obeisance

bowl basin, deep dish, vessel

box[1] carton, case, chest, container, pack, package, trunk

box[2] *v.* 1. exchange blows, fight, spar 2. buffet, clout (*Inf.*), cuff, hit, punch, slap, strike, wallop (*Inf.*), whack ~*n.* 3. blow, buffet, cuff, punch, slap, stroke, wallop (*Inf.*)

boxer fighter, prizefighter, pugilist, sparrer, sparring partner

boy fellow, junior, lad, schoolboy, stripling, youngster, youth

boycott ban, bar, black, blackball, blacklist, exclude, outlaw, prohibit, proscribe, refuse, reject, spurn

boyfriend admirer, date, follower, lover, man, steady, suitor, swain

bracing brisk, cool, crisp, energizing, exhilarating, fresh, invigorating, lively, refreshing, stimulating, tonic, vigorous

brain genius, highbrow, intellectual, prodigy, pundit, sage

brainless foolish, idiotic, inept, mindless, senseless, stupid, thoughtless, unintelligent, witless

brake 1. *n.* check, constraint, control, curb, rein, restraint 2. *v.* check, decelerate, halt, moderate, reduce speed, slacken, slow, stop

branch 1. arm, bough, limb, offshoot, prong, ramification, shoot, spray, sprig 2. chapter, department, division, local office, office, part, section, subdivision, subsection, wing

brand *n.* 1. cast, class, grade, kind, make, quality, sort, species, type, variety 2. hallmark, label, mark, sign, stamp, symbol, trademark ~*v.* 3. burn, burn in, label, mark, scar, stamp 4. denounce, disgrace, expose, mark, stigmatize

brandish display, exhibit, flourish, raise, shake, swing, wield

bravado bluster, boastfulness, bombast, brag, swagger

brave bold, courageous, daring, fearless, gallant, heroic, intrepid, plucky, resolute, valiant

bravery boldness, courage, daring, fortitude, gallantry, grit, guts (*Inf.*), hardiness, heroism, intrepidity, mettle, pluck, pluckiness, spirit, valour

bravura animation, audacity, boldness, brilliance, brio, daring, dash, display, élan, energy, exhibitionism, ostentation, panache, punch (*Inf.*), spirit, verve, vigour, virtuosity

brawl 1. *n.* argument, battle, broil, clash, disorder, dispute, fight, fracas, fray, free-for-all (*Inf.*), quarrel, row (*Inf.*), rumpus, scrap (*Inf.*), uproar, wrangle 2. *v.* battle, dispute, fight, quarrel, row (*Inf.*), scrap (*Inf.*), scuffle, wrangle, wrestle

breach 1. break, chasm, cleft, crack, fissure, gap, hole, opening, rent, rift, rupture, split 2. infringement, offence, transgression, trespass, violation

bread diet, fare, food, nourishment, nutriment, provisions, subsistence, sustenance, viands, victuals

breadth 1. latitude, span, spread, wideness, width 2. freedom, latitude, liberality, openness, permissiveness

break *v.* 1. batter, burst, crack, crash, demolish, destroy, divide, fracture, fragment, part, rend, separate, shatter, shiver, smash, snap, splinter, split, tear 2. breach, disobey, disregard, infringe, transgress, violate 3. demoralize, dispirit, enfeeble, impair, incapacitate, subdue, tame, undermine, weaken 4. *Of a record, etc.* beat, better, cap (*Inf.*), exceed, excel, go beyond, outdo, outstrip, surpass, top 5. appear, burst out, emerge, erupt, happen, occur 6. dash, escape, flee, fly, get away, run away ~*n.* 7. breach, cleft, crack, division, fissure, fracture, gap, gash, hole, opening, rent, rift, rupture, split, tear 8. breather (*Inf.*), halt, interlude, intermission, interruption, interval, let-up (*Inf.*), lull, pause, recess, respite, rest, suspension 9. alienation, breach, disaffection, estrangement, rift, rupture, separation, split

break away 1. escape, flee, fly, make off, run away 2. detach, part company, secede, separate

breakdown 1. collapse, disintegration, disruption, failure, stoppage 2. analysis, detailed list, diagnosis, dissection, itemization

break-in burglary, invasion, robbery

break in 1. barge in, butt in, interfere, interject, interpose, interrupt, intervene, intrude 2. burgle, invade, rob 3. accustom, condition, get used to, prepare, tame, train

break off 1. detach, divide, part, pull off, separate, snap off, splinter 2. cease, desist, discontinue, end, finish, halt, pause, stop, suspend, terminate

break out 1. appear, arise, begin, commence, emerge, happen, occur, set in, spring up, start 2. abscond, bolt, break loose, burst out, escape, flee, get free 3. burst out, erupt

breakthrough advance, development, discovery, find, gain, improvement, invention, leap, progress

break-up disintegration, dispersal, dissolution, divorce, ending, parting, rift, separation, split, splitting, termination

break up adjourn, disband, dismantle, disperse, disrupt, dissolve, divide, divorce, end, part, scatter, separate, sever, split, stop, suspend, terminate

breath 1. air, exhalation, gasp, gulp, inhalation, pant, respiration, wheeze 2. aroma, odour, smell, vapour, whiff 3. faint breeze, flutter, gust, puff, sigh, waft, zephyr 4. hint, murmur, suggestion, suspicion, undertone, whisper

breathe 1. draw in, gasp, gulp, inhale and exhale, pant, puff, respire, wheeze 2. articulate, express, murmur, say, sigh, utter, voice, whisper

breathless 1. exhausted, gasping, gulping, out of breath, panting, spent, wheezing, winded 2. agog, anxious, astounded, avid, eager, excited, with bated breath

breathtaking amazing, astonishing, awe-inspiring, awesome, exciting, impressive, magnificent, moving, overwhelming, stunning (*Inf.*), thrilling

breed *v.* 1. bear, beget, bring forth, engender, generate, hatch, multiply, originate, procreate, produce, propagate, reproduce 2. bring up, cultivate, develop, foster, instruct, nourish, nurture, raise, rear ~*n.* 3. brand, class, extraction, family, ilk, kind, line, lineage, pedigree, progeny, race, sort, species, stamp, stock, strain, type, variety

breeding 1. ancestry, lineage, nurture, raising, rearing, reproduction, training, upbringing 2. civility, conduct, courtesy, cultivation, culture, gentility, manners, polish, refinement, urbanity

breeze air, draught, flurry, gust, light wind, puff of air, waft, whiff, zephyr

brevity 1. conciseness, crispness, curtness, economy, pithiness, succinctness, terseness 2. ephemerality, impermanence, shortness, transience, transitoriness

brew *v.* 1. boil, ferment, infuse (*tea*), make (*beer*), seethe, soak, steep, stew 2. breed, concoct, contrive, develop, devise, excite, foment, form, gather, hatch, plan, plot, project, scheme, start, stir up

bribe 1. *n.* allurement, enticement, graft, hush money (*Sl.*), incentive, inducement, pay-off (*Inf.*) 2. *v.* buy off, corrupt, get at, grease the palm *or* hand of (*Sl.*), influence by gifts, lure, pay off (*Inf.*), reward, square, suborn

bribery buying off, corruption, graft, inducement

bridge *n.* 1. arch, flyover, overpass, span, viaduct 2. band, bond, connection, link, tie ~*v.* 3. arch over, attach, bind, connect, couple, cross, cross over, extend across, go over, join, link, reach across, span, traverse, unite

bridle *v.* 1. check, constrain, control, curb, govern, master, moderate, repress, restrain, subdue 2. be indignant, bristle, get angry, raise one's hackles, rear up

brief *adj.* 1. compressed, concise, crisp, curt, laconic, limited, pithy, short, succinct, terse, thumbnail, to the point 2. fast, fleeting, little, momentary, quick, short, short-lived, swift, transitory 3. abrupt, blunt, brusque, curt, sharp, short, surly ~*n.* 4. abstract, digest, epitome, outline, précis, sketch, summary, synopsis 5. case, contention, data, defence ~*v.* 6. advise, explain, fill in (*Inf.*), instruct, prepare, prime

briefing conference, guidance, information, instructions, meeting, preparation

briefly concisely, cursorily, curtly, hastily, hurriedly, in brief, in outline, in passing, momentarily, precisely, quickly, shortly

bright 1. beaming, blazing, brilliant, effulgent, flashing, gleaming, glistening, glittering, glowing, illuminated, intense, luminous, radiant, resplendent, shining, sparkling, twinkling, vivid 2. clear, clement, cloudless, fair, lucid, pleasant, sunny, unclouded 3. acute, astute, aware, brilliant, clear-headed, clever, ingenious, intelligent, inventive, keen, quick, quick-witted, sharp, smart, wide-awake 4. auspicious, encouraging, excellent, favourable, good, hopeful, optimistic, promising, propitious, prosperous, rosy 5. cheerful, gay, genial, glad, happy, jolly, joyful, joyous, lively, merry, vivacious

brighten 1. clear up, enliven, gleam, glow, illuminate, lighten, light up, make brighter, shine 2. become cheerful, gladden, hearten, perk up

brilliance, brilliancy 1. blaze, brightness, dazzle, gleam, glitter, intensity, radiance, sheen, sparkle, vividness 2. aptitude, braininess, cleverness, distinction, excellence, genius, giftedness, greatness, talent, wisdom 3. éclat, glamour, grandeur, magnificence, splendour

brilliant 1. ablaze, bright, dazzling, glittering, glossy, intense, luminous, radiant, refulgent, scintillating, shining, sparkling, vivid 2. celebrated, eminent, exceptional, famous, glorious, magnificent, outstanding, splendid, superb 3. accomplished, acute, astute, brainy, clever, discerning, expert, gifted, intellectual, intelligent, penetrating, profound, quick, talented

brim border, brink, circumference, edge, lip, margin, rim, skirt, verge

bring 1. accompany, bear, carry, conduct, convey, deliver, escort, fetch, gather, guide, import, lead, take, transfer, transport, usher 2. cause, contribute to, create, effect, engender, inflict, occasion, produce, result in, wreak

bring about accomplish, achieve, cause, compass, create, effect, make happen, manage, occasion, produce, realize

bring off accomplish, achieve, carry out, discharge, execute, perform, pull off, succeed

bring up develop, educate, form, nurture, raise, rear, support, teach, train

brink border, brim, edge, fringe, frontier, limit, margin, point, rim, skirt

brisk active, agile, alert, bustling, busy, energetic, lively, nimble, quick, speedy, spry, vigorous, vivacious

briskly actively, efficiently, energetically, firmly, incisively, nimbly, promptly, quickly, rapidly, readily, smartly, vigorously

bristle 1. *n.* barb, hair, prickle, spine, stubble, thorn, whisker 2. *v.* be angry, bridle, flare up, rage, see red, seethe

brittle breakable, crisp, crumbly, delicate, fragile, frail, shivery

broach bring up, hint at, introduce, mention, open up, propose, speak of, suggest, talk of, touch on

broad 1. ample, extensive, large, roomy, spacious, vast, voluminous, wide, widespread 2. comprehensive, far-reaching, general, inclusive, sweeping, universal, unlimited, wide, wide-ranging 3. liberal, open, permissive, progressive, tolerant, unbiased

broadcast *v.* 1. air, beam, radio, relay, show, televise, transmit 2. advertise, announce, circulate, disseminate, make public, proclaim, promulgate, publish, report, spread ~*n.* 3. programme, show, transmission

broaden develop, enlarge, expand, extend, increase, open up, spread, stretch, swell, widen

broad-minded catholic, flexible, indulgent, liberal, open-minded, permissive, responsive, tolerant, unbiased, unprejudiced

broadside abuse, assault, attack, censure, criticism, diatribe

brochure booklet, circular, folder, handbill, leaflet, pamphlet

broken 1. burst, demolished, destroyed, fractured, fragmented, ruptured, separated, severed, shattered 2. weak 3. disconnected, discontinuous, disturbed, erratic, fragmentary, incomplete, intermittent, interrupted, spasmodic 4. beaten, crippled, crushed, defeated, demoralized, humbled, oppressed, overpowered, subdued, tamed

broken-down collapsed, dilapidated, in disrepair, inoperative, old, out of commission, out of order, worn out

brokenhearted crestfallen, desolate, despairing, devastated, disappointed, disconsolate, grief-stricken, inconsolable, miserable, mournful, prostrated, sorrowful, wretched

broker agent, dealer, factor, go-between, intermediary, middleman

bronze brownish, chestnut, copper, reddish-brown, rust, tan

brood 1. *v.* agonize, dwell upon, fret, meditate, mope, muse, repine, ruminate, think upon 2. *n.* breed, chicks, children, clutch, family, hatch, infants, issue, litter, offspring, progeny, young

brook beck, burn, rill, rivulet, stream, streamlet, watercourse

brother 1. kin, kinsman, relation, relative, sibling 2. associate, colleague, companion, comrade, fellow member, mate, partner 3. cleric, friar, monk, regular, religious

brotherhood 1. camaraderie, companionship, comradeship, fellowship, friendliness, kinship 2. alliance, association, clan, clique, community, coterie, fraternity, guild, league, society, union

brotherly affectionate, amicable, benevolent, cordial, fraternal, friendly, kind, neighbourly, sympathetic

browbeat bulldoze (*Inf.*), bully, coerce, cow, domineer, dragoon, hector, intimidate, oppress, overawe, overbear, threaten, tyrannize

brown auburn, bronze, brunette, chestnut, chocolate, coffee, dark, dun, dusky, hazel, rust, sunburnt, tan, tanned, tawny, toasted, umber

browse 1. dip into, leaf through, look through, peruse, scan, skim, survey 2. crop, eat, feed, graze, nibble, pasture

bruise 1. *v.* blacken, blemish, contuse, crush, damage, deface, discolour, injure, mar, mark 2. *n.* blemish, contusion, discoloration, injury, mark, swelling

brunt burden, force, full force, impact, pressure, shock, strain, stress, thrust, violence

brush[1] *n.* 1. besom, broom, sweeper 2. clash, conflict, fight, fracas, scrap (*Inf.*), set-to (*Inf.*), skirmish, tussle ~*v.* 3. buff, clean, paint, polish, sweep, wash 4. contact, flick, glance, graze, kiss, scrape, stroke, sweep, touch

brush[2] *n.* bushes, copse, scrub, shrubs, thicket, undergrowth

brush aside dismiss, disregard, have no time for, ignore, override, sweep aside

brush up go over, polish up, read up, relearn, revise, study

brutal 1. bloodthirsty, cruel, ferocious, heartless, inhuman, merciless, pitiless, remorseless, ruthless, savage, uncivilized, vicious 2. beastly, bestial, brutish, coarse, crude

brute 1. animal, beast, creature, wild animal 2. barbarian, beast, devil, fiend, monster, ogre, sadist, savage, swine

bubble *n.* 1. bead, blister, drop, droplet, globule, vesicle ~*v.* 2. boil, effervesce, fizz, foam, froth, seethe, sparkle 3. babble, burble, gurgle, murmur

buccaneer pirate, privateer, sea-rover

buckle *n.* 1. catch, clasp, clip, fastener ~*v.* 2. catch, clasp, close, fasten, hook, secure 3. bend, bulge, cave in, collapse, crumple, fold, twist, warp

bud 1. *n.* germ, shoot, sprout 2. *v.* burgeon, develop, grow, shoot, sprout

budding beginning, burgeoning, fledgling, flowering, growing, incipient, nascent, potential, promising

budge 1. dislodge, give way, inch, move, propel, push, remove, roll, shift, slide, stir 2. bend, change, give way, persuade, sway, yield

budget 1. *n.* allowance, cost, finances, funds, means, resources 2. *v.* apportion, cost, cost out, estimate, plan, ration

buff addict, admirer, connoisseur, devotee, enthusiast, expert, fan

buffer bumper, cushion, fender, intermediary, safeguard, screen, shield

buffet[1] *n.* café, cafeteria, cold table, counter, cupboard, snack bar

buffet[2] 1. *v.* bang, batter, beat, box, bump, knock, pound, push, rap, shove, slap, strike, thump 2. *n.* bang, blow, bump, cuff, jolt, knock, push, rap, shove, slap, smack

buffoon clown, comedian, comic, droll, fool, harlequin, jester, joker, wag

bug *Inf. n.* 1. disease, germ, microorganism, virus ~*v.* 2. annoy, badger, bother, disturb, harass, irk, irritate, pester, plague, vex 3. eavesdrop, listen in, spy, tap, wiretap

build *v.* 1. assemble, construct, erect, fabricate, form, make, put up, raise 2. base, begin, constitute, establish, inaugurate, originate, set up, start ~*n.* 3. body, figure, form, frame, physique, shape

building 1. dwelling, edifice, fabric, house, pile, structure 2. construction, erection, raising

build-up 1. development, enlargement, escalation, expansion, gain, growth, increase 2. accretion, accumulation, heap, load, mass, stack, stockpile, store

bulge *n.* 1. bump, lump, protuberance, swelling 2. boost, increase, rise, surge ~*v.* 3. dilate, distend, enlarge, expand, project, protrude, puff out, sag, stand out, stick out, swell

bulk 1. immensity, largeness, magnitude, massiveness, size, substance, volume, weight 2. body, generality, lion's share, main part, majority, major part, mass, most, nearly all

bulldoze demolish, flatten, level, raze

bullet missile, pellet, projectile, shot, slug

bulletin announcement, communiqué, dispatch, message, news flash, notification, report, statement

bull-headed headstrong, inflexible, mulish, obstinate, pig-headed, stiff-necked, stubborn, stupid, tenacious, uncompromising, unyielding, wilful

bullish assured, bold, confident, expectant, improving, positive, rising

bulwark bastion, buttress, defence, fortification, rampart, redoubt

bumbling awkward, blundering, botching, bungling, clumsy, incompetent, inefficient, inept, lumbering, maladroit, muddled, stumbling

bump *v.* 1. bang, crash, hit, knock, slam, smash into, strike 2. bounce, jar, jerk, jolt, rattle, shake ~*n.* 3. bang, blow, crash, hit, impact, jar, jolt, knock, rap, shock, smash, thud, thump 4. bulge, contusion, knob, knot, lump, protuberance, swelling

bumper *adj.* abundant, bountiful, excellent, exceptional, massive, prodigal

bump into chance upon, come across, encounter, meet, run across, run into

bunch 1. *n.* batch, bouquet, bundle, clump, cluster, collection, heap, lot, mass, parcel, pile, quantity, sheaf, spray, stack, tuft 2. *v.* assemble, bundle, cluster, collect, crowd, flock, group, herd, mass, pack

bundle *n.* 1. assortment, batch, bunch, collection, group, heap, mass, pile, quantity 2. bag, bale, box, carton, crate, pack, package, packet, pallet, parcel, roll ~*v.* 3. bale, bind, fasten, pack, tie, tie up, truss, wrap

bungle blunder, butcher, make a mess of, mar, mess up, miscalculate, mismanage, muff, ruin, spoil

bungling awkward, blundering, incompetent, inept, maladroit

buoy beacon, float, guide, marker, signal

buoyant 1. afloat, floatable, floating, light 2. blithe, bouncy, breezy, bright, carefree, cheerful, happy, joyful, light-hearted, lively

burden 1. *n.* affliction, anxiety, care, clog, load, onus, sorrow, strain, stress, trial, trouble, weight, worry 2. *v.* bother, encumber, load, oppress, overload, saddle with, strain, tax, weigh down, worry

bureau 1. desk, writing desk 2. agency, branch, department, division, office, service

bureaucracy administration, civil service, government, ministry, officialdom

bureaucrat civil servant, mandarin, minister, officer, official, public servant

burglar housebreaker, pilferer, robber, sneak thief, thief

burial entombment, exequies, funeral, interment, obsequies

buried 1. entombed, interred, laid to rest 2. dead and buried, in the grave 3. covered, forgotten, hidden, suppressed 4. hidden, private, tucked away 5. caught up, committed, devoted, engrossed, immersed, intent, preoccupied, rapt

burlesque 1. *n.* caricature, mock, mockery, parody, satire 2. *v.* ape, caricature, exaggerate, imitate, lampoon, make fun of, mock, parody, ridicule, satirize, send up (*Brit. inf.*), take off (*Inf.*)

burly beefy, big, bulky, hefty, muscular, powerful, stocky, stout, strapping, strong, sturdy, well-built

burn 1. be ablaze, be on fire, blaze, flame, flare, flash, flicker, glow, smoke 2. char, ignite, incinerate, kindle, light, parch, scorch, set on fire, shrivel, singe, toast, wither

burning 1. blazing, fiery, flaming, flashing, gleaming, glowing, hot, illuminated, scorching 2. ardent, eager, earnest, fervent, frantic, intense, passionate, vehement, zealous

burnish 1. *v.* brighten, buff, furbish, glaze, polish, rub up, shine, smooth 2. *n.* gloss, lustre, patina, polish, sheen, shine

burrow 1. *n.* den, hole, lair, retreat, shelter, tunnel 2. *v.* delve, dig, excavate, hollow out, scoop out, tunnel

burst 1. *v.* blow up, break, crack, explode, fly open, fragment, puncture, rupture, shatter, shiver, split, tear apart 2. *n.* bang, blast, blowout, blow-up, breach, break, crack, discharge, explosion, rupture, split

bury 1. entomb, inearth, inhume, inter, lay to rest 2. conceal, cover, cover up, hide, secrete, stow away 3. embed, engulf, implant, sink, submerge

bush 1. hedge, plant, shrub, shrubbery, thicket 2. brush, scrub, the wild

busily actively, briskly, carefully, diligently, earnestly, energetically, industriously, intently, speedily, strenuously

business 1. calling, career, craft, employment, function, job, line, métier, occupation, profession, pursuit, trade, vocation, work 2. company, concern, enterprise, firm, organization, venture 3. commerce, dealings, industry, manufacturing, selling, trade, trading, transaction

businesslike correct, efficient, methodical, orderly, organized, practical, professional, regular, systematic, thorough, well-ordered

businessman, businesswoman capitalist, employer, entrepreneur, executive, financier, industrialist, merchant, tradesman, tycoon

bust bosom, breast, chest, torso

bustle 1. *v.* bestir, dash, fuss, hasten, hurry, rush, scamper, scramble, scurry, stir 2. *n.* activity, ado, agitation, commotion, excitement, flurry, fuss, haste, hurry, stir, to-do, tumult

busy 1. active, assiduous, brisk, diligent, employed, engaged, engrossed, hard at work, industrious, occupied, on duty, slaving, working 2. active, energetic, full, hectic, hustling, lively, restless, tireless, tiring

but 1. *sentence connector* further, however, moreover, nevertheless, on the contrary, on the other hand, still, yet 2. *conj.* bar, barring, except, excepting, excluding, notwithstanding, save, with the exception of 3. *adv.* just, merely, only, simply, singly, solely

butcher *n.* 1. destroyer, killer, murderer, slaughterer, slayer ~*v.* 2. carve, clean, cut, cut up, dress, joint, prepare, slaughter 3. assassinate, cut down, destroy, exterminate, kill, massacre, slaughter, slay 4. botch, destroy, mutilate, ruin, spoil, wreck

butt[1] handle, hilt, shaft, shank, stock

butt[2] dupe, mark, object, point, subject, target, victim

butt[3] *v./n. With or of the head or horns,* buck, buffet, bump, jab, knock, poke, prod, punch, push, ram, shove, thrust

buttonhole *v. Fig.* accost, bore, catch, grab, take aside, waylay

buttress 1. *n.* brace, mainstay, pier, prop, reinforcement, shore, stay, strut, support 2. *v.* back up, bolster, brace, prop, prop up, reinforce, shore, shore up, strengthen, support, sustain, uphold

buy 1. *v.* get, invest in, obtain, pay for, procure, purchase, shop for 2. *n.* acquisition, bargain, deal, purchase

by *prep.* 1. along, beside, by way of, close to, near, next to, over, past, via 2. through, through the agency of, under the aegis of ~*adv.* 3. aside, at hand, away, beyond, close, handy, in reach, near, past, to one side

bystander eyewitness, looker-on, observer, onlooker, passer-by, spectator, viewer, watcher, witness

C

cab minicab, taxi, taxicab

cabin 1. berth, chalet, cot, cottage, crib, hovel, hut, lodge, shack, shanty, shed 2. berth, compartment, deckhouse, quarters, room

cabinet 1. case, closet, commode, cupboard, dresser, locker 2. administration, assembly, council, counsellors, ministry

caddish despicable, ill-bred, low, ungentlemanly, unmannerly

café cafeteria, coffee bar, coffee shop, lunchroom, restaurant, snack bar, tearoom

cage *v.* confine, coop up, fence in, immure, impound, imprison, lock up, mew, restrain, shut up

cajole beguile, coax, decoy, entice, flatter, inveigle, lure, mislead, seduce, tempt, wheedle

cake bar, block, cube, loaf, lump, mass, slab

calamitous catastrophic, deadly, devastating, dire, disastrous, fatal, pernicious, ruinous, tragic, woeful

calamity affliction, cataclysm, catastrophe, disaster, distress, downfall, hardship, mischance, misfortune, mishap, reverse, ruin, scourge, tragedy, trial, woe

calculate adjust, compute, consider, count, determine, enumerate, estimate, figure, gauge, judge, rate, reckon, value, weigh, work out

calculation answer, computation, estimate, judgment, reckoning, result

calibre 1. bore, diameter, gauge, measure 2. *Fig.* ability, capacity, endowment, faculty, force, gifts, merit, parts, quality, scope, stature, talent, worth

call *v.* 1. announce, arouse, awaken, cry, cry out, hail, proclaim, rouse, shout, waken, yell 2. assemble, bid, collect, contact, convene, convoke, gather, invite, muster, phone, rally, ring up, summon, telephone **3.** christen, describe as, designate, dub, entitle, label, name, style, term ~*n.* **4.** cry, hail, shout, signal, whoop, yell **5.** announcement, appeal, command, demand, invitation, notice, order, plea, request, ring (*Brit. inf.*), summons, supplication, visit

call for demand, entail, need, occasion, require, suggest

calling employment, life's work, line, métier, mission, occupation, profession, province, pursuit, trade, vocation, work

callous cold, hard-bitten, hardened, hardhearted, heartless, indifferent, insensitive, obdurate, soulless, thick-skinned, uncaring, unfeeling, unresponsive, unsympathetic

calm *adj.* **1.** balmy, mild, pacific, peaceful, placid, quiet, restful, serene, smooth, still, tranquil, windless **2.** collected, composed, cool, equable, impassive, imperturbable, relaxed, sedate, self-possessed, unemotional, unexcited, unmoved, unruffled ~*v.* **3.** hush, mollify, placate, quieten, relax, soothe

calmness 1. calm, composure, equability, hush, peace, peacefulness, placidity, quiet, repose, serenity, smoothness, stillness, tranquillity **2.** composure, coolness, dispassion, equanimity, impassivity, imperturbability, self-possession

camouflage 1. *n.* blind, cloak, concealment, cover, deceptive markings, disguise, front, guise, mask, masquerade, mimicry, screen, subterfuge **2.** *v.* cloak, conceal, cover, disguise, hide, mask, obscure, screen, veil

camp bivouac, camp site

campaign attack, crusade, drive, expedition, offensive, push

cancel abolish, annul, blot out, call off, cross out, delete, efface, eliminate, erase, expunge, obliterate, quash, repeal, repudiate, rescind, revoke

cancellation abandonment, abolition, deletion, elimination, quashing, repeal, revocation

cancer blight, canker, carcinoma (*Pathol.*), corruption, evil, growth, malignancy, pestilence, rot, tumour

candid blunt, fair, frank, free, impartial, just, open, outspoken, plain, straightforward, truthful, unprejudiced

candidate applicant, aspirant, competitor, contender, contestant, entrant, nominee, runner

candour forthrightness, frankness, honesty, openness, outspokenness, truthfulness

canker bane, blight, cancer, corruption, infection, rot, ulcer

cannon big gun (*Inf.*), field gun, gun, mortar

canny acute, artful, astute, careful, cautious, circumspect, clever, judicious, knowing, prudent, sagacious, sharp, shrewd, subtle, wise

canopy awning, covering, shade, sunshade

cant 1. *n.* humbug, hypocrisy, insincerity, lip service, pretence, sanctimoniousness **2.** *v.* angle, incline, rise, slant, slope

cantankerous bad-tempered, captious, contrary, crabby, crotchety (*Inf.*), crusty, difficult, disagreeable, grumpy, irascible, irritable, peevish, perverse, quarrelsome, testy

canter *n./v.* amble, jog, lope

canvass 1. *v.* analyse, campaign, electioneer, examine, inspect, investigate, poll, scan, sift, solicit, study, ventilate **2.** *n.* examination, poll, scrutiny, survey

cap *v.* beat, better, cover, crown, exceed, excel, finish, outdo, outstrip, overtop, surpass, top, transcend

capability ability, capacity, facility, faculty, means, power, proficiency, wherewithal

capable able, accomplished, adapted, adept, apt, clever, competent, efficient, fitted, gifted, masterly, proficient, skilful, suited, talented

capacious ample, broad, commodious, expansive, extended, extensive, generous, liberal, roomy, sizable, spacious, substantial, vast, wide

capacity 1. amplitude, compass, extent, range, room, scope, size, space, volume **2.** ability, brains, cleverness, competence, competency, facility, faculty, forte, genius, gift, intelligence, power, readiness, strength **3.** function, office, position, post, province, role, service, sphere

cape head, headland, point, promontory

caper *v.* bounce, bound, cavort, dance, frisk, frolic, gambol, hop, jump, leap, romp, skip, spring

capital *adj.* **1.** cardinal, central, chief, foremost, important, leading, main, major, paramount, pre-eminent, prime, principal, vital **2.** excellent, fine, first, first-rate, prime, splendid, superb ~*n.* **3.** assets, cash, finances, funds, investment(s), means, money, principal, property, resources, stock, wealth, wherewithal

capitalism free enterprise, *laissez faire*, private enterprise, private ownership

capitulate give in, give up, relent, submit, succumb, surrender, yield

capsize keel over, overturn, tip over, turn over, turn turtle, upset

capsule lozenge, pill, tablet

captain boss, chief, commander, head, leader, master, officer, skipper

captivate allure, attract, beguile, bewitch, charm, dazzle, enchant, enslave, enthral, entrance, fascinate, infatuate, lure, mesmerize, seduce, win

captive 1. *n.* convict, detainee, hostage, internee, prisoner, slave **2.** *adj.* caged, confined, ensnared, imprisoned, incarcerated, locked up, restricted, subjugated

captivity confinement, custody, detention, imprisonment, incarceration, internment, servitude, slavery

capture 1. *v.* arrest, catch, secure, seize, take, take prisoner **2.** *n.* arrest, imprisonment, seizure

car automobile, machine, motor, motorcar, vehicle

carcass body, cadaver (*Medical*), corpse, dead body, hulk, remains, shell, skeleton

cardinal capital, central, chief, essential, first, foremost, greatest, highest, important, leading, main, pre-eminent, primary, prime, principal

care 1. anxiety, burden, concern, disquiet, interest, pressure, responsibility, solicitude, stress, trouble, vexation, woe, worry **2.** attention, caution, consideration, direction, forethought, heed, management, pains, prudence, regard, vigilance, watchfulness **3.** charge, control, custody, keeping, management, protection, supervision, ward

career *n.* calling, employment, life work, livelihood, occupation, pursuit, vocation

care for 1. attend, foster, look after, mind, minister to, nurse, protect, provide for, tend, watch over **2.** be fond of, desire, enjoy, like, love, prize, take to, want

careful 1. accurate, attentive, cautious, chary, circumspect, conscientious, discreet, fastidious, heedful, painstaking, precise, prudent, scrupulous, thoughtful, thrifty **2.** alert, concerned, judicious, mindful, particular, protective, solicitous, vigilant, wary, watchful

careless 1. absent-minded, forgetful, hasty, heedless, incautious, indiscreet, negligent, perfunctory, remiss, thoughtless, unconcerned, unguarded, unmindful, unthinking **2.** inaccurate, irresponsible, lackadaisical, neglectful, offhand, slapdash, slipshod, sloppy (*Inf.*)

carelessness inaccuracy, indiscretion, irresponsibility, neglect, negligence, omission, remissness, slackness, thoughtlessness

caress 1. *v.* cuddle, embrace, fondle, hug, kiss, pet, stroke **2.** *n.* cuddle, embrace, hug, kiss, pat, stroke

caretaker concierge, curator, custodian, janitor, keeper, porter, warden, watchman

cargo baggage, consignment, contents, freight, goods, lading, load, merchandise, shipment, tonnage, ware

caricature 1. *n.* burlesque, cartoon, farce, lampoon, parody, satire, takeoff (*Inf.*), travesty **2.** *v.* burlesque, distort, lampoon, mimic, mock, parody, ridicule, satirize, send up (*Brit. inf.*), take off (*Inf.*)

carnival celebration, fair, festival, fête, fiesta, gala, holiday, revelry

carol chorus, hymn, lay, song, strain

carp cavil, censure, complain, criticize, find fault, reproach

carpenter cabinet-maker, joiner, woodworker

carriage 1. conveyance, delivery, freight, transport **2.** cab, coach, vehicle **3.** *Fig.* air, bearing, behaviour, conduct, demeanour, gait, manner, mien, posture, presence

carry 1. bear, bring, conduct, convey, fetch, haul, lift, lug, move, relay, take, transfer, transmit, transport **2.** bear, hold up, maintain, shoulder, stand, suffer, support, sustain, underpin, uphold

carry on continue, endure, keep going, last, maintain, persevere, persist

carry out accomplish, achieve, carry through, discharge, effect, execute, fulfil, perform, realize

carton box, case, pack, package

cartoon animated film, animation, comic strip, lampoon, parody, satire, sketch, takeoff

cartridge charge, round, shell

carve chip, chisel, cut, divide, engrave, etch, form, hack, hew, mould, sculpt, sculpture, slash, slice, whittle

cascade *n.* cataract, deluge, falls, flood, fountain, outpouring, shower, torrent, waterfall

case 1. box, cabinet, capsule, carton, cartridge, casket, chest, compact, container, crate, holder, receptacle, shell, suitcase, tray, trunk **2.** circumstance(s), condition, context, dilemma, event, plight, position, predicament, situation, state **3.** example, illustration, instance, occasion, occurrence, specimen **4.** *Law* action, cause, dispute, lawsuit, proceedings, process, suit, trial

cash bullion, charge, coin, coinage, currency, dough (*Sl.*), funds, money, notes, payment, ready money, resources, wherewithal

cashier 1. *n.* bank clerk, banker, bursar, clerk, teller **2.** *v.* cast off, discard, discharge, dismiss, drum out, expel

cast *v.* **1.** chuck, drive, drop, fling, hurl, impel, launch, lob, pitch, project, shed, shy, sling, throw, thrust, toss ~*n.* **2.** fling, lob, throw, thrust, toss **3.** actors, characters, company, players

cast down deject, depress, desolate, discourage, dishearten, dispirit

castigate beat, cane, censure, chasten, chastise, correct, criticize, discipline, flay, flog, lash, rebuke, reprimand, scold, scourge, whip

castle chateau, citadel, fortress, keep, mansion, stronghold, tower

casual 1. accidental, chance, contingent, fortuitous, irregular, occasional, random, unexpected, unforeseen, unpremeditated **2.** blasé, indifferent, informal, nonchalant, offhand, perfunctory, relaxed, unconcerned

casualty loss, sufferer, victim

catalogue directory, index, inventory, list, record, register, roll, roster, schedule

catastrophe adversity, affliction, blow, calamity, cataclysm, devastation, disaster, failure, fiasco, ill, mischance, misfortune, mishap, reverse, tragedy, trial, trouble

catch *v.* **1.** apprehend, arrest, capture, clutch, ensnare, entrap, grab, grasp, grip, lay hold of, seize, snare, snatch, take **2.** detect, discover, expose, find out, surprise, unmask ~*n.* **3.** bolt, clasp, clip, fastener, hasp, hook, hook and eye, latch **4.** disadvantage, drawback, fly in the ointment, hitch, snag, stumbling block, trap, trick

catching contagious, infectious,

infective, transferable, transmittable

categorical absolute, direct, downright, emphatic, explicit, express, positive, unequivocal, unqualified

category class, department, division, grade, head, heading, list, order, rank, section, sort, type

cater furnish, outfit, provide, provision, purvey, supply, victual

cattle beasts, cows, livestock, stock

catty ill-natured, malevolent, malicious, mean, rancorous, spiteful, venomous

cause *n.* **1.** agent, beginning, creator, genesis, maker, origin, prime mover, producer, root, source, spring **2.** account, agency, aim, basis, consideration, end, grounds, incentive, inducement, motivation, motive, object, purpose, reason ~*v.* **3.** begin, bring about, compel, create, effect, engender, generate, give rise to, incite, induce, lead to, motivate, occasion, precipitate, produce, provoke, result in

caustic acrid, astringent, biting, burning, corroding, corrosive, keen, mordant

caution *n.* **1.** care, carefulness, circumspection, discretion, forethought, heed, prudence, vigilance, watchfulness **2.** admonition, advice, counsel, injunction, warning ~*v.* **3.** admonish, advise, tip off, urge, warn

cautious alert, cagey (*Inf.*), careful, chary, circumspect, discreet, guarded, heedful, judicious, prudent, tentative, vigilant, wary, watchful

cavalry horse, horsemen

cave cavern, den, grotto, hollow

cavern cave, hollow, pothole

cavity crater, hole, hollow, pit

cease come to an end, conclude, desist, die away, end, fail, finish, halt, leave off, refrain, stay, stop, terminate

ceaseless constant, continuous, endless, eternal, everlasting, incessant, never-ending, nonstop, perpetual, unending, untiring

cede allow, concede, grant, hand over, make over, renounce, resign, surrender, transfer, yield

celebrate commend, drink to, eulogize, exalt, extol, glorify, honour, keep, laud, observe, praise, proclaim, rejoice, reverence, toast

celebrated distinguished, eminent, famed, famous, glorious, illustrious, notable, popular, prominent, renowned, well-known

celebration carousal, festival, festivity, gala, jubilee, revelry

celebrity big name, dignitary, luminary, name, personage, personality, star, superstar, V.I.P.

cell **1.** cavity, chamber, compartment, cubicle, dungeon, stall **2.** coterie, group, unit

cement *v.* attach, bind, bond, glue, gum, join, plaster, seal, solder, stick together, unite, weld

cemetery burial ground, churchyard, graveyard

censure **1.** *v.* abuse, blame, castigate, condemn, criticize, denounce, rebuke, reprimand, reproach, reprove, scold, upbraid **2.** *n.* blame, castigation, condemnation, criticism, disapproval, rebuke, remonstrance, reprimand, reproach, reproof, stricture

central chief, essential, fundamental, inner, interior, main, mean, median, mid, middle, principal

centre core, crux, focus, heart, hub, mid, middle, pivot

ceremonial **1.** *adj.* formal, ritual, solemn, stately **2.** *n.* ceremony, formality, rite, ritual, solemnity

ceremony commemoration, function, observance, parade, rite, ritual, service, show

certain **1.** assured, confident, convinced, positive, satisfied, sure **2.** ascertained, conclusive, incontrovertible, indubitable, plain, true, undeniable, unmistakable, valid **3.** decided, definite, established, fixed, settled

certainty assurance, confidence, conviction, faith, inevitability, positiveness, sureness, trust, validity

certificate credential(s), diploma, document, licence, testimonial

certify assure, attest, authenticate, aver, avow, confirm, declare, endorse, guarantee, show, testify, validate, verify, witness

chaff *n.* dregs, husks, refuse, remains, rubbish, waste

chain *v.* **1.** bind, enslave, fetter, handcuff, manacle, restrain, shackle, tether ~*n.* **2.** coupling, fetter, link, manacle, shackle, union **3.** progression, sequence, series, set, string, succession, train

challenge *v.* brave, claim, dare, defy, demand, dispute, investigate, object to, provoke, question, require, stimulate, summon, tax, try

chamber bedroom, compartment, cubicle, enclosure, hall, hollow, room

champion conqueror, defender, guardian, hero, patron, protector, title holder, upholder, victor, warrior, winner

chance *n.* **1.** likelihood, occasion, odds, opening, opportunity, possibility, probability, prospect, scope, time **2.** accident, casualty, coincidence, destiny, fate, fortune, luck, misfortune, peril, providence **3.** gamble, hazard, risk, speculation, uncertainty ~*v.* **4.** befall, betide, come about, come to pass, fall out, happen, occur **5.** endanger, gamble, hazard, risk, stake, try, venture, wager

change *v.* **1.** alter, convert, diversify, fluctuate, metamorphose, moderate, modify, mutate, reform, remodel, reorganize, restyle, shift, transform, vary, veer **2.** barter, convert, displace, exchange, interchange, remove, replace, substitute, swap (*Inf.*), trade, transmit ~*n.* **3.** alteration, difference, innovation, metamorphosis, modification, mutation, permutation, revolution, transformation, transition **4.** conversion, exchange, interchange, substitution, trade

changeable capricious, erratic, fickle, fitful, fluid, inconstant, irregular, mercurial, mobile, protean, shifting, uncertain, unpredictable, unreliable, unsettled, unstable, unsteady, vacillating, variable, versatile, volatile, wavering

channel **1.** *n.* canal, duct, furrow, groove, gutter, main, passage, route, strait **2.** *v.* conduct, convey, direct, guide, transmit

chant **1.** *n.* carol, chorus, melody, psalm, song **2.** *v.* intone, recite, sing, warble

chaos anarchy, bedlam, confusion, disorder, pandemonium, tumult

chap character, customer, fellow, guy (*Inf.*), individual, person, sort, type

chapter clause, division, episode, part, period, phase, section, stage, topic

character **1.** calibre, cast, complexion, constitution, disposition, make-up, nature, personality, quality, reputation, temper, temperament, type **2.** honour, integrity, rectitude, strength, uprightness **3.** card (*Inf.*), eccentric, oddball (*Inf.*), oddity, original, queer fish (*Inf.*) **4.** part, persona, portrayal, role

characteristic **1.** *adj.* distinctive, distinguishing, individual, peculiar, representative, singular, special, specific, symbolic, typical **2.** *n.* attribute, faculty, feature, mark, peculiarity, property, quality, trait

charge *v.* **1.** accuse, arraign, blame, impeach, indict, involve **2.** bid, command, enjoin, exhort, instruct, order, require ~*n.* **3.** accusation, allegation, imputation, indictment **4.** assault, attack, onset, rush, sortie **5.** burden, care, concern, custody, duty, office, responsibility, safekeeping, trust, ward **6.** amount, cost, expenditure, expense, outlay, payment, price, rate

charity alms-giving, assistance, benefaction, donations, fund, gift, hand-out, philanthropy, relief

charm **1.** *v.* allure, attract, beguile, bewitch, cajole, captivate, delight, enchant, entrance, fascinate, mesmerize, please **2.** *n.* allure, appeal, attraction, desirability, enchantment, fascination, magic, magnetism, sorcery, spell

charming appealing, attractive, bewitching, captivating, delightful, engaging, lovely, pleasant, pleasing, seductive, winning, winsome

chart **1.** *n.* blueprint, diagram, graph, map, plan, table **2.** *v.* graph, map out, outline, plot, shape, sketch

charter *n.* contract, deed, document, franchise, indenture, privilege, right

chase course, drive, drive away, expel, follow, hound, hunt, pursue, put to flight, run after, track

chaste austere, decent, elegant, immaculate, incorrupt, innocent, modest, moral, neat, pure, quiet, refined, restrained, simple, unaffected, undefiled, virtuous, wholesome

chastise beat, castigate, censure, correct, flog, lash, punish, scold, scourge

chat **1.** *n.* chatter, gossip, talk, tête-à-tête **2.** *v.* chatter, gossip

chatter *n./v.* babble, blather, chat, gossip, natter, prattle

cheap **1.** bargain, cut-price, economical, inexpensive, keen, low-priced, reduced, sale **2.** common, inferior, paltry, poor, second-rate, shoddy, tatty, tawdry, worthless **3.** base, contemptible, despicable, low, mean, scurvy, sordid, vulgar

cheat *v.* **1.** beguile, deceive, defraud, double-cross (*Inf.*), dupe, fleece, fool, hoax, hoodwink, mislead, rip off (*Sl.*), swindle, thwart, trick, victimize **2.** baffle, check, defeat, deprive, foil, frustrate, prevent, thwart ~*n.* **3.** charlatan, cheater, con man (*Inf.*), deceiver, dodger, double-crosser (*Inf.*), impostor, rogue, shark, sharper, swindler, trickster

check *v.* **1.** compare, confirm, enquire into, examine, inspect, investigate, look at, look over, make sure, monitor, note, probe, scrutinize, study, test, tick, verify **2.** bar, bridle, control, curb, delay, halt, hinder, impede, inhibit, limit, obstruct, pause, repress, restrain, retard, stop, thwart ~*n.* **3.** examination, inspection, investigation, research, scrutiny, test **4.** constraint, control, curb, damper, hindrance, impediment, limitation, obstruction, restraint, stoppage

cheer *v.* **1.** brighten, buoy up, cheer up, comfort, console, elate, elevate, encourage, enliven, exhilarate, gladden, hearten, incite, inspirit, solace, uplift, warm **2.** acclaim, applaud, clap, hail, hurrah ~*n.* **3.** cheerfulness, comfort, gaiety, gladness, glee, hopefulness, joy, liveliness, merriment, merrymaking, mirth, optimism, solace

cheerful blithe, bright, buoyant, cheery, contented, enthusiastic, gay, glad, gladsome, happy, hearty, jaunty, jolly, joyful, light-hearted, merry, optimistic, pleasant, sparkling, sprightly, sunny

cheerfulness exuberance, gaiety, geniality, gladness, good cheer, good humour, high spirits, joyousness, light-heartedness

cheerless austere, bleak, comfortless, dark, dejected, depressed, desolate, disconsolate, dismal, drab, dreary, dull, forlorn, gloomy, grim, joyless, melancholy, miserable, mournful, sad, sombre, sorrowful, sullen, unhappy, woeful

cheery breezy, cheerful, happy, jovial, lively, pleasant, sunny

cherish care for, cling to, comfort, encourage, entertain, foster, harbour, hold dear, nourish, nurse, prize, shelter, support, sustain, treasure

chest box, case, casket, crate, trunk

chew bite, champ, crunch, gnaw, grind, masticate, munch

chide admonish, blame, censure, check, criticize, lecture, rebuke, reproach, reprove, scold, tell off (*Inf.*), upbraid

chief **1.** *adj.* capital, cardinal, central, especial, essential, foremost, grand, highest, key, leading, main, most important, outstanding, predominant, preeminent, premier, prevailing, principal, superior, supreme, uppermost, vital **2.** *n.* boss (*Inf.*), captain, commander, director, governor, head, leader, lord, manager, master, principal, ruler, superintendent

chiefly especially, essentially, in general, in the main, mainly, mostly, on the whole, principally, usually

child baby, brat, descendant, infant, issue, juvenile, kid (*Inf.*), little one, minor, offspring, progeny, toddler, tot, youngster (*Inf.*)

childhood boyhood, girlhood, immaturity, infancy, minority, schooldays, youth

childlike artless, credulous, guileless, ingenuous, innocent, naive, simple, trustful, trusting, unfeigned

chill **1.** *adj.* bleak, chilly, cold, freezing, raw, sharp, wintry **2.** *v.* congeal, cool, freeze, refrigerate

chilly **1.** breezy, brisk, cool, crisp, draughty, fresh, nippy, sharp **2.** hostile, unfriendly, unsympathetic, unwelcoming

china ceramics, crockery, porcelain, pottery, service, tableware, ware

chip *n.* dent, flake, flaw, fragment, nick, notch, paring, scrap, scratch, shaving, wafer

chivalrous bold, brave, courteous, courtly, gallant, gentlemanly, heroic, high-minded, honourable, knightly, true, valiant

chivalry courage, courtesy, courtliness, gallantry, politeness

choice **1.** *n.* alternative, election, option, pick, preference, say, selection, variety **2.** *adj.* best, dainty, elect, elite, excellent, exclusive, exquisite, handpicked, nice, precious, prize, rare, select, special, uncommon, valuable

choke bar, block, clog, close, congest, constrict, dam, obstruct, occlude, overpower, smother, stifle, stop, strangle, suffocate, suppress, throttle

choose adopt, designate, elect, fix on, opt for, pick, prefer, see fit, select, settle upon, single out, take, wish

chore burden, duty, job, task

chortle cackle, chuckle, crow, guffaw

chorus **1.** choir, choristers, ensemble, singers, vocalists **2.** burden, refrain, response, strain

christen baptize, call, dub, name, style, title

chronicle **1.** *n.* account, annals, diary, history, journal, narrative, record, story **2.** *v.* enter, narrate, record, recount, register, relate, report, set down, tell

chuck cast, discard, fling, heave, hurl, pitch, shy, sling, throw, toss

churlish boorish, crabbed, harsh, ill-tempered, impolite, morose, oafish, rude, sullen, surly, uncivil, unmannerly, vulgar

cinema big screen (*Inf.*), films, flicks (*Sl.*), movies, pictures

cipher **1.** nil, nothing, nought, zero **2.** character, digit, figure, number, numeral, symbol **3.** code, cryptograph

circle *n.* **1.** band, circumference, coil, cordon, cycle, disc, globe, lap, loop, orb, perimeter, revolution, ring, round, sphere, turn **2.** circuit, compass, domain, enclosure, field, orbit, province, range, realm, region, scene, sphere **3.** assembly, clique, club, company, coterie, crowd, fellowship, fraternity, group, set, society ~*v.* **4.** circumnavigate, coil, compass, curve, encircle, enclose, encompass, envelop, gird, hem in, revolve, ring, rotate, surround, tour

circuit area, compass, course, journey, orbit, revolution, round, route, tour, track

circulate broadcast, diffuse, distribute, issue, make known, promulgate, propagate, publicize, publish, spread

circulation **1.** currency, distribution, spread, transmission, vogue **2.** circling, flow, motion, rotation

circumference border, boundary, bounds, circuit, edge, extremity, fringe, limits, outline, perimeter, rim, verge

circumstance accident, condition, contingency, detail, element, event, fact, factor, happening, incident, item, occurrence, particular, position, respect, situation

circumstances life style, means, position, resources, situation, state, state of affairs, station, status, times

cistern basin, reservoir, sink, tank, vat

citadel bastion, fastness, fortification, fortress, keep, stronghold, tower

cite **1.** adduce, advance, allude to, enumerate, evidence, extract, mention, name, quote, specify **2.** *Law* call, subpoena, summon

citizen burgher, dweller, freeman, inhabitant, ratepayer, resident, townsman

city conurbation, megalopolis, metropolis, municipality

civil **1.** civic, domestic, home, interior, municipal, political **2.** affable, civilized, courteous, courtly, obliging, polished, polite, refined, urbane, well-bred, well-mannered

civilization **1.** culture, development, education, enlightenment, progress, refinement, sophistication **2.** community, nation, people, polity, society

civilize cultivate, educate, enlighten, improve, polish, refine, tame

civilized cultured, educated, enlightened, humane, polite, tolerant

claim **1.** *v.* allege, ask, assert, call for, collect, demand, exact, hold, insist, maintain, need, pick up, profess, require, take, uphold **2.** *n.* application, assertion, call, demand, petition, privilege, protestation, request, requirement, right, title

clan band, brotherhood, clique, faction, family, fraternity, group, race, sect, sept, set, society, tribe

clap acclaim, applaud, cheer

clarification elucidation, explanation, simplification

clarify clear up, elucidate, explain, make plain, resolve, simplify, shed light on

clarity definition, explicitness, intelligibility, lucidity, precision, simplicity, transparency

clash **1.** *v.* conflict, cross swords, feud, grapple, quarrel, war, wrangle **2.** *n.* brush, collision, conflict, confrontation, difference of opinion, disagreement, fight

clasp **1.** *v.* clutch, connect, embrace, enfold, fasten, grapple, grasp, grip, hold, hug, press, seize, squeeze **2.** *n.* brooch, buckle, catch, clip, grip, hasp, hook, pin, snap

class caste, category, collection, department, division, genus, grade, group, grouping, kind, league, order, rank, set, sort, species, sphere, status, type, value

classic *adj.* **1.** best, finest, first-rate, masterly **2.** archetypal, definitive, exemplary, ideal, master, model, standard **3.** abiding, ageless, deathless, enduring, immortal, lasting, undying ~*n.* **4.** exemplar, masterpiece, model, standard

classical **1.** chaste, elegant, pure, refined, restrained, symmetrical, well-proportioned **2.** Attic, Augustan, Grecian, Greek, Hellenic, Latin, Roman

classification analysis, arrangement, codification, grading, sorting, taxonomy

classify arrange, catalogue, codify, dispose, distribute, file, grade, rank, sort

clause **1.** article, chapter, condition, paragraph, part, passage, section **2.** heading, item, point, stipulation

claw nail, nipper, pincer, talon, tentacle

clean *adj.* **1.** faultless, fresh, hygienic, immaculate, pure, sanitary, spotless, unsoiled, unstained, unsullied, washed **2.** chaste, decent, exemplary, good, honourable, innocent, moral, pure, respectable, undefiled, upright, virtuous ~*v.* **3.** bath, cleanse, disinfect, do up, dust, launder, mop, purge, purify, rinse, scour, scrub, sponge, swab, sweep, wash, wipe

cleanser detergent, disinfectant, scourer, soap, soap powder, solvent

clear[1] *adj.* **1.** bright, cloudless, fair, fine, light, luminous, shining, sunny, unclouded, undimmed **2.** apparent, audible, coherent, definite, distinct, evident, explicit, express, lucid, manifest, obvious, palpable, patent, plain, pronounced, recognizable, unambiguous, unequivocal **3.** empty, free, open, smooth, unhampered, unhindered, unimpeded, unlimited, unobstructed **4.** certain, convinced, decided, definite, positive, resolved, satisfied, sure

clear[2] *v.* **1.** clean, erase, purify, refine, sweep away, tidy (up), wipe **2.** break up, brighten, clarify, lighten **3.** absolve, acquit, excuse, exonerate, justify, vindicate **4.** jump, leap, miss, pass over, vault

clear-cut definite, explicit, plain, precise, specific, straightforward, unambiguous, unequivocal

clearly beyond doubt, distinctly, evidently, obviously, openly, seemingly, undeniably, undoubtedly

clear up **1.** answer, clarify, elucidate, explain, resolve, solve, straighten out, unravel **2.** order, rearrange, tidy (up)

clergy clerics, ecclesiastics, holy orders, ministry, priesthood, the cloth

clergyman chaplain, cleric, curate, divine, father, minister, padre, parson, pastor, priest, rabbi, rector, reverend (*Inf.*), vicar

clever able, adroit, apt, astute, brainy (*Inf.*), bright, canny, capable, cunning, deep, discerning, expert, gifted, ingenious, intelligent, inventive, keen, knowing, quick, rational, sagacious, sensible, shrewd, skilful, smart, talented, witty

client applicant, buyer, consumer, customer, dependant, habitué, patient, protégé, shopper

clientele clients, customers, following, market, regulars, trade

cliff bluff, crag, escarpment, face, overhang, precipice, rock face, scar, scarp

climate **1.** region, temperature, weather **2.** ambience, feeling, mood, temper, trend

climax acme, apogee, culmination, head, height, highlight, high spot (*Inf.*), peak, summit, top, zenith

climb ascend, clamber, mount, rise, scale, shin up, soar, top

climb down **1.** descend, dismount **2.** back down, eat one's words, retract, retreat

cling adhere, be true to, clasp, cleave to, clutch, embrace, fasten, grasp, grip, hug, stick, twine round

clip[1] crop, curtail, cut, cut short, pare, prune, shear, shorten, snip, trim

clip[2] attach, fasten, fix, hold, pin, staple

cloak **1.** *v.* camouflage, conceal, cover, disguise, hide, mask, obscure, screen, veil **2.** *n.* blind, cape, coat, cover, front, mantle, mask, pretext, shield, wrap

clog block, burden, congest, dam up, hamper, hinder, impede, jam, obstruct, occlude, shackle, stop up

close[1] *v.* **1.** bar, block, choke, clog, confine, cork, fill, lock, obstruct, plug, seal, secure, shut, shut up, stop up **2.** cease, complete, conclude, discontinue, end, finish, shut down, terminate, wind up

close[2] **1.** adjacent, adjoining, approaching, at hand, handy, hard by, imminent, impending, near, nearby, neighbouring, nigh **2.** compact, congested, cramped, cropped, crowded, dense, impenetrable, jam-packed, packed, short, solid, thick, tight **3.** attached, confidential, dear, devoted, familiar, inseparable, intimate, loving **4.** airless, heavy, humid, muggy, oppressive, stale, stifling, stuffy, suffocating, sweltering, thick **5.** mean, mingy (*Inf.*), miserly, near, niggardly, parsimonious, stingy, tight-fisted, ungenerous

closed **1.** fastened, locked, out of service, sealed, shut **2.** concluded, decided, ended, finished, over, resolved, settled, terminated **3.** exclusive, restricted

cloth dry goods, fabric, material, stuff, textiles

clothe apparel, array, attire, cover, deck, drape, dress, endow, enwrap, equip, fit out, garb, habit, invest, outfit, rig, robe, swathe

clothes, clothing attire, costume, dress, ensemble, garb, garments, gear (*Inf.*), get-up (*Inf.*), habits, outfit, raiment, togs (*Inf.*), vestments, vesture, wardrobe, wear

cloud 1. *n.* billow, darkness, fog, gloom, haze, mist, murk, obscurity, vapour **2.** *v.* darken, dim, eclipse, obscure, overcast, overshadow, shade, shadow, veil

cloudy blurred, confused, dark, dim, dismal, dull, dusky, gloomy, hazy, indistinct, leaden, lowering, muddy, murky, nebulous, obscure, opaque, overcast, sombre, sullen, sunless

clown 1. *n.* buffoon, comedian, dolt, fool, harlequin, jester, joker, pierrot, prankster **2.** *v.* act the fool, jest, mess about

club 1. bat, bludgeon, cosh, cudgel, stick, truncheon **2.** association, circle, clique, company, fraternity, group, guild, lodge, order, set, society, union

clue evidence, hint, indication, inkling, intimation, lead, pointer, sign, suggestion, suspicion, tip, tip-off, trace

clumsy awkward, blundering, bumbling, bungling, gauche, gawky, heavy, ill-shaped, inept, lumbering, maladroit, ponderous, uncoordinated

cluster 1. *n.* batch, bunch, clump, collection, gathering, group, knot **2.** *v.* assemble, bunch, collect, flock, gather

clutch catch, clasp, cling to, embrace, grab, grapple, grasp, grip, seize

clutches claws, control, custody, grasp, grip, hands, keeping, power

coach *n.* **1.** bus, car, carriage, vehicle **2.** instructor, teacher, trainer, tutor ~*v.* **3.** cram, drill, instruct, prepare, train, tutor

coalesce blend, combine, come together, consolidate, fuse, integrate, merge, mix, unite

coalition alliance, amalgamation, association, bloc, combination, compact, confederacy, confederation, integration, league, merger, union

coarse boorish, brutish, foul-mouthed, gruff, loutish, rough, rude, uncivil

coarseness bawdiness, crudity, indelicacy, poor taste, ribaldry, roughness, smut, uncouthness, unevenness

coast 1. *n.* beach, border, coastline, seaside, shore, strand **2.** *v.* cruise, drift, freewheel, get by, glide, sail, taxi

coat *n.* **1.** fleece, fur, hair, hide, pelt, skin, wool **2.** coating, covering, layer, overlay ~*v.* **3.** apply, cover, plaster, smear, spread

coax allure, beguile, cajole, decoy, entice, flatter, persuade, prevail upon, soothe, talk into, wheedle

cocky arrogant, brash, cocksure, conceited, lordly, swaggering, vain

code 1. cipher **2.** canon, convention, custom, ethics, etiquette, manners, maxim, rules, system

cogitate consider, contemplate, deliberate, meditate, mull over, muse, ponder, reflect, ruminate, think

coil curl, entwine, loop, snake, spiral, twine, twist, wind, wreathe

coin 1. *v.* create, fabricate, forge, frame, invent, make up, mint, mould, originate, think up **2.** *n.* cash, change, copper, money, silver

coincide 1. be concurrent, coexist, synchronize **2.** accord, harmonize, match, square, tally

coincidence accident, chance, eventuality, fluke, luck, stroke of luck

cold *adj.* **1.** arctic, biting, bitter, bleak, chill, chilly, cool, freezing, frigid, frosty, frozen, icy, raw, wintry **2.** benumbed, chilled, chilly, freezing, numbed, shivery **3.** aloof, apathetic, dead, distant, frigid, indifferent, reserved, spiritless, standoffish, stony, unfeeling, unmoved, unresponsive, unsympathetic ~*n.* **4.** chill, chilliness, coldness, frigidity, frostiness, iciness, inclemency

collaborate cooperate, join forces, participate, team up, work together

collaborator associate, colleague, confederate, co-worker, partner, team-mate

collapse 1. *v.* break down, cave in, come to nothing, crumple, fail, faint, fall, fold, founder, give way, subside **2.** *n.* breakdown, cave-in, disintegration, downfall, exhaustion, failure, faint

collar *v.* apprehend, appropriate, capture, catch, grab, lay hands on, seize

colleague ally, assistant, associate, auxiliary, collaborator, companion, comrade, fellow worker, helper, partner, team-mate, workmate

collect 1. accumulate, amass, assemble, gather, heap, hoard, save, stockpile **2.** assemble, congregate, convene, converge, flock together, rally

collected calm, composed, cool, placid, poised, self-possessed, serene, unruffled

collection 1. accumulation, anthology, compilation, heap, hoard, mass, pile, set, stockpile, store **2.** assembly, assortment, cluster, company, crowd, gathering, group **3.** alms, contribution, offering, offertory

collide clash, conflict, crash, meet head-on

collision accident, bump, crash, impact, pile-up, smash

colony community, outpost, province, settlement, territory

colossal enormous, gigantic, huge, immense, massive, monstrous, monumental, mountainous, prodigious, titanic, vast

colour *n.* **1.** complexion, dye, hue, paint, pigment, shade, tincture, tinge, tint **2.** bloom, blush, brilliance, flush, glow, liveliness, rosiness, ruddiness, vividness ~*v.* **3.** dye, paint, stain, tinge, tint **4.** *Fig.* disguise, distort, embroider, falsify, garble, gloss over, misrepresent, pervert, prejudice, slant, taint **5.** blush, burn, crimson, flush, go crimson, redden

colourful 1. bright, brilliant, intense, motley, multicoloured, rich, variegated, vivid **2.** characterful, distinctive, graphic, interesting, lively, picturesque, rich, stimulating, unusual, vivid

colourless characterless, dreary, insipid, lacklustre, tame, uninteresting, vapid

column 1. cavalcade, file, line, list, procession, queue, rank, row, string, train **2.** pillar, post, shaft, support, upright

coma insensibility, oblivion, somnolence, stupor, trance, unconsciousness

comb *v.* **1.** dress, groom, untangle **2.** *Fig.* go through with a fine-tooth comb, hunt, rake, ransack, rummage, scour, screen, search, sift, sweep

combat action, battle, conflict, contest, encounter, engagement, fight, skirmish, struggle, war, warfare

combatant belligerent, contender, enemy, fighter, fighting man, opponent, serviceman, soldier, warrior

combination 1. amalgam, blend, coalescence, composite, mix, mixture **2.** alliance, association, cabal, cartel, coalition, compound, confederacy, consortium, federation, merger, syndicate, unification, union

combine amalgamate, bind, blend, bond, compound, connect, cooperate, fuse, incorporate, integrate, join (together), link, marry, merge, mix, pool, unify, unite

come 1. advance, appear, approach, arrive, become, draw near, enter, happen, materialize, move, move towards, near, occur, originate, turn out, turn up (*Inf.*) **2.** appear, arrive, attain, enter, materialize, reach, show up (*Inf.*), turn up (*Inf.*) **3.** fall, happen, occur, take place **4.** arise, emanate, emerge, end up, flow, issue, originate, result, turn out **5.** extend, reach

come about arise, befall, happen, occur, result, take place

come across chance upon, discover, encounter, find, happen upon, hit upon, meet, notice, unearth

come apart break, crumble, disintegrate, fall to pieces, separate, split, tear

comeback rally, rebound, recovery, resurgence, return, revival, triumph

come back reappear, recur, reenter, return

come between alienate, divide, estrange, meddle, part, separate

come by acquire, get, lay hold of, obtain, procure, secure, win

comedown anticlimax, blow, decline, demotion, disappointment, humiliation, reverse

comedy chaffing, drollery, facetiousness, farce, fun, hilarity, humour, jesting, joking, slapstick, witticisms

come forward offer one's services, present oneself, volunteer

come in appear, arrive, enter, finish, reach

come off go off, happen, occur, succeed, take place

come out 1. appear, be published **2.** conclude, end, result, terminate

come round accede, acquiesce, allow, concede, grant, mellow, relent, yield

come through 1. accomplish, achieve, prevail, succeed, triumph **2.** endure, survive, weather the storm, withstand

come up arise, crop up, happen, occur, rise, spring up, turn up

come up with advance, create, discover, furnish, offer, present, produce, propose, provide, submit, suggest

comfort *v.* **1.** cheer, commiserate with, console, ease, encourage, enliven, gladden, hearten, inspirit, invigorate, reassure, refresh, relieve, solace, soothe, strengthen ~*n.* **2.** aid, alleviation, cheer, consolation, ease, encouragement, help, relief, succour, support **3.** cosiness, creature comforts, ease, luxury, wellbeing

comfortable 1. agreeable, ample, commodious, convenient, cosy, delightful, easy, enjoyable, homely, loose, pleasant, relaxing, restful, roomy, snug **2.** affluent, prosperous, well-off, well-to-do

comforting cheering, consoling, encouraging, reassuring, soothing

comic *adj.* amusing, comical, droll, facetious, farcical, funny, humorous, joking, light, rich, waggish, witty

coming 1. *adj.* approaching, at hand, due, en route, forthcoming, future, imminent, impending, in store, in the wind, near, next, nigh **2.** *n.* accession, advent, approach, arrival

command *v.* **1.** bid, charge, compel, demand, direct, enjoin, order, require **2.** control, dominate, govern, head, lead, manage, reign over, rule, supervise, sway ~*n.* **3.** behest, bidding, decree, direction, directive, edict, fiat, injunction, instruction, mandate, order, precept, requirement

commander boss, captain, chief, C in C, C.O., commanding officer, director, head, leader, officer, ruler

commanding advantageous, controlling, decisive, dominant, dominating, superior

commemorate celebrate, honour, immortalize, keep, observe, pay tribute to, remember, salute

commemoration ceremony, honouring, memorial service, observance, remembrance, tribute

commence begin, embark on, enter upon, initiate, open, originate, start

commend acclaim, applaud, approve, compliment, eulogize, extol, praise, recommend

commendation acclaim, acclamation, approbation, approval, credit, good opinion, panegyric, praise, recommendation

comment *v.* **1.** mention, note, observe, opine, point out, remark, say **2.** criticize, elucidate, explain, interpret ~*n.* **3.** observation, remark, statement **4.** commentary, criticism, eluci-

dation, explanation, exposition, note
commentary analysis, critique, description, exegesis, explanation, narration, notes, review, treatise, voice-over
commentator 1. reporter, sportscaster 2. annotator, critic, expositor, interpreter, scholiast
commerce business, dealing, exchange, trade, traffic
commercial business, mercantile, sales, trade, trading
commission *n.* 1. appointment, authority, charge, duty, employment, errand, function, mandate, mission, task, trust, warrant 2. allowance, cut, fee, percentage, rake-off (*Sl.*) 3. board, committee, delegation, deputation, representative ~*v.* 4. appoint, authorize, contract, delegate, depute, empower, engage, nominate, order, select, send
commit carry out, do, enact, execute, perform, perpetrate
commitment 1. duty, engagement, liability, obligation, responsibility, tie 2. assurance, guarantee, pledge, promise, undertaking, vow, word
common 1. average, conventional, customary, daily, everyday, familiar, frequent, general, humdrum, obscure, ordinary, plain, regular, routine, run-of-the-mill, simple, standard, stock, usual, workaday 2. accepted, general, popular, prevailing, universal, widespread 3. coarse, hackneyed, inferior, low, pedestrian, plebeian, stale, trite, undistinguished, vulgar
common sense good sense, level-headedness, mother wit, native intelligence, practicality, prudence, soundness, wit
commotion ado, agitation, bustle, disorder, disturbance, excitement, ferment, furore, fuss, hubbub, racket, riot, rumpus, to-do, tumult, turmoil, uproar
communal collective, community, general, joint, public, shared
commune *n.* collective, community, cooperative, kibbutz
communicate acquaint, announce, be in contact, be in touch, connect, convey, correspond, declare, disclose, divulge, impart, inform, make known, pass on, phone, proclaim, publish, report, reveal, ring up, signify, spread, transmit, unfold
communication 1. connection, contact, conversation, correspondence, link, transmission 2. disclosure, dispatch, information, intelligence, message, news, report, statement, word
communiqué announcement, bulletin, dispatch, news flash, report
communism Bolshevism, collectivism, Marxism, socialism, state socialism
communist Bolshevik, collectivist, Marxist, socialist
community association, body politic, brotherhood, commonwealth, company, district, general public, locality, people, populace, population, public, residents, society, state
commuter daily traveller, straphanger, suburbanite
compact 1. close, compressed, condensed, dense, firm, impenetrable, impermeable, pressed together, solid, thick 2. brief, concise, epigrammatic, laconic, pithy, pointed, succinct, terse, to the point
companion 1. accomplice, ally, associate, colleague, comrade, confederate, consort, crony, friend, partner 2. complement, counterpart, fellow, match, mate, twin
companionship amity, company, conviviality, fellowship, fraternity, friendship, rapport, togetherness
company 1. assemblage, assembly, band, body, circle, collection, convention, coterie, crew, crowd, ensemble, gathering, group, league, party, set, throng, troop, troupe, turnout 2. association, business, concern, corporation, establishment, firm, house, partnership, syndicate
compare *With* **with** balance, collate, contrast, juxtapose, set against, weigh
comparison 1. contrast, distinction, juxtaposition 2. analogy, correlation, likeness, resemblance, similarity
compartment alcove, bay, berth, booth, carriage, cell, chamber, cubicle, locker, niche, pigeonhole, section
compass area, bound, boundary, circle, circuit, enclosure, extent, field, limit, range, reach, realm, round, scope, sphere, stretch, zone
compassion commiseration, condolence, fellow feeling, heart, humanity, kindness, mercy, soft-heartedness, sorrow, sympathy, tenderness
compel coerce, constrain, dragoon, drive, enforce, exact, force, impel, make, oblige, restrain, squeeze, urge
compensate 1. atone, indemnify, make good, make restitution, recompense, refund, reimburse, remunerate, repay, requite, reward, satisfy 2. balance, cancel (out), counteract, make up for, offset, redress
compensation amends, atonement, damages, indemnity, payment, remuneration, reparation, restitution, reward, satisfaction
compete be in the running, challenge, contend, contest, emulate, fight, pit oneself against, rival, strive, struggle, vie
competent able, adapted, appropriate, capable, clever, equal, fit, proficient, qualified, sufficient, suitable
competition 1. contention, contest, emulation, opposition, rivalry, strife, struggle 2. championship, contest, event, puzzle, quiz, tournament
competitor adversary, antagonist, challenger, competition, contestant, opponent, opposition, rival
compile amass, collect, cull, garner, gather, organize, put together
complacent contented, gratified, pleased, satisfied, self-assured, self-righteous, self-satisfied, serene, smug, unconcerned
complain bemoan, bewail, carp, deplore, find fault, fuss, grieve, groan, grouse, growl, grumble, lament, moan, whine
complaint 1. accusation, annoyance, charge, criticism, dissatisfaction, fault-finding, grievance, grouse, grumble, lament, moan, plaint, remonstrance, trouble, wail 2. affliction, ailment, disease, disorder, illness, malady, sickness
complete *adj.* 1. all, entire, full, intact, integral, unabridged, unbroken, undivided, whole 2. accomplished, achieved, concluded, ended, finished 3. consummate, perfect, thorough, total, utter ~*v.* 4. accomplish, achieve, cap, close, conclude, crown, discharge, do, end, execute, fill in, finalize, finish, fulfil, perfect, perform, realize, round off, settle, terminate
completely absolutely, altogether, en masse, entirely, from beginning to end, fully, heart and soul, in full, *in toto*, perfectly, quite, solidly, thoroughly, totally, utterly, wholly
complex circuitous, complicated, intricate, involved, knotty, labyrinthine, mingled, mixed, tangled, tortuous
complicate confuse, entangle, interweave, involve, make intricate, muddle, snarl up
complicated 1. complex, elaborate, intricate, involved 2. difficult, involved, perplexing, problematic, puzzling, troublesome
complication complexity, confusion, entanglement, intricacy, mixture, web
compliment 1. *n.* admiration, bouquet, commendation, congratulations, courtesy, eulogy, favour, flattery, honour, praise, tribute 2. *v.* commend, congratulate, extol, felicitate, flatter, laud, pay tribute to, praise, salute
comply accede, accord, acquiesce, adhere to, agree to, conform to, consent to, discharge, follow, fulfil, obey, observe, perform, respect, satisfy
component constituent, element, ingredient, item, part, piece, unit
compose build, compound, comprise, constitute, construct, fashion, form, make, make up, put together
composition 1. arrangement, configuration, constitution, design, form, formation, layout, make-up, structure 2. creation, essay, exercise, literary work, opus, piece, study, work, writing
composure aplomb, calm, calmness, collectedness, coolness, dignity, ease, equanimity, placidity, poise, sedateness, self-assurance, self-possession, serenity, tranquillity
compound 1. *v.* amalgamate, blend, coalesce, combine, concoct, fuse, intermingle, mingle, mix, synthesize, unite 2. *n.* alloy, amalgam, blend, combination, composite, composition, conglomerate, fusion, medley, mixture, synthesis 3. *adj.* complex, composite, conglomerate, intricate, multiple, not simple
comprehend assimilate, conceive, discern, fathom, grasp, know, make out, perceive, see, take in, understand
comprehension discernment, grasp, intelligence, judgment, knowledge, perception, realization, sense, understanding
compress compact, concentrate, condense, constrict, cram, crowd, crush, press, shorten summarize
comprise be composed of, consist of, contain, embrace, encompass, include, take in
compromise 1. *v.* adjust, agree, concede, give and take, go fifty-fifty (*Inf.*), meet halfway, settle, strike a balance 2. *n.* accommodation, accord, adjustment, agreement, concession, give-and-take, settlement, trade-off
compulsive compelling, driving, irresistible, obsessive, uncontrollable, urgent
compulsory binding, forced, imperative, mandatory, required, requisite
comrade ally, associate, colleague, companion, confederate, crony, fellow, friend, partner
conceal bury, cover, disguise, dissemble, hide, keep dark, keep secret, mask, obscure, screen, secrete, shelter
concede 1. acknowledge, admit, allow, confess, grant, own 2. cede, give up, hand over, surrender, yield
conceit arrogance, complacency, egotism, narcissism, pride, swagger, vainglory, vanity
conceited arrogant, cocky, egotistical, immodest, overweening, puffed up, self-important, swollen-headed, vain
conceivable believable, credible, imaginable, possible, thinkable
conceive 1. apprehend, believe, comprehend, envisage, fancy, grasp, imagine, realize, suppose, understand 2. create, design, devise, form, formulate, produce, project, purpose, think up
concentrate 1. consider closely, focus attention on, put one's mind to, rack one's brains 2. bring to bear, centre, cluster, converge, focus
concentrated 1. deep, hard, intense, intensive 2. condensed, reduced, rich, undiluted
concept hypothesis, idea, image, impression, notion, theory, view
concern *v.* 1. affect, apply to, bear on, be relevant to, interest, involve, pertain to, regard, touch 2. bother, disquiet, distress, disturb, make anxious, make uneasy, perturb, trouble, worry ~*n.* 3. affair, business, charge, field, interest, involvement, job, matter, mission, responsibility, task 4. anxiety, attention, burden, care, consideration, disquiet, distress, heed, responsibility, solicitude, worry 5. business, company, enterprise, establishment, firm, house, organization
concerned 1. active, implicated, interested, involved, mixed up, privy to 2. anxious, bothered, distressed, disturbed, exercised, troubled, uneasy, upset, worried
concerning about, apropos of, as regards, as to, in the matter of, on the subject of, re, regard-

ing, relating to, respecting, touching, with reference to

concise brief, compact, compressed, condensed, laconic, pithy, short, succinct, summary, terse, to the point

conclude 1. cease, close, come to an end, complete, end, finish, round off, terminate 2. assume, decide, deduce, gather, infer, judge, suppose, surmise

conclusion 1. close, completion, end, finale, finish, result 2. consequence, culmination, issue, outcome, result, upshot 3. agreement, conviction, decision, deduction, inference, judgment, opinion, resolution, settlement, verdict

conclusive clinching, convincing, decisive, definite, definitive, final, irrefutable, ultimate, unanswerable

concoction blend, brew, compound, creation, mixture, preparation

concrete *adj.* actual, definite, explicit, factual, material, real, sensible, specific, substantial, tangible

concur accord, acquiesce, agree, approve, assent, coincide, combine, consent, cooperate, harmonize, join

condemn 1. blame, censure, damn, denounce, disapprove, reproach, reprove, upbraid 2. convict, damn, doom, proscribe, sentence

condemnation 1. blame, censure, denouncement, denunciation, disapproval, reproach, reprobation, reproof, stricture 2. conviction, damnation, doom, judgment, proscription, sentence

condensation 1. abridgment, digest, précis, synopsis 2. concentration, crystallization, curtailment, reduction

condense abridge, compact, compress, concentrate, contract, curtail, epitomize, précis, shorten, summarize

condensed abridged, compressed, concentrated, curtailed, shortened, shrunken, slimmed down, summarized

condescend 1. bend, deign, lower oneself, see fit, stoop, submit, unbend (*Inf.*) 2. patronize, talk down to

condescending disdainful, lofty, lordly, patronizing, snobbish, snooty (*Inf.*), supercilious, superior

condition *n.* 1. case, circumstances, plight, position, predicament, shape, situation, state, state of affairs, *status quo* 2. arrangement, article, demand, limitation, modification, prerequisite, provision, proviso, qualification, requirement, requisite, restriction, rule, stipulation, terms 3. fettle, fitness, health, kilter, order, shape, state of health, trim ~*v.* 4. accustom, adapt, educate, equip, habituate, inure, make ready, prepare, ready, tone up, train, work out

conditional contingent, dependent, limited, provisional, qualified, subject to, with reservations

conditions circumstances, environment, milieu, situation, surroundings

conduct *n.* 1. administration, control, direction, guidance, leadership, management, organization, running, supervision 2. attitude, bearing, behaviour, carriage, comportment, demeanour, deportment, manners, mien (*Literary*), ways ~*v.* 3. administer, carry on, control, direct, govern, handle, lead, manage, organize, preside over, regulate, run, supervise

confederacy alliance, bund, coalition, compact, confederation, league, union

confer consult, converse, deliberate, discourse, parley, talk

conference congress, consultation, convention, convocation, discussion, forum, meeting, seminar, symposium, teach-in

confess 1. acknowledge, admit, allow, concede, confide, disclose, divulge, grant, own, own up, recognize 2. reveal

confession acknowledgment, admission, avowal, disclosure, revelation

confide admit, breathe, confess, disclose, divulge, impart, reveal, whisper

confidence 1. belief, credence, dependence, faith, reliance, trust 2. aplomb, assurance, boldness, courage, firmness, nerve, self-possession, self-reliance 3. **in confidence** confidentially, in secrecy, privately

confident 1. certain, convinced, counting on, positive, satisfied, secure, sure 2. assured, bold, dauntless, fearless, self-assured, self-reliant

confidential classified, intimate, off the record, private, privy, secret

confidentially between ourselves, in camera, in confidence, in secret, personally, privately

confine bind, bound, cage, enclose, hem in, hold back, imprison, incarcerate, intern, keep, limit, repress, restrain, restrict, shut up

confines boundaries, bounds, edge, limits

confirm 1. assure, buttress, clinch, establish, fix, fortify, reinforce, settle, strengthen 2. approve, authenticate, bear out, corroborate, endorse, ratify, sanction, substantiate, validate, verify

confirmation 1. evidence, proof, substantiation, testimony, verification 2. acceptance, agreement, approval, assent, endorsement, ratification, sanction

confirmed chronic, habitual, hardened, ingrained, inured, inveterate, long-established, rooted, seasoned

conflict *n.* 1. battle, clash, combat, contention, contest, encounter, engagement, fight, strife, war, warfare 2. antagonism, bad blood, difference, disagreement, discord, dissension, divided loyalties, friction, hostility, interference, opposition, strife, variance ~*v.* 3. be at variance, clash, collide, combat, contend, contest, differ, disagree, fight, interfere, strive, struggle

confound 1. amaze, astonish, astound, baffle, bewilder, confuse, dumbfound, mix up, mystify, nonplus, perplex, startle, surprise 2. demolish, destroy, explode, overthrow, overwhelm, refute, ruin

confuse 1. baffle, bemuse, bewilder, mystify, obscure, perplex, puzzle 2. abash, addle, demoralize, discomfit, discompose, disconcert, discountenance, disorient, embarrass, fluster, mortify, nonplus, shame, upset

confused 1. at a loss, at sea, baffled, bewildered, dazed, disorganized, flummoxed, muddled, nonplussed, perplexed, puzzled, taken aback, upset 2. chaotic, disarranged, disordered, disorderly, disorganized, in disarray, jumbled, mistaken, misunderstood, mixed up, out of order, untidy

confusion 1. bemusement, bewilderment, mystification, perplexity, puzzlement 2. bustle, chaos, clutter, commotion, disarrangement, disorder, disorganization, jumble, mess, muddle, shambles, tangle, turmoil, untidiness, upheaval

congenial adapted, agreeable, compatible, favourable, fit, friendly, genial, kindly, kindred, like-minded, pleasant, pleasing, suitable, sympathetic, well-suited

congested clogged, crammed, crowded, jammed, overcrowded, overfilled, overflowing, packed, stuffed, stuffed-up, teeming

congratulate compliment, felicitate

congratulations best wishes, compliments, felicitations, good wishes, greetings

congregate assemble, collect, come together, convene, converge, convoke, flock, forgather, gather, mass, meet, muster, rally, rendezvous, throng

congregation assembly, brethren, crowd, fellowship, flock, host, laity, multitude, parish, parishioners, throng

congress assembly, conclave, conference, convention, convocation, council, delegates, diet, legislature, meeting, parliament, representatives

conjecture 1. *v.* assume, fancy, guess, imagine, infer, suppose, surmise, suspect 2. *n.* assumption, conclusion, fancy, guess, guesswork, hypothesis, inference, notion, presumption, speculation, supposition, surmise, theorizing, theory

conjure juggle, play tricks

conjurer, conjuror magician, sorcerer, wizard

conjure up bring to mind, contrive, create, evoke, recall, recollect

connect affix, ally, cohere, combine, couple, fasten, join, link, relate, unite

connected akin, allied, associated, bracketed, combined, coupled, joined, linked, related, united

connection 1. alliance, attachment, coupling, fastening, junction, link, tie, union 2. bond, communication, correspondence, intercourse, link, marriage, relation, relationship, relevance, tie-in 3. acquaintance, ally, associate, contact, friend, sponsor

connoisseur aficionado, arbiter, authority, buff (*Inf.*), devotee, expert, judge, savant, specialist

conquer beat, crush, defeat, get the better of, humble, master, overcome, overpower, overthrow, quell, rout, subdue, succeed, surmount, triumph, vanquish

conqueror champion, hero, lord, master, vanquisher, victor, winner

conquest 1. defeat, discomfiture, mastery, overthrow, rout, triumph, victory 2. annexation, appropriation, coup, invasion, occupation, subjection, takeover

conscience moral sense, principles, scruples, still small voice

conscientious careful, diligent, exact, faithful, meticulous, painstaking, particular, punctilious, thorough

conscious 1. alert, alive to, awake, aware, cognizant, percipient, responsive, sensible, sentient, wise to (*Sl.*) 2. calculated, deliberate, intentional, knowing, premeditated, studied, wilful

consciousness apprehension, awareness, knowledge, realization, recognition, sensibility

consecrate dedicate, devote, exalt, hallow, ordain, sanctify, set apart

consecutive following, in sequence, in turn, running, sequential, successive, uninterrupted

consensus agreement, common consent, concord, harmony, unanimity

consent 1. *v.* accede, acquiesce, agree, allow, approve, assent, comply, concede, concur, permit, yield 2. *n.* agreement, approval, assent, compliance, go-ahead (*Inf.*), O.K. (*Inf.*), permission, sanction

consequence effect, end, event, issue, outcome, repercussion, result, upshot

consequently accordingly, ergo, hence, necessarily, therefore, thus

conservation custody, economy, maintenance, preservation, protection, safeguarding, safekeeping, saving, upkeep

conservative cautious, conventional, die-hard, guarded, hidebound, moderate, quiet, reactionary, right-wing, sober, tory, traditional

conserve hoard, husband, keep, nurse, preserve, protect, save, store up, take care of

consider 1. chew over, cogitate, consult, contemplate, deliberate, discuss, meditate, ponder, reflect, revolve, ruminate, study, weigh 2. bear in mind, care for, keep in view, make allowance for, regard, remember, respect

considerable 1. abundant, ample, appreciable, goodly, great, large, lavish, marked, much, plentiful, reasonable, substantial, tidy, tolerable 2. important, influential, noteworthy, renowned, significant

considerably appreciably, greatly, markedly, noticeably, remarkably, significantly, substantially, very much

considerate concerned, discreet, kind, kindly, mindful, obliging, patient, tactful, thoughtful, unselfish

consideration 1. attention, contemplation, deliberation, discussion, examination, reflection, regard, review, scrutiny, study, thought 2. concern, friendliness, kindliness, kindness, respect, solicitude, tact, thoughtfulness

considering all in all, in the light of, in view of

consignment batch, delivery, goods, shipment

consist *With* **of** be composed of, be made up of, amount to, comprise, contain, embody, include, incorporate, involve

consistent constant, dependable, regular, steady, true to type, unchanging, undeviating

consolation cheer, comfort, ease, encouragement, help, relief, solace, succour, support

console cheer, comfort, encourage, relieve, solace, soothe

consolidate fortify, reinforce, secure, stabilize, strengthen

consort 1. *n.* associate, companion, fellow, husband, partner, spouse (*of a reigning monarch*), wife 2. *v.* associate, fraternize, go around with, hang about *or* around with, keep company, mingle, mix

conspicuous clear, discernible, easily seen, evident, manifest, noticeable, obvious, patent, perceptible, visible

conspiracy collusion, confederacy, frame-up (*Sl.*), intrigue, machination, plot, scheme, treason

conspire contrive, devise, hatch treason, intrigue, machinate, manoeuvre, plot, scheme

constant 1. even, firm, fixed, habitual, immutable, invariable, permanent, perpetual, regular, stable, steadfast, steady, unbroken, unvarying 2. ceaseless, continuous, endless, eternal, everlasting, incessant, interminable, nonstop, perpetual, persistent, relentless, sustained, unrelenting, unremitting

constantly all the time, always, continually, endlessly, everlastingly, incessantly, interminably, invariably, nonstop, perpetually, relentlessly

consternation alarm, anxiety, awe, bewilderment, confusion, dismay, distress, dread, fear, fright, horror, panic, shock, terror

constituent 1. *adj.* basic, component, elemental, essential, integral 2. *n.* component, element, essential, factor, ingredient, part, principle, unit

constitute comprise, create, enact, establish, fix, form, found, make, make up, set up

constitution establishment, formation, organization

constitutional *adj.* 1. congenital, inborn, inherent, intrinsic, organic 2. chartered, statutory, vested ~*n.* 3. airing, stroll, turn, walk

constrain bind, compel, drive, force, impel, oblige, pressure, urge

constraint 1. compulsion, force, necessity, pressure, restraint 2. check, curb, damper, deterrent, hindrance, limitation, restriction

construct assemble, build, compose, create, design, erect, establish, fabricate, fashion, form, formulate, found, frame, make, manufacture, organize, put up, raise, set up, shape

construction assembly, building, composition, creation, edifice, erection, fabric, fabrication, figure, form, shape, structure

constructive helpful, positive, practical, productive, useful, valuable

consult ask, compare notes, confer, consider, debate, deliberate, interrogate, question, refer to, take counsel, turn to

consultant adviser, authority, specialist

consultation appointment, conference, council, deliberation, dialogue, discussion, examination, hearing, interview, meeting, session

consume absorb, deplete, drain, eat up, employ, exhaust, expend, finish up, lavish, lessen, spend, use, use up, utilize, vanish, waste, wear out

consumer buyer, customer, purchaser, shopper, user

contact *n.* 1. approximation, contiguity, junction, juxtaposition, touch, union 2. acquaintance, connection ~*v.* 3. approach, call, communicate with, get *or* be in touch with, get hold of, reach, ring (up), speak to, write to

contain accommodate, enclose, have capacity for, hold, incorporate, seat

container holder, receptacle, vessel

contemplate 1. brood over, consider, deliberate, meditate, observe, ponder, reflect upon study 2. consider, design, envisage, expect, foresee, intend, mean, plan, propose, think of

contemporary *adj.* 1. coexistent, synchronous 2. à la mode, current, in fashion, latest, modern, newfangled, present, present-day, recent, up-to-date ~*n.* 3. compeer, fellow, peer

contempt contumely, derision, disdain, disregard, disrespect, mockery, neglect, scorn, slight

contend 1. clash, compete, contest, cope, emulate, grapple, jostle, litigate, skirmish, strive, struggle, vie 2. affirm, allege, argue, assert, aver, avow, debate, dispute, hold, maintain

content[1] 1. *v.* appease, delight, gladden, gratify, humour, indulge, mollify, placate, please, reconcile, satisfy, suffice 2. *n.* comfort, ease, gratification, peace, peace of mind, pleasure, satisfaction 3. *adj.* agreeable, at ease, comfortable, contented, fulfilled, satisfied, willing to accept

content[2] burden, essence, gist, ideas, matter, meaning, significance, substance, text, thoughts

contented at ease, at peace, cheerful, comfortable, glad, gratified, happy, pleased, satisfied, serene, thankful

contentment comfort, ease, equanimity, fulfilment, gladness, gratification, happiness, peace, pleasure, repletion, satisfaction, serenity

contents 1. elements, ingredients, load 2. chapters, divisions, subject matter, subjects, themes, topics

contest *n.* 1. competition, game, match, tournament, trial ~*v.* 2. compete, contend, fight, fight over, strive, vie 3. argue, challenge, debate, dispute, doubt, litigate, oppose, question

contestant aspirant, candidate, competitor, contender, entrant, player

context background, connection, frame of reference, framework, relation

continual constant, endless, eternal, everlasting, frequent, incessant, interminable, perpetual, recurrent, regular, repeated, unceasing, unremitting

continually all the time, always, constantly, endlessly, eternally, everlastingly, incessantly, interminably, repeatedly

continuation extension, furtherance, sequel, supplement

continue abide, carry on, endure, last, live on, persist, remain, rest, stay, stay on, survive

continuing enduring, in progress, lasting, ongoing, sustained

continuity cohesion, connection, flow, progression, sequence, succession

continuous connected, constant, extended, prolonged, unbroken, unceasing, undivided, uninterrupted

contraband 1. *n.* black-marketing, smuggling, trafficking 2. *adj.* banned, black-market, forbidden, illegal, illicit, prohibited, smuggled, unlawful

contract *v.* 1. abridge, compress, condense, confine, constrict, curtail, dwindle, lessen, narrow, purse, reduce, shrink, shrivel, tighten, wither, wrinkle 2. agree, arrange, bargain, clinch, close, come to terms, covenant, engage, enter into, negotiate, pledge, stipulate ~*n.* 3. agreement, arrangement, bargain, bond, commitment, compact, convention, covenant, deal (*Inf.*), engagement, pact, settlement, treaty, understanding

contradict be at variance with, belie, challenge, contravene, counter, counteract, deny, dispute, negate, oppose

contradiction conflict, contravention, denial, inconsistency, opposite

contradictory antagonistic, antithetical, conflicting, contrary, incompatible, inconsistent, opposite, paradoxical

contraption apparatus, contrivance, device, gadget, mechanism, rig

contrary *adj.* adverse, anti, clashing, contradictory, counter, discordant, hostile, inimical, opposed, opposite

contrast 1. *n.* comparison, difference, disparity, dissimilarity, distinction, divergence, foil, opposition 2. *v.* compare, differ, differentiate, distinguish, oppose, set in opposition, set off

contribute add, afford, bestow, chip in, donate, furnish, give, provide, subscribe, supply

contribution addition, bestowal, donation, gift, grant, subscription

contributor 1. backer, bestower, donor, giver, patron, subscriber, supporter 2. freelance, journalist, reporter

contrite humble, penitent, regretful, remorseful, repentant, sorrowful, sorry

contrivance 1. artifice, design, dodge, expedient, formation, intrigue, measure, plan, plot, project, ruse, scheme, stratagem, trick 2. apparatus, appliance, contraption, device, equipment, gadget, gear, implement, invention, machine, mechanism

contrive concoct, construct, create, design, devise, engineer, fabricate, frame, improvise, invent

contrived artificial, elaborate, forced, laboured, overdone, unnatural

control *v.* 1. command, conduct, direct, dominate, govern, have charge of, lead, manage, manipulate, oversee, pilot, reign over, rule, steer, superintend, supervise 2. bridle, check, constrain, contain, curb, hold back, limit, master, rein in, repress, restrain, subdue ~*n.* 3. authority, charge, command, direction, discipline, government, guidance, jurisdiction, management, mastery, oversight, rule, supervision, supremacy 4. brake, check, curb, limitation, regulation, restraint

controversial at issue, contentious, debatable, disputable, disputed, open to question, under discussion

controversy argument, contention, debate, discussion, dispute, dissension, polemic, quarrel, squabble, strife, wrangle

convene assemble, bring together, call, come together, congregate, gather, meet, muster, rally, summon

convenience accessibility, appropriateness, availability, fitness, handiness, opportuneness, serviceability, suitability, usefulness, utility

convenient 1. appropriate, beneficial, commodious, fit, fitted, handy, helpful, labour-saving, opportune, seasonable, suitable, suited, timely, useful, well-timed 2. accessible, at hand, available, close at hand, handy

convention 1. assembly, conference, congress, convocation, council, delegates, meeting 2. code, custom, etiquette, formality, practice, propriety, protocol, tradition, usage

converge combine, come together, focus, gather, join, meet, merge, mingle

conversation chat, colloquy, communion, conference, converse, dialogue, discourse, discussion, exchange, gossip, talk, tête-à-tête

converse *n.* antithesis, contrary, obverse, opposite, reverse

conversion 1. change, transformation, transmutation 2. adaptation, alteration, modification, reconstruction, reorganization 3. change of heart, rebirth, reformation, regeneration

convert *v.* 1. alter, change,

transform, transmute, transpose, turn **2.** adapt, apply, modify, remodel, reorganize, restyle, revise

convey bear, bring, carry, conduct, fetch, forward, grant, guide, move, send, support, transmit, transport

convict 1. *v.* condemn, find guilty, imprison, sentence **2.** *n.* criminal, culprit, felon, malefactor, prisoner

conviction assurance, certainty, confidence, firmness, reliance

convince assure, bring round, persuade, satisfy, sway, win over

convulse agitate, derange, disorder, disturb, shake, shatter, twist, work

cool *adj.* **1.** chilled, chilly, nippy, refreshing **2.** calm, collected, composed, deliberate, imperturbable, level-headed, placid, quiet, relaxed, self-controlled, self-possessed, serene, unemotional, unexcited, unruffled **3.** aloof, distant, frigid, indifferent, lukewarm, offhand, reserved, unfriendly, uninterested, unresponsive, unwelcoming *~v.* **4.** chill, cool off, freeze, lose heat, refrigerate **5.** abate, allay, assuage, calm (down), dampen, lessen, moderate, quiet, temper

cooperate aid, assist, collaborate, combine, concur, conspire, contribute, help, join forces, pitch in, pull together, work together

cooperation assistance, collaboration, give-and-take, helpfulness, participation, responsiveness, teamwork, unity

cooperative accommodating, helpful, obliging, responsive, supportive

coordinate correlate, harmonize, integrate, match, mesh, organize, relate

cope 1. carry on, manage, struggle through, survive **2. cope with** deal, encounter, handle, struggle, tangle, tussle, weather, wrestle

copious abundant, ample, bountiful, extensive, exuberant, full, generous, lavish, liberal, luxuriant, overflowing, plenteous, plentiful, profuse, rich

copy *n.* **1.** counterfeit, duplicate, facsimile, forgery, image, imitation, likeness, model, pattern, photocopy, print, replica, replication, representation, reproduction *~v.* **2.** counterfeit, duplicate, photocopy, reproduce, transcribe **3.** ape, echo, emulate, follow, follow the example of, imitate, mimic, mirror, parrot, repeat, simulate

cord line, rope, string, twine

cordial affable, affectionate, agreeable, cheerful, friendly, genial, hearty, sociable, warm, warm-hearted, welcoming, wholehearted

cordon *n.* barrier, chain, line, ring

core centre, crux, essence, gist, heart, kernel, nub, nucleus, pith

corner *n.* **1.** angle, bend, crook, joint **2.** cavity, cranny, hideaway, hide-out, hole, niche, nook, recess, retreat *~v.* **3.** bring to bay, run to earth, trap

corny banal, commonplace, dull, feeble, hackneyed, maudlin, mawkish, old-fashioned, sentimental, stale, trite

corps band, body, company, contingent, crew, detachment, division, regiment, squad, squadron, team, troop, unit

corpse body, cadaver, carcass

correct *v.* **1.** adjust, amend, cure, improve, rectify, redress, reform, remedy, right **2.** admonish, chastise, chide, discipline, punish, reprimand, reprove *~adj.* **3.** accurate, exact, faultless, flawless, just, precise, regular, right, strict, true

correction 1. adjustment, alteration, amendment, improvement, modification **2.** admonition, castigation, chastisement, discipline, punishment, reproof

correctly accurately, perfectly, precisely, properly, rightly

correctness accuracy, exactitude, fidelity, preciseness, precision, regularity, truth

correspond 1. accord, agree, be consistent, coincide, conform, dovetail, fit, harmonize, match, square, tally **2.** communicate, exchange letters

correspondence 1. agreement, analogy, coincidence, comparison, conformity, congruity, correlation, fitness, harmony, match, relation, similarity **2.** communication, letters, mail, post, writing

correspondent *n.* **1.** letter writer, pen friend *or* pal **2.** contributor, journalist, reporter

corresponding analogous, answering, complementary, correlative, equivalent, interrelated, matching, reciprocal, similar

corridor aisle, hallway, passage, passageway

corrode canker, consume, corrupt, eat away, erode, gnaw, impair, rust, waste, wear away

corrosive 1. acrid, caustic, erosive, virulent, wasting, wearing **2.** caustic, cutting, incisive, mordant, sarcastic, trenchant

corrupt *adj.* **1.** dishonest, fraudulent, rotten, shady (*Inf.*), unethical, unprincipled, unscrupulous, venal **2.** altered, contaminated, decayed, defiled, distorted, doctored, falsified, rotten, tainted *~v.* **3.** bribe, debauch, demoralize, deprave, entice, fix (*Inf.*), lure, pervert, square (*Inf.*), suborn, subvert

corruption 1. breach of trust, bribery, bribing, demoralization, dishonesty, extortion, fraud, graft, jobbery, profiteering, shadiness, venality **2.** decadence, degeneration, depravity, evil, immorality, impurity, iniquity, perversion, sinfulness, vice, viciousness, wickedness

corset belt, bodice, girdle

cosmetic *adj.* beautifying, superficial, surface

cosmic huge, immense, infinite, limitless, measureless, universal, vast

cosmopolitan catholic, sophisticated, universal, urbane, well-travelled, worldly, worldly-wise

cost *n.* **1.** amount, charge, expenditure, expense, figure, outlay, payment, price, rate, worth **2.** damage, detriment, expense, harm, hurt, injury, loss, penalty, sacrifice, suffering *~v.* **3.** come to, sell at

costly 1. dear, excessive, expensive, extortionate, highly-priced, steep (*Inf.*), valuable **2.** gorgeous, lavish, luxurious, opulent, precious, priceless, rich, splendid, sumptuous

costume attire, clothing, dress, ensemble, garb, get-up (*Inf.*), livery, outfit, robes, uniform

cosy comfortable, homely, intimate, secure, sheltered, snug, warm

cottage but-and-ben (*Scot.*), cabin, chalet, cot, hut, lodge, shack

cough 1. *n.* bark, hack **2.** *v.* bark, clear one's throat, hack, hawk, hem

council assembly, board, cabinet, chamber, committee, conference, congress, convention, convocation, diet, ministry, panel, parliament, synod

counsel *n.* **1.** admonition, advice, caution, consideration, direction, forethought, guidance, information, recommendation, suggestion, warning **2.** advocate, attorney, barrister, lawyer, legal adviser, solicitor *~v.* **3.** admonish, advise, advocate, caution, exhort, instruct, recommend, urge, warn

count 1. add (up), calculate, cast up, check, compute, enumerate, estimate, number, reckon, score, tally, tot up **2.** carry weight, matter, rate, signify, tell, weigh

counter 1. *adv.* against, contrarily, conversely, in defiance of, versus **2.** *adj.* adverse, against, conflicting, contradictory, contrary, contrasting, obverse, opposing, opposite **3.** *v.* answer, hit back, meet, offset, parry, resist, respond, retaliate, return, ward off

counterbalance balance, compensate, make up for, offset, set off

counterfeit 1. *v.* copy, fabricate, fake, feign, forge, imitate, impersonate, pretend, sham, simulate **2.** *adj.* bogus, copied, faked, false, feigned, forged, fraudulent, imitation, phoney (*Sl.*), pseudo (*Inf.*), sham, simulated, spurious **3.** *n.* copy, fake, forgery, fraud, imitation, reproduction, sham

countermand annul, cancel, override, repeal, rescind, retract, reverse, revoke

counterpart complement, copy, duplicate, equal, fellow, match, mate, supplement, tally, twin

countless endless, incalculable, infinite, legion, limitless, measureless, myriad, uncounted, untold

count on *or* **upon** bank on, believe (in), depend on, lean on, reckon on, rely on, take on trust, trust

country 1. commonwealth, kingdom, nation, people, realm, sovereign state, state **2.** fatherland, homeland, motherland, nationality, native land **3.** land, part, region, terrain, territory **4.** citizens, community, electors, inhabitants, nation, people, populace, public, society, voters **5.** backwoods, farmland, green belt, outdoors, provinces, rural areas, wide open spaces (*Inf.*)

countryside country, farmland, green belt, outdoors, view, wide open spaces (*Inf.*)

count up add, sum, tally, total

county province, shire

coup action, deed, exploit, feat, manoeuvre, stratagem, stroke, stunt, *tour de force*

couple 1. *n.* brace, duo, pair, twosome **2.** *v.* buckle, clasp, conjoin, connect, hitch, join, link, marry, pair, unite, wed, yoke

coupon card, certificate, slip, ticket, token, voucher

courage boldness, bravery, daring, fearlessness, firmness, fortitude, gallantry, grit, guts (*Inf.*), heroism, mettle, nerve, pluck, resolution, valour

courageous audacious, bold, brave, daring, fearless, gallant, hardy, heroic, indomitable, intrepid, plucky, resolute, valiant, valorous

course 1. advance, continuity, development, flow, march, movement, order, progress, sequence, succession **2.** channel, direction, line, orbit, passage, path, road, route, tack, track, trail, trajectory, way **3.** lapse, passage, passing, sweep, term, time **4.** conduct, manner, method, mode, plan, policy, procedure, programme **5.** circuit, lap, race, racecourse, round **6.** classes, course of study, curriculum, lectures, programme, schedule, studies **7. of course** certainly, definitely, naturally, obviously, undoubtedly

court *n.* **1.** cloister, courtyard, piazza, plaza, quad (*Inf.*), quadrangle, square, yard **2.** hall, manor, palace **3.** attendants, retinue, royal household, suite, train **4.** bar, bench, court of justice, lawcourt, tribunal *~v.* **5.** chase, date, go (out) with, keep company with, make love to, pay court to, pursue, run after, serenade, take out, walk out with, woo **6.** cultivate, curry favour with, fawn upon, flatter, pander to, seek, solicit

courteous affable, attentive, civil, courtly, elegant, gallant, gracious, mannerly, polished, polite, refined, respectful, urbane, well-bred, well-mannered

courtesy affability, civility, elegance, gallantry, good breeding, good manners, graciousness, polish, politeness, urbanity

courtier attendant, follower, squire, train-bearer

courtly affable, ceremonious, chivalrous, civil, dignified, elegant, flattering, formal, gallant, lordly, polished, refined, stately, urbane

courtyard area, enclosure, playground, quad, quadrangle, yard

cove bay, creek, inlet, sound

covenant 1. bargain, commitment, compact, concordat, contract, convention, pact, promise, stipulation, treaty, trust **2.** bond, deed

cover *n.* **1.** cloak, cover-up, disguise, façade, front, mask, pretence, screen, smoke screen, veil **2.** concealment, defence, guard, hiding place, protection, refuge, sanctuary, shelter, shield **3.** compensation, indemnity, insurance, payment, protection *~v.* **4.** cloak, conceal, cover up, curtain, disguise, eclipse, hide, hood, house, mask, obscure, screen, secrete, shade, shroud, veil **5.** defend, guard, protect, reinforce, shelter, shield **6.** fill in for, relieve, stand in for, take over **7.** describe, detail, investigate, narrate, recount, relate, report, tell of, write up

covering 1. *n.* blanket, casing, clothing, coating, cover, housing, layer, overlay, protection, shelter, top, wrap, wrapper, wrapping **2.** *adj.* accompanying, descriptive, explanatory, introductory

cover up conceal, hide, hush up, keep dark, keep secret, keep silent about, repress, stonewall, suppress, whitewash (*Inf.*)

covet begrudge, crave, desire, envy, fancy (*Inf.*), hanker after, long for, lust after, thirst for, yearn for

covetous avaricious, envious, grasping, greedy, jealous, mercenary, yearning

coward craven, faint-heart, poltroon, renegade, sneak

cowardly base, craven, dastardly, faint-hearted, fearful, lily-livered, scared, shrinking, soft, spineless, timorous, weak, yellow (*Inf.*)

cower cringe, crouch, draw back, fawn, flinch, grovel, quail, shrink, skulk, sneak, tremble, truckle

coy arch, backward, bashful, demure, evasive, modest, prudish, reserved, retiring, self-effacing, shrinking, shy, skittish, timid

crack *v.* 1. break, burst, chip, chop, fracture, snap, splinter, split **2.** break down, collapse, give way, go to pieces, lose control, succumb, yield ~*n.* **3.** breach, break, chink, chip, cleft, cranny, crevice, fissure, fracture, gap, rift **4.** burst, clap, crash, explosion, pop, report, snap **5.** *Inf.* attempt, go, opportunity, stab, try **6.** *Sl.* dig, gag, insult, jibe, joke, quip, witticism ~*adj.* **7.** *Sl.* ace, choice, elite, excellent, first-class, first-rate, hand-picked, superior

cracked broken, chipped, crazed, damaged, defective, faulty, fissured, flawed, imperfect, split

crack up break down, collapse, go to pieces, have a breakdown

cradle *n.* 1. cot, crib, Moses basket **2.** *Fig.* beginning, birthplace, fount, origin, source, spring ~*v.* **3.** hold, lull, nestle, nurse, rock, support

craft 1. ability, aptitude, art, artistry, cleverness, dexterity, expertise, ingenuity, skill, technique, workmanship **2.** artfulness, contrivance, cunning, deceit, duplicity, guile, ruse, scheme, shrewdness, subtlety, trickery, wiles **3.** business, calling, employment, handicraft, handiwork, line, occupation, pursuit, trade, vocation, work **4.** aircraft, barque, boat, plane, ship, spacecraft, vessel

craftsman artificer, artisan, maker, master, skilled worker, smith, technician, wright

crafty artful, astute, calculating, canny, cunning, deceitful, designing, devious, foxy, fraudulent, guileful, knowing, scheming, sharp, shrewd, sly, subtle, tricky, wily

crag peak, pinnacle, rock, tor

cram compact, compress, crowd, crush, force, jam, overcrowd, overfill, pack, pack in, press, ram, shove, squeeze, stuff

cramp[1] *v.* check, clog, confine, encumber, hamper, handicap, hinder, impede, inhibit, obstruct, restrict, shackle

cramp[2] *n.* ache, crick, pain, pang, shooting pain, spasm, stiffness, twinge

cramped awkward, circumscribed, closed in, confined, congested, crowded, hemmed in, jammed in, narrow, overcrowded, packed, restricted, squeezed, uncomfortable

cranny breach, chink, cleft, crack, crevice, fissure, gap, hole, interstice, nook, opening

crash *n.* 1. bang, boom, clang, clash, din, racket, smash, thunder **2.** accident, bump, collision, jar, jolt, pile-up (*Inf.*), smash, thud, thump, wreck **3.** bankruptcy, collapse, debacle, depression, downfall, failure, ruin, smash ~*v.* **4.** come a cropper (*Inf.*), dash, fall, give way, hurtle, lurch, overbalance, pitch, plunge, precipitate oneself, sprawl, topple **5.** bang, bump (into), collide, crash-land (*an aircraft*), drive into, have an accident, hit, hurtle into, plough into, run together, wreck

crass asinine, boorish, bovine, coarse, dense, doltish, gross, insensitive, obtuse, stupid, unrefined

crate 1. *n.* box, case, container, packing case, tea chest **2.** *v.* box, case, encase, enclose, pack, pack up

crater depression, dip, hollow, shell hole

crave 1. cry out for (*Inf.*), desire, fancy (*Inf.*), hanker after, hunger after, long for, lust after, need, pant for, pine for, require, sigh for, thirst for, want, yearn for **2.** ask, beg, beseech, entreat, implore, petition, plead for, pray for, seek, solicit, supplicate

crawl 1. advance slowly, creep, drag, go on all fours, inch, pull *or* drag oneself along, slither, wriggle, writhe **2.** cringe, fawn, grovel, humble oneself, toady

craze enthusiasm, fad, fashion, infatuation, mania, mode, novelty, passion, rage, thing, trend, vogue

crazy 1. berserk, cracked (*Sl.*), cuckoo (*Inf.*), delirious, demented, deranged, idiotic, insane, mad, maniacal, mental (*Sl.*), not all there (*Inf.*), nuts (*Sl.*), nutty (*Sl.*), off one's head (*Sl.*), of unsound mind, potty (*Inf.*), round the bend (*Sl.*), touched, unbalanced, unhinged **2.** bizarre, eccentric, fantastic, odd, outrageous, peculiar, ridiculous, silly, strange, weird

creak *v.* grate, grind, groan, rasp, scrape, scratch, screech, squeak, squeal

cream 1. cosmetic, emulsion, liniment, lotion, oil, ointment, paste, salve, unguent **2.** best, *crème de la crème*, elite, flower, pick, prime

crease 1. *v.* crinkle, crumple, double up, fold, pucker, ridge, ruck up, rumple, screw up, wrinkle **2.** *n.* bulge, fold, groove, line, overlap, pucker, ridge, ruck, tuck, wrinkle

create beget, bring into being, coin, compose, concoct, design, develop, devise, form, formulate, generate, hatch, initiate, invent, make, originate, produce, spawn

creation 1. formation, generation, genesis, making, procreation, siring **2.** establishment, formation, foundation, inception, institution, laying down, origination, production, setting up **3.** achievement, brainchild (*Inf.*), concept, concoction, handiwork, invention, *magnum opus, pièce de résistance*, production

creative artistic, clever, fertile, gifted, imaginative, ingenious, inspired, inventive, original, productive, stimulating, visionary

creator architect, author, begetter, designer, father, framer, God, initiator, inventor, maker, originator, prime mover

creature animal, beast, being, brute, dumb animal, living thing, lower animal, quadruped

credentials authorization, card, certificate, deed, diploma, docket, licence, missive, passport, recommendation, reference(s), testimonial, title, voucher, warrant

credibility integrity, plausibility, reliability, tenability, trustworthiness

credible believable, conceivable, imaginable, likely, plausible, possible, probable, reasonable, tenable, thinkable

credit *n.* 1. acclaim, acknowledgment, approval, commendation, fame, glory, honour, kudos, merit, praise, recognition, thanks, tribute ~*v.* **2.** *With* **with** accredit, ascribe to, assign to, attribute to, impute to, refer to **3.** accept, bank on, believe, depend on, have faith in, rely on, trust

creditable admirable, commendable, deserving, estimable, exemplary, honourable, laudable, meritorious, praiseworthy, reputable, respectable, worthy

credulity blind faith, gullibility, naiveté, silliness, simplicity

creed articles of faith, belief, canon, catechism, confession, credo, doctrine, dogma, principles

creek bay, bight, cove, inlet

creep 1. crawl, glide, insinuate, slither, squirm, worm, wriggle, writhe **2.** skulk, slink, sneak, steal, tiptoe **3.** crawl, dawdle, drag, edge, inch

creeper climber, rambler, runner, vine

crescent half-moon, new moon, old moon, sickle, sickle-shape

crest apex, crown, head, height, highest point, peak, pinnacle, ridge, summit, top

crestfallen dejected, depressed, despondent, disappointed, disconsolate, downcast, downhearted

crevice chink, cleft, crack, cranny, fissure, fracture, gap, hole, rent, rift, slit, split

crew 1. hands, (ship's) company, (ship's) complement **2.** company, corps, gang, party, posse, squad, team, working party

crib *v. Inf.* cheat, pilfer, pirate, plagiarize, purloin, steal

crime fault, felony, misdeed, misdemeanour, offence, outrage, transgression, trespass, unlawful act, violation, wrong

criminal 1. *n.* convict, crook (*Inf.*), culprit, delinquent, evildoer, felon, jailbird, lawbreaker, malefactor, offender, sinner, transgressor **2.** *adj.* bent (*Sl.*), corrupt, crooked (*Inf.*), culpable, felonious, illegal, illicit, immoral, indictable, lawless, nefarious, unlawful, unrighteous, vicious, villainous, wicked, wrong

cripple *v.* disable, enfeeble, incapacitate, lame, maim, paralyse, weaken

crippled bedridden, deformed, disabled, enfeebled, handicapped, incapacitated, lame, paralysed

crisis 1. climax, crunch (*Inf.*), crux, height, turning point **2.** catastrophe, critical situation, dilemma, dire straits, disaster, emergency, exigency, extremity, mess, plight, predicament, quandary, strait, trouble

crisp 1. brittle, crispy, crumbly, crunchy, firm, fresh, unwilted **2.** bracing, brisk, fresh, invigorating, refreshing **3.** brief, brusque, clear, incisive, pithy, short, succinct, tart, terse

criterion canon, gauge, measure, norm, principle, rule, standard, test, yardstick

critic 1. analyst, arbiter, authority, commentator, connoisseur, expert, judge, pundit, reviewer **2.** carper, caviller, censor, detractor, fault-finder

critical 1. captious, carping, cavilling, censorious, derogatory, disapproving, disparaging, fault-finding, nagging, niggling **2.** accurate, analytical, diagnostic, discerning, discriminating, fastidious, judicious, penetrating, perceptive, precise **3.** crucial, dangerous, deciding, decisive, grave, momentous, perilous, pivotal, precarious, pressing, risky, serious, urgent, vital

criticism 1. bad press, censure, disapproval, disparagement, fault-finding, stricture **2.** analysis, appraisal, appreciation, assessment, comment, commentary, critique, elucidation, evaluation, judgment, notice, review

criticize carp, censure, condemn, disapprove of, disparage, nag at, pick to pieces, slate (*Inf.*)

croak *v.* caw, gasp, grunt, squawk, utter *or* speak harshly

crook cheat, criminal, racketeer, robber, rogue, shark, swindler, thief, villain

crooked 1. bent, bowed, crippled, curved, deformed, deviating, disfigured, distorted, hooked, irregular, misshapen, tortuous, twisted, twisting, warped, winding, zigzag **2.** askew, asymmetric, awry, lopsided, off-centre, slanted, slanting, squint **3.** *Inf.* bent (*Sl.*), corrupt, crafty, criminal, deceitful, dishonest, dishonourable, dubious, fraudulent, illegal, knavish, nefarious, questionable, shady (*Inf.*), shifty, underhand, unlawful, unscrupulous

croon breathe, hum, purr, sing, warble

crop 1. *n.* fruits, gathering, harvest, produce, reaping, season's growth, vintage, yield 2. *v.* clip, curtail, cut, lop, mow, pare, prune, reduce, shear, shorten, snip, top, trim

crop up appear, arise, emerge, happen, occur, spring up, turn up

cross *adj.* 1. angry, annoyed, captious, churlish, crusty, disagreeable, fractious, fretful, ill-humoured, ill-tempered, impatient, in a bad mood, irascible, irritable, out of humour, peevish, pettish, petulant, put out, querulous, short, snappish, snappy, sullen, surly, testy, vexed, waspish 2. crosswise, intersecting, oblique, transverse ~*v.* 3. bridge, cut across, extend over, ford, meet, pass over, ply, span, traverse, zigzag 4. crisscross, intersect, intertwine, lace 5. blend, crossbreed, hybridize, interbreed, mix ~*n.* 6. crucifix, rood 7. crossing, crossroads, intersection, junction 8. blend, combination, crossbreed, cur, hybrid, mixture, mongrel

cross-examine catechize, grill (*Inf.*), interrogate, pump, question, quiz

cross out *or* **off** blue-pencil, cancel, delete, eliminate, strike off *or* out

crouch bend down, bow, duck, hunch, kneel, squat, stoop

crow boast, brag, exult, gloat, glory in, strut, swagger, triumph, vaunt

crowd *n.* 1. army, assembly, company, flock, herd, horde, host, mass, mob, multitude, pack, press, rabble, swarm, throng, troupe 2. attendance, audience, gate, house, spectators ~*v.* 3. cluster, congregate, cram, flock, gather, huddle, mass, muster, press, push, stream, surge, swarm, throng

crowded busy, congested, cramped, crushed, full, huddled, mobbed, packed, populous, swarming, thronged

crown *n.* 1. chaplet, circlet, coronet, diadem, tiara 2. bays, distinction, garland, honour, kudos, laurels, prize, trophy 3. emperor, empress, king, monarch, monarchy, queen, *rex*, royalty, ruler, sovereign, sovereignty ~*v.* 4. adorn, dignify, festoon, honour, invest, reward 5. be the climax *or* culmination of, cap, complete, consummate, finish, fulfil, perfect, put the finishing touch to, round off, surmount, terminate, top

crucial central, critical, decisive, pivotal, searching, testing, trying

crucify execute, harrow, persecute, rack, torment, torture

crude 1. boorish, coarse, crass, dirty, gross, indecent, lewd, obscene, smutty, tactless, tasteless, uncouth, vulgar 2. natural, raw, unpolished, unprepared, unprocessed, unrefined 3. clumsy, makeshift, outline, primitive, rough, rough-hewn, rude, rudimentary, sketchy, undeveloped, unfinished, unformed, unpolished

crudely bluntly, clumsily, coarsely, impolitely, indecently, roughly, rudely, tastelessly, vulgarly

crudity coarseness, crudeness, impropriety, indelicacy, lewdness, loudness, lowness, obscenity, vulgarity

cruel 1. barbarous, bitter, brutal, callous, cold-blooded, ferocious, fierce, grim, hard, hard-hearted, harsh, heartless, hellish, implacable, inclement, inhuman, inhumane, malevolent, painful, ravening, raw, remorseless, sadistic, savage, severe, spiteful, unfeeling, unkind, vengeful, vicious 2. merciless, pitiless, ruthless, unrelenting

cruelly brutally, callously, ferociously, fiercely, heartlessly, in cold blood, mercilessly, pitilessly, sadistically, savagely, spitefully, unmercifully, viciously

cruelty bestiality, bloodthirstiness, brutality, callousness, depravity, ferocity, hardheartedness, harshness, inhumanity, sadism, savagery, severity, spite, spitefulness, venom

cruise 1. *v.* coast, sail, voyage 2. *n.* boat trip, sail, sea trip, voyage

crumb atom, bit, grain, mite, morsel, particle, scrap, shred, sliver, snippet, *soupçon*, speck

crumble 1. bruise, crumb, crush, fragment, granulate, grind, pound, powder 2. break up, collapse, come to dust, decay, decompose, degenerate, deteriorate, disintegrate, fall apart, go to pieces (*Inf.*), moulder, perish, tumble down

crumple 1. crease, crush, pucker, rumple, screw up, wrinkle 2. break down, cave in, collapse, fall, give way, go to pieces

crusade campaign, cause, drive, holy war, movement

crush 1. break, bruise, compress, crease, crumble, crumple, crunch, mash, pound, pulverize, rumple, smash, squeeze, wrinkle 2. conquer, overcome, overpower, overwhelm, put down, quell, stamp out, subdue, vanquish

crust coat, coating, covering, layer, outside, shell, skin, surface

crusty 1. brittle, crisp, crispy, friable, hard, short, well-baked, well-done 2. brusque, captious, choleric, crabby, cross, curt, gruff, irritable, peevish, prickly, snarling, surly, testy, touchy

cry *v.* 1. bawl, bewail, blubber, lament, shed tears, snivel, sob, wail, weep, whimper, whine, whinge (*Inf.*) 2. bawl, bellow, call, call out, exclaim, hail, howl, roar, scream, screech, shout, shriek, sing out, whoop, yell ~*n.* 3. blubbering, howl, keening, lament, lamentation, snivel, snivelling, sob, sobbing, sorrowing, wailing, weep, weeping

cry off back out, beg off, excuse oneself, quit, withdraw, withdraw from

cub 1. offspring, whelp, young 2. babe (*Inf.*), beginner, fledgling, lad, learner, recruit, trainee, youngster

cudgel baton, bludgeon, club, cosh, stick, truncheon

cue hint, key, nod, prompting, reminder, sign, signal, suggestion

culminate climax, close, conclude, end, end up, finish, terminate

culprit criminal, delinquent, felon, guilty party, miscreant, offender, rascal, sinner, wrongdoer

cult 1. body, church faction, clique, denomination, faith, following, party, religion, school, sect 2. admiration, craze, devotion, reverence, veneration, worship

cultivate 1. farm, harvest, plant, plough, prepare, tend, till, work 2. better, bring on, cherish, civilize, develop, discipline, elevate, enrich, foster, improve, polish, promote, refine, train

cultivation advancement, advocacy, development, encouragement, enhancement, fostering, furtherance, help, nurture, patronage, promotion, support

cultural artistic, broadening, civilizing, edifying, educational, educative, elevating, enriching, humane, humanizing, liberal

culture 1. civilization, customs, life style, mores, society, the arts, way of life 2. accomplishment, breeding, education, elevation, enlightenment, erudition, good taste, improvement, polish, politeness, refinement, urbanity

cultured accomplished, advanced, educated, enlightened, erudite, genteel, knowledgeable, polished, refined, scholarly, urbane, versed, well-bred, well-informed, well-read

culvert channel, conduit, drain, gutter, watercourse

cumbersome awkward, bulky, clumsy, heavy, incommodious, inconvenient, oppressive, unmanageable, unwieldy, weighty

cunning 1. *adj.* artful, astute, canny, crafty, devious, guileful, knowing, Machiavellian, sharp, shifty, shrewd, subtle, tricky, wily 2. *n.* artfulness, astuteness, craftiness, deceitfulness, deviousness, guile, shrewdness, slyness, trickery, wiliness

cup beaker, chalice, draught, drink, goblet, potion, teacup, trophy

curb 1. *v.* bite back, bridle, check, constrain, contain, control, hinder, impede, inhibit, moderate, muzzle, repress, restrain, restrict, retard, subdue, suppress 2. *n.* brake, bridle, check, control, deterrent, limitation, rein, restraint

cure *v.* 1. alleviate, correct, ease, heal, help, make better, mend, rehabilitate, relieve, remedy, restore, restore to health ~*n.* 2. antidote, healing, medicine, panacea, recovery, remedy, restorative, specific, treatment ~*v.* 3. dry, kipper, pickle, preserve, salt, smoke

curiosity 1. interest, prying 2. freak, marvel, novelty, oddity, phenomenon, rarity, sight, spectacle, wonder

curious 1. inquiring, inquisitive, interested, puzzled, questioning, searching 2. inquisitive, meddling, peeping, peering, prying, 3. bizarre, exotic, extraordinary, mysterious, novel, odd, peculiar, puzzling, quaint, queer, rare, singular, strange, unconventional, unique, unorthodox, unusual, wonderful

curl *v.* bend, coil, corkscrew, crimp, crinkle, crisp, curve, entwine, frizz, loop, meander, ripple, spiral, turn, twine, twirl, twist, wind, wreathe, writhe

currency bills, coinage, coins, money, notes

current *adj.* 1. accepted, circulating, common, customary, general, in circulation, in progress, in the air, in the news, ongoing, popular, present, prevailing, prevalent, rife, widespread 2. in, in fashion, in vogue, now (*Inf.*), present-day, up-to-date ~*n.* 3. course, draught, flow, jet, river, stream, tide

curse *n.* 1. blasphemy, expletive, oath, obscenity, swearing, swearword 2. ban, evil eye, excommunication, execration, imprecation, jinx, malediction 3. bane, burden, calamity, cross, disaster, evil, misfortune, ordeal, plague, scourge, torment, tribulation, trouble, vexation ~*v.* 4. blaspheme, swear, use bad language 5. damn, excommunicate, execrate, fulminate, imprecate

cursed 1. blighted, cast out, confounded, damned, doomed, execrable, ill-fated, unholy, unsanctified, villainous 2. abominable, damnable, detestable, devilish, fiendish, hateful, infamous, infernal, loathsome, odious, pernicious, pestilential, vile

curt abrupt, blunt, brief, brusque, gruff, offhand, pithy, rude, sharp, short, snappish, succinct, summary, tart, terse, unceremonious, uncivil, ungracious

curtail abbreviate, abridge, contract, cut, cut back, decrease, dock, lessen, lop, pare down, reduce, shorten, trim, truncate

curtain 1. *n.* drape (*Chiefly U.S.*), hanging 2. *v.* conceal, drape, hide, screen, shroud, shut off, shutter, veil

curve 1. *v.* arc, arch, bend, bow, coil, hook, inflect, turn, twist, wind 2. *n.* arc, bend, camber, half-moon, loop, turn

curved arched, bent, bowed, crooked, humped, rounded, sinuous, sweeping, turned, twisted

custody arrest, confinement, detention, imprisonment, incarceration

custom habit, manner, routine, way, wont

customary accepted, accustomed, acknowledged, common, confirmed, conventional, everyday, familiar, fashionable, general, normal, ordinary, popular, regular, routine, traditional, usual

customer buyer, client, consumer, habitué, patron, prospect, purchaser, regular (*Inf.*), shopper

customs duty, import charges, tariff, taxes, toll

cut *v.* 1. chop, cleave, divide, gash, incise, lacerate, nick, notch, penetrate, pierce, score, sever, slash, slice, slit, wound 2. carve, chip, chisel, chop, engrave, fashion, form, saw, sculpt, sculpture, shape, whittle

3. contract, cut back, decrease, ease up on, lower, rationalize, reduce, slash, slim (down) 4. abbreviate, abridge, condense, curtail, delete, edit out, excise, precis, shorten ~*n.* 5. gash, graze, groove, incision, laceration, nick, rent, rip, slash, slit, stroke, wound 6. cutback, decrease, economy, fall, lowering, reduction, saving

cutback cut, decrease, economy, lessening, reduction, retrenchment

cut down fell, hew, level, lop, raze

cut in break in, butt in, interpose, interrupt, intervene, intrude, move in

cut off 1. disconnect, intercept, interrupt, intersect 2. isolate, separate, sever

cut out cease, delete, extract, give up, refrain from, remove, sever, stop

cut-price bargain, cheap, reduced, sale

cut short break off, check, halt, interrupt, postpone, stop, terminate

cutting *adj.* biting, bitter, chill, keen, numbing, penetrating, piercing, raw, sharp, stinging

cut up 1. carve, chop, dice, divide, mince, slice 2. injure, knife, lacerate, slash, wound

cycle age, circle, era, period, phase, revolution, rotation

cynic doubter, pessimist, sceptic, scoffer

cynical derisive, ironic, misanthropical, mocking, pessimistic, sarcastic, sardonic, sceptical, scornful, sneering, unbelieving

D

dagger bayonet, dirk, poniard, skean, stiletto

daily *adj.* 1. diurnal, everyday, quotidian 2. common, commonplace, day-to-day, everyday, ordinary, regular, routine ~*adv.* 3. day after day, every day, often, once a day, regularly

dainty charming, delicate, elegant, fine, graceful, neat, petite, pretty

dam 1. *n.* barrage, barrier, hindrance, obstruction, wall 2. *v.* barricade, block, check, choke, confine, hold back, hold in, obstruct, restrict

damage *n.* 1. destruction, devastation, harm, hurt, injury, loss, mischief, suffering 2. *Plural* fine, indemnity, reimbursement, reparation, satisfaction ~*v.* 3. deface, harm, hurt, impair, injure, mar, mutilate, ruin, spoil, tamper with, weaken, wreck

damaging detrimental, harmful, hurtful, injurious, prejudicial, ruinous

dame baroness, dowager, lady, noblewoman, peeress

damn *v.* 1. blast, castigate, censure, condemn, criticize, denounce, denunciate, pan (*Inf.*), slam (*Sl.*), slate (*Inf.*) 2. abuse, curse, execrate, imprecate, revile, swear 3. condemn, doom, sentence ~*n.* 4. brass farthing, hoot, iota, jot, tinker's damn (*Sl.*), two hoots, whit

damned 1. accursed, condemned, doomed, infernal, lost, reprobate, unhappy 2. despicable, detestable, hateful, infamous, infernal, loathsome, revolting

damp *n.* 1. dampness, darkness, dew, drizzle, fog, humidity, mist, moisture, vapour ~*adj.* 2. clammy, dank, dewy, dripping, drizzly, humid, misty, moist, muggy, sodden, soggy, sopping, vaporous, wet ~*v.* 3. dampen, moisten, wet 4. *Fig.* allay, check, chill, cool, curb, dash, deaden, deject, depress, diminish, discourage, dispirit, dull, inhibit, moderate, restrain, stifle

dance 1. *v.* caper, frolic, gambol, hop, jig, prance, rock, skip, spin, sway, swing, whirl 2. *n.* ball, dancing party, social

danger hazard, insecurity, jeopardy, menace, peril, risk, threat, venture, vulnerability

dangerous alarming, breakneck, chancy (*Inf.*), exposed, hazardous, insecure, menacing, nasty, perilous, risky, threatening, treacherous, ugly, unsafe

dangerously alarmingly, carelessly, daringly, desperately, harmfully, hazardously, perilously, precariously, recklessly, riskily, unsafely, unsecurely

dangle 1. depend, flap, hang, hang down, sway, swing, trail 2. brandish, entice, flaunt, flourish, lure, tantalize, tempt, wave

dare *v.* 1. challenge, defy, goad, provoke, taunt 2. brave, gamble, hazard, make bold, presume, risk, stake, venture ~*n.* 3. challenge, defiance, provocation, taunt

daredevil 1. *n.* adventurer, desperado, madcap, show-off (*Inf.*), stunt man 2. *adj.* adventurous, audacious, bold, daring, death-defying, madcap, reckless

daring 1. *adj.* adventurous, bold, brave, fearless, game (*Inf.*), impulsive, intrepid, plucky, rash, reckless, valiant, venturesome 2. *n.* boldness, bravery, courage, fearlessness, grit, guts (*Inf.*), nerve (*Inf.*), pluck, rashness, spirit, temerity

dark *adj.* 1. black, dusky, ebony, sable, swarthy 2. cloudy, dim, dingy, indistinct, murky, overcast, pitch-black, pitchy, shadowy, shady, sunless, unlit 3. abstruse, arcane, concealed, cryptic, deep, enigmatic, hidden, mysterious, mystic, obscure, occult, recondite, secret 4. bleak, cheerless, dismal, doleful, drab, gloomy, grim, joyless, morbid, morose, mournful, sombre 5. angry, dour, forbidding, frowning, glowering, glum, ominous, scowling, sulky, sullen, threatening ~*n.* 6. darkness, dimness, dusk, gloom, murk, murkiness, obscurity, semi-darkness 7. evening, night, nightfall, night-time, twilight

darkness dark, dimness, dusk, gloom, murk, nightfall, obscurity, shade, shadiness, shadows

darling *n.* 1. beloved, dear, dearest, love, sweetheart 2. favourite, pet ~*adj.* 3. adored, beloved, cherished, dear, precious, treasured

darn mend, patch, repair, sew up, stitch

dart bound, dash, flash, flit, fly, race, run, rush, shoot, spring, sprint, start, tear, whiz

dash *v.* 1. break, crash, destroy, shatter, shiver, smash 2. cast, fling, hurl, slam, sling, throw 3. bolt, bound, dart, fly, haste, hasten, hurry, race, run, rush, speed, spring, sprint, tear 4. abash, chagrin, confound, dampen, disappoint, discomfort, discourage ~*n.* 5. brio, élan, flair, flourish, panache, spirit, style, verve, vigour, vivacity

dashing bold, daring, debonair, exuberant, gallant, lively, plucky, spirited, swashbuckling

data details, documents, facts, figures, information, input, materials, statistics

date 1. age, epoch, era, period, stage, time 2. appointment, assignation, engagement, meeting, rendezvous, tryst

dated antiquated, archaic, obsolete, old-fashioned, old hat, out, outdated, out of date, passé, unfashionable

daub *v.* coat, cover, paint, plaster, slap on (*Inf.*), smear

daunt alarm, appal, cow, dismay, frighten, intimidate, overawe, scare, subdue, terrify

dawdle dally, delay, hang about, idle, lag, loaf, loiter, potter, trail, waste time

dawn 1. *n.* daybreak, daylight, morning, sunrise 2. *v.* break, brighten, gleam, glimmer, grow light, lighten

day 1. daylight, daytime, twenty-four hours, working day 2. date, particular day, point in time, set time, time 3. **day after day** continually, monotonously, persistently, regularly, relentlessly 4. **day by day** daily, gradually, progressively, steadily

daydream *n.* 1. dream, musing, reverie, vision 2. dream, fancy, fantasy, fond hope, pipe dream, wish ~*v.* 3. dream, fancy, fantasize, imagine, muse

daylight 1. sunlight, sunshine 2. broad day, daytime 3. full view, openness, public attention

daze *v.* 1. benumb, numb, paralyse, shock, stun, stupefy 2. amaze, astonish, astound, befog, bewilder, blind, confuse, dazzle, perplex, stagger, startle, surprise ~*n.* 3. bewilderment, confusion, shock, stupor, trance

dazed baffled, bemused, bewildered, confused, dizzy, dopey (*Sl.*), fuddled, light-headed, muddled, numbed, perplexed, shocked, staggered, stunned, stupefied

dazzle 1. bedazzle, blind, blur, confuse, daze 2. amaze, astonish, awe, bowl over (*Inf.*), fascinate, impress, overawe, overpower, overwhelm, strike dumb, stupefy

dead 1. deceased, defunct, departed, extinct, gone, inanimate, late, lifeless, passed away, perished 2. callous, cold, dull, frigid, glassy, glazed, indifferent, inert, lukewarm, numb, paralysed, spiritless, torpid, unresponsive, wooden 3. boring, dull, flat, insipid, stale, tasteless, uninteresting, vapid

deadlock dead heat, draw, full stop, halt, impasse, stalemate, tie

deadly 1. baleful, baneful, dangerous, deathly, destructive, fatal, lethal, malignant, mortal, noxious, pernicious, poisonous, venomous 2. cruel, grim, implacable, mortal, ruthless 3. accurate, effective, exact, on target, precise, sure, true, unerring, unfailing

deaf 1. hard of hearing, stone deaf 2. oblivious, unconcerned, unhearing, unmoved

deafen din, drown out, make deaf, split *or* burst the eardrums

deafening booming, dinning, ear-splitting, intense, piercing, resounding, ringing

deal *v.* 1. bargain, buy and sell, do business, negotiate, sell, stock, trade, traffic, treat (with) 2. allot, apportion, assign, bestow, dispense, distribute, divide, dole out, give, reward, share ~*n.* 3. *Inf.* agreement, arrangement, bargain, contract, pact, transaction, understanding

dealer marketer, merchant, trader, tradesman, wholesaler

dear *adj.* 1. beloved, cherished, close, darling, esteemed, familiar, favourite, intimate, precious, prized, respected, treasured 2. costly, expensive, high-priced ~*n.* 3. angel, beloved, darling, loved one, precious, treasure

dearly extremely, greatly, profoundly, very much

death 1. bereavement, decease, demise, departure, dying, end, exit, expiration, loss, passing, quietus, release 2. destruction, downfall, extinction, finish, grave, ruin, undoing

deathless eternal, everlasting, immortal, imperishable, timeless

deathly 1. gaunt, ghastly, grim, haggard, pale, pallid, wan 2. deadly, extreme, fatal, intense, mortal, terrible

debase cheapen, degrade, demean, devalue, disgrace, dishonour, drag down, humble, lower, reduce, shame

debatable arguable, borderline, controversial, disputable, doubtful, dubious, in dispute, moot, open to question, questionable, uncertain, unsettled

debate *v.* 1. argue, contend, contest, discuss, dispute, question, wrangle ~*n.* 2. argument, contention, controversy, discussion, disputation, dispute 3. cogitation, consideration, deliberation, meditation, reflection

debris bits, dross, fragments, litter, pieces, remains, rubbish, rubble, ruins, waste, wreck, wreckage

debt arrears, bill, commitment, debit, due, duty, liability, obligation, score

debtor borrower, defaulter, insolvent

debunk cut down to size, deflate, disparage, expose, lampoon, mock, puncture, ridicule, show up

debut beginning, bow, coming out, entrance, inauguration, initiation, introduction, launching

decadent corrupt, debased, decaying, declining, degenerate, degraded, depraved, dissolute, immoral

decay *v.* 1. crumble, decline, degenerate, deteriorate, disintegrate, dissolve, dwindle, moulder, shrivel, sink, spoil, wane, wither 2. decompose, mortify, perish, putrefy, rot

decease death, demise, departure, dissolution, dying, release

deceased *adj.* dead, defunct, departed, expired, finished, former, gone, late, lifeless, lost

deceit artifice, cheating, cunning, dissimulation, double-dealing, duplicity, fraud, guile, hypocrisy, imposition, pretence, slyness, treachery, trickery

deceitful crafty, designing, dishonest, disingenuous, double-dealing, duplicitous, fallacious, false, fraudulent, guileful, hypocritical, illusory, insincere, treacherous, tricky, two-faced, underhand, untrustworthy

deceive beguile, betray, cheat, con (*Sl.*), cozen, delude, double-cross (*Inf.*), dupe, ensnare, entrap, fool, hoax, hoodwink, mislead, outwit, swindle, take in (*Inf.*), trick

decency correctness, courtesy, decorum, etiquette, good form, good manners, modesty, propriety, seemliness

decent becoming, chaste, comely, decorous, delicate, fit, modest, nice, polite, presentable, proper, pure, respectable, seemly, suitable

deception cunning, deceit, duplicity, fraud, fraudulence, guile, hypocrisy, imposition, insincerity, treachery, trickery

deceptive deceitful, delusive, dishonest, fake, false, fraudulent, illusory, misleading, mock, spurious, unreliable

decide adjudicate, choose, commit oneself, conclude, decree, determine, elect, end, purpose, resolve, settle

decipher construe, crack, decode, explain, interpret, make out, read, reveal, solve, understand, unfold, unravel

decision conclusion, finding, judgment, outcome, resolution, result, ruling, sentence, settlement, verdict

decisive 1. absolute, conclusive, critical, crucial, definite, definitive, fateful, final, influential, significant 2. determined, firm, forceful, incisive, resolute, strong-minded

deck *v.* adorn, array, attire, beautify, bedeck, bedight clothe, decorate, dress, embellish, festoon, grace, ornament

declaim harangue, hold forth, lecture, proclaim, rant, recite, speak

declaration 1. affirmation, assertion, disclosure, revelation, statement, testimony 2. announcement, edict, manifesto, notification, promulgation, pronouncement

declare affirm, announce, assert, attest, aver, avow, claim, confirm, maintain, proclaim, profess, pronounce, state, swear, testify

decline *v.* 1. avoid, deny, forgo, refuse, reject, say 'no', turn down 2. decrease, diminish, dwindle, ebb, fade, fail, fall, fall off, flag, lessen, shrink, sink, wane ~*n.* 3. downturn, dwindling, falling off, lessening, recession, slump

décor colour scheme, decoration, ornamentation

decorate 1. adorn, beautify, deck, embellish, enrich, grace, ornament, trim 2. colour, furbish, paint, paper, renovate 3. cite, honour

decoration 1. adornment, embellishment, enrichment, ornamentation, trimming 2. flounce, flourish, frill, garnish, ornament, scroll, spangle, trimmings, trinket 3. award, badge, colours, emblem, garter, medal, order, ribbon, star

decorum behaviour, breeding, decency, dignity, etiquette, gentility, good grace, good manners, gravity, politeness, propriety, protocol, respectability, seemliness

decoy 1. *n.* attraction, bait, enticement, inducement, lure, pretence, trap 2. *v.* allure, bait, deceive, ensnare, entice, entrap, inveigle, lure, seduce, tempt

decrease 1. *v.* abate, contract, curtail, cut down, decline, diminish, drop, dwindle, ease, fall off, lessen, lower, reduce, shrink, slacken, subside, wane 2. *n.* cutback, decline, ebb, falling off, loss, reduction, shrinkage, subsidence

decree 1. *n.* act, command, edict, enactment, law, mandate, order, precept, proclamation, regulation, ruling, statute 2. *v.* command, decide, determine, dictate, enact, lay down, ordain, order, prescribe, proclaim, rule

decrepit aged, crippled, debilitated, effete, feeble, frail, incapacitated, infirm, wasted, weak

dedicate commit, devote, give over to, pledge, surrender

dedicated committed, devoted, enthusiastic, purposeful, single-minded, wholehearted, zealous

deduce conclude, derive, draw, gather, glean, infer, reason, understand

deduct decrease by, reduce by, remove, subtract, take away, take from, withdraw

deduction 1. conclusion, consequence, finding, inference, reasoning, result 2. decrease, diminution, discount, reduction, subtraction

deed act, action, exploit, fact, feat, reality

deep *adj.* 1. bottomless, broad, far, profound, wide, yawning 2. extreme, grave, great, intense, profound 3. *Of a sound* bass, booming, full-toned, low, low-pitched, resonant, sonorous ~*adv.* 4. far down, far into, late

deeply completely, gravely, profoundly, seriously, thoroughly

de facto *adv.* actually, in effect, in fact, in reality, really

default 1. *n.* absence, defect, failure, lack, lapse, neglect, nonpayment, omission, want 2. *v.* bilk, defraud, dodge, evade, fail, neglect, rat, swindle

defeat 1. *v.* beat, conquer, crush, overpower, overthrow, overwhelm, quell, repulse, rout, subdue, subjugate, vanquish 2. *n.* conquest, debacle, overthrow, repulse, rout

defect 1. *n.* blemish, blotch, error, failing, fault, flaw, imperfection, mistake, spot, taint, want 2. *v.* change sides, desert, go over, rebel, revolt

defective broken, faulty, flawed, imperfect, inadequate, incomplete, insufficient, not working, out of order, scant, short

defence 1. armament, cover, deterrence, guard, immunity, protection, resistance, safeguard, security, shelter 2. apologia, argument, excuse, exoneration, explanation, justification, plea, vindication 3. *Law* alibi, case, declaration, denial, plea, pleading, rebuttal, testimony

defend 1. cover, fortify, guard, keep safe, preserve, protect, screen, secure, shelter, shield 2. assert, champion, endorse, espouse, justify, maintain, plead, speak up for, stand by, stand up for, support, sustain, uphold, vindicate

defender 1. bodyguard, escort, guard, protector 2. advocate, champion, patron, sponsor, supporter, vindicator

defer adjourn, delay, hold over, postpone, protract, put off, set aside, shelve, suspend, table

defiance challenge, contempt, disobedience, disregard, insolence, insubordination, opposition, rebelliousness, spite

deficiency defect, demerit, failing, fault, flaw, frailty, shortcoming, weakness

deficit arrears, default, deficiency, loss, shortage, shortfall

define describe, designate, detail, determine, explain, expound, interpret, specify, spell out

definite clear, clear-cut, determined, exact, explicit, express, fixed, marked, obvious, particular, precise, specific

definitely absolutely, categorically, certainly, clearly, easily, finally, indubitably, obviously, plainly, positively, surely, undeniably, unequivocally, unmistakably, unquestionably, without doubt, without question

definition clarification, description, elucidation, explanation, exposition, statement of meaning

deflate 1. collapse, contract, exhaust, flatten, puncture, shrink, void 2. chasten, dash, disconcert, dispirit, squash

deflect bend, diverge, glance off, shy, sidetrack, swerve, turn, twist, veer, wind

defraud beguile, bilk, cheat, delude, dupe, embezzle, fleece, outwit, pilfer, rob, rook (*Sl.*), swindle, trick

deft able, adept, adroit, agile, clever, dexterous, expert, handy, neat, nimble, proficient, skilful

defunct dead, deceased, departed, extinct, gone

defy beard, brave, challenge, confront, dare, despise, disregard, face, flout, provoke, scorn, slight, spurn

degenerate 1. *adj.* base, corrupt, debased, debauched, decadent, degraded, depraved, dissolute, fallen, immoral, low, mean 2. *v.* decay, decline, deteriorate, fall off, lapse, regress, rot, sink, slip, worsen

degrade cheapen, corrupt, debase, demean, discredit, disgrace, humble, humiliate, impair, injure, pervert, shame

degree 1. class, grade, level, order, position, rank, standing, station, status 2. calibre, extent, intensity, level, measure, proportion, quality, quantity, range, rate, ratio, scale, scope, standard

deity divinity, god, goddess, godhead, idol, immortal

dejected cast down, crestfallen, depressed, despondent, disconsolate, disheartened, dismal, doleful, down, downcast, gloomy, glum, low, low-spirited, melancholy, miserable, morose, sad, wretched

de jure by right, legally, rightfully

delay *v.* 1. defer, hold over, postpone, procrastinate, prolong, protract, put off, shelve, stall, suspend, table, temporize ~*n.* 2. deferment, postponement, procrastination, stay, suspension 3. check, detention, hindrance, hold-up, impediment, interruption, interval, obstruction, setback, stoppage, wait

delegate *n.* agent, ambassador, commissioner, deputy, envoy, legate, representative, vicar

delegation commission, contingent, deputation, embassy, envoys, legation, mission

delete blot out, cancel, cross out, cut out, dele, edit, efface, erase, expunge, obliterate, remove, rub out

deliberate 1. *v.* cogitate, consider, consult, debate, discuss, meditate, mull over, ponder, reflect, think, weigh 2. *adj.* calculated, conscious, considered, designed, intentional, planned, premeditated, purposeful, studied, thoughtful, wilful

deliberately by design, calculatingly, consciously, determinedly, emphatically, in cold blood, intentionally, knowingly, on purpose, wilfully

deliberation care, carefulness, caution, circumspection, consideration, coolness, forethought, meditation, prudence, purpose, reflection, speculation, study, thought, wariness

delicacy 1. elegance, exquisiteness, fineness, lightness, nicety, precision, subtlety 2. discrimination, finesse, purity, refinement, sensibility, sensitivity, tact, taste 3. *bonne bouche*, dainty, luxury, relish, savoury, titbit, treat

delicate 1. ailing, debilitated, flimsy, fragile, frail, sickly, slender, slight, tender, weak 2. accurate, deft, detailed, minute, precise, skilled 3. considerate, diplomatic, discreet, sensitive, tactful 4. critical, difficult, precarious, sensitive, ticklish, touchy

delicately carefully, deftly, elegantly, exquisitely, fastidiously, finely, gracefully, lightly, precisely, sensitively, skilfully, softly, subtly, tactfully

delicious appetizing, choice, dainty, luscious, mouthwatering, savoury, tasty, toothsome

delight 1. *n.* ecstasy, enjoyment, gladness, gratification, happiness, joy, pleasure, rapture, transport 2. *v.* amuse, charm, cheer, divert, enchant, gratify, please, ravish, rejoice, satisfy, thrill

delighted *adj.* captivated, charmed, enchanted, gladdened, happy, jubilant, overjoyed, pleased, thrilled

delightful agreeable, amusing,

captivating, charming, congenial, delectable, engaging, enjoyable, entertaining, fascinating, heavenly, pleasant, pleasurable, ravishing, thrilling

deliver 1. bear, bring, carry, cart, convey, distribute, transport 2. cede, commit, give up, grant, hand over, make over, relinquish, resign, surrender, transfer, turn over, yield 3. acquit, discharge, emancipate, free, liberate, loose, ransom, redeem, release, rescue, save

delivery 1. consignment, conveyance, dispatch, distribution, handing over, surrender, transfer, transmission, transmittal 2. escape, liberation, release, rescue

delude beguile, cheat, cozen, deceive, dupe, fool, gull (*Archaic*), hoax, hoodwink, impose on, misguide, mislead, take in (*Inf.*), trick

deluge cataclysm, downpour, flood, inundation, overflowing, spate, torrent

de luxe choice, costly, elegant, exclusive, expensive, grand, opulent, palatial, rich, select, special, splendid, sumptuous, superior

demagogue agitator, firebrand, rabble-rouser, soapbox orator

demand *v.* 1. ask, challenge, inquire, interrogate, question, request 2. call for, cry out for, involve, necessitate, need, require, take, want ~*n.* 3. bidding, charge, inquiry, interrogation, order, question, request, requisition

demanding challenging, difficult, exacting, exhausting, hard, taxing, tough, trying, wearing

demeanour air, bearing, behaviour, carriage, conduct, deportment, manner, mien

democracy commonwealth, government by the people, representative government, republic

democratic autonomous, egalitarian, popular, populist, representative, republican, self-governing

demolish 1. bulldoze, destroy, dismantle, flatten, knock down, level, overthrow, pulverize, raze, ruin, tear down 2. *Fig.* annihilate, defeat, destroy, overthrow, overturn, undo, wreck

demon 1. devil, evil spirit, fiend, goblin, malignant spirit 2. *Fig.* devil, fiend, monster, rogue, villain

demonstrable attestable, certain, evident, evincible, incontrovertible, indubitable, irrefutable, obvious, positive, self-evident, undeniable, unmistakable, verifiable

demonstrate 1. display, establish, evidence, exhibit, indicate, prove, show, testify to 2. describe, explain, illustrate, make clear, show how, teach 3. march, parade, picket, protest, rally

demonstration 1. confirmation, display, evidence, exhibition, expression, illustration, manifestation, proof, testimony, validation 2. explanation, exposition, presentation, test, trial 3. march, mass lobby, parade, picket, protest, rally, sit-in

demur *v.* balk, cavil, disagree, dispute, doubt, hesitate, object, pause, protest, refuse, take exception, waver

demure decorous, diffident, grave, modest, reserved, reticent, retiring, sedate, shy, sober, staid, unassuming

den 1. cave, cavern, haunt, hideout, hole, lair, shelter 2. cloister, cubbyhole, retreat, sanctum, snuggery, study

denial contradiction, disavowal, disclaimer, dismissal, dissent, negation, prohibition, rebuff, refusal, renunciation, repudiation, repulse, retraction, veto

denomination 1. belief, communion, creed, persuasion, religious group, school, sect 2. grade, size, unit, value

denote betoken, designate, express, imply, import, indicate, mark, mean, show, signify, typify

denounce accuse, attack, castigate, censure, condemn, decry, impugn, proscribe, revile, stigmatize, vilify

dense close, compact, compressed, condensed, heavy, impenetrable, opaque, solid, substantial, thick, thickset

dent 1. *n.* chip, crater, depression, dimple, dip, hollow, impression, indentation, pit 2. *v.* depress, dint, gouge, hollow, imprint, press in, push in

deny 1. contradict, disagree with, disprove, gainsay, oppose, rebuff, refute 2. abjure, disavow, discard, disclaim, disown, recant, renounce, repudiate, revoke

depart decamp, disappear, escape, exit, go, go away, leave, migrate, quit, remove, retire, retreat, set forth, start out, vanish, withdraw

department 1. district, division, province, region, sector 2. branch, bureau, division, office, section, station, subdivision, unit 3. domain, function, line, province, realm

departure 1. exit, exodus, going, leave-taking, leaving, removal, retirement, withdrawal 2. branching out, change, difference, innovation, novelty, shift

depend 1. bank on, build upon, calculate on, confide in, count on, lean on, reckon on, rely upon, trust in, turn to 2. be based on, be determined by, be subject to, hinge on, rest on

dependent 1. counting on, defenceless, helpless, immature, reliant, relying on, vulnerable, weak 2. conditional, contingent, depending, determined by, liable to, relative, subject to

deplete consume, decrease, drain, empty, evacuate, exhaust, expend, impoverish, lessen, milk, reduce, use up

deplorable 1. calamitous, dire, disastrous, distressing, grievous, lamentable, melancholy, miserable, pitiable, regrettable, sad, unfortunate, wretched 2. disgraceful, disreputable, execrable, opprobrious, reprehensible, scandalous, shameful

deplore 1. bemoan, bewail, grieve for, lament, mourn, regret, rue, sorrow over 2. abhor, censure, condemn, denounce, deprecate, disapprove of, object to

depose break, cashier, degrade, demote, dethrone, dismiss, displace, downgrade, remove from office

deposit 1. *v.* drop, lay, locate, place, precipitate, put, settle, sit down 2. *n.* down payment, instalment, money (*in bank*), part payment, pledge, retainer, security, stake, warranty

depot 1. repository, storehouse, warehouse 2. *Military* arsenal, dump 3. bus station, garage, terminus

deprave corrupt, debase, debauch, degrade, demoralize, pervert, seduce, vitiate

depraved corrupt, debased, debauched, degenerate, dissolute, evil, immoral, lewd, licentious, perverted, profligate, sinful, vicious, vile, wicked

depreciate decrease, deflate, devalue, lessen, lose value, lower, reduce

depreciation 1. depression, devaluation, drop, fall, slump 2. belittlement, derogation, detraction, disparagement

depress cast down, chill, damp, deject, desolate, discourage, dishearten, dispirit, oppress, sadden, weigh down

depressed blue, crestfallen, dejected, despondent, discouraged, dispirited, down, downcast, fed up, glum, low, melancholy, moody, morose, pessimistic, sad, unhappy

depressing black, bleak, discouraging, disheartening, dismal, distressing, dreary, gloomy, heartbreaking, hopeless, melancholy, sad, sombre

depression 1. dejection, despair, despondency, dolefulness, downheartedness, gloominess, hopelessness, low spirits, melancholy, sadness 2. *Commerce* dullness, economic decline, hard *or* bad times, inactivity, lowness, recession, slump, stagnation

deprive bereave, despoil, dispossess, divest, expropriate, rob, strip, wrest

deprived bereft, denuded, destitute, disadvantaged, forlorn, in need, in want, lacking, needy, poor

depth 1. abyss, deepness, drop, extent, measure, profundity 2. *Often plural* deepest (furthest, remotest) part, middle, midst

deputation commission, delegates, delegation, embassy, envoys, legation

deputize act for, stand in for, understudy

deputy agent, ambassador, commissioner, legate, lieutenant, proxy, representative, substitute, surrogate

deranged crazed, crazy, delirious, demented, distracted, frantic, frenzied, insane, irrational, lunatic, mad, maddened, unbalanced, unhinged

derelict abandoned, deserted, discarded, forsaken, neglected, ruined

deride chaff, disdain, disparage, flout, gibe, insult, jeer, mock, pooh-pooh, ridicule, scoff, scorn, sneer, taunt

derivation ancestry, basis, beginning, descent, etymology, foundation, genealogy, origin, root, source

derive collect, deduce, draw, elicit, extract, follow, gain, gather, get, glean, infer, obtain, procure, receive, trace

descend 1. alight, dismount, drop, fall, go down, move down, plunge, sink, subside, tumble 2. dip, incline, slant, slope 3. be handed down, be passed down, derive, issue, originate, proceed, spring

descent 1. coming down, drop, fall, plunge, swoop 2. ancestry, extraction, family tree, genealogy, heredity, lineage, origin, parentage

describe characterize, define, depict, detail, explain, express, illustrate, narrate, portray, recount, relate, report, specify, tell

description account, characterization, detail, explanation, narrative, portrayal, report, representation, sketch

desert[1] 1. *n.* solitude, waste, wasteland, wilderness, wilds 2. *adj.* arid, bare, barren, desolate, infertile, lonely, solitary, uncultivated, uninhabited, waste, wild

desert[2] *v.* abandon, abscond, betray, decamp, defect, forsake, give up, jilt, leave, leave stranded, maroon, quit, rat (on), relinquish, renounce, resign, throw over, vacate, walk out on (*Inf.*)

deserted abandoned, bereft, cast off, derelict, desolate, empty, forlorn, forsaken, isolated, lonely, neglected, solitary, unoccupied, vacant

deserter absconder, defector, escapee, fugitive, runaway, traitor, truant

deserve be entitled to, be worthy of, earn, gain, justify, merit, procure, rate, warrant, win

deserved condign, due, earned, fair, fitting, just, justifiable, justified, merited, proper, right, rightful, suitable, well-earned

design *v.* 1. describe, draft, draw, outline, plan, sketch, trace ~*n.* 2. blueprint, draft, drawing, model, outline, plan, scheme, sketch ~*v.* 3. conceive, create, fabricate, fashion, invent, originate, think up 4. aim, contrive, destine, devise, intend, make, mean, plan, project, propose, purpose, scheme, tailor ~*n.* 5. aim, end, goal, intent, intention, meaning, object, objective, point, purport, purpose, target, view

designation description, epithet, label, mark, name, title

designer artificer, creator, deviser, inventor, originator, stylist

desirable 1. advisable, agreeable, beneficial, eligible, enviable, good, pleasing, preferable, profitable, worthwhile 2. alluring, attractive, fascinating, fetching, seductive

desire *v.* 1. aspire to, covet, crave, fancy, hanker after, long for, want, wish for, yearn for 2. ask, entreat, importune, petition, request, solicit ~*n.* 3. appetite, craving, hankering, longing, need, want, wish 4. appetite, concupiscence, lasciviousness, lechery, libido, lust, lustfulness, passion

desist abstain, break off, cease, discontinue, end, forbear, give up, leave off, pause, refrain from, stop, suspend

desolate 1. bare, barren, bleak, desert, dreary, ruined, solitary, uninhabited, waste, wild 2. abandoned, bereft, comfortless, dejected, depressing, despondent, dismal, downcast, forlorn, forsaken, gloomy, lonely, melancholy, miserable, wretched

desolation destruction, devastation, havoc, ravages, ruin, ruination

despair 1. *v.* despond, give up, lose heart, lose hope 2. *n.* anguish, depression, desperation, gloom, hopelessness, melancholy, misery, wretchedness

despairing anxious, brokenhearted, dejected, depressed, desperate, despondent, disconsolate, downcast, frantic, griefstricken, hopeless, inconsolable, melancholy, miserable, suicidal, wretched

desperado bandit, criminal, cutthroat, gangster, gunman, lawbreaker, outlaw, ruffian, thug

desperate 1. dangerous, daring, determined, foolhardy, frantic, furious, hasty, headstrong, impetuous, madcap, rash, reckless, risky, violent, wild 2. despairing, forlorn, hopeless, irrecoverable, irretrievable, wretched

desperately badly, dangerously, gravely, perilously, seriously, severely

despise abhor, deride, detest, disdain, disregard, flout, loathe, look down on, neglect, revile, scorn, slight

despite *prep.* against, even with, in spite of, in the face of, notwithstanding, regardless of

despondent blue, dejected, depressed, despairing, disconsolate, discouraged, disheartened, doleful, down, downcast, gloomy, glum, hopeless, in despair, low, melancholy, miserable, morose, sad, sorrowful, wretched

despot autocrat, dictator, tyrant

despotism autarchy, autocracy, dictatorship, oppression, tyranny

destination harbour, haven, journey's end, landing-place, resting-place, station, stop, terminus

destine allot, appoint, assign, consecrate, decree, design, devote, doom, earmark, fate, intend, mark out, ordain, predetermine, purpose, reserve

destined bound, certain, designed, doomed, fated, foreordained, inescapable, inevitable, intended, meant, ordained, unavoidable

destiny doom, fate, fortune, lot, portion

destitute distressed, down and out, impecunious, impoverished, indigent, insolvent, moneyless, needy, penniless, penurious, poor

destroy annihilate, blow to bits, break down, crush, demolish, desolate, devastate, dismantle, dispatch, eradicate, extinguish, kill, ravage, raze, ruin, shatter, slay, smash, wipe out, wreck

destruction demolition, devastation, downfall, end, extermination, extinction, havoc, liquidation, massacre, overthrow, ruin, ruination, slaughter, wreckage, wrecking

destructive baleful, baneful, calamitous, cataclysmic, catastrophic, damaging, deadly, deleterious, detrimental, devastating, fatal, harmful, hurtful, injurious, lethal, pernicious, ruinous

detach cut off, disconnect, disengage, disentangle, disjoin, disunite, divide, free, isolate, loosen, remove, separate, sever, tear off, uncouple, unfasten

detachment aloofness, coolness, indifference, remoteness, unconcern

detail 1. *n.* aspect, component, count, element, fact, factor, feature, item, particular, point, respect, specific, technicality 2. *v.* allocate, appoint, assign, charge, commission, delegate, detach, send

detailed blow-by-blow, circumstantial, comprehensive, elaborate, exact, exhaustive, full, intricate, minute, particular, specific, thorough

detain 1. check, delay, hinder, hold up, impede, keep, keep back, retard, slow up (*or* down), stay, stop 2. arrest, confine, hold, intern, restrain

detect 1. catch, descry, distinguish, identify, note, notice, observe, recognize, scent, spot 2. catch, disclose, discover, expose, find, reveal, track down, uncover, unmask

detective C.I.D. man, constable, investigator, private eye, sleuth (*Inf.*)

detention confinement, custody, delay, hindrance, holding back, imprisonment, keeping in, restraint

deter caution, check, damp, daunt, debar, discourage, dissuade, frighten, hinder, inhibit from, intimidate, prevent, prohibit, put off, restrain, stop, talk out of

deteriorate 1. decline, degenerate, degrade, deprave, depreciate, go downhill (*Inf.*), lower, spoil, worsen 2. crumble, decay, decline, decompose, disintegrate, ebb, fade, fall apart, lapse, weaken, wear away

determination backbone, constancy, conviction, dedication, doggedness, drive, firmness, fortitude, perseverance, persistence, resolution, resolve, single-mindedness, steadfastness, tenacity, willpower

determine 1. arbitrate, conclude, decide, end, finish, fix upon, ordain, regulate, settle 2. ascertain, certify, check, detect, discover, find out, learn, verify, work out

determined bent on, constant, dogged, firm, fixed, intent, persistent, purposeful, resolute, set on, single-minded, steadfast, tenacious, unflinching, unwavering

deterrent check, curb, discouragement, disincentive, hindrance, impediment, obstacle, restraint

detest abominate, despise, dislike intensely, execrate, hate, loathe

detour bypass, byway, diversion

detract diminish, lessen, lower, reduce, take away from

detriment damage, disservice, harm, hurt, injury, loss, mischief, prejudice

detrimental adverse, baleful, deleterious, destructive, harmful, inimical, injurious, pernicious, prejudicial, unfavourable

devastate demolish, desolate, despoil, destroy, lay waste, level, pillage, plunder, ravage, raze, ruin, sack, spoil, waste, wreck

devastating caustic, deadly, effective, incisive, mordant, overpowering, overwhelming, sardonic, satirical, savage, stunning, trenchant, withering

develop 1. advance, cultivate, evolve, foster, grow, mature, progress, promote, prosper, ripen 2. amplify, augment, broaden, dilate upon, elaborate, enlarge, expand, unfold, work out 3. be a direct result of, break out, come about, ensue, follow, happen, result

development 1. advance, advancement, evolution, expansion, growth, improvement, increase, maturity, progress, progression, spread, unfolding 2. change, circumstance, event, happening, incident, issue, occurrence, outcome, result, situation, upshot

deviate avert, bend, deflect, depart, differ, digress, diverge, drift, err, part, stray, swerve, turn, turn aside, vary, veer, wander

deviation alteration, change, deflection, departure, digression, discrepancy, disparity, divergence, inconsistency, irregularity, shift, variance, variation

device 1. apparatus, appliance, contraption, contrivance, gadget, gimmick, implement, instrument, invention, tool, utensil 2. artifice, design, dodge, expedient, gambit, manoeuvre, plan, ploy, project, purpose, ruse, scheme, shift, stratagem, stunt, trick, wile

devil 1. demon, fiend, Satan 2. beast, brute, demon, monster, ogre, rogue, savage, terror, villain

devilish accursed, damnable, detestable, diabolic, diabolical, fiendish, hellish, infernal, satanic, wicked

devious calculating, deceitful, dishonest, evasive, indirect, insidious, insincere, scheming, sly, surreptitious, treacherous, tricky, underhand, wily

devise arrange, conceive, concoct, construct, contrive, design, dream up, form, formulate, frame, imagine, invent, plan, plot, prepare, project, scheme, think up

devoid barren, bereft, deficient, denuded, destitute, empty, free from, lacking, unprovided with, vacant, void, wanting, without

devote allot, apply, appropriate, assign, commit, concern oneself, dedicate, enshrine, give, pledge, reserve

devoted ardent, caring, committed, concerned, constant, dedicated, devout, faithful, fond, loving, loyal, staunch, steadfast, true

devour bolt, consume, cram, eat, gobble, gorge, gulp, guzzle, stuff, swallow, wolf

devout godly, holy, orthodox, pious, prayerful, pure, religious, reverent, saintly

dexterity adroitness, artistry, deftness, expertise, facility, finesse, handiness, knack, mastery, neatness, proficiency, skill, smoothness, touch

diagnose analyse, determine, distinguish, identify, interpret, pinpoint, pronounce, recognize

diagnosis 1. analysis, examination 2. conclusion, interpretation, opinion

diagonal *adj.* angled, cross, crossways, crosswise, oblique, slanting

diagonally aslant, at an angle, crosswise, obliquely

diagram chart, drawing, figure, layout, outline, plan, representation, sketch

dialect accent, idiom, jargon, language, patois, pronunciation, provincialism, speech, tongue, vernacular

dialogue 1. communication, conference, conversation, converse, discourse, discussion, interlocution 2. conversation, lines, script, spoken part

diary appointment book, chronicle, daily record, day-to-day account, engagement book, journal

dicky *adj.* fluttery, queer, shaky, unreliable, unsound, unsteady, weak

dictate 1. read out, say, speak, transmit, utter 2. command, decree, direct, enjoin, impose, lay down, ordain, order, prescribe

dictator absolute ruler, autocrat, despot, oppressor, tyrant

diction 1. language, phraseology, phrasing, style, usage 2. articulation, delivery, elocution, enunciation, inflection, intonation, pronunciation, speech

dictionary concordance, encyclopedia, glossary, lexicon, vocabulary, wordbook

die 1. decease, depart, expire, finish, pass away, perish 2. decay, decline, disappear, dwindle, ebb, end, fade, lapse, pass, sink, vanish, wane, wilt, wither 3. break down, fail, fizzle out, halt, lose power, peter out, run down, stop

die-hard 1. *n.* fanatic, old fogy, reactionary, zealot 2. *adj.* dyed-in-the-wool, immovable, inflexible, intransigent, reactionary, uncompromising

diet[1] *n.* 1. abstinence, dietary, fast, regime, regimen 2. commons, fare, food, nourishment, provisions, rations, subsistence, sustenance, viands, victuals ~*v.* 3. fast, lose weight, reduce, slim

diet[2] chamber, congress, council, legislature, meeting, parliament, sitting

differ be dissimilar, be distinct, contradict, contrast, depart from, diverge, run counter to, stand apart, vary

difference 1. alteration, change, contrast, deviation, differentiation, discrepancy, disparity, dissimilarity, distinction, divergence, diversity, unlikeness, variation, variety 2. distinction, exception, idiosyncrasy, peculiarity, singularity 3. argument, clash, conflict, contention, contretemps, controversy, debate, disagreement, discordance, dispute, quarrel, strife, tiff, wrangle

different 1. altered, at variance, changed, clashing, contrasting, deviating, disparate, dissimilar, divergent, diverse, inconsistent, opposed, unlike 2. assorted, diverse, manifold, many, miscellaneous, multifarious, numerous, several, some, sundry, varied, various
differentiate contrast, discern, discriminate, distinguish, mark off, separate, tell apart
difficult 1. arduous, demanding, formidable, hard, laborious, onerous, painful, strenuous, toilsome, uphill, wearisome 2. fastidious, fractious, fussy, hard to please, obstreperous, perverse, refractory, rigid, tiresome, troublesome, trying, unmanageable
difficulty 1. awkwardness, hardship, labour, pain, painfulness, strain, tribulation 2. deep water, dilemma, distress, embarrassment, fix (*Inf.*), hot water, jam (*Inf.*), mess, pickle (*Inf.*), plight, predicament, quandary, spot (*Inf.*), straits, trial, trouble
diffident backward, bashful, constrained, doubtful, hesitant, insecure, meek, modest, reluctant, reserved, self-conscious, sheepish, shrinking, shy, suspicious, timid, timorous, unobtrusive, unsure, withdrawn
dig *v.* 1. break up, burrow, delve, excavate, grub, hoe, hollow out, mine, penetrate, pierce, quarry, scoop, till, tunnel, turn over 2. delve, dig down, go into, investigate, probe, research, search ~*n.* 3. jab, poke, prod, punch, thrust 4. cutting remark, gibe, insult, jeer, quip, taunt, wisecrack (*Inf.*)
digest 1. absorb, assimilate, concoct, dissolve, incorporate 2. absorb, assimilate, consider, contemplate, grasp, master, meditate, ponder, study, take in, understand
digestion assimilation, conversion, incorporation, transformation
dig in defend, entrench, establish, fortify, maintain
dignified august, distinguished, exalted, formal, grave, honourable, imposing, lofty, lordly, noble, solemn, stately
dignitary notability, notable, personage, public figure, V.I.P., worthy
dignity courtliness, decorum, grandeur, gravity, hauteur, loftiness, majesty, nobility, propriety, solemnity, stateliness
digress depart, deviate, diverge, drift, expatiate, ramble, stray, turn aside, wander
dilapidated battered, broken-down, crumbling, decayed, decaying, decrepit, fallen in, falling apart, in ruins, neglected, ramshackle, rickety, ruined, run-down, shabby, shaky, tumble-down, uncared for, worn-out
dilemma difficulty, embarrassment, mess, perplexity, plight, predicament, problem, puzzle, quandary, spot (*Inf.*), strait
diligence activity, application, assiduity, attention, attentiveness, care, constancy, industry, perseverance
diligent active, assiduous, attentive, busy, careful, conscientious, constant, earnest, hard-working, indefatigable, industrious, laborious, persevering, persistent, studious, tireless
dilute *v.* adulterate, cut, thin (out), water down, weaken
dim *adj.* 1. cloudy, dark, darkish, dusky, grey, overcast, poorly lit, shadowy 2. bleary, blurred, faint, fuzzy, ill-defined, indistinct, obscured, shadowy, unclear 3. dense, doltish, dull, obtuse, slow, stupid, thick ~*v.* 4. blur, cloud, darken, dull, fade, lower, obscure, tarnish, turn down
diminish abate, contract, curtail, cut, decrease, lessen, lower, reduce, retrench, shrink, weaken
diminutive bantam, little, midget, miniature, minute, petite, pygmy, small, tiny, wee
din babel, clamour, clangour, clash, clatter, commotion, crash, hullabaloo, noise, outcry, pandemonium, racket, row, shout, uproar
dine banquet, eat, feast, lunch, sup
dingy colourless, dark, dim, dirty, discoloured, drab, dreary, dull, dusky, faded, gloomy, grimy, murky, obscure, seedy, shabby, soiled, sombre
dinner banquet, collation, feast, meal, refection, repast, spread
dip *v.* 1. bathe, douse, duck, dunk, immerse, plunge, rinse, souse 2. ladle, scoop, spoon 3. *With* **in** *or* **into** draw upon, reach into ~*n.* 4. douche, drenching, ducking, immersion, plunge, soaking 5. bathe, dive, plunge, swim 6. concoction, dilution, infusion, mixture, preparation, solution, suspension 7. basin, concavity, depression, hole, hollow, incline, slope 8. decline, fall, lowering, sag, slip, slump
diplomacy 1. statecraft, statesmanship 2. craft, delicacy, discretion, finesse, savoir faire, skill, subtlety, tact
diplomat go-between, mediator, moderator, negotiator, politician
diplomatic adept, discreet, polite, politic, prudent, sensitive, subtle, tactful
dire 1. alarming, awful, calamitous, cataclysmic, catastrophic, cruel, disastrous, horrible, ruinous, terrible, woeful 2. dismal, dreadful, fearful, gloomy, grim, ominous, portentous
direct[1] *v.* 1. administer, advise, conduct, control, dispose, govern, guide, handle, lead, manage, oversee, preside over, regulate, rule, run, superintend, supervise 2. bid, charge, command, dictate, enjoin, instruct, order 3. guide, indicate, lead, show
direct[2] *adj.* 1. candid, frank, honest, open, outspoken, plain-spoken, sincere, straight 2. absolute, blunt, categorical, downright, explicit, express, plain, unambiguous, unequivocal 3. nonstop, not crooked, shortest, straight, through, unbroken, uninterrupted
direction 1. administration, charge, command, control, government, guidance, leadership, management, order, oversight, supervision 2. aim, bearing, course, line, path, road, route, track, way
directive charge, command, decree, dictate, edict, injunction, instruction, notice, order, ordinance, ruling
directly 1. exactly, precisely, straight, unswervingly 2. candidly, face-to-face, honestly, in person, openly, personally, plainly, point-blank, straightforwardly, truthfully, unequivocally
director administrator, chairman, chief, controller, executive, governor, head, leader, manager, organizer, principal, producer
dirt 1. dust, filth, grime, impurity, mire, muck, mud, slime, smudge, stain, tarnish 2. clay, earth, loam, soil
dirty 1. filthy, foul, grimy, grubby, messy, mucky, muddy, nasty, polluted, soiled, sullied, unclean 2. corrupt, crooked, dishonest, fraudulent, illegal, treacherous, unfair, unscrupulous, unsporting
disability affliction, ailment, defect, disorder, handicap, impairment, infirmity, malady
disable cripple, damage, handicap, immobilize, impair, incapacitate, paralyse, prostrate, unfit, unman, weaken
disabled bedridden, crippled, handicapped, incapacitated, infirm, lame, mangled, mutilated, paralysed, weak
disadvantage damage, detriment, disservice, harm, hurt, injury, loss, prejudice
disagree 1. be discordant, be dissimilar, conflict, contradict, counter, depart, deviate, differ, diverge, vary 2. argue, bicker, clash, contend, contest, debate, dispute, dissent, object, oppose, quarrel, take issue with, wrangle
disagreeable bad-tempered, brusque, churlish, contrary, cross, difficult, disobliging, ill-natured, irritable, nasty, peevish, rude, surly, unfriendly, ungracious, unlikable, unpleasant
disagreement 1. difference, discrepancy, disparity, dissimilarity, divergence, diversity, incompatibility, incongruity, variance 2. argument, clash, conflict, debate, difference, discord, dispute, dissent, division, falling out, quarrel, squabble, strife, wrangle
disappear 1. be lost to view, depart, drop out of sight, ebb, escape, fade away, flee, fly, go, pass, recede, retire, wane, withdraw 2. cease, die out, dissolve, end, evaporate, expire, fade, pass away, perish, vanish
disappearance departure, desertion, eclipse, evanescence, evaporation, fading, flight, loss, passing, vanishing
disappoint dash, deceive, disenchant, dishearten, disillusion, dismay, dissatisfy, fail, let down, sadden, vex
disappointed depressed, despondent, discontented, discouraged, disenchanted, disgruntled, disillusioned, dissatisfied, distressed, downhearted, foiled, frustrated, let down, saddened, thwarted, upset
disappointment discontent, discouragement, disenchantment, disillusionment, displeasure, dissatisfaction, distress, failure, frustration, mortification, regret
disapproval censure, condemnation, criticism, deprecation, disapprobation, displeasure, dissatisfaction
disapprove 1. *Often with* **of** blame, censure, condemn, deplore, deprecate, dislike, frown on, object to, reject 2. disallow, set aside, spurn, turn down, veto
disarrange confuse, derange, discompose, disorder, disorganize, disturb, scatter, shuffle, unsettle, untidy
disarray 1. confusion, dismay, disorder, disunity, indiscipline, unruliness, upset 2. chaos, clutter, jumble, mess, mix-up, muddle, shambles, tangle, untidiness
disaster accident, adversity, blow, calamity, catastrophe, misadventure, mischance, misfortune, mishap, reverse, ruin, stroke, tragedy, trouble
disastrous adverse, catastrophic, destructive, detrimental, devastating, dire, dreadful, fatal, hapless, harmful, ill-fated, ill-starred, ruinous, terrible, tragic, unfortunate, unlucky
disbelief distrust, doubt, dubiety, incredulity, mistrust, scepticism, unbelief
discard abandon, cast aside, dispense with, dispose of, ditch (*Sl.*), drop, get rid of, jettison, reject, relinquish, remove, repudiate, scrap, shed
discharge *v.* 1. absolve, acquit, allow to go, clear, free, liberate, pardon, release, set free ~*n.* 2. acquittal, clearance, liberation, pardon, release, remittance ~*v.* 3. discard, dismiss, expel, oust 4. detonate, explode, fire, let off, set off, shoot ~*n.* 5. blast, burst, discharging, explosion, firing, report, salvo, shot, volley ~*v.* 6. accomplish, carry out, do, execute, fulfil, observe, perform 7. clear, honour, meet, pay, relieve, satisfy, settle, square up
disciple apostle, believer, convert, devotee, follower, learner, partisan, proselyte, pupil, student, supporter
disciplinarian despot, martinet, stickler, taskmaster, tyrant
discipline *n.* 1. drill, exercise, method, practice, regulation 2. conduct, control, orderliness, regulation, restraint, strictness 3. chastisement, correction, punishment ~*v.* 4. break in, bring up, check, control, drill, educate, exercise, form, govern, instruct, prepare, regulate, restrain, train
disclose broadcast, communicate, confess, divulge, impart, leak, let slip, make known, make public, publish, relate, reveal, tell, unveil, utter
discolour fade, mar, mark, rust, soil, stain, streak, tarnish, tinge
discomfort ache, annoyance, disquiet, distress, hardship, hurt, irritation, nuisance, pain, soreness, trouble, uneasiness, vexation
disconcert abash, agitate, bewilder, discompose, disturb, flurry, fluster, nonplus, perplex,

perturb, rattle (*Inf.*), ruffle, take aback, trouble, unbalance, unsettle, upset, worry
disconcerting alarming, awkward, baffling, bewildering, confusing, dismaying, distracting, disturbing, embarrassing, perplexing, upsetting
disconnect cut off, detach, divide, part, separate, sever, take apart, uncouple
disconsolate dejected, desolate, despairing, forlorn, gloomy, heartbroken, hopeless, inconsolable, melancholy, miserable, sad, unhappy, wretched
discontinue abandon, break off, cease, drop, end, finish, give up, halt, interrupt, leave off, pause, put an end to, quit, refrain from, stop, suspend, terminate
discord 1. clashing, conflict, contention, difference, dispute, dissension, disunity, division, friction, opposition, rupture, strife, variance, wrangling 2. cacophony, din, dissonance, harshness, jangle, jarring
discount *v.* 1. disbelieve, disregard, ignore, overlook, pass over 2. lower, mark down, rebate, reduce, take off ~*n.* 3. allowance, concession, cut, cut price, deduction, rebate, reduction
discourage abash, awe, cast down, damp, dampen, dash, daunt, deject, demoralize, depress, dishearten, dismay, frighten, intimidate, overawe, scare, unnerve
discouraged crestfallen, dashed, deterred, disheartened, dismayed, dispirited, downcast, glum, put off
discouragement dejection, depression, despair, despondency, disappointment, dismay, hopelessness, low spirits, pessimism
discouraging daunting, depressing, disappointing, dispiriting, unfavourable, unpropitious
discourse 1. *n.* chat, communication, conversation, converse, dialogue, discussion, speech, talk 2. *v.* confer, converse, debate, declaim, discuss, speak, talk
discourteous abrupt, badmannered, brusque, curt, illmannered, impolite, insolent, offhand, rude, uncivil, ungentlemanly, ungracious, unmannerly
discover 1. come across, come upon, dig up, find, light upon, locate, turn up, uncover, unearth 2. ascertain, descry, detect, determine, discern, disclose, espy, find out, learn, notice, perceive, realize, recognize, reveal, see, spot, uncover
discovery 1. ascertainment, detection, disclosure, exploration, finding, introduction, location, origination, revelation 2. breakthrough, coup, find, findings, innovation, invention, secret
discreet careful, cautious, circumspect, considerate, diplomatic, discerning, guarded, judicious, politic, prudent, reserved, tactful, wary
discrepancy conflict, difference, disagreement, disparity, dissimilarity, dissonance, divergence, incongruity, inconsistency, variance, variation
discretion acumen, care, carefulness, caution, consideration, diplomacy, discernment, good sense, judgment, maturity, prudence, sagacity, tact, wariness
discriminate 1. favour, show bias, show prejudice, single out, treat differently, victimize 2. assess, differentiate, discern, distinguish, evaluate, separate, sift
discriminating acute, astute, critical, cultivated, discerning, fastidious, keen, particular, refined, selective, sensitive, tasteful
discrimination bias, bigotry, favouritism, inequity, intolerance, prejudice, unfairness
discuss argue, confer, consider, converse, debate, deliberate, examine, go into, review, sift, thrash out, ventilate
discussion analysis, argument, colloquy, conference, consideration, consultation, conversation, debate, deliberation, dialogue, discourse, examination, exchange, review, scrutiny, symposium
disdain *n.* arrogance, contempt, derision, dislike, hauteur, indifference, scorn, sneering
disease affliction, ailment, complaint, condition, disorder, ill health, illness, indisposition, infection, infirmity, malady, sickness, upset
diseased infected, rotten, sick, sickly, tainted, unhealthy, unsound, unwell
disembark alight, arrive, get off, go ashore, land
disengage disentangle, ease, extricate, free, liberate, loosen, release, set free, unloose, untie
disentangle detach, disengage, extricate, free, loose, separate, sever, unfold, unravel, unsnarl, untangle, untwist
disfavour disapprobation, disapproval, dislike, displeasure
disfigure blemish, damage, deface, deform, distort, injure, maim, mutilate, scar
disgorge 1. belch, discharge, eject, empty, expel, regurgitate, spew, spit up, spout, throw up, vomit 2. cede, give up, relinquish, renounce, resign, surrender, yield
disgrace *n.* 1. baseness, degradation, dishonour, disrepute, ignominy, infamy, odium, opprobrium, shame 2. aspersion, blemish, blot, defamation, reproach, scandal, slur, stain, stigma 3. contempt, discredit, disesteem, disfavour, obloquy ~*v.* 4. abase, bring shame upon, defame, degrade, discredit, disfavour, dishonour, disparage, humiliate, reproach, shame, slur, stain, stigmatize, sully, taint
disgraceful contemptible, degrading, detestable, discreditable, dishonourable, disreputable, ignominious, infamous, low, mean, scandalous, shameful, shocking, unworthy
disgruntled annoyed, discontented, displeased, dissatisfied, grumpy, irritated, malcontent, peeved, peevish, petulant, put out, sulky, sullen, testy, vexed
disguise *v.* 1. cloak, conceal, cover, hide, mask, screen, secrete, shroud, veil 2. deceive, dissemble, dissimulate, fake, falsify, fudge, gloss over, misrepresent ~*n.* 3. cloak, costume, cover, mask, screen, veil
disguised cloaked, covert, fake, false, feigned, incognito, masked, pretend, unrecognizable
disgust 1. *v.* displease, nauseate, offend, outrage, put off, repel, revolt, sicken 2. *n.* abhorrence, abomination, antipathy, aversion, detestation, dislike, distaste, hatred, loathing, nausea, repugnance, repulsion, revulsion
disgusted appalled, nauseated, offended, outraged, repelled, repulsed, scandalized
disgusting abominable, distasteful, foul, gross, hateful, loathsome, nasty, nauseating, objectionable, obnoxious, odious, offensive, repellent, repugnant, revolting, shameless, sickening, stinking, vile, vulgar
dish 1. bowl, plate, platter, salver 2. fare, food, recipe
dishearten cast down, crush, damp, dampen, dash, daunt, deject, depress, deter, discourage, dismay, dispirit
dishonest corrupt, crafty, deceitful, deceiving, deceptive, designing, disreputable, double-dealing, false, fraudulent, guileful, lying, mendacious, perfidious, treacherous, unfair, unprincipled, unscrupulous, untrustworthy, untruthful
dishonesty corruption, craft, criminality, crookedness, deceit, duplicity, falsehood, falsity, fraud, fraudulence, graft, improbity, mendacity, perfidy, sharp practice, treachery, trickery, wiliness
dishonour 1. *v.* abase, blacken, corrupt, debase, debauch, defame, degrade, discredit, disgrace, shame, sully 2. *n.* discredit, disfavour, disgrace, disrepute, ignominy, infamy, obloquy, odium, opprobrium, reproach, scandal, shame
dishonourable base, despicable, discreditable, disgraceful, ignoble, infamous, scandalous, shameful
disillusioned disabused, disenchanted, indifferent, undeceived
disinclination antipathy, aversion, demur, dislike, hesitance, objection, opposition, reluctance, repugnance, resistance, unwillingness
disinclined antipathetic, averse, indisposed, loath, opposed, reluctant, resistant, unwilling
disinfect clean, cleanse, decontaminate, fumigate, purify, sterilize
disinfectant antiseptic, germicide, sterilizer
disinherit cut off, disown, dispossess, oust, repudiate
disintegrate break up, crumble, disunite, fall apart, fall to pieces, separate, shatter, splinter
disinterest detachment, equity, fairness, impartiality, justice, neutrality
disinterested detached, equitable, even-handed, impartial, impersonal, neutral, outside, unbiased, uninvolved, unprejudiced, unselfish
dislike 1. *n.* animosity, animus, antagonism, antipathy, aversion, detestation, disapproval, disgust, distaste, enmity, hatred, hostility, loathing, repugnance 2. *v.* abhor, abominate, be averse to, despise, detest, disapprove, disfavour, hate, loathe, object to, scorn, shun
disloyal disaffected, faithless, false, perfidious, seditious, subversive, traitorous, treacherous, two-faced, unfaithful, unpatriotic, untrustworthy
disloyalty deceitfulness, double-dealing, falseness, falsity, inconstancy, infidelity, perfidy, treachery, treason, unfaithfulness
dismal bleak, cheerless, dark, depressing, despondent, discouraging, dreary, forlorn, gloomy, gruesome, lowering, lugubrious, melancholy, sad, sombre, sorrowful
dismay 1. *v.* affright, alarm, appal, distress, frighten, horrify, paralyse, scare, terrify, unnerve 2. *n.* agitation, alarm, anxiety, apprehension, distress, dread, fear, fright, horror, panic, terror
dismember anatomize, disjoint, dislimb, dislocate, dissect, divide, rend, sever
dismiss 1. cashier, discharge, lay off, oust, remove 2. disband, disperse, dissolve, free, let go, release, send away
dismissal 1. adjournment, end, release 2. discharge, expulsion, notice, removal
disobedience insubordination, mutiny, noncompliance, recalcitrance, revolt, unruliness, waywardness
disobedient contrary, defiant, disorderly, insubordinate, intractable, mischievous, naughty, obstreperous, refractory, undisciplined, unruly, wilful
disobey defy, disregard, flout, ignore, infringe, overstep, rebel, resist, transgress, violate
disorderly 1. chaotic, confused, disorganized, indiscriminate, irregular, jumbled, messy, untidy 2. disruptive, lawless, obstreperous, rebellious, refractory, riotous, rowdy, tumultuous, turbulent, ungovernable, unlawful, unmanageable, unruly
disown cast off, deny, disallow, disavow, disclaim, reject, renounce, repudiate
dispassionate calm, collected, composed, cool, imperturbable, moderate, quiet, serene, sober, temperate, unemotional, unexcitable, unmoved
dispatch, despatch 1. *v.* conclude, discharge, dispose of, expedite, finish, perform, settle 2. *n.* account, bulletin, communication, communiqué, document, instruction, item, letter, message, missive, news, piece, report, story
dispense 1. allocate, allot, apportion, assign, deal out, disburse, distribute, dole out, mete out, share 2. administer, apply, carry out, direct, discharge, enforce, execute, implement, operate, undertake
disperse 1. broadcast, circulate, diffuse, disseminate, dissipate, distribute, scatter, spread, strew 2. disband, dismiss, dispel, dissolve, rout, scatter, send off, separate, vanish
dispirited crestfallen, dejected,

depressed, despondent, discouraged, disheartened, down, downcast, gloomy, glum, in the doldrums, low, morose, sad

displace 1. derange, disarrange, disturb, misplace, move, shift, transpose 2. crowd out, oust, replace, succeed, supersede, supplant, take the place of

display *v.* 1. betray, demonstrate, disclose, evidence, evince, exhibit, expose, manifest, open, present, reveal, show, unveil 2. expand, extend, model, open out, spread out, stretch out, unfold, unfurl ~*n.* 3. array, demonstration, exhibition, exposition, exposure, manifestation, presentation, revelation, show 4. flourish, ostentation, pageant, parade, pomp, show, spectacle

displease anger, annoy, disgust, dissatisfy, exasperate, incense, irk, irritate, nettle, offend, pique, provoke, put out, rile, upset, vex

displeasure anger, annoyance, disapproval, dislike, dissatisfaction, distaste, indignation, irritation, offence, pique, resentment, vexation, wrath

disposal 1. clearance, discarding, ejection, relinquishment, removal, riddance, scrapping, throwing away 2. arrangement, array, dispensation, disposition, distribution, grouping, placing, position

dispose adjust, arrange, array, determine, distribute, fix, group, marshal, order, place, put, range, rank, regulate, set, settle, stand

dispose of 1. deal with, decide, determine, end, finish with, settle 2. bestow, give, make over, part with, sell, transfer 3. destroy, discard, dump (*Inf.*), get rid of, jettison, scrap, unload

disposition character, constitution, make-up, nature, spirit, temper, temperament

disproportion asymmetry, disparity, imbalance, inequality, insufficiency, lopsidedness, unevenness

disproportionate excessive, incommensurate, inordinate, out of proportion, too much, unbalanced, unequal, uneven, unreasonable

disprove confute, controvert, discredit, expose, invalidate, negate, prove false, rebut, refute

dispute *v.* 1. argue, brawl, clash, contend, debate, discuss, quarrel, squabble, wrangle 2. challenge, contest, contradict, controvert, deny, doubt, impugn, question ~*n.* 3. argument, brawl, conflict, disagreement, discord, disturbance, feud, friction, quarrel, strife, wrangle

disqualification 1. disablement, incapacitation, unfitness 2. disenablement, disentitlement, elimination, exclusion, incompetence, ineligibility, rejection

disqualified debarred, eliminated, ineligible, knocked out

disqualify 1. disable, incapacitate, invalidate 2. debar, declare ineligible, disentitle, preclude, prohibit, rule out

disquiet alarm, anxiety, concern, disquietude, distress, fear, foreboding, fretfulness, restlessness, trouble, uneasiness, unrest, worry

disregard 1. discount, disobey, ignore, laugh off, make light of, neglect, overlook, pass over 2. brush off (*Sl.*), cold-shoulder, contemn, despise, disdain, disparage, slight, snub

disreputable base, contemptible, derogatory, discreditable, disgraceful, dishonourable, disorderly, ignominious, infamous, low, mean, notorious, scandalous, shameful, shocking, unprincipled, vicious, vile

disrepute disesteem, disfavour, disgrace, dishonour, ignominy, ill favour, ill repute, infamy, obloquy, shame, unpopularity

disrespect contempt, discourtesy, dishonour, disregard, impertinence, impoliteness, impudence, insolence, irreverence, lack of respect, rudeness

disrespectful bad-mannered, cheeky, contemptuous, discourteous, ill-bred, impertinent, impolite, impudent, insolent, insulting, irreverent, misbehaved, rude, uncivil

disrupt agitate, confuse, disorder, disorganize, disturb, spoil, throw into disorder, upset

dissatisfaction annoyance, disappointment, discontent, dismay, displeasure, distress, exasperation, frustration, irritation, regret, unhappiness

dissatisfied disappointed, discontented, disgruntled, displeased, fed up, frustrated, unfulfilled, ungratified, unhappy

dissect anatomize, cut up *or* apart, dismember, lay open

disseminate broadcast, circulate, diffuse, disperse, distribute, propagate, publish, scatter, sow, spread

dissension conflict, contention, difference, disagreement, discord, dispute, dissent, quarrel, strife

dissent 1. *v.* decline, differ, disagree, object, protest, refuse, withhold assent *or* approval 2. *n.* difference, disagreement, discord, nonconformity, objection, opposition, refusal, resistance

dissenter dissident, nonconformist, objector, protestant

dissertation discourse, essay, exposition, thesis, treatise

disservice bad turn, disfavour, harm, ill turn, injury, injustice, wrong

dissident 1. *adj.* differing, disagreeing, discordant, heterodox, nonconformist, schismatic 2. *n.* agitator, dissenter, rebel, recusant

dissimilar different, disparate, divergent, diverse

dissipate burn up, deplete, expend, fritter away, lavish, misspend, run through, spend, squander, waste

dissociate 1. break off, disband, disrupt, part company, quit 2. detach, disconnect, distance, divorce, isolate, segregate, separate, set apart

dissolute abandoned, corrupt, debauched, degenerate, depraved, immoral, lax, lewd, libertine, licentious, loose, profligate, vicious, wanton, wild

dissolution breaking up, disintegration, division, divorce, parting, resolution, separation

dissolve 1. flux, fuse, melt, soften, thaw 2. crumble, decompose, diffuse, disappear, disintegrate, disperse, dissipate, dwindle, evaporate, fade, melt away, perish, vanish, waste away

dissuade deter, discourage, disincline, divert, expostulate, put off, remonstrate, urge not to, warn

distance 1. *n.* absence, extent, gap, interval, lapse, length, range, reach, remoteness, remove, separation, space, span, stretch, width 2. *v.* dissociate oneself, separate oneself

distant 1. abroad, afar, far, faraway, far-flung, far-off, outlying, out-of-the-way, remote, removed 2. aloof, cold, cool, formal, haughty, reserved, restrained, standoffish, stiff, unapproachable, unfriendly, withdrawn

distaste abhorrence, antipathy, aversion, disfavour, disgust, disinclination, dislike, displeasure, horror, loathing, repugnance, revulsion

distasteful abhorrent, disagreeable, displeasing, obnoxious, offensive, repugnant, repulsive, undesirable, uninviting, unpalatable, unpleasant, unsavoury

distil condense, evaporate, express, purify, rectify, refine, vaporize

distinct 1. apparent, clear, clear-cut, decided, definite, evident, lucid, manifest, marked, noticeable, obvious, patent, plain, recognizable, sharp, well-defined 2. different, dissimilar, individual, separate, unconnected

distinction 1. discernment, discrimination, penetration, perception, separation 2. contrast, difference, differential, division, separation 3. celebrity, credit, eminence, excellence, fame, greatness, honour, importance, merit, name, note, prominence, quality, rank, renown, reputation, repute, superiority, worth

distinctly clearly, decidedly, definitely, evidently, manifestly, markedly, noticeably, obviously, plainly, precisely

distinguish 1. decide, determine, differentiate, discriminate, judge, tell apart 2. discern, know, make out, perceive, pick out, recognize, see, tell 3. celebrate, dignify, honour, immortalize

distinguished celebrated, conspicuous, eminent, famed, famous, illustrious, notable, noted, well-known

distort 1. bend, buckle, contort, deform, disfigure, misshape, twist, warp, wrench, wrest 2. bias, colour, falsify, garble, misrepresent, pervert, slant, twist

distract 1. divert, draw away, sidetrack, turn aside 2. agitate, bewilder, confound, confuse, disturb, harass, madden, perplex, puzzle, torment, trouble

distracted 1. agitated, bemused, bewildered, confused, flustered, harassed, puzzled, troubled 2. crazy, deranged, distraught, frantic, frenzied, insane, mad, raving, wild

distraction 1. agitation, bewilderment, commotion, confusion, discord, disorder, disturbance 2. amusement, beguilement, diversion, entertainment, pastime, recreation

distress 1. *n.* affliction, agony, anguish, anxiety, desolation, discomfort, grief, heartache, misery, pain, sadness, sorrow, torment, torture, woe, worry, wretchedness 2. *v.* afflict, agonize, bother, disturb, grieve, harass, harrow, pain, perplex, sadden, torment, trouble, upset, worry, wound

distressed agitated, anxious, distracted, distraught, saddened, tormented, troubled, upset, worried, wretched

distressing affecting, afflicting, disturbing, grievous, heartbreaking, hurtful, lamentable, painful, sad

distribute administer, allocate, allot, assign, deal, dispense, dispose, divide, dole out, give, measure out, mete, share

distribution 1. allocation, allotment, division, dole, partition, sharing 2. dealing, delivery, handling, mailing, marketing, trading, transport

district area, community, locality, neighbourhood, parish, quarter, region, sector, vicinity, ward

distrust 1. *v.* be sceptical of, be suspicious of, disbelieve, discredit, doubt, misbelieve, question, suspect 2. *n.* disbelief, doubt, misgiving, mistrust, qualm, question, scepticism, suspicion, wariness

disturb 1. bother, disrupt, interfere with, interrupt, intrude on, pester, rouse, startle 2. agitate, alarm, annoy, distract, distress, excite, fluster, harass, perturb, ruffle, shake, trouble, unsettle, upset, worry

disturbance 1. agitation, bother, confusion, disorder, distraction, hindrance, interruption, intrusion, perturbation, upset 2. brawl, commotion, disorder, fracas, fray, hubbub, riot, tumult, turmoil, uproar

disuse decay, discontinuance, idleness, neglect

ditch *n.* 1. channel, drain, dyke, furrow, gully, moat, trench, watercourse ~*v.* 2. dig, drain, excavate, gouge, trench 3. discard, dispose of, drop, get rid of, jettison, scrap

dither falter, haver, hesitate, oscillate, waver

dive 1. *v.* dip, disappear, drop, duck, fall, jump, leap, pitch, plummet, plunge, submerge, swoop 2. *n.* dash, jump, leap, lunge, plunge, spring

diverge branch, divide, fork, part, radiate, separate, split, spread

diverse 1. assorted, miscellaneous, several, sundry, varied, various 2. different, dissimilar, distinct, separate, unlike, varying

diversion 1. change, deflection, detour, deviation, digression, variation 2. amusement, delight, distraction, enjoyment, entertainment, game, pastime, play, pleasure, recreation, relaxation, sport

diversity assortment, difference, heterogeneity, medley, multiplicity, range, variance, variegation, variety

divert deflect, redirect, switch, turn aside
diverting amusing, enjoyable, entertaining, fun, humorous, pleasant
divide 1. cut (up), detach, disconnect, part, partition, segregate, separate, sever, shear, split, subdivide 2. allocate, allot, apportion, deal out, dispense, distribute, dole out, measure out, portion, share
dividend bonus, extra, gain, plus, portion, share, surplus
divine *adj.* 1. celestial, godlike, heavenly, holy, spiritual, superhuman, supernatural 2. *Inf.* beautiful, excellent, glorious, marvellous, perfect, splendid, wonderful ~*v.* 3. conjecture, deduce, discern, foretell, guess, infer, intuit, perceive, suppose, surmise, suspect, understand
diviner augur, oracle, prophet, seer, sibyl, soothsayer
divinity 1. deity, divine nature, godliness, holiness, sanctity 2. deity, genius, god, goddess, guardian spirit, spirit 3. religion, religious studies, theology
divisible fractional, separable, splittable
division 1. cutting up, detaching, dividing, partition, separation 2. allotment, apportionment, distribution, sharing 3. boundary, demarcation, divide, divider, partition 4. branch, category, class, compartment, department, group, head, part, portion, section, sector, segment
divorce 1. *n.* breach, break, decree nisi, dissolution, disunion, rupture, separation, severance, split-up 2. *v.* annul, disconnect, dissociate, disunite, divide, part, separate, sever, split up, sunder
divulge betray, confess, declare, disclose, exhibit, expose, impart, leak, let slip, make known, proclaim, publish, reveal, tell, uncover
dizzy faint, giddy, reeling, shaky, staggering, swimming, wobbly
do *v.* 1. accomplish, achieve, act, carry out, complete, conclude, discharge, end, execute, perform, produce, work 2. be adequate, be enough, be of use, be sufficient, pass muster, satisfy, serve, suffice, suit 3. adapt, render, translate, transpose 4. behave, carry oneself, conduct oneself 5. fare, get along, get on, make out, manage, proceed 6. bring about, cause, create, effect, produce 7. *Sl.* cheat, deceive, defraud, dupe, fleece, hoax, swindle, trick ~*n.* 8. *Inf.* affair, event, function, gathering, occasion, party
do away with 1. destroy, exterminate, kill, liquidate, murder, slay 2. abolish, discard, discontinue, eliminate, get rid of, remove
docile biddable, compliant, manageable, obedient, pliant, submissive, tractable
docility compliance, manageability, meekness, obedience, pliancy, submissiveness, tractability
dock 1. *n.* harbour, pier, quay, waterfront, wharf 2. *v.* anchor, berth, drop anchor, land, moor, put in, tie up
doctor *n.* 1. general practitioner, G.P., medical practitioner, physician ~*v.* 2. treat 3. botch, cobble, fix, mend, patch up, repair 4. alter, change, disguise, falsify, fudge, pervert, tamper with
doctrinaire *adj.* biased, dogmatic, fanatical, inflexible, insistent, opinionated, rigid
doctrine article, belief, canon, concept, conviction, creed, dogma, opinion, precept, principle, teaching, tenet
document 1. *n.* certificate, legal form, paper, record, report 2. *v.* authenticate, back up, certify, cite, corroborate, detail, instance, substantiate, support, validate, verify
dodge *v.* 1. dart, duck, shift, sidestep, swerve, turn aside 2. avoid, deceive, elude, evade, fend off, fudge, get out of, hedge, parry, shirk, shuffle, trick ~*n.* 3. device, feint, ploy, ruse, scheme, stratagem, subterfuge, trick, wile
dog 1. *n.* bitch, canine, cur, hound, man's best friend, mongrel, pup, puppy, tyke 2. *v.* haunt, hound, plague, pursue, shadow, track, trail, trouble
dogged determined, firm, persevering, persistent, resolute, staunch, steadfast, steady, tenacious, unflagging, unshakable
dogma article, belief, creed, doctrine, precept, principle, tenet
dogmatic arbitrary, arrogant, assertive, categorical, dictatorial, downright, emphatic, imperious, obdurate, overbearing, peremptory
doldrums blues, boredom, depression, dullness, ennui, gloom, inertia, listlessness, malaise, stagnation, tedium
dole 1. *n.* allowance, alms, benefit, gift, grant, parcel, pittance, portion, quota, share 2. *v. Usually with* **out** administer, allocate, allot, assign, deal, dispense, distribute, divide, give, hand out, share
dolt ass, chump (*Inf.*), dullard, dunce, fool, idiot, ignoramus, nitwit, simpleton, thickhead
domestic 1. family, home, household, private 2. house, house-trained, pet, tame, trained 3. indigenous, internal, native, not foreign
dominant ascendant, assertive, commanding, controlling, governing, leading, presiding, ruling, superior, supreme
dominate 1. control, direct, govern, lead, master, monopolize, overbear, rule, tyrannize 2. bestride, loom over, overlook, stand over, survey, tower above
domination authority, command, control, influence, mastery, power, rule, superiority, supremacy, sway
domineer bluster, browbeat, bully, hector, intimidate, menace, overbear, swagger, threaten, tyrannize
dominion ascendancy, authority, command, control, government, mastery, power, rule, sovereignty, supremacy, sway
don dress in, get into, pull on, put on
donate bestow, gift, give, present, subscribe
donation alms, benefaction, boon, contribution, gift, grant, gratuity, largess, offering, present, subscription
done 1. accomplished, completed, concluded, consummated, ended, executed, finished, over, perfected, realized, terminated, through 2. cooked, ready 3. depleted, exhausted, finished, spent, used up 4. acceptable, conventional, *de rigueur*, proper
donor almsgiver, benefactor, contributor, donator, giver
doom 1. *n.* catastrophe, death, destiny, destruction, downfall, fate, fortune, lot, portion, ruin 2. *v.* condemn, consign, damn, decree, destine, judge, sentence
doomed condemned, cursed, fated, hopeless, ill-fated, ill-omened, luckless
door egress, entrance, entry, exit, ingress, opening
dope drugs, narcotic, opiate
dormant asleep, inactive, inert, latent, quiescent, sleeping, sluggish, slumbering, suspended
dose draught, drench, measure, portion, potion, prescription, quantity
dot *n.* atom, circle, dab, fleck, full stop, iota, jot, mark, mite, mote, point, speck, spot
dotage feebleness, imbecility, old age, second childhood, senility, weakness
dote on *or* **upon** admire, adore, hold dear, prize, treasure
double 1. *adj.* coupled, doubled, dual, duplicate, in pairs, paired, twice, twin, twofold 2. *v.* duplicate, enlarge, fold, grow, increase, magnify, multiply, plait, repeat
double-cross betray, cheat, defraud, hoodwink, mislead, swindle, trick
doubt *v.* 1. discredit, distrust, fear, misgive, mistrust, query, question, suspect 2. be dubious, be uncertain, demur, fluctuate, hesitate, scruple, vacillate, waver ~*n.* 3. apprehension, disquiet, distrust, fear, incredulity, lack of faith, misgiving, mistrust, qualm, scepticism, suspicion 4. ambiguity, confusion, difficulty, dilemma, perplexity, problem, quandary
doubtful 1. ambiguous, debatable, dubious, equivocal, hazardous, indefinite, obscure, problematic, questionable, unclear, unconfirmed, unsettled, vague 2. hesitating, irresolute, perplexed, sceptical, suspicious, tentative, uncertain, unconvinced, undecided, unresolved, unsettled, unsure, vacillating, wavering
doubtless 1. assuredly, certainly, clearly, of course, precisely, surely, truly, unquestionably 2. apparently, most likely, ostensibly, presumably, probably, seemingly
dour dismal, dreary, forbidding, gloomy, grim, morose, sour, sullen, unfriendly
dowdy dingy, drab, old-fashioned, shabby, unfashionable
do without abstain from, dispense with, forgo, give up
down *adj.* blue, dejected, depressed, disheartened, downcast, low, miserable, sad, unhappy
down and out derelict, destitute, impoverished, penniless, ruined
downcast cheerless, dejected, depressed, despondent, disconsolate, discouraged, disheartened, dismayed, dispirited, miserable, sad, unhappy
downfall breakdown, collapse, debacle, descent, destruction, disgrace, fall, overthrow, ruin, undoing
downgrade degrade, demote, humble
downhearted crestfallen, dejected, depressed, despondent, discouraged, disheartened, dismayed, downcast, low-spirited, sad, sorrowful, unhappy
downpour cloudburst, deluge, flood, inundation, rainstorm
down-to-earth common-sense, hard-headed, matter-of-fact, plain-spoken, practical, realistic, sane, sensible
downward *adj.* declining, descending, earthward, heading down, slipping
doze *v.* catnap, drowse, nap, nod, sleep, slumber, zizz (*Inf.*)
drab cheerless, colourless, dingy, dismal, dreary, dull, flat, gloomy, grey, lacklustre, shabby, sombre, uninspired
draft 1. *v.* compose, design, draw, draw up, formulate, outline, plan, sketch 2. *n.* outline, plan, rough, sketch, version
drag draw, hale, haul, lug, pull, tow, trail, tug, yank
dragoon bully, coerce, compel, constrain, drive, force, impel, intimidate
drain *v.* 1. bleed, draw off, dry, empty, milk, remove, tap, withdraw 2. consume, deplete, dissipate, empty, exhaust, sap, strain, tax, use up, weary ~*n.* 3. channel, conduit, culvert, ditch, duct, outlet, pipe, sewer, sink, trench, watercourse 4. depletion, drag, exhaustion, reduction, sap, strain, withdrawal
drama 1. play, show 2. acting, dramaturgy, stagecraft, theatre 3. crisis, excitement, scene, spectacle, theatrics, turmoil
dramatic 1. theatrical 2. breathtaking, electrifying, emotional, exciting, melodramatic, sensational, startling, sudden, tense, thrilling
dramatist playwright, scriptwriter
dramatize act, overdo, overstate, play-act
drastic desperate, dire, extreme, forceful, harsh, radical, severe, strong
draught 1. *Of air* current, flow, movement 2. cup, dose, drench, drink, potion, quantity
draw *v.* 1. drag, haul, pull, tow, tug 2. depict, design, map out, mark out, outline, paint, portray, sketch, trace 3. allure, attract, bring forth, call forth, elicit, engage, entice, evoke, induce, influence, invite, persuade 4. elongate, extend, lengthen, stretch 5. breathe in, drain, inhale, inspire, pull, respire, suck 6. compose, draft, formulate, frame, prepare, write ~*n.* 7. *Inf.* attraction, enticement, lure 8. dead heat, stalemate, tie
drawback defect, difficulty, disadvantage, fault, flaw, handicap, hindrance, hitch, impedi-

ment, nuisance, obstacle, snag, stumbling block, trouble
draw back recoil, retract, retreat, shrink, start back, withdraw
drawing cartoon, depiction, illustration, outline, picture, portrayal, representation, sketch, study
drawn fatigued, fraught, harassed, harrowed, pinched, sapped, strained, stressed, taut, tense, tired, worn
draw on exploit, extract, fall back on, rely on
draw out drag out, extend, lengthen, prolong, protract, stretch
draw up compose, draft, formulate, frame, prepare, write out
dread 1. *v.* fear, quail, shrink from, shudder, tremble 2. *n.* alarm, apprehension, aversion, awe, dismay, fear, fright, horror, terror, trepidation
dreadful alarming, appalling, awful, distressing, fearful, formidable, frightful, ghastly, hideous, horrible, monstrous, shocking, terrible, tragic
dream *n.* 1. daydream, delusion, fantasy, illusion, imagination, reverie, speculation, trance, vision 2. ambition, aspiration, design, desire, goal, hope, notion, wish ~*v.* 3. daydream, envisage, fancy, imagine, stargaze, think, visualize
dreamy 1. chimerical, fantastic, misty, shadowy, unreal 2. absent, abstracted, daydreaming, faraway, musing, pensive, preoccupied
dreary 1. bleak, cheerless, comfortless, depressing, dismal, doleful, downcast, drear, forlorn, gloomy, glum, lonely, melancholy, mournful, sad, solitary, sombre, sorrowful, wretched 2. boring, drab, dull, lifeless, monotonous, routine, tedious, uneventful, wearisome
dregs deposit, dross, grounds, lees, residue, scum, sediment, trash, waste
drench drown, flood, inundate, saturate, soak, souse, steep, wet
dress *n.* 1. costume, ensemble, frock, garment, gown, outfit, robe, suit 2. attire, clothes, clothing, costume, garb, garments, guise, ~*v.* 3. attire, change, clothe, don, garb, put on, robe 4. bandage, bind up, plaster, treat
dressmaker couturier, seamstress, tailor
dress up beautify, embellish, gild, improve, titivate
dribble drip, drop, leak, ooze, run, seep, trickle
drift coast, float, meander, stray, waft, wander
drill *v.* 1. exercise, instruct, practise, rehearse, teach, train ~*n.* 2. discipline, exercise, practice, preparation, repetition, training ~*v.* 3. bore, pierce, puncture, sink in ~*n.* 4. bit, borer, gimlet
drink *v.* 1. drain, gulp, guzzle, imbibe, partake of, quaff, sip, suck, sup, swallow, swig, swill, wash down 2. revel, tipple, tope ~*n.* 3. beverage, liquid, potion, refreshment 4. alcohol, liquor, spirits
drip 1. *v.* drop, exude, filter, splash, sprinkle, trickle 2. *n.* dribble, drop, leak, trickle
drive *v.* 1. herd, hurl, impel, propel, push, send, urge 2. direct, go, guide, handle, manage, motor, operate, ride, steer, travel ~*n.* 3. excursion, jaunt, journey, outing, ride, run, trip, turn 4. effort, energy, enterprise, initiative, vigour
driving compelling, dynamic, energetic, forceful, vigorous
drizzle 1. *n.* fine rain, Scotch mist 2. *v.* rain, shower, spray, sprinkle
droll amusing, comic, comical, diverting, eccentric, entertaining, farcical, funny, humorous, jocular, ludicrous, odd, quaint, ridiculous, risible, whimsical
droop bend, drop, fall down, hang (down), sag, sink
drop *n.* 1. bead, drip, globule, pearl, tear 2. dab, dash, mouthful, nip, pinch, sip, spot, taste, tot, trace, trickle 3. decline, decrease, downturn, fall-off, reduction ~*v.* 4. decline, depress, descend, diminish, dive, droop, fall, lower, plunge, sink, tumble 5. abandon, cease, desert, discontinue, forsake, give up, leave, relinquish, terminate
drop off decline, decrease, diminish, dwindle, fall off, lessen, slacken
drop out abandon, back out, forsake, give up, leave, quit, renege, stop, withdraw
drought dry spell, dry weather
drove collection, company, crowd, flock, gathering, herd, horde, mob, multitude, press, swarm, throng
drown deluge, drench, engulf, flood, go down, go under, immerse, inundate, sink, submerge, swamp
drudge factotum, hack, menial, plodder, servant, slave, toiler, worker
drudgery chore, hack work, hard work, labour, slavery, slog, toil
drug *n.* 1. medicine, physic, poison, remedy 2. narcotic, opiate ~*v.* 3. dose, medicate, treat
drum *v.* beat, pulsate, rap, reverberate, tap, tattoo, throb
drunk 1. *adj.* drunken, fuddled, inebriated, intoxicated, maudlin, merry (*Inf.*), tight (*Inf.*), tipsy, well-oiled (*Sl.*) 2. *n.* drunkard, inebriate, sot, toper
drunkenness alcoholism, dipsomania, insobriety, intemperance, intoxication, tipsiness
dry *adj.* 1. arid, barren, dehydrated, dried up, parched, sapless, thirsty, torrid, waterless 2. *Fig.* boring, dreary, dull, monotonous, plain, tedious, tiresome, uninteresting ~*v.* 3. dehydrate, desiccate, drain, make dry, parch, sear
dual coupled, double, duplicate, matched, paired, twin, twofold
dubious 1. doubtful, hesitant, uncertain, unconvinced, undecided, unsure, wavering 2. ambiguous, debatable, doubtful, equivocal, indefinite, obscure, problematical, unclear, unsettled 3. questionable, suspect, suspicious
duck 1. bend, bow, crouch, dodge, drop, lower, stoop 2. *Inf.* avoid, dodge, escape, evade, shirk, sidestep
dudgeon ire, resentment, umbrage, wrath
due *adj.* 1. outstanding, owed, owing, payable, unpaid 2. appropriate, becoming, bounden, deserved, fit, fitting, just, justified, merited, obligatory, proper, right, rightful, suitable 3. expected, expected to arrive, scheduled ~*adv.* 4. dead, direct, directly, exactly, straight
duel 1. affair of honour, single combat 2. clash, competition, contest, encounter, engagement, fight, rivalry
dues charge, charges, fee, levy
dull 1. dense, dim, slow, stolid, stupid, thick, unintelligent 2. apathetic, blank, callous, dead, empty, heavy, indifferent, lifeless, listless, slow, sluggish 3. boring, commonplace, dreary, dry, flat, plain, prosaic, tedious, tiresome, unimaginative, uninteresting 4. cloudy, dim, gloomy, overcast
duly 1. accordingly, befittingly, correctly, deservedly, fittingly, properly, rightfully, suitably 2. on time, punctually
dumb inarticulate, mute, silent, soundless, speechless, tongue-tied, voiceless, wordless
dummy *n.* 1. figure, form, model 2. copy, counterfeit, duplicate, imitation, sham, substitute ~*adj.* 3. artificial, bogus, fake, false, imitation, mock, sham, simulated
dump *v.* 1. deposit, drop, fling down, let fall, throw down ~*n.* 2. junkyard, refuse heap, rubbish heap, rubbish tip, tip 3. hovel, mess, pigsty, shack, shanty, slum
dungeon cage, cell, lockup, prison
duplicate 1. *adj.* corresponding, identical, matched, twin, twofold 2. *n.* carbon copy, copy, double, likeness, match, mate, replica, reproduction, twin 3. *v.* copy, double, echo, photocopy, repeat, reproduce
durability endurance, imperishability, permanence, persistence
durable abiding, constant, dependable, enduring, fast, firm, hard-wearing, persistent, reliable, resistant, sound, stable, strong, sturdy, substantial, tough
dusk dark, evening, nightfall, sundown, sunset, twilight
dusky dark, dark-hued, sable, swarthy
dust *n.* 1. grime, grit, particles, powder 2. dirt, earth, ground, soil
dusty dirty, grubby, sooty, unclean, undusted, unswept
dutiful compliant, conscientious, devoted, docile, obedient, punctilious, respectful, submissive
duty 1. business, calling, charge, engagement, function, mission, obligation, office, onus, responsibility, role, service, task, work 2. customs, excise, impost, levy, tariff, tax, toll 3. **off duty** at leisure, free, off, off work, on holiday 4. **on duty** at work, busy, engaged
dwarf 1. *n.* bantam, midget, pygmy 2. *adj.* baby, diminutive, miniature, petite, pocket, small, tiny, undersized 3. *v.* dominate, overshadow, tower above *or* over
dwell abide, inhabit, live, lodge, remain, reside, rest, settle, sojourn, stay, stop
dwelling abode, domicile, establishment, habitation, home, house, quarters, residence
dye 1. *n.* colour, colouring, pigment, stain, tinge, tint 2. *v.* colour, pigment, stain, tincture, tinge, tint
dying ebbing, expiring, fading, failing, final, going, *in extremis*, moribund, mortal, passing, perishing, sinking
dynamic active, driving, energetic, forceful, go-ahead, high-powered, lively, magnetic, powerful, vigorous, vital
dynasty ascendancy, dominion, empire, government, house, regime, rule, sovereignty, sway

E

each 1. *adj.* every 2. *pron.* every one, one and all 3. *adv.* apiece, from each, individually, per capita, per head, per person, respectively, singly
eager agog, anxious, ardent, athirst, earnest, enthusiastic, fervent, greedy, hungry, intent, keen, longing, raring, zealous
ear *Fig.* 1. attention, hearing, heed, notice, regard 2. discrimination, sensitivity, taste
early 1. *adj.* forward, premature, untimely 2. *adv.* beforehand, in advance, in good time, prematurely, too soon
earn 1. collect, draw, gain, get, gross, make, net, obtain, procure, reap, receive 2. deserve, merit, rate, warrant, win
earnest close, constant, determined, firm, fixed, grave, intent, resolute, serious, sincere, solemn, stable, staid, steady
earnings gain, income, pay, proceeds, profits, receipts, remuneration, return, reward, salary, stipend, wages
earth 1. globe, orb, planet, sphere, world 2. clay, dirt, ground, land, loam, sod, soil, topsoil, turf
earthenware ceramics, crockery, crocks, pots, pottery, terra cotta
earthly 1. mundane, terrestrial, worldly 2. human, material, mortal, profane, secular, temporal, worldly
ease 1. *n.* affluence, calmness, comfort, contentment, enjoyment, happiness, leisure, peace, quiet, relaxation, repose, rest, serenity, tranquillity 2. *v.* abate, allay, alleviate, assuage, calm, comfort, disburden, lessen, lighten, moderate, pacify, palliate, quiet, relax, relent, relieve, slacken, soothe, still
easily comfortably, effortlessly, readily, simply, smoothly, with ease, without difficulty
easy child's play, clear, effortless, facile, light, no bother, not difficult, no trouble, painless, simple, smooth, straightforward, uncomplicated, undemanding
easy-going amenable, calm, carefree, casual, complacent, easy, even-tempered, flexible, indulgent, lenient, liberal, mild, moderate, nonchalant, permissive, placid, relaxed, serene, tolerant, uncritical, undemanding, unhurried

eat **1.** chew, consume, devour, munch, swallow **2.** dine, feed, have a meal, take food

eavesdrop listen in, monitor, overhear, spy

ebb *v.* **1.** abate, fall away, flow back, go out, recede, retire, retreat, sink, subside, wane, withdraw **2.** decay, decline, decrease, degenerate, deteriorate, diminish, drop, dwindle, fade away, fall away, flag, lessen, peter out, shrink, sink, slacken, weaken

eccentric abnormal, anomalous, bizarre, capricious, erratic, freakish, idiosyncratic, irregular, odd, outlandish, peculiar, singular, strange, uncommon, unconventional, weird

eccentricity abnormality, anomaly, caprice, foible, idiosyncrasy, irregularity, nonconformity, oddity, peculiarity, quirk, singularity, strangeness, unconventionality, waywardness, weirdness

ecclesiastic churchman, clergyman, cleric, divine, holy man, minister, parson, priest

echo *v.* **1.** repeat, resound, reverberate ~*n.* **2.** answer, repetition, reverberation **3.** copy, imitation, parallel, reflection, reproduction, ringing

eclipse *v.* **1.** blot out, cloud, darken, dim, obscure, overshadow, shroud, veil ~*n.* **2.** dimming, extinction, shading **3.** decline, diminution, failure, fall, loss

economic **1.** business, commercial, financial, industrial, mercantile, trade **2.** productive, profitable, profit-making, remunerative, solvent, viable **3.** budgetary, financial, fiscal, material, monetary, pecuniary

economical **1.** cost-effective, efficient, money-saving, sparing, time-saving, unwasteful, work-saving **2.** careful, frugal, prudent, saving, scrimping, sparing, thrifty

economize be economical, be frugal, be sparing, cut back, husband, retrench, save, scrimp, tighten one's belt

economy frugality, husbandry, parsimony, providence, prudence, restraint, saving, thrift

ecstasy bliss, delight, elation, enthusiasm, euphoria, exaltation, fervour, frenzy, joy, rapture, trance, transport

ecstatic blissful, delirious, elated, enthusiastic, euphoric, fervent, frenzied, joyful, joyous, overjoyed, rapturous, transported

eddy **1.** *n.* swirl, vortex, whirlpool **2.** *v.* swirl, whirl

edge **1.** border, bound, boundary, brim, brink, fringe, limit, line, lip, margin, outline, perimeter, rim, side, threshold, verge **2.** bite, force, incisiveness, interest, keenness, point, pungency, sharpness, sting, urgency, zest

edgy ill at ease, irascible, irritable, keyed up, nervous, on edge, restive, tense, touchy

edible eatable, fit to eat, good, harmless, palatable, wholesome

edict act, command, decree, dictate, dictum, fiat, injunction, law, mandate, manifesto, order, pronouncement, regulation, ruling, statute

edifice building, erection, habitation, house, pile, structure

edify educate, elevate, enlighten, guide, improve, inform, instruct, nurture, school, teach, uplift

edit adapt, annotate, censor, check, condense, correct, emend, polish, revise, rewrite

edition copy, impression, issue, number, printing, version, volume

educate civilize, coach, cultivate, develop, discipline, drill, edify, enlighten, exercise, foster, improve, inform, instruct, school, teach, train

educated civilized, cultivated, cultured, enlightened, experienced, informed, knowledgeable, learned, lettered, literary, polished, refined, tasteful

education breeding, civilization, cultivation, culture, development, discipline, edification, enlightenment, erudition, improvement, indoctrination, instruction, knowledge, scholarship, training, tutoring

eerie awesome, fearful, frightening, ghostly, mysterious, spectral, strange, uncanny, unearthly, weird

efface blot out, cancel, cross out, delete, destroy, dim, erase, excise, expunge, obliterate, raze, rub out, wipe out

effect *n.* **1.** conclusion, consequence, event, fruit, issue, outcome, result, upshot **2. in effect** actually, effectively, essentially, for practical purposes, in actuality, in fact, in reality, in truth, really, virtually **3. take effect** become operative, begin, come into force, produce results, work ~*v.* **4.** accomplish, achieve, bring about, carry out, cause, complete, create, execute, fulfil, give rise to, initiate, make, perform, produce

effective **1.** able, active, capable, competent, effectual, efficient, energetic, operative, productive, serviceable, useful **2.** active, current, in force, in operation, operative, real

effects belongings, chattels, gear, goods, movables, paraphernalia, possessions, property, things

effervesce ferment, fizz, foam, sparkle

effervescent **1.** bubbling, bubbly, foaming, foamy, frothing, sparkling **2.** animated, buoyant, ebullient, enthusiastic, excited, exhilarated, exuberant, gay, in high spirits, irrepressible, lively, merry, vital, vivacious

effete corrupt, debased, decadent, decayed, decrepit, degenerate, dissipated, feeble, ineffectual, spoiled, weak

efficacious active, capable, competent, effective, effectual, efficient, energetic, operative, potent, powerful, successful, useful

efficiency adeptness, capability, competence, economy, effectiveness, power, skill

efficient able, adept, businesslike, capable, competent, economic, powerful, productive, proficient, ready, skilful, workmanlike

effluent effluvium, pollutant, sewage, waste

effort endeavour, energy, exertion, force, labour, pains, power, strain, stress, stretch, striving, struggle, toil, trouble, work

effortless easy, facile, painless, simple, smooth, uncomplicated, undemanding

effusion discharge, emission, gush, outflow, outpouring, shedding, stream

effusive ebullient, enthusiastic, extravagant, exuberant, fulsome, gushing, lavish, profuse, talkative, unreserved, wordy

egocentric egotistic, self-centred, selfish

egoism egocentricity, narcissism, self-absorption, self-centredness, self-importance, self-love, self-regard

egotist boaster, braggart, egoist, egomaniac, self-admirer

egress escape, exit, exodus, issue, outlet, passage out, vent, way out, withdrawal

eject **1.** cast out, discharge, disgorge, emit, expel, throw out **2.** discharge, dislodge, dismiss, get rid of, oust, throw out

elaborate *adj.* **1.** careful, detailed, exact, intricate, laboured, minute, painstaking, precise, skilful, thorough **2.** complex, complicated, detailed, fussy, involved, ornamented, showy ~*v.* **3.** add detail, amplify, decorate, develop, devise, enhance, enlarge, garnish, improve, polish, produce, refine

elapse glide by, go, go by, lapse, pass, pass by, roll by, slip away

elastic flexible, plastic, pliable, resilient, rubbery, springy, supple, yielding

elated cheered, delighted, ecstatic, elevated, euphoric, excited, exhilarated, exultant, gleeful, joyful, jubilant, overjoyed, proud, roused

elbow **1.** *n.* angle, bend, corner, joint, turn **2.** *v.* bump, crowd, hustle, jostle, knock, nudge, push, shoulder, shove

elder **1.** *adj.* ancient, first-born, older, senior **2.** *n.* older person, senior

elect appoint, choose, decide upon, determine, opt for, pick, pick out, prefer, select, settle on, vote

election choice, choosing, decision, judgment, preference, selection, vote

elector constituent, voter

electric *Fig.* charged, dynamic, rousing, stimulating, stirring, tense, thrilling

electrify *Fig.* amaze, animate, astonish, astound, excite, fire, invigorate, jolt, rouse, shock, startle, stimulate, stir, thrill

elegance beauty, courtliness, dignity, gentility, grace, gracefulness, grandeur, luxury, polish, politeness, refinement, sumptuousness

elegant artistic, beautiful, chic, choice, comely, courtly, cultivated, delicate, exquisite, fashionable, fine, genteel, graceful, handsome, luxurious, nice, refined, stylish, sumptuous, tasteful

element basis, component, constituent, factor, feature, hint, ingredient, member, part, section, trace, unit

elementary **1.** clear, easy, facile, plain, rudimentary, simple, straightforward, uncomplicated **2.** basic, fundamental, initial, original, rudimentary

elements basics, essentials, foundations, fundamentals, principles, rudiments

elevate **1.** heighten, hoist, lift, lift up, raise, uplift, upraise **2.** advance, aggrandize, exalt, prefer, promote, upgrade

elevation **1.** altitude, height **2.** eminence, height, hill, hillock, mountain, rise **3.** exaltedness, grandeur, loftiness, nobility, nobleness, sublimity

elicit bring out, call forth, cause, derive, draw out, educe, evoke, evolve, exact, extort, extract, obtain, wrest

eligible fit, preferable, proper, qualified, suitable, suited, worthy

eliminate cut out, dispose of, do away with, exterminate, get rid of, remove, stamp out, take out

elite aristocracy, best, cream, elect, flower, gentry, high society, nobility, pick, upper class

elocution articulation, delivery, diction, enunciation, oratory, public speaking, rhetoric, speech, utterance

elongate draw out, extend, lengthen, make longer, prolong, protract, stretch

elope abscond, bolt, decamp, disappear, escape, leave, run away, run off, slip away, steal away

eloquence expressiveness, fluency, oratory, persuasiveness, rhetoric

eloquent articulate, fluent, forceful, graceful, moving, persuasive, well-expressed

elsewhere abroad, absent, away, not here

elucidate clarify, clear up, explain, expound, gloss, illuminate, make plain, spell out, unfold

elude avoid, dodge, escape, evade, flee, get away from, shirk, shun

elusive shifty, slippery, tricky

emaciated attenuated, cadaverous, gaunt, haggard, lank, lean, meagre, pinched, thin, wasted

emanate arise, derive, emerge, flow, issue, originate, proceed, spring, stem

emancipate deliver, discharge, enfranchise, free, liberate, release, set free, unshackle

emancipation deliverance, enfranchisement, freedom, liberation, liberty

embargo ban, bar, barrier, blockage, check, hindrance, impediment, interdict, prohibition, restraint, restriction, stoppage

embark **1.** board ship, go aboard, take ship **2.** *With* **on** *or* **upon** begin, broach, commence, engage, enter, initiate, launch, plunge into, set about, set out, start, take up, undertake

embarrass chagrin, discompose, disconcert, distress, fluster, mortify

embarrassing awkward, disconcerting, distressing, humiliating, sensitive, shameful, touchy, tricky, uncomfortable

embarrassment awkwardness, bashfulness, chagrin, confusion, distress, humiliation, mortification, shame

embellish adorn, beautify, bedeck, deck, decorate, dress up, elaborate, embroider, enhance, enrich, garnish, gild, grace, ornament

embezzle abstract, appropriate, filch, misapply, misappropriate, misuse, peculate, pilfer, purloin, steal

embitter anger, disaffect, disillusion, envenom, poison, sour

emblem badge, crest, device, figure, image, insignia, mark, representation, sign, symbol, token, type

embolden cheer, encourage, fire, hearten, inflame, inspirit, invigorate, nerve, reassure, rouse, stimulate, vitalize

embrace *v.* **1.** clasp, cuddle, encircle, enfold, grasp, hold, hug, seize, squeeze **2.** accept, adopt, espouse, grab, receive, seize, take up, welcome *~n.* **3.** clasp, cuddle, hug, squeeze

embroil complicate, confound, confuse, disorder, disturb, enmesh, entangle, implicate, incriminate, involve, mire, mix up, perplex, trouble

embryo germ, nucleus, root

emend amend, correct, edit, improve

emerge **1.** appear, arise, come forth, come out, come up, emanate, issue, proceed, rise, spring up, surface **2.** come out, crop up, develop, materialize, transpire, turn up

emergency crisis, danger, difficulty, extremity, necessity, pass, pinch, plight, predicament, quandary, strait

emigrate migrate, move, move abroad, remove

eminence celebrity, dignity, distinction, esteem, fame, greatness, importance, notability, note, prestige, rank, renown, reputation, repute, superiority

eminent celebrated, distinguished, esteemed, exalted, famous, grand, great, high, illustrious, important, notable, noted, noteworthy, outstanding, prestigious, renowned, signal, superior, well-known

emission diffusion, discharge, ejection, exhalation, issuance, issue, radiation

emit diffuse, discharge, eject, emanate, exhale, exude, give off, give out, issue, radiate, send out, shed, throw out, transmit, utter, vent

emolument benefit, earnings, fee, gain, hire, pay, payment, profits, recompense, remuneration, return, reward, salary, stipend, wages

emotion ardour, excitement, feeling, fervour, passion, sensation, sentiment, warmth

emotional **1.** demonstrative, excitable, hot-blooded, passionate, sensitive, susceptible, temperamental, tender, warm **2.** ardent, enthusiastic, fervent, fervid, fiery, heated, passionate, roused, stirred, zealous

emphasis accent, attention, force, importance, insistence, intensity, moment, power, preeminence, priority, prominence, significance, strength, stress, weight

emphasize accent, dwell on, highlight, insist on, play up, press home, stress, underline, underscore, weight

emphatic absolute, certain, decided, definite, direct, distinct, earnest, forceful, forcible, important, impressive, insistent, marked, positive, powerful, resounding, significant, striking, strong, telling, vigorous

empire commonwealth, kingdom, realm

employ **1.** engage, enlist, hire, retain, take on **2.** engage, fill, occupy, spend, take up, use up

employed active, busy, engaged, in employment, in work, occupied, working

employee hand, staff member, wage-earner, worker, workman

employer business, company, establishment, firm, organization, owner, patron, proprietor

employment **1.** engagement, enlistment, hire **2.** application, exercise, exertion, use **3.** business, calling, craft, employ, job, line, métier, occupation, profession, pursuit, service, trade, vocation, work

empower allow, authorize, commission, delegate, enable, entitle, license, permit, qualify, sanction, warrant

emptiness **1.** bareness, blankness, desolation, vacancy, vacuum, void, waste **2.** cheapness, hollowness, idleness, insincerity, triviality

empty *adj.* **1.** bare, blank, clear, deserted, desolate, hollow, unfurnished, uninhabited, unoccupied, vacant, void, waste **2.** aimless, banal, frivolous, fruitless, futile, hollow, inane, ineffective, meaningless, purposeless, silly, unreal, vain, valueless, worthless **3.** absent, blank, vacant, vacuous *~v.* **4.** clear, consume, deplete, discharge, drain, evacuate, exhaust, pour out, unburden, unload, use up, vacate, void

enable allow, authorize, commission, empower, fit, license, permit, prepare, qualify, sanction, warrant

enact authorize, command, decree, legislate, ordain, order, pass, proclaim, ratify, sanction

enamour bewitch, charm, enchant, endear, enrapture, entrance, fascinate

enamoured bewitched, charmed, enchanted, enraptured, entranced, fascinated, fond, in love

enchant beguile, bewitch, captivate, charm, delight, enamour, enrapture, enthral, fascinate, hypnotize, spellbind

enchanter conjurer, magician, sorcerer, spellbinder, witch, wizard

enchanting alluring, appealing, attractive, bewitching, captivating, charming, delightful, entrancing, fascinating, pleasant

enclose **1.** bound, cover, encase, encircle, encompass, fence, hedge, hem in, pen, shut in, wall in, wrap **2.** include, insert, put in, send with

encompass **1.** circle, encircle, enclose, envelop, girdle, hem in, ring, surround **2.** bring about, cause, contrive, devise, effect, manage

encounter *v.* **1.** chance upon, come upon, confront, experience, face, meet, run across **2.** attack, combat, come into conflict with, contend, engage, fight, grapple with, strive, struggle *~n.* **3.** brush, confrontation, meeting

encourage buoy up, cheer, comfort, console, embolden, hearten, incite, inspire, rally, reassure, rouse, stimulate

encouragement aid, boost, cheer, consolation, favour, help, inspiration, reassurance, stimulation, stimulus, succour, support, urging

encouraging bright, cheerful, good, hopeful, promising, reassuring, rosy, stimulating

encroach impinge, infringe, intrude, invade, make inroads, overstep, trench, trespass, usurp

encumber burden, clog, cramp, embarrass, hamper, handicap, hinder, impede, inconvenience, obstruct, oppress, overload, retard, saddle, slow down, trammel, weigh down

end *n.* **1.** boundary, edge, extent, extremity, limit, point, terminus, tip **2.** close, closure, completion, conclusion, consequence, culmination, denouement, ending, expiry, finale, finish, issue, outcome, resolution, result, stop, termination, wind-up **3.** aim, aspiration, design, drift, goal, intention, object, objective, point, purpose, reason **4.** death, demise, destruction, dissolution, doom, extinction, ruin, ruination *~v.* **5.** cease, close, complete, conclude, culminate, dissolve, expire, finish, resolve, stop, terminate, wind up

endanger compromise, hazard, imperil, jeopardize, put at risk, risk, threaten

endeavour **1.** *n.* aim, attempt, effort, enterprise, essay, go, trial, try, venture **2.** *v.* aim, aspire, attempt, essay, strive, struggle, try, undertake

ending close, completion, conclusion, denouement, finale, finish, resolution, termination, wind-up

endless **1.** ceaseless, constant, continual, eternal, everlasting, immortal, incessant, infinite, interminable, perpetual, unbounded, unbroken, undying, unlimited **2.** interminable, monotonous, overlong **3.** continuous, unbroken, undivided, whole

endorse advocate, affirm, approve, authorize, back, champion, confirm, favour, ratify, recommend, sanction, support, sustain, warrant

endorsement **1.** countersignature, qualification, signature **2.** advocacy, affirmation, approval, authorization, backing, confirmation, favour, fiat, ratification, recommendation, sanction, support, warrant

endow award, bequeath, bestow, confer, donate, endue, enrich, favour, finance, fund, furnish, give, grant, invest, leave, make over, provide, settle on, supply, will

endowment award, benefaction, bequest, bestowal, boon, donation, fund, gift, grant, income, largess, legacy, presentation, property, provision, revenue

endurable bearable, sufferable, supportable, sustainable, tolerable

endurance bearing, fortitude, patience, perseverance, resignation, resolution, stamina, staying power, strength, submission, sufferance, tenacity, toleration

endure **1.** bear, brave, cope with, experience, go through, stand, suffer, support, sustain, undergo, weather, withstand **2.** abide, allow, bear, brook, countenance, permit, stand, stomach, suffer, swallow, take patiently, tolerate

enemy adversary, antagonist, competitor, foe, opponent, rival

energetic active, brisk, dynamic, forceful, forcible, indefatigable, lively, potent, powerful, spirited, strenuous, strong, tireless, vigorous

energy activity, ardour, drive, efficiency, élan, exertion, fire, force, intensity, life, liveliness, pluck, power, spirit, stamina, strength, verve, vigour, vitality, vivacity, zeal, zest

enforce apply, carry out, coerce, compel, constrain, exact, execute, impose, insist on, oblige, prosecute, reinforce, require, urge

enfranchise **1.** give the vote to **2.** emancipate, free, liberate, manumit, release, set free

engage **1.** appoint, commission, employ, enlist, enrol, hire, retain, take on **2.** bespeak, book, charter, hire, lease, prearrange, rent, reserve, secure **3.** absorb, busy, engross, grip, involve, occupy, preoccupy, tie up **4.** assail, attack, combat, fall on, fight with, give battle to, meet, take on **5.** activate, apply, bring into operation, energize, set going, switch on **6.** dovetail, interact, interlock, join, mesh

engaged affianced, pledged, promised, spoken for

engagement **1.** betrothal, bond, compact, contract, oath, obligation, pact, pledge, promise, vow, word **2.** appointment, commitment, date, meeting **3.** action, battle, combat, conflict, contest, fight

engine **1.** machine, mechanism, motor **2.** agency, agent, apparatus, appliance, contrivance, device, implement, instrument, means, tool, weapon

engineer **1.** *n.* contriver, designer, deviser, director, inventor, manipulator, originator, planner, schemer **2.** *v.* bring about, cause, concoct, contrive, control, create, devise, effect, encompass, manage, mastermind, originate, plan, plot, scheme

engrave carve, chase, chisel, cut, etch, inscribe

engrossed absorbed, caught up, deep, enthralled, fascinated, intent, preoccupied, rapt, riveted

enigma conundrum, mystery, problem, puzzle, riddle

enjoy **1.** appreciate, delight in, like, rejoice in, relish, revel in take joy in 2. experience, own, possess, use

enjoyable agreeable, amusing, delicious, delightful, entertaining, pleasant, pleasing, pleasurable, satisfying

enjoyment amusement, delight, entertainment, fun, gladness, gratification, gusto, happiness, indulgence, joy, pleasure, recreation, relish, satisfaction, zest

enlarge add to, augment, broaden, diffuse, dilate, distend, elongate, expand, extend, grow, heighten, increase, inflate, lengthen, magnify, multiply, stretch, swell, wax, widen

enlighten advise, apprise, civilize, counsel, edify, educate, inform, instruct, make aware, teach

enlist engage, enrol, gather, join, join up, muster, obtain, procure, recruit, register, secure, sign up

enliven brighten, buoy up, cheer up, excite, exhilarate, fire, gladden, hearten, inspire, inspirit, invigorate, quicken, rouse, spark, stimulate, vitalize, wake up

enmity animosity, animus, antagonism, antipathy, aversion, bad blood, bitterness, hate, hatred, hostility, ill will, malevolence, malice, rancour, spite, venom

enormity atrocity, depravity, disgrace, evilness, outrageousness, turpitude, viciousness, villainy, wickedness

enormous astronomic, colossal, gigantic, gross, huge, immense, mammoth, massive, monstrous, prodigious, tremendous, vast

enough 1. *adj.* abundant, adequate, ample, plenty, sufficient 2. *adv.* abundantly, adequately, amply, fairly, moderately, passably, reasonably, satisfactorily, sufficiently, tolerably

enquire 1. ask, query, question 2. *Also* **inquire** conduct an inquiry, examine, explore, inspect, investigate, look into, make inquiry, probe, scrutinize, search

enquiry examination, exploration, inquest, inspection, investigation, probe, research, scrutiny, search, study, survey

enrage anger, exasperate, incense, incite, inflame, infuriate, irritate, provoke

enrolment acceptance, admission, enlistment, recruitment, registration

en route in transit, on the way

ensign badge, banner, colours, flag, pennant, pennon, standard, streamer

ensue arise, attend, be consequent on, befall, come after, derive, flow, follow, issue, proceed, result, stem, succeed, supervene

entail bring about, call for, cause, demand, give rise to, impose, involve, lead to, necessitate, occasion, require, result in

entangle 1. catch, embroil, enmesh, ensnare, implicate, involve, knot, mix up, snag, snare, tangle, trap 2. complicate, confuse, mix up, muddle, perplex, puzzle, snarl, twist

enter 1. arrive, come *or* go in *or* into, insert, introduce, penetrate, pierce 2. begin, commence, embark upon, enlist, enrol, join, sign up, start, take up 3. list, log, note, record, register, set down, take down 4. offer, present, proffer, register, submit, tender

enterprise 1. adventure, effort, endeavour, essay, operation, plan, programme, project, undertaking, venture 2. activity, daring, dash, drive, energy, enthusiasm, initiative, readiness, resource, spirit, vigour, zeal 3. business, company, concern, establishment, firm, operation

enterprising active, adventurous, bold, daring, dashing, eager, go-ahead, intrepid, keen, ready, resourceful, spirited, stirring, vigorous, zealous

entertain 1. amuse, charm, cheer, delight, divert, occupy, please 2. be host to, harbour, have company, lodge, put up, treat

entertaining amusing, charming, delightful, diverting, funny, humorous, pleasant, witty

entertainment amusement, cheer, distraction, diversion, enjoyment, fun, good time, play, pleasure, recreation, satisfaction, sport, treat

enthusiasm ardour, eagerness, earnestness, excitement, fervour, frenzy, interest, keenness, passion, relish, vehemence, warmth, zeal, zest

enthusiast admirer, aficionado, devotee, fan, fanatic, follower, lover, zealot

enthusiastic ardent, avid, devoted, eager, earnest, ebullient, excited, fervent, fervid, hearty, keen, lively, spirited, unstinting, vigorous, warm, wholehearted, zealous

entice allure, attract, beguile, cajole, coax, decoy, draw, inveigle, lead on, lure, persuade, seduce, tempt, wheedle

entire complete, full, total, whole

entirely absolutely, altogether, completely, fully, perfectly, thoroughly, totally, unreservedly, utterly, wholly, without exception, without reservation

entitle 1. allow, authorize, empower, enable, fit for, license, permit, qualify for, warrant 2. call, christen, designate, dub, label, name, style, term, title

entrance[1] *n.* 1. access, door, doorway, entry, gate, inlet, opening, passage, way in 2. arrival, entry, ingress, introduction 3. access, admission, admittance, entrée, entry, ingress

entrance[2] *v.* bewitch, captivate, charm, delight, enchant, enthral, fascinate, ravish, transport

entrant 1. beginner, convert, initiate, newcomer, novice, probationer, tyro 2. candidate, competitor, contestant, entry, participant, player

entrust assign, charge, commend, commit, confide, consign, delegate, deliver, hand over, invest, trust

entry 1. appearance, initiation, introduction 2. access, door, doorway, entrance, gate, inlet, opening, passageway, portal, way in 3. access, admission, entrance, entrée 4. attempt, candidate, competitor, contestant, effort, entrant, participant, player, submission

enumerate 1. cite, detail, itemize, list, mention, name, quote, recite, recount, rehearse, relate, specify, spell out, tell 2. add up, calculate, count, number, reckon, sum up, tally, total

envelop blanket, cloak, conceal, cover, embrace, encase, enclose, enfold, engulf, hide, obscure, sheathe, shroud, surround, swathe, veil, wrap

envelope case, casing, coating, cover, covering, jacket, sheath, shell, skin, wrapping

enviable blessed, desirable, favoured, fortunate, lucky, privileged

envious covetous, grudging, jaundiced, jealous, malicious, resentful, spiteful

environment atmosphere, background, conditions, context, element, habitat, locale, medium, milieu, scene, setting, situation, surroundings

environs district, locality, neighbourhood, outskirts, precincts, vicinity

envisage 1. contemplate, fancy, imagine, picture, think up, visualize 2. anticipate, envision, foresee, predict, see

envoy agent, ambassador, courier, delegate, diplomat, emissary, intermediary, messenger, minister, representative

envy 1. *n.* covetousness, grudge, hatred, ill will, jealousy, malice, resentment, spite 2. *v.* begrudge, be jealous (of), covet, grudge, resent

epidemic 1. *adj.* general, prevailing, rampant, rife, sweeping, wide-ranging, widespread 2. *n.* outbreak, plague, rash, spread, wave

epigram bon mot, quip, witticism

epilogue coda, conclusion, postscript

episode 1. adventure, affair, event, experience, happening, incident, matter, occurrence 2. chapter, instalment, part, passage, scene, section

epistle communication, letter, message, missive, note

epithet description, designation, name, nickname, tag, title

epitome embodiment, essence, exemplar, personification, type

epoch age, date, era, period, time

equable 1. agreeable, calm, composed, easy-going, placid, serene, temperate, unexcitable 2. consistent, constant, even, regular, smooth, stable, steady, temperate, tranquil, unchanging, uniform, unvarying

equal *adj.* 1. alike, commensurate, equivalent, identical, like, proportionate, tantamount, uniform 2. balanced, egalitarian, even, evenly matched, matched, regular, symmetrical, uniform 3. able, adequate, capable, competent, fit, ready, suitable, up to ~*n.* 4. brother, compeer, equivalent, fellow, match, mate, peer, rival, twin

equality balance, egalitarianism, equivalence, evenness, fairness, identity, likeness, parity, sameness, similarity, uniformity

equate agree, balance, compare, correspond with, liken, match, offset, pair, square, tally

equation agreement, balancing, comparison, correspondence, equivalence, likeness, match, pairing, parallel

equilibrium 1. balance, counterpoise, equipoise, evenness, rest, stability, steadiness 2. calm, calmness, composure, coolness, equanimity, poise, self-possession, stability, steadiness

equip accoutre, arm, array, attire, endow, fit out, furnish, kit out, outfit, prepare, provide, rig, stock, supply

equipment accoutrements, apparatus, baggage, furnishings, gear, outfit, stuff, supplies, tackle, tools

equivalence agreement, conformity, correspondence, evenness, identity, likeness, match, parity, similarity, synonymy

equivalent alike, commensurate, comparable, corresponding, equal, even, interchangeable, of a kind, same, similar, synonymous, tantamount

equivocal ambiguous, ambivalent, doubtful, dubious, evasive, indefinite, indeterminate, misleading, obscure, questionable, suspicious, uncertain

era age, cycle, date, day *or* days, epoch, generation, period, stage, time

eradicate annihilate, destroy, efface, eliminate, erase, expunge, extinguish, obliterate, remove, root out, stamp out, uproot, weed out, wipe out

erect 1. *adj.* firm, raised, rigid, standing, stiff, straight, upright, vertical 2. *v.* build, construct, lift, mount, pitch, put up

erode consume, corrode, destroy, deteriorate, eat away, grind down, spoil

err be inaccurate, be incorrect, blunder, go wrong, make a mistake, miscalculate, misjudge, mistake

errand charge, commission, job, message, mission, task

erratic aberrant, abnormal, capricious, changeable, desultory, fitful, inconsistent, irregular, shifting, unreliable, unstable, variable, wayward

erroneous amiss, fallacious, false, inaccurate, incorrect, inexact, invalid, mistaken, spurious, untrue, wrong

error blunder, delusion, erratum, fallacy, fault, flaw, inaccuracy, miscalculation, mistake, oversight, slip, solecism

erstwhile bygone, former, late, old, one-time, past, previous, sometime

erudite cultivated, educated, knowledgeable, learned, lettered, literate, scholarly, well-educated, well-read

erupt belch forth, blow up, break out, burst forth, burst out, discharge, explode, flare up, gush, pour forth, out, spit out, spout, throw off, vent, vomit

eruption discharge, ejection, explosion, flare-up, outbreak, outburst

escalate ascend, be increased, enlarge, expand, extend, grow, heighten, increase, intensify, mount, raise, rise

escapade adventure, antic, caper, fling, mischief, spree, stunt, trick

escape *v.* 1. bolt, break free, decamp, flee, fly, get away, run away *or* off, skip, slip away ~*n.* 2. break, break-out, flight, getaway ~*v.* 3. avoid, dodge, duck, elude, evade, pass, shun, slip ~*n.* 4. elusion, evasion ~*v.* 5. drain, emanate, flow, gush, issue, leak, seep, spurt ~*n.* 6. drain, efflux, emission, gush, leak, leakage, outflow, outpour, seepage, spurt

escort 1. *n.* bodyguard, company, convoy, cortege, entourage, guard, protection, retinue, safeguard, train 2. *v.* accompany, conduct, convoy, guard, guide, lead, partner, protect, squire, usher

especial chief, exceptional, extraordinary, marked, notable, noteworthy, outstanding, principal, signal, special, uncommon, unusual

especially chiefly, conspicuously, exceptionally, extraordinarily, mainly, markedly, notably, principally, remarkably, specially, strikingly, supremely, uncommonly, unusually

espousal advocacy, backing, championship, defence, embracing, maintenance, support, taking up

espouse adopt, advocate, back, champion, defend, embrace, maintain, stand up for, support, take up

essay article, composition, discourse, disquisition, dissertation, paper, piece, tract

essence 1. being, core, entity, heart, kernel, life, lifeblood, nature, pith, principle, soul, spirit, substance 2. concentrate, distillate, extract, spirits, tincture

essential *adj.* 1. crucial, important, indispensable, necessary, needed, requisite, vital 2. basic, cardinal, fundamental, inherent, innate, intrinsic, key, main, principal ~*n.* 3. basic, fundamental, necessity, requisite, rudiment, *sine qua non*

establish base, constitute, create, decree, enact, entrench, fix, form, found, ground, implant, inaugurate, install, institute, plant, root, secure, settle, set up, start

establishment 1. business, company, concern, enterprise, firm, house, institution, organization, outfit (*Inf.*), setup (*Inf.*), structure, system 2. **the Establishment** established order, ruling class

estate area, domain, holdings, lands, manor, property

esteem 1. *v.* admire, be fond of, cherish, honour, like, love, prize, respect, revere, reverence, treasure, value 2. *n.* credit, good opinion, honour, regard, respect, reverence

estimate *v.* 1. assess, calculate roughly, evaluate, gauge, guess, judge, number, reckon, value 2. assess, believe, conjecture, consider, guess, judge, rank, rate, reckon, surmise, think ~*n.* 3. approximate calculation, assessment, evaluation, guess, judgment, reckoning, valuation

estrange alienate, antagonize, disunite, divide, part, separate, set at odds, withdraw, withhold

estuary creek, firth, fjord, inlet, mouth

et cetera and others, and so forth, and so on, and the like, and the rest

eternal abiding, ceaseless, constant, deathless, endless, everlasting, immortal, infinite, interminable, never-ending, perennial, perpetual, timeless, unceasing, undying, unending, without end

ethical correct, fitting, good, honest, honourable, just, moral, principled, proper, right, upright

ethics conscience, moral code, morality, moral philosophy, moral values, principles, standards

etiquette civility, code, convention, courtesy, customs, decorum, manners, politeness, propriety, protocol, rules, usage

evacuate abandon, clear, decamp, depart, desert, forsake, leave, move out, pull out, quit, relinquish, remove, vacate, withdraw

evade avoid, circumvent, decline, dodge, duck, elude, escape, shirk, shun, sidestep

evaluate appraise, assay, assess, estimate, gauge, judge, rank, rate, reckon, value, weigh

evaporate 1. dry, dry up, vaporize 2. dematerialize, disappear, disperse, dissipate, dissolve, fade away, melt, vanish

evasion avoidance, cunning, dodge, equivocation, escape, evasiveness, excuse, prevarication, ruse, shift, shuffling, sophistry, subterfuge, trickery

eve day before, night before, vigil

even *adj.* 1. flat, flush, level, plane, plumb, smooth, steady, straight, true, uniform 2. cool, equable, imperturbable, peaceful, placid, serene, stable, steady, tranquil, undisturbed, unexcitable, unruffled, well-balanced 3. balanced, disinterested, dispassionate, equitable, fair, impartial, just, unbiased, unprejudiced ~*adv.* 4. all the more, much, still, yet

event affair, business, circumstance, episode, experience, fact, happening, incident, matter, milestone, occasion, occurrence

eventful active, busy, critical, crucial, decisive, exciting, fateful, full, historic, important, lively, memorable, momentous, notable, significant

eventually after all, finally, in the end, in the long run, one day, some day, some time, sooner or later, ultimately

ever 1. at all, at any time (period, point), in any case, on any occasion 2. always, at all times, constantly, continually, endlessly, eternally, incessantly, perpetually, relentlessly, to the end of time, unceasingly, unendingly

everlasting abiding, deathless, endless, eternal, immortal, imperishable, infinite, interminable, never-ending, perpetual, timeless, undying

evermore always, eternally, ever, for ever, *in perpetuum*, to the end of time

everyday accustomed, common, commonplace, conventional, dull, familiar, frequent, habitual, informal, mundane, ordinary, routine, stock, usual, wonted

evict boot out (*Inf.*), chuck out (*Inf.*), dislodge, dispossess, eject, expel, kick out (*Inf.*), oust, put out, remove, show the door (to), throw on to the streets, throw out, turf out (*Inf.*), turn out

evidence affirmation, confirmation, data, declaration, demonstration, grounds, indication, mark, proof, sign, substantiation, testimony, token, witness

evident apparent, clear, incontestable, indisputable, manifest, noticeable, obvious, patent, perceptible, plain, visible

evidently apparently, it seems, ostensibly, outwardly, seemingly

evil *adj.* 1. bad, base, corrupt, depraved, malicious, malignant, sinful, vicious, vile, villainous, wicked, wrong 2. calamitous, catastrophic, destructive, dire, harmful, hurtful, injurious, mischievous, painful, pernicious, ruinous, sorrowful, unfortunate, unlucky, woeful ~*n.* 3. badness, baseness, corruption, immorality, vice, villainy, wickedness, wrong, wrongdoing

evoke 1. arouse, awaken, call, excite, induce, recall, stimulate, stir up, summon up 2. call forth, elicit, produce, provoke

evolution development, enlargement, expansion, growth, increase, progress, unrolling

evolve develop, disclose, educe, elaborate, enlarge, expand, grow, increase, mature, open, progress, unfold, unroll, work out

exact *adj.* 1. accurate, careful, correct, definite, explicit, faithful, faultless, identical, literal, methodical, orderly, particular, precise, right, specific, true, unequivocal, unerring, veracious, very 2. careful, meticulous, painstaking, punctilious, rigorous, scrupulous, severe, strict ~*v.* 3. call for, claim, command, compel, demand, extort, extract, force, impose, insist upon, require

exactly 1. accurately, carefully, correctly, definitely, explicitly, faithfully, faultlessly, literally, precisely, severely, strictly, truly, truthfully, veraciously 2. absolutely, expressly, indeed, just, particularly, precisely, quite, specifically

exactness carefulness, correctness, exactitude, faultlessness, nicety, precision, promptitude, regularity, rigorousness, scrupulousness, strictness, truth, veracity

exaggerate amplify, embroider, emphasize, enlarge, exalt, inflate, magnify, overdo, overestimate, overstate

exaggeration embellishment, emphasis, enlargement, excess, hyperbole, inflation, magnification, overstatement, pretension, pretentiousness

exalt advance, dignify, elevate, ennoble, honour, promote, raise, upgrade

exaltation advancement, dignity, elevation, eminence, ennoblement, grandeur, high rank, honour, loftiness, prestige, promotion, rise, upgrading

exalted august, dignified, elevated, eminent, grand, high, honoured, lofty, prestigious

examination analysis, catechism, checkup, exploration, inquiry, inquisition, inspection, interrogation, investigation, perusal, probe, questioning, quiz, review, scrutiny, search, study, survey, test, trial

examine analyse, appraise, check out, consider, explore, inspect, investigate, look over, peruse, ponder, probe, review, scan, scrutinize, sift, study, survey, test, vet, weigh

example 1. case, illustration, instance, sample, specimen 2. **for example** e.g., *exempli gratia*, for instance, to illustrate

exasperate anger, annoy, embitter, enrage, exacerbate, excite, gall, incense, inflame, infuriate, irk, irritate, madden, nettle, pique, provoke, rankle, rouse, vex

exasperation anger, annoyance, fury, irritation, passion, pique, rage, vexation, wrath

excavate burrow, delve, dig, dig out, dig up, gouge, hollow, mine, quarry, scoop, trench, tunnel, uncover, unearth

exceed beat, better, eclipse, excel, outdistance, outdo, outreach, outrun, outshine, outstrip, overtake, pass, surmount, surpass, top, transcend

exceedingly enormously, especially, exceptionally, extremely, greatly, highly, hugely, inordinately, superlatively, unusually, vastly, very

excel beat, be superior, better, eclipse, exceed, go beyond, outdo, outrival, outshine, pass, surmount, surpass, top, transcend

excellence distinction, eminence, goodness, greatness, high quality, merit, perfection, superiority, supremacy, virtue, worth

excellent admirable, capital, champion, choice, distinguished, exemplary, exquisite, fine, first-class, first-rate, good, great, meritorious, notable, noted, outstanding, prime, select, superb, superior, superlative, worthy

except, except for apart from, bar, barring, besides, but, excepting, excluding, exclusive of, omitting, other than

exception anomaly, deviation, freak, irregularity, oddity, peculiarity, quirk, special case

exceptional excellent, extraordinary, marvellous, outstanding, phenomenal, prodigious, remarkable, special, superior

excess *n.* 1. glut, leftover, overdose, overflow, plethora, remainder, superfluity, surfeit, surplus, too much 2. debauchery, dissipation, dissoluteness, extravagance, intemperance, overindulgence, prodigality ~*adj.* 3. extra, leftover, redundant, remaining, residual, spare, surplus

excessive enormous, exaggerated, extravagant, extreme, inordinate, needless, overdone, overmuch, prodigal, profligate, superfluous, too much, undue, unreasonable

exchange 1. *v.* bandy, barter,

change, commute, switch, trade, truck **2.** *n.* barter, dealing, substitution, switch, trade, traffic, truck

excitable edgy, hasty, highly strung, hot-headed, nervous, passionate, sensitive, temperamental, testy, touchy, violent, volatile

excite agitate, arouse, awaken, disturb, evoke, fire, foment, galvanize, incite, inflame, inspire, move, provoke, quicken, rouse, stimulate, stir up, thrill, waken

excitement action, ado, adventure, agitation, animation, commotion, elation, ferment, fever, flurry, furore, heat, passion, thrill, tumult, warmth

exciting exhilarating, inspiring, intoxicating, moving, provocative, rousing, sensational, stimulating, stirring, thrilling

exclaim call, call out, cry, cry out, declare, proclaim, shout, utter, yell

exclamation call, cry, expletive, interjection, outcry, shout, utterance, yell

exclude 1. ban, bar, debar, disallow, forbid, interdict, keep out, ostracize, prohibit, proscribe, refuse, shut out, veto **2.** eliminate, except, ignore, leave out, omit, pass over, preclude, reject, repudiate, rule out

exclusive 1. aristocratic, chic, choice, clannish, closed, elegant, fashionable, limited, narrow, private, restricted, select, selfish, snobbish **2.** confined, limited, peculiar, restricted, unique

excommunicate anathematize, ban, banish, cast out, denounce, eject, exclude, expel, proscribe, remove, repudiate, unchurch

exculpate absolve, acquit, clear, discharge, dismiss, excuse, exonerate, free, justify, pardon, release, vindicate

excursion airing, day trip, expedition, jaunt, journey, outing, pleasure trip, tour, trip

excuse *v.* **1.** absolve, acquit, bear with, exculpate, exonerate, forgive, indulge, overlook, pardon, pass over, tolerate, wink at **2.** absolve, discharge, exempt, free, let off, liberate, release, relieve, spare *~n.* **3.** apology, defence, explanation, grounds, justification, mitigation, plea, pretext, reason, vindication

execute behead, electrocute, guillotine, hang, kill, put to death, shoot

execution 1. accomplishment, achievement, administration, carrying out, completion, discharge, effect, enactment, enforcement, implementation, performance, prosecution, realization, rendering **2.** hanging, killing

executive *n.* **1.** administrator, director, manager, official **2.** administration, directorate, directors, government, leadership, management *~adj.* **3.** administrative, controlling, decision-making, directing, governing, managerial

exemplary admirable, commendable, correct, estimable, excellent, good, ideal, laudable, meritorious, model, praiseworthy, sterling

exemplify demonstrate, depict, display, embody, evidence, exhibit, illustrate, instance, represent, show

exempt 1. *v.* absolve, discharge, except, excuse, exonerate, free, let off, liberate, release, relieve, spare **2.** *adj.* absolved, clear, discharged, excused, favoured, free, immune, liberated, not liable, not subject, privileged, released, spared

exercise *v.* **1.** apply, bring to bear, employ, enjoy, exert, practise, put to use, use, utilize, wield **2.** drill, inure, practise, train, work out *~n.* **3.** action, activity, discipline, drill, drilling, effort, labour, toil, training, work, work-out **4.** drill, lesson, practice, problem, schooling, task, work

exert bring into play, bring to bear, employ, exercise, expend, use, utilize, wield

exertion action, application, attempt, effort, industry, strain, stretch, struggle, toil, trial, use

exhaust 1. bankrupt, cripple, debilitate, disable, drain, enervate, fatigue, impoverish, prostrate, sap, tire, weaken, wear out **2.** consume, deplete, dissipate, expend, finish, run through, spend, squander, use up, waste **3.** drain, dry, empty, strain, void

exhausted 1. debilitated, disabled, drained, enervated, enfeebled, fatigued, jaded, sapped, spent, tired out, wasted, weak, worn out **2.** at an end, consumed, depleted, dissipated, done, expended, finished, gone, spent, squandered, used up, wasted

exhausting arduous, crippling, difficult, fatiguing, gruelling, hard, laborious, sapping, strenuous, taxing, testing, tiring

exhibit 1. *v.* display, expose, express, indicate, manifest, offer, parade, present, put on view, reveal, show **2.** *n.* display, exhibition, model, show

exhort advise, beseech, bid, call upon, encourage, entreat, goad, incite, persuade, spur, urge, warn

exigency 1. constraint, demand, necessity, need, requirement **2.** crisis, difficulty, emergency, extremity, hardship, pass, pinch, plight, predicament, quandary, strait

exile *n.* **1.** banishment, expatriation, expulsion, ostracism, proscription, separation **2.** émigré, expatriate, outcast, refugee *~v.* **3.** banish, deport, drive out, eject, expel, oust, proscribe

exist abide, be, be living, be present, breathe, endure, happen, last, live, occur, prevail, remain, stand, survive

existence actuality, animation, being, breath, continuance, continuation, duration, endurance, life, subsistence, survival

exit door, egress, gate, outlet, passage out, vent, way out

exodus departure, evacuation, migration, retirement, retreat, withdrawal

exonerate absolve, acquit, clear, discharge, dismiss, excuse, justify, pardon, vindicate

expand amplify, augment, bloat, blow up, broaden, develop, dilate, distend, enlarge, extend, fatten, fill out, grow, heighten, increase, inflate, lengthen, magnify, multiply, prolong, protract, swell, thicken, wax, widen

expanse area, breadth, extent, field, plain, range, space, stretch, sweep, tract

expansive affable, communicative, effusive, free, friendly, garrulous, genial, loquacious, open, outgoing, sociable, talkative, warm

expect 1. assume, believe, calculate, conjecture, forecast, foresee, imagine, presume, reckon, suppose, surmise, think, trust **2.** anticipate, await, contemplate, envisage, hope for, look ahead to, look for, look forward to, predict, watch for

expectation assumption, assurance, belief, calculation, confidence, conjecture, forecast, likelihood, presumption, probability, supposition, surmise, trust

expediency, expedience advisability, appropriateness, aptness, benefit, convenience, effectiveness, fitness, helpfulness, meetness, pragmatism, profitability, propriety, prudence, suitability, usefulness, utility

expedient advantageous, advisable, appropriate, beneficial, convenient, desirable, effective, fit, helpful, meet, opportune, politic, practical, pragmatic, profitable, proper, prudent, suitable, useful, worthwhile

expedition enterprise, excursion, exploration, journey, mission, quest, safari, tour, trek, trip, undertaking, voyage

expel 1. cast out, discharge, dislodge, drive out, eject, remove, throw out **2.** ban, banish, bar, blackball, discharge, dismiss, evict, exclude, exile, oust, proscribe, throw out

expend consume, disburse, dissipate, employ, exhaust, go through, pay out, spend, use (up)

expendable inessential, replaceable, unimportant

expenditure charge, cost, disbursement, expense, outgoings, outlay, output, payment, spending, use

expense charge, cost, disbursement, loss, outlay, output, payment, sacrifice, spending, toll, use

expensive costly, dear, excessive, exorbitant, high-priced, inordinate, lavish, overpriced, rich, stiff

experience *n.* **1.** contact, doing, evidence, exposure, familiarity, knowledge, observation, participation, practice, proof, training, trial, understanding **2.** affair, encounter, episode, event, happening, incident, ordeal, test, trial *~v.* **3.** behold, encounter, endure, face, feel, go through, have, know, live through, meet, observe, perceive, sample, sense, suffer, sustain, taste, try, undergo

experienced accomplished, adept, capable, competent, expert, familiar, knowledgeable, practised, professional, qualified, seasoned, skilful, tested, trained, tried, veteran, well-versed

experiment 1. *n.* assay, attempt, investigation, procedure, proof, research, test, trial, trial run, venture **2.** *v.* examine, investigate, research, sample, test, try, verify

experimental empirical, exploratory, pilot, preliminary, provisional, speculative, tentative, test, trial

expert 1. *n.* adept, authority, master, past master, professional, specialist, virtuoso, wizard **2.** *adj.* able, adept, adroit, apt, clever, deft, experienced, handy, knowledgeable, masterly, practised, proficient, qualified, skilful, trained

expertise aptness, cleverness, command, deftness, dexterity, facility, judgment, knack, knowledge, mastery, proficiency, skilfulness, skill

expire 1. cease, close, come to an end, conclude, end, finish, lapse, run out, stop, terminate **2.** depart, die, perish

explain clarify, clear up, define, demonstrate, describe, disclose, elucidate, expound, interpret, resolve, solve, teach, unfold

explanation 1. elucidation, exposition, interpretation, resolution **2.** account, answer, cause, excuse, meaning, motive, reason, sense, vindication

explicit categorical, certain, clear, definite, direct, distinct, exact, express, frank, open, patent, plain, positive, precise, specific, stated, unqualified, unreserved

explode 1. blow up, burst, detonate, discharge, go off, set off, shatter, shiver **2.** debunk, discredit, disprove, invalidate, refute, repudiate

exploit 1. *n.* achievement, adventure, attainment, deed, feat, stunt **2.** *v.* abuse, manipulate, misuse, play on *or* upon, take advantage of

exploration examination, inquiry, inspection, investigation, probe, research, scrutiny, search, study

explore analyse, examine, inquire into, inspect, investigate, look into, probe, prospect, research, scrutinize, search

explosion bang, blast, burst, clap, crack, detonation, discharge, outburst, report

explosive 1. unstable, volatile **2.** fiery, stormy, touchy, vehement, violent

exponent advocate, backer, champion, defender, promoter, spokesman, supporter, upholder

expose 1. display, exhibit, manifest, present, put on view, reveal, show, uncover, unveil **2.** air, betray, bring to light, denounce, detect, disclose, divulge, lay bare, let out, make known, reveal, show up, uncover, unmask

exposed 1. bare, exhibited, laid bare, on display, on show, on view, revealed, shown, unconcealed, uncovered **2.** open, unprotected

exposure 1. baring, display, manifestation, publicity, revelation, showing, uncovering, unveiling **2.** airing, denunciation, detection, disclosure, divulgence, revelation, unmasking

expound describe, elucidate, explain, illustrate, interpret, spell out

express *v.* 1. articulate, assert, asseverate, communicate, couch, declare, phrase, pronounce, put, say, speak, state, tell, utter, voice, word ~*adj.* 2. clearcut, especial, particular, singular, special 3. direct, fast, high-speed, nonstop, quick, rapid, speedy, swift

expression 1. assertion, communication, declaration, mention, pronouncement, speaking, statement, utterance 2. demonstration, exhibition, indication, representation, show, sign, symbol, token 3. choice of words, delivery, diction, execution, language, phrasing, speech, style, wording 4. idiom, locution, phrase, remark, term, turn of phrase, word

expressly especially, exactly, intentionally, on purpose, particularly, precisely, purposely, specially, specifically

expulsion banishment, discharge, dismissal, ejection, eviction, exclusion, exile, proscription, removal

exquisite 1. beautiful, dainty, delicate, elegant, fine, lovely, precious 2. attractive, beautiful, charming, comely, lovely, pleasing, striking

extempore ad lib, freely, impromptu, improvised, offhand, on the spot, unprepared

extend 1. carry on, continue, drag out, draw out, lengthen, prolong, protract, spin out, spread out, stretch, unfurl, unroll 2. add to, augment, broaden, develop, dilate, enhance, enlarge, expand, increase, spread, widen

extension addendum, addition, adjunct, annexe, branch, supplement, wing

extensive broad, capacious, commodious, comprehensive, far-flung, far-reaching, general, great, huge, large, lengthy, long, prevalent, protracted, spacious, sweeping, thorough, universal, vast, wholesale, wide, widespread

extent 1. bounds, compass, play, range, reach, scope, sphere, sweep 2. amount, amplitude, area, breadth, bulk, degree, duration, expanse, expansion, length, magnitude, measure, quantity, size, stretch, term, time, volume, width

exterior 1. *n.* appearance, aspect, coating, covering, façade, face, finish, outside, shell, skin, surface 2. *adj.* external, outer, outermost, outside, outward, superficial, surface

exterminate abolish, annihilate, destroy, eliminate, eradicate, extirpate

external apparent, exterior, outer, outermost, outside, outward, superficial, surface, visible

extinct dead, defunct, gone, lost, vanished

extinction abolition, annihilation, death, dying out, excision, extermination, obliteration, oblivion

extinguish 1. blow out, douse, put out, quench, smother, snuff out, stifle 2. abolish, destroy, eliminate, end, expunge, exterminate, kill, obscure, remove, suppress, wipe out

extol acclaim, applaud, celebrate, commend, eulogize, exalt, glorify, laud, praise

extort blackmail, bully, exact, extract, force, squeeze, wrest, wring

extra 1. *adj.* accessory, added, additional, auxiliary, fresh, further, more, new, other, supplemental, supplementary 2. *n.* addendum, addition, appurtenance, attachment, bonus, complement, extension, supernumerary, supplement 3. *adv.* especially, exceptionally, extraordinarily, extremely, particularly, remarkably, uncommonly, unusually

extract *v.* 1. draw, pluck out, pull, pull out, remove, take out, uproot, withdraw 2. derive, draw, elicit, evoke, exact, gather, get, glean, obtain, reap, wrest, wring ~*n.* 3. concentrate, decoction, distillate, distillation, essence, juice 4. abstract, citation, clipping, cutting, excerpt, passage, quotation, selection

extraordinary amazing, bizarre, curious, exceptional, fantastic, odd, outstanding, particular, peculiar, phenomenal, rare, remarkable, singular, special, strange, surprising, uncommon, unfamiliar, unheard-of, unique, unprecedented, unusual, unwonted, weird, wonderful

extravagance improvidence, lavishness, overspending, prodigality, profligacy, profusion, squandering, waste

extravagant 1. excessive, improvident, imprudent, lavish, prodigal, profligate, spendthrift, wasteful 2. costly, excessive, exorbitant, expensive, extortionate, inordinate, overpriced, steep (*Inf.*), unreasonable

extreme *adj.* 1. acute, great, greatest, high, highest, intense, maximum, severe, supreme, ultimate, utmost, uttermost, worst 2. faraway, far-off, farthest, final, last, most distant, outermost, remotest, terminal, ultimate, utmost, uttermost ~*n.* 3. acme, apex, boundary, climax, depth, edge, end, excess, extremity, height, limit, maximum, minimum, nadir, pinnacle, pole, termination, top, ultimate, zenith

extremely acutely, exceedingly, exceptionally, excessively, extraordinarily, greatly, highly, inordinately, intensely, markedly, quite, severely, uncommonly, unusually, utterly, very

extremity acme, apex, apogee, border, bound, boundary, brim, brink, edge, end, frontier, limit, margin, maximum, minimum, nadir, pinnacle, pole, rim, terminal, tip, top, ultimate, verge, zenith

extricate clear, deliver, disengage, disentangle, free, get out, liberate, release, relieve, remove, rescue, withdraw

exuberance 1. cheerfulness, eagerness, ebullience, effervescence, energy, enthusiasm, excitement, exhilaration, high spirits, life, liveliness, spirit, sprightliness, vigour, vitality, vivacity, zest 2. abundance, lavishness, lushness, luxuriance, profusion, rankness, richness, superabundance

exuberant 1. animated, buoyant, cheerful, eager, ebullient, effervescent, elated, energetic, enthusiastic, excited, exhilarated, high-spirited, lively, sparkling, spirited, sprightly, vigorous, vivacious, zestful 2. abundant, copious, lavish, lush, overflowing, plenteous, plentiful, profuse, rank, rich, teeming

exult be delighted, be elated, be joyful, be jubilant, be overjoyed, celebrate, jubilate, make merry, rejoice

eye *n.* 1. eyeball 2. appreciation, discernment, discrimination, judgment, perception, recognition, taste 3. **keep an** *or* **one's eye on** guard, keep in view, look after, look out for, monitor, observe, regard, scrutinize, supervise, survey, watch over 4. **see eye to eye** accord, agree, back, coincide, concur, fall in, get on, go along, subscribe to 5. **up to one's eyes** busy, caught up, engaged, inundated, overwhelmed, wrapped up in ~*v.* 6. contemplate, gaze at, glance at, inspect, look at, peruse, regard, scan, scrutinize, stare at, study, survey, view, watch

eyesight perception, sight, vision

eyesore atrocity, blemish, blight, blot, disfigurement, disgrace, horror, mess, monstrosity, ugliness

eyewitness looker-on, observer, onlooker, spectator, viewer, witness

F

fabric 1. cloth, material, stuff, textile, web 2. constitution, framework, make-up, organization, structure

fabulous 1. amazing, astounding, breathtaking, fictitious, inconceivable, incredible, legendary, phenomenal, unbelievable 2. fictitious, imaginary, invented, legendary, made-up, mythical, unreal

façade appearance, exterior, face, front, frontage, guise, mask, pretence, semblance, show, veneer

face *n.* 1. countenance, features, physiognomy, visage 2. appearance, aspect, expression, frown, grimace, look, pout, scowl, smirk 3. **face to face** *à deux*, confronting, in confrontation, opposite, tête-à-tête, vis-à-vis 4. **on the face of it** apparently, at first sight, seemingly, to the eye ~*v.* 5. brave, confront, cope with, deal with, defy, encounter, experience, meet, oppose 6. be opposite, front onto, give towards *or* onto, look onto, overlook

facet angle, aspect, face, part, phase, plane, side, slant, surface

facetious amusing, comical, droll, flippant, frivolous, funny, humorous, jesting, jocular, merry, playful, pleasant, waggish, witty

face up to accept, acknowledge, come to terms with, confront, cope with, deal with, meet head-on

facile adept, adroit, easy, effortless, fluent, light, quick, ready, simple, skilful, smooth, uncomplicated

facilitate ease, expedite, forward, further, help, make easy, promote, speed up

facility ability, adroitness, dexterity, ease, efficiency, effortlessness, fluency, knack, proficiency, quickness, readiness, skilfulness, skill, smoothness

facing opposite, partnering

facsimile copy, duplicate, photocopy, print, replica, reproduction, transcript

fact 1. act, deed, event, *fait accompli*, happening, incident, occurrence, performance 2. actuality, certainty, reality, truth 3. **in fact** actually, indeed, in reality, in truth, really, truly

faction bloc, cabal, camp, caucus, clique, coalition, confederacy, division, gang, group, junta, lobby, minority, party, pressure group, section, sector, set, splinter group

factor aspect, cause, circumstance, component, consideration, element, influence, item, part, point, thing

factory mill, plant, works

facts data, details, information, the whole story

factual accurate, authentic, close, correct, credible, exact, faithful, genuine, literal, objective, precise, real, sure, true, true-to-life, unadorned, unbiased, veritable

faculties intelligence, powers, reason, senses, wits

faculty 1. branch of learning, department, discipline, profession, school, teaching staff 2. authorization, licence, prerogative, privilege, right

fad affectation, craze, fancy, fashion, mania, mode, rage, trend, vogue, whim

fade 1. blanch, bleach, blench, dim, discolour, dull, grow dim, lose colour, lose lustre, pale, wash out 2. decline, die out, dim, disperse, dissolve, droop, dwindle, ebb, fail, fall, flag, languish, melt away, perish, shrivel, vanish, waste away, wilt, wither

faded bleached, dim, discoloured, dull, indistinct, pale, washed out

fading declining, decreasing, disappearing, dying, on the decline, vanishing

fail 1. be defeated, be unsuccessful, break down, come to grief, come to naught, come to nothing, fall short, founder, go astray, go down, miscarry, misfire, miss, run aground, turn out badly 2. abandon, desert, disappoint, forget, forsake, let down, neglect, omit

failing *n.* blemish, blind spot, defect, deficiency, drawback, error, failure, fault, flaw, imperfection, lapse, misfortune, shortcoming, weakness

failure 1. breakdown, collapse, defeat, downfall, fiasco, miscarriage, overthrow, wreck 2. disappointment, incompetent, loser, no-good, nonstarter 3. default, neglect, negligence, nonsuccess, omission, remissness, shortcoming 4. breakdown, decay, decline, failing, loss 5. bankruptcy, crash, downfall, insolvency, ruin

aint *adj.* 1. delicate, dim, distant, dull, faltering, feeble, hazy, hushed, ill-defined, indistinct, light, low, muted, soft, subdued, thin, vague, whispered 2. feeble, remote, slight, weak 3. dizzy, drooping, exhausted, fatigued, giddy, lethargic, lightheaded, muzzy, vertiginous, weak ~*v.* 4. black out, collapse, fade, fail, languish, pass out, weaken

aintly feebly, in a whisper, indistinctly, softly, weakly

air[1] *adj.* 1. above board, clean, disinterested, dispassionate, equal, even-handed, honest, honourable, impartial, just, lawful, legitimate, objective, proper, square, unbiased, upright 2. blonde, light 3. adequate, all right, average, decent, mediocre, middling, moderate, not bad, passable, reasonable, respectable, satisfactory, tolerable 4. beautiful, comely, handsome, lovely, pretty, well-favoured

air[2] *n.* bazaar, carnival, festival, fête, gala, market, show

airly 1. adequately, moderately, pretty well, quite, rather, reasonably, somewhat, tolerably 2. deservedly, equitably, honestly, justly, objectively, properly

airness decency, equity, impartiality, justice, legitimacy, rightfulness, uprightness

airy brownie, elf, hob, sprite

airy tale *or* **fairy story** 1. folk tale, romance 2. fantasy, fiction, invention, lie, tall story, untruth

aith 1. assurance, confidence, conviction, credence, credit, reliance, trust 2. allegiance, constancy, faithfulness, fealty, fidelity, loyalty, truth, truthfulness

aithful 1. constant, dependable, devoted, loyal, reliable, staunch, steadfast, true, trusty, truthful, unwavering 2. accurate, close, exact, just, precise, strict, true

aithless disloyal, doubting, false, fickle, inconstant, perfidious, traitorous, treacherous, unbelieving, unfaithful, unreliable, untrue, untrustworthy, untruthful

ake 1. *v.* copy, counterfeit, fabricate, feign, forge, pretend, put on, sham, simulate 2. *n.* charlatan, copy, forgery, fraud, hoax, imitation, impostor, mountebank, reproduction, sham

all *v.* 1. cascade, collapse, crash, descend, dive, drop, drop down, keel over, nose-dive, pitch, plummet, plunge, settle, sink, stumble, subside, topple, trip, trip over, tumble 2. abate, decline, decrease, depreciate, diminish, dwindle, ebb, fall off, flag, go down, lessen, slump, subside 3. be taken, capitulate, give in *or* up, give way, go out of office, resign, succumb, surrender, yield ~*n.* 4. descent, dive, drop, plummet, plunge, slip, spill, tumble 5. cut, decline, decrease, dip, drop, dwindling, falling off, lessening, lowering, reduction, slump 6. capitulation, collapse, death, defeat, downfall, failure, overthrow, resignation, ruin, surrender 7. declivity, descent, incline, slant, slope

fallacy deceit, deception, delusion, error, falsehood, flaw, illusion, misconception, mistake, sophism, untruth

fall apart break up, crumble, disband, disintegrate, disperse, dissolve, shatter

fall asleep doze off, go to sleep

fall back on call upon, employ, resort to

fall behind drop back, lag, trail

fall down disappoint, fail, go wrong

fallen *adj.* 1. collapsed, decayed, flat, ruinous, sunken 2. disgraced, immoral, loose, lost, ruined, shamed, sinful 3. dead, killed, lost, perished, slain

fallible erring, frail, ignorant, imperfect, mortal, uncertain, weak

fall in with accept, agree with, assent, concur with, cooperate with, go along with, support

fall out argue, clash, differ, disagree, fight, quarrel, squabble

fallow dormant, idle, inert, resting, uncultivated, undeveloped, unplanted

false 1. concocted, erroneous, faulty, fictitious, improper, inaccurate, incorrect, inexact, invalid, mistaken, unfounded, unreal, wrong 2. lying, mendacious, unreliable, unsound, untrue, untrustworthy, untruthful 3. artificial, bogus, feigned, forged, imitation, mock, pretended, sham

falsehood 1. deceit, deception, dishonesty, mendacity, perjury, prevarication, untruthfulness 2. fib, fiction, lie, story, untruth

falsify alter, belie, counterfeit, distort, doctor, fake, forge, misrepresent, pervert

falter hesitate, shake, stammer, stutter, tremble, waver

fame celebrity, credit, eminence, glory, honour, name, prominence, renown, reputation, repute, stardom

familiar 1. common, conventional, customary, domestic, everyday, frequent, household, mundane, ordinary, recognizable, repeated, routine, stock, well-known 2. **familiar with** acquainted with, at home with, aware of, conscious of, introduced, knowledgeable, versed in, well up in 3. amicable, close, confidential, cordial, easy, free, friendly, informal, intimate, near, open, relaxed, unreserved

familiarity 1. acquaintance, awareness, experience, grasp 2. closeness, ease, fellowship, freedom, friendliness, informality, intimacy, naturalness, openness, sociability

family brood, children, household, issue, kin, offspring, people, progeny, relations, relatives

famine dearth, hunger, scarcity, starvation

famous celebrated, conspicuous, eminent, glorious, honoured, illustrious, legendary, notable, noted, prominent, remarkable, renowned, well-known

fanatic *n.* addict, bigot, devotee, enthusiast, extremist, visionary, zealot

fancy *v.* 1. believe, conceive, guess, imagine, infer, reckon, suppose, surmise, think, think likely 2. crave, desire, dream of, long for, relish, wish for, would like, yearn for ~*adj.* 3. decorated, elaborate, elegant, intricate, ornamented, ornate

fantastic eccentric, exotic, fanciful, freakish, grotesque, imaginative, odd, peculiar, quaint, queer, rococo, strange, unreal, weird, whimsical

fantasy apparition, daydream, delusion, dream, fancy, hallucination, illusion, mirage, nightmare, pipe dream, reverie, vision

far *adv.* 1. afar, a good way, a great distance, a long way, deep 2. considerably, decidedly, extremely, greatly, incomparably, much 3. **so far** thus far, to date, until now, up to now, up to the present ~*adj.* 4. distant, long, outlying, remote, removed

farce 1. buffoonery, comedy, satire, slapstick 2. absurdity, joke, mockery, nonsense, parody, ridiculousness, sham, travesty

fare *n.* 1. charge, price, ticket money, transport cost 2. diet, eatables, food, meals, menu, provisions, rations ~*v.* 3. do, get along, get on, make out, manage, prosper

farewell adieu, departure, goodbye, parting, valediction

far-fetched doubtful, dubious, improbable, incredible, preposterous, strained, unbelievable, unconvincing, unlikely, unnatural, unrealistic

farm 1. *n.* grange, holding, homestead, land, plantation, smallholding 2. *v.* cultivate, operate, plant, work

far-reaching broad, extensive, important, significant, sweeping, widespread

fascinate absorb, allure, beguile, bewitch, captivate, charm, delight, enchant, engross, enravish, enthral, entrance, hypnotize, infatuate, intrigue, rivet, transfix

fascination allure, attraction, charm, enchantment, glamour, lure, magic, magnetism, pull, sorcery, spell

fashion *n.* 1. convention, craze, custom, fad, latest, latest style, look, mode, prevailing taste, rage, style, trend, usage, vogue 2. attitude, demeanour, manner, method, mode, style, way ~*v.* 3. construct, contrive, create, design, forge, form, make, manufacture, mould, shape, work

fashionable à la mode, chic, current, customary, genteel, in vogue, latest, modern, modish, popular, prevailing, smart, stylish, up-to-date, usual

fast[1] *adj.* 1. brisk, fleet, flying, hasty, hurried, nippy, quick, rapid, speedy, swiftly, winged 2. dissolute, giddy, intemperate, licentious, loose, profligate, promiscuous, wild ~*adv.* 3. quickly, rapidly, speedily, swiftly, with all haste 4. extravagantly, intemperately, loosely, wildly

fast[2] 1. *v.* abstain, deny oneself, go hungry, go without food, practise abstention, refrain from food *or* eating 2. *n.* abstinence, fasting

fasten affix, anchor, attach, bind, bolt, chain, connect, fix, grip, join, lace, link, lock, make fast, make firm, seal, secure, tie, unite

fat *adj.* 1. corpulent, fleshy, gross, heavy, obese, overweight, plump, podgy, portly, rotund, solid, stout, tubby 2. adipose, fatty, greasy, oily, suety ~*n.* 3. blubber, bulk, corpulence, flesh, obesity, overweight, paunch

fatal 1. deadly, final, incurable, killing, lethal, malignant, mortal, pernicious 2. baleful, baneful, calamitous, catastrophic, disastrous, lethal, ruinous

fate 1. chance, destiny, divine will, fortune, predestination, providence 2. end, future, issue, outcome, upshot

fated destined, doomed, foreordained, marked down, predestined, preordained, sure, written

fateful critical, crucial, decisive, important, significant

father *n.* 1. begetter, pater, patriarch, sire 2. ancestor, forebear, forefather, predecessor, progenitor 3. abbé, confessor, curé, pastor, priest ~*v.* 4. beget, get, procreate, sire

fatherly benevolent, benign, indulgent, kind, kindly, paternal, protective, supportive, tender

fathom 1. divine, estimate, gauge, measure, penetrate, plumb, probe, sound 2. comprehend, get to the bottom of, grasp, interpret, understand

fatigue 1. *v.* drain, exhaust, jade, overtire, tire, weaken, wear out, weary 2. *n.* debility, heaviness,guor, lethargy, overtiredness, tiredness

fatuous absurd, brainless, dense, dull, foolish, idiotic, inane, ludicrous, mindless, silly, stupid, witless

fault *n.* 1. blemish, defect, drawback, failing, flaw, imperfection, lack, shortcoming, snag, weakness, weak point 2. lapse, misconduct, misdeed, misdemeanour, offence, sin, trespass, wrong

fault-finding *adj.* captious, carping, censorious, critical, pettifogging

faultless 1. accurate, classic, correct, exemplary, faithful, foolproof, impeccable, model, perfect 2. above reproach, blameless, guiltless, immaculate, innocent, pure, sinless, spotless, stainless

faulty bad, broken, damaged, defective, erroneous, impaired, imperfect, inaccurate, incorrect, invalid, malfunctioning, unsound, weak, wrong

favour *n.* 1. approval, backing, bias, esteem, good opinion, good will, grace, kindness, partiality, patronage, support 2. benefit, boon, courtesy, good turn, indulgence, kindness, service 3. **in favour of** backing, for, pro, supporting ~*v.* 4. be partial to, esteem, indulge, pamper, reward, smile upon, spoil, value

favourable advantageous, appropriate, auspicious, beneficial, convenient, fair, fit, good, helpful, hopeful, opportune, promising, propitious, suitable, timely

favourably advantageously, auspiciously, conveniently, fortunately, opportunely, profitably, well

favourite 1. *adj.* best-loved, choice, dearest, esteemed, preferred 2. *n.* choice, darling, dear, idol, pet, pick, preference

fawn[1] *adj.* beige, buff, neutral

fawn[2] *v. Often with* **on** *or* **upon** be obsequious, be servile, court, crawl, creep, cringe, flatter, grovel, kneel, kowtow, toady

fear *n.* 1. alarm, awe, consternation, dismay, dread, fright, horror, panic, qualms, terror, timidity, tremors, trepidation 2. bogey, bugbear, horror, nightmare, phobia, spectre ~*v.* 3. dare not, dread, shudder at, take fright, tremble at

fearful 1. afraid, alarmed, anxious, apprehensive, diffident, frightened, hesitant, intimidated, nervous, panicky, scared, shrinking, tense, timid, timorous, uneasy 2. appalling, awful, dire, dreadful, frightful, ghastly, grievous, grim, hideous, horrible, monstrous, shocking, terrible

fearfully apprehensively, diffidently, nervously, timidly, timorously, uneasily

fearless bold, brave, confident, courageous, daring, gallant, heroic, indomitable, intrepid, plucky, unafraid, valiant, valorous

feasible attainable, likely, possible, practicable, reasonable, viable, workable

feast *n.* banquet, carousal, dinner, entertainment, junket, repast, revels, treat

feat achievement, act, attainment, deed, exploit, performance

feathers down, plumage, plumes

feature *n.* 1. aspect, attribute, characteristic, facet, factor, hallmark, mark, peculiarity, point, property, quality, trait 2. article, column, comment, item, piece, report, story ~*v.* 3. accentuate, emphasize, headline, play up, present, promote, set off, spotlight, star

feckless aimless, feeble, futile, hopeless, incompetent, ineffectual, shiftless, useless, weak, worthless

federation alliance, amalgamation, association, coalition, combination, confederacy, entente, federacy, league, syndicate, union

fed up (with) annoyed, bored, depressed, discontented, dismal, dissatisfied, down, gloomy, glum, weary of

fee account, bill, charge, compensation, emolument, hire, pay, payment, remuneration, reward, toll

feeble delicate, doddering, effete, enervated, enfeebled, exhausted, failing, faint, frail, infirm, languid, powerless, puny, shilpit (*Scot.*), sickly, weak, weakened

feebleness debility, delicacy, exhaustion, frailty, incapacity, infirmity, languor, lassitude, sickliness, weakness

feed *v.* 1. cater for, nourish, provide for, supply, sustain, victual 2. *Sometimes with* **on** devour, eat, fare, graze, live on, nurture, pasture, subsist

feel *v.* 1. caress, finger, fondle, handle, manipulate, maul, paw, stroke, touch 2. be aware of, endure, enjoy, experience, go through, have, know, notice, observe, perceive, suffer, undergo 3. explore, fumble, grope, sound, test, try 4. be convinced, intuit, sense 5. believe, be of the opinion that, consider, deem, hold, judge, think 6. appear, resemble, seem 7. **feel like** desire, fancy, want

feeler antenna, tentacle, whisker

feeling 1. feel, perception, sensation, sense, sense of touch, touch 2. consciousness, hunch, idea, impression, inkling, notion, presentiment, sense, suspicion 3. inclination, instinct, opinion, view

feelings ego, emotions, self-esteem, sensitivities, susceptibilities

fell *v.* cut, cut down, demolish, flatten, floor, hew, knock down, level, raze

fellow *n.* 1. boy, character, individual, man, person 2. associate, colleague, companion, compeer, comrade, co-worker, equal, friend, member, partner, peer

fellowship brotherhood, camaraderie, communion, familiarity, intercourse, intimacy, kindliness, sociability

feminine delicate, gentle, girlish, graceful, ladylike, modest, soft, tender, womanly

fen bog, marsh, morass, quagmire, slough, swamp

fence 1. *n.* barricade, barrier, defence, guard, hedge, paling, palisade, railings, rampart, shield, stockade, wall 2. *v. Often with* **in** *or* **off** bound, confine, coop, defend, enclose, guard, hedge, pen, protect, restrict, secure, separate, surround

ferment *v.* 1. boil, brew, bubble, concoct, foam, froth, heat, leaven, rise, seethe, work 2. *Fig.* agitate, boil, excite, fester, foment, heat, incite, inflame, provoke, rouse, seethe, smoulder, stir up ~*n.* 3. *Fig.* agitation, commotion, excitement, fever, frenzy, glow, heat, stew, stir, tumult, turmoil, unrest, uproar

ferocious fierce, predatory, rapacious, ravening, savage, violent, wild

ferocity bloodthirstiness, brutality, cruelty, inhumanity, rapacity, ruthlessness, savagery, wildness

ferret out dig up, disclose, discover, drive out, elicit, get at, nose out, root out, search out, smell out, trace, track down, unearth

ferry 1. *n.* ferryboat, packet 2. *v.* carry, convey, ship, shuttle, transport

fertile abundant, fat, fecund, flowering, fruitful, luxuriant, plenteous, plentiful, productive, prolific, rich, teeming, yielding

fertility abundance, fecundity, fruitfulness, luxuriance, productiveness, richness

fertilizer compost, dressing, dung, guano, manure, marl

fervent, fervid ardent, devout, eager, earnest, emotional, enthusiastic, excited, fiery, heartfelt, impassioned, intense, vehement, warm

fervour ardour, eagerness, earnestness, enthusiasm, excitement, intensity, passion, vehemence, warmth, zeal

festival 1. commemoration, feast, fête, fiesta, holiday, saint's day 2. carnival, celebration, festivities, fête, field day, gala, jubilee, treat

festive back-slapping, carnival, celebratory, cheery, convivial, festal, gala, gay, happy, hearty, holiday, jolly, jovial, joyful, jubilant, light-hearted, merry, mirthful, sportive

festoon array, bedeck, deck, decorate, drape, garland, hang, swathe, wreathe

fetch 1. bring, carry, conduct, convey, deliver, escort, get, go for, lead, obtain, retrieve, transport 2. draw forth, elicit, give rise to, produce 3. bring in, earn, go for, make, realize, sell for, yield

feud 1. *n.* argument, bad blood, broil, conflict, disagreement, discord, dissension, enmity, faction, grudge, hostility, quarrel, rivalry, strife, vendetta 2. *v.* bicker, brawl, clash, contend, dispute, duel, fall out, quarrel, row, squabble, war

fever *Fig.* agitation, delirium, ecstasy, excitement, ferment, fervour, flush, frenzy, heat, passion, turmoil, unrest

few 1. *adj.* inconsiderable, infrequent, insufficient, meagre, negligible, rare, scant, scanty, scarce, scattered, sparse, sporadic, thin 2. *pron.* handful, scarcely any, scattering, small number, some

fiancé, fiancée betrothed, intended, wife- *or* husband-to-be

fiasco catastrophe, debacle, disaster, failure, mess, rout, ruin

fib *n.* fiction, lie, prevarication, story, untruth, white lie

fibre 1. pile, staple, strand, texture, thread 2. *Fig.* essence, nature, quality

fickle capricious, changeable, faithless, fitful, flighty, inconstant, irresolute, mercurial, unfaithful, unstable, unsteady, vacillating, volatile

fiction 1. fable, fantasy, legend, myth, novel, romance, story, tale 2. fabrication, falsehood, fancy, fantasy, imagination, improvisation, invention, lie, tall story, untruth

fictitious apocryphal, artificial, assumed, bogus, false, fanciful, feigned, imaginary, imagined, improvised, invented, made-up, mythical, spurious, unreal, untrue

fiddling futile, petty, trifling, trivial

fidelity 1. constancy, devotion, faithfulness, integrity, loyalty, staunchness, trustworthiness 2. accuracy, adherence, closeness, correspondence, exactness, precision

fidget bustle, chafe, fret, squirm, twitch, worry

fidgety impatient, jerky, nervous, on edge, restive, restless, uneasy

field 1. *n.* grassland, green, meadow, pasture 2. *v.* catch, pick up, retrieve, return, stop

fiend 1. demon, devil, evil spirit 2. addict, enthusiast, fanatic

fierce brutal, cruel, dangerous, feral, ferocious, menacing, murderous, passionate, savage, threatening, truculent, uncontrollable, untamed, vicious, wild

fiercely frenziedly, furiously, menacingly, passionately, savagely, tempestuously, tigerishly, viciously

fight *v.* 1. assault, battle, box, brawl, clash, close, combat, conflict, contend, engage, feud, grapple, joust, spar, struggle, take the field, tilt, tussle, war, wrestle 2. contest, defy, dispute, oppose, resist, strive, struggle, withstand 3. argue, bicker, dispute, squabble, wrangle 4. carry on, conduct, engage in, prosecute, wage ~*n.* 5. altercation, battle, bout, brawl, brush, clash, combat, conflict, contest, dispute, duel, encounter, engagement, fracas, fray, hostilities, joust, melee, riot, row, scuffle, skirmish, struggle, tussle, war

fighter 1. fighting man, soldier, warrior 2. boxer, pugilist

fighting *adj.* aggressive, belligerent, combative, contentious, disputatious, hawkish, martial, militant, pugnacious, truculent, warlike

fight off beat off, repel, repress, repulse, resist, stave off, ward off

figure *n.* 1. character, cipher, digit, number, numeral, symbo[l] 2. amount, cost, price, sum, total, value 3. form, outline, shadow, shape, silhouette 4. body, build, frame, physique, proportions, shape, torso 5. celebrity, character, dignitary, force, leader, notability, notable, personage, personality, presence, worthy

figurehead cipher, dummy, mouthpiece, name, nonentity, puppet

figure out 1. calculate, compute, reckon, work out 2. comprehend, decipher, fathom, resolve, see, understand

filch abstract, embezzle, misappropriate, pilfer, purloin, steal, take, thieve

file[1] *v.* abrade, burnish, furbish, polish, rasp, refine, rub, rub down, scrape, shape, smooth

file[2] 1. *n.* case, data, documents, dossier, folder, information, portfolio 2. *v.* enter, record, register, slot in

fill brim over, cram, crowd, furnish, glut, gorge, pack, pervade, replenish, sate, satiate, satisfy, stock, store, stuff, supply, swell

fill in 1. answer, complete, fill up 2. replace, represent, stand in, sub

filling 1. *n.* contents, insides, padding, stuffing, wadding 2. *adj.* ample, heavy, satisfying, square, substantial

film *n.* 1. coating, covering, gauze, layer, membrane, scum, skin, tissue 2. motion picture, movie (*U.S. inf.*) ~*v.* 3. photograph, shoot, take

filter 1. *v.* clarify, filtrate, purify, refine, screen, sieve, sift, strain, winnow 2. *n.* gauze, mesh, riddle, sieve, strainer

filth 1. contamination, defilement, dirt, dung, excrement, excreta, faeces, filthiness, foulness, garbage, grime, muck, nastiness, ordure, pollution, refuse, sewage, slime, sludge, squalor, uncleanness 2. corruption, dirty-mindedness, impurity, indecency, obscenity, po[rnography]

nography, smut, vileness, vulgarity

filthy 1. dirty, faecal, feculent, foul, nasty, polluted, putrid, slimy, squalid, unclean, vile 2. begrimed, black, blackened, grimy, grubby, miry, mucky, muddy, smoky, sooty, unwashed 3. bawdy, coarse, corrupt, depraved, foul, impure, indecent, lewd, licentious, obscene, pornographic, smutty, suggestive

final 1. closing, end, eventual, last, latest, terminating, ultimate 2. absolute, conclusive, decided, decisive, definite, definitive, determinate, finished, incontrovertible, irrevocable, settled

finalize agree, complete, conclude, decide, settle, tie up, work out

finally at last, at length, at long last, at the last, eventually, in the end, lastly, ultimately

finance 1. *n.* accounts, banking, business, commerce, economics, investment, money 2. *v.* back, float, fund, guarantee, pay for, subsidize, support, underwrite

finances affairs, assets, capital, cash, funds, money, resources, wherewithal

financial budgeting, economic, fiscal, monetary, money, pecuniary

find *v.* 1. chance upon, come across, descry, discover, encounter, espy, expose, ferret out, hit upon, locate, meet, recognize, spot, turn up, uncover, unearth 2. get back, recover, regain, repossess, retrieve ~*n.* 3. acquisition, asset, bargain, catch, discovery, good buy

find out detect, discover, learn, note, observe, perceive, realize

fine[1] *adj.* 1. admirable, beautiful, choice, excellent, exceptional, exquisite, first-class, first-rate, great, magnificent, masterly, ornate, outstanding, rare, select, skilful, splendid, superior, supreme 2. balmy, bright, clear, cloudless, dry, fair, pleasant, sunny 3. dainty, delicate, elegant, exquisite, fragile 4. abstruse, acute, critical, discriminating, fastidious, hairsplitting, intelligent, keen, minute, nice, precise, quick, refined, sensitive, sharp, subtle, tasteful, tenuous 5. clear, pure, refined, solid, sterling, unadulterated, unalloyed, unpolluted 6. acceptable, agreeable, all right, convenient, good, satisfactory, suitable

fine[2] 1. *v.* mulct, penalize, punish 2. *n.* damages, forfeit, penalty, punishment

finesse 1. adroitness, artfulness, cleverness, craft, delicacy, diplomacy, discretion, polish, quickness, savoir-faire, skill, subtlety, tact 2. artifice, bluff, feint, manoeuvre, ruse, trick, wile

finger *v.* feel, handle, manipulate, maul, meddle with, touch, toy with

finish *v.* 1. accomplish, achieve, cease, close, complete, conclude, deal with, discharge, do, end, execute, finalize, fulfil, get done, round off, settle, stop, terminate 2. *Often with* **off** annihilate, best, bring down, defeat, destroy, dispose of, exterminate, get rid of, kill, overcome, overpower, rout, ruin, worst ~*n.* 3. cessation, close, closing, completion, conclusion, culmination, dénouement, end, ending, finale 4. annihilation, bankruptcy, death, defeat, end, liquidation, ruin ~*v.* 5. elaborate, perfect, polish, refine ~*n.* 6. cultivation, culture, elaboration, perfection, polish, refinement ~*v.* 7. coat, face, gild, lacquer, polish, smooth off, stain, texture, veneer, wax ~*n.* 8. appearance, grain, lustre, patina, polish, shine, smoothness, surface, texture

finished 1. classic, consummate, cultivated, elegant, expert, flawless, impeccable, masterly, perfected, polished, professional, proficient, refined, skilled, smooth, urbane 2. accomplished, achieved, closed, complete, completed, concluded, done, ended, entire, final, finalized, full, in the past, over, over and done with, shut, terminated, through, tied up 3. done, drained, empty, exhausted, gone, spent, used up 4. bankrupt, defeated, devastated, doomed, gone, liquidated, lost, ruined, through, undone, wound up, wrecked

finite bounded, conditioned, limited, restricted, terminable

fire *n.* 1. blaze, combustion, conflagration, flames, inferno 2. barrage, hail, salvo, shelling, sniping, volley 3. **on fire** a. ablaze, aflame, alight, blazing, burning, fiery, flaming, in flames b. ardent, eager, enthusiastic, excited, inspired, passionate ~*v.* 4. ignite, kindle, light, set ablaze, set aflame, set alight, set fire to, set on fire 5. detonate, discharge, eject, explode, hurl, launch, let off, loose, set off, shell, shoot

firm[1] *adj.* 1. close-grained, compact, compressed, concentrated, dense, hard, inelastic, inflexible, rigid, set, solid, solidified, stiff, unyielding 2. braced, embedded, fast, fastened, fixed, immovable, motionless, riveted, robust, rooted, secure, secured, stable, stationary, steady, strong, sturdy, taut, tight, unshakable 3. adamant, constant, definite, fixed, inflexible, obdurate, resolute, resolved, set on, settled, staunch, steadfast, strict, true, unflinching, unshakable, unswerving, unwavering, unyielding

firm[2] *n.* association, business, company, concern, corporation, enterprise, house, organization, partnership

firmly 1. immovably, motionlessly, securely, steadily, tightly, unshakably 2. determinedly, resolutely, staunchly, steadfastly, strictly, unchangeably, unwaveringly

firmness 1. density, fixedness, hardness, inelasticity, inflexibility, resistance, rigidity, solidity, stiffness 2. immovability, soundness, stability, steadiness, strength, tautness, tension, tightness 3. constancy, inflexibility, obduracy, resolution, resolve, staunchness, steadfastness, strictness

first *adj.* 1. chief, foremost, head, highest, leading, pre-eminent, prime, principal, ruling 2. earliest, initial, maiden, opening, original, premier, primitive, primordial, pristine 3. basic, cardinal, elementary, fundamental, key, primary ~*adv.* 4. beforehand, firstly, initially

first-rate admirable, elite, excellent, exceptional, first class, outstanding, prime, superb, superlative, tiptop, top

fissure breach, break, chink, crack, cranny, crevice, fault, fracture, gap, hole, opening, rent, rift, rupture, slit, split

fit *adj.* 1. able, adequate, appropriate, apt, becoming, capable, competent, convenient, correct, deserving, equipped, expedient, good enough, prepared, proper, qualified, ready, right, seemly, suitable, trained, worthy 2. hale, healthy, robust, strapping, toned up, trim, well ~*v.* 3. accord, agree, belong, concur, conform, correspond, dovetail, go, interlock, join, match, meet, suit, tally 4. adapt, adjust, alter, arrange, dispose, fashion, modify, place, position, shape

fitful broken, desultory, erratic, fluctuating, haphazard, impulsive, intermittent, irregular, spasmodic, sporadic, variable

fitness 1. adaptation, applicability, appropriateness, aptness, competence, eligibility, pertinence, preparedness, propriety, qualifications, readiness, seemliness, suitability 2. good condition, good health, health, robustness, strength, vigour

fitting 1. *adj.* appropriate, becoming, correct, decent, decorous, desirable, proper, right, seemly, suitable 2. *n.* attachment, component, connection, part, piece, unit

fix *v.* 1. anchor, embed, establish, implant, install, locate, place, plant, position, root, set, settle 2. attach, bind, cement, connect, couple, fasten, glue, link, pin, secure, stick, tie 3. agree on, appoint, arrange, arrive at, conclude, decide, define, determine, establish, limit, name, resolve, set, settle, specify ~*n.* 4. *Inf.* difficulty, dilemma, embarrassment, mess, plight, predicament, quandary

fixed 1. attached, established, immovable, made fast, permanent, rigid, rooted, secure, set 2. agreed, arranged, decided, definite, established, planned, resolved, settled

fix up agree on, arrange, fix, organize, plan, settle, sort out

flabbergasted amazed, astonished, astounded, confounded, dazed, disconcerted, dumbfounded, overcome, overwhelmed, speechless, staggered, stunned

flag[1] *v.* abate, decline, die, droop, ebb, fade, fail, faint, fall, fall off, languish, pine, sag, sink, slump, succumb, wane, weaken, weary, wilt

flag[2] banner, colours, ensign, jack, pennant, pennon, standard, streamer

flagging declining, decreasing, ebbing, fading, failing, sinking, tiring, waning, weakening, wilting

flagrant awful, barefaced, blatant, bold, brazen, crying, dreadful, egregious, enormous, flaunting, glaring, immodest, infamous, notorious, open, ostentatious, outrageous, scandalous, shameless

flagstone block, flag, slab

flail *v.* beat, thrash, thresh, windmill

flair 1. ability, aptitude, faculty, feel, genius, gift, knack, mastery, talent 2. chic, dash, discernment, elegance, panache, style, stylishness, taste

flamboyant 1. elaborate, florid, ornate, rich, rococo, showy, theatrical 2. brilliant, colourful, dashing, glamorous, swashbuckling

flame *v.* 1. blaze, burn, flare, flash, glare, glow, shine ~*n.* 2. blaze, fire, light 3. *Fig.* affection, ardour, fervency, fervour, fire, intensity, keenness, passion, warmth

flaming 1. ablaze, afire, blazing, brilliant, burning, fiery, glowing, raging, red-hot 2. angry, aroused, hot, impassioned, intense, raging, scintillating, vehement, vivid

flap 1. *v.* agitate, beat, flail, flutter, shake, swing, swish, thrash, thresh, vibrate, wag, wave 2. *n.* apron, cover, fly, fold, lapel, skirt, tab, tail

flare blaze, burn up, dazzle, flicker, flutter, glare, waver

flare up blaze, boil over, break out, explode, fire up, lose control, lose one's temper

flash *v.* 1. blaze, flare, flicker, glare, gleam, glint, glisten, glitter, light, shimmer, sparkle, twinkle 2. bolt, dart, fly, race, shoot, speed, sprint, streak, sweep, zoom ~*n.* 3. blaze, burst, dazzle, flare, flicker, gleam, ray, shaft, shimmer, spark, sparkle, streak, twinkle 4. instant, moment, second, shake, split second, trice, twinkling

flashy cheap, flaunting, garish, gaudy, glittery, loud, meretricious, ostentatious, showy, tasteless, tawdry, tinselly

flat[1] 1. even, horizontal, level, levelled, low, plane, smooth, unbroken 2. laid low, outstretched, prostrate, reclining, recumbent, supine 3. boring, dead, dull, insipid, lacklustre, lifeless, monotonous, prosaic, spiritless, stale, tedious, uninteresting, vapid, watery, weak

flat[2] apartment, rooms

flatly absolutely, categorically, completely, positively, unhesitatingly

flatness 1. evenness, smoothness, uniformity 2. dullness, emptiness, insipidity, monotony, staleness, tedium, vapidity

flatten compress, even out, iron out, level, plaster, raze, roll, squash, trample

flatter blandish, butter up, cajole, compliment, court, fawn, humour, inveigle, praise, puff, wheedle

flattering complimentary, fawning, fulsome, gratifying, honeyed, ingratiating, laudatory, sugary

flattery blandishment, cajolery, fawning, obsequiousness, servility

flavour 1. *n.* aroma, essence, extract, odour, piquancy, relish, savour, seasoning, smack, tang, taste, zest 2. v. imbue, infuse, lace, leaven, season, spice

flaw 1. blemish, defect, failing, fault, imperfection, speck, spot, weakness, weak spot 2. breach, break, cleft, crack, crevice, fissure, fracture, rent, rift, split, tear

flawed broken, chipped, cracked, damaged, defective, faulty, unsound

flee avoid, bolt, decamp, depart, escape, fly, get away, leave, shun, take flight, vanish

fleet n. flotilla, naval force, navy, sea power, squadron, task force, vessels, warships

fleeting brief, ephemeral, flying, fugitive, momentary, passing, short, short-lived, temporary, transient, transitory

flesh 1. body, brawn, fatness, food, meat, tissue, weight 2. body, human nature, sensuality

flexibility adaptability, complaisance, elasticity, resilience, springiness

flexible 1. ductile, elastic, limber, lithe, plastic, pliable, springy, stretchy, supple 2. adaptable, adjustable, open, variable 3. amenable, biddable, docile, gentle, manageable, responsive, tractable

flicker v. 1. flutter, quiver, vibrate, waver ~n. 2. flare, flash, gleam, glimmer, spark 3. breath, drop, glimmer, spark, trace, vestige

flight[1] 1. mounting, soaring, winging 2. journey, trip, voyage 3. cloud, flock, formation, squadron, swarm, unit, wing

flight[2] escape, exit, exodus, fleeing, getaway, retreat

flimsy 1. delicate, fragile, frail, insubstantial, makeshift, rickety, shaky, shallow, slight, superficial, unsubstantial 2. feeble, frivolous, implausible, inadequate, poor, thin, transparent, trivial, unconvincing, unsatisfactory, weak

flinch baulk, blench, cower, cringe, duck, flee, quail, recoil, retreat, shirk, shrink, start, swerve, wince, withdraw

fling v. cast, heave, hurl, jerk, pitch, precipitate, propel, send, shy, sling, throw, toss

flippancy cheekiness, frivolity, impertinence, irreverence, levity, pertness

flippant disrespectful, frivolous, glib, impertinent, impudent, irreverent, pert, rude

flirt 1. v. coquet, dally, make advances, philander 2. n. coquette, heart-breaker, philanderer, tease

float v. 1. be buoyant, hang, hover, poise 2. bob, drift, glide, move gently, sail, slide, slip along 3. launch, promote, set up

floating 1. buoyant, sailing, swimming, unsinkable 2. fluctuating, free, migratory, movable, unattached, uncommitted, variable, wandering

flock v. 1. collect, congregate, converge, crowd, gather, group, herd, huddle, mass, throng, troop ~n. 2. drove, flight, gaggle, herd, skein 3. collection, company, congregation, convoy, crowd, gathering, group, herd, host, mass, multitude, throng

flog 1. beat, chastise, flay, lash, scourge, thrash, trounce, whack, whip 2. drive, oppress, overtax, punish, push, strain, tax

flood v. 1. deluge, drown, immerse, inundate, overflow, submerge, swamp 2. engulf, flow, gush, overwhelm, rush, surge, swarm, sweep 3. choke, fill, glut, oversupply, saturate ~n. 4. deluge, downpour, flash flood, inundation, overflow, spate, tide, torrent 5. abundance, flow, glut, profusion, rush, stream, torrent

floor 1. n. level, stage, storey, tier 2. v. Fig. baffle, beat, bewilder, confound, conquer, defeat, discomfit, disconcert, dumbfound, nonplus, overthrow, perplex, prostrate, puzzle, stump

floral flower-patterned, flowery

florid 1. flushed, high-coloured, rubicund, ruddy 2. baroque, busy, embellished, flamboyant, flowery, fussy, high-flown, ornate

flotsam debris, jetsam, junk, sweepings, wreckage

flounder v. blunder, fumble, grope, muddle, plunge, struggle, stumble, toss, tumble, wallow

flourish 1. v. bear fruit, be successful, bloom, blossom, boom, burgeon, develop, flower, increase, prosper, succeed, thrive 2. n. dash, display, fanfare, parade, shaking, show, twirling, wave

flourishing blooming, lush, luxuriant, prospering, rampant, successful, thriving

flow circulate, course, glide, gush, move, pour, purl, ripple, roll, run, rush, slide, surge, sweep, swirl, whirl

flower n. 1. bloom, blossom, efflorescence 2. Fig. best, cream, elite, freshness, height, pick, vigour ~v. 3. bloom, blossom, burgeon, effloresce, flourish, mature, open, unfold

flowery embellished, fancy, figurative, florid, ornate, rhetorical

flowing continuous, cursive, easy, fluent, smooth, unbroken, uninterrupted

fluctuate alternate, change, hesitate, oscillate, seesaw, shift, swing, undulate, vacillate, vary, veer, waver

fluency assurance, command, control, ease, facility, glibness, slickness, smoothness

fluent articulate, easy, effortless, facile, flowing, natural, ready, smooth, voluble

fluid adj. 1. flowing, liquefied, liquid, melted, molten, runny, watery 2. adaptable, adjustable, changeable, flexible, floating, indefinite, mercurial, mobile, mutable, shifting ~n. 3. liquid, liquor, solution

flurry agitation, bustle, commotion, disturbance, excitement, ferment, flap, fluster, flutter, furore, fuss, hurry, stir, to-do, tumult, whirl

flush[1] 1. v. blush, burn, colour, colour up, crimson, flame, glow, go red, redden, suffuse 2. n. bloom, blush, colour, freshness, glow, redness, rosiness

flush[2] adj. 1. even, flat, level, plane, square, true 2. abundant, affluent, full, generous, lavish, liberal, overflowing, prodigal ~adv. 3. hard against, level with, squarely, touching

fluster 1. v. agitate, bother, bustle, confound, confuse, disturb, excite, flurry, heat, hurry, perturb, ruffle, upset 2. n. bustle, commotion, disturbance, dither, flurry, flutter, furore, ruffle, turmoil

flutter 1. v. agitate, beat, flap, flicker, fluctuate, hover, palpitate, quiver, ripple, ruffle, shiver, tremble, vibrate, waver 2. n. palpitation, quiver, shiver, shudder, tremble, tremor, twitching, vibration

fly v. 1. flit, flutter, hover, mount, sail, soar, take wing, wing 2. aviate, control, manoeuvre, operate, pilot 3. display, float, show, wave 4. elapse, flit, glide, pass, pass swiftly, roll on, run its course, slip away 5. bolt, career, dart, dash, hare, hasten, hurry, race, rush, scamper, scoot, shoot, speed, sprint, tear

flying adj. 1. brief, fleeting, hasty, hurried, rushed 2. express, fast, fleet, mercurial, mobile, rapid, speedy, winged

foam 1. n. bubbles, froth, head, lather, spray, spume, suds 2. v. boil, bubble, effervesce, fizz, froth, lather

focus n. centre, core, cynosure, headquarters, heart, hub, meeting place, target

foe adversary, antagonist, enemy, opponent, rival

fog n. gloom, miasma, mist, murk, murkiness, smog

foggy blurred, cloudy, dim, grey, hazy, indistinct, misty, murky, nebulous, obscure, vaporous

foil[1] v. baffle, balk, check, counter, defeat, elude, frustrate, nullify, outwit, stop, thwart

foil[2] antithesis, background, complement, contrast, setting

fold v. 1. bend, crease, crumple, double, gather, intertwine, overlap, pleat, tuck, turn under 2. do up, enclose, enfold, entwine, envelop, wrap, wrap up ~n. 3. bend, crease, furrow, layer, overlap, pleat, turn, wrinkle

folder binder, envelope, file, portfolio

folk clan, family, kin, people, race, tribe

follow 1. succeed, supersede, supplant 2. chase, dog, hound, hunt, pursue, shadow, stalk, tail, track, trail 3. comply, conform, heed, mind, note, obey, observe, regard, watch

follower adherent, admirer, apostle, backer, believer, convert, devotee, disciple, fan, fancier, habitué, partisan, pupil, supporter, votary, worshipper

following adj. consequent, ensuing, later, next, specified, subsequent, succeeding, successive

folly absurdity, foolishness, idiocy, imbecility, imprudence, indiscretion, irrationality, lunacy, madness, nonsense, recklessness, silliness, stupidity

fond adoring, affectionate, amorous, caring, devoted, doting, indulgent, loving, tender, warm

fondle caress, cuddle, dandle, pat, pet, stroke

fondly affectionately, dearly, indulgently, lovingly, possessively, tenderly

fondness attachment, fancy, liking, love, partiality, penchant, predilection, preference, soft spot, susceptibility, taste, weakness

food board, bread, commons, cooking, cuisine, diet, edibles, fare, foodstuffs, larder, meat, menu, nourishment, nutrition, provender, provisions, rations, refreshment, stores, sustenance, table, victuals

fool n. 1. ass, dolt, dunce, dunderhead, halfwit, idiot, ignoramus, illiterate, jackass, loon, moron, nitwit, numskull, silly, simpleton 2. buffoon, clown, comic, harlequin, jester, motley, pierrot ~v. 3. beguile, bluff, cheat, deceive, delude, dupe, hoax, hoodwink, mislead, take in, trick 4. act the fool, cut capers, feign, jest, joke, pretend, tease

foolhardy bold, hot-headed, impetuous, imprudent, incautious, irresponsible, madcap, precipitate, rash, reckless, venturesome, venturous

foolish 1. absurd, ill-advised, ill-judged, imprudent, incautious, indiscreet, injudicious, senseless, short-sighted, silly, unintelligent, unreasonable, unwise 2. brainless, crazy, doltish, fatuous, half-witted, harebrained, idiotic, imbecilic, ludicrous, mad, ridiculous, senseless, silly, simple, stupid, weak, witless

foolishly absurdly, idiotically, ill-advisedly, imprudently, incautiously, indiscreetly, injudiciously, mistakenly, short-sightedly, stupidly, unwisely

foolishness absurdity, folly, imprudence, inanity, indiscretion, irresponsibility, silliness, stupidity, weakness

foolproof certain, guaranteed, infallible, safe, unassailable

footing basis, establishment, foot-hold, foundation, ground, groundwork, installation, settlement

footling fiddling, fussy, immaterial, insignificant, irrelevant, minor, niggly, petty, pointless, silly, time-wasting, trifling, trivial, unimportant

footstep 1. footfall, step, tread 2. footmark, footprint, trace, track

forage n. feed, fodder, food, foodstuffs, provender

forbear abstain, avoid, cease, decline, desist, eschew, omit, pause, refrain, stop, withhold

forbearance indulgence, leniency, lenity, mildness, moderation, patience, resignation, restraint, self-control, temperance, tolerance

forbearing easy, forgiving, indulgent, lenient, long-suffering, merciful, mild, moderate, patient, tolerant

forbid ban, debar, disallow, exclude, hinder, inhibit, outlaw, preclude, prohibit, proscribe, rule out, veto

forbidden banned, outlawed, prohibited, proscribed, taboo, vetoed

force n. 1. energy, impact, impulse, life, might, muscle, potency, power, pressure, stimulus, strength, stress, vigour 2. coercion, compulsion, constraint, duress, enforcement, pressure, violence 3. bite, cogency, effect, effectiveness, efficacy, influence, power, strength, validity, weight 4.

drive, emphasis, fierceness, intensity, persistence, vehemence, vigour ~*v.* 5. coerce, compel, constrain, drive, impel, impose, make, necessitate, obligate, oblige, overcome, press, press-gang, pressure, pressurize, urge 6. blast, break open, prise, propel, push, thrust, use violence on, wrench, wrest 7. drag, exact, extort, wring

forced 1. compulsory, involuntary, mandatory, obligatory, slave, unwilling 2. affected, artificial, contrived, false, insincere, laboured, stiff, strained, unnatural, wooden

forceful cogent, compelling, convincing, dynamic, effective, pithy, potent, powerful, telling, vigorous, weighty

forcible active, cogent, compelling, effective, efficient, energetic, forceful, impressive, mighty, potent, powerful, strong, telling, valid, weighty

forebear ancestor, father, forefather, forerunner, predecessor, progenitor

forebode augur, betoken, foreshadow, foreshow, foretell, foretoken, forewarn, indicate, portend, predict, presage, prognosticate, promise, warn of

foreboding anxiety, apprehension, apprehensiveness, chill, dread, fear, misgiving, premonition, presentiment

forecast 1. *v.* augur, calculate, divine, estimate, foresee, foretell, plan, predict, prophesy 2. *n.* anticipation, conjecture, foresight, forethought, guess, outlook, planning, prediction, prognosis, projection, prophecy

forefather ancestor, father, forebear, forerunner, predecessor

foregoing above, antecedent, former, preceding, previous, prior

foreign alien, borrowed, distant, exotic, external, imported, outlandish, outside, overseas, remote, strange, unfamiliar, unknown

foreigner alien, immigrant, incomer, newcomer, outlander, stranger

foremost chief, first, front, highest, initial, leading, preeminent, principal, supreme

forerunner ancestor, envoy, forebear, foregoer, harbinger, herald, precursor, predecessor, progenitor, prototype

foresee anticipate, divine, envisage, forebode, forecast, foretell, predict, prophesy

foreshadow augur, betoken, bode, forebode, imply, indicate, portend, predict, presage, promise, signal

foresight anticipation, care, caution, forethought, precaution, preparedness, prescience, provision

foretell adumbrate, augur, forecast, foreshadow, forewarn, portend, predict, presage, prophesy, signify

forethought anticipation, precaution, providence, provision, prudence

forewarn admonish, advise, alert, caution, tip off

forfeit 1. *n.* damages, fine, loss, penalty 2. *v.* be deprived of, be stripped of, give up, lose, relinquish, surrender

forge coin, copy, counterfeit, fake, falsify, feign, imitate

forget lose sight of, omit, overlook

forgive absolve, acquit, condone, excuse, exonerate, pardon, remit

forgiving clement, humane, lenient, merciful, mild, soft-hearted, tolerant

forgo, forego abandon, cede, do without, give up, relinquish, renounce, resign, sacrifice, surrender, waive, yield

forgotten buried, bygone, lost, obliterated, omitted, past, unremembered

forlorn abandoned, cheerless, comfortless, deserted, desolate, destitute, disconsolate, helpless, homeless, hopeless, lonely, lost, miserable, pathetic, pitiable, pitiful, unhappy, wretched

form[1] *v.* 1. assemble, bring about, build, concoct, construct, contrive, create, devise, establish, fabricate, fashion, forge, found, invent, make, model, mould, produce, set up, shape 2. arrange, combine, design, dispose, draw up, frame, organize, pattern, plan

form[2] *n.* 1. appearance, cast, cut, fashion, formation, model, mould, pattern, shape, structure 2. format, framework, harmony, order, orderliness, organization, plan, proportion, structure, symmetry 3. application, document, paper, sheet

formal approved, ceremonial, explicit, express, fixed, lawful, legal, methodical, official, prescribed, regular, rigid, ritualistic, set, solemn, strict

formality 1. ceremony, convention, custom, gesture, procedure, red tape, rite, ritual 2. correctness, decorum, etiquette, protocol, punctilio

formation 1. accumulation, composition, development, establishment, evolution, generation, genesis, manufacture, organization, production 2. arrangement, configuration, design, disposition, figure, grouping, pattern, rank, structure

formative impressionable, malleable, mouldable, pliant, susceptible

former 1. ancient, bygone, departed, of yore, old, old-time, past 2. above, aforesaid, foregoing, preceding

formerly already, before, lately, once, previously

formidable 1. daunting, dreadful, fearful, frightful, horrible, intimidating, menacing, shocking, terrifying, threatening 2. arduous, challenging, colossal, difficult, onerous, overwhelming, toilsome

formula 1. rite, ritual, rubric 2. blueprint, method, precept, prescription, principle, procedure, recipe, rule, way

formulate codify, define, detail, express, frame, specify, systematize

forsake abandon, cast off, desert, disown, jilt, leave, quit, repudiate, throw over

forsaken abandoned, cast off, deserted, destitute, disowned, forlorn, friendless, ignored, isolated, jilted, left behind, left in the lurch, lonely, marooned, outcast, solitary

fort blockhouse, camp, castle, citadel, fortress, garrison, redoubt, station, stronghold

forte gift, métier, speciality, strength, strong point, talent

forth ahead, away, forward, onward, out, outward

forthcoming 1. approaching, coming, expected, future, imminent, impending, prospective 2. chatty, communicative, expansive, free, informative, open, sociable, talkative, unreserved

forthright above-board, blunt, candid, direct, frank, open, outspoken, straightforward

forthwith at once, directly, immediately, instantly, quickly, right away, straightaway

fortification bulwark, castle, citadel, defence, fastness, fort, fortress, keep, protection, stronghold

fortify brace, cheer, confirm, embolden, encourage, hearten, invigorate, reassure, stiffen, strengthen, sustain

fortress castle, citadel, fort, redoubt

fortunate bright, favoured, golden, happy, lucky, prosperous, rosy, successful, well-off

fortunately by good luck, happily, luckily, providentially

fortune 1. affluence, gold mine, possessions, property, prosperity, riches, treasure, wealth 2. accident, chance, destiny, fate, hazard, kismet, luck, providence

forward 1. *adj.* advanced, early, onward, precocious, premature, progressive, well-developed 2. *adv.* *Also* **forwards** ahead, forth, on, onward 3. *v.* advance, aid, assist, back, encourage, expedite, favour, foster, further, hasten, help, hurry, promote, speed, support

foster 1. cultivate, encourage, feed, nurture, promote, stimulate, support, uphold 2. bring up, mother, nurse, raise, rear, take care of 3. cherish, entertain, harbour, nourish, sustain

foul *adj.* 1. contaminated, dirty, disgusting, fetid, filthy, impure, loathsome, nasty, nauseating, noisome, offensive, polluted, putrid, rank, repulsive, revolting, rotten, squalid, stinking, sullied, tainted, unclean 2. bad, blustery, disagreeable, foggy, murky, rainy, rough, stormy, wet, wild ~*v.* 3. besmear, besmirch, contaminate, defile, dirty, pollute, smear, soil, stain, sully, taint

found constitute, construct, create, endow, erect, establish, fix, inaugurate, institute, organize, originate, plant, raise, settle, set up, start

foundation 1. base, basis, bedrock, bottom, footing, substructure, underpinning 2. endowment, establishment, inauguration, institution, settlement

founder[1] *n.* author, beginner, benefactor, builder, designer, establisher, father, framer, generator, initiator, inventor, maker, organizer, originator

founder[2] *v.* be lost, go down, go to the bottom, sink, submerge

foundling orphan, outcast, stray, waif

fountain fount, jet, reservoir, spout, spray, spring, well

foyer anteroom, entrance hall, lobby, vestibule

fracas brawl, disturbance, fight, melee, quarrel, riot, row, rumpus, scrimmage, scuffle, trouble, uproar

fractious awkward, captious, crabby, cross, fretful, irritable, peevish, recalcitrant, testy, touchy, unruly

fracture 1. *n.* breach, break, cleft, crack, fissure, gap, opening, rent, rift, rupture, schism, split 2. *v.* break, crack, rupture, splinter, split

fragile breakable, brittle, dainty, delicate, feeble, fine, flimsy, frail, infirm, slight, weak

fragment bit, chip, fraction, morsel, part, piece, portion, remnant, scrap, shiver, sliver

fragmentary bitty, broken, disconnected, discrete, disjointed, incoherent, incomplete, partial, piecemeal

fragrance aroma, balm, bouquet, perfume, scent, smell

fragrant aromatic, balmy, odorous, perfumed, sweet-scented, sweet-smelling

frail breakable, brittle, decrepit, delicate, feeble, flimsy, fragile, infirm, insubstantial, puny, slight, tender, unsound, vulnerable, weak

frailty feebleness, puniness, susceptibility, weakness

frame *v.* 1. assemble, build, constitute, construct, fabricate, fashion, forge, form, institute, invent, make, model, mould, set up 2. compose, contrive, devise, draft, draw up, form, formulate, hatch, plan, shape, sketch 3. case, enclose, mount, surround ~*n.* 4. casing, fabric, form, scheme, shell, structure, system 5. anatomy, body, build, physique, skeleton 6. mount, mounting, setting

framework core, fabric, foundation, groundwork, plan, schema, shell, skeleton, structure

franchise charter, exemption, freedom, immunity, right, suffrage, vote

frank artless, blunt, candid, direct, downright, forthright, free, honest, open, outright, outspoken, plain, sincere, straightforward, transparent, truthful, unconcealed, undisguised, unreserved, unrestricted

frankness bluntness, candour, forthrightness, openness, outspokenness, plain speaking

frantic berserk, distracted, distraught, frenetic, frenzied, furious, hectic, mad, overwrought, raging, raving, wild

fraternity association, brotherhood, circle, clan, club, companionship, company, comradeship, fellowship, guild, kinship, league, set, sodality, union

fraud 1. artifice, cheat, chicanery, craft, deceit, deception, double-dealing, duplicity, guile, hoax, humbug, imposture, spuriousness, stratagems, swindling, treachery, trickery 2. bluffer, charlatan, cheat, counterfeit, double-dealer, fake, forgery, hoax, hoaxer, impostor, mountebank, pretender, quack, sham, swindler

fraudulent crafty, criminal, deceitful, deceptive, dishonest, false, knavish, sham, spurious, swindling, treacherous

fray *v.* chafe, fret, rub, wear, wear away, wear thin

freak 1. *n.* aberration, abnormality, anomaly, malformation, monster, oddity 2. *adj.* aberrant, abnormal, atypical, bizarre, erratic, exceptional, fortuitous, odd, queer, unexpected, unforeseen, unpredictable, unusual

free *adj.* 1. complimentary, for nothing, gratis, gratuitous, unpaid 2. at large, at liberty, footloose, independent, liberated, loose, uncommitted, unconstrained, unfettered, unrestrained 3. able, allowed, clear, disengaged, loose, open, permitted, unattached, unhampered, unimpeded, unobstructed, unregulated, unrestricted, untrammelled 4. *With* **of** above, beyond, deficient in, devoid of, exempt from, immune to, lacking (in), not liable to, safe from, unaffected by, untouched by, without 5. autarchic, autonomous, democratic, emancipated, independent, self-governing, self-ruling, sovereign 6. available, empty, extra, idle, not tied down, spare, unemployed, uninhabited, unoccupied, unused, vacant 7. big (*Inf.*), bounteous, bountiful, charitable, eager, generous, hospitable, lavish, liberal, munificent, open-handed, prodigal, unsparing, unstinting, willing 8. **free and easy** casual, easy-going, informal, lax, lenient, liberal, relaxed, tolerant, unceremonious ~*adv.* 9. at no cost, for love, gratis, without charge 10. abundantly, copiously, freely, idly, loosely ~*v.* 11. deliver, discharge, emancipate, let go, let out, liberate, loose, manumit, release, turn loose, uncage, unchain, unfetter, unleash, untie 12. clear, cut loose, deliver, disengage, disentangle, exempt, extricate, ransom, redeem, relieve, rescue, rid, unburden, undo

freedom 1. autonomy, deliverance, emancipation, home rule, independence, liberty, release, self-government 2. exemption, immunity, impunity, privilege 3. ability, carte blanche, discretion, elbowroom, facility, flexibility, free rein, latitude, leeway, licence, opportunity, play, power, range, scope

freely 1. of one's own accord, spontaneously, voluntarily, willingly 2. candidly, frankly, openly, plainly, unreservedly 3. unchallenged 4. abundantly, amply, bountifully, copiously, extravagantly, lavishly, liberally, open-handedly, unstintingly

freeze 1. benumb, chill, congeal, glaciate, harden, ice over *or* up, stiffen 2. fix, hold up, inhibit, peg, stop, suspend

freezing arctic, biting, bitter, chill, chilled, cutting, frosty, glacial, icy, numbing, penetrating, raw, wintry

freight *n.* bales, bulk, burden, cargo, consignment, contents, goods, haul, lading, load, merchandise, payload, tonnage

French Gallic

frenzied agitated, convulsive, distracted, distraught, excited, frantic, frenetic, furious, hysterical, mad, maniacal, rabid, uncontrolled, wild

frequent[1] *adj.* common, constant, continual, customary, everyday, familiar, habitual, numerous, persistent, recurrent, repeated, usual

frequent[2] *v.* attend, be found at, haunt, patronize, resort, visit

frequently commonly, habitually, much, often, repeatedly, very often

fresh 1. different, latest, modern, new, novel, original, recent, unusual, up-to-date 2. added, additional, extra, further, more, other, renewed 3. bracing, bright, brisk, clean, clear, cool, crisp, invigorating, pure, refreshing, sparkling, stiff, sweet 4. blooming, clear, fair, florid, glowing, good, hardy, healthy, rosy, wholesome 5. artless, callow, green, inexperienced, natural, new, raw, untrained, untried, youthful

freshen enliven, liven up, refresh, restore, revitalize, rouse, spruce up, titivate

freshness 1. inventiveness, newness, novelty, originality 2. bloom, brightness, cleanness, clearness, dewiness, glow, shine, sparkle, vigour

fret affront, agonize, anguish, annoy, brood, chagrin, goad, grieve, harass, irritate, provoke, ruffle, torment, worry

friction abrasion, erosion, fretting, grating, irritation, resistance, rubbing, scraping

friend chum, companion, comrade, confidant, crony, familiar, intimate, pal, partner, playmate, soul mate

friendliness amiability, congeniality, conviviality, geniality, kindliness, sociability, warmth

friendly affectionate, amiable, amicable, attentive, beneficial, benevolent, benign, close, companionable, comradely, convivial, cordial, familiar, favourable, fond, genial, good, helpful, intimate, kind, kindly, neighbourly, outgoing, peaceable, propitious, receptive, sociable, sympathetic, welcoming, well-disposed

friendship affection, affinity, alliance, amity, attachment, benevolence, closeness, concord, familiarity, fondness, good-fellowship, good will, harmony, intimacy, love, rapport, regard

fright alarm, apprehension, dismay, dread, fear, horror, panic, quaking, scare, shock, terror, trepidation

frighten alarm, appal, cow, daunt, dismay, intimidate, petrify, scare, shock, startle, terrify, terrorize, unman, unnerve

frightened afraid, alarmed, dismayed, frozen, panicky, petrified, scared, startled, terrified, terrorized, unnerved

frightening alarming, appalling, dismaying, dreadful, fearful, fearsome, hair-raising, horrifying, intimidating, menacing, shocking, terrifying, unnerving

frightful appalling, awful, dire, dreadful, fearful, ghastly, grim, grisly, gruesome, harrowing, hideous, horrible, lurid, macabre, petrifying, shocking, terrible, terrifying, traumatic, unnerving, unspeakable

frigid 1. arctic, chill, cold, cool, frost-bound, frosty, frozen, gelid, glacial, hyperboreal, icy, Siberian, wintry 2. aloof, austere, forbidding, formal, icy, lifeless, passionless, passive, repellent, rigid, stiff, unapproachable, unbending, unfeeling, unloving, unresponsive

frills additions, affectation(s), decoration(s), embellishment(s), extras, finery, frippery, fuss, mannerisms, ornamentation, ostentation, superfluities, tomfoolery, trimmings

fringe 1. binding, border, edging, hem, tassel, trimming 2. borderline, edge, limits, march, marches, margin, outskirts, perimeter, periphery

frisk bounce, caper, cavort, dance, frolic, gambol, hop, jump, play, prance, rollick, romp, skip, sport, trip

fritter (**away**) dissipate, idle (away), misspend, run through, squander, waste

frivolity childishness, flippancy, folly, fun, gaiety, giddiness, jest, levity, lightness, nonsense, puerility, shallowness, silliness, superficiality, trifling, triviality

frivolous childish, dizzy, empty-headed, flighty, flippant, foolish, giddy, idle, juvenile, light-minded, puerile, silly, superficial

frolic *v.* 1. caper, cavort, cut capers, frisk, gambol, lark, make merry, play, rollick, romp, sport ~*n.* 2. antic, escapade, gambol, game, lark, prank, revel, romp, spree 3. amusement, fun, gaiety, high jinks, merriment, sport

frolicsome coltish, frisky, gay, kittenish, lively, merry, playful, sportive, sprightly

front *n.* 1. exterior, façade, face, facing, foreground, forepart, frontage, obverse 2. beginning, fore, forefront, head, lead, top, van, vanguard 3. blind, cover, cover-up, disguise, façade, mask, pretext, show 4. **in front** ahead, before, first, in advance, in the lead, in the van, leading, preceding, to the fore ~*adj.* 5. first, foremost, head, headmost, lead, leading, topmost ~*v.* 6. face (onto), look over *or* onto, overlook

frontier borderland, borderline, bound, boundary, confines, edge, limit, marches, perimeter, verge

frost freeze, hoarfrost, rime

frosty 1. chilly, cold, frozen, icy, rimy, wintry 2. discouraging, frigid, off-putting, standoffish, unenthusiastic, unfriendly, unwelcoming

frown 1. glare, glower, lower, scowl 2. *With* **on** *or* **upon** disapprove of, discourage, dislike

frozen 1. arctic, chilled, frigid, frosted, icebound, ice-cold, icy, numb 2. fixed, petrified, rooted, stock-still, stopped, suspended

frugal abstemious, careful, economical, meagre, niggardly, parsimonious, prudent, saving, sparing, thrifty

fruit 1. crop, harvest, produce, product, yield 2. advantage, benefit, consequence, effect, outcome, profit, result, return, reward

fruitful 1. fecund, fertile 2. abundant, copious, flush, plenteous, plentiful, productive, profuse, prolific, rich, spawning

fruition attainment, completion, consummation, enjoyment, fulfilment, materialization, maturity, perfection, realization, ripeness

fruitless abortive, barren, futile, idle, ineffectual, in vain, pointless, profitless, unavailing, unproductive, unprofitable, unsuccessful, useless, vain

frustrate baffle, balk, block, check, confront, counter, defeat, disappoint, foil, forestall, inhibit, neutralize, nullify, stymie, thwart

frustrated disappointed, discontented, discouraged, disheartened, embittered, foiled, irked, resentful

fudge *v.* avoid, dodge, equivocate, evade, fake, falsify, hedge, misrepresent, patch up, shuffle, slant, stall

fuel ammunition, encouragement, fodder, food, incitement, material, means, nourishment, provocation

fugitive runaway

fulfil accomplish, achieve, answer, carry out, complete, conclude, conform to, discharge, effect, execute, fill, finish, keep, meet, obey, observe, perfect, perform, realise, satisfy

fulfilment accomplishment, achievement, attainment, completion, consummation, crowning, discharge, end, implementation, observance, perfection, realization

full 1. brimful, complete, entire, filled, gorged, intact, loaded, replete, sated, satiated, satisfied, saturated, stocked, sufficient 2. abundant, ample, broad, comprehensive, copious, detailed, exhaustive, extensive, generous, maximum, plenary, plenteous, plentiful, thorough, unabridged 3. chock-full, crammed, crowded, in use, jammed, occupied, packed, taken

full-grown adult, developed, marriageable, mature, nubile, of age, ripe

fullness broadness, completeness, comprehensiveness, entirety, extensiveness, plenitude, totality, vastness, wealth, wholeness

full-scale all-out, comprehensive, exhaustive, extensive, full-dress, in-depth, major, proper, sweeping, thorough, thorough-going, wide-ranging

fully 1. absolutely, altogether, completely, entirely, intimately, perfectly, positively, thoroughly, totally, utterly, wholly 2. abundantly, adequately, amply, enough, plentifully, satisfactorily, sufficiently

fulsome adulatory, excessive, extravagant, fawning, gross, ingratiating, inordinate, insincere, nauseating, saccharine, sickening, sycophantic, unctuous

fumble botch, bungle, make a hash of (*Inf.*), mess up, misfield, mishandle, mismanage, muff, spoil

fume boil, chafe, rage, rant, rave, seethe, smoulder, storm

fumes exhaust, gas, haze, pollution, reek, smog, smoke, stench, vapour

fumigate cleanse, disinfect, purify, sterilize

fun amusement, cheer, distraction, diversion, enjoyment, entertainment, frolic, gaiety, good time, jollity, joy, junketing, merriment, mirth, pleasure, recreation, romp, sport, treat

function *n.* **1.** activity, business, capacity, charge, concern, duty, employment, exercise, job, mission, occupation, office, operation, part, post, province, purpose, responsibility, role, situation, task ~*v.* **2.** act, behave, do duty, go, officiate, operate, perform, run, serve, work ~*n.* **3.** affair, do (*Inf.*), gathering, reception, social occasion

functional practical, serviceable, useful, utilitarian, utility, working

fund *n.* **1.** capital, endowment, foundation, kitty, pool, reserve, stock, store, supply **2.** hoard, mine, repository, reserve, reservoir, source, storehouse, treasury, vein ~*v.* **3.** capitalize, endow, finance, float, pay for, promote, stake, subsidize, support

fundamental *adj.* basic, cardinal, central, crucial, elementary, essential, first, important, indispensable, integral, intrinsic, key, necessary, prime, principal, underlying, vital

fundamentally at heart, basically, essentially, intrinsically, primarily

funds capital, cash, finance, hard cash, money, ready money, resources, savings

funeral burial, interment, obsequies

funnel *v.* channel, conduct, convey, direct, filter, move, pass, pour

funny 1. absurd, amusing, comic, comical, diverting, droll, entertaining, facetious, farcical, hilarious, humorous, jocular, jolly, laughable, ludicrous, rich, ridiculous, riotous, risible, silly, slapstick, waggish, witty **2.** curious, dubious, mysterious, odd, peculiar, perplexing, puzzling, queer, remarkable, strange, suspicious, unusual, weird

furious angry, beside oneself, boiling, enraged, frantic, frenzied, fuming, incensed, infuriated, mad, maddened, raging, wrathful

furnish 1. appoint, decorate, equip, fit (out, up), outfit, provide, rig, stock, store, supply **2.** afford, bestow, endow, give, grant, offer, present, provide, reveal, supply

furniture appointments, chattels, effects, equipment, fittings, furnishings, goods, household goods, movable property, possessions

furore commotion, disturbance, excitement, frenzy, fury, outburst, outcry, stir, uproar

furrow channel, crease, fluting, groove, hollow, line, rut, seam, trench, wrinkle

further 1. *adj.* additional, extra, fresh, more, new, other, supplementary **2.** *adv.* additionally, also, as well as, besides, furthermore, in addition, moreover, on top of, what's more, yet **3.** *v.* advance, aid, assist, champion, encourage, expedite, facilitate, forward, foster, hasten, help, patronize, promote, push, speed, succour, work for

furthermore additionally, as well, besides, in addition, moreover, to boot, too

furthest extreme, farthest, most distant, outermost, outmost, remotest, ultimate, uttermost

furtive clandestine, cloaked, covert, hidden, secret, secretive, skulking, slinking, sly, sneaking, sneaky, stealthy, surreptitious, underhand

fury 1. anger, frenzy, ire, madness, passion, rage, wrath **2.** ferocity, force, intensity, power, savagery, severity, turbulence, vehemence, violence

fuss *n.* **1.** ado, agitation, bother, bustle, commotion, confusion, excitement, fidget, flurry, fluster, flutter, hurry, stir, to-do, upset, worry **2.** argument, bother, complaint, difficulty, display, furore, objection, row, squabble, trouble, unrest, upset ~*v.* **3.** bustle, fidget, fret, fume

fussy choosy, difficult, exacting, faddy, fastidious, finicky, old-maidish, old-womanish, overparticular, particular, pernickety, squeamish

futile abortive, barren, bootless, empty, forlorn, fruitless, hollow, ineffectual, nugatory, profitless, sterile, unavailing, unproductive, unprofitable, unsuccessful, useless, vain, valueless, worthless

future 1. *n.* expectation, hereafter, outlook, prospect, time to come **2.** *adj.* approaching, coming, destined, eventual, expected, fated, forthcoming, impending, later, prospective, subsequent, to come, ultimate, unborn

G

gadget appliance, contrivance, device, gimmick, invention, novelty, tool

gaffe blunder, faux pas, gaucherie, howler, indiscretion, mistake, slip, solecism

gag *v.* curb, muffle, muzzle, quiet, silence, stifle, still, stop up, suppress, throttle

gaiety blitheness, cheerfulness, elation, glee, good humour, high spirits, hilarity, *joie de vivre*, jollity, joviality, joyousness, liveliness, merriment, mirth, vivacity

gaily blithely, cheerfully, gleefully, happily, joyfully, lightheartedly, merrily

gain *v.* **1.** achieve, acquire, advance, attain, build up, capture, collect, enlist, gather, get, glean, harvest, improve, increase, net, obtain, pick up, procure, profit, realize, reap, secure, win, win over **2.** acquire, bring in, clear, earn, get, make, net, obtain, produce, realize, win, yield ~*n.* **3.** acquisition, advance, advantage, attainment, benefit, dividend, earnings, emolument, growth, headway, improvement, income, increase, increment, lucre, proceeds, produce, profit, return, rise, winnings, yield

gains booty, earnings, prize, proceeds, profits, revenue, winnings

gainsay contradict, controvert, deny, disaffirm, dispute

gait bearing, carriage, pace, step, stride, tread, walk

gala carnival, celebration, festival, festivity, fête, jamboree, pageant, party

gale blast, hurricane, squall, storm, tempest, tornado, typhoon

gallant *adj.* **1.** bold, brave, courageous, daring, dashing, dauntless, doughty, fearless, heroic, honourable, intrepid, lionhearted, manful, manly, noble, plucky, valiant, valorous **2.** attentive, chivalrous, courteous, courtly, gentlemanly, gracious, magnanimous, noble, polite ~*n.* **3.** admirer, beau, boyfriend, escort, lover, paramour, suitor, wooer

gallantry audacity, boldness, bravery, courage, daring, fearlessness, heroism, intrepidity, manliness, mettle, nerve, pluck, prowess, spirit, valiance, valour

galling aggravating (*Inf.*), annoying, bitter, bothersome, exasperating, harassing, humiliating, irksome, irritating, nettlesome, plaguing, provoking, rankling, vexatious, vexing

gallop bolt, career, dart, dash, fly, hasten, hurry, race, run, rush, shoot, speed, sprint

galvanize arouse, awaken, electrify, excite, fire, inspire, invigorate, jolt, move, provoke, quicken, shock, spur, startle, stimulate, stir, thrill

gamble *v.* **1.** back, bet, game, play, punt, stake, wager **2.** back, chance, hazard, risk, speculate, stake, venture ~*n.* **3.** chance, lottery, risk, speculation, uncertainty, venture **4.** bet, punt, wager

gambol caper, cavort, frisk, frolic, hop, jump, prance, rollick, skip

game[1] *n.* **1.** amusement, distraction, diversion, entertainment, frolic, fun, jest, joke, lark, merriment, pastime, play, recreation, romp, sport **2.** contest, event, match, meeting, round **3.** chase, prey, quarry, wild animals

game[2] *adj.* bold, brave, courageous, dogged, fearless, gallant, heroic, intrepid, persistent, plucky, resolute, spirited, valiant, valorous

gamut compass, field, range, scale, scope, series, sweep

gang band, circle, clique, club, company, coterie, crowd, group, herd, horde, lot, mob, pack, party, ring, set, shift, squad, team, troupe

gangster bandit, brigand, desperado, hoodlum, racketeer, robber, ruffian, thug, tough

gap blank, breach, break, chink, cleft, crack, cranny, crevice, divide, hiatus, hole, intermission, interruption, interstice, interval, lacuna, lull, opening, pause, recess, rent, rift, space, void

gape 1. gawk, goggle, stare, wonder **2.** crack, open, split, yawn

gaping broad, cavernous, great, open, vast, wide, wide open, yawning

garbage debris, detritus, junk, litter, rubbish, scraps

garble 1. confuse, jumble, mix up **2.** doctor, falsify, misquote, misreport, misrepresent, mistranslate, mutilate, pervert, slant, tamper with, twist

garish brassy, cheap, flashy, gaudy, glaring, glittering, loud, raffish, showy, tasteless, vulgar

garland bays, chaplet, crown, festoon, honours, laurels, wreath

garments apparel, array, attire, clothes, clothing, costume, dress, garb, habit, outfit, robes, togs, uniform, vestments, wear

garner accumulate, amass, assemble, collect, deposit, gather, hoard, put by, reserve, save, stockpile, store, treasure

garnish adorn, beautify, bedeck, deck, decorate, embellish, enhance, grace, ornament, set off, trim

garrison 1. armed force, command, detachment, troops, unit **2.** base, camp, encampment, fort, fortification, fortress, post, station, stronghold

garrulous 1. babbling, chattering, chatty, effusive, glib, gossiping, gushing, loquacious, prattling, talkative, verbose, voluble **2.** diffuse, long-winded, prolix, prosy, verbose, windy, wordy

gash 1. *v.* cleave, cut, incise, lacerate, rend, slash, slit, split, tear, wound **2.** *n.* cleft, cut, incision, laceration, rent, slash, slit, split, tear, wound

gasp 1. *v.* blow, choke, gulp, pant, puff **2.** *n.* blow, ejaculation, exclamation, gulp, pant, puff

gate access, barrier, door, doorway, egress, entrance, exit, passage, portal

gather 1. accumulate, amass, assemble, collect, congregate, convene, flock, garner, group, heap, hoard, marshal, mass, muster, pile up, round up, stack up, stockpile **2.** assume, conclude, deduce, draw, hear, infer, learn, make, surmise, understand **3.** crop, cull, garner, glean, harvest, pick, pluck, reap, select

gathering assembly, company, conclave, concourse, congregation, congress, convention, convocation, crowd, flock, group, knot, meeting, muster, party, rally, throng, turnout

gauche awkward, clumsy, graceless, ignorant, ill-bred, ill-mannered, inelegant, inept, insensitive, maladroit, tactless, uncultured, unpolished, unsophisticated

gaudy bright, brilliant, flashy, florid, garish, gay, glaring, loud, ostentatious, raffish, showy, tasteless, tawdry, vulgar

gauge *v.* **1.** ascertain, calculate, check, compute, count, determine, measure, weigh **2.** adjudge, appraise, assess, estimate, evaluate, guess, judge, rate, reckon, value ~*n.* **3.** basis, example, guide, indicator, measure, meter, model, pattern, rule, sample, standard, test, yardstick **4.** bore, capacity, degree, depth, extent, height, magnitude, measure, scope, size, span, thickness, width

gaunt angular, attenuated, bony, cadaverous, emaciated, haggard, lank, lean, meagre, pinched, rawboned, scraggy, scrawny, skinny, spare, thin, wasted

gawky awkward, clownish, clumsy, gauche, loutish, lumbering, lumpish, maladroit, oafish, uncouth, ungainly

gay 1. animated, blithe, carefree, cheerful, debonair, glad, gleeful, happy, hilarious, jolly, jovial, joyful, joyous, lively, merry, sparkling, sunny, vivacious 2. bright, brilliant, colourful, flamboyant, flashy, fresh, garish, gaudy, rich, showy, vivid

gaze 1. *v.* contemplate, gape, look, regard, stare, view, watch, wonder 2. *n.* fixed look, look, stare

gazette journal, newspaper, news-sheet, organ, paper, periodical

gear 1. cog, cogwheel, toothed wheel 2. accessories, accoutrements, apparatus, equipment, harness, instruments, outfit, rigging, supplies, tackle, tools, trappings 3. baggage, belongings, effects, kit, luggage, stuff, things

gelatinous gluey, glutinous, gummy, jelly-like, mucilaginous, sticky, viscid, viscous

gelid arctic, chilly, cold, freezing, frigid, frosty, frozen, glacial, ice-cold, icy, polar

gem 1. jewel, precious stone, stone 2. flower, jewel, masterpiece, pearl, pick, prize, treasure

general 1. accepted, broad, common, extensive, popular, prevailing, prevalent, public, universal, widespread 2. accustomed, conventional, customary, everyday, habitual, normal, ordinary, regular, typical, usual 3. approximate, ill-defined, imprecise, inaccurate, indefinite, inexact, loose, undetailed, unspecific, vague

generally 1. almost always, as a rule, by and large, conventionally, customarily, habitually, mainly, normally, ordinarily, regularly, typically, usually 2. commonly, extensively, popularly, publicly, universally, widely

generate beget, breed, cause, create, engender, form, initiate, make, originate, procreate, produce, propagate, spawn, whip up

generation 1. begetting, breeding, creation, formation, genesis, procreation, production, propagation, reproduction 2. age, day, days, epoch, era, period, time, times

generosity benevolence, bounty, charity, kindness, liberality, munificence, open-handedness

generous 1. benevolent, bounteous, bountiful, charitable, free, hospitable, kind, lavish, liberal, munificent, open-handed, princely, ungrudging, unstinting 2. big-hearted, disinterested, good, high-minded, lofty, magnanimous, noble, unselfish

genial affable, agreeable, amiable, cheerful, cheery, convivial, cordial, easygoing, enlivening, friendly, happy, hearty, jolly, jovial, joyous, kind, kindly, merry, pleasant, sunny, warm

genius 1. adept, expert, maestro, master, virtuoso 2. ability, aptitude, bent, brilliance, capacity, endowment, faculty, flair, gift, inclination, knack, talent, turn

genteel aristocratic, civil, courteous, courtly, cultured, elegant, fashionable, formal, gentlemanly, ladylike, mannerly, polished, polite, refined, respectable, stylish, urbane, well-mannered

gentility civility, courtesy, courtliness, culture, decorum, elegance, etiquette, formality, good manners, polish, politeness, propriety, refinement, respectability

gentle 1. amiable, benign, bland, humane, kind, kindly, lenient, meek, merciful, mild, peaceful, placid, quiet, soft, tender 2. balmy, calm, clement, easy, light, low, mild, moderate, muted, placid, quiet, serene, slight, smooth, soft, soothing, temperate, tranquil, untroubled

gentlemanly civil, courteous, cultivated, gallant, genteel, honourable, mannerly, noble, obliging, polished, polite, refined, well-bred, well-mannered

genuine actual, authentic, honest, legitimate, natural, original, pure, real, sound, sterling, true, veritable

germ 1. microbe, microorganism, virus 2. beginning, bud, cause, embryo, origin, root, rudiment, seed, source, spark

germinate bud, develop, grow, originate, shoot, sprout, swell

gesticulate gesture, indicate, motion, sign, signal, wave

gesture 1. *n.* action, indication, motion, sign, signal 2. *v.* indicate, motion, sign, signal, wave

get 1. achieve, acquire, attain, bring, come by, earn, fetch, gain, glean, inherit, make, net, obtain, pick up, procure, realize, reap, receive, secure, succeed to, win 2. arrest, capture, grab, lay hold of, seize, take, trap 3. become, come to be, grow, turn, wax 4. arrive, come, reach 5. arrange, contrive, fix, manage, succeed 6. coax, convince, induce, influence, persuade, sway, wheedle, win over

get across 1. cross, ford, negotiate, pass over, traverse 2. communicate, convey, impart, put over, transmit

get ahead advance, be successful, do well, flourish, make good, progress, prosper, succeed, thrive

get along 1. agree, be friendly, harmonize 2. cope, develop, fare, manage, progress, shift

get at 1. acquire, attain, reach 2. hint, imply, intend, lead up to, mean, suggest 3. annoy, attack, blame, carp, criticize, nag, pick on, taunt

get back 1. recoup, recover, regain, repossess, retrieve 2. arrive home, return, revert, revisit

get by circumvent, go around, go past, overtake, pass, round

get down alight, bring down, climb down, descend, disembark, dismount, lower, step down

get in alight, appear, arrive, come, embark, enter, infiltrate, insert, land, mount

get off alight, depart, descend, disembark, dismount, escape, exit, leave

get on 1. ascend, board, climb, embark, mount 2. advance, cope, fare, manage, progress, prosper, succeed 3. agree, be compatible, be friendly, concur, harmonize

get out alight, break out, decamp, escape, evacuate, leave, vacate, withdraw

get over 1. cross, ford, pass, surmount, traverse 2. come round, mend, recover, revive, survive 3. communicate, convey, impart

get round 1. bypass, circumvent, edge, evade, skirt 2. cajole, coax, convert, persuade, prevail upon

get together accumulate, assemble, collect, congregate, convene, converge, gather, join, meet, muster, rally, unite

get up arise, ascend, climb, increase, mount, rise, scale, stand

ghastly ashen, deathlike, dreadful, frightful, grim, grisly, gruesome, hideous, horrible, livid, loathsome, pale, pallid, repellent, shocking, spectral, terrible, terrifying, wan

ghost apparition, phantom, revenant, soul, spectre, spirit, wraith

ghostly eerie, illusory, insubstantial, phantom, spectral, supernatural, uncanny, unearthly, weird

giant 1. *n.* colossus, leviathan, monster, titan 2. *adj.* colossal, elephantine, enormous, gargantuan, gigantic, huge, immense, jumbo (*Inf.*), large, mammoth, monstrous, prodigious, vast

gibberish babble, balderdash, blather, double talk, drivel, gabble, jabber, jargon, nonsense, prattle, twaddle

gibe, jibe 1. *v.* deride, flout, jeer, mock, ridicule, scoff, scorn, sneer, taunt, twit 2. *n.* derision, dig, jeer, mockery, ridicule, sarcasm, scoffing, sneer, taunt

giddiness dizziness, faintness, vertigo

giddy dizzy, faint, light-headed, reeling, unsteady, vertiginous

gift 1. benefaction, bequest, bounty, contribution, donation, grant, gratuity, largess, legacy, offering, present 2. ability, aptitude, attribute, bent, capability, capacity, faculty, flair, genius, knack, power, talent

gifted able, accomplished, adroit, brilliant, capable, clever, expert, ingenious, intelligent, masterly, skilled, talented

gigantic colossal, elephantine, enormous, giant, huge, immense, mammoth, monstrous, prodigious, stupendous, tremendous, vast

giggle *v./n.* chortle, chuckle, laugh, snigger, titter

gild adorn, beautify, bedeck, brighten, coat, deck, dress up, embellish, embroider, enhance, enrich, garnish, grace

gimmick contrivance, device, dodge, gadget, gambit, ploy, scheme, stratagem, stunt, trick

gingerly carefully, cautiously, charily, circumspectly, delicately, hesitantly, reluctantly, squeamishly, suspiciously, timidly, warily

gird 1. belt, bind, girdle 2. encircle, enclose, enfold, environ, hem in, pen, ring, surround

girdle 1. *n.* band, belt, cummerbund, fillet, sash, waistband 2. *v.* bind, bound, encircle, enclose, encompass, environ, hem, ring, surround

girl damsel, daughter, female child, lass, maid, maiden, miss, wench

girth bulk, measure, size

gist core, drift, essence, force, idea, import, marrow, meaning, nub, pith, point, sense, substance

give 1. accord, administer, allow, award, bestow, commit, confer, consign, contribute, deliver, donate, entrust, furnish, grant, permit, present, provide, supply 2. demonstrate, display, evidence, indicate, manifest, offer, proffer, provide, set forth, show 3. allow, cede, concede, devote, grant, hand over, lend, relinquish, surrender, yield

give away betray, disclose, divulge, expose, leak, let out, reveal, uncover

give in capitulate, collapse, comply, concede, quit, submit, surrender, yield

given addicted, apt, disposed, inclined, liable, likely, prone

give off discharge, emit, exhale, exude, produce, release, vent

give out 1. discharge, emit, exhale, exude, produce, release, send out, smell of, throw out, vent 2. announce, broadcast, communicate, disseminate, impart, make known, notify, publish, utter

give up abandon, capitulate, cease, cede, cut out, desist, despair, forswear, hand over, leave off, quit, relinquish, renounce, resign, stop, surrender, waive

glad cheerful, contented, delighted, gay, gleeful, gratified, happy, jocund, jovial, joyful, overjoyed, pleased, willing

gladden cheer, delight, enliven, exhilarate, hearten, please, rejoice

gladly cheerfully, freely, gaily, gleefully, happily, joyfully, merrily, readily, willingly

gladness blitheness, cheerfulness, delight, felicity, gaiety, glee, happiness, high spirits, hilarity, jollity, joy, joyousness, mirth, pleasure

glamorous alluring, attractive, beautiful, captivating, charming, dazzling, elegant, enchanting, entrancing, exciting, fascinating, glittering, glossy, lovely, prestigious, smart

glamour allure, appeal, attraction, beauty, charm, enchantment, fascination, prestige

glance *v.* 1. gaze, glimpse, look, peep, scan, view ~*n.* 2. glimpse, look, peek, peep, quick look, squint, view 3. gleam, glimmer, glint, reflection, sparkle, twinkle 4. allusion, passing mention, reference

glare *v.* 1. frown, glower, lower, scowl, stare angrily ~*n.* 2. black look, dirty look, frown, glower, lower, scowl 3. blaze, brilliance, dazzle, flame, glow

glaring audacious, blatant, conspicuous, flagrant, gross, manifest, obvious, open, outstanding, overt, patent, rank, visible

glassy clear, glossy, icy, shiny, slick, slippery, smooth, transparent

glaze 1. *v.* burnish, coat, enam-

el, gloss, lacquer, polish, varnish **2.** *n.* coat, enamel, finish, gloss, lacquer, lustre, patina, polish, shine, varnish
gleam 1. *n.* beam, flash, glow, ray, sparkle **2.** *v.* flare, flash, glance, glimmer, glint, glisten, glitter, glow, shimmer, shine, sparkle
glee cheerfulness, delight, elation, exultation, fun, gaiety, gladness, hilarity, jollity, joy, joyfulness, liveliness, merriment, mirth, triumph, verve
gleeful cheerful, delighted, elated, exuberant, gay, happy, jocund, jovial, joyful, jubilant, merry, mirthful, overjoyed, pleased, triumphant
glib artful, easy, fluent, plausible, quick, ready, slick, smooth, suave, voluble
glide coast, drift, float, flow, fly, roll, run, sail, skate, skim, slide, slip, soar
glimmer 1. *v.* blink, flicker, gleam, glisten, glitter, glow, shimmer, shine, sparkle, twinkle **2.** *n.* blink, flicker, gleam, glow, shimmer, sparkle, twinkle
glimpse 1. *n.* brief view, glance, look, peek, peep, quick look, sight, sighting **2.** *v.* espy, sight, spot, spy, view
glint 1. *v.* flash, gleam, glimmer, glitter, shine, sparkle, twinkle **2.** *n.* flash, gleam, glimmer, glitter, shine, sparkle
glisten flash, gleam, glimmer, glint, glitter, shimmer, shine, sparkle, twinkle
glitter 1. *v.* coruscate, flare, flash, gleam, glimmer, glint, glisten, scintillate, shimmer, shine, sparkle, twinkle **2.** *n.* beam, brightness, flash, glare, gleam, lustre, radiance, sheen, shimmer, shine, sparkle
gloat crow, exult, glory, relish, revel in, triumph, vaunt
global 1. international, planetary, universal, worldwide **2.** all-inclusive, all-out, comprehensive, encyclopedic, exhaustive, general, thorough, total, unbounded, unlimited
globe ball, earth, orb, planet, round, sphere, world
globule bead, bubble, drop, droplet, particle
gloom 1. blackness, cloud, cloudiness, dark, darkness, dimness, dullness, dusk, murk, murkiness, obscurity, shade, shadow, twilight **2.** blues, dejection, depression, despair, despondency, low spirits, melancholy, misery, sadness, sorrow, unhappiness, woe
gloomy 1. black, dark, dim, dismal, dreary, dull, dusky, murky, obscure, overcast, shadowy, sombre **2.** bad, black, cheerless, comfortless, depressing, disheartening, dispiriting, dreary, joyless, sad, saddening, sombre **3.** blue, cheerless, dejected, despondent, dismal, dispirited, downcast, downhearted, glum, melancholy, miserable, moody, morose, pessimistic, sad
glorify 1. adorn, augment, dignify, elevate, enhance, ennoble, illuminate, immortalize, lift up, magnify, raise **2.** celebrate, eulogize, extol, hymn, laud, lionize, magnify, praise
glorious 1. celebrated, distinguished, elevated, eminent, excellent, famed, famous, grand, honoured, illustrious, magnificent, majestic, noble, noted, renowned, sublime, triumphant **2.** delightful, enjoyable, excellent, fine, great, marvellous, pleasurable, splendid, wonderful
glory *n.* **1.** celebrity, dignity, distinction, eminence, exaltation, fame, honour, immortality, kudos, praise, prestige, renown **2.** adoration, blessing, gratitude, homage, praise, veneration, worship **3.** grandeur, greatness, magnificence, majesty, nobility, pageantry, pomp, splendour, sublimity, triumph ~*v.* **4.** boast, crow, exult, gloat, relish, revel, triumph
gloss[1] **1.** *n.* brightness, brilliance, burnish, gleam, lustre, polish, sheen, shine, varnish, veneer **2.** *v.* camouflage, conceal, cover up, disguise, hide, mask, veil
gloss[2] annotation, commentary, explanation, footnote, note, scholium, translation
glossy bright, brilliant, burnished, glassy, glazed, lustrous, polished, shining, shiny, sleek, smooth
glow *n.* **1.** burning, gleam, glimmer, light **2.** brightness, brilliance, effulgence, radiance, splendour, vividness **3.** ardour, enthusiasm, excitement, fervour, gusto, intensity, passion, vehemence, warmth ~*v.* **4.** brighten, burn, gleam, glimmer, redden, shine, smoulder **5.** blush, colour, fill, flush, radiate, thrill, tingle
glower frown, glare, lower, scowl
glowing aglow, beaming, bright, flaming, florid, flushed, red, rich, suffused, vivid, warm
glue 1. *n.* adhesive, gum, paste **2.** *v.* affix, fix, gum, paste, seal, stick
glum crestfallen, crusty, dejected, doleful, down, gloomy, gruff, grumpy, ill-humoured, low, moody, morose, saturnine, sour, sulky, sullen
glut excess, oversupply, saturation, superfluity, surfeit, surplus
glutton gobbler, gorger, gormandizer, gourmand
gluttony greed, rapacity, voraciousness, voracity
gnaw 1. bite, chew, munch, nibble, worry **2.** consume, devour, erode, fret
go *v.* **1.** advance, decamp, depart, journey, leave, move, pass, proceed, repair, set off, travel, withdraw **2.** function, move, operate, perform, run, work **3.** develop, eventuate, fall out, fare, happen, proceed, result, turn out, work out **4.** die, expire, perish **5.** elapse, expire, flow, lapse, pass, slip away ~*n.* **6.** attempt, bid, effort, essay, try, turn
goad 1. *n.* impetus, incentive, incitement, irritation, motivation, pressure, spur, stimulation, stimulus, urge **2.** *v.* annoy, arouse, drive, egg on, exhort, harass, hound, impel, incite, instigate, irritate, lash, prick, prod, prompt, propel, spur, stimulate, sting, urge, worry
goal aim, ambition, design, destination, end, intention, limit, mark, object, objective, purpose, target
go along acquiesce, agree, assent, concur, cooperate, follow
go away decamp, depart, exit, leave, move out, recede, withdraw
go back return, revert
gobble bolt, cram, devour, gorge, gulp, guzzle, stuff, swallow, wolf
go-between agent, broker, dealer, factor, intermediary, liaison, mediator
go by 1. elapse, exceed, flow on, pass, proceed **2.** adopt, be guided by, follow, heed, judge from, observe
godforsaken abandoned, backward, bleak, deserted, desolate, dismal, dreary, forlorn, gloomy, lonely, remote
godless depraved, evil, impious, profane, ungodly, wicked
godly devout, good, holy, pious, religious, righteous, saintly
godsend blessing, windfall
go far advance, be successful, do well, progress, succeed
go for 1. clutch at, fetch, obtain, reach, seek, stretch for **2.** assail, assault, attack
go in (for) adopt, embrace, engage in, enter, espouse, practise, pursue, take up
go into analyse, consider, discuss, examine, investigate, probe, pursue, review, scrutinize, study
golden 1. bright, brilliant, flaxen, shining, yellow **2.** best, blissful, flourishing, glorious, happy, joyful, joyous, precious, prosperous, rich, successful **3.** auspicious, excellent, favourable, opportune, promising, propitious, rosy, valuable
gone 1. elapsed, ended, finished, over, past **2.** absent, astray, away, lacking, lost, missing, vanished **3.** dead, deceased, defunct, departed, extinct, no more **4.** consumed, done, finished, spent, used up
good *adj.* **1.** acceptable, admirable, agreeable, capital, choice, excellent, fine, first-class, first-rate, great, pleasant, pleasing, positive, precious, satisfactory, splendid, superior, tiptop, valuable, worthy **2.** admirable, estimable, ethical, exemplary, honest, honourable, moral, praiseworthy, right, righteous, upright, virtuous, worthy **3.** able, accomplished, adept, adroit, capable, clever, competent, dexterous, efficient, expert, first-rate, proficient, reliable, satisfactory, serviceable, skilled, sound, suitable, talented, thorough, trustworthy, useful **4.** authentic, bona fide, dependable, genuine, honest, legitimate, proper, real, reliable, sound, true, trustworthy, valid **5.** decorous, dutiful, mannerly, obedient, orderly, polite, proper, seemly, well-behaved **6.** adequate, ample, complete, considerable, entire, extensive, full, large, long, sizable, solid, substantial, sufficient, whole ~*n.* **7.** advantage, avail, behalf, benefit, gain, interest, profit, service, use, usefulness, welfare, wellbeing, worth **8.** excellence, goodness, merit, morality, probity, rectitude, right, righteousness, uprightness, virtue, worth
goodbye adieu, farewell, parting
good-for-nothing 1. *n.* idler, layabout, profligate, scapegrace, waster, wastrel **2.** *adj.* feckless, idle, irresponsible, useless, worthless
good-humoured amiable, cheerful, congenial, genial, happy, pleasant
good-looking attractive, handsome, personable, pretty
good-natured agreeable, benevolent, friendly, helpful, kind, tolerant, well-disposed, willing to please
goodness 1. excellence, merit, quality, superiority, value, worth **2.** benevolence, friendliness, generosity, good will, graciousness, kindness, mercy **3.** honesty, honour, integrity, merit, morality, probity, rectitude, righteousness, uprightness, virtue
goods 1. belongings, chattels, effects, furniture, gear, movables, possessions, property, things, trappings **2.** merchandise, stock, stuff, wares
good will favour, friendship, heartiness, kindliness, zeal
go off 1. blow up, detonate, explode **2.** *Inf.* go bad, go stale, rot
go on continue, endure, happen, last, occur, persist, proceed, stay
go out 1. depart, exit, leave **2.** die out, expire, fade out
go over 1. examine, inspect, review, revise, study **2.** peruse, read, scan, skim
gorge[1] *n.* canyon, cleft, defile, fissure, pass, ravine
gorge[2] *v.* bolt, cram, devour, feed, fill, glut, gobble, gulp, guzzle, overeat, surfeit, swallow, wolf
gorgeous beautiful, brilliant, dazzling, elegant, glittering, grand, luxuriant, magnificent, opulent, ravishing, showy, splendid, sumptuous, superb
gossamer *adj.* airy, delicate, diaphanous, fine, flimsy, gauzy, light, sheer, silky, thin, transparent
gossip *n.* **1.** chitchat, hearsay, idle talk, prattle, scandal, small talk, tittle-tattle **2.** babbler, blether, busybody, chatterer, scandalmonger, tattler, telltale ~*v.* **3.** blether, chat, gabble, prate, prattle, tattle
go through 1. bear, brave, endure, experience, suffer, tolerate, undergo, withstand **2.** consume, exhaust, squander, use **3.** check, examine, explore, hunt, look, search
govern 1. administer, command, conduct, control, direct, guide, hold sway, lead, manage, order, oversee, pilot, reign, rule, steer, supervise **2.** sway, underlie
government 1. administration, authority, dominion, law, rule, sovereignty, state, statecraft **2.** administration, executive, ministry, regime **3.** authority, command, control, direction, domination, guidance, management, regulation, restraint, supervision, sway
governor administrator, chief, commander, controller, director, executive, head, leader, manager, overseer, ruler, supervisor
go with accompany, agree, blend, complement, concur,

correspond, fit, harmonize, match, suit

go without abstain, be denied, be deprived of, deny oneself, do without, go short, lack, want

gown costume, dress, frock, garb, garment, habit, robe

grab bag, capture, catch, clutch, grasp, grip, pluck, seize, snap up, snatch

grace *n.* **1.** beauty, charm, ease, elegance, finesse, loveliness, pleasantness, poise, polish, refinement **2.** benefaction, beneficence, benevolence, favour, generosity, goodness, good will, kindliness, kindness **3.** cultivation, decency, decorum, etiquette, manners, propriety, tact **4.** charity, clemency, compassion, forgiveness, indulgence, leniency, lenity, mercy, pardon, quarter, reprieve **5.** benediction, blessing, prayer, thanks, thanksgiving ~*v.* **6.** adorn, beautify, bedeck, deck, decorate, dignify, distinguish, elevate, embellish, enhance, enrich, favour, garnish, glorify, honour, ornament, set off

graceful agile, beautiful, becoming, charming, comely, easy, elegant, fine, flowing, natural, pleasing, smooth, tasteful

gracious affable, amiable, beneficent, benevolent, benign, charitable, chivalrous, civil, compassionate, considerate, cordial, courteous, friendly, hospitable, indulgent, kind, lenient, loving, merciful, mild, obliging, pleasing, polite, well-mannered

grade 1. *n.* brand, category, class, condition, degree, echelon, group, level, mark, notch, order, place, position, quality, rank, rung, size, stage, station, step **2.** *v.* arrange, brand, class, classify, evaluate, group, order, range, rank, rate, sort, value

gradient bank, grade, hill, incline, rise, slope

gradual even, gentle, graduated, moderate, piecemeal, progressive, regular, slow, steady, unhurried

gradually bit by bit, by degrees, evenly, gently, moderately, piecemeal, progressively, slowly, steadily

graduate *v.* calibrate, grade, mark off, measure out, proportion, regulate

grain 1. cereals, corn **2.** grist, kernel, seed

grand 1. ambitious, august, dignified, elevated, eminent, exalted, fine, glorious, great, haughty, illustrious, imposing, impressive, large, lofty, lordly, luxurious, magnificent, majestic, noble, opulent, palatial, pompous, pretentious, princely, regal, splendid, stately, striking, sumptuous **2.** admirable, excellent, fine, first-class, first-rate, outstanding, splendid, superb, wonderful

grandeur dignity, greatness, importance, loftiness, magnificence, majesty, nobility, pomp, splendour, state

grandiose affected, ambitious, bombastic, extravagant, flamboyant, pompous, pretentious, showy

grant 1. *v.* accede to, accord, acknowledge, admit, agree to, allocate, allot, allow, assign, award, bestow, cede, concede, confer, consent to, donate, give, impart, permit, present, yield **2.** *n.* admission, allocation, allotment, allowance, award, bequest, bounty, concession, donation, endowment, gift, present, subsidy

grasp *v.* **1.** catch, clasp, clinch, clutch, grab, grapple, grip, hold, lay *or* take hold of, seize, snatch **2.** comprehend, follow, realize, see, take in, understand ~*n.* **3.** clasp, clutches, embrace, grip, hold, possession, tenure **4.** comprehension, knowledge, mastery, perception, realization, understanding

grasping acquisitive, avaricious, close-fisted, covetous, greedy, mean, miserly, rapacious, selfish, stingy, tightfisted, venal

grate 1. creak, grind, rasp, rub, scrape, scratch **2.** annoy, chafe, exasperate, fret, gall, irk, irritate, jar, nettle, peeve, rankle, vex

grateful appreciative, indebted, obliged, thankful

gratify delight, favour, fulfil, give pleasure, gladden, humour, indulge, please, recompense, thrill

gratitude appreciation, indebtedness, obligation, recognition, thanks

gratuitous free, unasked-for, unpaid, unrewarded, voluntary

gratuity benefaction, bonus, bounty, donation, gift, largess, perquisite, present, reward, tip

grave[1] *n.* crypt, mausoleum, pit, sepulchre, tomb, vault

grave[2] **1.** dignified, dour, dull, earnest, gloomy, heavy, leaden, long-faced, muted, quiet, serious, sober, solemn, sombre, staid, subdued, thoughtful, unsmiling **2.** acute, critical, crucial, dangerous, hazardous, important, momentous, perilous, pressing, serious, severe, threatening, vital, weighty

graveyard burial ground, cemetery, churchyard, necropolis

gravity acuteness, exigency, importance, moment, seriousness, severity, significance, urgency, weightiness

greasy 1. fatty, oily, slick, slimy, slippery **2.** fawning, glib, ingratiating, oily, slick, smooth, toadying, unctuous

great 1. big, bulky, colossal, enormous, extensive, gigantic, huge, immense, large, mammoth, stupendous, tremendous, vast, voluminous **2.** extended, lengthy, long, prolonged, protracted **3.** capital, chief, grand, leading, main, major, paramount, primary, principal, prominent, superior **4.** considerable, decided, excessive, extravagant, extreme, grievous, high, inordinate, pronounced, strong **5.** consequential, critical, crucial, grave, heavy, important, momentous, serious, significant, weighty **6.** celebrated, distinguished, eminent, exalted, excellent, famed, famous, glorious, illustrious, notable, outstanding, prominent, remarkable, renowned **7.** august, chivalrous, dignified, distinguished, exalted, fine, glorious, grand, heroic, impressive, lofty, magnanimous, noble, sublime **8.** active, devoted, enthusiastic, keen, zealous **9.** able, adept, adroit, expert, good, masterly, proficient, skilful, skilled **10.** admirable, excellent, fine, first-rate, good, wonderful

greatly abundantly, by much, considerably, enormously, exceedingly, extremely, highly, hugely, immensely, mightily, much, notably, powerfully, remarkably, vastly, very much

greatness 1. bulk, enormity, hugeness, immensity, largeness, length, magnitude, mass, size **2.** gravity, heaviness, import, importance, moment, seriousness, significance, urgency, weight **3.** celebrity, distinction, eminence, fame, glory, grandeur, note, renown

greed, greediness 1. gluttony, hunger, ravenousness, voracity **2.** avidity, covetousness, cupidity, desire, eagerness, longing, rapacity, selfishness

greedy 1. gluttonous, hungry, insatiable, ravenous, voracious **2.** acquisitive, avaricious, avid, covetous, craving, desirous, eager, grasping, hungry, impatient, rapacious, selfish

green *adj.* **1.** blooming, budding, fresh, grassy, leafy, new, undecayed, verdant **2.** fresh, immature, new, raw, recent, unripe ~*n.* **3.** common, grassplot, lawn, sward, turf

greet accost, address, hail, meet, receive, salute, welcome

greeting address, hail, reception, salute, welcome

gregarious affable, convivial, cordial, friendly, outgoing, sociable, social

grey 1. ashen, bloodless, colourless, livid, pale, pallid, wan **2.** cheerless, cloudy, dark, depressing, dim, dismal, drab, dreary, dull, foggy, gloomy, misty, murky, overcast, sunless **3.** aged, ancient, elderly, mature, old, venerable

grief agony, anguish, bereavement, dejection, distress, grievance, heartache, heartbreak, misery, mourning, pain, regret, remorse, sadness, sorrow, suffering, trial, tribulation, trouble, woe

grievance complaint, damage, distress, hardship, injury, injustice, resentment, sorrow, trial, tribulation, trouble, wrong

grieve 1. ache, bemoan, bewail, complain, deplore, lament, mourn, regret, rue, sorrow, suffer, wail, weep **2.** afflict, agonize, crush, distress, hurt, injure, pain, sadden, wound

grievous 1. calamitous, damaging, distressing, dreadful, grave, harmful, heavy, hurtful, injurious, lamentable, oppressive, painful, severe **2.** deplorable, dreadful, flagrant, glaring, heinous, intolerable, lamentable, monstrous, offensive, outrageous, shameful, shocking, unbearable

grim cruel, ferocious, fierce, forbidding, formidable, frightful, ghastly, grisly, gruesome, harsh, hideous, horrible, horrid, merciless, morose, relentless, resolute, ruthless, severe, shocking, sinister, stern, sullen, surly, terrible

grimace face, frown, mouth, scowl, sneer, wry face

grime dirt, filth, smut, soot

grimy begrimed, besmeared, besmirched, dirty, filthy, foul, grubby, smutty, soiled, sooty, unclean

grind *v.* **1.** crush, granulate, grate, mill, pound, powder, pulverize **2.** gnash, grate, grit, scrape ~*n.* **3.** chore, drudgery, hard work, labour, task, toil

grip *n.* **1.** clasp, purchase **2.** control, domination, grasp, hold, influence, mastery, perception, possession, power, tenure, understanding ~*v.* **3.** clasp, clutch, grasp, hold, seize **4.** catch up, compel, engross, enthral, entrance, fascinate, hold, involve, mesmerize, rivet, spellbind

gripping compulsive, enthralling, exciting, fascinating, riveting, thrilling

grisly abominable, appalling, awful, dreadful, frightful, ghastly, grim, gruesome, hideous, horrid, macabre, terrible

grit 1. dust, gravel, sand **2.** backbone, courage, fortitude, gameness, mettle, nerve, perseverance, pluck, resolution, spirit, tenacity, toughness

groan 1. *n.* cry, moan, sigh, whine **2.** *v.* cry, grumble, moan, sigh, whine

groggy confused, dazed, dizzy, faint, reeling, shaky, stunned, unsteady, weak

groom *n.* **1.** stableboy, stableman ~*v.* **2.** clean, dress, smarten up, tidy, turn out **3.** coach, drill, educate, make ready, nurture, prepare, prime, ready, train

groove channel, cutting, flute, furrow, gutter, hollow, rut, score, trench

grope feel, finger, fish, flounder, fumble, grabble, search

gross *adj.* **1.** big, bulky, corpulent, dense, fat, great, heavy, hulking, large, massive, obese, overweight, thick **2.** aggregate, entire, total, whole **3.** coarse, crude, improper, impure, indecent, indelicate, lewd, low, obscene, offensive, rude, sensual, unseemly, vulgar **4.** boorish, callous, coarse, crass, dull, ignorant, imperceptive, insensitive, tasteless, unrefined

grotesque deformed, distorted, fantastic, freakish, incongruous, malformed, misshapen, odd, outlandish, ridiculous, strange, unnatural, weird

ground *n.* **1.** clod, dirt, dry land, dust, earth, field, land, mould, sod, soil, terrain, turf **2.** *Often plural* area, country, district, domain, estate, fields, gardens, land, property, realm, terrain, tract **3.** arena, field, pitch, stadium ~*v.* **4.** base, establish, fix, found, set, settle **5.** coach, inform, initiate, instruct, prepare, teach, train, tutor

groundless baseless, empty, false, idle, imaginary, unfounded, unjustified, unwarranted

groundwork base, basis, footing, foundation, fundamentals, preliminaries, preparation, spadework

group 1. *n.* association, band, batch, bunch, category, circle, class, clique, clump, cluster, collection, company, coterie, crowd, faction, formation, gang, gathering, organization, pack, party, set, troop **2.** *v.* arrange, assemble, associate, assort, bracket, class, classify, dispose, gather, marshal, order, organize, put together, range, sort

grouse **1.** *v.* carp, complain, grumble, moan, whine **2.** *n.* complaint, grievance, grumble, moan, objection

grow **1.** develop, enlarge, expand, extend, fill out, heighten, increase, multiply, spread, stretch, swell, thicken, widen **2.** develop, flourish, shoot, spring up, sprout, vegetate **3.** advance, expand, improve, progress, prosper, succeed, thrive **4.** breed, cultivate, farm, produce, raise

grown-up adult, fully-grown, mature

growth **1.** development, enlargement, evolution, expansion, extension, growing, increase, multiplication **2.** crop, cultivation, development, produce, shooting, sprouting, vegetation **3.** advance, expansion, improvement, progress, prosperity, rise, success

grub *v.* **1.** burrow, dig up, probe, pull up, search for, uproot **2.** ferret, forage, hunt, rummage, scour, search, uncover, unearth ~*n.* **3.** caterpillar, larva, maggot **4.** food, rations, sustenance, victuals

grubby dirty, filthy, grimy, mean, messy, mucky, scruffy, seedy, shabby, slovenly, smutty, soiled, sordid, squalid, unkempt, untidy, unwashed

grudge **1.** *n.* animus, antipathy, aversion, bitterness, dislike, enmity, grievance, hate, ill will, malevolence, malice, pique, rancour, resentment, spite, venom **2.** *v.* begrudge, complain, covet, envy, mind, resent, stint

gruelling arduous, brutal, crushing, demanding, difficult, fierce, grinding, hard, harsh, laborious, punishing, severe, stiff, strenuous, taxing, tiring, trying

gruesome abominable, awful, fearful, ghastly, grim, grisly, horrendous, macabre, repugnant, repulsive, shocking, terrible

gruff bearish, blunt, brusque, churlish, crabbed, crusty, curt, discourteous, grumpy, ill-humoured, ill-natured, impolite, rough, rude, sour, sullen, surly, uncivil, ungracious, unmannerly

grumble **1.** *v.* carp, complain, find fault, grouse, moan, whine **2.** *n.* complaint, grievance, grouse, moan, objection

guarantee **1.** *n.* assurance, bond, certainty, covenant, earnest, pledge, promise, security, surety, undertaking, warranty, word **2.** *v.* answer for, assure, certify, insure, maintain, pledge, promise, protect, secure, swear, vouch for, warrant

guard *v.* **1.** cover, defend, escort, keep, mind, oversee, patrol, police, protect, safeguard, save, screen, secure, shelter, shield, tend, watch, watch over ~*n.* **2.** custodian, defender, lookout, picket, sentinel, sentry, warder, watch, watchman **3.** buffer, bulwark, bumper, defence, pad, protection, rampart, safeguard, screen, security, shield **4.** attention, care, caution, heed, vigilance, wariness, watchfulness

guardian champion, curator, custodian, defender, escort, guard, keeper, preserver, protector, trustee, warden, warder

guerrilla freedom fighter, irregular, partisan, underground fighter

guess **1.** *v.* conjecture, estimate, fathom, predict, solve, speculate, work out **2.** *n.* conjecture, feeling, hypothesis, judgment, notion, prediction, reckoning, speculation, supposition, surmise, suspicion, theory

guest boarder, company, lodger, visitor

guidance advice, conduct, control, counsel, direction, government, help, instruction, intelligence, leadership, management, teaching

guide *v.* **1.** accompany, attend, conduct, convoy, direct, escort, lead, pilot, shepherd, steer, usher **2.** command, control, direct, handle, manage, manoeuvre, steer **3.** advise, counsel, educate, govern, influence, instruct, regulate, rule, superintend, supervise, sway, teach, train ~*n.* **4.** adviser, attendant, conductor, counsellor, director, escort, leader, mentor, monitor, pilot, steersman, teacher, usher **5.** catalogue, directory, handbook, instructions, key, manual, vade mecum

guild brotherhood, club, company, corporation, fellowship, fraternity, league, lodge, order, society, union

guile art, artifice, cleverness, craft, craftiness, cunning, deceit, deception, duplicity, knavery, ruse, slyness, treachery, trickery

guilt **1.** blame, delinquency, iniquity, misconduct, responsibility, sinfulness, wickedness, wrong, wrongdoing **2.** bad conscience, contrition, disgrace, dishonour, infamy, regret, remorse, self-reproach, shame, stigma

guiltless blameless, clear, impeccable, innocent, pure, sinless, spotless, unimpeachable, untainted, untarnished

guilty at fault, convicted, criminal, culpable, delinquent, erring, evil, felonious, offending, responsible, sinful, to blame, wicked, wrong

gulf **1.** bay, bight, sea inlet **2.** breach, chasm, cleft, gap, rent, rift, split, void

gullible credulous, foolish, green, innocent, naive, silly, simple, trusting, unsophisticated, unsuspecting

gully channel, ditch, gutter

gulp **1.** *v.* bolt, devour, gobble, quaff, swallow, swill, toss off, wolf **2.** *n.* draught, mouthful, swallow

gum adhesive, exudate, glue, mucilage, paste, resin

gumption ability, acumen, common sense, enterprise, initiative, resourcefulness, sagacity, shrewdness, spirit

gurgle **1.** *v.* babble, bubble, burble, crow, lap, murmur, plash, purl, ripple, splash **2.** *n.* murmur, ripple

gush **1.** *v.* burst, cascade, flood, flow, jet, pour, run, rush, spout, spurt, stream **2.** *n.* burst, cascade, flood, flow, jet, outburst, outflow, rush, spout, spurt, stream, torrent

gust blast, blow, breeze, flurry, gale, puff, rush, squall

gusto appetite, brio, delight, enjoyment, enthusiasm, fervour, liking, pleasure, relish, verve, zeal, zest

guts backbone, boldness, courage, daring, grit, mettle, nerve, pluck, spirit

gutter channel, conduit, ditch, drain, duct, pipe, sluice, trench, trough, tube

guttural deep, gruff, hoarse, husky, low, rasping, rough, thick, throaty

guy **1.** *n.* chap, fellow, lad, man, person, youth **2.** *v.* caricature, mock, ridicule

H

habit **1.** bent, custom, disposition, manner, practice, propensity, quirk, tendency, way **2.** custom, mode, practice, routine, rule, second nature, usage, wont **3.** dress, garb, garment, riding dress

habitation abode, domicile, dwelling, home, house, living quarters, lodging, quarters, residence

habitual accustomed, common, customary, familiar, fixed, natural, normal, ordinary, regular, routine, standard, traditional, usual, wonted

hack[1] chop, cut, gash, hew, kick, lacerate, mangle, mutilate, notch, slash

hack[2] *adj.* **1.** banal, mediocre, pedestrian, poor, tired, undistinguished, uninspired, unoriginal ~*n.* **2.** penny-a-liner, scribbler **3.** drudge, plodder, slave

hackneyed banal, common, commonplace, overworked, pedestrian, stale, stereotyped, stock, threadbare, timeworn, tired, trite, unoriginal, worn-out

hag crone, fury, harridan, shrew, termagant, virago, vixen, witch

haggard careworn, drawn, emaciated, gaunt, ghastly, pinched, shrunken, thin, wan, wasted, wrinkled

haggle **1.** bargain, barter **2.** bicker, dispute, quarrel, squabble, wrangle

hail[1] *Fig.* **1.** *n.* barrage, pelting, rain, shower, storm, volley **2.** *v.* barrage, batter, beat down upon, pelt, rain, shower, storm, volley

hail[2] acclaim, acknowledge, applaud, cheer, exalt, glorify, greet, honour, salute, welcome

hair **1.** locks, mane, mop, shock, tresses **2. split hairs** cavil, find fault, overrefine, pettifog, quibble

hair-raising alarming, exciting, frightening, horrifying, shocking, startling, terrifying, thrilling

hale blooming, fit, flourishing, healthy, hearty, robust, sound, strong, vigorous

half **1.** *n.* division, equal part, fifty per cent, fraction, portion, section **2.** *adj.* divided, fractional, halved, incomplete, limited, moderate, partial **3.** *adv.* all but, barely, inadequately, incompletely, in part, partially, partly, slightly

half-hearted cool, indifferent, listless, lukewarm, neutral, passive, perfunctory, spiritless, tame, uninterested

halfway *adv.* **1.** midway **2.** incompletely, moderately, nearly, partially, partly, rather ~*adj.* **3.** central, equidistant, intermediate, mid, middle, midway

half-witted crazy, doltish, dull, feeble-minded, foolish, idiotic, moronic, silly, simple, stupid

hall **1.** corridor, entry, foyer, lobby, passage, vestibule **2.** auditorium, chamber, meeting place

halo aura, corona, nimbus, radiance

halt[1] *v.* **1.** break off, cease, close down, desist, draw up, pull up, rest, stand still, stop, wait **2.** arrest, block, check, curb, cut short, end, hold back, impede, obstruct, stem, terminate ~*n.* **3.** arrest, break, close, end, pause, stand, standstill, stop, stoppage, termination

halt[2] **1.** falter, hobble, limp, stumble **2.** be unsure, dither, haver, hesitate, pause, stammer, waver

halting awkward, faltering, hesitant, laboured, stumbling, stuttering

halve bisect, cut in half, divide equally, split in two

hammer *v.* **1.** bang, beat, drive, hit, knock, strike, tap **2.** beat out, fashion, forge, form, make, shape

hammer out accomplish, bring about, complete, finish, negotiate, produce, settle, sort out, work out

hamper *v.* bind, cramp, curb, embarrass, encumber, entangle, fetter, frustrate, handicap, hinder, hold up, impede, interfere with, obstruct, prevent, restrict, slow down, thwart

hand *n.* **1.** fist, palm, **2.** direction, influence, part, participation, share **3.** aid, assistance, help, support **4.** artisan, craftsman, employee, hired man, labourer, operative, worker, workman **5. in hand a.** in order, under control **b.** in reserve, put by, ready ~*v.* **6.** deliver, pass **7.** aid, assist, conduct, convey, give, guide, help, lead, present, transmit

handbook guide, instruction book, manual

handcuff fetter, manacle, shackle

hand down *or* **on** bequeath, give, grant, transfer, will

handful few, small number, small quantity, smattering, sprinkling

handicap **1.** barrier, block, disadvantage, drawback, encumbrance, hindrance, impediment, limitation, obstacle, restriction, shortcoming **2.** advantage, edge, head start, odds, penalty, upper hand **3.** defect, disability, impairment

handicraft art, craft, handiwork, skill, workmanship

handiwork achievement, artefact, craft, creation, design, invention, product, production, result

handle *n.* **1.** grip, haft, helve, hilt, knob, stock ~*v.* **2.** feel, finger, fondle, grasp, hold, maul, poke, touch **3.** control, direct, guide, manage, manipulate, manoeuvre, operate, steer, use, wield **4.** administer, conduct, cope with, deal with, manage, supervise, treat

handling administration, approach, direction, management, treatment

hand-out 1. alms, charity, dole **2.** bulletin, circular, leaflet

hand out deal out, disburse, dispense, distribute, give out, mete

hand over deliver, donate, present, release, surrender, turn over, yield

handsome admirable, attractive, becoming, comely, elegant, fine, good-looking, graceful, majestic, personable, stately, well-proportioned

handsomely abundantly, amply, bountifully, generously, liberally, munificently, plentifully, richly

handwriting calligraphy, fist, hand, longhand, scrawl, script

handy 1. accessible, available, close, convenient, near, nearby, within reach **2.** convenient, helpful, manageable, neat, practical, serviceable, useful **3.** adept, adroit, clever, deft, expert, nimble, ready, skilful, skilled

hang 1. dangle, depend, droop, incline, suspend **2.** execute **3.** adhere, cling, hold, rest, stick **4.** attach, cover, deck, decorate, drape, fasten, fix, furnish

hang about *or* **around** dally, linger, loiter, roam, tarry, waste time

hang back demur, hesitate, recoil

hangdog *adj.* abject, browbeaten, cowed, cringing, downcast, furtive, guilty, shamefaced, wretched

hanger-on dependant, follower, lackey, leech, minion, parasite, sycophant

hanging *adj.* dangling, drooping, flapping, floppy, loose, pendent, suspended, swinging, unattached, unsupported

hang on carry on, continue, endure, go on, hold on, hold out, persevere, persist, remain

hang over be imminent, impend, loom, menace, threaten

hank coil, length, loop, piece, roll, skein

hankering craving, desire, hunger, itch, longing, urge, wish, yearning

haphazard 1. accidental, arbitrary, chance, random **2.** aimless, careless, casual, disorderly, indiscriminate, slipshod, unsystematic

happen 1. appear, arise, come about, come to pass, develop, ensue, follow, materialize, occur, result, transpire **2.** befall, betide **3.** chance, fall out, supervene, turn out

happening accident, adventure, affair, case, chance, episode, event, experience, incident, occurrence, phenomenon

happily 1. agreeably, contentedly, delightedly, enthusiastically, freely, gladly, heartily, willingly, with pleasure **2.** blithely, cheerfully, gaily, gleefully, joyfully, joyously, merrily **3.** auspiciously, favourably, fortunately, luckily, propitiously **4.** appropriately, aptly, felicitously, gracefully, successfully

happiness beatitude, blessedness, bliss, cheer, cheerfulness, cheeriness, contentment, delight, ecstasy, elation, enjoyment, felicity, gaiety, gladness, high spirits, joy, jubilation, merriment, pleasure, prosperity, satisfaction

happy blessed, blithe, cheerful, content, contented, delighted, ecstatic, elated, glad, gratified, jolly, joyful, jubilant, merry, overjoyed, pleased, thrilled

happy-go-lucky blithe, carefree, casual, easy-going, heedless, improvident, insouciant, nonchalant, untroubled

harangue 1. *n.* address, diatribe, exhortation, lecture, oration, screed, speech, tirade **2.** *v.* address, declaim, exhort, hold forth, lecture, rant

harass annoy, badger, bait, beleaguer, bother, disturb, exasperate, exhaust, fatigue, harry, hound, perplex, persecute, pester, plague, tease, tire, torment, trouble, vex, weary, worry

harbour *n.* **1.** destination, haven, port **2.** covert, haven, refuge, retreat, sanctuary, security, shelter ~*v.* **3.** conceal, hide, lodge, protect, provide refuge, relieve, secrete, shelter, shield

hard *adj.* **1.** compact, dense, firm, inflexible, rigid, rocklike, solid, stiff, stony, strong, tough, unyielding **2.** arduous, backbreaking, exacting, exhausting, fatiguing, formidable, laborious, rigorous, strenuous, tough, uphill, wearying **3.** baffling, complex, complicated, difficult, intricate, involved, knotty, perplexing, puzzling, tangled, thorny **4.** callous, cold, cruel, exacting, grim, harsh, implacable, obdurate, pitiless, ruthless, severe, stern, strict, stubborn, unjust, unkind, unsympathetic ~*adv.* **5.** energetically, fiercely, forcefully, forcibly, heavily, intensely, powerfully, severely, sharply, strongly, vigorously, violently **6.** assiduously, determinedly, diligently, doggedly, earnestly, industriously, intently, persistently, steadily, strenuously, untiringly **7.** agonizingly, badly, distressingly, harshly, laboriously, painfully, roughly, severely **8.** bitterly, hardly, keenly, rancorously, reluctantly, resentfully, slowly, sorely

hard and fast binding, immutable, incontrovertible, inflexible, invariable, rigid, set, strict, stringent, unalterable

harden 1. bake, cake, freeze, set, solidify, stiffen **2.** brace, buttress, fortify, gird, indurate, nerve, reinforce, steel, strengthen, toughen

hardened 1. chronic, fixed, habitual, inveterate, irredeemable, reprobate, set, shameless **2.** accustomed, habituated, inured, seasoned, toughened

hard-headed astute, cool, practical, pragmatic, realistic, sensible, shrewd, tough

hardhearted callous, cold, cruel, hard, heartless, indifferent, insensitive, intolerant, merciless, pitiless, stony, uncaring, unfeeling, unkind, unsympathetic

hard-hitting critical, tough, unsparing, vigorous

hardiness boldness, courage, fortitude, resilience, resolution, robustness, ruggedness, toughness

hardly almost not, barely, by no means, faintly, infrequently, just, not at all, not quite, no way, only, only just, scarcely, with difficulty

hardship adversity, affliction, austerity, burden, calamity, destitution, difficulty, fatigue, grievance, labour, misery, misfortune, need, suffering, toil, torment, tribulation, trouble, want

hard up bankrupt, impecunious, impoverished, penniless, poor

hard-wearing durable, resilient, rugged, stout, strong, tough, well-made

hard-working assiduous, busy, diligent, energetic, industrious, zealous

hardy firm, fit, hale, healthy, hearty, in fine fettle, lusty, robust, rugged, sound, stalwart, stout, strong, sturdy, tough, vigorous

harm 1. *n.* abuse, damage, detriment, hurt, ill, impairment, injury, loss, mischief, misfortune **2.** *v.* abuse, blemish, damage, hurt, ill-treat, ill-use, impair, injure, maltreat, mar, molest, ruin, spoil, wound

harmful baleful, baneful, destructive, detrimental, evil, hurtful, injurious, noxious, pernicious

harmless gentle, innocent, innocuous, inoffensive, safe

harmonious agreeable, compatible, concordant, congruous, coordinated, dulcet, euphonious, harmonizing, matching, melodious, musical, tuneful

harmony 1. accord, agreement, amicability, amity, compatibility, concord, conformity, cooperation, friendship, like-mindedness, peace, rapport, sympathy, unity **2.** euphony, melody, tune, tunefulness

harness *n.* **1.** equipment, gear, tack, tackle, trappings ~*v.* **2.** couple, hitch up, saddle, yoke **3.** apply, channel, control, employ, exploit, utilize

harry annoy, badger, chivvy, disturb, fret, harass, molest, pester, plague, tease, torment, trouble, vex, worry

harsh 1. coarse, croaking, crude, discordant, dissonant, glaring, grating, guttural, jarring, rasping, raucous, rough, strident **2.** abusive, austere, bitter, bleak, brutal, cruel, dour, grim, hard, relentless, ruthless, severe, sharp, stern, unfeeling, unkind, unpleasant

harshly brutally, cruelly, grimly, roughly, severely, sharply, sternly, strictly

harshness acerbity, acrimony, asperity, austerity, bitterness, brutality, hardness, ill-temper, rigour, severity

harvest 1. ingathering, reaping **2.** crop, produce, yield

hash hotchpotch, jumble, mess, mix-up, muddle, shambles

haste 1. briskness, celerity, dispatch, expedition, fleetness, quickness, rapidity, speed, swiftness, urgency **2.** bustle, hurry, hustle, impetuosity, rashness, recklessness, rush

hasten bolt, dash, fly, haste, race, run, rush, scurry, scuttle, speed, sprint

hastily 1. apace, fast, promptly, quickly, rapidly, speedily **2.** hurriedly, impetuously, impulsively, precipitately, rashly, recklessly, too quickly

hasty 1. brisk, eager, fast, fleet, hurried, prompt, rapid, speedy, swift, urgent **2.** foolhardy, headlong, heedless, impetuous, impulsive, precipitate, rash, reckless

hatch 1. breed, brood, incubate **2.** *Fig.* conceive, concoct, contrive, design, devise, plan, plot, project, scheme

hate 1. *v.* abhor, abominate, despise, detest, dislike, execrate **2.** *n.* abhorrence, abomination, antagonism, antipathy, aversion, detestation, dislike, enmity, execration, hatred, hostility, loathing, odium

hateful abominable, despicable, detestable, disgusting, execrable, foul, horrible, loathsome, obnoxious, odious, offensive, repellent, repugnant, repulsive, revolting, vile

hatred animosity, animus, antagonism, antipathy, aversion, detestation, dislike, enmity, execration, hate, ill will, odium, repugnance, revulsion

haughty arrogant, conceited, disdainful, high, imperious, lofty, overweening, proud, scornful, snobbish, supercilious

haul 1. *v.* drag, draw, hale, heave, lug, pull, tow, trail, tug **2.** *n.* booty, catch, find, gain, harvest, loot, spoils, takings, yield

haunt *v.* **1.** visit, walk **2.** beset, come back, obsess, plague, possess, prey on, recur, torment, trouble **3.** frequent, repair, resort, visit ~*n.* **4.** rendezvous, resort

haunting eerie, evocative, nostalgic, poignant, recurrent, unforgettable

have 1. hold, keep, obtain, occupy, own, possess, retain **2.** endure, enjoy, experience, feel, meet with, suffer, sustain, undergo **3. have to** be bound, be compelled, be forced, be obliged, have got to, must, ought, should

haven 1. harbour, port **2.** *Fig.* asylum, refuge, retreat, sanctuary, shelter

havoc 1. damage, desolation, destruction, devastation, ravages, ruin, slaughter, waste, wreck **2.** chaos, confusion, disorder, disruption, mayhem, shambles

hazardous dangerous, difficult, insecure, perilous, precarious, risky, unsafe

haze cloud, film, fog, mist, obscurity, smokiness, steam, vapour

hazy 1. blurry, cloudy, dim, dull, faint, foggy, misty, nebulous, obscure, overcast, smoky, veiled **2.** *Fig.* fuzzy, indefinite, indistinct, loose, muddled, nebulous, uncertain, unclear, vague

head *n.* **1.** pate, skull **2.** captain, chief, chieftain, commander, director, leader, manager, master, principal, supervisor **3.** apex, crest, crown, height, peak, pitch, summit, tip, top, vertex **4.** ability, aptitude, brain, capacity, faculty, flair, intellect, mind, talent, thought **5.** branch, category, class, department, division, heading, section, subject, topic ~*adj.* **6.** arch, chief, first, foremost, front, highest, leading, main, premier, prime, principal, supreme, topmost ~*v.* **7.** be *or* go first, cap, crown, lead, precede, top **8.** command, control, direct, govern, guide, lead, manage, rule, run, supervise

headache bane, bother, inconvenience, nuisance, problem, trouble, vexation, worry

heading 1. caption, headline, name, rubric, title **2.** category, class, division, section

headlong 1. *adj.* dangerous, hasty, impetuous, impulsive, precipitate, reckless, thoughtless **2.** *adv.* hastily, heedlessly, helter-skelter, hurriedly, pell-mell, precipitately, rashly, wildly

headstrong contrary, heedless, impulsive, intractable, obstinate, perverse, rash, reckless, self-willed, stubborn, ungovernable, unruly, wilful

headway advance, improvement, progress, way

heal 1. cure, make well, mend, remedy, restore, treat **2.** compose, harmonize, patch up, reconcile, settle, soothe

health fitness, robustness, soundness, strength, vigour, wellbeing

healthy active, blooming, fit, flourishing, hale, hardy, robust, sound, strong, sturdy, vigorous, well

heap 1. *n.* accumulation, collection, hoard, lot, mass, mound, mountain, pile, stack, store **2.** *v.* accumulate, amass, augment, bank, collect, gather, hoard, increase, mound, pile, stack, stockpile, store

hear 1. attend, catch, eavesdrop, hark, heed, listen to, overhear **2.** ascertain, be informed, discover, find out, gather, learn, pick up, understand **3.** *Law* examine, investigate, judge, try

hearing 1. audition, ear, perception **2.** audience, audition, interview **3.** earshot, range, reach, sound **4.** inquiry, investigation, review, trial

hearsay buzz, gossip, report, rumour, talk

heart 1. affection, benevolence, compassion, concern, humanity, love, pity, tenderness, understanding **2.** boldness, bravery, courage, mettle, mind, nerve, pluck, purpose, resolution, spirit, will **3.** centre, core, crux, essence, hub, kernel, marrow, middle, nucleus, pith, quintessence, root **4. by heart** by memory, by rote, off pat, parrot-fashion (*Inf.*), pat, word for word **5. take heart** be comforted, be encouraged, brighten up, cheer up, perk up, revive

heartbreaking agonizing, bitter, disappointing, distressing, grievous, pitiful, poignant, sad, tragic

heartbroken crushed, dejected, desolate, despondent, disappointed, disconsolate, dispirited, downcast, grieved, miserable

heartfelt ardent, cordial, deep, devout, earnest, fervent, genuine, honest, profound, sincere, unfeigned, warm

heartily cordially, deeply, feelingly, genuinely, profoundly, sincerely, unfeignedly, warmly

heartless brutal, callous, cold, cruel, hard, harsh, inhuman, merciless, pitiless, uncaring, unfeeling, unkind

hearty 1. affable, ardent, cordial, eager, effusive, friendly, generous, genial, jovial, unreserved, warm **2.** active, energetic, hale, hardy, healthy, robust, sound, strong, vigorous, well

heat *n.* **1.** fever, sultriness, swelter, torridity, warmness, warmth **2.** *Fig.* agitation, ardour, excitement, fervour, fever, fury, intensity, passion, vehemence, violence, warmth, zeal ~*v.* **3.** flush, glow, grow hot, make hot, reheat, warm up **4.** animate, excite, impassion, inflame, inspirit, rouse, stimulate, stir, warm

heated angry, bitter, excited, fierce, fiery, frenzied, furious, intense, passionate, raging, stormy, vehement, violent

heathen *n.* **1.** idolater, infidel, pagan, unbeliever **2.** barbarian, philistine, savage ~*adj.* **3.** godless, heathenish, idolatrous, infidel, irreligious, pagan **4.** barbaric, philistine, savage, uncivilized

heave 1. drag, elevate, haul, hoist, lever, lift, pull, raise, tug **2.** cast, fling, hurl, pitch, send, sling, throw, toss

heaven *Fig.* bliss, dreamland, ecstasy, enchantment, happiness, paradise, rapture, transport, utopia

heavenly *Inf.* beautiful, blissful, delightful, entrancing, exquisite, glorious, lovely, rapturous, ravishing, sublime, wonderful

heavily 1. awkwardly, clumsily, ponderously **2.** laboriously, painfully **3.** completely, decisively, roundly, thoroughly, utterly

heaviness 1. gravity, weight **2.** grievousness, oppressiveness, severity, weightiness **3.** deadness, dullness, languor, lassitude, numbness, sluggishness, torpor

heavy 1. bulky, massive, ponderous, portly, weighty **2.** burdensome, difficult, grievous, hard, harsh, intolerable, laborious, onerous, oppressive, severe, tedious, vexatious, wearisome **3.** apathetic, drowsy, dull, inactive, indolent, inert, listless, slow, sluggish, stupid, torpid, wooden **4.** burdened, encumbered, laden, loaded, oppressed, weighted

heckle disrupt, interrupt, jeer, pester, shout down, taunt

hectic boisterous, chaotic, excited, fevered, feverish, flurrying, frantic, frenetic, frenzied, heated, riotous, turbulent, wild

hedge *n.* **1.** hedgerow, quickset **2.** barrier, boundary, screen, windbreak ~*v.* **3.** border, edge, enclose, fence, surround **4.** block, confine, hem in, hinder, obstruct, restrict **5.** dodge, duck, equivocate, evade, prevaricate, quibble, sidestep, temporize

heed 1. *n.* attention, care, caution, consideration, ear, mind, note, notice, regard, respect, thought, watchfulness **2.** *v.* attend, consider, follow, listen to, mark, mind, note, obey, observe, regard

heedless careless, imprudent, inattentive, incautious, negligent, oblivious, rash, reckless, thoughtless, unmindful

heel 1. crust, end, remainder, rump, stub, stump **2. down at heel** dowdy, impoverished, rundown, seedy, shabby, slipshod, slovenly, worn

height 1. altitude, elevation, highness, loftiness, stature **2.** apex, apogee, crest, crown, hill, mountain, peak, pinnacle, summit, top, vertex, zenith **3.** acme, dignity, eminence, exaltation, grandeur, loftiness, prominence

heighten add to, aggravate, amplify, augment, enhance, improve, increase, intensify, magnify, sharpen, strengthen

hell 1. abyss, bottomless pit, infernal regions, inferno, lower world, nether world, underworld **2.** agony, anguish, martyrdom, misery, nightmare, ordeal, suffering, torment, trial, wretchedness

hellish damnable, damned, devilish, diabolical, fiendish, infernal

help *v.* **1.** abet, aid, assist, back, befriend, cooperate, promote, relieve, save, second, serve, stand by, succour, support **2.** alleviate, ameliorate, cure, ease, facilitate, heal, improve, mitigate, relieve, remedy, restore ~*n.* **3.** advice, aid, assistance, avail, benefit, cooperation, guidance, service, support, use, utility

helper aide, ally, assistant, attendant, auxiliary, collaborator, colleague, deputy, helpmate, mate, partner, right-hand man, second, supporter

helpful 1. beneficial, constructive, favourable, fortunate, practical, productive, profitable, serviceable, timely, useful **2.** beneficent, benevolent, caring, friendly, kind, supportive, sympathetic

helping *n.* piece, plateful, portion, ration, serving

helpless 1. abandoned, defenceless, dependent, destitute, exposed, forlorn, vulnerable **2.** disabled, feeble, impotent, incapable, incompetent, infirm, paralysed, powerless, unfit, weak

hem border, edge, fringe, margin, trimming

hence ergo, therefore, thus

henceforth from now on, hence, hereafter, hereinafter, in the future

herald *n.* **1.** crier, messenger **2.** forerunner, harbinger, indication, omen, precursor, sign, signal, token

herd 1. *n.* collection, crowd, crush, drove, flock, horde, mass, mob, multitude, press, swarm, throng **2.** *v.* assemble, associate, collect, congregate, flock, gather, huddle, muster, rally

hereafter after this, from now on, henceforth, in future

hereditary family, genetic, inborn, inbred, inheritable

heredity constitution, genetics, inheritance

heresy apostasy, error, impiety, schism, unorthodoxy

heretic apostate, dissenter, renegade, sectarian, separatist

heritage bequest, birthright, endowment, estate, inheritance, legacy, lot, patrimony, portion, share, tradition

hermit anchorite, eremite, monk, recluse, solitary

hero 1. celebrity, champion, exemplar, great man, idol, star, superstar, victor **2.** leading man, male lead, protagonist

heroic bold, brave, courageous, daring, doughty, fearless, gallant, intrepid, undaunted, valiant

heroine 1. celebrity, goddess, ideal **2.** diva, female lead, leading lady, prima donna

heroism boldness, bravery, courage, daring, fearlessness, fortitude, gallantry, prowess, spirit, valour

hesitant diffident, doubtful, half-hearted, halting, irresolute, reluctant, sceptical, shy, timid, uncertain, unsure, vacillating, wavering

hesitate be uncertain, delay, dither, doubt, pause, vacillate, wait, waver

hesitation delay, doubt, indecision, irresolution, uncertainty, vacillation

hew 1. axe, chop, cut, hack, lop, split **2.** carve, fashion, form, make, model, sculpt, sculpture, shape, smooth

heyday bloom, flowering, pink, prime

hidden abstruse, close, concealed, covert, cryptic, dark, masked, mysterious, mystic, mystical, obscure, occult, recondite, secret, shrouded, unseen, veiled

hide 1. cache, conceal, hole up, lie low, secrete, take cover **2.** bury, cloak, conceal, cover, disguise, eclipse, mask, obscure, screen, shelter, shroud, veil

hidebound conventional, narrow-minded, rigid, set

hideous ghastly, grim, grisly, grotesque, gruesome, monstrous, repulsive, revolting, ugly, unsightly

hiding *n.* beating, caning, drubbing, flogging, spanking, thrashing, whipping

high *adj.* **1.** elevated, lofty, soaring, steep, tall, towering **2.** excessive, extreme, great, sharp, strong **3.** arch, chief, eminent, exalted, important, influential, leading, powerful, prominent, ruling, significant, superior **4.** costly, dear, expensive, high-priced **5.** acute, penetrating, piercing, piping, sharp, shrill, soprano, strident, treble **6. high and dry** abandoned, bereft, destitute, helpless, stranded **7. high and low** all over, everywhere, exhaustively ~*adv.* **8.** aloft, at great height, far up, way up

highbrow 1. *n.* aesthete, intellectual, mastermind, savant, scholar **2.** *adj.* bookish, cultivated, cultured, deep

high-flown elaborate, extravagant, florid, grandiose, lofty, overblown, pretentious

high-handed arbitrary, autocratic, despotic, domineering, imperious, oppressive, overbearing

highlight 1. *n.* climax, feature, focus, peak 2. *v.* accent, emphasize, feature, set off, show up, spotlight, stress, underline

highly decidedly, eminently, extraordinarily, extremely, greatly, immensely, supremely, tremendously, vastly, very, very much

high-powered aggressive, driving, dynamic, effective, energetic, forceful, go-ahead, vigorous

high-speed brisk, express, fast, quick, rapid, swift

high-spirited boisterous, bold, bouncy, daring, dashing, energetic, exuberant, frolicsome, fun-loving, gallant, lively, mettlesome, spirited, vibrant, vital, vivacious

high spirits abandon, exhilaration, exuberance, good cheer, hilarity

hijack commandeer, expropriate, seize, skyjack, take over

hike 1. *v.* back-pack, ramble, tramp, walk 2. *n.* march, ramble, tramp, trek, walk

hilarious amusing, comical, convivial, entertaining, funny, gay, happy, humorous, jolly, jovial, joyful, merry, noisy

hilarity amusement, boisterousness, cheerfulness, conviviality, exhilaration, exuberance, gaiety, glee, high spirits, jollification, jollity, joviality, joyousness, laughter, levity, merriment, mirth

hill elevation, eminence, fell, height, knoll, mound, mount, prominence, tor

hilt grip, haft, handgrip, handle, helve

hinder arrest, check, debar, delay, deter, encumber, hamper, handicap, impede, interrupt, obstruct, oppose, prevent, retard, stop, thwart

hindmost concluding, final, furthest, last, trailing, ultimate

hindrance bar, barrier, check, deterrent, difficulty, drag, drawback, encumbrance, handicap, hitch, impediment, limitation, obstacle, snag, stoppage

hinge *v.* depend, hang, pivot, rest, turn

hint *n.* 1. clue, implication, indication, inkling, innuendo, intimation, mention, reminder, suggestion, tip-off 2. advice, help, pointer, suggestion, tip 3. breath, dash, *soupçon*, speck, suggestion, suspicion, taste, tinge, touch, trace, whiff, whisper ~*v.* 4. allude, cue, imply, indicate, intimate, mention, prompt, suggest, tip off

hire *v.* 1. appoint, employ, engage, sign up, take on 2. charter, engage, lease, let, rent ~*n.* 3. charge, cost, fee, price, rent, rental

hiss *n.* 1. buzz, hissing, sibilance 2. boo, catcall, contempt, derision, jeer ~*v.* 3. rasp, shrill, sibilate, wheeze, whirr, whistle, whiz 4. boo, catcall, condemn, damn, decry, deride, hoot, jeer, mock, revile, ridicule

historic celebrated, extraordinary, famous, momentous, notable, outstanding, remarkable, significant

history account, annals, chronicle, memoirs, narration, narrative, recital, record, relation, saga, story

hit *v.* 1. bang, batter, beat, cuff, flog, knock, lob, punch, slap, smack, sock (*Sl.*), strike, swat, thump, whack 2. bang into, bump, collide with, crash against, run into, smash into ~*n.* 3. blow, bump, clash, cuff, impact, knock, rap, shot, slap, smack, stroke 4. *Inf.* sellout, sensation, success, triumph, winner

hitch 1. *v.* attach, connect, couple, fasten, harness, join, make fast, tether, tie, unite, yoke 2. *n.* catch, check, delay, difficulty, drawback, hindrance, hold-up, impediment, mishap, problem, snag, stoppage, trouble

hitherto heretofore, previously, so far, thus far, till now, until now, up to now

hit off capture, catch, impersonate, mimic, represent

hit on *or* **upon** arrive at, chance upon, discover, guess, invent, realize, stumble on

hit or miss aimless, casual, cursory, haphazard, indiscriminate, random, uneven

hit out (at) assail, attack, castigate, condemn, denounce, lash out

hoard 1. *n.* cache, fund, heap, mass, pile, reserve, stockpile, store, supply 2. *v.* accumulate, amass, buy up, cache, collect, deposit, garner, gather, hive, lay up, put by, save, stockpile, store, treasure

hoarse croaky, grating, gravelly, growling, gruff, guttural, harsh, husky, rasping, raucous, rough, throaty

hoax cheat, deception, fraud, imposture, joke, practical joke, prank, ruse, swindle, trick

hobby activity, diversion, pastime, relaxation, sideline

hoist 1. *v.* elevate, erect, heave, lift, raise, rear 2. *n.* crane, elevator, lift, tackle, winch

hold *v.* 1. have, keep, maintain, occupy, own, possess, retain 2. adhere, clasp, cleave, clinch, cling, clutch, cradle, embrace, enfold, grasp, grip, stick 3. arrest, bind, check, confine, curb, detain, imprison, restrain, stay, stop, suspend 4. assume, believe, consider, deem, entertain, esteem, judge, maintain, presume, reckon, regard, think, view 5. continue, endure, last, persevere, persist, remain, resist, stay, wear 6. assemble, call, carry on, celebrate, conduct, convene, have, run 7. bear, brace, carry, prop, shoulder, support, sustain, take 8. accommodate, comprise, contain, seat, take ~*n.* 9. clasp, clutch, grasp, grip 10. footing, leverage, prop, purchase, stay, support, vantage

hold back check, control, curb, inhibit, repress, restrain, suppress

holder bearer, custodian, incumbent, keeper, occupant, owner, possessor, proprietor, purchaser

hold forth declaim, descant, discourse, harangue, lecture, orate, preach, speak, speechify

hold off 1. avoid, defer, delay, keep from, postpone, put off, refrain 2. fend off, keep off, rebuff, repel, repulse

hold out 1. extend, give, offer, present, proffer 2. carry on, continue, endure, hang on, last, persevere, persist, stand fast, withstand

hold over adjourn, defer, delay, postpone, put off, suspend, waive

hold-up bottleneck, delay, difficulty, hitch, obstruction, setback, snag, stoppage, trouble, wait

hold up 1. delay, detain, hinder, impede, retard, set back, slow down, stop 2. brace, buttress, jack up, prop, shore up, support, sustain

hold with agree to *or* with, approve of, countenance, subscribe to, support

hole 1. breach, break, crack, fissure, gap, opening, outlet, puncture, rent, split, tear, vent 2. defect, error, fallacy, fault, flaw

holiday 1. break, leave, recess, time off, vacation 2. celebration, feast, festival, fête, gala, saint's day

holiness devoutness, divinity, godliness, piety, purity, sanctity, spirituality

hollow *adj.* 1. empty, unfilled, vacant, void 2. concave, depressed, indented, sunken 3. deep, dull, flat, low, muffled, muted, rumbling, toneless 4. empty, fruitless, futile, pointless, useless, vain, worthless ~*n.* 5. basin, bowl, cave, cavern, cavity, crater, cup, dent, depression, hole, indentation, pit, trough 6. bottom, dale, dell, dingle, glen, valley

holy devout, divine, faithful, godly, hallowed, pious, pure, religious, righteous, saintly, sublime, virtuous

home 1. abode, dwelling, habitation, house, residence 2. birthplace, family, fireside, hearth, homestead, home town, household 3. element, habitat, haunt, range, territory 4. **at home** at ease, comfortable, familiar, relaxed 5. **at home in, on,** *or* **with** conversant with, knowledgeable, proficient, skilled, well-versed

homeland fatherland, motherland, native land

homespun artless, coarse, homely, inelegant, plain, rough, rude, rustic, unpolished

homicidal deadly, lethal, mortal, murderous

homicide bloodshed, killing, manslaughter, murder, slaying

homogeneity comparability, consistency, oneness, sameness, similarity, uniformity

homogeneous akin, alike, cognate, comparable, consistent, identical, kindred, similar, uniform, unvarying

honest 1. decent, ethical, high-minded, honourable, law-abiding, reliable, reputable, scrupulous, trustworthy, trusty, truthful, upright, veracious, virtuous 2. equitable, fair, impartial, just 3. candid, direct, forthright, frank, open, outright, plain, sincere

honestly 1. by fair means, cleanly, ethically, honourably, in good faith, lawfully, legally, legitimately, on the level (*Inf.*), with clean hands 2. candidly, frankly, in all sincerity, in plain English, plainly, straight (out), to one's face, truthfully

honesty fidelity, honour, integrity, morality, probity, rectitude, reputability, straightness, trustworthiness, truthfulness, uprightness, veracity, virtue

honour *n.* 1. credit, dignity, distinction, esteem, fame, glory, prestige, rank, renown, reputation, repute 2. acclaim, accolade, commendation, deference, homage, kudos, praise, recognition, regard, respect, reverence, tribute 3. decency, fairness, goodness, integrity, morality, probity, rectitude, uprightness 4. compliment, credit, favour, pleasure, privilege 5. chastity, innocence, modesty, purity, virginity, virtue ~*v.* 6. admire, adore, appreciate, esteem, exalt, glorify, hallow, prize, respect, revere, reverence, value, venerate, worship

honourable 1. ethical, fair, honest, just, moral, principled, true, trustworthy, trusty, upright, upstanding, virtuous 2. eminent, great, illustrious, noble, notable, noted, prestigious, renowned, venerable

honours awards, decorations, dignities, distinctions, laurels, titles

hoodwink befool, cheat, cozen, delude, dupe, fool, hoax, impose, mislead, swindle, trick

hook *n.* 1. catch, clasp, fastener, hasp, holder, link, lock, peg 2. noose, snare, springe, trap ~*v.* 3. catch, clasp, fasten, fix, hasp, secure 4. catch, enmesh, ensnare, entrap, snare, trap

hooligan delinquent, rowdy, ruffian, tough, vandal

hoop band, circlet, girdle, loop, ring, wheel

hoot *n.* 1. call, cry, toot 2. boo, catcall, hiss, jeer, yell ~*v.* 3. boo, catcall, condemn, decry, denounce, hiss, howl down, jeer, yell at 4. cry, scream, shout, shriek, toot, whoop, yell

hop 1. *v.* bound, caper, dance, jump, leap, skip, spring, vault 2. *n.* bounce, bound, jump, leap, skip, spring, step, vault

hope 1. *n.* ambition, anticipation, assumption, belief, confidence, desire, dream, expectancy, faith, longing 2. *v.* anticipate, aspire, await, believe, desire, expect, foresee, long, rely, trust

hopeful 1. assured, buoyant, confident, expectant, optimistic, sanguine 2. auspicious, bright, cheerful, encouraging, heartening, promising, propitious, reassuring, rosy

hopefully 1. confidently, expectantly, optimistically, sanguinely 2. conceivably, expectedly, feasibly, probably

hopeless 1. defeatist, dejected, desperate, despondent, disconsolate, downhearted, forlorn, pessimistic 2. helpless, incurable, irremediable, irreparable, irreversible, lost 3. forlorn, futile, impossible, impracticable, pointless, unattainable, useless, vain

horde band, crew, crowd, drove, gang, host, mob, multitude, pack, press, swarm, throng, troop

horizon 1. skyline, vista 2. compass, perspective, prospect, purview, range, realm, scope, sphere, stretch

horrible 1. abominable, appalling, awful, dreadful, fearful, frightful, ghastly, grim, grisly, gruesome, heinous, hideous, horrid, repulsive, revolting, shameful, shocking, terrible 2. awful, cruel, disagreeable, dreadful, mean, nasty, terrible, unkind, unpleasant

horrid 1. awful, disgusting, dreadful, horrible, nasty, offensive, terrible, unpleasant 2. appalling, formidable, frightening, harrowing, hideous, horrific, odious, repulsive, revolting, shocking, terrifying

horrify 1. alarm, frighten, intimidate, petrify, scare, terrify 2. appal, disgust, dismay, outrage, shock, sicken

horror 1. alarm, apprehension, awe, consternation, dismay, dread, fear, fright, panic, terror 2. aversion, detestation, disgust, hatred, loathing, repugnance, revulsion

horseman cavalier, dragoon, equestrian, rider

hospitable amicable, bountiful, cordial, friendly, generous, genial, gracious, kind, liberal, sociable, welcoming

hospitality cheer, conviviality, cordiality, friendliness, sociability, warmth, welcome

host[1] entertainer, innkeeper, landlord, proprietor

host[2] army, array, drove, horde, legion, multitude, myriad, swarm, throng

hostage captive, gage, pawn, pledge, prisoner, security, surety

hostile 1. antagonistic, contrary, inimical, malevolent, opposed, unkind, warlike 2. adverse, alien, unfriendly, unsympathetic, unwelcoming

hostilities conflict, fighting, state of war, war, warfare

hostility animosity, animus, antagonism, antipathy, aversion, detestation, enmity, hatred, ill will, malevolence, malice, opposition, unfriendliness

hot 1. boiling, burning, fiery, flaming, heated, roasting, scalding, scorching, searing, steaming, sultry, sweltering, torrid, warm 2. acrid, biting, peppery, piquant, pungent, sharp, spicy

hotchpotch farrago, hash, jumble, medley, *mélange*, mess, mishmash, mixture, olio, potpourri

hothead daredevil, desperado, tearaway

hot-headed fiery, foolhardy, hasty, impetuous, precipitate, rash, reckless, unruly, volatile

hound *v.* chase, drive, give chase, hunt, hunt down, pursue

house *n.* 1. abode, building, dwelling, edifice, home, residence 2. family, household, ménage 3. ancestry, clan, dynasty, kindred, line, lineage, race, tribe 4. business, company, concern, establishment, firm, organization 5. hotel, inn, public house, tavern *~v.* 6. accommodate, billet, board, domicile, harbour, lodge, put up, quarter, take in

household *n.* family, home, house, ménage

housing dwellings, homes, houses

hovel cabin, den, hole, hut, shack, shanty, shed

hover 1. drift, float, flutter, fly, hang, poise 2. linger

however after all, anyhow, but, nevertheless, nonetheless, notwithstanding, still, though, yet

howl 1. *n.* bay, bellow, clamour, cry, groan, hoot, outcry, roar, scream, shriek, wail, yelp, yowl 2. *v.* bellow, cry, cry out, lament, roar, scream, shout, shriek, wail, weep, yell, yelp

howler blunder, error, malapropism, mistake

huddle *n.* 1. crowd, disorder, heap, jumble, mass, mess, muddle 2. conference, discussion, meeting *~v.* 3. cluster, converge, crowd, flock, gather, press, throng 4. crouch, cuddle, curl up, nestle, snuggle

hue colour, dye, shade, tincture, tinge, tint, tone

hug *v.* 1. clasp, cuddle, embrace, enfold, hold close, squeeze 2. cherish, cling, hold onto, nurse, retain *~n.* 3. bear hug, clasp, clinch (*Sl.*), embrace, squeeze

huge colossal, enormous, gargantuan, giant, gigantic, great, immense, large, massive, mountainous, prodigious, stupendous, tremendous, vast

hulk derelict, frame, hull, shell, shipwreck, wreck

hull *n.* 1. body, casing, covering, frame, framework, skeleton 2. husk, peel, pod, rind, shell, shuck, skin

hum 1. buzz, drone, mumble, murmur, purr, sing, throb, thrum, vibrate, whir 2. be active, be busy, bustle, buzz, move, pulsate, pulse, stir, vibrate

human 1. fleshly, manlike, mortal 2. compassionate, considerate, fallible, forgivable, humane, kind, kindly, natural

humane benign, charitable, clement, compassionate, forbearing, forgiving, gentle, good, kind, lenient, merciful, mild, sympathetic, tender, understanding

humanity flesh, man, mankind, men, mortality, people

humble 1. meek, modest, submissive, unostentatious 2. common, commonplace, insignificant, low, low-born, lowly, mean, modest, obscure, ordinary, poor, simple

humbug 1. bluff, cheat, deceit, dodge, feint, fraud, hoax, ruse, sham, swindle, trick, trickery, wile 2. charlatan, cheat, fraud, impostor, quack, swindler, trickster

humdrum boring, dreary, dull, mundane, ordinary, repetitious, routine, tedious, tiresome, unvaried

humid clammy, damp, dank, moist, muggy, steamy, sticky, sultry, wet

humiliate abase, bring low, chagrin, chasten, crush, debase, degrade, discomfit, disgrace, embarrass, humble, shame, subdue

humility diffidence, lowliness, meekness, modesty, servility, submissiveness

humorist comedian, comic, droll, jester, joker, wag, wit

humorous amusing, comic, comical, entertaining, facetious, farcical, funny, hilarious, laughable, ludicrous, merry, playful, pleasant, witty

humour *n.* 1. amusement, comedy, drollery, facetiousness, fun, funniness, wit 2. comedy, farce, jesting, jests, jokes, joking, pleasantry, wit, wittiness 3. mood, spirits, temper 4. bent, bias, fancy, freak, mood, propensity, quirk, vagary, whim *~v.* 5. accommodate, cosset, favour, flatter, gratify, indulge, mollify, pamper, spoil

hump bulge, bump, knob, mound, projection, swelling

hunch feeling, idea, impression, inkling, intuition, premonition, presentiment, suspicion

hunger *n.* 1. appetite, emptiness, famine, ravenousness, starvation, voracity 2. appetite, craving, desire, itch, lust, yearning *~v.* 3. crave, desire, hanker, itch, long, pine, starve, thirst, want, wish, yearn

hungry 1. empty, famishing, hollow, ravenous, starved, starving, voracious 2. avid, covetous, craving, desirous, eager, greedy, keen, yearning

hunk block, chunk, lump, mass, piece, slab, wedge

hunt *v.* 1. chase, hound, pursue, stalk, track, trail 2. ferret about, forage, look, scour, search, seek, try to find *~n.* 3. chase, hunting, investigation, pursuit, quest, search

hurdle *n.* 1. barricade, barrier, fence, hedge, wall 2. barrier, difficulty, hindrance, impediment, obstacle, snag

hurl cast, fire, fling, heave, launch, pitch, project, propel, send, shy, sling, throw, toss

hurricane cyclone, gale, storm, tempest, tornado, typhoon, windstorm

hurried brief, cursory, hasty, hectic, perfunctory, precipitate, quick, rushed, short, slapdash, speedy, superficial, swift

hurry *v.* 1. dash, fly, rush, scurry 2. accelerate, expedite, goad, hasten, hustle, push on, quicken, urge *~n.* 3. bustle, celerity, commotion, dispatch, expedition, flurry, haste, quickness, rush, speed, urgency

hurt *v.* 1. bruise, damage, disable, harm, impair, injure, mar, spoil, wound 2. ache, be sore, burn, pain, smart, sting, throb 3. afflict, aggrieve, annoy, distress, grieve, pain, sadden, sting, upset, wound *~n.* 4. discomfort, distress, pain, pang, soreness, suffering 5. bruise, sore, wound

husbandry agriculture, cultivation, farming, tillage

hush *v.* 1. mute, quieten, silence, still, suppress 2. allay, appease, calm, compose, mollify, soothe *~n.* 3. calm, peace, quiet, silence, stillness, tranquillity

husky croaking, croaky, gruff, guttural, harsh, hoarse, rasping, raucous, rough, throaty

hustle bustle, crowd, elbow, force, haste, hasten, hurry, impel, jog, jostle, push, rush, shove, thrust

hut cabin, den, hovel, lean-to, refuge, shanty, shed, shelter

hygiene cleanliness, sanitation

hygienic aseptic, clean, germ-free, healthy, pure, sanitary, sterile

hypnotize 1. mesmerize 2. entrance, fascinate, magnetize, spellbind

hypocrisy cant, deceit, deception, dissembling, duplicity, falsity, insincerity, pharisaism, pretence, two-facedness

hypocrite charlatan, deceiver, dissembler, fraud, impostor, pharisee, pretender

hypocritical canting, deceitful, deceptive, dissembling, duplicitous, false, fraudulent, hollow, insincere, sanctimonious, specious, spurious, two-faced

hypothesis assumption, postulate, premise, proposition, theory, thesis

hypothetical academic, assumed, conjectural, imaginary, putative

hysteria agitation, delirium, frenzy, hysterics, madness, panic, unreason

hysterical berserk, convulsive, crazed, distracted, distraught, frantic, frenzied, mad, overwrought, raving, uncontrollable

I

icy 1. arctic, biting, bitter, chilly, cold, freezing, frosty, frozen over, ice-cold, raw 2. *Fig.* aloof, cold, distant, forbidding, frigid, frosty, glacial, hostile, indifferent, steely, stony, unfriendly

idea 1. concept, conclusion, fancy, impression, judgment, perception, thought, understanding 2. belief, conviction, doctrine, interpretation, notion, opinion, teaching, view, viewpoint

ideal *n.* 1. archetype, criterion, epitome, example, exemplar, last word, model, paradigm, paragon, pattern, perfection, prototype, standard, standard of perfection *~adj.* 2. classic, complete, model, perfect, quintessential, supreme 3. abstract, conceptual, hypothetical, intellectual, mental, theoretical, transcendental

idealist *n.* romantic, visionary

identical alike, duplicate, equal, equivalent, indistinguishable, interchangeable, like, self-same, the same, twin

identification 1. cataloguing, labelling, naming, pinpointing, recognition 2. credentials, papers

identify catalogue, classify, diagnose, label, make out, name, pick out, pinpoint, place, recognize, spot, tag

identity distinctiveness, existence, individuality, oneness, particularity, personality, self, selfhood, singularity, uniqueness

idiocy fatuity, fatuousness, foolishness, imbecility, insanity, lunacy

idiom 1. expression, locution, phrase 2. jargon, language, parlance, style, talk, usage, vernacular

idiosyncrasy characteristic, eccentricity, habit, mannerism, peculiarity, quirk, trick

idiot ass, cretin, dunderhead, fool, halfwit, imbecile, moron, nitwit, simpleton

idiotic asinine, crazy, fatuous, foolish, halfwitted, imbecile, insane, lunatic, moronic, senseless, stupid

idle *adj.* 1. dead, empty, inactive, jobless, out of work, redundant, stationary, unemployed, unoccupied, unused, vacant 2. indolent, lazy, shiftless, slothful, sluggish 3. frivolous, insignificant, irrelevant, superficial, trivial, unhelpful ~*v.* 4. coast, drift, mark time, shirk, slack, slow down, vegetate

idleness 1. inaction, inactivity, leisure, unemployment 2. hibernation, inertia, laziness, shiftlessness, sloth, sluggishness, torpor 3. lazing, loafing, pottering, time-wasting, trifling

idol deity, god, graven image, image, pagan symbol

idolater 1. heathen, pagan 2. admirer, adorer, devotee, idolizer, votary, worshipper

idolatry adoration, adulation, apotheosis, exaltation, glorification

idolize admire, adore, deify, dote upon, exalt, glorify, hero-worship, look up to, love, revere, reverence, venerate, worship

ignite burn, catch fire, fire, inflame, kindle, light, set fire to

ignominious abject, disgraceful, dishonourable, disreputable, humiliating, indecorous, inglorious, scandalous, shameful, sorry, undignified

ignominy contempt, disgrace, dishonour, disrepute, infamy, obloquy, odium, reproach, shame, stigma

ignorance benightedness, blindness, illiteracy, unenlightenment, unintelligence

ignorant 1. benighted, blind to, inexperienced, innocent, oblivious, unaware, unconscious, unenlightened, uninformed, unknowing, unwitting 2. green, illiterate, naive, unaware, uneducated, unlettered, unread, untaught, untrained, untutored

ignore cold-shoulder, disregard, neglect, overlook, pass over, reject

ill *adj.* 1. ailing, diseased, indisposed, infirm, off-colour, queasy, queer, sick, unwell 2. bad, damaging, evil, foul, harmful, injurious, ruinous, unfortunate, unlucky, vile, wicked, wrong 3. disturbing, ominous, sinister, threatening, unhealthy, unlucky, unpropitious, unwholesome ~*n.* 4. affliction, harm, hurt, injury, misery, misfortune, pain, trial, tribulation, trouble, unpleasantness, woe 5. ailment, complaint, disease, disorder, infirmity, malady, malaise, sickness 6. abuse, badness, cruelty, damage, destruction, evil, malice, mischief, suffering, wickedness ~*adv.* 7. badly, hard, poorly, unfavourably, unfortunately, unluckily

ill-advised foolish, impolitic, imprudent, inappropriate, incautious, indiscreet, injudicious, misguided, overhasty, rash, reckless, unseemly, unwise

ill-bred bad-mannered, boorish, churlish, coarse, crass, discourteous, impolite, indelicate, rude, uncivil, uncouth, ungallant, ungentlemanly, unladylike, unmannerly, unrefined, vulgar

illegal banned, black-market, bootleg, criminal, felonious, forbidden, illicit, lawless, outlawed, prohibited, proscribed, unauthorized, unconstitutional, unlawful, unlicensed, unofficial, wrongful

illegality crime, felony, illicitness, lawlessness, unlawfulness, wrong, wrongness

illegible faint, indecipherable, obscure, scrawled, unreadable

illegitimate 1. illegal, illicit, improper, unconstitutional, unlawful 2. bastard, fatherless, natural

ill-fated blighted, doomed, hapless, ill-omened, luckless, unfortunate, unhappy, unlucky

ill feeling animus, antagonism, bitterness, dissatisfaction, enmity, frustration, hostility, ill will, indignation, offence, rancour, resentment

ill-founded baseless, empty, groundless, idle, unjustified, unproven, unreliable, unsubstantiated, unsupported

ill-humoured acrimonious, crabbed, cross, disagreeable, grumpy, huffy, impatient, irascible, irritable, moody, morose, petulant, sharp, snappish, snappy, sulky, sullen, tart, testy, thin-skinned, touchy, waspish

illicit 1. bootleg, contraband, criminal, felonious, illegal, prohibited, unlawful, unlicensed 2. forbidden, furtive, guilty, immoral, improper, wrong

illiterate benighted, ignorant, uncultured, uneducated

ill-judged foolish, injudicious, misguided, overhasty, rash, unwise

ill-mannered boorish, churlish, coarse, discourteous, impolite, insolent, loutish, rude, uncivil, uncouth, unmannerly

illness affliction, ailment, attack, complaint, disability, disease, disorder, indisposition, infirmity, malady, malaise, poor health, sickness

illogical absurd, fallacious, faulty, inconsistent, incorrect, invalid, irrational, meaningless, senseless, specious, spurious, unreasonable, unsound

ill-treat abuse, damage, harass, harm, harry, injure, maltreat, mishandle, misuse, oppress, wrong

illuminate 1. brighten, light, light up 2. clarify, clear up, elucidate, enlighten, explain, instruct, make clear

illuminating explanatory, helpful, informative, instructive, revealing

illumination awareness, clarification, enlightenment, perception, revelation, understanding

illusion 1. chimera, daydream, fantasy, hallucination, mirage, mockery, phantasm, semblance 2. delusion, error, fallacy, fancy

illusory *or* **illusive** apparent, beguiling, deceitful, delusive, fallacious, false, misleading, mistaken, sham, unreal, untrue

illustrate 1. bring home, clarify, demonstrate, elucidate, emphasize, exhibit, explain, interpret, show 2. adorn, decorate, depict, draw, picture, sketch

illustrated decorated, graphic, pictorial, pictured

illustration 1. analogy, case, clarification, demonstration, elucidation, example, explanation, instance, specimen 2. adornment, decoration, figure, picture, plate, sketch

illustrious brilliant, celebrated, distinguished, eminent, famous, glorious, great, noble, notable, noted, prominent, remarkable, renowned, signal, splendid

ill will acrimony, animosity, antagonism, antipathy, aversion, dislike, enmity, envy, grudge, hatred, hostility, malice, rancour, resentment, spite, unfriendliness, venom

image 1. appearance, effigy, figure, icon, idol, likeness, picture, portrait, reflection, statue 2. conceit, concept, figure, idea, impression, perception

imaginable conceivable, credible, likely, plausible, possible, thinkable

imaginary assumed, dreamlike, fanciful, fictional, ideal, illusive, illusory, imagined, invented, legendary, made-up, mythological, nonexistent, shadowy, supposed, unreal, unsubstantial, visionary

imagination creativity, enterprise, fancy, ingenuity, insight, inspiration, inventiveness, originality, vision, wit

imaginative clever, creative, dreamy, enterprising, fanciful, ingenious, inspired, inventive, original, poetical, visionary, vivid

imagine conceive, conjure up, create, devise, envisage, frame, invent, picture, plan, project, scheme, think of, think up, visualize

imbecile 1. *n.* bungler, dolt, dotard, fool, halfwit, idiot, moron 2. *adj.* asinine, fatuous, foolish, idiotic, inane, moronic, simple, stupid, thick

imbibe consume, drink, quaff, suck, swallow

imitate affect, ape, burlesque, copy, counterfeit, duplicate, echo, emulate, follow, impersonate, mimic, mirror, mock, parody, personate, repeat, simulate

imitation *n.* 1. aping, copy, counterfeit, echoing, likeness, mimicry, resemblance, simulation 2. fake, forgery, impersonation, impression, mockery, parody, reflection, reproduction, sham, substitution, travesty ~*adj.* 3. artificial, dummy, ersatz, mock, reproduction, sham, simulated, synthetic

imitative copied, derivative, mock, onomatopoeic, parrotlike, plagiarized, put-on, secondhand, simulated, unoriginal

imitator echo, follower, impersonator, impressionist, mimic, parrot, shadow

immaculate 1. clean, impeccable, neat, spruce, trim, unexceptionable 2. faultless, flawless, guiltless, incorrupt, innocent, perfect, pure, sinless, spotless, stainless, unpolluted, unsullied, untarnished, virtuous

immaterial extraneous, impertinent, inapposite, inconsequential, inessential, insignificant, irrelevant, trifling, trivial, unimportant

immature 1. adolescent, crude, green, premature, raw, undeveloped, unformed, unripe, unseasonable, untimely, young 2. callow, childish, inexperienced, infantile, jejune, juvenile, puerile

immaturity crudeness, crudity, greenness, imperfection, rawness, unpreparedness, unripeness

immediate 1. instant, instantaneous 2. adjacent, close, direct, near, nearest, next, recent

immediately at once, directly, forthwith, instantly, now, promptly, right away, this instant, unhesitatingly, without delay

immense colossal, elephantine, enormous, extensive, giant, gigantic, great, huge, infinite, large, mammoth, massive, monumental, prodigious, stupendous, titanic, tremendous, vast

immigrant incomer, newcomer, settler

imminent at hand, close, coming, forthcoming, gathering, impending, looming, menacing, near, threatening

immobile fixed, frozen, immovable, motionless, rigid, riveted, rooted, stable, static, stationary, stiff, still, stolid, unmoving

immobilize cripple, disable, freeze, halt, paralyse, stop, transfix

immoderate enormous, excessive, exorbitant, extreme, inordinate, intemperate, profligate, uncontrolled, undue, unjustified, unreasonable, unrestrained, unwarranted

immodesty 1. coarseness, impurity, indelicacy, lewdness, obscenity 2. audacity, boldness, impudence, shamelessness, temerity

immoral abandoned, bad, corrupt, debauched, degenerate, depraved, evil, impure, indecent, lewd, licentious, nefarious, obscene, profligate, reprobate, sinful, unchaste, unethical, unprincipled, vicious, vile, wicked, wrong

immorality corruption, debauchery, depravity, dissoluteness, evil, licentiousness, profligacy, sin, vice, wickedness

immortal *adj.* 1. abiding, constant, deathless, endless, enduring, eternal, everlasting, imperishable, incorruptible, indestructible, lasting, perennial, perpetual, timeless, undying, unfading ~*n.* 2. god, goddess 3. hero

immortality 1. deathlessness, endlessness, eternity, indestructibility, perpetuity 2. celebrity, fame, glorification, greatness, renown

immovable 1. fast, firm, fixed, jammed, rooted, secure, set, stable, stationary, stuck 2. adamant, constant, inflexible, obdurate, resolute, steadfast, unshakable, unwavering

immune clear, exempt, free, invulnerable, proof (against), protected, resistant, safe, unaffected

immunity amnesty, charter, exemption, franchise, freedom, indemnity, liberty, prerogative, privilege, release, right

impact bang, blow, bump, collision, contact, crash, force, jolt, knock, shock, smash, stroke, thump

impair blunt, damage, deteriorate, diminish, enfeeble, harm,

hinder, injure, lessen, mar, reduce, spoil, undermine, weaken, worsen
impart communicate, convey, disclose, discover, divulge, make known, pass on, relate, reveal, tell
impartial detached, disinterested, equal, equitable, even-handed, fair, just, neutral, objective, open-minded, unbiased, unprejudiced
impartiality detachment, disinterest, dispassion, equality, equity, fairness, neutrality, objectivity
impasse deadlock, stalemate
impassioned ardent, blazing, excited, fervent, fiery, furious, glowing, heated, inflamed, inspired, intense, passionate, rousing, stirring, violent, vivid, warm
impatience haste, heat, impetuosity, intolerance, shortness, vehemence
impatient 1. abrupt, brusque, curt, demanding, edgy, hasty, intolerant, irritable, sudden, testy 2. agog, chafing, eager, fretful, headlong, impetuous
impeach accuse, arraign, blame, censure, charge, denounce, indict, tax
impeccable exact, exquisite, faultless, flawless, incorrupt, innocent, perfect, precise, pure, sinless, stainless
impecunious destitute, indigent, insolvent, penniless
impede bar, block, brake, check, clog, curb, delay, hamper, hinder, obstruct, restrain, retard, stop
impediment bar, barrier, block, check, clog, curb, defect, difficulty, hindrance, obstacle, snag
impel drive, force, incite, induce, influence, instigate, motivate, move, oblige, power, prod, prompt, propel, push, require, spur, stimulate, urge
impending approaching, coming, gathering, imminent, looming, menacing, near, nearing, threatening
imperative compulsory, crucial, essential, insistent, obligatory, pressing, urgent, vital
imperceptible faint, fine, gradual, inaudible, infinitesimal, insensible, invisible, microscopic, minute, shadowy, slight, small, subtle, tiny
imperfect broken, damaged, defective, faulty, flawed, immature, impaired, incomplete, inexact, limited, partial, patchy, sketchy, unfinished
imperfection blemish, defect, deficiency, failing, fault, flaw, frailty, infirmity, shortcoming, stain, taint, weakness
imperial 1. kingly, majestic, princely, queenly, regal, royal, sovereign 2. august, exalted, grand, great, high, lofty, magnificent, noble, superior, supreme
imperil endanger, expose, hazard, jeopardize, risk
impersonal cold, detached, dispassionate, formal, inhuman, neutral, remote
impersonate act, ape, enact, imitate, mimic, personate
impertinence audacity, boldness, brazenness, disrespect, effrontery, impudence, incivility, insolence, rudeness
impertinent bold, brazen, disrespectful, impolite, impudent, insolent, rude, uncivil, unmannerly
imperturbable calm, collected, complacent, composed, cool, sedate, self-possessed, tranquil, unmoved, unruffled
impetuous ardent, eager, fierce, furious, hasty, headlong, impulsive, precipitate, rash, spontaneous, unplanned, unthinking, vehement, violent
impetus 1. goad, impulse, incentive, push, spur, stimulus 2. energy, force, momentum, power
impious godless, irreligious, irreverent, profane, sacrilegious, sinful, ungodly, unholy, wicked
impish elfin, mischievous, puckish, rascally, roguish, sportive, waggish
implant inculcate, infix, infuse, instil, sow
implement 1. *n.* apparatus, appliance, device, gadget, instrument, tool 2. *v.* bring about, carry out, complete, effect, enforce, execute, fulfil, perform, realize
implicate associate, compromise, concern, embroil, entangle, imply, include, incriminate, involve, mire
implication 1. association, connection, entanglement, involvement 2. inference, innuendo, meaning, overtone, presumption, significance, signification, suggestion
implicit contained, implied, inferred, inherent, latent, tacit, understood, unspoken
implied implicit, indirect, inherent, insinuated, suggested, tacit, undeclared, unspoken
implore beg, beseech, crave, entreat, importune, plead with, pray, solicit, supplicate
imply 1. connote, hint, insinuate, intimate, signify, suggest 2. betoken, denote, entail, evidence, import, include, indicate, involve, mean, point to, presuppose
impolite bad-mannered, churlish, discourteous, ill-bred, ill-mannered, indecorous, insolent, loutish, rough, rude, uncivil, ungentlemanly, ungracious, unladylike, unmannerly
impoliteness bad manners, boorishness, discourtesy, insolence, rudeness, unmannerliness
import 1. *n.* bearing, drift, gist, implication, intention, meaning, message, purport, sense, significance, thrust 2. *v.* bring in, introduce, land
importance 1. concern, consequence, import, interest, moment, significance, substance, value, weight 2. distinction, eminence, esteem, influence, mark, pre-eminence, prestige, prominence, standing, status, usefulness, worth
important 1. far-reaching, grave, large, material, momentous, primary, salient, serious, signal, significant, substantial, urgent, weighty 2. eminent, foremost, high-level, high-ranking, influential, leading, notable, noteworthy, outstanding, powerful, pre-eminent, prominent, seminal
importunate clamorous, demanding, dogged, earnest, exigent, insistent, persistent, pressing, urgent
impose decree, establish, exact, fix, institute, introduce, lay, levy, ordain, place, promulgate, put, set
imposing august, commanding, dignified, effective, grand, impressive, majestic, stately, striking
imposition 1. application, decree, laying on, levying, promulgation 2. encroachment, intrusion, liberty, presumption 3. artifice, cheating, deception, fraud, hoax, stratagem, trickery
impossible hopeless, impracticable, inconceivable, unattainable, unobtainable, unthinkable
impostor charlatan, cheat, deceiver, fake, fraud, hypocrite, pretender, quack, rogue, sham, trickster
impotence disability, feebleness, frailty, inability, inadequacy, incapacity, incompetence, ineffectiveness, infirmity, paralysis, powerlessness, uselessness, weakness
impotent disabled, feeble, frail, helpless, incapable, ineffective, infirm, nerveless, paralysed, powerless, unable, weak
impoverish 1. bankrupt, beggar, break, ruin 2. deplete, diminish, drain, exhaust, reduce, sap
impoverished bankrupt, destitute, distressed, impecunious, indigent, necessitous, needy, penurious, poverty-stricken, ruined, straitened
impracticable 1. impossible, unattainable, unfeasible, unworkable 2. awkward, inapplicable, inconvenient, unsuitable, useless
impractical 1. impossible, unrealistic, unserviceable, unworkable, visionary, wild 2. idealistic, romantic, unrealistic, visionary
imprecise careless, equivocal, estimated, fluctuating, hazy, ill-defined, inaccurate, indefinite, indeterminate, inexact, loose, rough, vague
impress affect, excite, influence, inspire, move, stir, strike, sway, touch
impression 1. effect, feeling, impact, influence, reaction, sway 2. belief, concept, conviction, fancy, feeling, hunch, idea, memory, notion, opinion, sense, suspicion 3. imitation, impersonation, parody
impressive exciting, forcible, moving, powerful, stirring, touching
imprint 1. *n.* impression, mark, print, sign, stamp 2. *v.* engrave, establish, etch, fix, impress, print, stamp
imprison confine, constrain, detain, immure, jail, lock up, put away
imprisoned behind bars, captive, confined, immured, incarcerated, in irons, in jail, jailed, locked up, put away
imprisonment confinement, custody, detention, duress, incarceration
improbability doubt, dubiety, uncertainty, unlikelihood
improbable doubtful, dubious, fanciful, far-fetched, implausible, questionable, unbelievable, uncertain, unconvincing, unlikely, weak
impromptu ad-lib, extempore, improvised, offhand, spontaneous, unpremeditated, unprepared, unrehearsed, unscripted
improper 1. impolite, indecent, indecorous, indelicate, risqué, smutty, suggestive, unfitting, unseemly, untoward, vulgar 2. abnormal, false, inaccurate, incorrect, irregular, wrong
impropriety 1. bad taste, indecency, indecorum, unsuitability, vulgarity 2. blunder, faux pas, gaffe, gaucherie, mistake, slip, solecism
improve 1. advance, amend, augment, better, correct, help, mend, polish, rectify, touch up, upgrade 2. develop, enhance, gain strength, increase, pick up, progress, rally, reform, rise
improvement 1. amelioration, amendment, betterment, correction, gain, rectification 2. advance, development, enhancement, increase, progress, rally, recovery, rise
improvisation ad-lib, expedient, impromptu, invention, makeshift
improvise 1. ad-lib, extemporize, invent 2. concoct, contrive, devise, make do
imprudent careless, foolish, heedless, ill-advised, ill-judged, impolitic, improvident, incautious, indiscreet, irresponsible, rash, reckless, unthinking, unwise
impudence audacity, boldness, effrontery, impertinence, insolence, presumption, rudeness, sauciness, shamelessness
impudent audacious, bold, bold-faced, brazen, forward, impertinent, insolent, presumptuous, rude
impulse force, impetus, momentum, movement, pressure, push, stimulus, surge, thrust
impulsive emotional, hasty, headlong, impetuous, instinctive, intuitive, passionate, precipitate, quick, rash
impure 1. adulterated, alloyed, debased, mixed, unrefined 2. contaminated, defiled, dirty, filthy, foul, infected, polluted, sullied, tainted, unclean
impurity 1. adulteration, mixture 2. contamination, defilement, dirtiness, filth, foulness, infection, pollution, taint, uncleanness
imputation accusation, attribution, blame, censure, charge, insinuation, reproach, slander, slur
inability impotence, inadequacy, incapability, incapacity, incompetence, ineptitude, powerlessness
inaccessible impassable, remote, unapproachable, unattainable
inaccuracy 1. imprecision, inexactness, unfaithfulness, unreliability 2. blunder, defect, erratum, error, fault, miscalculation, mistake, slip
inaccurate careless, defective, faulty, imprecise, incorrect, in error, inexact, mistaken, out, unfaithful, unreliable, unsound, wild, wrong

inaction dormancy, idleness, inertia, rest, torpor
inactive abeyant, dormant, idle, immobile, inert, inoperative, jobless, latent, unemployed, unoccupied, unused
inactivity 1. dormancy, hibernation, immobility, inaction, passivity, unemployment 2. dullness, heaviness, indolence, inertia, lassitude, sloth, stagnation, vegetation
inadequacy 1. dearth, deficiency, insufficiency, meagreness, paucity, poverty, scantiness, shortage, skimpiness 2. faultiness, inability, inaptness, incompetence, incompetency, inefficacy, unfitness, unsuitableness
inadequate 1. defective, deficient, faulty, imperfect, incomplete, insubstantial, insufficient, meagre, niggardly, scanty, short, sketchy, skimpy, sparse 2. inapt, incapable, incompetent, unequal, unfitted, unqualified
inadmissible immaterial, inappropriate, incompetent, irrelevant, unacceptable, unallowable, unqualified
inadvisable impolitic, imprudent, inexpedient, injudicious, unwise
inane empty, fatuous, frivolous, futile, idiotic, mindless, puerile, senseless, silly, stupid, trifling, unintelligent, vacuous, vain, vapid, worthless
inanimate cold, dead, defunct, extinct, inactive, inert, lifeless, quiescent, soulless, spiritless
inapplicable inapposite, inappropriate, inapt, irrelevant, unsuitable, unsuited
inappropriate ill-suited, ill-timed, improper, incongruous, malapropos, tasteless, unbecoming, unbefitting, unfit, unfitting, unseemly, unsuitable, untimely
inapt 1. ill-fitted, ill-suited, inappropriate, unsuitable, unsuited 2. awkward, clumsy, dull, gauche, inept, slow, stupid
inarticulate 1. blurred, indistinct, muffled, mumbled, unclear, unintelligible 2. dumb, mute, silent, unspoken, unvoiced, voiceless, wordless 3. faltering, halting, hesitant, poorly spoken
inattentive absent-minded, careless, distracted, distrait, dreamy, heedless, negligent, preoccupied, remiss, thoughtless, vague
inaudible indistinct, low, stifled
inaugural dedicatory, first, initial, introductory, maiden, opening
inaugurate 1. begin, commence, initiate, institute, introduce, launch, originate, set in motion, set up 2. induct, install, instate, invest
inauguration initiation, institution, launch, launching, opening
inauspicious bad, black, discouraging, ill-omened, ominous, unfortunate, unlucky, unpropitious
incalculable boundless, countless, enormous, immense, inestimable, infinite, limitless, measureless, numberless, untold, vast
incapable feeble, incompetent, ineffective, inept, insufficient, unfit, unfitted, unqualified, weak
incapacitate cripple, disable, disqualify, immobilize, paralyse, prostrate
incapacity disqualification, feebleness, impotence, inability, inadequacy, incapability, incompetency, ineffectiveness, powerlessness, unfitness, weakness
incarcerate commit, confine, detain, gaol, immure, impound, imprison, intern, jail, lock up, restrain, restrict
incautious careless, hasty, heedless, improvident, imprudent, impulsive, indiscreet, negligent, precipitate, rash, reckless, thoughtless
incense *v.* anger, enrage, exasperate, excite, inflame, infuriate, irritate, madden, provoke
incensed angry, enraged, exasperated, fuming, furious, indignant, infuriated, irate
incentive bait, encouragement, goad, impetus, impulse, inducement, lure, motivation, motive, spur, stimulus
inception beginning, birth, dawn, initiation, origin, outset, rise, start
incessant ceaseless, constant, continuous, endless, eternal, everlasting, interminable, perpetual, persistent, relentless, unending, unrelenting, unremitting
incident 1. adventure, circumstance, episode, event, fact, happening, matter, occurrence 2. brush, clash, commotion, mishap, scene, skirmish
incidental accidental, casual, chance, fortuitous, odd, random
incipient beginning, developing, embryonic, inceptive, inchoate, starting
incision cut, gash, slash, slit
incisive 1. acute, keen, piercing, trenchant 2. acid, biting, caustic, cutting, mordant, sarcastic, sardonic, satirical, severe, sharp
incite animate, drive, egg on, encourage, excite, goad, impel, inflame, instigate, prompt, provoke, rouse, spur, stimulate, urge
incitement encouragement, goad, impetus, impulse, instigation, motivation, motive, provocation, spur, stimulus
incivility bad manners, discourteousness, disrespect, impoliteness, rudeness
inclement bitter, boisterous, foul, harsh, intemperate, rigorous, rough, severe, stormy, tempestuous
inclination affection, aptitude, bent, bias, desire, disposition, fancy, fondness, leaning, liking, partiality, penchant, predilection, predisposition, proclivity, propensity, stomach, taste, tendency, turn, wish
incline *v.* 1. be disposed, bias, influence, persuade, prejudice, sway, tend, turn 2. bend, bevel, cant, deviate, diverge, lean, slant, slope, tend, tilt, tip, veer ~*n.* 3. ascent, descent, dip, grade, gradient, ramp, rise, slope
inclined apt, disposed, given, liable, likely, minded, prone, willing
inclose *see* ENCLOSE
include comprehend, comprise, contain, cover, embody, embrace, encompass, incorporate, involve, take in
inclusion incorporation, insertion
inclusive all in, all together, blanket, comprehensive, full, general, overall, sweeping, umbrella
incoherent confused, disjointed, inarticulate, inconsistent, loose, muddled, rambling, uncoordinated, unintelligible, wandering, wild
income earnings, gains, interest, means, pay, proceeds, profits, receipts, revenue, salary, takings, wages
incoming approaching, arriving, entering, homeward, landing, new
incomparable inimitable, matchless, paramount, peerless, superlative, supreme, unequalled, unmatched, unrivalled
incompatible antipathetic, conflicting, contradictory, discordant, disparate, incongruous, inconsistent, mismatched, uncongenial, unsuitable
incompetent incapable, ineffectual, inept, inexpert, insufficient, unable, unfit, unfitted, unskilful, useless
incomplete defective, deficient, fragmentary, imperfect, insufficient, lacking, partial, short, undeveloped, undone, unfinished, wanting
incomprehensible baffling, enigmatic, impenetrable, inconceivable, inscrutable, mysterious, obscure, opaque, perplexing, puzzling, unfathomable, unintelligible
inconceivable impossible, incredible, unbelievable, unheard-of, unimaginable, unknowable, unthinkable
inconclusive ambiguous, indecisive, indeterminate, open, uncertain, undecided, unsettled, vague
incongruous absurd, conflicting, contradictory, contrary, discordant, extraneous, improper, inapt, incoherent, inconsistent, unbecoming, unsuitable, unsuited
inconsiderate careless, insensitive, intolerant, rude, self-centred, selfish, tactless, thoughtless, unkind, unthinking
inconsistency disagreement, discrepancy, disparity, divergence, paradox, variance
inconsistent 1. at odds, at variance, conflicting, contradictory, contrary, discordant, incoherent, incompatible, incongruous, irreconcilable 2. capricious, changeable, erratic, fickle, inconstant, irregular, unpredictable, unstable, unsteady, variable
inconspicuous hidden, insignificant, modest, muted, ordinary, plain, quiet, retiring, unassuming, unobtrusive, unostentatious
incontrovertible certain, established, incontestable, indisputable, indubitable, irrefutable, positive, sure, undeniable, unquestionable
inconvenience *n.* annoyance, awkwardness, bother, difficulty, disadvantage, disruption, disturbance, drawback, fuss, hindrance, nuisance, trouble, uneasiness, upset, vexation
inconvenient annoying, awkward, bothersome, disturbing, embarrassing, inopportune, tiresome, troublesome, unseasonable, unsuitable, untimely, vexatious
incorporate absorb, amalgamate, assimilate, blend, coalesce, combine, consolidate, embody, fuse, include, integrate, merge, mix, unite
incorrect false, faulty, flawed, improper, inaccurate, inexact, mistaken, out, specious, unfitting, unsuitable, untrue, wrong
incorrigible hardened, hopeless, incurable, intractable, inveterate
incorruptible honest, honourable, just, straight, trustworthy, unbribable, upright
increase 1. *v.* add to, advance, amplify, augment, boost, build up, develop, dilate, enhance, enlarge, escalate, expand, extend, grow, heighten, inflate, intensify, magnify, mount, multiply, proliferate, prolong, raise, snowball, spread, strengthen, swell, wax 2. *n.* addition, boost, development, enlargement, escalation, expansion, extension, gain, growth, increment, intensification, rise, upsurge, upturn
incredible absurd, beyond belief, far-fetched, implausible, impossible, improbable, inconceivable, preposterous, unbelievable, unimaginable, unthinkable
incredulous disbelieving, doubtful, doubting, dubious, sceptical, suspicious, unbelieving
increment accretion, addition, advancement, augmentation, enlargement, gain, increase
incriminate accuse, arraign, blame, charge, impeach, implicate, indict, involve
incumbent binding, compulsory, mandatory, necessary, obligatory
incur arouse, contract, draw, earn, gain, induce, meet with, provoke
incurable *adj.* 1. hopeless, incorrigible, inveterate 2. fatal, irrecoverable, irremediable, terminal
indebted beholden, grateful, obligated, obliged
indecency coarseness, crudity, foulness, grossness, immodesty, impurity, indecorum, indelicacy, lewdness, obscenity, pornography, smut, smuttiness, vileness, vulgarity
indecent blue, coarse, crude, dirty, filthy, foul, gross, improper, impure, indelicate, lewd, licentious, pornographic, salacious, scatological, smutty, vile
indecision doubt, hesitancy, irresolution, uncertainty, vacillation
indecisive doubtful, faltering, hesitating, irresolute, tentative, uncertain, undecided, undetermined, wavering
indeed actually, certainly, doubtlessly, positively, really, strictly, truly, undeniably, undoubtedly, veritably
indefensible faulty, inexcusable, unforgivable, unpardonable, unwarrantable, wrong

indefinite confused, doubtful, equivocal, evasive, general, imprecise, indeterminate, indistinct, inexact, loose, obscure, uncertain, unclear, undetermined, unfixed, unknown, unlimited, unsettled, vague
indelible enduring, indestructible, ineffaceable, ineradicable, permanent
indelicacy bad taste, coarseness, crudity, grossness, immodesty, impropriety, indecency, obscenity, offensiveness, vulgarity
indelicate blue, coarse, crude, embarrassing, gross, immodest, improper, indecent, low, obscene, off-colour, offensive, risqué, rude, suggestive, tasteless, vulgar
indemnify 1. endorse, insure, protect, secure, underwrite 2. compensate, pay, repair, repay, requite, satisfy
independence autarchy, autonomy, freedom, home rule, liberty, self-government, self-rule, sovereignty
independent absolute, free, liberated, separate, unconnected, uncontrolled, unrelated
independently alone, autonomously, individually, solo, unaided
indescribable ineffable, inexpressible, unutterable
indestructible abiding, durable, enduring, everlasting, immortal, imperishable, indelible, indissoluble, lasting, permanent
indeterminate imprecise, inconclusive, indefinite, inexact, uncertain, undefined, unfixed, unspecified, vague
index 1. clue, guide, indication, mark, sign, symptom, token 2. director, forefinger, hand, indicator, needle, pointer
indicate betoken, denote, evince, imply, manifest, point to, reveal, show, signify, suggest
indication clue, evidence, explanation, hint, index, manifestation, mark, note, omen, portent, sign, signal, symptom, warning
indicator display, gauge, guide, index, mark, marker, meter, pointer, sign, signal, signpost, symbol
indictment accusation, allegation, charge, impeachment, prosecution, summons
indifference aloofness, apathy, callousness, carelessness, coldness, coolness, detachment, disregard, unconcern
indifferent 1. aloof, apathetic, callous, careless, cold, cool, detached, distant, heedless, inattentive, regardless, unconcerned, unimpressed, unresponsive 2. average, fair, mediocre, middling, moderate, ordinary, passable, perfunctory, undistinguished, uninspired
indignant angry, annoyed, disgruntled, exasperated, furious, heated, incensed, irate, resentful, riled, scornful, wrathful
indignation anger, fury, rage, resentment, scorn, umbrage, wrath
indirect circuitous, crooked, devious, meandering, oblique, rambling, roundabout, tortuous, wandering, winding, zigzag
indiscreet foolish, hasty, ill-advised, ill-considered, ill-judged, impolitic, imprudent, incautious, injudicious, naive, rash, reckless, tactless, unwise
indiscriminate aimless, careless, desultory, general, random, sweeping, uncritical, unselective, unsystematic, wholesale
indispensable crucial, essential, imperative, key, necessary, needed, needful, requisite, vital
indisposed ailing, ill, sick, unwell
indisposition ailment, ill health, illness, sickness
indisputable absolute, beyond doubt, certain, evident, incontestable, incontrovertible, positive, sure, undeniable
indistinct ambiguous, bleary, blurred, confused, dim, doubtful, faint, hazy, indefinite, indeterminate, indiscernible, misty, obscure, out of focus, shadowy, unclear, unintelligible, vague, weak
indistinguishable alike, identical, twin
individual 1. *adj.* characteristic, discrete, distinct, exclusive, identical, own, particular, peculiar, personal, proper, respective, separate, several, single, singular, special, specific, unique 2. *n.* being, character, creature, mortal, party, person, soul, type, unit
individuality character, distinction, originality, personality, uniqueness
indolent idle, inactive, inert, lackadaisical, languid, lazy, lethargic, listless, slack, slothful, slow, sluggish, torpid
indomitable invincible, resolute, staunch, steadfast
indubitable certain, evident, incontrovertible, obvious, sure, unarguable, undeniable, undoubted
induce actuate, convince, draw, encourage, get, impel, incite, influence, move, persuade, press, prompt
inducement attraction, bait, cause, consideration, encouragement, impulse, incentive, incitement, influence, lure, motive, reward, spur, stimulus, urge
indulge 1. cater to, give way to, gratify, pander to, regale, satiate, satisfy, yield to 2. With **in** bask in, luxuriate in, revel in, wallow in
indulgence 1. excess, fondness, intemperance, kindness, leniency, partiality, profligacy, spoiling 2. courtesy, forbearance, good will, patience, tolerance, understanding
indulgent compliant, easy-going, favourable, fond, forbearing, gentle, kind, lenient, liberal, mild, permissive, tender, tolerant
industrialist boss, capitalist, magnate, manufacturer, producer, tycoon
industrious active, busy, diligent, energetic, hard-working, laborious, persistent, productive, purposeful, steady, tireless, zealous
industry 1. business, commerce, manufacturing, production, trade 2. activity, application, assiduity, determination, diligence, effort, labour, perseverance, persistence, toil, vigour, zeal
ineffective barren, bootless, feeble, fruitless, futile, idle, impotent, inadequate, inefficient, unavailing, unproductive, useless, vain, weak, worthless
ineffectual bootless, emasculate, feeble, fruitless, futile, idle, impotent, inadequate, incompetent, inept, lame, powerless, unavailing, useless, vain, weak
inefficient disorganized, feeble, inept, inexpert, slipshod, wasteful, weak
ineligible disqualified, ruled out, unacceptable, undesirable, unfit, unqualified, unsuitable
inept awkward, bungling, clumsy, gauche, maladroit, unskilful
ineptitude clumsiness, gaucheness, incapacity, unfitness, unhandiness
inequality bias, disparity, diversity, imparity, prejudice
inequitable biased, one-sided, partial, prejudiced, unfair, unjust
inert dead, dormant, dull, idle, immobile, inactive, inanimate, leaden, lifeless, motionless, passive, quiescent, slack, sluggish, static, still, torpid, unresponsive
inertia apathy, deadness, drowsiness, dullness, idleness, immobility, laziness, lethargy, listlessness, passivity, sloth, stillness, stupor, torpor
inescapable certain, destined, fated, inevitable, inexorable, sure
inestimable incalculable, invaluable, precious, priceless, prodigious
inevitable assured, certain, decreed, destined, fixed, necessary, ordained, settled, sure, unavoidable
inevitably automatically, certainly, necessarily, perforce, surely, unavoidably
inexcusable outrageous, unforgivable, unpardonable, unwarrantable
inexpensive bargain, budget, cheap, economical, low-cost, low-priced, modest, reasonable
inexperience greenness, ignorance, newness, rawness, unfamiliarity
inexperienced amateur, fresh, green, immature, new, raw, unacquainted, unfamiliar, unpractised, unskilled, untrained, unversed
inexpert awkward, bungling, clumsy, inept, maladroit, unpractised, unprofessional, unskilful
inexplicable baffling, enigmatic, inscrutable, insoluble, mysterious, strange, unaccountable
infallible 1. faultless, impeccable, perfect, unerring, unimpeachable 2. certain, dependable, foolproof, reliable, sure, trustworthy, unfailing
infamous base, disgraceful, dishonourable, disreputable, hateful, heinous, ignominious, ill-famed, iniquitous, loathsome, monstrous, nefarious, notorious, odious, outrageous, scandalous, scurvy, shameful, shocking, vile, villainous, wicked
infancy 1. babyhood, early childhood 2. beginnings, cradle, dawn, early stages, emergence, inception, origins, outset, start
infant *n.* baby, child, suckling, toddler, tot
infantile babyish, childish, immature, puerile, tender, weak, young
infatuate befool, beguile, besot, bewitch, captivate, delude, enchant, fascinate, mislead, obsess, stupefy
infatuated beguiled, besotted, bewitched, captivated, enraptured, fascinated, inflamed, intoxicated, obsessed, possessed, spellbound
infect blight, contaminate, corrupt, defile, influence, poison, pollute, taint, touch
infection contagion, contamination, corruption, poison, pollution
infectious catching, communicable, contagious, contaminating, corrupting, infective, pestilential, poisoning
infer conclude, conjecture, deduce, derive, gather, presume, understand
inference assumption, conclusion, conjecture, consequence, corollary, deduction, presumption, surmise
inferior junior, lesser, lower, menial, minor, secondary, subordinate, subsidiary, underneath
inferiority imperfection, inadequacy, meanness, mediocrity, shoddiness
infertile barren, sterile, unfruitful
infest beset, flood, invade, overrun, ravage, swarm, throng
infiltrate creep in, penetrate, percolate, permeate, pervade
infinite *adj.* absolute, all-embracing, boundless, enormous, eternal, immense, inestimable, inexhaustible, interminable, limitless, measureless, numberless, perpetual, stupendous, total, unbounded, uncounted, untold, vast, wide, without end, without number
infinity boundlessness, endlessness, eternity, immensity, vastness
infirm decrepit, doddering, doddery, failing, feeble, frail, lame, weak
inflame anger, arouse, embitter, enrage, excite, fire, heat, ignite, impassion, incense, infuriate, kindle, madden, provoke, rile, rouse, stimulate
inflamed angry, festering, fevered, heated, hot, red, septic, sore, swollen
inflammable combustible, flammable, incendiary
inflate amplify, balloon, blow up, boost, dilate, distend, enlarge, escalate, exaggerate, expand, increase, swell
inflated exaggerated, ostentatious, overblown, swollen
inflation blowing up, distension, enlargement, escalation, expansion, increase, rise, spread, swelling
inflection 1. bend, bow, crook, curvature, intonation, modulation 2. *Gram.* conjugation, declension
inflexibility 1. hardness, inelasticity, rigidity, stiffness, stringency 2. fixity, intransigence, obstinacy
inflexible adamant, firm, fixed, immovable, implacable, inexo-

rable, intractable, iron, obdurate, relentless, resolute, rigorous, set, steadfast, steely, strict, stringent, stubborn, unbending, unyielding

inflict apply, deliver, exact, impose, levy, visit, wreak

influence *n.* 1. agency, authority, control, credit, direction, domination, effect, guidance, mastery, power, pressure, rule, spell, sway, weight 2. hold, importance, leverage, power, prestige, weight ~*v.* 3. affect, arouse, bias, control, count, direct, dispose, guide, impel, impress, incite, incline, induce, instigate, manipulate, modify, move, persuade, predispose, prompt, rouse, sway

influx arrival, flow, incursion, inflow, inrush, invasion, rush

inform acquaint, advise, apprise, communicate, enlighten, instruct, notify, teach, tell, tip off

informal casual, easy, familiar, natural, relaxed, simple

information advice, counsel, data, facts, instruction, intelligence, knowledge, material, message, news, notice, report, tidings, word

informed abreast, acquainted, briefed, conversant, enlightened, erudite, expert, familiar, knowledgeable, learned, posted, primed, reliable, up, versed, well-read

informer accuser, betrayer, sneak, stool pigeon

infrequent occasional, rare, sporadic, uncommon, unusual

infringe break, contravene, disobey, transgress, violate

infuriate anger, enrage, exasperate, incense, irritate, madden, provoke, rile

infuriating aggravating (*Inf.*), annoying, exasperating, galling, maddening, mortifying, pestilential, provoking, vexatious

ingenious adroit, bright, brilliant, clever, crafty, creative, dexterous, fertile, inventive, masterly, original, ready, resourceful, shrewd, skilful, subtle

ingenuous artless, candid, childlike, frank, guileless, honest, innocent, naive, open, plain, simple, sincere, trustful, unreserved, unsophisticated

ingenuousness artlessness, candour, frankness, innocence, naivety, openness

ingratiate blandish, crawl, fawn, flatter, grovel

ingratitude thanklessness, ungratefulness

ingredient component, constituent, element, part

inhabit abide, dwell, live, lodge, occupy, people, populate, possess, reside, tenant

inhabitant aborigine, citizen, denizen, dweller, indweller, inmate, native, occupant, occupier, resident, tenant

inhabited colonized, developed, held, occupied, peopled, populated, settled, tenanted

inherit accede to, be left, fall heir to, succeed to

inheritance bequest, birthright, heritage, legacy, patrimony

inhibit arrest, bar, bridle, check, constrain, curb, debar, discourage, forbid, frustrate, hinder, impede, obstruct, prevent, restrain, stop

inhibition bar, check, embargo, hindrance, interdict, obstacle, prohibition, reserve, restraint, restriction, reticence, shyness

inhospitable 1. unfriendly, ungenerous, unkind, unsociable, unwelcoming 2. bare, barren, bleak, desolate, empty, hostile, lonely, sterile

inhuman animal, barbaric, bestial, brutal, cruel, diabolical, fiendish, heartless, merciless, pitiless, remorseless, ruthless, savage, unfeeling, vicious

inhumane brutal, cruel, heartless, pitiless, unfeeling, unkind

iniquitous atrocious, base, criminal, evil, heinous, immoral, infamous, nefarious, reprehensible, sinful, unjust, unrighteous, vicious, wicked

initial *adj.* beginning, early, first, inaugural, introductory, opening, primary

initially at *or* in the beginning, at first, first, firstly, originally, primarily

initiate 1. begin, break the ice, inaugurate, institute, launch, open, originate, pioneer, start 2. indoctrinate, induct, instate, instruct, introduce, invest, teach, train

initiative advantage, beginning, first move, first step, lead

inject 1. inoculate, vaccinate 2. infuse, insert, instil, interject, introduce

injudicious foolish, hasty, ill-advised, ill-judged, ill-timed, imprudent, indiscreet, inexpedient, rash, unthinking, unwise

injunction command, dictate, mandate, order, precept, ruling

injure abuse, blemish, blight, break, damage, deface, disable, harm, hurt, impair, maltreat, mar, ruin, spoil, tarnish, undermine, vitiate, weaken, wound, wrong

injured broken, disabled, hurt, lamed, undermined, weakened, wounded

injury abuse, damage, evil, grievance, harm, hurt, ill, injustice, mischief, ruin, wound, wrong

injustice bias, favouritism, inequality, oppression, partiality, prejudice, unfairness, unlawfulness, wrong

inkling clue, glimmering, hint, idea, indication, intimation, notion, suggestion, suspicion, whisper

inland *adj.* domestic, interior, internal

inlet arm (of the sea), bay, bight, cove, creek, entrance, ingress, passage

inmost *or* **innermost** basic, buried, central, deep, deepest, essential, intimate, personal, private, secret

innate congenital, essential, inborn, inbred, inherent, inherited, instinctive, intrinsic, intuitive, native, natural

inner central, essential, inside, interior, internal, intestinal, inward, middle

innkeeper host, hostess, hotelier, landlady, landlord, publican

innocence 1. blamelessness, chastity, probity, purity, righteousness, uprightness, virginity, virtue 2. artlessness, freshness, gullibility, naiveté, simplicity

innocent 1. blameless, clear, faultless, guiltless, honest, uninvolved, unoffending 2. chaste, immaculate, impeccable, incorrupt, pristine, pure, righteous, sinless, spotless, stainless, upright, virginal 3. artless, childlike, credulous, frank, guileless, gullible, ingenuous, naive, open, simple, unworldly

innovation change, departure, introduction, novelty, variation

innuendo aspersion, hint, implication, insinuation, suggestion, whisper

innumerable countless, incalculable, infinite, many, myriad, untold

inoffensive harmless, humble, innocent, mild, peaceable, quiet, retiring, unobtrusive, unoffending

inopportune ill-timed, inauspicious, malapropos, mistimed, unpropitious, untimely

inordinate disproportionate, excessive, exorbitant, extravagant, immoderate, intemperate, undue, unreasonable

inquest inquiry, inquisition, investigation, probe

inquire examine, explore, inspect, investigate, make inquiries, probe, scrutinize, search

inquiry examination, exploration, inquest, investigation, probe, research, scrutiny, search, study, survey

inquisition cross-examination, examination, inquest, inquiry, investigation, question

inquisitive curious, inquiring, intrusive, peering, probing, prying, questioning, scrutinizing

insane crazed, crazy, demented, deranged, mad, unhinged

insanitary dirty, disease-ridden, filthy, impure, infected, infested, noxious, polluted, unclean, unhealthy, unhygienic

insanity dementia, frenzy, madness

insatiable greedy, intemperate, rapacious, ravenous, voracious

inscribe 1. carve, cut, engrave, etch, impress, imprint 2. address, dedicate

inscription dedication, engraving, label, legend, lettering, saying, words

inscrutable 1. blank, deadpan, enigmatic 2. hidden, mysterious, unexplainable, unfathomable, unintelligible

insecure 1. afraid, anxious, uncertain, unconfident, unsure 2. flimsy, frail, insubstantial, loose, precarious, rickety, rocky, shaky, unreliable, unsound, unstable, unsteady, weak

insecurity anxiety, fear, uncertainty, unsureness, worry

insensible benumbed, dull, inert, numbed, stupid, torpid

insensitive callous, crass, hardened, imperceptive, indifferent, obtuse, tactless, thick-skinned, tough, unfeeling

inseparable 1. indissoluble, indivisible, inseverable 2. bosom, close, devoted, intimate

insert enter, interpolate, interpose, introduce, place, put, set, stick in, tuck in

insertion addition, implant, inclusion, inset, interpolation, introduction

inside *n.* 1. contents, inner part, interior 2. *Often plural. Inf.* belly, bowels, entrails, gut, guts, stomach, vitals ~*adv.* 3. indoors, under cover, within ~*adj.* 4. inner, innermost, interior, internal, inward

insidious artful, crafty, cunning, deceptive, designing, duplicitous, guileful, slick, sly, smooth, sneaking, stealthy, subtle, tricky, wily

insight awareness, discernment, intuition, judgment, observation, perception, understanding, vision

insignia badge, crest, emblem, ensign, symbol

insignificance inconsequence, irrelevance, paltriness, pettiness, triviality, unimportance, worthlessness

insignificant flimsy, inconsiderable, irrelevant, meaningless, minor, negligible, nugatory, paltry, petty, scanty, trifling, trivial, unimportant, unsubstantial

insincere devious, dishonest, dissembling, double-dealing, duplicitous, evasive, faithless, false, hollow, hypocritical, lying, perfidious, two-faced, unfaithful, untrue, untruthful

insincerity deviousness, dishonesty, dissimulation, duplicity, hypocrisy, mendacity, perfidy, pretence, untruthfulness

insinuate 1. allude, hint, imply, indicate, intimate, suggest 2. infiltrate, infuse, inject, instil, introduce

insinuation allusion, aspersion, hint, implication, innuendo, slur, suggestion

insipid 1. banal, bland, colourless, drab, dry, dull, flat, lifeless, limp, pointless, prosaic, stale, stupid, tame, tedious, trite, vapid, weak, wearisome 2. bland, flavourless, tasteless, unappetizing, watery

insist 1. be firm, demand, persist, require 2. aver, claim, contend, hold, maintain, reiterate, repeat, swear, urge, vow

insistence assertion, contention, emphasis, reiteration, stress, urging

insistent demanding, dogged, emphatic, exigent, forceful, incessant, unrelenting, urgent

insolence abuse, audacity, boldness, disrespect, effrontery, gall (*Inf.*), impertinence, impudence, insubordination, rudeness

insolent abusive, bold, contemptuous, impertinent, impudent, insubordinate, insulting, pert, rude, saucy, uncivil

insoluble baffling, inexplicable, mysterious, mystifying, obscure, unfathomable

insolvency bankruptcy, failure, liquidation, ruin

insolvent bankrupt, failed, ruined

insomnia sleeplessness, wakefulness

inspect check, examine, investigate, look over, oversee, scan, scrutinize, search, supervise, survey, vet

inspection check, examination, investigation, look-over, review, scan, scrutiny, search, supervision, surveillance, survey

inspector censor, checker, critic, examiner, investigator, overseer, scrutineer, supervisor
inspiration arousal, awakening, encouragement, influence, muse, spur, stimulus
inspire animate, encourage, enliven, galvanize, hearten, imbue, influence, infuse, inspirit, instil, spark off, spur, stimulate
inspired brilliant, dazzling, enthralling, exciting, impressive, memorable, outstanding, superlative, thrilling, wonderful
inspiring affecting, encouraging, exciting, exhilarating, heartening, moving, rousing, stimulating, stirring, uplifting
instability fickleness, fluctuation, fluidity, frailty, imbalance, insecurity, restlessness, unsteadiness, vacillation, variability, volatility, weakness
install, instal 1. fix, lay, lodge, place, position, put in, set up, station 2. establish, induct, institute, introduce, invest, set up
installation 1. inauguration, induction, investiture 2. equipment, machinery, plant, system
instalment chapter, division, episode, part, portion, repayment, section
instance 1. *n.* case, example, illustration, occasion, occurrence, precedent, situation, time 2. *v.* adduce, cite, mention, name, quote, specify
instant 1. *n.* flash, moment, second, split second, trice, twinkling 2. *adj.* direct, immediate, instantaneous, prompt, quick, urgent
instantaneous direct, immediate, instant, on-the-spot
instantaneously at once, forthwith, immediately, instantly, promptly, straight away
instantly at once, directly, forthwith, immediately, instantaneously, now, without delay
instead alternatively, preferably, rather
instigate actuate, encourage, impel, incite, influence, initiate, kindle, move, prompt, provoke, rouse, set on, spur, start, stimulate, stir up, urge, whip up
instil, instill engender, implant, impress, infix, infuse, insinuate
instinct aptitude, faculty, feeling, gift, impulse, intuition, knack, proclivity, talent, tendency, urge
instinctive inborn, inherent, innate, intuitional, intuitive, natural, reflex
institute[1] *v.* appoint, begin, enact, establish, fix, found, induct, initiate, install, introduce, invest, ordain, organize, pioneer, settle, set up, start
institute[2] *n.* academy, college, conservatory, foundation, guild, school, seminary, society
institution 1. creation, establishment, foundation, investiture 2. academy, college, foundation, hospital, institute, school, seminary, society, university 3. custom, fixture, law, practice, ritual, rule, tradition
instruct 1. bid, charge, direct, enjoin, order, tell 2. coach, discipline, drill, educate, ground, guide, inform, school, teach, train, tutor
instruction coaching, discipline, drilling, education, grounding, guidance, information, lesson(s), schooling, teaching, training, tuition
instructions advice, directions, guidance, information, orders, rules
instructor adviser, coach, guide, master, mentor, mistress, pedagogue, teacher, trainer, tutor
instrument appliance, contrivance, device, gadget, implement, mechanism, tool, utensil
instrumental active, assisting, auxiliary, conducive, helpful, involved, of help *or* service, subsidiary, useful
insubordinate defiant, disobedient, disorderly, rebellious, recalcitrant, riotous, seditious, turbulent, undisciplined, unruly
insubordination defiance, disobedience, indiscipline, insurrection, mutiny, rebellion, revolt, riotousness, sedition
insufferable detestable, impossible, intolerable, outrageous, unbearable, unendurable, unspeakable
insufficient inadequate, lacking, short
insular *Fig.* blinkered, closed, illiberal, isolated, limited, narrow, parochial, petty, provincial
insulate *Fig.* close off, cut off, isolate, protect
insult 1. *n.* abuse, indignity, insolence, outrage, rudeness, slight, snub 2. *v.* abuse, injure, offend, outrage, revile, slander, slight
insupportable insufferable, intolerable, past bearing, unbearable, unendurable
insurance cover, guarantee, indemnity, protection, provision, safeguard, security, warranty
insure assure, cover, guarantee, indemnify, underwrite, warrant
insurgent *n.* insurrectionist, rebel, revolutionary, rioter
intact complete, entire, perfect, sound, together, unbroken, undamaged, unharmed, unhurt, untouched, unviolated, virgin, whole
integral 1. basic, component, constituent, essential 2. complete, entire, full, intact, undivided, whole
integrate accommodate, assimilate, blend, coalesce, combine, fuse, harmonize, join, knit, merge, mesh, unite
integrity goodness, honesty, honour, principle, probity, purity, rectitude, righteousness, uprightness, virtue
intellect brains (*Inf.*), intelligence, judgment, mind, reason, sense, understanding
intellectual 1. *adj.* bookish, highbrow, intelligent, mental, rational, scholarly, studious, thoughtful 2. *n.* academic, highbrow
intelligence 1. acumen, alertness, brightness, capacity, cleverness, discernment, intellect, mind, perception, quickness, reason, understanding 2. advice, data, disclosure, facts, findings, information, knowledge, news, notice, report, rumour, tidings, tip-off, word
intelligent acute, alert, apt, bright, clever, discerning, knowing, perspicacious, quick, rational, sharp, smart
intelligentsia highbrows, illuminati, intellectuals, literati
intelligible clear, distinct, lucid, open, plain, understandable
intemperate excessive, extreme, immoderate, incontinent, inordinate, prodigal, profligate, self-indulgent, severe, unrestrained, violent, wild
intend aim, contemplate, determine, mean, meditate, plan, propose, purpose, scheme
intense 1. acute, close, concentrated, deep, extreme, fierce, forceful, great, harsh, powerful, profound, protracted, severe, strained 2. ardent, burning, eager, earnest, fanatical, fervent, fierce, heightened, impassioned, keen, passionate, vehement
intensify add to, aggravate, boost, concentrate, deepen, emphasize, enhance, heighten, increase, magnify, quicken, reinforce, set off, sharpen, strengthen
intensity ardour, concentration, depth, emotion, energy, excess, fervour, fierceness, fire, force, keenness, passion, potency, power, severity, strain, strength, tension, vehemence, vigour
intensive all-out, concentrated, demanding, exhaustive, thorough
intent absorbed, alert, attentive, committed, concentrated, determined, eager, earnest, fixed, occupied, preoccupied, rapt, resolute, resolved, steadfast, steady, watchful, wrapped up
intention aim, design, end, goal, idea, object, objective, point, purpose, scope, target, view
intentional deliberate, designed, meant, planned, premeditated, purposed, studied
inter bury, lay to rest, sepulchre
intercede interpose, intervene, mediate, plead, speak
intercept arrest, block, catch, check, cut off, deflect, head off, stop, take
interchangeable equivalent, identical, reciprocal, synonymous, the same
intercourse 1. association, commerce, communion, connection, contact, converse, dealings, trade, traffic, truck 2. carnal knowledge, coition, coitus, congress, copulation, intimacy
interest *n.* 1. affection, attention, attraction, concern, curiosity, notice, regard, suspicion, sympathy 2. concern, consequence, importance, moment, note, significance, weight 3. activity, diversion, hobby, pastime, pursuit, relaxation 4. advantage, benefit, gain, good, profit ~*v.* 5. amuse, attract, divert, engross, fascinate 6. affect, concern, engage, involve
interested 1. affected, attentive, attracted, curious, drawn, excited, fascinated, intent, keen, moved, stimulated 2. concerned, implicated, involved, partial, partisan
interesting absorbing, amusing, appealing, attractive, compelling, curious, engaging, engrossing, entertaining, gripping, intriguing, pleasing, stimulating, suspicious, unusual
interfere butt in, intervene, intrude, meddle, tamper
interference 1. intervention, intrusion, meddling 2. collision, conflict, obstruction, opposition
interim *adj.* acting, caretaker, improvised, makeshift, provisional, stopgap, temporary
interior *adj.* 1. inner, inside, internal, inward 2. *Geog.* central, inland, remote 3. hidden, inner, personal, private, secret, spiritual ~*n.* 4. *Geog.* centre, heartland, upcountry
interloper intruder, trespasser
interlude break, delay, episode, halt, hiatus, intermission, interval, pause, respite, rest, spell, stop, stoppage, wait
intermediate halfway, intervening, mean, mid, middle, midway
interment burial, burying, funeral
interminable ceaseless, dragging, endless, everlasting, infinite, limitless, long, protracted, unbounded, unlimited, wearisome
intermittent broken, discontinuous, fitful, irregular, occasional, periodic, punctuated, recurrent, spasmodic, sporadic
intern confine, detain, hold
internal inner, inside, interior, intimate, private
international cosmopolitan, global, intercontinental, universal, worldwide
interpose 1. interfere, intervene, intrude, step in 2. insert, interject, introduce
interpret adapt, clarify, construe, decipher, decode, define, elucidate, explain, expound, paraphrase, read, render, solve, take, translate
interpretation analysis, clarification, construction, diagnosis, elucidation, exegesis, explanation, explication, meaning, performance, reading, rendering, sense, translation, version
interpreter annotator, exponent, scholiast, translator
interrogate ask, cross-examine, enquire, examine, inquire, investigate, pump, question, quiz
interrogation cross-examination, cross-questioning, enquiry, examination, inquisition, probing, questioning
interrupt break in, butt in, check, cut off, delay, disconnect, discontinue, disturb, divide, heckle, hinder, hold up, intrude, obstruct, separate, sever, stay, stop, suspend
interruption break, disconnection, disruption, disturbance, division, halt, hiatus, hitch, impediment, intrusion, obstacle, obstruction, pause, stop, stoppage
intersection crossing, crossroads, interchange, junction
interval break, delay, gap, interlude, intermission, meantime, meanwhile, opening, pause, period, playtime, rest, season, space, spell, term, time, wait

intervene arbitrate, intercede, interfere, intrude, mediate
intervention agency, interference, intrusion, mediation
interview 1. *n.* audience, conference, consultation, dialogue, meeting, talk 2. *v.* examine, interrogate, question, talk to
interviewer examiner questioner, reporter
intimacy closeness, confidence, familiarity, understanding
intimate[1] *adj.* 1. bosom, cherished, close, confidential, dear, friendly, near, warm 2. personal, private, privy, secret 3. cosy, friendly, informal, snug, warm ~*n.* 4. bosom friend, comrade, confidant, companion, crony, familiar, friend, pal
intimate[2] *v.* allude, communicate, declare, hint, impart, imply, indicate, insinuate, remind, state, suggest, warn
intimately 1. closely, confidentially, warmly 2. fully, thoroughly, very well
intimidate alarm, appal, bully, coerce, dishearten, dismay, frighten, overawe, scare, subdue, terrify, terrorize, threaten
intimidation browbeating, bullying, fear, menaces, pressure, terror, threat
intolerable excruciating, impossible, insufferable, insupportable, painful, unbearable, unendurable
intolerance chauvinism, fanaticism, narrow-mindedness, prejudice, racialism, racism
intolerant chauvinistic, fanatical, narrow, narrow-minded, one-sided, prejudiced, racist, small-minded, uncharitable
intoxicated drunk, drunken, fuddled, inebriated
intoxication drunkenness, inebriation, tipsiness
intrepid bold, brave, courageous, daring, doughty, fearless, gallant, heroic, plucky, resolute, stalwart, unafraid, unflinching, valiant, valorous
intricacy complexity, involvement, knottiness
intricate baroque, complex, complicated, difficult, elaborate, fancy, involved, knotty, obscure, perplexing, tangled, tortuous
intrigue *v.* 1. attract, charm, fascinate, interest, rivet, titillate 2. connive, conspire, machinate, plot, scheme ~*n.* 3. collusion, conspiracy, double-dealing, knavery, manipulation, manoeuvre, plot, ruse, scheme, stratagem, trickery, wile 4. affair, amour, liaison, romance
intriguing diverting, exciting, fascinating, interesting, tantalizing, titillating
intrinsic basic, built-in, central, congenital, essential, genuine, inborn, inbred, inherent, native, natural, real, true
introduce 1. acquaint, familiarize, make known, present 2. begin, bring in, commence, establish, found, inaugurate, initiate, institute, launch, organize, pioneer, set up, start, usher in 3. announce, open, preface
introduction 1. baptism, debut, inauguration, induction, initiation, institution, launch, presentation 2. foreword, lead-in, opening, overture, preamble, preface, prelude, proem, prologue
introductory early, elementary, first, inaugural, initial, opening, prefatory, preliminary, preparatory, starting
intrude encroach, infringe, interfere, interrupt, obtrude, trespass, violate
intruder burglar, interloper, invader, prowler, raider, thief, trespasser
intrusion infringement, interruption, invasion, trespass, violation
intuition hunch, insight, instinct, perception, presentiment
inundate deluge, drown, engulf, flood, glut, overflow, overrun, overwhelm, submerge, swamp
invade assail, assault, attack, burst in, encroach, infringe, occupy, raid, violate
invader aggressor, attacker, plunderer, raider, trespasser
invalid[1] *adj.* ailing, disabled, feeble, frail, ill, infirm, sick, sickly
invalid[2] *adj.* baseless, false, ill-founded, illogical, irrational, null and void, unfounded, unsound, untrue, void, worthless
invaluable costly, inestimable, precious, priceless, valuable
invariable changeless, consistent, constant, fixed, immutable, inflexible, regular, rigid, set, unchanging, unfailing, unvarying, unwavering
invariably always, consistently, customarily, ever, habitually, perpetually, regularly
invasion assault, attack, foray, incursion, inroad, irruption, offensive, onslaught, raid
invective abuse, censure, contumely, diatribe, obloquy, reproach, sarcasm, tirade, vituperation
invent coin, conceive, contrive, create, design, devise, discover, formulate, imagine, improvise, originate, think up
invention 1. contraption, contrivance, creation, design, development, device, discovery, gadget 2. deceit, fabrication, fake, falsehood, fantasy, fiction, forgery, lie, prevarication, sham, story, untruth
inventive creative, fertile, gifted, imaginative, ingenious, resourceful
inventor author, coiner, creator, designer, father, maker, originator
inventory *n.* account, catalogue, list, record, register, roll, roster, schedule
inverse *adj.* contrary, inverted, opposite, reverse, transposed
invert capsize, overturn, reverse, transpose, upset, upturn
invest 1. advance, devote, lay out, put in, sink, spend 2. endow, endue, provide, supply 3. *Mil.* beleaguer, beset, besiege, enclose, surround
investigate consider, enquire into, examine, explore, inspect, probe, scrutinize, search, sift, study
investigation analysis, enquiry, examination, exploration, hearing, inquest, inquiry, inspection, probe, research, review, scrutiny, search, study, survey
investigator examiner, inquirer, (private) detective, researcher, reviewer, sleuth
investiture admission, enthronement, inauguration, induction, installation
investment asset, speculation, transaction, venture
inveterate chronic, confirmed, deep-dyed, entrenched, established, hardened, incorrigible, ineradicable, long-standing
invigorate brace, energize, enliven, exhilarate, fortify, galvanize, harden, quicken, refresh, rejuvenate, stimulate, strengthen
invincible indestructible, insuperable, unassailable, unbeatable, unconquerable
invisible 1. indiscernible, out of sight, unseen 2. concealed, disguised, hidden, inconspicuous
invitation 1. asking, begging, bidding, call, request, solicitation, summons 2. coquetry, enticement, incitement, inducement, overture, provocation, temptation
invite 1. ask, beg, bid, call, request, solicit, summon 2. allure, attract, bring on, court, draw, encourage, entice, lead, provoke, solicit, tempt, welcome
inviting alluring, appealing, attractive, captivating, delightful, engaging, fascinating, pleasing, seductive, tempting, warm, welcoming
invocation appeal, entreaty, petition, prayer, supplication
invoke adjure, beg, beseech, call upon, conjure, entreat, implore, petition, pray, solicit, supplicate
involuntary compulsory, forced, obligatory, reluctant, unwilling
involve 1. entail, imply, mean, necessitate, presuppose, require 2. affect, associate, concern, connect, draw in, implicate, incriminate, inculpate, touch 3. absorb, bind, commit, engage, engross, grip, hold, rivet, wrap up
involvement association, commitment, concern, connection, interest, responsibility
inward *adj.* 1. entering, incoming, ingoing, penetrating 2. confidential, hidden, inmost, innermost, inside, interior, internal, personal, private, secret
inwardly at heart, inside, privately, secretly, within
irksome annoying, boring, burdensome, disagreeable, exasperating, tedious, tiresome, troublesome, unwelcome, vexatious, vexing, wearisome
iron *adj. Fig.* adamant, cruel, hard, heavy, immovable, implacable, inflexible, obdurate, rigid, steel, strong, tough, unbending, unyielding
ironic, ironical 1. mocking, sarcastic, sardonic, satirical, sneering, wry 2. incongruous, paradoxical
iron out clear up, eliminate, erase, expedite, harmonize, put right, reconcile, resolve, settle, simplify, sort out, unravel
irony 1. mockery, sarcasm, satire 2. contrariness, incongruity, paradox
irrational absurd, crazy, foolish, illogical, silly, unreasonable, unsound, unthinking, unwise
irrefutable certain, incontestable, incontrovertible, indisputable, indubitable, invincible, sure, unanswerable, undeniable
irregular *adj.* 1. eccentric, erratic, fitful, fluctuating, fragmentary, haphazard, intermittent, occasional, patchy, random, shifting, spasmodic, sporadic, uncertain, unpunctual, unsteady, unsystematic, variable, wavering 2. asymmetrical, broken, bumpy, craggy, crooked, elliptic, jagged, lopsided, pitted, ragged, rough, unequal, uneven ~*n.* 3. guerrilla, partisan, volunteer
irregularity 1. asymmetry, bumpiness, crookedness, lopsidedness, patchiness, raggedness, roughness, unevenness 2. aberration, anomaly, breach, deviation, eccentricity, freak, malfunction, malpractice, oddity, peculiarity, singularity, unorthodoxy
irrelevance, irrelevancy inappositeness, inappropriateness
irrelevant extraneous, immaterial, impertinent, inapplicable, inappropriate, unrelated
irreparable beyond repair, irremediable, irretrievable, irreversible
irrepressible boisterous, buoyant, ebullient, uncontrollable, unmanageable
irreproachable blameless, faultless, guiltless, impeccable, innocent, perfect, pure, unimpeachable
irresistible 1. compelling, imperative, overpowering, overwhelming, potent, urgent 2. alluring, enchanting, fascinating, ravishing, seductive, tempting
irresponsible careless, flighty, giddy, immature, reckless, shiftless, thoughtless, unreliable, untrustworthy, wild
irreverent derisive, disrespectful, flippant, impertinent, impious, mocking, saucy
irreversible final, incurable, irrevocable
irrevocable changeless, fated, fixed, irreversible, predestined, settled, unalterable, unreversible
irrigate flood, inundate, moisten, water, wet
irritability bad temper, impatience, peevishness, petulance, prickliness, testiness, tetchiness, touchiness
irritable bad-tempered, cantankerous, choleric, crabbed, cross, dyspeptic, exasperated, fiery, fretful, hasty, hot, ill-humoured, ill-tempered, irascible, peevish, petulant, prickly, snappish, snarling, tense, testy, touchy
irritate 1. anger, annoy, bother, enrage, exasperate, fret, harass, incense, inflame, infuriate, nettle, offend, pester, provoke, ruffle, vex 2. aggravate, chafe, fret, inflame, intensify, pain, rub
irritated angry, annoyed, cross, displeased, exasperated, harassed, impatient, nettled, ruffled, vexed

irritating annoying, displeasing, irksome, maddening, nagging, pestilential, provoking, troublesome, trying, upsetting, vexatious
irritation anger, annoyance, displeasure, exasperation, impatience, indignation, irritability, resentment, testiness, vexation, wrath
isolate cut off, detach, disconnect, divorce, insulate, quarantine, segregate, separate, sequester, set apart
isolated hidden, lonely, outlying, remote, retired, secluded, unfrequented
isolation aloofness, detachment, disconnection, exile, loneliness, quarantine, retirement, seclusion, separation, solitude, withdrawal
issue *n.* **1.** affair, argument, concern, matter, point, problem, question, subject, topic **2.** copy, edition, instalment, number **3.** children, descendants, heirs, offspring, progeny, scions ~*v.* **4.** announce, broadcast, circulate, deliver, distribute, emit, give out, promulgate, publish, release **5.** arise, emanate, emerge, flow, originate, proceed, rise, spring, stem
itch *v.* **1.** crawl, irritate, prickle, tickle, tingle **2.** ache, burn, crave, hanker, hunger, long, lust, pant, pine, yearn ~*n.* **3.** irritation, prickling, tingling **4.** craving, desire, hunger, longing, lust, passion, yearning
item **1.** article, aspect, component, consideration, detail, entry, matter, particular, point, thing **2.** account, article, bulletin, dispatch, feature, note, paragraph, piece, report
itinerant *adj.* ambulatory, migratory, nomadic, peripatetic, roaming, roving, travelling, unsettled, vagabond, vagrant
itinerary circuit, journey, line, programme, route, schedule, tour

J

jab *v./n.* dig, lunge, nudge, poke, prod, punch, stab, tap, thrust
jacket case, casing, coat, covering, envelope, folder, sheath, skin, wrapper
jackpot award, bonanza, kitty, pool, pot, prize, reward, winnings
jack up elevate, heave, hoist, lift, lift up, raise, rear
jade harridan, hussy, nag, shrew, slattern, slut, trollop, vixen, wench
jaded **1.** exhausted, fatigued, spent, tired, weary **2.** bored, dulled, glutted, gorged, sated, surfeited
jagged barbed, broken, cleft, craggy, notched, pointed, ragged, ridged, rough, serrated, spiked, toothed, uneven
jail, gaol **1.** *n.* borstal, prison, reformatory **2.** *v.* confine, detain, immure, impound, imprison, incarcerate, lock up
jailer, gaoler captor, guard, keeper, warder
jam *v.* **1.** cram, crowd, crush, force, pack, press, squeeze, stuff, throng, wedge **2.** block, clog, congest, halt, obstruct, stall, stick ~*n.* **3.** crowd, crush, horde, mass, mob, multitude, pack, press, swarm, throng **4.** bind, dilemma, plight, predicament, quandary, strait, trouble
jangle **1.** *v.* chime, clank, clash, rattle, vibrate **2.** *n.* clang, clangour, clash, din, dissonance, jar, racket, rattle
janitor caretaker, concierge, custodian, doorkeeper, porter
jar[1] *n.* crock, flagon, jug, pitcher, pot, urn, vase, vessel
jar[2] *v.* **1.** bicker, clash, contend, disagree, interfere, oppose, quarrel, wrangle **2.** agitate, disturb, grate, irritate, jolt, offend, rasp, rock, shake, vibrate **3.** annoy, clash, grate, grind, irk, irritate, nettle
jargon argot, cant, dialect, idiom, parlance, patois, slang, tongue, usage
jaunt airing, excursion, expedition, outing, ramble, stroll, tour, trip
jaunty airy, breezy, buoyant, carefree, dapper, gay, high-spirited, lively, perky, showy, smart, sprightly, spruce, trim
jaw **1.** *v.* babble, chat, chatter, gossip, lecture, talk **2.** *n.* chat, conversation, gossip, natter, talk
jealous covetous, desirous, envious, green, grudging, intolerant, resentful, rival
jealousy covetousness, distrust, envy, ill-will, mistrust, resentment, spite
jeer *v.* banter, barrack, deride, flout, gibe, heckle, hector, mock, ridicule, scoff, sneer, taunt
jeopardize chance, endanger, gamble, hazard, imperil, risk, stake, venture
jeopardy danger, exposure, hazard, peril, risk, venture
jerk *v./n.* jolt, lurch, pull, throw, thrust, tug, tweak, twitch, wrench, yank
jest **1.** *n.* banter, bon mot, fun, hoax, jape, joke, play, prank, quip, sally, sport, witticism **2.** *v.* banter, chaff, deride, gibe, jeer, joke, mock, quip, scoff, sneer, tease
jester **1.** comedian, comic, humorist, joker, wag, wit **2.** buffoon, clown, fool, madcap, mummer, pantaloon
jet[1] black, ebony, inky, raven, sable
jet[2] *n.* **1.** flow, fountain, gush, spout, spray, spring, stream **2.** nozzle, rose, spout, sprinkler ~*v.* **3.** flow, gush, issue, rush, shoot, spout, squirt, stream, surge
jettison abandon, discard, dump, eject, expel, heave, scrap, unload
jetty breakwater, dock, mole, pier, quay, wharf
jewel **1.** brilliant, ornament, precious stone, trinket **2.** charm, gem, paragon, pearl, prize, rarity, wonder
jib balk, recoil, refuse, retreat, shrink
jig *v.* bounce, caper, prance, shake, skip, twitch, wobble
jingle *v.* **1.** chime, clatter, clink, rattle, ring, tinkle ~*n.* **2.** clang, clink, rattle, ringing, tinkle **3.** chorus, ditty, doggerel, melody, song, tune
jinx **1.** *n.* curse, evil eye, plague, voodoo **2.** *v.* bewitch, curse
job **1.** affair, charge, chore, concern, duty, errand, function, pursuit, responsibility, role, stint, task, undertaking, venture, work **2.** business, calling, capacity, career, craft, employment, function, livelihood, métier, occupation, office, position, post, profession, situation, trade, vocation
jobless idle, inactive, out of work, unemployed, unoccupied
jocular amusing, comical, droll, facetious, funny, humorous, jolly, jovial, playful, roguish, sportive, teasing, waggish, witty
jog **1.** arouse, nudge, prod, prompt, push, remind, shake, stimulate, stir, suggest **2.** canter, lope, run, trot **3.** lumber, plod, tramp, trudge
join **1.** accompany, add, adhere, annex, append, attack, cement, combine, connect, couple, fasten, knit, link, marry, splice, tie, unite, yoke **2.** enlist, enrol, enter, sign up
joint **1.** *n.* connection, hinge, junction, knot, nexus, node, seam, union **2.** *adj.* collective, combined, communal, concerted, cooperative, joined, mutual, shared, united
jointly as one, collectively, mutually, together, unitedly
joke **1.** *n.* frolic, fun, jape, jest, lark, play, pun, quip, quirk, sally, sport, witticism, yarn **2.** *v.* banter, chaff, deride, frolic, gambol, jest, mock, quip, ridicule, taunt, tease
jolly carefree, cheerful, convivial, festive, funny, gay, gladsome, hilarious, jocund, jovial, joyful, joyous, jubilant, merry, mirthful, playful
jolt *v.* **1.** jar, jerk, knock, push, shake, shove **2.** astonish, disturb, perturb, stagger, startle, stun, surprise, upset ~*n.* **3.** bump, jar, jerk, jump, quiver, shake, start **4.** blow, bombshell, reversal, setback, shock, surprise
jostle bump, butt, crowd, elbow, jog, jolt, press, push, shove, squeeze, throng, thrust
journal **1.** daily, gazette, magazine, monthly, newspaper, paper, periodical, record, register, review, tabloid, weekly **2.** diary, log, record
journalist broadcaster, columnist, commentator, contributor, correspondent, hack, newspaperman, pressman, reporter, stringer
journey excursion, expedition, jaunt, odyssey, outing, passage, pilgrimage, progress, ramble, tour, travel, trek, trip, voyage
jovial airy, blithe, buoyant, cheery, convivial, cordial, gay, glad, happy, jolly, jubilant, merry, mirthful
joy bliss, delight, ecstasy, elation, exultation, felicity, festivity, gaiety, gladness, glee, pleasure, rapture, ravishment, satisfaction, transport
joyful blithesome, delighted, glad, gratified, happy, jubilant, light-hearted, merry, pleased, satisfied
joyless cheerless, dejected, depressed, dismal, dispirited, downcast, dreary, gloomy, miserable, sad, unhappy
jubilant elated, enraptured, excited, exuberant, exultant, glad, joyous, overjoyed, rejoicing, thrilled, triumphant
judge *n.* **1.** adjudicator, arbiter, moderator, referee, umpire **2.** arbiter, assessor, authority, connoisseur, critic, evaluator, expert **3.** justice, magistrate ~*v.* **4.** adjudge, adjudicate, arbitrate, ascertain, conclude, decide, determine, discern, mediate, referee, umpire **5.** appreciate, assess, consider, criticize, esteem, estimate, evaluate, examine, review, value
judgment **1.** acumen, common sense, discernment, discrimination, intelligence, perspicacity, prudence, sagacity, sense, shrewdness, taste, understanding, wisdom **2.** arbitration, award, conclusion, decision, decree, finding, order, result, ruling, sentence, verdict **3.** appraisal, assessment, conviction, deduction, diagnosis, estimate, finding, opinion, valuation, view
judicious acute, astute, careful, cautious, circumspect, considered, diplomatic, discerning, discreet, expedient, informed, politic, prudent, rational, sage, sane, sensible, shrewd, skilful, sober, sound, thoughtful, well-judged, wise
jug carafe, crock, ewer, jar, pitcher, urn, vessel
juggle alter, change, disguise, falsify, manipulate, manoeuvre, misrepresent, modify
juice fluid, liquid, liquor, nectar, sap
juicy **1.** lush, moist, succulent, watery **2.** colourful, interesting, racy, risqué, sensational, spicy, suggestive
jumble **1.** *v.* confound, confuse, disarrange, dishevel, disorder, disorganize, entangle, mix, muddle, shuffle, tangle **2.** *n.* chaos, clutter, confusion, disarray, disorder, litter, medley, *mélange*, mess, miscellany, mixture, muddle
jumbo giant, huge, immense, large
jump *v.* **1.** bounce, bound, caper, clear, gambol, hop, hurdle, leap, skip, spring, vault **2.** avoid, digress, evade, miss, omit, overshoot, skip, switch ~*n.* **3.** bound, caper, hop, leap, skip, spring, vault **4.** advance, boost, increase, increment, rise, upsurge, upturn
jumper pullover, sweater, woolly
jumpy agitated, anxious, fidgety, jittery, nervous, restless, tense
junction alliance, combination, connection, coupling, joint, juncture, linking, seam, union
junior inferior, lesser, lower, minor, secondary, subordinate, younger
junk clutter, debris, leavings, litter, oddments, refuse, rubbish, rummage, scrap, trash, waste
jurisdiction authority, command, control, dominion, influence, power, prerogative, rule, say, sway
just *adj.* **1.** blameless, decent, equitable, fair, good, honest, honourable, impartial, lawful, pure, right, righteous, unbiased, upright, virtuous **2.** appropriate, apt, deserved, due, fitting, justified, merited, proper, reasonable, suitable ~*adv.* **3.** absolute-

ly, completely, entirely, exactly, perfectly, precisely **4.** hardly, lately, only now, recently, scarcely

justice **1.** equity, fairness, honesty, impartiality, integrity, justness, law, legality, legitimacy, rectitude, right **2.** amends, correction, penalty, redress, reparation

justifiable acceptable, defensible, excusable, fit, lawful, legitimate, proper, right, sound, tenable, valid, warrantable, well-founded

justification apology, approval, defence, excuse, explanation, extenuation, plea, vindication

justify absolve, acquit, approve, confirm, defend, establish, excuse, exonerate, explain, legalize, maintain, substantiate, support, sustain, uphold, validate, vindicate, warrant

juvenile adolescent, boy, child, girl, infant, minor, youth

juxtaposition adjacency, closeness, contact, nearness, vicinity

K

keen **1.** ardent, avid, eager, earnest, enthusiastic, fervid, fierce, intense, zealous **2.** acid, acute, biting, caustic, cutting, edged, incisive, piercing, pointed, sardonic, satirical, sharp, tart, trenchant

keenness ardour, avidity, diligence, eagerness, enthusiasm, fervour, impatience, intensity, passion, zeal, zest

keep *v.* **1.** conserve, control, hold, maintain, possess, preserve, retain **2.** amass, carry, deal in, deposit, furnish, garner, heap, hold, pile, place, stack, stock, store, trade in **3.** care for, defend, guard, look after, maintain, manage, mind, operate, protect, safeguard, shelter, shield, tend, watch over **4.** board, feed, maintain, nourish, subsidize, support, sustain, victual **5.** adhere to, celebrate, fulfil, hold, honour, obey, observe, perform, respect, solemnize ~*n.* **6.** board, food, livelihood, living, maintenance, means, nourishment, subsistence, support **7.** castle, citadel, dungeon, fastness, stronghold, tower

keep back check, constrain, control, curb, delay, hold back, limit, prohibit, restrain, restrict, retard, withhold

keeper attendant, caretaker, curator, custodian, defender, gaoler, governor, guard, jailer, overseer, preserver, steward, warden, warder

keeping care, charge, custody, patronage, possession, protection, safekeeping, trust

keep on continue, endure, last, persevere, persist, prolong

keepsake emblem, favour, memento, relic, remembrance, reminder, souvenir, symbol, token

keep up balance, compete, contend, continue, maintain, match, persevere, preserve, rival, sustain, vie

key *n.* **1.** latchkey, opener **2.** *Fig.* answer, clue, cue, explanation, guide, interpretation, lead, means, pointer, sign, solution, translation ~*adj.* **3.** basic, chief, crucial, decisive, essential, fundamental, important, leading, main, major, pivotal, principal

keynote centre, core, essence, gist, kernel, marrow, pith, substance

kick **1.** *v.* boot, punt **2.** *n.* force, intensity, pep, power, punch, pungency, sparkle, strength, tang, verve, vitality, zest

kick off begin, commence, initiate, open, start

kick out discharge, dismiss, eject, evict, expel, oust, reject, remove, sack, toss out

kid **1.** *n.* baby, bairn, boy, child, girl, infant, lad, little one, stripling, teenager, tot, youngster, youth **2.** *v.* bamboozle, beguile, cozen, delude, fool, hoax, hoodwink, jest, joke, mock, plague, pretend, ridicule, tease, trick

kidnap abduct, capture, hijack, remove, seize, skyjack, steal

kill **1.** annihilate, assassinate, butcher, destroy, dispatch, execute, exterminate, extirpate, massacre, murder, neutralize, obliterate, slaughter, slay **2.** *Fig.* cancel, cease, deaden, defeat, halt, quash, quell, ruin, scotch, smother, stifle, stop, suppress, veto

killer assassin, butcher, executioner, exterminator, gunman, murderer, slaughterer, slayer

killing bloodshed, carnage, extermination, fatality, homicide, manslaughter, massacre, murder, slaughter, slaying

kin affinity, blood, connection, consanguinity, extraction, kinship, lineage, relationship, stock

kind[1] *n.* brand, breed, class, family, genus, race, set, sort, species, variety

kind[2] *adj.* affectionate, amiable, beneficent, benevolent, benign, bounteous, charitable, compassionate, congenial, considerate, cordial, courteous, friendly, generous, gentle, good, gracious, humane, indulgent, lenient, loving, mild, neighbourly, obliging, propitious, tender-hearted, thoughtful

kindle fire, ignite, inflame, light, set fire to

kindliness amiability, benevolence, charity, compassion, friendliness, gentleness, humanity, sympathy

kindly **1.** *adj.* benevolent, compassionate, cordial, favourable, genial, gentle, good-natured, hearty, helpful, kind, mild, pleasant, polite, sympathetic, warm **2.** *adv.* agreeably, graciously, politely, tenderly, thoughtfully

kindness **1.** affection, benevolence, charity, compassion, fellow-feeling, generosity, goodness, grace, humanity, indulgence, tenderness, tolerance, understanding **2.** aid, assistance, benefaction, bounty, favour, generosity, good deed, help, service

king emperor, majesty, monarch, overlord, prince, ruler, sovereign

kingdom **1.** dominion, dynasty, empire, monarchy, realm, reign, sovereignty **2.** county, division, nation, province, state, territory, tract

kink **1.** bend, coil, entanglement, knot, tangle, twist, wrinkle **2.** crotchet, eccentricity, fetish, foible, quirk, singularity, vagary, whim

kiosk bookstall, booth, counter, newsstand, stall, stand

kiss *v.* greet, osculate, salute

kit apparatus, effects, equipment, gear, outfit, rig, supplies, tackle, tools

knack ability, aptitude, bent, capacity, dexterity, expertise, flair, forte, genius, gift, handiness, ingenuity, skill, talent, trick

knave blackguard, cheat, rascal, reprobate, rogue, scamp, scoundrel, swindler, villain

knavery chicanery, corruption, deceit, dishonesty, fraud, roguery, trickery, villainy

kneel bow, curtsey, genuflect, kowtow, stoop

knell **1.** *v.* chime, herald, peal, resound, ring, sound, toll **2.** *n.* chime, peal, toll

knickers bloomers, briefs, drawers, panties, smalls, underwear

knick-knack bauble, bric-a-brac, plaything, trifle, trinket

knife blade, cutter, cutting tool

knit affix, ally, bind, connect, contract, fasten, heal, intertwine, join, link, loop, mend, secure, tie, unite, weave

knob boss, bulk, bump, bunch, knot, lump, nub, projection, protrusion, snag, stud, swelling, tumour

knock **1.** *v.* buffet, clap, cuff, hit, punch, rap, slap, smack, strike, thump, thwack **2.** *n.* blow, box, clip, clout, cuff, hammering, rap, slap, smack, thump

knockout hit, sensation, smash, success, triumph, winner

knot **1.** *v.* bind, entangle, knit, loop, secure, tether, tie, weave **2.** *n.* bond, bow, braid, connection, joint, ligature, loop, rosette, tie

know **1.** apprehend, experience, fathom, feel certain, learn, notice, perceive, realize, recognize, see, undergo, understand **2.** be acquainted with, be familiar with, fraternize with, have dealings with, have knowledge of, recognize **3.** discern, distinguish, identify, make out, perceive, recognize, see, tell

knowing astute, clever, competent, discerning, experienced, expert, intelligent, qualified, skilful, well-informed

knowledge **1.** enlightenment, erudition, instruction, intelligence, learning, scholarship, science, tuition, wisdom **2.** ability, cognition, consciousness, discernment, grasp, judgment, recognition, understanding

knowledgeable acquainted, *au fait*, aware, cognizant, conscious, experienced, familiar, understanding, well-informed

known admitted, avowed, celebrated, common, confessed, familiar, famous, manifest, noted, obvious, patent, plain, popular, published, recognized, well-known

L

label *n.* **1.** marker, sticker, tag, tally, ticket **2.** brand, company, mark, trademark ~*v.* **3.** mark, stamp, sticker, tag, tally **4.** brand, call, class, classify, define, describe, designate, identify, name

labour *n.* **1.** industry, toil, work **2.** employees, hands, labourers, workers, work force, workmen **3.** drudgery, effort, exertion, industry, pains, toil **4.** childbirth, contractions, delivery, labour pains, pains, parturition, throes, travail ~*v.* **5.** dwell on, elaborate, overdo, overemphasize, strain

laboured awkward, difficult, forced, heavy, stiff, strained

labourer blue-collar worker, drudge, hand, labouring man, manual worker, worker, workman

lacerate claw, cut, gash, jag, maim, mangle, rend, rip, slash, tear, wound

lack **1.** *n.* absence, dearth, deficiency, deprivation, destitution, need, scantiness, scarcity, shortage, want **2.** *v.* miss, need, require, want

lackadaisical apathetic, dull, half-hearted, indifferent, limp, listless, spiritless

lacking defective, flawed, impaired, inadequate, missing, needing, wanting, without

lacklustre boring, dim, drab, dry, dull, flat, leaden, lifeless, muted, prosaic, sombre, vapid

laconic brief, compact, concise, crisp, curt, pithy, short, succinct, terse

lad boy, fellow, juvenile, kid, schoolboy, stripling, youngster, youth

laden burdened, charged, full, hampered, loaded, oppressed, taxed

ladylike courtly, cultured, decorous, elegant, genteel, modest, polite, proper, refined, respectable, well-bred

lag dawdle, delay, idle, linger, loiter, saunter, straggle, tarry, trail

laggard dawdler, idler, loiterer, lounger, straggler

laid-back at ease, casual, easy-going, relaxed, unhurried

lame **1.** crippled, disabled, game, hobbling, limping **2.** *Fig.* feeble, flimsy, inadequate, poor, thin, unconvincing, weak

lament **1.** *v.* bemoan, bewail, complain, deplore, grieve, mourn, regret, sorrow, wail, weep **2.** *n.* complaint, moan, moaning, plaint, wail, wailing

lamentable **1.** distressing, grievous, mournful, regrettable, sorrowful, tragic, unfortunate, woeful **2.** low, meagre, mean, miserable, pitiful, poor, wretched

lampoon **1.** *n.* burlesque, parody, satire, skit, squib **2.** *v.* burlesque, caricature, mock, parody, ridicule, satirize

land *n.* **1.** earth, ground, terra firma **2.** dirt, ground, loam, soil **3.** acres, estate, grounds, property, realty **4.** country, district, nation, province, region, territory, tract ~*v.* **5.** alight, arrive, berth, debark, disembark, dock, touch down

landlord host, hotelier, hotelkeeper, innkeeper

landmark **1.** feature, monument **2.** crisis, milestone, turning point, watershed

landscape countryside, outlook, panorama, prospect, scene, scenery, view, vista

language 1. conversation, discourse, expression, parlance, speech, talk, vocalization 2. argot, cant, dialect, idiom, jargon, patois, speech, tongue, vernacular, vocabulary 3. diction, expression, phrasing, style, wording

languid 1. drooping, faint, feeble, limp, pining, sickly, weak, weary 2. lazy, listless, spiritless, unenthusiastic, uninterested 3. dull, heavy, inactive, inert, lethargic, sluggish, torpid

languish decline, droop, fade, fail, faint, flag, sicken, waste, weaken, wilt, wither

lank 1. dull, lifeless, limp, long, straggling 2. emaciated, gaunt, lanky, lean, scrawny, skinny, slender, slim, spare, thin

lanky angular, bony, gaunt, rangy, spare, tall, thin

lap 1. *n.* circle, circuit, course, loop, orbit, round, tour 2. *v.* cover, enfold, fold, swathe, turn, twist, wrap

lapse *n.* 1. error, failing, fault, indiscretion, mistake, omission, oversight, slip ~*v.* 2. decline, drop, fail, fall, sink, slide, slip 3. end, expire, run out, stop, terminate

lapsed discontinued, ended, expired, finished, invalid

large 1. big, bulky, enormous, giant, goodly, great, huge, immense, king-size, massive, monumental, sizable, substantial, vast 2. ample, broad, capacious, copious, extensive, full, generous, grand, liberal, plentiful, roomy, spacious, sweeping, wide

largely chiefly, generally, mainly, mostly, predominantly, primarily, principally, widely

largess 1. benefaction, bounty, charity, generosity, liberality, philanthropy 2. bequest, bounty, donation, gift, grant, present

lark antic, caper, fling, frolic, fun, gambol, game, jape, mischief, prank, revel, rollick, romp, spree

lash[1] *n.* 1. blow, hit, stripe, stroke ~*v.* 2. beat, birch, flog, horsewhip, lam (*Sl.*), scourge, thrash, whip 3. beat, buffet, dash, drum, hammer, hit, knock, pound, smack, strike

lash[2] bind, fasten, join, make fast, rope, secure, strap, tie

lass damsel, girl, maid, maiden, miss, young woman

last[1] *adj.* 1. aftermost, hindmost, rearmost 2. latest, most recent 3. closing, concluding, extreme, final, furthest, remotest, ultimate, utmost ~*adv.* 4. after, behind

last[2] *v.* abide, continue, endure, keep, persist, remain, survive, wear

lasting abiding, continuing, durable, enduring, long-term, permanent, perpetual, unceasing, undying, unending

latch bar, bolt, catch, clamp, fastening, hasp, hook, lock

late 1. behind, belated, delayed, overdue, slow, tardy, unpunctual 2. advanced, fresh, modern, new, recent 3. dead, deceased, defunct, departed, ex-, former, old, past

lately just now, latterly, of, late, recently

lateness belatedness, delay, retardation, unpunctuality

later *adv.* after, afterwards, in time, later on, next, subsequently, thereafter

lateral edgeways, flanking, sideways

latest *adj.* current, fashionable, in, modern, most recent, newest, now

lather bubbles, foam, froth, soap, soapsuds, suds

latitude 1. breadth, compass, extent, range, room, scope, space, span, spread, sweep, width 2. freedom, indulgence, leeway, liberty, unrestrictedness

latter closing, concluding, last, later, latest, modern, recent, second

latterly hitherto, lately, recently

lattice fretwork, grating, grid, grille, mesh, network, trellis, web

laudable admirable, creditable, excellent, meritorious, praiseworthy, worthy

laugh *v.* 1. chortle, chuckle, giggle, guffaw, snigger, titter 2. **laugh at** deride, jeer, lampoon, mock, ridicule, scoff at, taunt ~*n.* 3. belly laugh (*Inf.*), chortle, chuckle, giggle, guffaw, snigger, titter

laughable absurd, derisory, ludicrous, nonsensical, preposterous, ridiculous

laughter amusement, glee, hilarity, merriment, mirth

launch 1. cast, discharge, dispatch, fire, project, propel, throw 2. begin, commence, embark upon, inaugurate, initiate, instigate, introduce, open, start

laurels acclaim, awards, bays, commendation, credit, distinction, fame, glory, honour, praise, renown, reward

lavatory bathroom, convenience, loo, powder room, (public) convenience, toilet, washroom, water closet

lavish 1. copious, exuberant, lush, opulent, plentiful, profuse, prolific, sumptuous 2. bountiful, free, generous, liberal, munificent, open-handed

law 1. charter, code, jurisprudence 2. act, code, commandment, covenant, decree, edict, enactment, order, ordinance, rule, statute

law-abiding compliant, dutiful, good, honest, lawful, obedient, orderly, peaceful

lawbreaker convict, criminal, culprit, delinquent, miscreant, offender, sinner, trespasser, wrongdoer

lawful allowable, authorized, constitutional, just, legal, legalized, legitimate, licit, permissible, proper, rightful, valid

lawless anarchic, chaotic, disorderly, insubordinate, insurgent, mutinous, rebellious, reckless, riotous, seditious, unruly, wild

lawsuit action, argument, case, cause, contest, dispute, litigation, proceedings, prosecution, suit, trial

lawyer advocate, attorney, barrister, legal adviser, solicitor

lax careless, casual, easy-going, lenient, negligent, remiss, slack, slipshod

lay[1] 1. deposit, establish, leave, place, plant, posit, put, set, set down, settle, spread 2. arrange, dispose, locate, organize, position, set out 3. bear, deposit, produce 4. allot, ascribe, assign, attribute, charge, impute 5. concoct, contrive, design, devise, hatch, plan, plot, prepare, work out 6. bet, gamble, hazard, risk, stake, wager

lay[2] 1. laic, nonclerical, secular 2. amateur, inexpert

layabout good-for-nothing, idler, laggard, loafer, lounger, shirker, vagrant, wastrel

lay down discard, drop, give, surrender, yield

layer bed, ply, row, seam, stratum, thickness, tier

lay in amass, build up, collect, hoard, stockpile

layman amateur, lay person, nonprofessional, outsider

lay-off discharge, dismissal, unemployment

lay off discharge, dismiss, drop, let go, oust, pay off

lay on cater (for), furnish, give, provide, supply

layout arrangement, design, draft, outline, plan

lay out arrange, design, display, exhibit, plan, spread out

laziness idleness, inactivity, indolence, slackness, sloth, slowness, tardiness

lazy 1. idle, inactive, indolent, inert, slack, slothful, slow 2. drowsy, languid, lethargic, sleepy, sluggish, somnolent, torpid

leach drain, extract, filter, filtrate, lixiviate (*Chem.*), percolate, seep, strain

lead *v.* 1. conduct, escort, guide, pilot, precede, steer, usher 2. cause, dispose, draw, incline, induce, influence, persuade, prevail, prompt 3. command, direct, govern, head, manage, supervise 4. be ahead (of), exceed, excel, outdo, outstrip, surpass, transcend 5. have, live, pass, spend, undergo ~*n.* 6. advantage, edge, first place, margin, precedence, priority, start, supremacy, van 7. direction, example, guidance, leadership, model 8. clue, guide, hint, indication, suggestion, tip 9. leading role, principal, protagonist, star part

leader captain, chief, chieftain, commander, conductor, director, guide, head, principal, ruler, superior

leadership 1. direction, domination, guidance, management, running 2. authority, command, control, influence, initiative, pre-eminence, supremacy, sway

leading chief, first, foremost, greatest, highest, main, outstanding, principal, ruling, superior

leaf *n.* 1. blade, flag, needle, pad 2. folio, page, sheet

leaflet bill, booklet, circular, handbill, pamphlet

league alliance, association, band, coalition, combination, compact, confederacy, fellowship, fraternity, group, guild, partnership, union

leak *n.* 1. chink, crack, crevice, fissure, hole, opening, puncture 2. drip, leakage, percolation, seepage 3. disclosure, divulgence ~*v.* 4. discharge, drip, escape, exude, pass, percolate, seep, spill, trickle 5. disclose, divulge

lean[1] *v.* 1. be supported, prop, recline, repose, rest 2. bend, incline, slant, slope, tilt, tip

lean[2] *adj.* 1. bony, emaciated, gaunt, lank, rangy, skinny, slender, slim, spare, thin, wiry 2. bare, barren, meagre, pitiful, poor, scanty, sparse

leaning aptitude, bent, bias, inclination, liking, partiality, penchant, proneness, taste, tendency

leap 1. *v.* bounce, bound, caper, cavort, frisk, gambol, hop, jump, skip, spring 2. *n.* bound, caper, frisk, hop, jump, skip, spring, vault

learn 1. acquire, attain, grasp, imbibe, master, pick up 2. get off, pat, learn by heart, memorize 3. detect, discern, discover, find out, gain, gather, hear, understand

learned academic, cultured, erudite, expert, highbrow, lettered, literate, scholarly, skilled, versed, well-read

learner beginner, disciple, novice, pupil, scholar, student, trainee, tyro

learning culture, education, erudition, information, knowledge, letters, lore, research, schooling, study, tuition, wisdom

lease *v.* charter, hire, let, loan, rent

least fewest, last, lowest, meanest, minimum, poorest, smallest, tiniest

leave[1] *v.* 1. abandon, decamp, depart, desert, disappear, exit, forsake, go, move, quit, relinquish, retire, withdraw 2. abandon, cease, desert, desist, drop, forbear, give up, refrain, relinquish, renounce, stop 3. allot, assign, cede, commit, consign, entrust, refer 4. bequeath, transmit, will

leave[2] *n.* 1. allowance, concession, consent, freedom, liberty, permission, sanction 2. furlough, holiday, sabbatical, time off, vacation

leave out bar, cast aside, count out, disregard, except, exclude, ignore, neglect, omit, overlook, reject

lecture *n.* 1. address, discourse, harangue, instruction, lesson, speech, talk ~*v.* 2. address, discourse, expound, harangue, speak, talk, teach ~*n.* 3. censure, chiding, rebuke, reprimand, reproof, scolding ~*v.* 4. admonish, castigate, censure, chide, rate, reprimand, reprove, scold

lees deposit, dregs, grounds, sediment

leeway latitude, margin, play, room, scope, space

left-handed awkward, careless, clumsy, fumbling, gauche, maladroit

leg 1. limb, member 2. brace, prop, support, upright 3. lap, part, portion, section, segment, stage, stretch

legacy 1. bequest, estate, gift, heirloom, inheritance 2. heritage, patrimony, tradition

legal allowed, authorized, lawful, legalized, legitimate, licit, permissible, proper, rightful, sanctioned, valid

legalize allow, approve, license, permit, sanction, validate

legend 1. fable, fiction, folk tale, myth, narrative, saga, story, tale 2. caption, device, motto

legendary fabled, fabulous, fanciful, fictitious, mythical, romantic, storied, traditional

legibility clarity, neatness, plainness, readability

legible clear, distinct, neat, plain, readable

legion *n.* 1. army, brigade, company, division, force, troop 2. drove, horde, host, mass, multitude, myriad, number, throng ~*adj.* 3. countless, myriad

legislate enact, establish, ordain, prescribe

legislation 1. enactment, prescription, regulation 2. act, bill, charter, law, measure

legislative *adj.* congressional, judicial, ordaining, parliamentary

legislator lawgiver, parliamentarian

legislature assembly, chamber, congress, diet, parliament, senate

legitimate authentic, genuine, lawful, legal, licit, proper, real, rightful, sanctioned, statutory, true

leisure ease, freedom, holiday, liberty, opportunity, pause, quiet, recreation, relaxation, respite, rest, retirement, spare time, vacation

leisurely comfortable, easy, gentle, lazy, relaxed, restful, slow, unhurried

lend 1. advance, loan 2. add, afford, bestow, confer, contribute, furnish, give, grant, impart, present, provide, supply

length 1. *Of linear extent* distance, extent, measure, reach, span 2. *Of time* duration, period, space, span, stretch, term

lengthen continue, draw out, elongate, expand, extend, increase, prolong, protract, stretch

lengthy diffuse, extended, interminable, long, prolix, tedious, verbose

leniency, lenience clemency, forbearance, gentleness, indulgence, mercy, mildness, tolerance

lenient forbearing, forgiving, gentle, indulgent, kind, merciful, mild, tender, tolerant

less *adj.* 1. shorter, slighter, smaller 2. inferior, minor, secondary, subordinate ~*adv.* 3. barely, little, meagrely

lessen abate, abridge, contract, curtail, decrease, die down, diminish, ease, impair, lighten, lower, moderate, narrow, reduce, shrink, slacken, weaken

lesser inferior, lower, minor, secondary, slighter, subordinate

lesson 1. class, coaching, instruction, period, schooling, teaching, tutoring 2. deterrent, example, exemplar, message, model, moral, precept

let *v.* 1. allow, authorize, give leave, grant, permit, sanction, tolerate, warrant 2. hire, lease, rent

let down disappoint, fail, leave stranded

lethal baneful, deadly, destructive, devastating, fatal, mortal, murderous, pernicious, virulent

lethargic apathetic, comatose, drowsy, dull, heavy, inactive, inert, languid, lazy, listless, sleepy, slothful, slow, sluggish, somnolent, torpid

lethargy apathy, inaction, inertia, languor, lassitude, listlessness, sloth, stupor, torpidity, torpor

let in admit, greet, include, incorporate, receive, take in, welcome

let off 1. discharge, emit, explode, fire, give off, leak, release 2. absolve, discharge, excuse, exempt, exonerate, forgive, pardon, release, spare

let out 1. emit, produce 2. discharge, free, liberate, release 3. betray, disclose, leak, reveal

letter 1. character, sign, symbol 2. acknowledgment, answer, communication, dispatch, epistle, line, message, missive, note, reply

let-up abatement, break, cessation, interval, lull, pause, recess, respite

let up abate, decrease, diminish, moderate, slacken, stop, subside

level *adj.* 1. even, flat, horizontal, plain, plane, smooth, uniform 2. balanced, comparable, equivalent, even, flush, in line, on a line, on a par, proportionate 3. calm, equable, even, even-tempered, stable, steady ~*v.* 4. flatten, plane, smooth 5. bulldoze, demolish, destroy, flatten, raze, smooth, wreck ~*n.* 6. altitude, elevation, height 7. bed, floor, layer, storey, stratum

level-headed balanced, calm, collected, composed, cool, dependable, reasonable, sane, sensible, steady

lever 1. *n.* bar, crowbar, handle 2. *v.* force, move, prise, purchase, raise

levity facetiousness, flightiness, frivolity, giddiness, silliness, skittishness, triviality

levy 1. *v.* charge, collect, demand, exact, gather, impose, tax 2. *n.* assessment, collection, exaction, gathering, imposition

lewd bawdy, blue, dirty, impure, indecent, libidinous, licentious, loose, obscene, pornographic, salacious, smutty, unchaste, vile, vulgar, wanton

lewdness crudity, depravity, impurity, indecency, lechery, licentiousness, obscenity, profligacy, smut, unchastity, vulgarity

liability 1. accountability, duty, obligation, onus, responsibility 2. arrear, debit, debt, obligation 3. burden, disadvantage, drag, drawback, encumbrance, handicap, hindrance, impediment, millstone, nuisance

liable 1. accountable, answerable, bound, responsible 2. exposed, open, subject, susceptible, vulnerable

liaison 1. communication, connection, contact, go-between, hook-up, interchange 2. affair, amour, intrigue, romance

liar fibber, perjurer, prevaricator

libel 1. *n.* aspersion, calumny, defamation, slander, smear 2. *v.* blacken, calumniate, defame, malign, revile, slander, slur, smear, traduce, vilify

libellous aspersive, defamatory, derogatory, false, injurious, malicious, scurrilous, slanderous, traducing, untrue, vituperative

liberal 1. advanced, libertarian, progressive, radical, reformist 2. altruistic, bountiful, charitable, free-handed, generous, kind, open handed, unstinting 3. abundant, ample, bountiful, copious, handsome, lavish, munificent, plentiful, profuse, rich

liberality 1. altruism, bounty, charity, generosity, kindness, largess, munificence, openhandedness, philanthropy 2. breadth, broad-mindedness, candour, impartiality, latitude, magnanimity, toleration

liberalize broaden, ease, expand, extend, loosen, moderate, relax, slacken, soften, stretch

liberate deliver, discharge, emancipate, free, redeem, release, rescue, set free

liberation deliverance, emancipation, freedom, release

liberator deliverer, rescuer, saviour

libertine debauchee, lecher, rake, reprobate, roué, seducer, womanizer

liberty 1. autonomy, emancipation, freedom, immunity, independence, release, self-determination, sovereignty 2. carte blanche, dispensation, franchise, freedom, leave, licence, permission, privilege, right, sanction

licence *n.* 1. authority, carte blanche, certificate, charter, dispensation, entitlement, exemption, immunity, leave, liberty, permission, permit, privilege, right, warrant 2. abandon, anarchy, disorder, excess, indulgence, lawlessness, laxity, unruliness

license *v.* accredit, allow, authorize, certify, commission, empower, permit, sanction, warrant

licentious abandoned, debauched, disorderly, dissolute, immoral, impure, lascivious, lax, lewd, profligate, sensual, uncontrolled, unruly, wanton

lick brush, lap, taste, tongue, touch, wash

lie[1] 1. *v.* equivocate, fabricate, falsify, fib, invent, misrepresent, perjure, prevaricate 2. *n.* deceit, fabrication, falsehood, fib, fiction, invention, mendacity, prevarication, untruth

lie[2] *v.* 1. be prone, be recumbent, be supine, couch, loll, lounge, recline, repose, rest, sprawl, stretch out 2. be interred, be located, belong, be placed, be situated, exist, extend, remain

life 1. being, breath, entity, growth, vitality 2. being, career, course, duration, existence, span, time 3. human, individual, mortal, person, soul 4. autobiography, biography, career, confessions, history, memoirs, story 5. behaviour, conduct 6. activity, brio, energy, go (*Inf.*), high spirits, liveliness, sparkle, spirit, verve, vigour, vitality, vivacity, zest

lifeless 1. cold, dead, deceased, defunct, extinct, inanimate, inert 2. comatose, inert, insensate, insensible

lifelike authentic, exact, faithful, natural, real, realistic, vivid

lifelong constant, enduring, lasting, long-lasting, long-standing, perennial, permanent, persistent

lift *v.* 1. elevate, hoist, pick up, raise, rear, upheave, uplift, upraise 2. annul, cancel, end, relax, remove, rescind, revoke, stop, terminate 3. ascend, be dispelled, climb, disappear, disperse, dissipate, mount, rise, vanish ~*n.* 4. car ride, drive, ride, run, transport 5. boost, encouragement, fillip, pick-me-up, reassurance, uplift

light[1] *n.* 1. blaze, brilliance, flash, glare, gleam, glint, glow, illumination, radiance, ray, shine, sparkle 2. beacon, bulb, candle, flare, lamp, lantern, star, taper, torch 3. cockcrow, dawn, daybreak, daylight, daytime, morning, sun, sunbeam, sunrise, sunshine 4. example, exemplar, model, paragon 5. flame, lighter, match 6. **bring to light** disclose, discover, expose, reveal, show, uncover, unearth, unveil 7. **come to light** appear, transpire, turn up 8. **in (the) light of** because of, considering, in view of ~*adj.* 9. aglow, bright, glowing, shining, sunny 10. blond, faded, fair, pale, pastel ~*v.* 11. fire, ignite, inflame, kindle 12. brighten, clarify, illuminate, irradiate, put on, switch on, turn on 13. animate, brighten, cheer, irradiate, lighten

light[2] *adj.* 1. airy, delicate, easy, flimsy, portable, slight 2. faint, gentle, indistinct, mild, moderate, slight, soft, weak 3. inconsiderable, minute, scanty, slight, small, thin, tiny, trifling, trivial 4. easy, effortless, manageable, moderate, simple, untaxing 5. agile, airy, graceful, lithe, nimble 6. entertaining, frivolous, funny, gay, humorous, pleasing, superficial, trifling, trivial, witty 7. airy, blithe, carefree, cheerful, cheery, fickle, frivolous, gay, lively, merry, sunny 8. frugal, modest, restricted, small ~*v.* 9. alight, land, perch, settle

lighten[1] brighten, flash, gleam, illuminate, irradiate, make bright, shine

lighten[2] 1. ease, unload 2. alleviate, assuage, ease, lessen, mitigate, reduce, relieve

light-headed fickle, flighty, flippant, foolish, frivolous, giddy, inane, shallow, silly, superficial, trifling

light-hearted blithe, bright, carefree, cheerful, gay, glad, gleeful, insouciant, jolly, merry, playful, sunny, untroubled

lightly airily, delicately, faintly, gently, gingerly, slightly, softly, timidly

lightweight *adj.* insignificant, paltry, petty, slight, trifling, trivial, unimportant, worthless

likable, likeable agreeable, amiable, attractive, charming, engaging, friendly, genial, nice, pleasant, pleasing, sympathetic, winning, winsome

like[1] *adj.* akin, alike, allied, analogous, corresponding, identical, relating, resembling, same, similar

like[2] *v.* **1.** delight in, enjoy, love, relish, revel in **2.** admire, appreciate, approve, cherish, esteem, prize

likelihood chance, liability, likeliness, possibility, probability, prospect

likely 1. *adj.* anticipated, apt, disposed, expected, inclined, liable, possible, probable, prone, tending **2.** *adv.* doubtlessly, no doubt, presumably, probably

liken compare, match, parallel, relate

likeness 1. affinity, resemblance, similarity **2.** copy, depiction, effigy, facsimile, image, model, picture, portrait, replica, study

liking affection, appreciation, attraction, bent, bias, desire, fondness, love, penchant, preference, stomach, taste, tendency, weakness

limb appendage, arm, extension, extremity, leg, member, part, wing

limelight attention, fame, prominence, publicity, recognition, stardom

limit *n.* **1.** bound, deadline, end, termination, ultimate, utmost **2.** *Often plural* border, boundary, edge, end, extent, frontier, perimeter, periphery **3.** ceiling, check, curb, maximum, restraint, restriction ~*v.* **4.** bound, check, confine, curb, fix, hinder, ration, restrain, restrict, specify

limitation block, check, condition, constraint, control, curb, drawback, impediment, qualification, restraint, restriction, snag

limited bounded, checked, confined, curbed, defined, finite, fixed, hampered, restricted

limitless boundless, countless, endless, immense, infinite, numberless, unbounded, undefined, unending, untold, vast

limp[1] *v.* falter, hobble, hop, shamble, shuffle

limp[2] *adj.* drooping, flabby, flaccid, floppy, lax, loose, relaxed, slack, soft

line *n.* **1.** band, bar, channel, dash, groove, mark, rule, score, scratch, streak, stripe, stroke **2.** crease, furrow, mark, wrinkle **3.** border, boundary, demarcation, edge, frontier, limit, mark **4.** contour, figure, profile, silhouette **5.** cable, cord, filament, rope, strand, string, thread, wire **6.** axis, course, direction, path, route, track **7.** approach, avenue, belief, course, ideology, method, policy, position, practice, procedure, scheme, system **8.** activity, area, business, calling, department, employment, field, forte, interest, job, occupation, profession, pursuit, trade, vocation **9.** column, file, procession, queue, rank, row, sequence, series **10.** ancestry, breed, family, race, stock, strain, succession **11.** card, letter, message, note, postcard, report, word **12. draw the line** object, prohibit, restrict ~*v.* **13.** crease, cut, draw, furrow, inscribe, mark, rule, score, trace **14.** border, bound, edge, fringe, rank, rim, skirt, verge

lined 1. feint, ruled **2.** worn, wrinkled

lines 1. configuration, contour, cut, outline, shape, style **2.** convention, example, model, pattern, plan, principle, procedure **3.** part, script, words

line-up arrangement, array, row, selection, team

line up 1. fall in, form ranks, queue up **2.** assemble, obtain, organize, prepare, procure, produce, secure

linger 1. loiter, remain, stay, stop, tarry, wait **2.** abide, continue, endure, persist, remain, stay

lingering dragging, persistent, remaining, slow

link *n.* **1.** component, element, member, part, piece **2.** association, attachment, bond, connection, joint, knot, tie, tie-up, vinculum ~*v.* **3.** attach, bind, connect, couple, fasten, join, tie, unite, yoke **4.** associate, bracket, connect, identify

lip 1. brim, brink, edge, margin, rim **2.** *Sl.* effrontery, insolence, rudeness

liquid *n.* **1.** fluid, juice, liquor ~*adj.* **2.** fluid, melted, molten, running, runny, thawed, wet **3.** brilliant, clear, limpid, shining, translucent **4.** dulcet, fluent, mellifluent, mellifluous, melting, smooth, soft, sweet **5.** *Of assets* convertible, negotiable

liquidate 1. clear, discharge, pay, settle, square **2.** abolish, annul, cancel, dissolve, terminate **3.** cash, realize **4.** annihilate, destroy, dispatch, eliminate, exterminate, kill, murder, remove, silence

liquor alcohol, drink, grog, intoxicant, spirits, strong drink

list[1] **1.** *n.* catalogue, directory, file, index, inventory, invoice, register, roll, schedule, tally **2.** *v.* bill, book, catalogue, enrol, enter, enumerate, file, index, itemize, note, record, register, schedule

list[2] **1.** *v.* cant, heel over, incline, lean, tilt, tip **2.** *n.* cant, tilt

listen 1. attend, hark, hear **2.** concentrate, heed, mind, obey, observe

listless apathetic, heavy, indolent, inert, languid, lethargic, limp, sluggish, supine, torpid

literacy articulacy, education, learning, proficiency, scholarship

literal 1. close, exact, faithful, strict, verbatim **2.** actual, genuine, plain, real, simple, true

literally actually, exactly, faithfully, plainly, precisely, really, simply, strictly, truly, verbatim

literary bookish, erudite, formal, learned, literate, well-read

literate cultivated, educated, erudite, informed, learned, lettered, scholarly

literature letters, lore, writings

lithe flexible, lissom, pliable, pliant, supple

litigant claimant, contestant, disputant, party, plaintiff

litigate go to law, prosecute, sue

litigation action, case, contending, disputing, lawsuit, process

litter *n.* **1.** debris, fragments, muck, refuse, rubbish, shreds **2.** clutter, confusion, disarray, disorder, jumble, mess **3.** brood, family, offspring, progeny, young **4.** bedding, couch **5.** palanquin, stretcher ~*v.* **6.** clutter, derange, disorder, scatter, strew

little *adj.* **1.** diminutive, dwarf, elfin, infinitesimal, mini, miniature, minute, petite, pygmy, short, slender, small, tiny, wee **2.** infant, junior, undeveloped, young **3.** insufficient, meagre, scant, skimpy, small, sparse **4.** brief, fleeting, hasty, passing, short, short-lived **5.** insignificant, minor, negligible, paltry, trifling, trivial **6.** base, cheap, mean, petty, small-minded ~*adv.* **7.** barely, hardly **8.** rarely, scarcely, seldom

live[1] *v.* **1.** be, breathe, exist, have life **2.** last, persist, prevail **3.** abide, dwell, inhabit, lodge, occupy, reside, settle **4.** endure, fare, feed, lead, pass, remain, subsist, survive

live[2] *adj.* **1.** alive, animate, breathing, existent, living, vital **2.** active, burning, current, hot, pressing, prevalent, topical, unsettled, vital **3.** alert, brisk, dynamic, earnest, energetic, vivid

livelihood job, living, maintenance, means, occupation, subsistence, work

liveliness activity, boisterousness, briskness, dynamism, energy, gaiety, smartness, spirit, vitality, vivacity

lively 1. active, agile, alert, brisk, chirpy, energetic, keen, nimble, perky, quick, sprightly, spry, vigorous **2.** blithe, cheerful, frisky, gay, merry, spirited, vivacious **3.** astir, bustling, busy, crowded, eventful, moving, stirring **4.** bright, colourful, exciting, forceful, invigorating, racy, refreshing, stimulating, vivid

liven animate, brighten, enliven, rouse, stir, vitalize, vivify

liverish 1. bilious, queasy **2.** crusty, disagreeable, grumpy, ill-humoured, irritable, peevish, snappy

livery attire, clothing, costume, dress, garb, regalia, suit, uniform

livid 1. angry, black-and-blue, bruised, contused, discoloured, purple **2.** ashen, bloodless, greyish, leaden, pale, pallid, pasty, wan, waxen **3.** enraged, fuming, furious, incensed, indignant

living *adj.* **1.** active, alive, breathing, existing, strong, vigorous, vital ~*n.* **2.** being, existence, life, subsistence **3.** job, livelihood, maintenance, occupation, subsistence, sustenance, work

load *n.* **1.** bale, cargo, freight, lading, shipment **2.** burden, incubus, millstone, onus, oppression, pressure, trouble, weight, worry ~*v.* **3.** cram, fill, freight, heap, lade, pack, pile, stack, stuff **4.** burden, hamper, oppress, trouble, worry **5.** charge, prime

loaded 1. burdened, charged, full, laden, weighted **2.** biased, distorted, weighted **3.** charged, primed **4.** *Sl.* affluent, moneyed, rich, wealthy, well off, well-to-do

loaf block, cake, cube, lump, slab

loan *n.* advance, credit, mortgage

loathing abhorrence, antipathy, aversion, disgust, hatred, horror, odium, repugnance, repulsion, revulsion

loathsome abhorrent, disgusting, execrable, hateful, horrible, nasty, odious, offensive, repugnant, revolting, vile

lobby *n.* **1.** corridor, foyer, hall, hallway, passage, porch, vestibule **2.** pressure group ~*v.* **3.** campaign for, influence, persuade, pressure, promote

local *adj.* **1.** community, district, parish, regional **2.** confined, limited, narrow, parish, parochial, provincial, restricted ~*n.* **3.** inhabitant, native, resident

locality area, district, region, vicinity

locate detect, discover, find, pinpoint, unearth

location bearings, locale, place, point, site, situation, spot, venue

lock 1. *n.* bolt, clasp, padlock **2.** *v.* bolt, close, fasten, latch, seal, secure, shut

lockup cell, gaol, jail

lock up cage, confine, detain, imprison, incarcerate, jail

lodge *n.* **1.** cabin, chalet, cottage, gatehouse, house, hut, shelter **2.** association, branch, club, group, society ~*v.* **3.** accommodate, billet, board, entertain, harbour, put up, shelter, stay, stop **4.** catch, imbed, implant, stick

lodger boarder, guest, paying guest, resident, tenant

lodging abode, accommodation, boarding, dwelling, habitation, residence, rooms, shelter

lofty 1. high, raised, soaring, tall, towering **2.** distinguished, elevated, grand, illustrious, imposing, majestic, noble, stately, superior **3.** condescending, haughty, lordly, patronizing, proud, supercilious

log *n.* **1.** block, chunk, stump, trunk **2.** account, chart, journal, listing, record, tally ~*v.* **3.** book, chart, note, record, register, tally

loggerhead at loggerheads estranged, feuding, opposed, quarrelling

logic 1. reason, sense, sound judgment **2.** link, rationale, relationship

logical clear, cogent, coherent, consistent, rational, relevant, sound, valid

loiter dally, dawdle, delay, idle, lag, linger, loaf, stroll

lone isolated, one, only, separate, single, sole, unaccompanied

loneliness desolation, isolation, seclusion, solitude

lonely 1. abandoned, estranged, forlorn, forsaken, friendless, outcast **2.** alone, apart, single, solitary, withdrawn **3.** deserted, remote, secluded, solitary, uninhabited

long[1] *adj.* expanded, extended, lengthy, stretched

long[2] *v.* covet, crave, desire, hanker, hunger, itch, lust, pine, want, yearn

longing ambition, aspiration, coveting, craving, desire, hungering, itch, thirst, urge, wish

long-standing enduring, established, fixed, time-honoured
long-suffering easygoing, patient, resigned, stoical, tolerant
long-winded garrulous, lengthy, prolix, rambling, repetitious, tedious, verbose, wordy
look *v.* **1.** consider, contemplate, examine, eye, gaze, glance, inspect, observe, peep, regard, scan, scrutinize, see, study, survey, view, watch **2.** appear, display, evidence, exhibit, present, seem, show **3.** forage, hunt, search, seek ~*n.* **4.** gaze, glance, glimpse, inspection, observation, review, sight, survey, view **5.** air, appearance, aspect, bearing, cast, complexion, demeanour, effect, expression, face, fashion, guise, manner
look after guard, mind, nurse, protect, tend, watch
look down on *or* **upon** despise, disdain, scorn, sneer, spurn
look forward to anticipate, await, expect
look into check out, delve into, examine, explore, inspect, investigate, probe, research, scrutinize, study
lookout 1. guard, vigil, watch **2.** guard, sentinel, sentry **3.** beacon, citadel, post, watchtower
look out be careful, be vigilant, beware, watch out
look over check, examine, inspect, monitor, peruse, scan, view
look up 1. find, research **2.** ameliorate, improve, progress
loom appear, bulk, emerge, hover, impend, menace, take shape, threaten
loop 1. *n.* bend, circle, coil, curl, curve, eyelet, kink, noose, ring, spiral, twirl, twist **2.** *v.* bend, circle, coil, connect, curl, encircle, fold, join, knot, roll, turn, twist
loophole 1. aperture, opening, slot **2.** *Fig.* avoidance, escape, evasion, excuse, plea, pretext
loose *adj.* **1.** floating, free, insecure, movable, released, unattached, unfastened, unsecured, untied, wobbly **2.** baggy, easy, relaxed, slack, sloppy **3.** diffuse, ill-defined, imprecise, inaccurate, indefinite, inexact, rambling, random, vague **4.** abandoned, disreputable, dissipated, dissolute, fast, immoral, lewd, licentious, promiscuous, unchaste, wanton ~*v.* **5.** detach, disengage, ease, free, release, slacken, unbind, undo, unfasten, unloose, untie
loosen 1. detach, separate, slacken, undo, unstick, untie **2.** deliver, free, liberate, release
loot booty, goods, haul, plunder, prize, spoils
lopsided askew, awry, crooked, off balance, squint, tilting, unbalanced, uneven
lord 1. commander, governor, leader, master, potentate, prince, ruler, seigneur, sovereign, superior **2.** earl, noble, nobleman, peer, viscount
lordly arrogant, despotic, dictatorial, disdainful, haughty, imperious, lofty, patronizing, proud, supercilious
lore beliefs, doctrine, folk-wisdom, teaching, wisdom
lose 1. displace, drop, forget, mislay, misplace, miss **2.** capitulate, default, fail, forfeit, miss, yield **3.** be defeated
loser also-ran, failure, underdog
loss 1. deprivation, failure, losing, misfortune, privation, waste **2.** cost, damage, defeat, destruction, detriment, harm, hurt, injury, ruin
lost 1. disappeared, forfeited, mislaid, misplaced, missing, strayed, vanished, wayward **2.** adrift, astray, at sea, disoriented, off-course **3.** baffled, bewildered, confused, helpless, ignorant, mystified, perplexed, puzzled **4.** absent, absorbed, distracted, dreamy, entranced, preoccupied, rapt, spellbound **5.** bygone, dead, extinct, forgotten, gone, lapsed, obsolete, past **6.** abandoned, corrupt, damned, depraved, fallen
lot 1. batch, collection, crowd, group, quantity, set **2.** accident, chance, destiny, doom, fate, fortune, hazard, plight, portion **3.** allowance, parcel, part, piece, portion, quota, ration, share **4. a lot** *or* **lots** abundance, a great deal, heap(s), numbers, piles, plenty, quantities, scores
lotion balm, cream, liniment, solution
lottery 1. draw, raffle, sweepstake **2.** chance, gamble, hazard, risk
loud 1. blaring, blatant, deafening, ear-piercing, noisy, piercing, resounding, rowdy, sonorous, stentorian, strident, strong, thundering, tumultuous, turbulent, vehement **2.** *Fig.* brassy, flamboyant, flashy, garish, gaudy, glaring, lurid, ostentatious, showy, tasteless, vulgar **3.** brash, brazen, coarse, crass, crude, raucous, vulgar
loudly deafeningly, noisily, shrilly, vigorously
lounge *v.* laze, loaf, loiter, recline, relax, saunter, sprawl
lout bear, boor, churl, clod, dolt, gawk, lubber, oaf, yahoo
lovable amiable, attractive, charming, cuddly, delightful, enchanting, endearing, lovely, pleasing, sweet, winning
love *v.* **1.** cherish, hold dear, idolize, prize, treasure, worship **2.** appreciate, desire, enjoy, fancy, like, relish, savour **3.** caress, cuddle, embrace, fondle, kiss, pet ~*n.* **4.** adulation, affection, ardour, devotion, fondness, friendship, infatuation, liking, passion, rapture, regard, tenderness, warmth
lovely 1. attractive, beautiful, charming, comely, exquisite, graceful, handsome, pretty, sweet **2.** agreeable, delightful, enjoyable, gratifying, nice, pleasant
lover admirer, beau, beloved, boyfriend, girlfriend, mistress, paramour, suitor, sweetheart
loving affectionate, ardent, cordial, dear, devoted, doting, fond, friendly, kind, tender, warm
low 1. little, short, small, squat, stunted **2.** deep, shallow, subsided, sunken **3.** depleted, little, meagre, paltry, reduced, scant, small, sparse, trifling **4.** deficient, inadequate, inferior, mediocre, poor, puny, second-rate, shoddy, worthless **5.** coarse, common, crude, disgraceful, dishonourable, disreputable, gross, obscene, rough, rude, unrefined, vulgar **6.** humble, lowborn, lowly, meek, obscure, plain, plebeian, poor, simple **7.** blue, dejected, depressed, despondent, disheartened, down, forlorn, gloomy, glum, miserable, morose, sad, unhappy **8.** gentle, hushed, muffled, muted, quiet, soft, subdued, whispered **9.** cheap, economical, inexpensive, moderate, modest, reasonable **10.** abject, base, dastardly, degraded, depraved, despicable, ignoble, mean, nasty, sordid, unworthy, vile, vulgar
lower *adj.* **1.** inferior, junior, lesser, minor, secondary, smaller, subordinate ~*v.* **2.** depress, drop, fall, sink, submerge **3.** abase, belittle, debase, degrade, deign, demean, devalue, disgrace, humiliate
low-grade bad, inferior, poor, substandard
lowly 1. ignoble, inferior, mean, obscure, plebeian, subordinate **2.** docile, dutiful, gentle, meek, modest, unassuming
low-spirited apathetic, blue, dejected, depressed, despondent, down, gloomy, low, miserable, moody, sad, unhappy
loyal attached, constant, dependable, devoted, dutiful, faithful, staunch, steadfast, true, trustworthy, unswerving, unwavering
loyalty allegiance, faithfulness, fidelity, patriotism, staunchness, steadfastness, trustiness
lubricate grease, oil, smear
lucid 1. clear, distinct, evident, explicit, intelligible, limpid, obvious, plain, transparent **2.** beaming, bright, brilliant, effulgent, gleaming, radiant, shining **3.** clear, diaphanous, limpid, pure, transparent
luck 1. accident, chance, destiny, fate, fortune **2.** advantage, blessing, fluke, prosperity, stroke, success, windfall
luckily favourably, fortunately, happily, opportunely
luckless cursed, disastrous, doomed, hapless, hopeless, jinxed, unfortunate, unhappy, unpropitious, unsuccessful
lucky blessed, charmed, favoured, fortunate, prosperous, successful
lucrative fat, fruitful, gainful, paying, productive, profitable, remunerative, well-paid
lucre gain, mammon, money, profit, riches, spoils, wealth
ludicrous absurd, burlesque, comic, crazy, droll, funny, laughable, odd, preposterous, ridiculous, silly
luggage baggage, bags, cases, gear, suitcases, trunks
lugubrious dismal, doleful, dreary, funereal, gloomy, melancholy, mournful, sad, serious, sombre, woebegone, woeful
lukewarm apathetic, cold, cool, half-hearted, indifferent, unenthusiastic, uninterested
lull 1. *v.* allay, calm, compose, hush, pacify, quell, quiet, soothe, still, subdue **2.** *n.* calm, calmness, hush, pause, quiet, respite, silence
lullaby berceuse, cradlesong
lumber[1] *n.* clutter, discards, junk, refuse, rubbish, trash
lumber[2] *v.* clump, plod, shamble, shuffle, stump, trudge, trundle
lumbering awkward, blundering, bovine, clumsy, heavy, hulking, overgrown, ponderous, ungainly, unwieldy
luminous bright, brilliant, glowing, lighted, lit, lustrous, radiant, resplendent, shining, vivid
lump *n.* **1.** ball, bunch, cake, chunk, gob, group, hunk, mass, piece, spot, wedge **2.** bulge, bump, growth, protrusion, protererance, swelling, tumour ~*v.* **3.** bunch, collect, combine, group, mass, pool, unite
lunacy 1. derangement, idiocy, insanity, madness **2.** absurdity, craziness, folly, foolishness, idiocy, madness, stupidity
lunatic 1. *adj.* crazy, daft, demented, deranged, insane, irrational, mad, unhinged **2.** *n.* madman, maniac, psychopath
lunge 1. *n.* charge, cut, jab, pass, spring, stab, swing, swipe, thrust **2.** *v.* bound, charge, cut, dash, dive, jab, leap, poke, stab, thrust
lure 1. *v.* attract, beckon, decoy, draw, ensnare, entice, inveigle, invite, lead on, seduce, tempt **2.** *n.* attraction, bait, decoy, magnet, temptation
lurid 1. graphic, melodramatic, sensational, shocking, startling, unrestrained, vivid **2.** disgusting, ghastly, gory, grim, gruesome, macabre, revolting, savage, violent
lurk crouch, hide, prowl, skulk, slink, sneak, snoop
luscious appetizing, delectable, delicious, honeyed, juicy, mouth-watering, palatable, rich, savoury, succulent, sweet
lush abundant, dense, green, lavish, prolific, rank, teeming, verdant
lust *n.* **1.** carnality, lechery, lewdness, libido, salaciousness, sensuality, wantonness **2.** appetite, avidity, craving, cupidity, desire, greed, longing, passion, thirst ~*v.* **3.** covet, crave, desire, need, want, yearn
lustre 1. burnish, gleam, glint, glitter, gloss, glow, sheen, shimmer, shine, sparkle **2.** brightness, brilliance, dazzle, radiance, resplendence **3.** distinction, fame, glory, honour, prestige, renown
lusty hale, healthy, hearty, powerful, robust, stalwart, stout, strapping, strong, sturdy, vigorous, virile
luxurious comfortable, costly, expensive, lavish, opulent, rich, splendid, sumptuous
luxury 1. affluence, opulence, richness, splendour **2.** comfort, delight, enjoyment, gratification, indulgence, pleasure, satisfaction, wellbeing **3.** extra, extravagance, treat
lying 1. *n.* deceit, dishonesty, duplicity, fabrication, falsity, guile, mendacity, perjury, untruthfulness **2.** *adj.* deceitful, dishonest, false, guileful, mendacious, perfidious, treacherous, untruthful

M

macabre deathly, dreadful, frightening, frightful, ghastly, ghostly, grim, grisly, gruesome, hideous, horrid, unearthly, weird

machine 1. apparatus, appliance, contraption, contrivance, device, engine, instrument, tool 2. agency, organization, party, structure, system

machinery 1. apparatus, equipment, gear, tackle, tools, works 2. agency, channels, organization, procedure, structure, system

mad 1. crazed, delirious, demented, deranged, distracted, frantic, frenzied, insane, lunatic, psychotic, raving, unbalanced, unhinged 2. absurd, foolhardy, foolish, imprudent, irrational, ludicrous, preposterous, senseless, unreasonable, unsafe, unsound, wild

madden annoy, craze, enrage, exasperate, inflame, infuriate, provoke, upset, vex

made-up fabricated, false, fictional, imaginary, invented, mythical, specious, unreal, untrue

madly 1. crazily, dementedly, distractedly, frantically, frenziedly, hysterically, insanely 2. absurdly, foolishly, irrationally, unreasonably, wildly 3. energetically, excitedly, furiously, hastily, hurriedly, quickly, rapidly, recklessly, speedily, violently, wildly

madness 1. aberration, craziness, delusion, dementia, derangement, distraction, insanity, lunacy, mania, mental illness, psychopathy, psychosis 2. absurdity, daftness (*Inf.*), folly, foolhardiness, foolishness, nonsense, preposterousness, wildness 3. anger, exasperation, frenzy, fury, ire, rage, raving, wildness, wrath 4. ardour, craze, enthusiasm, fanaticism, fondness, infatuation, keenness, passion, rage, zeal 5. abandon, agitation, excitement, frenzy, furore, intoxication, riot, unrestraint, uproar

magazine 1. journal, pamphlet, paper, periodical 2. arsenal, depot, store, warehouse

magic *n.* 1. enchantment, occultism, sorcery, spell, witchcraft 2. conjuring, illusion, legerdemain, trickery 3. allurement, charm, enchantment, fascination, glamour, magnetism, power ~*adj.* 4. *Also* **magical** charming, enchanting, entrancing, fascinating, magnetic, marvellous, miraculous

magistrate judge, justice

magnanimity charitableness, generosity, munificence, nobility, selflessness, unselfishness

magnanimous big, charitable, free, generous, handsome, kind, munificent, noble, selfless, ungrudging, unselfish

magnate 1. baron, chief, leader, mogul, plutocrat, tycoon 2. baron, grandee, magnifico, merchant, notable, personage, prince

magnetic alluring, attractive, captivating, charming, enchanting, entrancing, hypnotic, irresistible, seductive

magnetism allure, appeal, attraction, charisma, charm, draw, enchantment, fascination, magic, power, pull, spell

magnificence brilliance, glory, grandeur, luxury, majesty, nobility, opulence, pomp, splendour, sublimity

magnificent brilliant, elegant, elevated, exalted, excellent, fine, glorious, gorgeous, grand, imposing, impressive, lavish, noble, opulent, princely, regal, rich, splendid, stately, sumptuous, superb, superior

magnify 1. amplify, augment, boost, deepen, dilate, enlarge, expand, heighten, increase, intensify 2. blow up, dramatize, enhance, exaggerate, inflate, overdo

magnitude 1. consequence, eminence, grandeur, greatness, importance, mark, moment, note, significance, weight 2. amount, amplitude, bulk, capacity, dimensions, expanse, extent, hugeness, immensity, largeness, mass, measure, quantity, size, space, strength, volume

maid 1. damsel, girl, maiden, miss, nymph, wench 2. housemaid, servant

maiden *n.* 1. damsel, girl, maid, miss, nymph, virgin, wench ~*adj.* 2. chaste, intact, pure, virgin 3. first, initial, introductory 4. fresh, new, untapped, untried, unused

mail *n.* 1. letters, packages, parcels, post 2. post, postal service ~*v.* 3. dispatch, forward, post, send

maim cripple, disable, hurt, impair, incapacitate, injure, lame, mangle, mar, mutilate, wound

main 1. *adj.* capital, cardinal, central, chief, critical, crucial, essential, foremost, head, leading, necessary, paramount, particular, pre-eminent, primary, prime, principal, special, supreme, vital 2. *n.* cable, channel, conduit, duct, line, pipe

mainly chiefly, generally, largely, mostly, overall, predominantly, primarily

mainstay anchor, backbone, bulwark, linchpin, pillar, prop

maintain 1. conserve, continue, finance, keep, prolong, look after, nurture, perpetuate, preserve, provide, retain, supply, support, sustain, uphold 2. affirm, allege, assert, asseverate, aver, avow, claim, contend, declare, hold, insist, profess, state 3. back, champion, defend, justify, plead for, uphold, vindicate

maintenance 1. care, conservation, continuation, nurture, perpetuation, preservation, provision, repairs, supply, support, upkeep 2. aliment, alimony, allowance, food, keep, living, subsistence, support, upkeep

majestic awesome, elevated, exalted, grand, imperial, imposing, impressive, kingly, lofty, magnificent, monumental, noble, princely, regal, royal, splendid, stately, sublime, superb

majesty dignity, glory, grandeur, kingliness, magnificence, nobility, pomp, royalty, splendour, state, sublimity

major better, bigger, chief, elder, greater, higher, larger, leading, main, most, senior, superior, supreme, uppermost

majority 1. best part, bulk, mass, more, most, plurality, preponderance, superiority 2. manhood, maturity, seniority

make *v.* 1. assemble, build, compose, constitute, construct, create, fabricate, fashion, forge, form, frame, manufacture, originate, produce, shape, synthesize 2. accomplish, beget, cause, create, effect, generate, occasion, produce 3. cause, coerce, compel, constrain, dragoon, drive, force, impel, induce, oblige, press, require 4. appoint, assign, create, designate, elect, install, invest, nominate, ordain 5. draw up, enact, establish, fix, form, frame, pass 6. compose, constitute, embody, form, represent 7. calculate, estimate, gauge, judge, reckon, suppose, think 8. acquire, clear, earn, gain, get, net, obtain, realize, secure, take in, win ~*n.* 9. brand, build, character, composition, construction, cut, designation, form, kind, mark, model, shape, sort, structure, style, type, variety

make-believe *n.* charade, dream, fantasy, imagination, pretence, unreality

make believe dream, enact, imagine, play, pretend

make do cope, improvise, manage

make off abscond, bolt, decamp, flee, fly

make out 1. detect, discern, discover, espy, perceive, recognize, see 2. decipher, fathom, follow, grasp, perceive, realize, see, understand 3. complete, inscribe

maker author, builder, director, framer, manufacturer, producer

makeshift 1. *adj.* expedient, provisional, stopgap, substitute, temporary 2. *n.* expedient, shift, stopgap, substitute

make-up 1. cosmetics, powder 2. arrangement, assembly, composition, configuration, constitution, construction, format, formation, organization, structure

make up 1. compose, comprise, constitute, form 2. coin, compose, concoct, construct, create, devise, fabricate, formulate, frame, hatch, invent, originate 3. complete, fill, meet, supply

maladjusted disturbed, neurotic, unstable

malady ailment, complaint, disease, illness, indisposition, infirmity, sickness

malcontent agitator, complainer, grouser, grumbler, rebel, troublemaker

male manlike, manly, masculine, virile

malefactor convict, criminal, culprit, delinquent, felon, lawbreaker, offender, outlaw, villain, wrongdoer

malevolence hate, ill will, malice, malignity, rancour, spite, vindictiveness

malevolent baleful, evil-minded, hostile, malicious, malignant, pernicious, spiteful, vengeful, vicious, vindictive

malformation deformity, distortion, misshape

malfunction 1. *v.* break down, fail 2. *n.* breakdown, defect, failure, fault, flaw

malice animosity, bitterness, enmity, hate, hatred, rancour, spite, venom, vindictiveness

malicious baleful, bitter, hateful, injurious, malevolent, pernicious, rancorous, resentful, spiteful, vengeful, vicious

malign 1. *adj.* bad, baleful, baneful, evil, harmful, hostile, hurtful, pernicious, vicious, wicked 2. *v.* abuse, defame, denigrate, disparage, harm, injure, libel, revile, slander, smear, traduce

malignant baleful, bitter, harmful, hostile, hurtful, malevolent, malicious, pernicious, spiteful, vicious

malpractice misbehaviour, misconduct, misdeed, offence

maltreat abuse, damage, harm, hurt, injure, mistreat

mammoth colossal, enormous, giant, huge, immense, massive, mighty, prodigious, titanic, vast

man *n.* 1. gentleman, male 2. adult, being, body, human being, individual, one, person, personage, somebody, soul 3. humanity, human race, mankind, mortals, people 4. attendant, employee, hand, retainer, servant, soldier, subject, valet, vassal, worker, workman ~*v.* 5. crew, fill, garrison, occupy, people, staff

manacle bond, chain, fetter, handcuff, iron, shackle, tie

manage 1. administer, command, concert, conduct, direct, govern, oversee, rule, run, supervise 2. accomplish, arrange, contrive, deal with, effect, engineer, succeed 3. control, guide, handle, influence, manipulate, operate, pilot, ply, steer, train, use, wield

manageable compliant, controllable, docile, easy, handy, submissive, tractable, wieldy

management administration, board, directorate, employers

manager conductor, controller, director, executive, governor, head, organizer, proprietor, supervisor

mandate authority, bidding, charge, command, decree, directive, edict, fiat, instruction, order, sanction, warrant

mandatory binding, compulsory, obligatory, required, requisite

mangle butcher, crush, cut, deform, destroy, distort, hack, maim, mar, mutilate, spoil, tear, wreck

mangy dirty, mean, scruffy, seedy, shabby, shoddy, squalid

manhandle 1. maul, pull, push 2. carry, haul, heave, lift, manoeuvre, pull, push, shove, tug

manhood bravery, courage, firmness, masculinity, maturity, mettle, resolution, spirit, strength, valour, virility

mania craziness, delirium, derangement, disorder, frenzy, insanity, lunacy, madness

maniac lunatic, madman, psychopath

manifest *adj.* apparent, clear, distinct, evident, glaring, noticeable, obvious, open, patent, plain, visible

manifestation disclosure, display, exhibition, exposure, instance, mark, materialization, revelation, show, sign, symptom, token

manifold abundant, assorted,

diverse, many, multiple, numerous, varied, various
manipulate 1. employ, handle, operate, ply, use, wield, work 2. direct, guide, influence, negotiate, steer
mankind humanity, human race, man, people
manliness boldness, bravery, courage, heroism, masculinity, valour, vigour, virility
manly bold, brave, courageous, daring, fearless, gallant, hardy, heroic, male, masculine, noble, powerful, resolute, robust, strong, valiant, valorous, vigorous, virile
man-made artificial, manufactured, synthetic
manner 1. air, appearance, aspect, bearing, behaviour, conduct, demeanour, deportment, look, presence, tone 2. approach, custom, genre, habit, line, method, mode, practice, process, routine, style, tenor, usage, way, wont
mannerism foible, habit, peculiarity, quirk, trait, trick
mannerly civil, civilized, courteous, genteel, gracious, polished, polite, refined, well-bred
manners 1. bearing, behaviour, breeding, carriage, conduct, demeanour, deportment 2. courtesy, decorum, etiquette, polish, politeness, protocol, refinement
manoeuvre *n.* 1. action, artifice, dodge, intrigue, machination, move, plan, plot, ploy, ruse, scheme, subterfuge, tactic, trick ~*v.* 2. contrive, devise, engineer, intrigue, manage, plan, plot, scheme 3. direct, drive, guide, handle, navigate, pilot, steer
mansion abode, dwelling, habitation, hall, manor, residence, seat, villa
manual 1. *adj.* hand-operated, human, physical 2. *n.* bible, guide, handbook, instructions
manufacture 1. *v.* assemble, build, compose, construct, create, forge, form, make, mould, process, produce, shape, think up, trump up 2. *n.* assembly, construction, fabrication, production
manure compost, droppings, dung, muck, ordure
many *adj.* abundant, copious, countless, frequent, manifold, myriad, numerous, profuse, sundry, varied, various
mar blemish, blight, blot, damage, deface, harm, hurt, injure, ruin, scar, spoil, stain, taint, tarnish, vitiate
maraud forage, foray, loot, pillage, plunder, raid, ransack, ravage, sack
march *v.* 1. file, pace, parade, stalk, stride, strut, tramp, tread, walk ~*n.* 2. tramp, trek, walk 3. demonstration, parade, procession
margin 1. border, bound, brim, brink, confine, edge, limit, rim, side, verge 2. allowance, extra, latitude, leeway, play, room, scope, space
marginal borderline, peripheral
marine maritime, nautical, naval, oceanic, seafaring
mariner bluejacket, hand, sailor, salt, seafarer, seaman, tar
marital conjugal, married, matrimonial, nuptial, wedded
maritime marine, nautical, naval, oceanic, sea, seafaring
mark *n.* 1. blot, bruise, dent, impression, line, nick, scar, scratch, smudge, spot, stain, streak 2. badge, blaze, brand, emblem, evidence, feature, hallmark, indication, label, note, print, proof, seal, sign, stamp, symbol, symptom, token 3. aim, end, goal, object, objective, purpose, target 4. footprint, sign, trace, track, trail, vestige ~*v.* 5. blemish, blot, blotch, brand, bruise, dent, impress, imprint, nick, scar, scratch, smudge, stain, streak 6. brand, identify, label, stamp 7. attend, mind, note, notice, observe, regard, remark, watch
marked apparent, clear, conspicuous, decided, distinct, evident, manifest, notable, noted, obvious, patent, remarkable, signal, striking
markedly clearly, conspicuously, decidedly, distinctly, evidently, greatly, manifestly, notably, obviously, patently, remarkably, signally, strikingly
market 1. *n.* bazaar, fair, mart 2. *v.* retail, sell, vend
maroon abandon, cast away, desert, leave, strand
marriage 1. match, matrimony, wedding, wedlock 2. alliance, association, coupling, link, merger, union
married 1. joined, one, united, wed, wedded 2. conjugal, connubial, marital, matrimonial, nuptial, wifely
marrow core, cream, essence, gist, heart, kernel, pith, quick, substance
marry 1. espouse, wed 2. ally, bond, join, knit, link, match, merge, tie, unite, yoke
marsh bog, fen, quagmire, slough, swamp
marshal align, arrange, array, assemble, collect, deploy, dispose, gather, group, muster, order, rank
marshy boggy, miry, spongy, swampy, wet
martial bellicose, heroic, military
martinet disciplinarian, stickler
martyrdom agony, anguish, ordeal, persecution, suffering, torment, torture
marvel 1. *v.* gape, gaze, goggle, wonder 2. *n.* genius, miracle, phenomenon, portent, prodigy, wonder
marvellous amazing, astounding, breathtaking, extraordinary, miraculous, prodigious, remarkable, stupendous, wondrous
masculine 1. male, manful, manlike, manly, virile 2. bold, brave, gallant, hardy, powerful, resolute, robust, strong, vigorous
mass *n.* 1. block, chunk, hunk, lump, piece 2. body, collection, entirety, sum, totality, whole 3. batch, bunch, collection, combination, heap, load, lot, pile, quantity, stack 4. assemblage, band, body, crowd, group, horde, host, lot, mob, number, throng, troop 5. body, bulk, majority, preponderance 6. bulk, greatness, magnitude, size ~*adj.* 7. extensive, indiscriminate, large-scale, pandemic, popular, wholesale, widespread ~*v.* 8. accumulate, assemble, collect, forgather, gather, mob, muster, rally, swarm, throng
massacre 1. *n.* butchery, carnage, killing, murder, slaughter 2. *v.* butcher, exterminate, kill, mow down, murder, slaughter, slay
massage 1. *n.* manipulation, rub-down 2. *v.* manipulate, rub down
massive big, bulky, enormous, extensive, gigantic, great, heavy, huge, hulking, immense, imposing, impressive, ponderous, solid, substantial, vast, weighty
master *n.* 1. captain, chief, commander, controller, director, employer, governor, head, lord, manager, overlord, overseer, owner, principal, ruler 2. adept, expert, genius, maestro, virtuoso, wizard ~*adj.* 3. adept, expert, masterly, proficient, skilful, skilled ~*v.* 4. acquire, grasp, learn 5. bridle, check, conquer, curb, defeat, overcome, quash, quell, subdue, subjugate, suppress, tame, vanquish
masterful 1. adept, adroit, clever, deft, expert, first-rate, skilful, skilled, superior, supreme 2. arrogant, dictatorial, domineering, high-handed
masterly adept, adroit, clever, fine, first-rate, skilful, superior
masterpiece classic, jewel, *tour de force*
mastery 1. command, familiarity, grasp, knowledge, understanding 2. ability, attainment, expertise, prowess, skill
match *n.* 1. bout, contest, game, test, trial 2. counterpart, equal, equivalent, peer, rival 3. copy, double, duplicate, equal, replica, twin 4. affiliation, alliance, combination, couple, duet, marriage, pair, pairing, partnership, union ~*v.* 5. ally, combine, couple, join, link, marry, mate, pair, unite, yoke 6. adapt, agree, blend, correspond, fit, go with, harmonize, suit, tally 7. compare, contend, equal, oppose, pit against, rival, vie
matching comparable, corresponding, double, duplicate, equal, identical, like, paired, same, twin
matchless consummate, incomparable, inimitable, peerless, perfect, superlative, supreme, unequalled, unique, unrivalled
mate *n.* 1. husband, partner, spouse, wife 2. colleague, companion, fellow-worker 3. assistant, helper, subordinate ~*v.* 4. breed, copulate, couple, pair 5. marry, match, wed 6. couple, join, match, pair, yoke
material *n.* 1. body, element, matter, stuff, substance 2. data, evidence, facts, information, notes, work 3. cloth, fabric, stuff ~*adj.* 4. bodily, concrete, fleshly, physical, substantial, tangible, worldly 5. essential, grave, important, key, meaningful, momentous, serious, significant, vital, weighty
materialize appear, happen, occur, turn up
materially considerably, essentially, gravely, greatly, much, seriously, significantly, substantially
matrimonial conjugal, marital, married, nuptial, wedding
matrimony marriage, nuptials, wedlock
matrix forge, mould, origin, source
matter *n.* 1. body, stuff, substance 2. affair, business, concern, episode, event, incident, occurrence, question, situation, subject, topic 3. importance, moment, note, significance, weight ~*v.* 4. signify
matter-of-fact deadpan, dry, dull, flat, lifeless, mundane, plain, prosaic, sober
mature 1. *adj.* adult, fit, grown, matured, mellow, of age, perfect, prepared, ready, ripe, seasoned 2. *v.* age, bloom, develop, mellow, perfect, ripen, season
maturity adulthood, experience, fullness, majority, manhood, perfection, ripeness, wisdom
maudlin lachrymose, sentimental, tearful
maul 1. abuse, ill-treat, manhandle, molest, paw 2. batter, beat, claw, lacerate, mangle, pummel, thrash
maxim adage, aphorism, axiom, byword, motto, proverb, rule, saw, saying
maximum 1. *n.* ceiling, crest, extremity, height, most, peak, pinnacle, summit, top, utmost, uttermost, zenith 2. *adj.* greatest, highest, most, topmost, utmost
maybe perchance, perhaps, possibly
mayhem chaos, commotion, confusion, destruction, disorder, fracas, havoc, trouble, violence
maze 1. intricacy, labyrinth, meander 2. *Fig.* imbroglio, perplexity, puzzle, snarl, tangle, web
meadow field, grassland, pasture
meagre deficient, inadequate, little, paltry, poor, puny, scanty, short, slender, slight, small, spare, sparse
mean[1] *v.* 1. betoken, convey, denote, express, imply, indicate, purport, represent, say, signify, spell, suggest, symbolize 2. aim, aspire, design, desire, intend, plan, propose, purpose, set out, want, wish
mean[2] *adj.* 1. beggarly, close, mercenary, miserly, parsimonious, stingy, tight, ungenerous 2. abject, base, callous, contemptible, degraded, despicable, ignoble, low-minded, petty, scurvy, shabby, shameful, sordid, vile, wretched 3. beggarly, insignificant, miserable, paltry, petty, poor, scruffy, seedy, shabby, sordid, squalid, tawdry, wretched
mean[3] 1. *n.* average, balance, median, middle, mid-point, norm 2. *adj.* average, intermediate, medial, median, medium, middle, standard
meander 1. *v.* ramble, snake, stray, stroll, turn, wander, wind 2. *n.* bend, coil, curve, loop, turn, twist, zigzag
meaning 1. drift, explanation, gist, implication, import, interpretation, message, purport, sense, significance, substance,

upshot, value 2. aim, design, end, goal, idea, intention, object, plan, point, purpose, trend 3. effect, force, point, thrust, use, validity, value, worth

meaningful 1. important, material, purposeful, relevant, serious, significant, valid 2. eloquent, expressive, meaning, pointed, speaking

meaningless aimless, empty, futile, hollow, inane, insignificant, nonsensical, pointless, trifling, trivial, useless, vain, worthless

meanness 1. miserliness, parsimony, selfishness, tightfistedness 2. bad temper, churlishness, hostility, ill temper, malice, nastiness, rudeness, unpleasantness 3. baseness, degradation, narrow-mindedness, pettiness, shabbiness, vileness 4. baseness, humbleness, lowliness, servility

means 1. agency, avenue, course, instrument, medium, method, mode, process, way 2. affluence, estate, fortune, funds, income, money, property, resources, riches, substance, wealth

measurable determinable, material, perceptible, quantifiable, significant

measure *n.* 1. allowance, amount, amplitude, capacity, degree, extent, proportion, quantity, quota, range, ration, reach, scope, share, size 2. gauge, metre, rule, scale 3. method, standard, system 4. criterion, example, model, norm, standard, test 5. act, action, course, deed, expedient, means, procedure, step 6. act, bill, enactment, law, resolution, statute 7. beat, cadence, foot, metre, rhythm, verse ~*v.* 8. assess, calculate, calibrate, compute, determine, estimate, evaluate, gauge, judge, quantify, rate, size, sound, survey, value, weigh

measurement assessment, calculation, calibration, estimation, evaluation, mensuration, survey, valuation

measure up (to) be adequate, be fit, compare, equal, match, meet, rival

meat aliment, cheer, comestibles, fare, flesh, food, nourishment, provender, provisions, rations, subsistence, viands, victuals

mechanical 1. automatic 2. automatic, cold, cursory, dead, habitual, impersonal, instinctive, lacklustre, lifeless, perfunctory, routine, unconscious, unfeeling

mechanism 1. apparatus, appliance, contrivance, device, instrument, structure, system, tool 2. agency, execution, means, medium, method, operation, performance, procedure, system, technique

meddle interfere, intervene, intrude, pry

mediate arbitrate, conciliate, intercede, intervene, reconcile, referee, resolve, settle, umpire

mediator advocate, arbiter, go-between, intermediary, judge, negotiator, peacemaker, referee, umpire

medicine cure, drug, physic, remedy

medieval antiquated, archaic, old-fashioned, primitive

mediocre average, indifferent, inferior, mean, middling, ordinary, passable, pedestrian, tolerable, undistinguished, uninspired

mediocrity 1. indifference, insignificance, poorness 2. nobody, nonentity

meditate cogitate, consider, contemplate, deliberate, muse, ponder, reflect, study, think

medium *adj.* 1. average, fair, intermediate, mean, mediocre, middle ~*n.* 2. average, centre, mean, middle 3. agency, avenue, channel, form, instrument, means, mode, organ, vehicle, way

medley jumble, miscellany, mishmash, mixture, pastiche, patchwork

meek 1. deferential, docile, gentle, humble, mild, modest, patient, peaceful, soft, submissive, unpretentious, yielding 2. acquiescent, compliant, resigned, tame, timid, weak

meekness 1. deference, docility, gentleness, humbleness, humility, mildness, modesty, patience, softness, submission 2. acquiescence, compliance, tameness, timidity, weakness

meet 1. confront, contact, encounter, find 2. abut, adjoin, connect, converge, cross, intersect, join, touch, unite 3. answer, comply, discharge, equal, fulfil, gratify, handle, match, perform, satisfy 4. assemble, collect, come together, gather, muster, rally

meeting 1. assignation, encounter, engagement, introduction, rendezvous 2. assembly, audience, company, conference, congregation, convention, gathering, rally, reunion, session 3. concourse, confluence, convergence, crossing, intersection, junction, union

melancholy 1. *n.* dejection, depression, despondency, gloom, sadness, sorrow, unhappiness, woe 2. *adj.* gloomy, glum, joyless, low, lugubrious, miserable, mournful, pensive, sad, sombre, sorrowful, unhappy

mellow *adj.* 1. delicate, juicy, mature, perfect, rich, ripe, soft, sweet 2. dulcet, full, melodious, rich, rounded, smooth, sweet, tuneful 3. cheerful, cordial, elevated, expansive, genial, happy, jolly, jovial, relaxed ~*v.* 4. develop, improve, mature, perfect, ripen, season, soften, sweeten

melodious dulcet, musical, silvery, sweet-sounding, tuneful

melodramatic extravagant, histrionic, overdramatic, theatrical

melody air, descant, music, refrain, song, strain, theme, tune

melt 1. diffuse, dissolve, flux, fuse, liquefy, soften, thaw 2. disarm

member 1. fellow, representative 2. arm, component, constituent, element, leg, limb, organ, part, portion

memoir account, biography, essay, journal, life, narrative

memoirs autobiography, diary, experiences, journals, life, life story, memories, recollections

memorable celebrated, distinguished, famous, historic, illustrious, important, notable, remarkable, significant, striking, unforgettable

memorial 1. *adj.* commemorative, monumental 2. *n.* monument, plaque, record, souvenir

memorize learn, learn by heart, learn by rote, remember

memory 1. recall, recollection, reminiscence 2. honour, remembrance

menace *v.* 1. alarm, browbeat, bully, frighten, impend, intimidate, loom, lour, lower, terrorize, threaten ~*n.* 2. scare, threat, warning 3. danger, hazard, jeopardy, peril

menacing alarming, dangerous, frightening, intimidating, looming, louring, lowering, ominous, threatening

mend *v.* 1. cure, darn, fix, heal, patch, rectify, refit, reform, remedy, renew, repair, restore 2. amend, better, correct, emend, improve, rectify, reform, revise ~*n.* 3. darn, patch, repair, stitch

menial *adj.* boring, dull, humdrum, routine, unskilled

mental cerebral, intellectual

mentality 1. brains, comprehension, intellect, mind, understanding, wit 2. attitude, disposition, outlook, personality

mentally intellectually, inwardly, rationally, subjectively

mention *v.* 1. adduce, broach, cite, communicate, declare, disclose, divulge, impart, intimate, name, recount, refer to, report, reveal, state, tell, touch upon ~*n.* 2. citation, recognition, tribute 3. allusion, indication, remark

mentor adviser, coach, counsellor, guide, instructor, teacher, tutor

mercantile commercial, trading

mercenary *adj.* 1. avaricious, covetous, grasping, greedy, sordid, venal 2. bought, hired, paid, venal ~*n.* 3. hireling

merchandise goods, produce, stock, wares

merchant broker, dealer, retailer, salesman, seller, shopkeeper, trader, tradesman, trafficker, vendor, wholesaler

merciful compassionate, forbearing, forgiving, generous, gracious, humane, kind, lenient, liberal, soft, sparing, sympathetic

merciless callous, cruel, hardhearted, heartless, inexorable, relentless, severe, unfeeling, unsympathetic

mercy 1. charity, clemency, compassion, favour, forbearance, forgiveness, grace, kindness, pity, quarter 2. boon, godsend, piece of luck, relief

mere *adj.* absolute, bare, common, entire, plain, pure, sheer, simple, stark, unmixed, utter

merge amalgamate, blend, combine, fuse, intermix, join, meet, mingle, mix, unite

merger amalgamation, coalition, fusion, incorporation, union

merit *n.* 1. asset, excellence, good, goodness, integrity, quality, talent, value, virtue, worth, worthiness 2. claim, credit, desert, due, right ~*v.* 3. deserve, earn, incur, warrant

merriment amusement, conviviality, festivity, frolic, fun, gaiety, laughter, mirth, revelry, sport

merry 1. blithe, carefree, cheerful, convivial, festive, gay, glad, gleeful, happy, jolly, joyful, joyous, light-hearted, mirthful, rollicking, sportive, vivacious 2. amusing, comic, comical, facetious, funny, hilarious, humorous

mesh *n.* 1. net, network, web 2. entanglement, snare, tangle, toils, trap, web ~*v.* 3. catch, ensnare, entangle, net, snare, tangle, trap 4. combine, connect, dovetail, engage, harmonize, knit

mess *n.* 1. botch, chaos, clutter, confusion, dirtiness, disarray, disorder, jumble, litter, shambles, turmoil, untidiness 2. difficulty, muddle, perplexity, plight, predicament ~*v.* 3. *Often with* **up** botch, bungle, clutter, dirty, disarrange, dishevel, foul, litter, pollute, scramble

message 1. bulletin, communication, dispatch, letter, missive, note, notice, tidings, word 2. idea, import, moral, point, theme

messenger agent, bearer, carrier, courier, emissary, envoy, go-between, herald, runner

messy chaotic, cluttered, confused, dirty, dishevelled, disordered, disorganized, grubby, littered, muddled

metaphor allegory, analogy, image, symbol

meteoric brief, brilliant, ephemeral, fast, flashing, fleeting, momentary, rapid, sudden, swift

method 1. approach, course, fashion, form, manner, mode, plan, practice, procedure, programme, routine, rule, scheme, style, system, technique, way 2. design, form, order, pattern, planning, structure

methodical businesslike, deliberate, disciplined, efficient, meticulous, neat, organized, planned, precise, regular, structured, tidy

meticulous detailed, exact, fastidious, painstaking, precise, scrupulous, strict, thorough

microscopic imperceptible, infinitesimal, tiny

midday noon, noonday, twelve o'clock

middle 1. *adj.* central, halfway, inner, inside, mean, medial, median, medium, mid 2. *n.* centre, focus, heart, inside, mean, midpoint, midst, thick

middling adequate, all right, average, fair, indifferent, mediocre, medium, moderate, modest, ordinary, passable, tolerable, unremarkable

midget dwarf, gnome, pygmy

midst bosom, centre, core, depths, heart, hub, interior, middle, thick

might ability, capability, efficacy, energy, force, potency, power, prowess, strength, sway, valour, vigour

mighty forceful, hardy, potent, powerful, robust, stalwart, stout, strong, sturdy, vigorous

migrant drifter, gypsy, itiner-

ant, nomad, rover, tinker, transient, vagrant, wanderer
migrate journey, move, roam, rove, shift, travel, trek, wander
migration journey, movement, roving, shift, travel, trek, voyage
migratory gypsy, itinerant, nomadic, roving, shifting, transient, unsettled, vagrant
mild amiable, balmy, bland, calm, docile, easy, forbearing, forgiving, gentle, indulgent, kind, meek, mellow, merciful, moderate, peaceable, placid, pleasant, serene, smooth, soft, temperate, tender, tranquil, warm
mildness blandness, calmness, docility, gentleness, indulgence, kindness, leniency, meekness, placidity, smoothness, softness, tenderness, warmth
militant 1. active, aggressive, assertive, combative 2. belligerent, fighting
military 1. *adj.* armed, martial, soldierly, warlike 2. *n.* armed forces, army, forces, services
milk *v.* drain, express, extract, press, tap
mill *n.* 1. factory, foundry, plant, shop, works 2. crusher, grinder
mime 1. *n.* dumb show, gesture 2. *v.* gesture, represent, simulate
mimic 1. *v.* ape, caricature, imitate, impersonate, parody 2. *n.* caricaturist, imitator, impersonator, parodist, parrot
mind *n.* 1. intellect, mentality, reason, sense, spirit, understanding, wits 2. memory, recollection, remembrance 3. brain, head, imagination, psyche 4. bent, desire, disposition, fancy, inclination, intention, leaning, notion, purpose, tendency, urge, will, wish 5. attention, concentration, thinking, thoughts 6. **make up one's mind** choose, decide, determine, resolve 7. **bear** *or* **keep in mind** remember, take note of ~*v.* 8. care, disapprove, dislike, object, resent 9. attend, follow, heed, mark, note, notice, obey, observe, regard, respect, watch 10. ensure, make certain 11. guard, look after, take care of, tend, watch
mindful alert, attentive, aware, careful, chary, cognizant, conscious, heedful, wary, watchful
mine *n.* 1. colliery, deposit, lode, pit, shaft, vein 2. fund, hoard, reserve, source, stock, store, supply ~*v.* 3. delve, excavate, extract, hew, quarry, unearth
mingle 1. alloy, blend, combine, compound, intermix, join, marry, merge, mix, unite 2. associate, circulate, fraternize, hobnob, socialize
miniature *adj.* baby, diminutive, dwarf, little, midget, pocket, reduced, small, tiny, toy, wee
minimal least, littlest, nominal, slightest, smallest, token
minimize 1. attenuate, curtail, decrease, diminish, prune, reduce, shrink 2. belittle, decry, deprecate, discount, underestimate, underrate
minimum 1. *n.* bottom, depth, least, lowest, nadir, slightest 2. *adj.* least, lowest, slightest, smallest
minion creature, flatterer, flunky, follower, hanger-on, henchman, hireling, lackey, pet, toady, yes man
minister *n.* 1. churchman, clergyman, cleric, divine, ecclesiastic, parson, pastor, preacher, priest, vicar 2. ambassador, delegate, diplomat, envoy, executive, office-holder, official, plenipotentiary ~*v.* 3. attend, tend
ministry administration, cabinet, council, government, holy orders
minor inconsiderable, inferior, junior, lesser, light, paltry, petty, secondary, slight, small, subordinate, trivial, younger
mint 1. *adj.* brand-new, excellent, first-class, fresh, perfect 2. *v.* cast, coin, make, produce, stamp, strike
minute[1] *n.* flash, instant, moment, second
minute[2] *adj.* fine, little, slender, small, tiny
minutes notes, proceedings, record(s), transcript
minx coquette, flirt, hoyden, hussy, jade, tomboy, wanton
miracle marvel, prodigy, wonder
miraculous amazing, astonishing, astounding, extraordinary, incredible, magical, marvellous, phenomenal, supernatural, wonderful
mirage illusion, phantasm
mire bog, marsh, morass, quagmire, swamp
mirror *n.* 1. glass, reflector 2. double, image, likeness, reflection ~*v.* 3. copy, depict, echo, emulate, follow, reflect, represent, show
mirth amusement, cheerfulness, festivity, frolic, fun, gaiety, glee, laughter, levity, merriment, pleasure, rejoicing, revelry, sport
mirthful amusing, blithe, cheerful, cheery, festive, funny, gay, glad, happy, jolly, jovial, laughable, light-hearted, merry, playful, sportive
misadventure accident, calamity, catastrophe, debacle, disaster, failure, mischance, misfortune, mishap, reverse, setback
misappropriate embezzle, misapply, misuse, pocket, steal, swindle
misbehaviour impropriety, indiscipline, insubordination, misconduct
miscalculate blunder, err, go wrong, misjudge, overrate, underrate
miscellaneous assorted, diverse, indiscriminate, jumbled, many, mingled, mixed, motley, promiscuous, sundry, varied, various
miscellany anthology, assortment, collection, jumble, medley, mixture, variety
mischance accident, calamity, disaster, misadventure, misfortune, mishap
mischief 1. devilment, impishness, misbehaviour, naughtiness, roguery, trouble, waywardness 2. damage, detriment, disruption, evil, harm, hurt, injury, trouble
mischievous 1. arch, bad, badly behaved, impish, naughty, playful, puckish, roguish, sportive, teasing, vexatious, wayward 2. bad, damaging, destructive, evil, harmful, hurtful, injurious, malignant, pernicious, sinful, spiteful, wicked
misconception delusion, error, misunderstanding
misconduct delinquency, immorality, impropriety, malpractice, misbehaviour, transgression, wrongdoing
misdemeanour fault, misconduct, offence, peccadillo, transgression
miser niggard, skinflint
miserable 1. afflicted, crestfallen, dejected, depressed, despondent, distressed, downcast, forlorn, gloomy, melancholy, mournful, sorrowful, unhappy, woebegone, wretched 2. destitute, meagre, needy, penniless, poor, poverty-stricken, scanty 3. abject, bad, contemptible, despicable, disgraceful, low, mean, pathetic, piteous, pitiable, shabby, shameful, sordid, sorry, squalid, vile, worthless, wretched
miserly avaricious, close, covetous, grasping, illiberal, mean, niggardly, parsimonious, sordid, stingy
misery 1. agony, anguish, depression, desolation, despair, discomfort, distress, gloom, grief, hardship, melancholy, sadness, sorrow, suffering, torment, torture, unhappiness, woe 2. affliction, burden, calamity, curse, disaster, load, misfortune, ordeal, sorrow, trial, tribulation, trouble, woe
misfire fail, fall through, miscarry
misfit eccentric, nonconformist
misfortune 1. bad luck, infelicity 2. accident, adversity, affliction, blow, calamity, disaster, hardship, harm, loss, misadventure, misery, reverse, setback, tragedy, trouble
misgiving anxiety, distrust, doubt, hesitation, reservation, suspicion, uncertainty, unease, worry
misguided deluded, foolish, ill-advised, imprudent, misled, misplaced, mistaken, unreasonable, unwise
mishandle botch, bungle, mismanage
mishap accident, adversity, bad luck, calamity, contretemps, disaster, hard luck, misadventure, mischance, misfortune
misinform deceive, misdirect, misguide, mislead
misinterpret distort, misapprehend, misconstrue, misjudge, misread, mistake, misunderstand
mislead beguile, bluff, deceive, delude, fool, hoodwink, misdirect, misguide, misinform
misleading ambiguous, confusing, deceitful, delusory, evasive, false, spurious
mismanage botch, bungle, maladminister, misdirect, misgovern, mishandle
misquote distort, falsify, garble, mangle, misreport, muddle, pervert, twist
misrepresent disguise, distort, falsify, garble, pervert, twist
misrule 1. maladministration, mismanagement 2. anarchy, disorder, lawlessness, tumult, turmoil
miss[1] *v.* 1. avoid, blunder, err, escape, evade, fail, forego, lack, lose, miscarry, mistake, omit, overlook, skip, slip, trip 2. need, pine for, want, wish ~*n.* 3. blunder, error, failure, fault, loss, mistake, omission, oversight, want
miss[2] damsel, girl, maid, spinster
misshapen contorted, crippled, crooked, deformed, distorted, grotesque, twisted, ugly, ungainly, warped
missile projectile, rocket, weapon
missing absent, astray, gone, lacking, lost, mislaid, misplaced
mission 1. aim, assignment, business, calling, charge, duty, errand, goal, job, office, operation, purpose, pursuit, quest, task, trust, undertaking, vocation, work 2. delegation, deputation, task force
missionary converter, evangelist, preacher
missive dispatch, epistle, letter, message, note, report
mist cloud, dew, drizzle, film, fog, haze, smog, spray, steam, vapour
mistake 1. *n.* blunder, error, fault, gaffe, oversight, slip, solecism 2. *v.* misconceive, misconstrue, misjudge, misread, misunderstand
mistaken fallacious, false, faulty, inaccurate, incorrect, misguided, misinformed, unfounded, wrong
mistress concubine, girlfriend, kept woman, lover, paramour
mistrust 1. *v.* beware, doubt, fear, suspect 2. *n.* doubt, fear, misgiving, scepticism, suspicion, uncertainty
misty bleary, cloudy, dark, dim, foggy, hazy, indistinct, obscure, vague
misunderstand misconceive, misconstrue, mishear, misinterpret, misjudge, mistake
misunderstanding error, misconstruction, misjudgment, misreading, mistake, mix-up
misuse 1. *n.* abuse, corruption, malapropism, perversion, profanation, solecism, waste 2. *v.* abuse, corrupt, desecrate, dissipate, misapply, pervert, profane, prostitute, squander, waste
mitigate abate, allay, appease, assuage, blunt, calm, check, dull, ease, extenuate, lessen, lighten, modify, mollify, pacify, palliate, placate, quiet, remit, soften, soothe, subdue, temper, weaken
mix 1. alloy, amalgamate, blend, coalesce, combine, compound, cross, fuse, incorporate, intermingle, join, merge, mingle, unite 2. associate, consort, fraternize, join, mingle, socialize
mixed 1. alloyed, amalgamated, blended, combined, composite, compound, fused, incorporated, joint, mingled, united 2. assorted, diverse, motley, varied 3. ambivalent, equivocal, indecisive, uncertain
mixture alloy, amalgam, association, assortment, blend, brew, combine, compound, concoction, conglomeration, cross, fusion, medley, miscellany, mix, union, variety

mix-up confusion, disorder, jumble, mess, mistake, muddle

mix up 1. blend, combine, mix 2. confound, confuse, muddle

moan 1. *n.* groan, lament, sigh, sob, sough, wail, whine 2. *v.* bewail, deplore, grieve, groan, lament, mourn, sigh, sob, whine

mob 1. *n.* body, collection, crowd, drove, flock, gang, gathering, herd, horde, host, mass, pack, press, swarm, throng 2. *v.* jostle, overrun, surround

mobile 1. itinerant, migrant, movable, peripatetic, portable, travelling, wandering 2. changeable, ever-changing, expressive

mobilize call up, marshal, muster, organize, prepare, rally, ready

mock *v.* 1. chaff, deride, flout, insult, jeer, ridicule, scoff, scorn, sneer, taunt, tease ~*n.* 2. banter, derision, gibe, jeering, ridicule, scorn, sneer 3. fake, forgery, fraud, imitation, sham ~*adj.* 4. artificial, bogus, counterfeit, dummy, fake, false, feigned, forged, fraudulent, imitation, pretended, sham, spurious

mockery 1. contempt, contumely, derision, disdain, jeering, ridicule, scorn 2. burlesque, caricature, deception, farce, imitation, lampoon, mimicry, parody, pretence, sham, travesty

mocking contemptuous, derisive, disdainful, insulting, irreverent, satirical, scornful, taunting

model *n.* 1. copy, facsimile, image, imitation, mock-up, replica, representation 2. archetype, design, epitome, example, exemplar, gauge, ideal, mould, original, paradigm, paragon, pattern, prototype, standard, type 3. poser, sitter, subject 4. mannequin ~*v.* 5. base, carve, cast, design, fashion, form, mould, pattern, plan, sculpt, shape 6. display, show off, wear ~*adj.* 7. copy, dummy, facsimile, imitation, miniature 8. archetypal, exemplary, ideal, illustrative, paradigmatic, perfect, standard, typical

moderate 1. *adj.* calm, cool, deliberate, equable, gentle, limited, mild, modest, peaceable, reasonable, restrained, sober, steady, temperate 2. *v.* abate, allay, appease, assuage, calm, control, curb, decrease, diminish, lessen, mitigate, modulate, pacify, quiet, regulate, repress, restrain, soften, subdue, tame, temper

moderately fairly, gently, passably, quite, rather, reasonably, slightly, somewhat, tolerably

moderation calmness, composure, coolness, equanimity, fairness, justice, mildness, reasonableness, restraint, sedateness, temperance

modern contemporary, current, fresh, late, latest, new, novel, present, recent

modernize bring up to date, rejuvenate, remake, remodel, renew, renovate, revamp, update

modest 1. bashful, coy, demure, discreet, humble, meek, quiet, reserved, reticent, retiring, shy, simple 2. fair, limited, ordinary, small

modesty demureness, diffidence, humility, meekness, propriety, reserve, reticence, shyness, timidity

modification adjustment, refinement, revision, variation

modify adapt, adjust, alter, change, convert, recast, reform, reorganize, reshape, revise, transform, vary

mogul baron, lord, magnate, notable, personage, tycoon

moist clammy, damp, dank, dewy, drizzly, humid, rainy, wet, wettish

moisten damp, soak, water, wet

moisture damp, dew, humidity, liquid, sweat, water

molecule atom, mite, particle

molest abuse, afflict, annoy, badger, bother, disturb, harass, harry, hector, irritate, persecute, pester, torment, upset, vex, worry

moment 1. flash, instant, minute, second, twinkling 2. hour, instant, juncture, point, stage, time

momentous critical, crucial, decisive, fateful, grave, historic, important, serious, significant, vital

momentum drive, energy, force, impetus, power, push, thrust

monarch king, potentate, prince, princess, queen, ruler, sovereign

monastery abbey, cloister, convent, friary, house, nunnery, priory

monastic ascetic, austere, cloistered, recluse, secluded, withdrawn

monetary capital, cash, financial, fiscal

money banknotes, capital, cash, coin, currency, funds, hard cash, legal tender

mongrel 1. *n.* cross, crossbreed, hybrid 2. *adj.* crossbred, half-breed, hybrid

monitor 1. *n.* guide, overseer, supervisor, watchdog 2. *v.* check, follow, observe, record, scan, supervise, survey, watch

monk brother, monastic, religious

monkey *n.* 1. primate, simian 2. devil, imp, rascal, rogue, scamp ~*v.* 3. fool, interfere, meddle, mess, play, tamper, tinker, trifle

monolithic colossal, giant, gigantic, huge, immovable, massive, monumental, solid, substantial

monologue harangue, lecture, sermon, speech

monopolize control, corner, dominate, engross, take up

monotonous boring, colourless, droning, dull, flat, humdrum, plodding, repetitious, repetitive, samey (*Inf.*), soporific, tedious, tiresome, toneless, unchanging, uniform, uninflected, unvaried, wearisome

monotony boredom, dullness, flatness, repetitiveness, routine, sameness, tedium, uniformity

monster 1. *n.* barbarian, beast, brute, demon, devil, fiend, ogre, savage, villain 2. *adj.* colossal, enormous, giant, huge, immense, massive, tremendous

monstrosity atrocity, evil, frightfulness, horror, obscenity

monstrous 1. abnormal, dreadful, fiendish, freakish, frightful, grotesque, gruesome, hellish, hideous, horrible, obscene, terrible, unnatural 2. atrocious, cruel, devilish, diabolical, disgraceful, evil, fiendish, foul, horrifying, infamous, inhuman, intolerable, loathsome, odious, outrageous, satanic, scandalous, shocking, vicious, villainous 3. colossal, enormous, giant, gigantic, great, huge, immense, massive, prodigious, stupendous, tremendous, vast

monument cairn, gravestone, marker, mausoleum, memorial, obelisk, pillar, shrine, statue, tombstone

monumental awesome, classic, enduring, enormous, historic, immortal, important, lasting, majestic, memorable, outstanding, prodigious, significant, unforgettable

mood 1. disposition, humour, spirit, temper, tenor, vein 2. blues, depression, doldrums, melancholy, sulk

moody angry, broody, crabbed, crestfallen, cross, crusty, curt, dismal, doleful, dour, downcast, frowning, gloomy, glum, ill-tempered, irritable, lugubrious, melancholy, miserable, morose, offended, pensive, petulant, sad, saturnine, sulky, sullen, temperamental, testy, touchy

moon 1. *n.* satellite 2. *v.* daydream, idle, languish

moor[1] heath, moorland

moor[2] anchor, berth, dock, fasten, fix, lash, secure

moot *adj.* arguable, contestable, controversial, debatable, doubtful, unsettled

mop up 1. sponge, swab, wash, wipe 2. *Military* clear, eliminate, pacify, secure

moral *adj.* 1. ethical 2. blameless, chaste, decent, good, honest, innocent, just, noble, principled, proper, pure, right, righteous, upright, virtuous ~*n.* 3. lesson, meaning, message, point, significance

morale confidence, heart, mettle, spirit, temper

morality chastity, decency, goodness, honesty, integrity, justice, principle, righteousness, virtue

morals conduct, integrity, manners, principles, scruples, standards

moratorium freeze, halt, respite, standstill, stay, suspension

morbid 1. brooding, gloomy, grim, pessimistic, sick, sombre, unhealthy, unwholesome 2. dreadful, ghastly, grisly, gruesome, hideous, horrid, macabre

more 1. *adj.* added, extra, fresh, further, new, other, spare, supplementary 2. *adv.* better, further, longer

moreover additionally, also, besides, further

moribund 1. doomed, dying, fading fast, failing 2. declining, forceless, stagnant, waning, weak

morning dawn, daybreak, forenoon, sunrise

moron ass, blockhead, cretin, dolt, dunce, fool, halfwit, idiot, imbecile, numskull, simpleton, thickhead

morose churlish, crabbed, cross, depressed, dour, down, gloomy, glum, gruff, ill-tempered, low, melancholy, moody, mournful, perverse, pessimistic, saturnine, sour, sulky, sullen, surly, taciturn

morsel bit, bite, crumb, fraction, fragment, grain, mouthful, piece, scrap, segment, slice, soupçon, taste

mortal *adj.* 1. earthly, ephemeral, human, temporal, transient, worldly 2. deadly, destructive, fatal, killing, lethal, murderous ~*n.* 3. being, body, earthling, human, individual, man, person, woman

mortality 1. humanity, transience 2. bloodshed, carnage, death, destruction, fatality, killing

mortified abashed, affronted, annoyed, ashamed, confounded, crushed, deflated, displeased, embarrassed, humbled, shamed, vexed

mortify abase, abash, annoy, chasten, confound, crush, disappoint, displease, embarrass, humble, shame, vex

mostly chiefly, customarily, generally, largely, mainly, particularly, predominantly, principally, usually

moth-eaten antiquated, decrepit, outdated, outworn, ragged, seedy, shabby, stale, tattered, threadbare

mother *n.* 1. dam, mater ~*adj.* 2. inborn, innate, native, natural ~*v.* 3. bear, produce 4. cherish, nurse, nurture, protect, raise, rear, tend

motherly affectionate, caring, fond, gentle, kind, loving, maternal, tender

motion *n.* 1. action, change, flow, move, movement, passage, progress, travel 2. proposal, proposition, submission, suggestion ~*v.* 3. beckon, direct, gesture, nod, signal, wave

motionless calm, frozen, halted, immobile, lifeless, static, stationary, still, unmoving

motivate actuate, arouse, bring, cause, draw, drive, impel, induce, inspire, inspirit, instigate, lead, move, persuade, prompt, stimulate, stir

motivation ambition, desire, drive, hunger, inspiration, interest, wish

motive *n.* cause, design, ground(s), incentive, inducement, influence, inspiration, intention, occasion, purpose, reason, spur, stimulus

motley assorted, dissimilar, diversified, mingled, mixed, unlike, varied

mottled blotchy, chequered, dappled, flecked, marbled, piebald, pied, speckled, stippled, streaked, variegated

motto adage, cry, maxim, precept, proverb, rule, saw, saying, slogan

mould *n.* 1. cast, die, form, pattern, shape 2. brand, build, cut, design, fashion, form, format, frame, kind, line, make, pattern, shape, style ~*v.* 3. carve, cast, construct, create, fashion, forge, form, make, model, sculpt, shape, stamp, work

mouldy bad, decaying, rotten, spoiled, stale
mound 1. heap, pile, stack 2. bank, dune, hill, hillock, knoll, rise
mount *v.* 1. ascend, climb, escalade, scale 2. bestride, jump on 3. arise, ascend, rise, soar, tower 4. build, grow, increase, intensify, multiply, pile up, swell 5. display, frame, set 6. exhibit, prepare, produce, put on, stage ~*n.* 7. backing, base, fixture, foil, frame, mounting, setting, stand, support 8. horse
mountain alp, elevation, eminence, height, mount, peak
mountainous alpine, high, highland, rocky, soaring, steep, towering, upland
mourn bewail, deplore, grieve, lament, miss, rue, sorrow, wail, weep
mournful afflicting, distressing, grievous, lamentable, melancholy, painful, piteous, plaintive, sad, sorrowful, tragic, unhappy, woeful
mourning grief, lamentation, weeping, woe
mouth *n.* 1. jaws, lips 2. door, entrance, gateway, inlet, opening, orifice, rim 3. **down in** *or* **at the mouth** blue, dejected, depressed, dispirited, down, melancholy, sad, unhappy
mouthpiece agent, delegate, representative
move *v.* 1. advance, budge, drift, go, march, proceed, progress, shift, stir, walk 2. carry, change, shift, switch, transfer, transport, transpose 3. leave, migrate, quit, relocate, remove 4. activate, drive, impel, motivate, operate, propel, push, shift, shove, start, turn 5. affect, agitate, cause, excite, incite, induce, influence, inspire, lead 6. advocate, propose, recommend, suggest, urge ~*n.* 7. act, action, deed, measure, motion, ploy, shift, step, stratagem, stroke, turn
movement 1. act, action, activity, advance, agitation, change, exercise, flow, gesture, motion, operation, progress, shift, steps, stir, stirring, transfer 2. campaign, crusade, drive, faction, front, group, party 3. *Music* division, part, passage, section 4. beat, cadence, measure, metre, pace, rhythm, swing, tempo
moving affecting, arousing, emotional, exciting, inspiring, poignant, stirring, touching
mow crop, cut, scythe, shear, trim
much 1. *adj.* abundant, ample, considerable, copious, great, plenteous, substantial 2. *adv.* a lot, considerably, decidedly, exceedingly, frequently, greatly, indeed, often, regularly
muck up botch, bungle, ruin, spoil
mud clay, dirt, mire, ooze, silt, sludge
muddle *v.* 1. confuse, disorder, mess, scramble, spoil, tangle 2. bewilder, confound, confuse, daze, perplex, stupefy ~*n.* 3. chaos, clutter, confusion, daze, disarray, disorder, mess, mixup, tangle
muddy boggy, dirty, marshy, soiled
muffle cloak, conceal, cover, disguise, envelop, hood, mask, shroud
muffled dim, dull, faint, muted, stifled, strangled
mug beaker, cup, flagon, jug, pot, tankard
muggy close, damp, humid, sticky, stuffy, sultry
multifarious different, diversified, legion, manifold, many, numerous, sundry, varied
multiple collective, many, several, sundry, various
multiply augment, breed, expand, extend, increase, reproduce, spread
multitude army, assembly, collection, congregation, crowd, horde, host, legion, lot, mass, mob, myriad, sea, swarm, throng
mundane banal, everyday, humdrum, ordinary, prosaic, routine, workaday
municipal borough, city, civic, community, public, town, urban
municipality borough, city, district, town, township
munificence benevolence, bigheartedness, bounty, generosity, largess, liberality, philanthropy
munificent big-hearted, bountiful, generous, lavish, liberal, philanthropical, princely, rich
murder 1. *n.* assassination, bloodshed, butchery, carnage, homicide, killing, manslaughter, massacre, slaying 2. *v.* assassinate, butcher, destroy, dispatch, kill, massacre, slaughter
murderer assassin, butcher, cutthroat, killer, slayer
murderous barbarous, bloodthirsty, bloody, brutal, cruel, deadly, fatal, internecine, lethal, sanguinary, savage
murky cheerless, cloudy, dark, dim, dreary, dull, dusky, foggy, gloomy, grey, misty, obscure, overcast
murmur 1. *n.* babble, drone, humming, mumble, muttering, purr, rumble, undertone, whisper 2. *v.* babble, buzz, drone, hum, mumble, mutter, purr, rumble, whisper
muscle 1. sinew, tendon, thew 2. brawn, force, might, potency, power, stamina, strength, weight
muscular athletic, lusty, powerful, robust, sinewy, stalwart, strapping, strong, vigorous
muse brood, cogitate, deliberate, dream, meditate, ponder, reflect, ruminate, speculate, think, weigh
musical dulcet, lilting, lyrical, melodious, tuneful
must *n.* duty, essential, imperative, necessity, obligation, requirement, requisite, *sine qua non*
muster 1. *v.* assemble, call up, collect, congregate, convene, convoke, enrol, gather, group, marshal, meet, mobilize, rally, summon 2. *n.* assembly, collection, concourse, congregation, convention, gathering, meeting, rally
musty airless, dank, decayed, frowsty, fusty, mildewed, mouldy, old, smelly, stale, stuffy
mutable adaptable, alterable, changeable, fickle, flexible, uncertain, unreliable, variable, volatile
mute 1. *adj.* dumb, silent, speechless, unspoken, wordless 2. *v.* dampen, deaden, lower, moderate, soften, subdue
mutilate butcher, cripple, damage, disable, disfigure, dismember, hack, injure, lacerate, lame, maim, mangle
mutinous disobedient, insubordinate, rebellious, refractory, revolutionary, seditious, subversive, unruly
mutiny 1. *n.* disobedience, insubordination, insurrection, rebellion, resistance, revolt, revolution, riot, rising, strike, uprising 2. *v.* disobey, rebel, resist, revolt, strike
mutter complain, mumble, murmur, rumble
mutual common, interactive, joint, reciprocal, returned, shared
muzzle censor, choke, curb, restrain, silence, stifle, suppress
myopic near-sighted, short-sighted
myriad 1. *adj.* countless, incalculable, innumerable, untold 2. *n.* army, flood, horde, host, millions, scores, swarm, thousands
mysterious abstruse, arcane, baffling, concealed, cryptic, curious, dark, furtive, hidden, inexplicable, inscrutable, obscure, recondite, secret, strange, uncanny, unknown, weird
mystery conundrum, enigma, problem, puzzle, question, riddle, secrecy, secret
mystify baffle, bewilder, confound, confuse, escape, perplex, puzzle, stump
myth allegory, fable, fiction, legend, parable, saga, story, tradition
mythical 1. fabled, fairy-tale, legendary 2. fabricated, fanciful, fictitious, invented, pretended, unreal, untrue
mythology folklore, legend, stories, tradition

N

nadir bottom, depths, zero
nag[1] 1. *v.* annoy, badger, chivvy, goad, harass, harry, henpeck, pester, plague, provoke, scold, vex, worry 2. *n.* harpy, scold, shrew, termagant, virago
nag[2] hack, horse, jade
nail *v.* attach, beat, fasten, fix, hammer, join, pin, secure, tack
naive artless, candid, childlike, guileless, ingenuous, innocent, open, simple, trusting, unaffected, unpretentious, unsophisticated
naïveté artlessness, candour, frankness, inexperience, ingenuousness, innocence, naturalness, simplicity
naked 1. bare, divested, exposed, nude, stripped, unclothed, unconcealed, uncovered, undraped, undressed 2. defenceless, helpless, unarmed, unguarded, unprotected, vulnerable
nakedness bareness, nudity, undress
name *n.* 1. denomination, designation, epithet, nickname, sobriquet, term, title 2. distinction, eminence, esteem, fame, honour, note, praise, renown, repute 3. credit, reputation ~*v.* 4. baptize, call, christen, dub, entitle, label, style, term 5. appoint, choose, commission, designate, identify, nominate, select, specify
named baptized, called, christened, dubbed, labelled, styled, termed
nameless 1. anonymous, untitled 2. incognito, obscure, unknown, unsung 3. horrible, indescribable, unmentionable, unspeakable
namely specifically, to wit, viz.
nap 1. *v.* doze, drowse, nod, rest, sleep 2. *n.* rest, siesta, sleep
narcotic analgesic, anodyne, drug, opiate, painkiller, sedative, tranquillizer
narrate describe, detail, recite, recount, rehearse, relate, repeat, report, tell
narration description, explanation, reading, recital, relation, storytelling
narrative account, chronicle, detail, history, report, statement, story, tale
narrator author, bard, chronicler, commentator, reporter, storyteller
narrow *adj.* 1. close, confined, cramped, limited, meagre, near, pinched, restricted, scanty, straitened, tight 2. biased, bigoted, dogmatic, illiberal, intolerant, partial, prejudiced, small-minded ~*v.* 3. diminish, limit, reduce, simplify, straiten, tighten
narrowly barely, just, scarcely
narrow-minded biased, bigoted, hidebound, illiberal, insular, intolerant, parochial, petty, strait-laced
nastiness 1. defilement, filth, foulness, impurity, pollution, squalor, uncleanliness 2. indecency, licentiousness, obscenity, pollution, pornography 3. malice, meanness, spitefulness, unpleasantness
nasty 1. dirty, disagreeable, disgusting, filthy, foul, horrible, nauseating, obnoxious, odious, offensive, polluted, repellent, repugnant, sickening, unpleasant, vile 2. blue, foul, gross, impure, indecent, lewd, licentious, obscene, pornographic, ribald, smutty 3. abusive, annoying, despicable, disagreeable, distasteful, malicious, mean, spiteful, unpleasant, vicious, vile
nation community, country, people, race, realm, society, state
national 1. civil, countrywide, governmental, public, state 2. domestic, internal, social
nationalism allegiance, chauvinism, loyalty, patriotism
nationality birth, race
native *adj.* 1. congenital, endemic, hereditary, inborn, inbred, indigenous, inherited, innate, instinctive 2. genuine, original, real 3. domestic, home, home-made, indigenous, local, mother ~*n.* 4. aborigine, citizen, countryman, dweller, inhabitant
natty chic, dapper, elegant, neat, smart, spruce, stylish, trim
natural 1. common, everyday, logical, normal, ordinary, regu-

lar, typical, usual **2.** characteristic, essential, inborn, inherent, innate, instinctive, intuitive **3.** artless, candid, frank, genuine, ingenuous, open, real, simple, spontaneous, unaffected, unpretentious

naturalist biologist, botanist, ecologist, zoologist

naturalize acclimatize, accustom, adapt, familiarize, habituate

naturally customarily, genuinely, informally, normally, simply, spontaneously, typically, unaffectedly, unpretentiously

nature **1.** character, complexion, essence, features, make-up, quality, traits **2.** category, description, kind, sort, species, style, type, variety **3.** creation, earth, environment, universe, world **4.** disposition, humour, mood, outlook, temper, temperament **5.** country, landscape

naughty annoying, bad, disobedient, exasperating, impish, misbehaved, mischievous, perverse, playful, roguish, sinful, teasing, wayward, wicked, worthless

nausea **1.** biliousness, qualm(s), sickness, vomiting **2.** aversion, disgust, loathing, repugnance, revulsion

nauseate disgust, horrify, offend, repel, repulse, revolt, sicken

nautical maritime, naval, seafaring, yachting

naval marine, maritime, nautical

navigable clear, negotiable, passable, unobstructed

navigate cross, cruise, direct, drive, guide, handle, journey, manoeuvre, pilot, plan, plot, sail, steer, voyage

navigation cruising, pilotage, sailing, seamanship, steering, voyaging

navy fleet, flotilla, warships

near *adj.* **1.** adjacent, adjoining, alongside, beside, bordering, close, contiguous, nearby, neighbouring, nigh, touching **2.** forthcoming, imminent, impending, looming, next **3.** akin, allied, attached, connected, dear, familiar, intimate, related

nearby adjacent, adjoining, convenient, handy, neighbouring

nearly about, all but, almost, approaching, approximately, closely, not quite, practically, roughly, virtually, well-nigh

nearness **1.** accessibility, availability, closeness, handiness, proximity, vicinity **2.** immediacy, imminence

neat **1.** accurate, dainty, fastidious, methodical, nice, orderly, shipshape, smart, spruce, straight, systematic, tidy, trim **2.** adept, adroit, agile, apt, clever, deft, dexterous, efficient, effortless, elegant, expert, graceful, handy, nimble, precise, skilful, stylish **3.** *Of alcoholic drinks* pure, straight, undiluted, unmixed

neatly accurately, daintily, fastidiously, methodically, nicely, smartly, sprucely, systematically, tidily

neatness **1.** accuracy, daintiness, fastidiousness, orderliness, smartness, tidiness **2.** agility, aptness, cleverness, dexterity, efficiency, elegance, grace, gracefulness, precision, skill, style

nebulous cloudy, confused, dim, hazy, imprecise, indefinite, indistinct, misty, murky, obscure, shadowy, uncertain, unclear, vague

necessarily automatically, by definition, certainly, compulsorily, consequently, inevitably, inexorably, naturally, of course, perforce, willy-nilly

necessary compulsory, essential, imperative, mandatory, needful, obligatory, required, vital

necessitate call for, coerce, compel, constrain, demand, force, oblige, require

necessity **1.** demand, exigency, need, requirement **2.** fundamental, need, prerequisite, requirement, requisite, *sine qua non*, want

need *v.* **1.** call for, demand, lack, miss, necessitate, require, want ~*n.* **2.** longing, requisite, want, wish **3.** destitution, distress, extremity, inadequacy, insufficiency, lack, neediness, paucity, penury, poverty, privation, shortage **4.** exigency, obligation, urgency, want **5.** demand, desideratum, essential, requirement, requisite

needless dispensable, excessive, expendable, groundless, pointless, redundant, superfluous, unwanted, useless

needy deprived, destitute, impoverished, penniless, poor, underprivileged

nefarious atrocious, base, criminal, depraved, dreadful, evil, execrable, horrible, infamous, infernal, odious, shameful, sinful, vicious, vile, wicked

negate annul, cancel, invalidate, neutralize, nullify, repeal, rescind, retract, reverse, revoke, void, wipe out

negation antithesis, contrary, converse, denial, disavowal, disclaimer, inverse, opposite, rejection, reverse

negative *adj.* **1.** contrary, denying, dissenting, opposing, refusing, resisting **2.** invalidating, neutralizing, nullifying **3.** antagonistic, colourless, contrary, cynical, gloomy, jaundiced, neutral, pessimistic, unenthusiastic, uninterested, unwilling, weak ~*n.* **4.** denial, refusal

neglect *v.* **1.** disdain, disregard, ignore, overlook, rebuff, scorn, slight, spurn **2.** be remiss, evade, forget, omit, procrastinate, shirk, skimp ~*n.* **3.** disdain, disregard, disrespect, indifference, slight, unconcern **4.** carelessness, default, failure, forgetfulness, laxity, oversight, remissness, slackness

neglected abandoned, derelict, overgrown

negligence carelessness, default, disregard, failure, inadvertence, inattention, indifference, laxity, omission, oversight, shortcoming, slackness, thoughtlessness

negligent careless, forgetful, heedless, inadvertent, inattentive, indifferent, offhand, regardless, remiss, slack, thoughtless, unthinking

negligible insignificant, minor, minute, petty, small, trifling, trivial, unimportant

negotiate arbitrate, arrange, bargain, confer, consult, contract, deal, debate, discuss, handle, manage, mediate, parley, settle, transact, work out

negotiation arbitration, bargaining, debate, diplomacy, discussion

neighbourhood community, district, environs, locality, precincts, proximity, quarter, region, vicinity

neighbouring adjacent, adjoining, bordering, near, nearby, nearest, next, surrounding

nerve **1.** bravery, coolness, courage, daring, endurance, energy, fearlessness, firmness, force, fortitude, gameness, mettle, might, pluck, resolution, spirit, vigour, will **2.** *Inf.* audacity, boldness, brazenness, effrontery, gall, impertinence, impudence, insolence

nerves anxiety, nervousness, strain, stress, tension

nervous agitated, anxious, apprehensive, edgy, fearful, fidgety, hysterical, jumpy, neurotic, ruffled, shaky, tense, timid, uneasy, weak, worried

nervousness agitation, anxiety, disquiet, excitability, fluster, tension, timidity, worry

nest **1.** den, haunt, refuge, resort, retreat **2.** breeding-ground, den

nestle cuddle, huddle, snuggle

nestling **1.** chick, fledgling **2.** babe, baby, infant

net[1] **1.** *n.* lattice, mesh, tracery, web **2.** *v.* bag, capture, catch, enmesh, ensnare, entangle, trap

net[2], **nett** *adj.* **1.** clear, final, take-home **2.** closing, conclusive, final ~*v.* **3.** clear, earn, gain, make, realize, reap

nether below, beneath, bottom, inferior, lower, under

nettle annoy, goad, harass, irritate, pique, provoke, ruffle, sting, tease, vex

network arrangement, channels, complex, grid, grill, maze, mesh, organization, structure, system, web

neurosis abnormality, deviation, instability, obsession, phobia

neurotic abnormal, anxious, compulsive, disordered, disturbed, nervous, unstable

neuter *v.* castrate, geld, spay

neutral disinterested, dispassionate, impartial, noncombatant, unaligned, unbiased, uncommitted, undecided, unprejudiced

neutrality detachment, impartiality

neutralize cancel, counteract, frustrate, nullify, offset, undo

never-ending boundless, ceaseless, constant, continual, eternal, everlasting, incessant, nonstop, perpetual, relentless, unbroken, unceasing, uninterrupted, unremitting

nevertheless but, however, notwithstanding, regardless, still, yet

new **1.** advanced, contemporary, current, different, fresh, latest, modern, newfangled, novel, original, recent, topical, unfamiliar, unknown, unused, unusual, up-to-date, virgin **2.** added, extra, more **3.** altered, changed, improved, modernized, redesigned, renewed, restored

newcomer alien, arrival, beginner, foreigner, incomer, novice, outsider

newfangled contemporary, modern, new, new-fashioned, novel, recent

newly anew, freshly, just, lately, latterly, recently

news account, advice, bulletin, dispatch, exposé, gossip, hearsay, information, intelligence, leak, release, report, revelation, rumour, scandal, statement, story, tidings, word

next *adj.* **1.** consequent, ensuing, following, later, subsequent, succeeding **2.** adjacent, adjoining, closest, nearest, neighbouring ~*adv.* **3.** afterwards, closely, following, later, subsequently, thereafter

nice **1.** agreeable, amiable, attractive, charming, courteous, friendly, good, kind, pleasant, polite, refined, well-mannered **2.** dainty, fine, neat, tidy, trim **3.** accurate, careful, critical, delicate, exact, fastidious, fine, meticulous, precise, rigorous, scrupulous, strict, subtle

nicely **1.** acceptably, agreeably, amiably, attractively, charmingly, courteously, kindly, pleasantly, politely, well **2.** daintily, finely, neatly, tidily, trimly **3.** critically, delicately, exactly, fastidiously, finely, meticulously, precisely, rigorously, scrupulously, strictly, subtly

nicety accuracy, exactness, meticulousness, minuteness, precision

niche alcove, corner, hollow, nook, opening, recess

nick chip, cut, damage, dent, mark, notch, scar, score, scratch

nickname diminutive, epithet, label, pet name, sobriquet

niggardly close, covetous, frugal, grudging, mean, mercenary, miserly, parsimonious, penurious, sparing, stingy, tightfisted

niggle **1.** carp, cavil, criticize, find fault, fuss **2.** annoy, irritate, rankle, worry

niggling **1.** cavilling, finicky, fussy, insignificant, minor, nitpicking (*Inf.*), pettifogging, petty, piddling (*Inf.*), quibbling, trifling, unimportant **2.** gnawing, irritating, persistent, troubling, worrying

night dark, night-time

nightfall dusk, evening, sunset, twilight

nightmare **1.** hallucination **2.** horror, ordeal, torment, trial, tribulation

nil duck, love, none, nothing, zero

nimble active, agile, alert, brisk, deft, lively, prompt, quick, ready, smart, sprightly, spry, swift

nip[1] *v.* bite, catch, clip, grip, pinch, snag, snap, snip, tweak, twitch

nip[2] *n.* dram, draught, drop, finger, portion, sip, *soupçon*, taste

nipple breast, dug, pap, teat, tit, udder

nippy biting, chilly, sharp, stinging
nitty-gritty basics, core, crux, essence, facts, gist, reality, substance
nobble 1. disable, handicap, incapacitate, weaken 2. bribe, get at, influence, intimidate, outwit
nobility 1. aristocracy, elite, lords, nobles, peerage 2. dignity, eminence, excellence, grandeur, greatness, majesty, nobleness, superiority, worthiness 3. honour, integrity, uprightness, virtue
noble *n.* 1. lord, nobleman, peer ~*adj.* 2. aristocratic, highborn, lordly 3. august, dignified, distinguished, elevated, eminent, grand, great, imposing, impressive, lofty, splendid, stately 4. generous, honourable, upright, virtuous, worthy
nobody 1. no-one 2. cipher, menial, nonentity
nocturnal night, nightly, nighttime
nod *v.* 1. bow, dip, duck, gesture, indicate, salute, signal 2. agree, assent, concur 3. doze, droop, drowse, nap, sleep, slump ~*n.* 4. beck, gesture, greeting, salute, sign, signal
noise babble, blare, clamour, clatter, commotion, cry, din, fracas, hubbub, outcry, pandemonium, racket, row, sound, talk, tumult, uproar
noiseless hushed, mute, quiet, silent, soundless, still
noisy boisterous, chattering, deafening, loud, piercing, riotous, strident, turbulent, uproarious, vociferous
nomad drifter, migrant, rambler, rover, vagabond, wanderer
nomadic itinerant, migrant, pastoral, peripatetic, roaming, roving, travelling, vagrant, wandering
nom de plume alias, pseudonym
nomenclature classification, codification, locution, vocabulary
nominal formal, ostensible, pretended, professed, puppet, self-styled, so-called, supposed, theoretical, titular
nominate appoint, assign, choose, designate, elect, elevate, name, present, propose, recommend, select, submit, suggest, term
nomination appointment, choice, election, proposal, selection, suggestion
nominee aspirant, candidate, contestant, entrant, runner
nonchalance calm, composure, equanimity, indifference, unconcern
nonchalant airy, apathetic, calm, careless, casual, collected, cool, detached, indifferent, offhand, unconcerned
noncommittal careful, cautious, discreet, evasive, guarded, indefinite, neutral, politic, reserved, tactful, vague, wary
non compos mentis crazy, deranged, insane, mentally ill, of unsound mind
nonconformist dissenter, eccentric, heretic, maverick, protester, radical, rebel
nondescript characterless, dull, indeterminate, mousy, ordinary, undistinguished, uninspiring, uninteresting, unremarkable, vague
none nil, nobody, no-one, nothing, not one, zero
nonentity cipher, mediocrity, nobody
nonessential dispensable, extraneous, inessential, superfluous, unimportant, unnecessary
nonetheless despite that, even so, however, nevertheless, yet
nonexistent chimerical, fancied, fictional, hypothetical, illusory, imaginary, insubstantial, legendary, missing, unreal
nonsense absurdity, balderdash, blather, bombast, drivel, folly, gibberish, inanity, jest, rot, rubbish, silliness, stuff, stupidity, trash, twaddle
nonstop 1. *adj.* ceaseless, constant, continuous, direct, endless, steady, unbroken, unending, uninterrupted 2. *adv.* constantly, directly, endlessly, steadily
nook alcove, cavity, corner, cranny, crevice, niche, opening, recess, retreat
norm average, criterion, mean, model, pattern, rule, standard, type
normal accustomed, average, common, natural, ordinary, popular, regular, routine, standard, typical, usual
normality naturalness, popularity, regularity
normally commonly, ordinarily, regularly, typically, usually
nose *v.* detect, scent, smell, sniff
nosegay bouquet, posy
nostalgia homesickness, longing, yearning
nostalgic homesick, longing, regretful
nostrum cure, drug, elixir, medicine, potion, remedy, specific
notability celebrity, distinction, eminence, esteem, fame, renown
notable 1. *adj.* celebrated, distinguished, eminent, famous, manifest, marked, memorable, noteworthy, noticeable, pre-eminent, pronounced, rare, remarkable, renowned, striking, uncommon, unusual, well-known 2. *n.* celebrity, dignitary, personage
notably distinctly, especially, markedly, outstandingly, particularly, remarkably
notation characters, code, script, signs, symbols, system
notch cleft, cut, incision, mark, nick, score
note *n.* 1. comment, epistle, gloss, letter, memo, message, minute, record, remark, reminder 2. indication, mark, sign, symbol, token 3. heed, notice, observation, regard ~*v.* 4. designate, indicate, mark, mention, notice, observe, record, register, remark, see
noted acclaimed, celebrated, distinguished, eminent, famous, illustrious, prominent, recognized, well-known
noteworthy exceptional, important, remarkable, significant, unusual
nothing cipher, naught, nonentity, nonexistence, nought, nullity, trifle, void, zero
notice *v.* 1. detect, discern, distinguish, heed, mark, mind, note, observe, perceive, remark, see, spot ~*n.* 2. heed, note, observation, regard 3. advice, announcement, instruction, intelligence, intimation, news, order, warning 4. criticism, poster, review, sign
noticeable clear, conspicuous, distinct, evident, manifest, obvious, perceptible, plain, striking
notification advice, alert, declaration, information, intelligence, message, notice, publication, statement
notify acquaint, advise, alert, announce, declare, inform, tell, warn
notion 1. belief, concept, idea, impression, inkling, judgment, knowledge, opinion, view 2. caprice, desire, fancy, impulse, whim, wish
notoriety dishonour, disrepute, scandal
notorious 1. disreputable, infamous, scandalous 2. blatant, flagrant, glaring, obvious, open, overt, patent
notoriously disreputably, infamously
notwithstanding although, despite, however, nevertheless, nonetheless, though, yet
nought naught, nil, nothing, zero
nourish attend, feed, nurse, nurture, supply, sustain, tend
nourishing healthful, nutritious, wholesome
nourishment diet, food, nutrition, sustenance, victuals
novel 1. *adj.* different, fresh, new, original, rare, singular, strange, uncommon, unfamiliar, unusual 2. *n.* fiction, romance, story, tale
novelty 1. freshness, newness, oddity, strangeness, surprise 2. bauble, curiosity, gadget, gewgaw, gimcrack, gimmick, memento, souvenir, trifle, trinket
novice amateur, apprentice, beginner, learner, newcomer, probationer, proselyte, pupil, tyro
now at once, immediately, instantly, promptly, straightaway
nucleus basis, centre, core, heart, kernel, pivot
nude bare, disrobed, exposed, naked, stripped, unclad, unclothed, undressed
nudge *v.* bump, dig, elbow, jog, poke, prod, push, shove, touch
nudity bareness, nakedness, undress
nugget chunk, clump, hunk, lump
nuisance bore, bother, irritation, offence, pest, plague, problem, trouble, vexation
nullify abolish, annul, cancel, invalidate, negate, neutralize, quash, repeal, rescind, revoke, veto, void
numb 1. *adj.* dead, deadened, frozen, insensible, paralysed, stupefied, torpid 2. *v.* benumb, deaden, dull, freeze, paralyse, stun, stupefy
number *n.* 1. count, digit, figure, integer, numeral, sum, total, unit 2. amount, collection, company, crowd, horde, many, multitude, quantity, throng 3. copy, edition ~*v.* 4. account, add, calculate, compute, count, reckon, tell, total
numbered contained, counted, fixed, included, limited, specified, totalled
numberless countless, endless, infinite, untold
numbness deadness, dullness, insensibility, paralysis, torpor
numeral character, cipher, digit, figure, integer, number, symbol
numerous abundant, copious, many, plentiful, profuse, several
nunnery abbey, cloister, convent, house, monastery
nurse *v.* 1. tend, treat 2. feed, nourish, nurture, suckle 3. *Fig.* cherish, encourage, foster, preserve, promote, succour, support
nurture *n.* 1. diet, food ~*v.* 2. feed, nourish, nurse, support, sustain, tend 3. bring up, develop, educate, instruct, rear, school, train
nutrition food, nourishment, sustenance
nutritious beneficial, healthful, nourishing, wholesome

O

oasis *Fig.* haven, island, refuge, retreat, sanctuary, sanctum
oath 1. affirmation, avowal, bond, pledge, promise, vow, word 2. curse, expletive, imprecation, profanity
obdurate adamant, callous, dogged, firm, fixed, hard, implacable, inexorable, inflexible, iron, mulish, obstinate, pigheaded, relentless, stubborn, unbending, unshakable
obedience acquiescence, agreement, compliance, deference, docility, duty, observance, respect, submissiveness
obedient acquiescent, amenable, biddable, compliant, docile, duteous, dutiful, regardful, respectful, submissive, well-trained
obelisk column, monolith, monument, needle, pillar, shaft
obese corpulent, fat, fleshy, gross, heavy, outsize, plump, podgy, portly, rotund, stout, tubby
obesity bulk, corpulence, fatness, fleshiness, grossness, overweight, portliness, stoutness
obey 1. comply, conform, discharge, execute, follow, fulfil, heed, keep, mind, observe, perform, respond, serve 2. bow to, submit, yield
object[1] *n.* 1. article, body, fact, item, reality, thing 2. aim, butt, focus, target, victim 3. design, end, goal, idea, intent, motive, objective, point, purpose, reason
object[2] *v.* demur, expostulate, oppose, protest
objection cavil, censure, demur, doubt, exception, opposition, protest, remonstrance, scruple
objectionable deplorable, distasteful, indecorous, insufferable, intolerable, obnoxious, offensive, regrettable, repugnant, undesirable, unpleasant
objective 1. *adj.* detached, dis-

passionate, fair, impartial, impersonal, judicial, just, unemotional, unprejudiced **2.** *n.* aim, ambition, aspiration, design, end, goal, mark, object, purpose, target
objectively dispassionately, even-handedly, impartially
obligation burden, charge, compulsion, duty, liability, must, onus, requirement, responsibility, trust
obligatory binding, compulsory, essential, imperative, mandatory, necessary, required
oblige 1. bind, compel, force, impel, make, require **2.** accommodate, benefit, favour, gratify, indulge, please, serve
obliged 1. appreciative, beholden, grateful, gratified, indebted, thankful **2.** bound, compelled, forced, required
obliging agreeable, amiable, civil, considerate, cooperative, courteous, friendly, good-natured, helpful, kind, polite, willing
oblique angled, aslant, inclined, slanted, slanting, sloped, sloping
obliterate cancel, delete, destroy, efface, eradicate, erase, expunge, extirpate, wipe out
oblivion 1. forgetfulness, insensibility, neglect, unawareness, unconsciousness, (waters of) Lethe **2.** blackness, darkness, eclipse, limbo, void
oblivious blind, careless, deaf, forgetful, heedless, ignorant, neglectful, regardless, unaware
obnoxious abominable, detestable, disgusting, foul, hateful, horrid, insufferable, nasty, odious, offensive, repellent, repugnant, repulsive, revolting, unpleasant
obscene bawdy, blue, coarse, dirty, disgusting, filthy, foul, gross, immoral, improper, impure, indecent, lewd, offensive, pornographic, prurient, ribald, salacious, shameless, suggestive
obscenity 1. bawdiness, coarseness, dirtiness, filthiness, grossness, immodesty, impurity, lewdness, pornography, salacity, suggestiveness, vileness **2.** impropriety, indecency, indelicacy, profanity, swearword, vulgarism
obscure *adj.* **1.** ambiguous, arcane, confusing, cryptic, deep, doubtful, esoteric, hazy, hidden, involved, mysterious, occult, opaque, recondite, unclear, vague **2.** blurred, cloudy, dim, dusky, faint, gloomy, indistinct, murky, shadowy, shady, sombre, tenebrous, unlit, veiled ~*v.* **3.** conceal, cover, disguise, hide, screen, veil **4.** bedim, befog, block, blur, cloak, cloud, darken, dim, dull, eclipse, mask, overshadow, shade, shroud
obscurity 1. ambiguity, complexity, intricacy, vagueness **2.** darkness, dimness, dusk, gloom, haze, haziness, murkiness, shadows **3.** insignificance, lowliness, unimportance
observable apparent, clear, discernible, evident, noticeable, obvious, open, patent, perceptible, recognizable, visible
observance 1. attention, celebration, discharge, notice, observation, performance **2.** ceremonial, custom, fashion, form, practice, rite, ritual, tradition
observant alert, attentive, heedful, mindful, perceptive, quick, vigilant, watchful
observation attention, consideration, examination, experience, information, inspection, knowledge, notice, review, scrutiny, study, surveillance
observe 1. detect, discern, discover, espy, note, notice, perceive, see, spot, witness **2.** monitor, regard, scrutinize, study, survey, view, watch **3.** comment, declare, mention, note, opine, remark, say, state **4.** comply, follow, fulfil, heed, honour, keep, mind, obey, respect **5.** keep, remember, solemnize
observer commentator, eyewitness, onlooker, spectator, viewer, witness
obsessive compulsive, consuming, fixed, unforgettable
obsolescent ageing, declining, waning
obsolete ancient, antiquated, archaic, bygone, dated, *démodé*, extinct, musty, old, outmoded, outworn, passé
obstacle bar, barrier, check, hindrance, hitch, hurdle, interruption, obstruction, snag
obstinacy firmness, inflexibility, intransigence, persistence, pertinacity, resoluteness, stubbornness, tenacity, wilfulness
obstinate determined, dogged, firm, immovable, inflexible, intractable, opinionated, pertinacious, perverse, recalcitrant, refractory, self-willed, steadfast, stubborn, tenacious
obstreperous boisterous, disorderly, loud, noisy, rackety, restive, riotous, rough, rowdy, tumultuous, turbulent, uncontrolled, undisciplined, unruly, wild
obstruct arrest, bar, block, check, choke, clog, cumber, curb, cut off, frustrate, hamper, hamstring, hide, hinder, impede, inhibit, interrupt, mask, obscure, prevent, restrict, stop
obstruction bar, barrier, blockage, check, hindrance, impediment, snag, stop, stoppage
obstructive awkward, preventative, restrictive, unhelpful
obtain achieve, acquire, earn, gain, get, procure, secure
obtrusive forward, meddling, nosy, officious, prying
obvious apparent, clear, conspicuous, distinct, evident, manifest, open, overt, palpable, patent, perceptible, plain, pronounced, recognizable, self-evident, straightforward, transparent, unmistakable, unsubtle, visible
obviously certainly, clearly, distinctly, palpably, patently, plainly
occasion 1. chance, incident, moment, occurrence, opening, time **2.** affair, event, experience, occurrence **3.** call, cause, excuse, ground(s), motive, prompting, provocation, reason
occasional casual, desultory, incidental, infrequent, irregular, odd, rare, sporadic
occasionally irregularly, periodically, sometimes
occupant holder, indweller, inhabitant, inmate, lessee, occupier, resident, tenant, user
occupation 1. activity, business, calling, craft, employment, job, post, profession, pursuit, trade, vocation, work **2.** control, holding, occupancy, possession, residence, tenancy, tenure, use **3.** conquest, invasion
occupied 1. busy, employed, engaged, working **2.** engaged, full, taken, unavailable
occupy 1. *Often passive* absorb, amuse, busy, divert, employ, engage, engross, entertain, immerse, interest, involve, monopolize, preoccupy **2.** capture, hold, invade, keep, seize
occur arise, befall, betide, chance, eventuate, happen, materialize, result
occurrence affair, circumstance, episode, event, happening, incident, proceeding
odd 1. abnormal, bizarre, curious, deviant, different, eccentric, extraordinary, freak, funny, irregular, peculiar, quaint, queer, rare, remarkable, singular, strange, uncommon, unusual, weird, whimsical **2.** lone, remaining, single, solitary, spare, unpaired
oddity abnormality, anomaly, freak, irregularity, peculiarity, phenomenon, quirk, rarity
odds 1. edge, lead, superiority **2.** balance, chances, likelihood, probability **3.** difference, distinction
odious abominable, detestable, disgusting, execrable, foul, hateful, horrible, loathsome, offensive, repellent, repugnant, repulsive, revolting, unpleasant
odour aroma, bouquet, essence, fragrance, perfume, scent, smell, stink
off *adj.* **1.** absent, cancelled, finished, gone, inoperative, postponed, unavailable **2.** bad, disappointing, disheartening, displeasing, poor, quiet, slack, substandard, unrewarding, unsatisfactory **3.** bad, decomposed, high, mouldy, rancid, rotten, sour, turned
off and on intermittently, occasionally, sometimes
offbeat bizarre, eccentric, idiosyncratic, novel, strange, uncommon, unconventional, unorthodox, unusual, weird
off colour ill, peaky, queasy, sick, unwell
offence 1. crime, fault, lapse, misdeed, misdemeanour, peccadillo, sin, transgression, trespass, wrong **2.** anger, annoyance, displeasure, pique, resentment, umbrage, wrath
offend 1. affront, annoy, displease, fret, gall, insult, irritate, outrage, pain, pique, provoke, rile, slight, snub, upset, vex, wound **2.** disgust, repel, repulse, sicken
offended displeased, huffy, outraged, pained, piqued, resentful, smarting, stung, upset
offender criminal, culprit, lawbreaker, malefactor, miscreant, transgressor
offensive *adj.* **1.** abusive, annoying, detestable, displeasing, insolent, insulting, irritating, rude, uncivil, unmannerly **2.** disagreeable, disgusting, grisly, loathsome, nasty, noisome, obnoxious, odious, repellent, revolting, sickening, unpleasant, unsavoury, vile **3.** aggressive, attacking, invading ~*n.* **4.** attack, drive, onslaught
offer *v.* **1.** bid, extend, give, proffer, tender **2.** afford, furnish, present, provide, show **3.** advance, extend, move, propose, submit, suggest **4.** volunteer ~*n.* **5.** attempt, bid, essay, overture, proposal, suggestion, tender
offering contribution, gift, present, sacrifice
offhand abrupt, aloof, brusque, careless, casual, cavalier, curt, glib, offhanded, perfunctory, uninterested
office appointment, business, capacity, charge, commission, duty, employment, obligation, occupation, place, post, responsibility, role, service, situation, station, trust, work
officer agent, bureaucrat, executive, representative
official 1. *adj.* authentic, authoritative, bona fide, certified, ex officio, formal, legitimate, licensed, proper **2.** *n.* agent, bureaucrat, executive, representative
officiate chair, conduct, manage, preside, serve
officious bustling, forward, impertinent, interfering, intrusive, meddlesome, mischievous, obtrusive, opinionated, overbusy, overzealous
off-load discharge, dump, jettison, shift, transfer, unburden, unload
off-putting discouraging, disturbing, formidable, frustrating, unnerving, unsettling
offset counteract, counterbalance, counterpoise, countervail, neutralize
offshoot adjunct, appendage, branch, by-product, development, sprout
often frequently, generally, much, repeatedly
oil *v.* grease, lubricate
old 1. aged, ancient, decrepit, elderly, grey, mature, senile, venerable **2.** antiquated, antique, cast-off, crumbling, dated, decayed, done, obsolete, old-fashioned, outdated, passé, stale, timeworn, unoriginal, worn-out **3.** antique, archaic, bygone, early, immemorial, original, primeval, primitive, pristine, remote **4.** experienced, familiar, hardened, practised, skilled, time-honoured, traditional, versed, veteran, vintage
old-fashioned ancient, antiquated, archaic, dated, dead, *démodé*, obsolescent, past
old-world archaic, courtly, gallant, picturesque, quaint, traditional
omen augury, foreboding, indication, portent, presage, sign
ominous dark, fateful, menacing, portentous, sinister, threatening
omission default, failure, gap, lack, leaving out, neglect, oversight
omit disregard, drop, eliminate, exclude, fail, forget, miss (out), neglect, overlook, skip
omnipotent all-powerful, supreme
once 1. long ago, previously **2.**

at once directly, forthwith, immediately, instantly, now, right away

onerous burdensome, crushing, demanding, difficult, exacting, grave, hard, heavy, laborious, oppressive, taxing, weighty

one-sided biased, coloured, lopsided, partial, partisan, prejudiced, unfair, unjust

onlooker bystander, eyewitness, observer, spectator, witness

only 1. *adv.* exclusively, just, merely, purely 2. *adj.* exclusive, individual, lone, single, sole, solitary, unique

onslaught assault, attack, offensive

onus burden, liability, load, obligation, responsibility, task

ooze bleed, discharge, drain, drop, emit, escape, filter, leach, leak, seep, strain, sweat, weep

opaque clouded, cloudy, dim, dull, filmy, hazy, muddied, murky

open *adj.* 1. agape, ajar, extended, gaping, revealed, unclosed, uncovered, unfastened, unfurled, unlocked, unsealed, yawning 2. airy, bare, clear, exposed, extensive, free, navigable, passable, rolling, spacious, sweeping, unfenced, wide 3. available, free, general, public, unengaged, unoccupied, unqualified, unrestricted, vacant 4. apparent, avowed, barefaced, blatant, clear, conspicuous, downright, evident, manifest, obvious, plain, visible 5. arguable, debatable, moot, undecided, unresolved, unsettled 6. artless, candid, fair, frank, guileless, honest, innocent, natural, sincere, transparent 7. exposed, unprotected ~*v.* 8. begin, commence, inaugurate, initiate, kick off (*Inf.*), launch, start 9. clear, crack, unbar, unblock, unclose, uncork, uncover, undo, unfasten, unlock, unseal, untie, unwrap 10. expand, unfold, unfurl, unroll

open-air alfresco, outdoor

opening *n.* 1. aperture, breach, break, cleft, crack, gap, hole, rent, rupture, slot, space, split, vent 2. chance, occasion, opportunity, place, vacancy 3. beginning, birth, dawn, inception, initiation, launch, onset, outset, start ~*adj.* 4. beginning, early, first, inaugural, initial, introductory, primary

openly 1. candidly, forthrightly, frankly, plainly, unhesitatingly, unreservedly 2. blatantly, brazenly, publicly, shamelessly, unashamedly, wantonly

open-minded broad, catholic, dispassionate, enlightened, free, impartial, liberal, reasonable, receptive, tolerant, unbiased, unprejudiced

operate act, function, go, perform, run, work

operation 1. action, affair, course, exercise, motion, movement, procedure, process, use, working 2. **in operation** effective, functioning 3. activity, agency, effect, effort, force, influence 4. affair, business, deal, enterprise, proceeding, transaction, undertaking 5. assault, campaign, exercise, manoeuvre

operational functional, going, ready, usable, viable, working

operator conductor, driver, handler, mechanic, practitioner, technician, worker

opinion assessment, belief, conjecture, feeling, idea, judgment, mind, notion, persuasion, sentiment, theory, view

opinionated bigoted, cocksure, dictatorial, doctrinaire, dogmatic, inflexible, obstinate, prejudiced, stubborn

opponent adversary, antagonist, challenger, competitor, contestant, disputant, enemy, foe, rival

opportune appropriate, apt, auspicious, convenient, favourable, felicitous, fitting, happy, lucky, proper, propitious, seasonable, suitable, timely, well-timed

opportunity chance, hour, moment, occasion, opening, scope, time

oppose bar, check, combat, counter, defy, face, fight, hinder, obstruct, prevent, resist, take on, withstand

opposed against, conflicting, contrary, dissentient, hostile, inimical, opposing

opposite *adj.* 1. corresponding, facing, fronting 2. adverse, conflicting, contradictory, contrary, contrasted, diverse, hostile, inimical, irreconcilable, opposed, reverse, unlike ~*n.* 3. antithesis, contradiction, contrary, converse, inverse, reverse

opposition 1. antagonism, competition, disapproval, hostility, prevention, resistance 2. antagonist, foe, other side, rival

oppress 1. afflict, burden, dispirit, harass, sadden, torment, vex 2. abuse, crush, harry, maltreat, overpower, persecute, subdue, subjugate, suppress, wrong

oppression abuse, brutality, cruelty, harshness, injury, injustice, misery, persecution, severity, tyranny

oppressive 1. brutal, cruel, despotic, grinding, harsh, heavy, onerous, repressive, severe, tyrannical, unjust 2. airless, close, heavy, stifling, stuffy, sultry, torrid

oppressor autocrat, despot, persecutor, scourge, tormentor, tyrant

opt (for) choose, elect, prefer

optimistic assured, bright, buoyant, cheerful, confident, expectant, hopeful, positive

optimum *adj.* best, highest, ideal, peak, perfect, superlative

option alternative, choice, election, preference, selection

optional extra, open, possible, voluntary

opulence affluence, fortune, luxury, plenty, prosperity, riches, richness

opulent affluent, luxurious, moneyed, prosperous, rich, sumptuous, wealthy

oracle 1. prophet, seer, sibyl, soothsayer 2. divination, prediction, prognostication, prophecy, revelation, vision

oral spoken, verbal, viva voce, vocal

oration address, discourse, harangue, lecture, speech

orator declaimer, lecturer, rhetorician, speaker

oratorical declamatory, eloquent, high-flown, rhetorical, sonorous

oratory declamation, eloquence, rhetoric

orb ball, circle, globe, ring, round, sphere

orbit *n.* 1. circle, course, cycle, path, revolution, rotation, track, trajectory 2. *Fig.* ambit, compass, course, domain, influence, range, reach, scope, sphere, sweep ~*v.* 3. circle, encircle, revolve around

orchestrate 1. arrange, score 2. arrange, concert, coordinate, present

ordain 1. anoint, appoint, call, consecrate, destine, elect, frock, invest, nominate 2. fate, intend, predestine 3. decree, dictate, enact, enjoin, fix, lay down, order, prescribe, rule, set, will

ordeal affliction, agony, anguish, nightmare, suffering, test, torture, trial

order *n.* 1. arrangement, method, neatness, pattern, plan, regularity, symmetry, system, tidiness 2. array, disposal, disposition, grouping, layout, line, placement, progression, sequence, series, structure, succession 3. calm, control, discipline, law, peace, quiet, tranquillity 4. caste, class, degree, grade, hierarchy, position, rank, status 5. breed, cast, class, family, genre, genus, ilk, kind, sort, species, tribe, type 6. behest, command, decree, dictate, direction, directive, injunction, instruction, law, precept, regulation, rule, stipulation 7. application, booking, commission, request, reservation 8. brotherhood, community, company, fraternity, guild, league, lodge, sect, sisterhood, society, union ~*v.* 9. adjure, bid, charge, command, decree, direct, enact, enjoin, instruct, ordain, prescribe, require 10. book, call for, contract for, engage, prescribe, request, reserve 11. adjust, align, arrange, catalogue, class, classify, conduct, control, dispose, group, manage, marshal, neaten, organize, regulate, systematize, tabulate, tidy

orderly *adj.* 1. businesslike, in order, methodical, neat, regular, shipshape, systematic, tidy, trim 2. controlled, decorous, disciplined, law-abiding, quiet, restrained, well-behaved

ordinarily commonly, customarily, generally, habitually, normally, usually

ordinary 1. accustomed, common, customary, established, everyday, normal, prevailing, regular, routine, settled, standard, stock, typical, usual, wonted 2. conventional, familiar, homespun, household, humble, modest, plain, prosaic, simple, unpretentious, workaday 3. average, commonplace, fair, indifferent, inferior, pedestrian, stereotyped, undistinguished, uninspired, unremarkable

organ 1. device, implement, instrument, tool 2. element, member, part, process, structure, unit 3. agency, channel, forum, medium, mouthpiece, newspaper, publication, vehicle, voice

organism animal, being, body, creature, entity, structure

organization 1. assembly, construction, disposal, formation, management, regulation, running, standardization 2. arrangement, chemistry, composition, constitution, design, format, framework, grouping, make-up, method, organism, pattern, plan, structure, system, unity, whole 3. association, body, combine, company, concern, consortium, group, institution, league, syndicate

organize arrange, catalogue, classify, codify, constitute, construct, coordinate, dispose, establish, form, frame, group, marshal, pigeonhole, set up, shape

orgy 1. debauch, revelry 2. bout, excess, indulgence, spree, surfeit

orientation bearings, direction, location, position

orifice aperture, cleft, hole, mouth, opening, perforation, pore, rent, vent

origin 1. base, cause, derivation, fountain, occasion, roots, source, spring 2. beginning, birth, dawning, emergence, foundation, genesis, inauguration, inception, launch, outset, start

original *adj.* 1. earliest, first, initial, introductory, opening, primary, pristine, rudimentary, starting 2. creative, fertile, fresh, ingenious, inventive, new, novel, resourceful, untried, unusual 3. archetypal, authentic, first, genuine, master, primary ~*n.* 4. archetype, master, model, pattern, precedent, prototype, standard, type

originality boldness, break with tradition, cleverness, creativeness, creative spirit, creativity, daring, freshness, imagination, imaginativeness, individuality, ingenuity, innovation, innovativeness, inventiveness, new ideas, newness, novelty, resourcefulness, unconventionality, unorthodoxy

originate 1. arise, begin, come, derive, emerge, flow, issue, result, rise, spring, start, stem 2. conceive, create, discover, evolve, formulate, generate, initiate, institute, introduce, invent, launch, pioneer, produce

ornament 1. adornment, bauble, decoration, frill, garnish, trinket 2. flower, honour, jewel, pride, treasure

ornamental attractive, decorative, showy

ornate beautiful, bedecked, busy, decorated, elaborate, elegant, fancy, florid, rococo

orthodox accepted, approved, conformist, conventional, doctrinal, established, official, received, sound, traditional, true

orthodoxy authenticity, authority, conformity, inflexibility, soundness

ostensible alleged, apparent, manifest, outward, plausible, professed, seeming, specious

ostentation affectation, boasting, display, exhibitionism, flourish, parade, pomp, pretentiousness, show, window-dressing

ostentatious boastful, conspicuous, extravagant, flamboyant, gaudy, loud, pompous, pretentious, showy, vulgar

other *adj.* 1. added, alternative, extra, further, more, spare, supplementary 2. different, dissimilar, distinct, diverse, remaining, separate

otherwise if not, or else, or then

out *adj.* 1. impossible, ruled out, unacceptable 2. abroad, absent, away, elsewhere, gone, not at home, outside

out-and-out absolute, complete, outright, perfect, total, unqualified, utter

outbreak burst, explosion, flare-up, flash, outburst, rash, spasm

outcast *n.* castaway, exile, leper, pariah, refugee, untouchable, wretch

outclass beat, eclipse, exceed, excel, outdistance, outdo, outrank, outstrip, surpass

outcome aftermath, consequence, end, issue, result, upshot

outcry clamour, complaint, cry, howl, noise, outburst, protest, scream, screech, uproar, yell

outdated antiquated, archaic, obsolete, old-fashioned, unfashionable

outdoor alfresco, open-air, outside

outer exposed, exterior, external, outward, remote, superficial, surface

outfit 1. *n.* clothes, costume, ensemble, garb, gear, kit, suit, trappings 2. *v.* appoint, equip, furnish, provision, stock, supply

outflow discharge, drainage, effluence, gush, jet, outfall, outpouring, rush, spout

outgoing departing, former, last, leaving, past, retiring

outgoings costs, expenditure, expenses, outlay, overheads

outing excursion, jaunt, trip

outlandish alien, barbarous, eccentric, exotic, foreign, grotesque, queer, strange, weird

outlaw 1. *n.* bandit, brigand, highwayman, marauder, robber 2. *v.* ban, banish, bar, condemn, forbid, prohibit, proscribe

outlay *n.* cost, expenses, investment, outgoings

outlet avenue, channel, opening, release, vent

outline *n.* 1. draft, drawing, frame, layout, plan, rough, skeleton, sketch, tracing 2. résumé, rundown, summary, synopsis 3. contour, figure, form, profile, shape, silhouette ~*v.* 4. adumbrate, delineate, draft, plan, summarize, trace

outlook 1. angle, attitude, perspective, slant, viewpoint, views 2. forecast, future, prospect

output manufacture, production, yield

outrage *n.* 1. atrocity, enormity, evil, inhumanity 2. abuse, affront, indignity, injury, insult, offence, shock, violation, violence 3. anger, fury, hurt, indignation, resentment, shock, wrath ~*v.* 4. affront, incense, offend, scandalize, shock

outrageous 1. atrocious, beastly, flagrant, horrible, infamous, inhuman, scandalous, shocking, villainous, violent, wicked 2. disgraceful, offensive, scandalous, shocking, unreasonable

outright *adj.* 1. absolute, arrant, complete, perfect, pure, thorough, total, unconditional, utter, wholesale 2. definite, direct, flat ~*adv.* 3. absolutely, completely, explicitly, openly, overtly, straightforwardly, thoroughly 4. cleanly, immediately, instantly

outset beginning, inception, opening, start

outshine eclipse, outclass, outstrip, surpass, top

outside *adj.* 1. exterior, external, extramural, extreme, outdoor, outer, outward, surface 2. distant, faint, marginal, negligible, remote, slight, slim, small, unlikely ~*n.* 3. exterior, façade, face, front, skin, surface, topside

outskirts borders, boundary, edge, environs, suburbs, vicinity

outspoken abrupt, blunt, candid, direct, explicit, frank, free, open, round

outstanding 1. celebrated, distinguished, eminent, excellent, exceptional, great, important, impressive, special, superior, well-known 2. arresting, conspicuous, marked, memorable, notable, prominent, salient, striking 3. due, ongoing, open, owing, payable, pending, unpaid, unsettled

outward *adj.* apparent, evident, exterior, external, obvious, ostensible, outer, outside, perceptible, superficial, surface, visible

outwardly apparently, externally, officially, ostensibly

outweigh compensate for, eclipse, override, predominate

outwit cheat, deceive, defraud, dupe, outjockey, outmanoeuvre, swindle

outworn abandoned, antiquated, disused, obsolete, outdated, rejected, stale, threadbare, tired, worn-out

ovation acclaim, applause, cheers, plaudits, tribute

over *adj.* 1. accomplished, by, bygone, closed, completed, concluded, finished, gone, past ~*adj./adv.* 2. beyond, extra, left over, remaining, superfluous, surplus, unused ~*prep.* 3. above, on, on top of, upon 4. above, exceeding, in excess of, more than ~*adv.* 5. above, aloft, on high, overhead

overact exaggerate, ham *or* ham up (*Inf.*), overdo, overplay

overall *adj.* blanket, complete, general, inclusive, umbrella

overbalance capsize, overturn, slip, tumble, upset

overbearing arrogant, despotic, dogmatic, domineering, lordly, officious, oppressive, overweening, peremptory, superior

overcast clouded, darkened, dismal, dreary, dull, grey, hazy, lowering, murky, sombre, threatening

overcharge cheat, fleece, short change, surcharge

overcome beat, best, conquer, crush, defeat, master, overpower, prevail, subdue, subjugate, surmount, survive, vanquish, worst

overcrowded choked, congested, crammed full, overloaded, swarming

overdo belabour, exaggerate, overindulge, overplay

overdone 1. exaggerated, excessive, fulsome, inordinate, undue 2. burnt, charred, overcooked

overdue behindhand, belated, late, owing, tardy, unpunctual

overemphasize belabour

overflow 1. *v.* cover, deluge, drown, flood, inundate, soak, submerge, swamp 2. *n.* flood, inundation, spill, surplus

overflowing abounding, copious, plentiful, profuse, rife, superabundant, swarming, teeming, thronged

overhaul *v.* 1. check, do up (*Inf.*), examine, inspect, recondition, re-examine, repair, restore, service, survey 2. overtake, pass ~*n.* 3. checkup, examination, inspection, service

overhead 1. *adv.* above, skyward, up above, upward 2. *adj.* overhanging, roof, upper

overheads burden, running cost(s)

overindulgence excess, intemperance, overeating, surfeit

overjoyed delighted, elated, joyful, jubilant, rapturous, thrilled

overload burden, encumber, oppress, strain

overlook 1. disregard, forget, ignore, miss, neglect, omit, pass, slight 2. condone, disregard, excuse, forgive

overpower beat, conquer, crush, defeat, master, overcome, overwhelm, quell, subdue, subjugate, vanquish

overrate exaggerate, overestimate, overpraise, oversell, overvalue

override annul, cancel, disregard, ignore, nullify, outweigh, quash, reverse, set aside, supersede, upset, vanquish

overriding cardinal, compelling, final, major, paramount, predominant, primary, prime, ruling, supreme, ultimate

overrule alter, annul, cancel, invalidate, override, overturn, recall, repeal, rescind, reverse, revoke, veto

overrun 1. invade, occupy, rout, swamp 2. choke, infest, inundate, overgrow, permeate, ravage 3. exceed, overshoot

overseer chief, foreman, master, manager, supervisor

overshadow 1. dominate, dwarf, eclipse, excel, outshine, surpass 2. bedim, cloud, darken, dim, obfuscate, obscure, veil

oversight 1. blunder, error, fault, lapse, laxity, mistake, neglect, omission, slip 2. care, charge, control, custody, direction, management, surveillance

overtake outdistance, outdo, outstrip, overhaul, pass

overthrow *v.* 1. abolish, beat, conquer, crush, defeat, depose, dethrone, master, oust, overwhelm, topple, unseat 2. demolish, destroy, level, overturn, raze, ruin, subvert, upend, upset ~*n.* 3. defeat, discomfiture, displacement, dispossession, downfall, end, fall, ousting, rout, ruin, undoing

overture *Often plural* advance, approach, invitation, offer, proposal, signal, tender

overturn 1. capsize, overbalance, reverse, spill, topple, tumble, upend, upset, upturn 2. abolish, annul, countermand, depose, destroy, invalidate, overthrow, repeal, rescind, reverse

overwhelm 1. bury, crush, deluge, engulf, flood, inundate, submerge, swamp 2. confuse, devastate, prostrate, stagger

overwhelming crushing, devastating, overpowering, shattering, stunning, vast

overwork burden, exhaust, exploit, fatigue, oppress, overtax, overuse, prostrate, strain, weary

overwrought agitated, distracted, excited, frantic, keyed up, on edge, tense

owing *adj.* due, outstanding, overdue, owed, payable, unpaid, unsettled

own *adj.* 1. individual, particular, personal, private 2. **on one's own** alone, independently, isolated, unaided 3. **hold one's own** compete ~*v.* 4. enjoy, have, hold, keep, possess, retain 5. **own up (to)** admit, confess 6. acknowledge, admit, allow, avow, concede, confess, disclose, grant, recognize

owner holder, landlord, lord, master, mistress, possessor, proprietor

ownership dominion, possession, proprietorship, title

P

pace *n.* 1. gait, measure, step, stride, tread, walk 2. momentum, motion, movement, progress, rate, speed, tempo, time, velocity ~*v.* 3. march, patrol, pound, stride 4. count, determine, mark out, measure, step

pacifist dove, peace lover, peacemonger

pack *n.* 1. bale, bundle, burden, kit, kitbag, knapsack, load, package, packet, parcel, rucksack, truss 2. band, bunch, collection, company, crew, crowd, deck, drove, flock, gang, group, herd, lot, mob, set, troop ~*v.* 3. bundle, burden, load, package, store, stow 4. charge, compact, compress, cram, crowd, fill, jam, mob, press, ram, stuff, tamp, throng, wedge

package *n.* 1. box, carton, container, parcel 2. combination, entity, unit, whole ~*v.* 3. batch, box, pack, wrap

packed brimful, chock-full, congested, crammed, crowded, filled, full, jammed, overflowing, overloaded, seething, swarming

packet bag, carton, container, package, parcel

pack up 1. put away, store, tidy up 2. finish, give up 3. break down, fail, give out, stall, stop

pact agreement, alliance, bargain, bond, concord, contract, covenant, deal, league, protocol, treaty, understanding

pad *n.* 1. buffer, cushion, protection, stiffening, stuffing, wad 2. block, jotter, notepad, tablet, writing pad 3. foot, paw, sole ~*v.* 4. cushion, pack, protect, shape, stuff **5.** *Often with* **out** amplify, augment, eke, inflate, lengthen, protract, stretch

padding filling, packing, stuffing, wadding

paddle[1] **1.** *n.* oar, scull, sweep **2.** *v.* oar, propel, pull, row, scull

paddle[2] dabble, plash, slop, wade

pagan 1. *n.* heathen, infidel, unbeliever **2.** *adj.* heathen, infidel

page[1] folio, leaf, sheet, side

page[2] **1.** *n.* attendant, footboy, pageboy, servant, squire **2.** *v.* call, seek, summon

pageant display, parade, procession, ritual, show, spectacle, tableau

pain *n.* **1.** ache, cramp, hurt, irritation, pang, soreness, spasm, tenderness, throb, trouble, twinge **2.** agony, anguish, bitterness, distress, grief, heartache, misery, suffering, torment, torture, woe ~*v.* **3.** ail, chafe, harm, hurt, inflame, injure, smart, sting, throb **4.** afflict, aggrieve, agonize, disquiet, distress, grieve, hurt, sadden, torment, torture, vex, worry, wound

pained aggrieved, distressed, hurt, injured, offended, reproachful, stung, upset, wounded

painful 1. disagreeable, distasteful, grievous, unpleasant **2.** agonizing, harrowing, inflamed, raw, smarting, sore, tender **3.** arduous, difficult, hard, laborious, severe, tedious, troublesome, trying, vexatious

painfully clearly, deplorably, distressingly, dreadfully, markedly, sadly, unfortunately

painkiller anaesthetic, analgesic, drug, remedy, sedative

painless easy, effortless, fast, pain-free, quick, simple

pains bother, care, diligence, effort, industry, labour, trouble

painstaking assiduous, careful, conscientious, diligent, earnest, meticulous, punctilious, scrupulous, sedulous, strenuous, thorough

paint *n.* **1.** colour, colouring, dye, emulsion, pigment, stain, tint ~*v.* **2.** delineate, depict, draw, figure, picture, portray, represent, sketch **3.** apply, coat, colour, cover, daub, decorate

pair 1. *n.* brace, couple, doublet, duo, match, span, twins **2.** *v.* bracket, couple, join, marry, match, mate, team, twin, wed, yoke

palatable appetizing, delicious, luscious, mouthwatering, savoury, tasty

palate 1. appetite, heart, stomach, taste **2.** appreciation, enjoyment, gusto, liking, relish, zest

palatial de luxe, grand, illustrious, imposing, magnificent, majestic, opulent, regal, spacious, splendid, stately, sumptuous

pale 1. ashen, ashy, bleached, colourless, faded, light, pasty, sallow, wan, white **2.** dim, faint, feeble, inadequate, poor, thin, weak

palm *Fig.* bays, crown, fame, glory, honour, laurels, merit, prize, success, triumph, trophy, victory

palmy fortunate, glorious, golden, halcyon, happy, joyous, prosperous, thriving

palpable apparent, blatant, clear, conspicuous, evident, manifest, obvious, open, patent, plain, visible

palpitate beat, flutter, pound, pulsate, quiver, shiver, throb, tremble, vibrate

paltry base, beggarly, derisory, despicable, insignificant, low, meagre, mean, minor, miserable, petty, pitiful, poor, puny, slight, small, sorry, trifling, trivial, unimportant, worthless, wretched

pamper baby, coddle, cosset, fondle, gratify, humour, indulge, pet, spoil

pamphlet booklet, brochure, circular, folder, leaflet, tract

pan 1. *n.* container, pot, saucepan, vessel **2.** *v. Inf.* censure, criticize, flay

panacea cure-all, elixir, nostrum

panache dash, élan, flamboyance, flourish, spirit, style, verve

pandemonium babel, bedlam, chaos, confusion, din, racket, rumpus, tumult, turmoil, uproar

pang ache, agony, distress, gripe, pain, prick, spasm, stab, sting, stitch, twinge

panic agitation, alarm, dismay, fear, fright, horror, scare, terror

panoply array, attire, dress, garb, regalia, show

panorama 1. prospect, scenery, view, vista **2.** perspective, survey

pant blow, breathe, gasp, heave, huff, puff, throb, wheeze

paper *n.* **1.** *Often plural* certificate, deed, documents, instrument, record **2.** *Plural* diaries, dossier, file, letters, records **3.** daily, gazette, journal, news, organ ~*v.* **4.** hang, line, wallpaper

par *n.* average, level, mean, norm, standard, usual

parable allegory, exemplum, fable, lesson, moral tale, story

parade *n.* **1.** array, ceremony, column, march, pageant, procession, review, spectacle, train **2.** array, display, ostentation, pomp, show, spectacle, vaunting ~*v.* **3.** march, process **4.** air, brandish, display, exhibit, flaunt, show, strut, swagger, vaunt

paradise bliss, delight, felicity, heaven

paradox ambiguity, anomaly, contradiction, enigma, oddity, puzzle

paragon archetype, criterion, exemplar, ideal, jewel, model, pattern, prototype

paragraph clause, item, notice, part, passage, portion, section, subdivision

parallel *adj.* **1.** alongside, equidistant **2.** akin, analogous, complementary, like, matching, resembling, similar, uniform ~*n.* **3.** analogue, corollary, counterpart, duplicate, equal, equivalent, match, twin **4.** analogy, comparison, correlation, likeness, resemblance, similarity

paralyse 1. cripple, disable, incapacitate, lame **2.** arrest, benumb, freeze, halt, numb, petrify, stun, stupefy, transfix

paralysis 1. immobility, palsy **2.** arrest, breakdown, halt, standstill

paralytic *adj.* crippled, disabled, immobile, incapacitated, lame, numb, palsied, paralysed

paramount capital, cardinal, chief, dominant, eminent, first, foremost, main, outstanding, pre-eminent, primary, principal, superior, supreme

paraphernalia apparatus, baggage, belongings, effects, gear, material, stuff, tackle, things, trappings

parasite hanger-on, leech

parcel 1. *n.* bundle, carton, package **2.** *v. Often with* **up** do up, pack, package, tie up, wrap

parch blister, burn, dry up, evaporate, scorch, sear, shrivel, wither

parched arid, dry, scorched, thirsty, waterless, withered

pardon 1. *v.* absolve, acquit, amnesty, condone, exculpate, excuse, exonerate, forgive, free, overlook, release, remit, reprieve **2.** *n.* absolution, acquittal, allowance, amnesty, discharge, excuse, grace, indulgence, release, remission, reprieve

pardonable excusable, forgivable, minor, understandable, venial

parent father, guardian, mother, sire

parentage ancestry, birth, descent, family, line, lineage, origin, pedigree, race, stock

parish church, community, congregation, flock, fold

parity consistency, equality, par, uniformity, unity

park estate, garden, grounds, parkland, woodland

parliament assembly, congress, convocation, council, diet, legislature, senate

parliamentary deliberative, governmental, lawmaking, legislative

parlour front room, lounge, sitting room

parlous dangerous, desperate, difficult, dire, hazardous, risky

parody 1. *n.* burlesque, caricature, imitation, satire, skit **2.** *v.* burlesque, caricature, mimic, satirize, travesty

parry 1. block, deflect, rebuff, repel, repulse **2.** avoid, dodge, evade, fence, shun, sidestep

parsimonious close, frugal, grasping, mean, miserable, miserly, niggardly, penny-pinching (*Inf.*), penurious, saving, scrimpy, sparing, stingy, tightfisted

parson churchman, clergyman, cleric, divine, incumbent, minister, pastor, preacher, priest, rector, vicar

part *n.* **1.** bit, fraction, fragment, lot, piece, portion, scrap, section, share, slice **2.** branch, constituent, division, element, ingredient, limb, member, organ, piece, unit **3.** cause, concern, faction, interest, party, side **4.** bit, business, capacity, charge, duty, function, place, role, say, share, task, work **5.** *Theat.* character, lines, role **6. in good part** cheerfully, cordially, well **7. in part** a little, in some measure, partially, partly, slightly, somewhat ~*v.* **8.** break, cleave, come apart, detach, disunite, divide, rend, separate, sever, split, tear **9.** depart, go, go away, leave, quit, separate, withdraw

partake *With* **in** engage, participate, share, take part

partial 1. imperfect, incomplete, limited, unfinished **2.** biased, influenced, interested, one-sided, partisan, prejudiced, tendentious, unfair, unjust

partiality 1. bias, preference, prejudice **2.** fondness, inclination, liking, love, penchant, predilection, proclivity, taste, weakness

partially fractionally, halfway, incompletely, in part, moderately, partly, piecemeal, somewhat

participant associate, contributor, member, party, shareholder

participate enter into, join in, perform, share, take part

particle atom, bit, crumb, grain, iota, jot, mite, mote, piece, scrap, shred, speck, tittle, whit

particular *adj.* **1.** distinct, exact, express, peculiar, precise, special, specific **2.** especial, marked, notable, remarkable, singular, uncommon, unusual **3.** critical, dainty, demanding, discriminating, exacting, fastidious, finicky, fussy ~*n.* **4.** *Usually plural* circumstance, detail, fact, feature, item, specification **5. in particular** distinctly, especially, exactly, expressly, specifically

particularly especially, exceptionally, markedly, singularly, surprisingly, uncommonly, unusually

parting 1. adieu, farewell, going, goodbye **2.** breaking, division, partition, rift, rupture, separation, split

partisan *n.* **1.** backer, devotee, stalwart, supporter, upholder, votary **2.** guerrilla, irregular ~*adj.* **3.** biased, factional, interested, one-sided, partial, prejudiced, sectarian

partition *n.* **1.** division, segregation, separation **2.** barrier, screen, wall **3.** allotment, distribution, portion, share ~*v.* **4.** apportion, cut up, divide, separate, share, split up, subdivide

partly partially, relatively, slightly, somewhat

partner 1. ally, associate, bedfellow, colleague, companion, comrade, helper, mate, teammate **2.** consort, helpmate, husband, mate, spouse, wife

partnership alliance, combine, company, cooperative, firm, house, society, union

party 1. celebration, festivity, function, gathering, reception, social **2.** band, body, company, crew, gang, group, squad, team, unit **3.** alliance, cabal, clique, coalition, confederacy, coterie, faction, grouping, league, set, side **4.** individual, person

pass[1] *v.* **1.** depart, elapse, flow, go, leave, move, proceed, roll, run **2.** beat, exceed, excel, outdo, outstrip, surmount, surpass **3.** answer, graduate, qualify, succeed, suffice, suit **4.** befall, develop, happen, occur **5.** convey, deliver, exchange, give, hand, kick, reach, send, throw, transfer **6.** accept, adopt, approve, decree, enact, legislate, ordain, ratify

pass[2] *n.* 1. canyon, col, defile, gap, gorge, ravine 2. identification, licence, passport, permission, permit, safe-conduct, ticket, warrant

passable adequate, average, fair, mediocre, middling, moderate, ordinary, presentable, tolerable

passage 1. avenue, channel, course, lane, path, road, route, thoroughfare, way 2. corridor, doorway, entrance, hall, lobby, vestibule 3. extract, paragraph, piece, quotation, section, sentence, text, verse 4. crossing, journey, tour, trek, trip, voyage 5. allowance, freedom, permission, right, visa, warrant

passenger fare, rider, traveller

passing *adj.* 1. brief, fleeting, momentary, short, temporary, transient, transitory 2. casual, cursory, glancing, hasty, quick, shallow, short, slight, superficial

passion 1. ardour, eagerness, emotion, excitement, feeling, fire, heat, intensity, joy, rapture, spirit, transport, warmth, zeal 2. ardour, concupiscence, desire, fondness, infatuation, itch, keenness, love, lust 3. bug (*Inf.*), craving, craze, enthusiasm, fancy, fascination, idol, infatuation, mania, obsession 4. anger, fit, flare-up (*Inf.*), frenzy, fury, indignation, ire, outburst, paroxysm, rage, resentment, storm

passionate 1. amorous, ardent, aroused, desirous, erotic, hot, loving, lustful, sensual 2. animated, ardent, eager, emotional, excited, fierce, frenzied, heartfelt, impassioned, intense, strong, vehement, warm, wild

passive compliant, docile, enduring, inactive, inert, lifeless, nonviolent, patient, receptive, resigned, submissive

pass over disregard, ignore, omit, overlook

past *adj.* 1. completed, done, elapsed, ended, extinct, finished, forgotten, gone, over, spent 2. ancient, bygone, early, foregoing, former, late, olden, recent ~*n.* 3. background, experience, history, life, past life ~*adv.* 4. across, beyond, by, on, over

pastel delicate, light, soft

pastiche blend, hotchpotch, medley, miscellany, mixture, motley

pastime activity, amusement, diversion, entertainment, game, hobby, leisure, play, recreation, sport

pastor churchman, clergyman, divine, minister, parson, priest, rector, vicar

pastoral *adj.* 1. bucolic, idyllic, rural, rustic, simple 2. clerical, ministerial, priestly

pasture grass, grazing, meadow, pasturage

pat 1. *v.* caress, dab, fondle, pet, slap, stroke, tap, touch 2. *n.* clap, dab, light blow, slap, stroke, tap

patch *n.* 1. reinforcement 2. bit, scrap, shred, small piece, spot, stretch 3. area, ground, land, plot, tract ~*v.* 4. cover, fix, mend, repair, sew up

patchwork hash, jumble, medley, mixture, pastiche

patchy bitty, erratic, fitful, irregular, random, sketchy, spotty, uneven

patent 1. *adj.* blatant, clear, downright, evident, flagrant, glaring, manifest, obvious, open 2. *n.* copyright, invention, licence

paternal concerned, fatherly, protective, solicitous, vigilant

path 1. footway, track, trail 2. avenue, course, direction, passage, procedure, road, route, track, walk, way

pathetic affecting, distressing, melting, moving, pitiable, plaintive, poignant, sad, tender, touching

pathos pitifulness, plaintiveness, poignancy, sadness

patience 1. calmness, forbearance, restraint, serenity, sufferance, tolerance, toleration 2. constancy, diligence, endurance, fortitude, resignation, stoicism, submission

patient *adj.* 1. calm, composed, long-suffering, philosophical, quiet, resigned, serene, stoical, submissive, uncomplaining 2. even-tempered, forbearing, forgiving, indulgent, lenient, mild, tolerant ~*n.* 3. case, invalid, sufferer

patriot chauvinist, loyalist, nationalist

patriotic chauvinistic, loyal, nationalistic

patrol *n.* 1. guarding, policing, protecting, vigilance, watching 2. garrison, guard, patrolman, sentinel, watchman ~*v.* 3. cruise, guard, inspect, police, pound, range, safeguard

patron 1. advocate, backer, benefactor, champion, defender, friend, guardian, helper, sponsor, supporter 2. buyer, client, customer, habitué, shopper

patronage 1. aid, assistance, backing, encouragement, help, promotion, sponsorship, support 2. business, clientele, commerce, custom, trade, trading, traffic

patronize 1. look down on 2. assist, back, befriend, foster, fund, help, sponsor, support 3. deal with, frequent

patronizing condescending, disdainful, gracious, haughty, lofty, snobbish, supercilious, superior

patter *n.* 1. line, pitch 2. chatter, nattering, prattle 3. argot, cant, jargon, patois, slang, vernacular ~*v.* 4. chatter, prate, tattle

pattern *n.* 1. decoration, decorative design, design, device, figure 2. method, order, plan, sequence, system 3. kind, shape, sort, style, type, variety 4. design, diagram, guide, instructions, original, plan, stencil, template 5. example, guide, model, norm, original, paragon, prototype, sample, specimen, standard ~*v.* 6. copy, emulate, follow, form, imitate, model, mould, order, shape, style

paucity dearth, lack, poverty, rarity, scarcity, shortage

pauper bankrupt, beggar, insolvent, mendicant

pause 1. *v.* break, cease, delay, desist, discontinue, halt, hesitate, interrupt, rest, wait, waver 2. *n.* break, cessation, delay, gap, halt, hesitation, interlude, interval, lull, respite, rest, stay, stoppage, wait

pawn deposit, hazard, mortgage, pledge, stake, wager

pay *v.* 1. clear, compensate, cough up (*Inf.*), discharge, foot, give, honour, liquidate, meet, offer, recompense, reimburse, remit, remunerate, render, requite, reward, settle 2. benefit, repay, serve 3. bestow, extend, give, grant, present, proffer, render 4. bring in, produce, profit, return, yield ~*n.* 5. allowance, earnings, emoluments, fee, hire, income, recompense, remuneration, reward, salary, stipend, takings, wages

payable due, mature, outstanding, owed, owing

pay back reciprocate, recompense, retaliate

payment 1. discharge, outlay, paying, remittance, settlement 2. fee, hire, remuneration, reward, wage

pay off 1. discharge, dismiss, fire 2. clear, discharge, settle, square 3. be effective, succeed, work

pay out disburse, expend, spend

peace 1. accord, agreement, concord, harmony 2. conciliation, treaty, truce 3. calm, composure, contentment, relaxation, repose, serenity 4. calm, calmness, hush, quiet, repose, rest, silence, tranquillity

peaceable 1. friendly, gentle, mild, pacific, placid, unwarlike 2. balmy, calm, peaceful, quiet, restful, serene, still, tranquil, undisturbed

peaceful 1. amicable, friendly, harmonious 2. calm, gentle, placid, quiet, restful, serene, still, tranquil 3. pacific, placatory

peak *n.* 1. apex, brow, crest, pinnacle, point, summit, tip, top 2. acme, apogee, climax, crown, zenith ~*v.* 3. climax, culminate

peal 1. *n.* blast, chime, clang, clap, crash, reverberation, ring, roar, rumble, sound 2. *v.* chime, crack, crash, resonate, resound, ring, roar, roll, rumble, sound, toll

peasant 1. countryman, rustic 2. boor, churl, lout, provincial, yokel

peccadillo error, indiscretion, lapse, misdeed

peculiar abnormal, bizarre, curious, eccentric, freakish, funny, odd, offbeat, outlandish, quaint, queer, singular, strange, uncommon, unusual, weird

peculiarity abnormality, eccentricity, foible, mannerism, oddity, quirk

pedagogue instructor, schoolmaster, schoolmistress, teacher

pedantic abstruse, academic, bookish, didactic, donnish, formal, fussy, overnice, particular, pedagogic, pompous, precise, priggish, stilted

peddle hawk, market, sell, trade, vend

pedestal base, foot, foundation, mounting, pier, plinth, stand, support

pedestrian 1. *n.* foot-traveller, walker 2. *adj.* banal, boring, commonplace, dull, flat, humdrum, mediocre, mundane, ordinary, plodding, prosaic

pedigree ancestry, blood, breed, derivation, descent, extraction, family, family tree, genealogy, heritage, line, lineage, race, stemma, stirps, stock

peek spy

peel flake off, pare, scale, skin

peephole chink, crack, crevice, fissure, hole, keyhole, slit

peer[1] *n.* 1. baron, count, duke, earl, lord, marquess, nobleman, viscount 2. equal, fellow, like, match

peer[2] *v.* gaze, inspect, peep, scan, snoop, spy

peerage aristocracy, lords and ladies, nobility, peers

peerless excellent, incomparable, matchless, outstanding, unmatched, unrivalled

peevish acrimonious, captious, childish, churlish, cross, crusty, fractious, fretful, grumpy, irritable, petulant, sulky, sullen, surly, testy, touchy, waspish

peg *v.* attach, fasten, fix, join, secure

pelt assail, batter, cast, hurl, pepper, shower, sling, strike, thrash, throw

pen[1] *v.* compose, draft, jot down, write

pen[2] 1. *n.* cage, coop, fold, hutch, sty 2. *v.* cage, confine, enclose, hedge, hurdle

penal corrective, disciplinary, punitive, retributive

penalize discipline, handicap, punish

penalty fine, forfeit, handicap, price, punishment, retribution

penance atonement, penalty, reparation

penchant bent, bias, fondness, inclination, leaning, partiality, predilection, proclivity, propensity, taste, tendency, turn

pending awaiting, imminent, undecided, undetermined, unsettled

penetrate 1. bore, enter, pierce, prick, probe, stab 2. diffuse, enter, get in, infiltrate, permeate, pervade, seep, suffuse

penetration 1. entrance, incision, inroad, piercing, puncturing 2. astuteness, discernment, insight, keenness, perception, shrewdness, wit

penitence contrition, regret, remorse, repentance, shame, sorrow

penitent *adj.* abject, contrite, regretful, remorseful, sorrowful, sorry

pennant banner, ensign, flag, jack, streamer

penniless bankrupt, destitute, needy, poor, ruined

pension allowance, annuity, benefit, superannuation

pensive contemplative, dreamy, grave, melancholy, mournful, musing, preoccupied, reflective, ruminative, sad, serious, sober, solemn, sorrowful, thoughtful, wistful

people *n.* 1. humanity, mankind, mortals, persons 2. citizens, clan, community, family, folk, nation, population, public, race, tribe 3. crowd, masses, mob, multitude, populace, rabble, the herd ~*v.* 4. colonize, inhabit, occupy, populate, settle

perceive behold, descry, discern, discover, espy, note, notice, observe, recognize, remark, see, spot

perceptible appreciable, clear, detectable, discernible, distinct, evident, noticeable, obvious, recognizable, tangible, visible

perception awareness, conception, discernment, feeling, grasp, idea, insight, notion, recognition, sensation, sense, taste, understanding

perceptive acute, alert, astute, aware, discerning, observant, percipient, perspicacious, quick, responsive, sharp

perch 1. *n.* branch, pole, post, roost 2. *v.* alight, balance, land, rest, roost, settle, sit on

percussion blow, brunt, bump, clash, concussion, crash, impact, jolt, knock, shock, smash, thump

peremptory 1. binding, compelling, decisive, final, imperative, obligatory, undeniable 2. arbitrary, dictatorial, dogmatic, domineering, intolerant, overbearing

perennial abiding, constant, continual, enduring, incessant, inveterate, lifelong, persistent, recurrent, unchanging

perfect *adj.* 1. absolute, complete, consummate, entire, finished, full, sheer, unadulterated, unalloyed, unmitigated, utter, whole 2. blameless, excellent, faultless, flawless, ideal, impeccable, pure, splendid, sublime, superb, supreme, unblemished, unmarred, untarnished ~*v.* 3. achieve, complete, consummate, effect, finish, fulfil, perform, realize

perfection 1. achievement, completion, consummation, evolution, fulfilment, realization 2. completeness, exactness, excellence, faultlessness, integrity, maturity, precision, purity, sublimity, superiority, wholeness 3. acme, crown, ideal, paragon

perfectly 1. altogether, completely, entirely, fully, quite, thoroughly, totally, utterly, wholly 2. admirably, exquisitely, faultlessly, superbly, supremely, wonderfully

perform 1. accomplish, achieve, act, complete, discharge, do, effect, execute, fulfil, satisfy, transact, work 2. act, depict, enact, play, present, produce, render, represent, stage

performance 1. achievement, act, carrying out, completion, conduct, discharge, execution, exploit, feat, fulfilment, work 2. acting, appearance, exhibition, play, portrayal, presentation, production, show

performer actor, actress, artiste, player

perfume aroma, bouquet, fragrance, incense, odour, scent, smell

perfunctory careless, cursory, heedless, indifferent, mechanical, offhand, routine, sketchy, slipshod, slovenly, superficial

perhaps conceivably, feasibly, maybe, possibly

peril danger, hazard, insecurity, jeopardy, menace, pitfall, risk, uncertainty

perimeter ambit, border, bounds, circumference, confines, edge, limit

period interval, season, space, span, spell, stretch, term, time, while

periodical *n.* journal, magazine, monthly, organ, paper, publication, quarterly, review, serial, weekly

perish 1. die, expire, pass away 2. collapse, decline, disappear, fall, vanish 3. decay, decompose, disintegrate, moulder, rot, waste, wither

perishable decaying, short-lived, unstable

perjury false statement, forswearing, oath breaking

permanence constancy, continuance, duration, endurance, finality, fixedness, indestructibility, lastingness, perpetuity, stability, survival

permanent abiding, constant, durable, enduring, fixed, immutable, indestructible, invariable, lasting, perpetual, persistent, stable, steadfast

permeate charge, fill, impregnate, infiltrate, penetrate, percolate, pervade, saturate

permissible acceptable, allowable, authorized, lawful, legal, permitted, proper

permission allowance, approval, assent, authorization, consent, dispensation, freedom, go-ahead (*Inf.*), green light, leave, liberty, licence, permit, sanction, sufferance, tolerance

permissive easy-going, forbearing, free, indulgent, lax, lenient, liberal, tolerant

permit 1. *v.* agree, allow, authorize, consent, empower, enable, give leave *or* permission, grant, let, license, sanction, suffer, tolerate, warrant 2. *n.* liberty, licence, pass, passport, permission, sanction, warrant

pernicious bad, baleful, damaging, deadly, deleterious, destructive, detrimental, evil, fatal, harmful, hurtful, offensive, pestilent, poisonous, ruinous, wicked

pernickety carping, exacting, fastidious, finicky, fussy, nice, particular

peroration conclusion, recapitulation

perpendicular at right angles to, straight, upright, vertical

perpetrate commit, do, effect, enact, execute, inflict, perform, wreak

perpetual abiding, endless, enduring, eternal, everlasting, immortal, infinite, lasting, permanent, unchanging, unending

perpetuate maintain, preserve, sustain

perplex 1. baffle, bewilder, confound, confuse, mystify, puzzle, stump 2. complicate, entangle, involve, tangle

perplexing baffling, complex, complicated, confusing, difficult, enigmatic, hard, intricate, involved, knotty, mysterious, puzzling, strange, thorny, weird

perquisite benefit, bonus, dividend, extra, plus

persecute 1. afflict, distress, harass, hound, hunt, ill-treat, injure, maltreat, martyr, molest, oppress, pursue, torment, torture, victimize 2. annoy, badger, bait, bother, pester, tease, vex, worry

perseverance dedication, diligence, endurance, persistence, pertinacity, resolution, stamina, tenacity

persevere carry on, continue, endure, go on, hang on, hold fast, maintain, persist, pursue, remain

persist 1. continue, insist, persevere 2. abide, continue, endure, keep up, last, linger, remain

persistence constancy, diligence, endurance, grit, perseverance, pertinacity, pluck, resolution, tenacity

persistent determined, dogged, immovable, indefatigable, obdurate, obstinate, persevering, pertinacious, resolute, steadfast, steady, stubborn, tenacious, tireless

person being, body, human, individual, soul

personage celebrity, dignitary, luminary, notable, somebody, V.I.P., worthy

personal exclusive, individual, intimate, own, particular, peculiar, private, special

personality 1. character, disposition, identity, make-up, nature, temperament 2. celebrity, notable, personage, star

personally 1. alone, independently, solely 2. individually, privately, specially, subjectively

personification embodiment, image, incarnation, likeness, portrayal, recreation, representation, semblance

personify embody, epitomize, exemplify, express, mirror, represent, symbolize, typify

personnel employees, helpers, liveware, members, people, staff, workers

perspective 1. angle, attitude, context, outlook, proportion, relation, relativity 2. outlook, panorama, prospect, scene, view, vista

perspire drip, exude, glow, secrete, sweat, swelter

persuade actuate, advise, allure, coax, counsel, entice, impel, induce, influence, prompt, sway, urge

persuasion 1. cajolery, conversion, enticement, inducement, wheedling 2. cogency, force, potency, power 3. belief, conviction, credo, creed, faith, opinion, tenet, views

persuasive cogent, convincing, credible, effective, eloquent, forceful, impressive, influential, logical, moving, plausible, sound, telling, touching, valid, weighty, winning

pertain apply, befit, belong, concern, refer, regard, relate

pertinent admissible, applicable, apposite, appropriate, apt, fit, fitting, germane, material, proper, relevant, suitable

perturb agitate, alarm, bother, disconcert, disquiet, disturb, fluster, trouble, unsettle, upset, vex, worry

perturbed agitated, alarmed, anxious, disturbed, fearful, flurried, flustered, nervous, restless, shaken, troubled, uncomfortable, uneasy, upset, worried

peruse browse, check, examine, inspect, read, scan, scrutinize, study

pervade affect, charge, diffuse, extend, fill, imbue, infuse, penetrate, percolate, permeate, suffuse

pervasive common, extensive, general, inescapable, prevalent, rife, universal, widespread

perverse 1. abnormal, contradictory, deviant, improper, incorrect, miscreant, rebellious, refractory, troublesome, unhealthy, unreasonable 2. contrary, dogged, headstrong, intractable, intransigent, obdurate, wilful, wrong-headed 3. contrary, mulish, obstinate, stubborn, wayward

pervert *v.* 1. abuse, distort, falsify, garble, misuse, twist, warp 2. corrupt, debase, debauch, degrade, deprave, subvert ~*n.* 3. debauchee, degenerate, deviant

perverted aberrant, abnormal, corrupt, debased, debauched, depraved, deviant, evil, immoral, sick, unnatural, vicious, vitiated, warped, wicked

pessimism cynicism, depression, despair, despondency, distrust, gloom, hopelessness, melancholy

pessimist cynic, defeatist, worrier

pessimistic bleak, cynical, dark, dejected, depressed, distrustful, gloomy, glum, hopeless, morose, resigned, sad

pest 1. annoyance, bother, irritation, nuisance, thorn in one's flesh, trial, vexation 2. bane, blight, bug, curse, epidemic, infection, pestilence, plague, scourge

pester annoy, badger, bother, disturb, fret, get at, harass, harry, irk, nag, pick on, plague, torment, worry

pestilence 1. epidemic, plague, visitation 2. blight, cancer, curse, scourge

pestilential annoying, dangerous, destructive, evil, foul, harmful, injurious, pernicious, ruinous

pet *n.* 1. darling, favourite, idol, jewel, treasure ~*adj.* 2. cherished, dearest, favourite, preferred, special ~*v.* 3. baby, coddle, cosset, pamper, spoil 4. caress, fondle, pat, stroke

peter out dwindle, ebb, evaporate, fade, fail, stop, wane

petition 1. *n.* address, appeal, entreaty, plea, prayer, request, suit, supplication 2. *v.* adjure, appeal, ask, beg, beseech, crave, entreat, plead, pray, press, solicit, sue, urge

petty 1. inferior, insignificant, little, negligible, paltry, slight, small, trifling 2. cheap, grudging, mean, shabby, spiteful, stingy, ungenerous

petulance ill humour, irritability, peevishness, pique, sulkiness, sullenness

petulant bad-tempered, captious, crabbed, cross, crusty, fretful, impatient, irritable, moody, peevish, querulous, sour, sulky, sullen

phantom apparition, ghost, spectre, spirit, wraith

phase aspect, chapter, juncture, period, point, position, stage, state, step, time

phase out close, ease off, eliminate, pull out, remove, replace, terminate, wind down, withdraw

phenomenal fantastic, marvellous, miraculous, prodigious, remarkable, sensational, singular, unique, unusual, wondrous

phenomenon 1. circumstance, episode, event, fact, happening, incident, occurrence 2. marvel, miracle, prodigy, rarity, sensation, sight, spectacle

philanthropic altruistic, benevolent, benignant, charitable, gracious, humanitarian, kind, munificent

philanthropist alms-giver, altruist, benefactor, contributor, donor, patron

philanthropy altruism, benevolence, benignity, bounty, charitableness, charity, generosity, kind-heartedness, liberality, munificence, patronage

philistine 1. *n.* barbarian, bourgeois, lout, lowbrow, vulgarian, yahoo 2. *adj.* anti-intellectual, crass, ignorant, lowbrow, tasteless, uneducated, unrefined

philosopher logician, metaphysician, sage, theorist, thinker

philosophical, philosophic 1. abstract, erudite, learned, logical, rational, theoretical, thoughtful, wise 2. calm, collected, composed, cool, impassive, imperturbable, patient, resigned, serene, stoical, tranquil, unruffled

philosophy 1. knowledge, logic, metaphysics, rationalism, reason, reasoning, thinking, thought, wisdom 2. beliefs, doctrine, ideology, principle, tenets, thinking, values, viewpoint

phlegmatic apathetic, cold, dull, frigid, heavy, impassive, listless, placid, sluggish, stoical, stolid, unemotional

phobia aversion, dislike, distaste, dread, fear, hatred, horror, obsession, repulsion, revulsion, terror

phone *n.* 1. telephone 2. call, ring ~*v.* 3. ring, ring up, telephone

phoney 1. *adj.* affected, assumed, bogus, fake, false, forged, imitation, sham, trick 2. *n.* fake, forgery, fraud, humbug, impostor, pretender, sham

photograph 1. *n.* image, likeness, picture, print, shot, slide, snapshot 2. *v.* film, record, shoot, take

phrase 1. *n.* expression, idiom, locution, motto, remark, saying, tag, utterance 2. *v.* couch, express, formulate, frame, present, put, say, term, utter, voice, word

physical 1. bodily, corporal, earthly, fleshly, incarnate, mortal 2. material, natural, real, sensible, solid, substantial, visible

physique body, build, constitution, figure, form, frame, make-up, shape

pick *v.* 1. choose, elect, handpick, mark out, opt for, select, sort out 2. collect, cull, cut, gather, harvest, pluck, pull ~*n.* 3. choice, decision, option, preference, selection 4. elect, elite, flower, pride, prize

picket *n.* 1. pale, paling, post, stake, stanchion, upright 2. protester 3. guard, lookout, patrol, scout, sentinel, sentry, spotter, watch ~*v.* 4. blockade, boycott, demonstrate

pick-me-up drink, refreshment, restorative, stimulant, tonic

pick-up *n.* 1. acceleration, response, revving (*Inf.*), speed-up 2. change for the better, gain, improvement, rally, recovery, revival, strengthening, upswing, upturn

pick up 1. gather, grasp, hoist, lift, raise, take up, uplift 2. buy, find, garner, happen upon, obtain, purchase 3. gain, improve, mend, rally, recover 4. call for, collect, get 5. acquire, learn, master

picnic excursion, outing

pictorial graphic, picturesque, scenic, striking, vivid

picture *n.* 1. drawing, effigy, engraving, illustration, image, likeness, painting, photograph, portrait, portrayal, print, sketch 2. account, description, image, impression, report 3. copy, double, duplicate, image, likeness, replica, twin 4. film, movie ~*v.* 5. visualize

picturesque attractive, beautiful, charming, colourful, graphic, pretty, quaint, scenic, striking, vivid

piece 1. bit, chunk, division, fraction, fragment, length, morsel, part, portion, quantity, scrap, section, segment, share, shred, slice 2. article, composition, creation, item, production, study, work

pier 1. jetty, quay, wharf 2. buttress, column, pile, piling, pillar, support, upright

pierce bore, drill, enter, prick, probe, puncture, spike, stab, stick into, transfix

piety devotion, dutifulness, duty, faith, grace, holiness, religion, reverence, veneration

pig boar, hog, piglet, sow, swine

pigeonhole 1. *n.* compartment, locker, niche, place, section 2. *v.* defer, file, postpone, put off, shelve

pig-headed contrary, inflexible, mulish, obstinate, perverse, self-willed, stubborn, stupid, wilful

pigment colour, dye, dyestuff, paint, stain, tincture, tint

pile *n.* 1. collection, heap, hoard, mass, mound, mountain, stack, stockpile 2. building, edifice, erection, structure ~*v.* 3. amass, assemble, collect, gather, heap, hoard, load up, mass, stack, store

pile-up accident, collision, crash, smash

pilfer appropriate, embezzle, filch, purloin, rob, steal, take, thieve

pilgrim crusader, traveller, wanderer, wayfarer

pilgrimage crusade, excursion, expedition, journey, mission, tour, trip

pillage 1. *v.* despoil, loot, maraud, plunder, raid, ransack, ravage, rifle, rob, sack, strip 2. *n.* depredation, plunder, rapine, robbery, sack

pillar 1. column, pier, post, prop, shaft, support, upright 2. leader, mainstay, rock, supporter, upholder, worthy

pillory *v.* brand, denounce, lash, show up, stigmatize

pilot 1. *n.* airman, aviator, captain, coxswain, director, flier, guide, helmsman, leader, navigator, steersman 2. *v.* conduct, control, direct, drive, fly, guide, handle, lead, manage, navigate, operate, steer 3. *adj.* model, test, trial

pin *v.* 1. affix, attach, fasten, fix, join, secure 2. fix, hold down, hold fast, immobilize, pinion, press, restrain

pinch *v.* 1. grasp, nip, press, squeeze, tweak 2. chafe, confine, cramp, crush, hurt, pain ~*n.* 3. nip, squeeze, tweak 4. bit, dash, jot, mite, small quantity, *soupçon*, speck, taste 5. crisis, hardship, necessity, pass, plight, predicament, pressure, strait, stress

pin down 1. constrain, force, make, press, pressurize 2. bind, confine, constrain, fix, hold, immobilize

pinion *v.* bind, chain, fasten, manacle, shackle, tie

pink 1. *n.* best, height, peak, summit 2. *adj.* flesh, flushed, reddish, rose, roseate, rosy, salmon

pinnacle acme, apex, crest, crown, height, meridian, peak, summit, top, vertex, zenith

pinpoint define, distinguish, identify, locate, spot

pioneer *n.* 1. colonist, explorer, settler 2. developer, founder, innovator, leader, trailblazer ~*v.* 3. create, develop, discover, establish, initiate, instigate, institute, invent, launch, originate, prepare, start

pious 1. dedicated, devoted, devout, godly, holy, religious, reverent, saintly, spiritual 2. pietistic, religiose, sanctimonious, unctuous

pipe *n.* 1. conduit, duct, hose, line, main, passage, tube 2. briar, clay, meerschaum 3. fife, horn, tooter, whistle ~*v.* 4. cheep, peep, play, sing, sound, warble, whistle

pipe down hush, shush, silence

piquant biting, peppery, pungent, savoury, sharp, spicy, tart

pique 1. *n.* annoyance, displeasure, grudge, huff, irritation, offence, resentment, umbrage, vexation 2. *v.* affront, annoy, displease, incense, irk, mortify, nettle, offend, provoke, rile, sting, vex, wound

piracy freebooting, hijacking, plagiarism, rapine, stealing, theft

pirate *n.* 1. corsair, freebooter, marauder, raider, rover 2. infringer, plagiarist ~*v.* 3. borrow, copy, plagiarize, poach, reproduce, steal

pit abyss, cavity, chasm, coal mine, crater, dent, depression, dimple, gulf, hole, hollow, mine, pothole

pitch *v.* 1. cast, fling, hurl, launch, sling, throw, toss 2. erect, fix, locate, place, plant, put up, raise, settle, set up, station ~*n.* 3. angle, dip, gradient, incline, slope, tilt 4. degree, height, level, point, summit 5. harmonic, modulation, sound, timbre, tone 6. line, patter, sales talk 7. ground, sports field

pitch-black dark, ebony, inky, jet, jet-black, pitch-dark, raven, sable, unlit

piteous affecting, deplorable, distressing, grievous, lamentable, miserable, mournful, moving, plaintive, poignant, sad, sorrowful, woeful, wretched

pitfall catch, danger, difficulty, drawback, hazard, peril, snag, trap

pith 1. core, crux, essence, gist, heart, kernel, marrow, meat, nub, point, salient point 2. consequence, depth, force, import, importance, matter, moment, power, significance, strength, substance, value, weight

pitiful 1. distressing, grievous, lamentable, miserable, pathetic, sad, woeful, wretched 2. abject, base, beggarly, inadequate, low, mean, miserable, paltry, shabby, sorry, vile, worthless

pitiless brutal, callous, cruel, harsh, heartless, implacable, inhuman, merciless, relentless, ruthless, unmerciful

pittance allowance, drop, mite, modicum, ration, slave wages, trifle

pity 1. *n.* charity, compassion, condolence, fellow feeling, forbearance, kindness, mercy, sympathy, tenderness, understanding 2. *v.* commiserate with, feel for, grieve for, weep for

pivot *n.* 1. axis, spindle, swivel 2. centre, heart, hinge, hub, kingpin ~*v.* 3. revolve, rotate, spin, swivel, turn, twirl 4. depend, hang, hinge, rely, turn

placard advertisement, bill, poster, sticker

placate appease, calm, conciliate, humour, mollify, pacify, satisfy, soothe

place *n.* 1. area, location, locus, point, position, site, situation, spot, station, venue, whereabouts 2. city, district, hamlet, locale, locality, neighbourhood, quarter, region, town, vicinity, village 3. grade, position, rank, station, status 4. appointment, billet (*Inf.*), employment, job, position, post 5. accommodation, room, space, stead 6. affair, charge, concern, duty, function, prerogative, responsibility, right, role 7. **take place** befall, betide, go on, happen, occur, transpire (*Inf.*) ~*v.* 8. deposit, dispose, establish, fix, install, lay, locate, plant, position, put, rest, set, settle, situate, stand, station, stick 9. arrange, class, classify, grade, group, order, rank, sort 10. allocate, appoint, assign, charge, entrust, give

placid calm, collected, composed, cool, even, gentle, mild, peaceful, quiet, serene, still, tranquil

plague *n.* 1. disease, epidemic, infection, pestilence 2. *Fig.* bane, blight, calamity, cancer, curse, evil, scourge, torment, trial 3. *Inf.* bother, irritant, nuisance, pest, problem, vexation ~*v.* 4. afflict, annoy, badger, bedevil, bother, disturb, fret, harass, harry, haunt, molest, pain, persecute, pester, tease, torment, torture, trouble, vex

plain *adj.* 1. apparent, clear, comprehensible, distinct, evident, legible, lucid, manifest, obvious, patent, transparent, unmistakable, visible 2. artless, blunt, candid, direct, downright, forthright, frank, guileless, honest, ingenuous, open, outspoken, sincere **3.** common, commonplace, everyday, frugal, homely, lowly, modest, ordinary, simple, workaday **4.** austere, bare, basic, discreet, modest, muted, pure, restrained, severe, simple, stark, unembellished, unornamented, unvarnished **5.** ill-favoured, ordinary, ugly, unattractive, unprepossessing **6.** even, flat, level, plane, smooth ~*n.* **7.** flatland, grassland, lowland, plateau, prairie, tableland

plain-spoken blunt, candid, direct, explicit, forthright, frank, open, outright, outspoken

plaintive disconsolate, doleful, grief-stricken, grievous, melancholy, mournful, pathetic, piteous, pitiful, rueful, sad, sorrowful, wistful, woeful

plan *n.* **1.** design, device, idea, method, plot, procedure, programme, project, proposal, proposition, scenario, scheme, strategy, suggestion, system **2.** blueprint, chart, delineation, diagram, drawing, layout, map, representation, scale drawing, sketch ~*v.* **3.** arrange, concoct, contrive, design, devise, draft, invent, organize, outline, plot, prepare, represent, scheme, think out **4.** aim, contemplate, envisage, foresee, intend, mean, propose, purpose

plane *n.* **1.** flat surface, level surface **2.** condition, degree, footing, level, position, stratum ~*adj.* **3.** even, flat, flush, horizontal, level, regular, smooth, uniform

plant *n.* **1.** bush, flower, herb, shrub, vegetable, weed **2.** factory, foundry, mill, shop, works, yard **3.** equipment, gear, machinery ~*v.* **4.** scatter, seed, set out, sow, transplant

plaster *n.* **1.** mortar, stucco **2.** bandage, dressing ~*v.* **3.** bedaub, besmear, coat, cover, daub, overlay, smear, spread

plastic *adj.* **1.** docile, malleable, manageable, pliable, receptive, responsive, tractable **2.** ductile, fictile, flexible, mouldable, pliable, pliant, soft, supple

plate 1. dish, platter **2.** course, dish, helping, portion, serving **3.** layer, panel, sheet, slab

plateau highland, table, upland

platform dais, podium, rostrum, stage, stand

platitude bromide, cliché, commonplace, stereotype, truism

plausible believable, credible, glib, possible, probable, reasonable, smooth, specious, tenable

play *v.* **1.** caper, frisk, frolic, gambol, revel, romp, sport, trifle **2.** challenge, compete, participate, rival, take on, take part, vie with **3.** act, execute, impersonate, perform, personate, portray, represent **4. play by ear** ad lib, improvise, rise to the occasion, take it as it comes **5. play for time** delay, filibuster, stall, temporize ~*n.* **6.** comedy, drama, dramatic piece, entertainment, farce, masque, performance, piece, radio play, show, tragedy **7.** diversion, entertainment, frolic, fun, gambol, game, recreation, romp, sport **8.** foolery, fun, humour, jest, sport, teasing

playboy philanderer, rake, roué, socialite, womanizer

player 1. competitor, contestant, team member **2.** actor, actress, entertainer, performer **3.** artist, musician, performer, virtuoso

playful cheerful, frolicsome, gay, impish, lively, merry, mischievous, puckish, rollicking, spirited, sprightly, vivacious

playmate companion, comrade, friend

plaything amusement, game, pastime, toy, trifle, trinket

play up emphasize, highlight, stress, underline

plea appeal, entreaty, overture, petition, prayer, request, suit, supplication

plead 1. ask, beg, beseech, crave, entreat, implore, petition, request, solicit **2.** adduce, allege, argue, assert, maintain

pleasant 1. agreeable, amusing, delectable, delightful, enjoyable, fine, gratifying, lovely, nice, refreshing, satisfying, welcome **2.** affable, agreeable, amiable, charming, cheerful, congenial, engaging, friendly, likable, nice

pleasantry badinage, banter, jest, joke, quip, sally, witticism

please amuse, charm, cheer, content, delight, gladden, gratify, humour, indulge, rejoice, satisfy, suit, tickle, tickle pink

pleased contented, delighted, euphoric, glad, gratified, happy, satisfied, thrilled

pleasing agreeable, amiable, amusing, attractive, charming, delightful, enjoyable, entertaining, gratifying, polite, satisfying

pleasure bliss, comfort, contentment, delight, ease, enjoyment, gladness, happiness, joy, recreation, satisfaction, solace

plebeian *adj.* base, coarse, common, ignoble, low, mean, proletarian, unrefined, vulgar, working-class

pledge *n.* **1.** covenant, oath, promise, undertaking, vow, warrant, word **2.** bail, bond, collateral, deposit, earnest, gage, guarantee, pawn, security, surety **3.** health, toast ~*v.* **4.** contract, engage, promise, swear, undertake, vouch, vow

plentiful abundant, ample, bountiful, complete, copious, generous, infinite, lavish, liberal, profuse

plenty 1. enough, fund, mass, mine, mountain(s), plethora, quantity, store, sufficiency **2.** abundance, affluence, copiousness, fertility, luxury, opulence, profusion, prosperity, wealth

plethora excess, glut, profusion, superabundance, surfeit, surplus

pliable 1. ductile, flexible, limber, lithe, plastic, pliant, supple **2.** adaptable, compliant, docile, pliant, receptive, responsive, susceptible, tractable, yielding

plight *n.* case, condition, difficulty, dilemma, extremity, predicament, situation, state, straits, trouble

plod clump, drag, lumber, slog, tramp, tread, trudge

plot[1] *n.* **1.** conspiracy, intrigue, plan, scheme, stratagem **2.** action, narrative, outline, scenario, story, subject, theme, thread ~*v.* **3.** collude, conspire, contrive, hatch, intrigue, manoeuvre, plan, scheme **4.** chart, draft, draw, locate, map, mark, outline **5.** concoct, contrive, design, devise, frame, hatch, lay, project

plot[2] *n.* area, ground, lot, patch

plough *v.* cultivate, dig, furrow, ridge, till, turn over

pluck[1] *n.* boldness, bravery, courage, grit, heart, mettle, nerve, resolution, spirit

pluck[2] *v.* **1.** catch, clutch, snatch, tug, tweak, yank **2.** finger, pick

plucky bold, brave, daring, game, gritty, valiant

plug *n.* **1.** bung, cork, spigot, stopper **2.** mention, publicity, puff, push ~*v.* **3.** block, bung, choke, close, cork, cover, fill, pack, seal, stop, stopper, stopple, stop up, stuff **4.** mention, promote, publicize, puff, push

plum *Fig.* **1.** *n.* bonus, cream, find, pick, prize **2.** *adj.* best, choice

plumb *n.* **1.** lead, weight ~*adv.* **2.** perpendicularly, vertically **3.** bang, exactly, precisely, slap ~*v.* **4.** delve, explore, fathom, gauge, measure, probe, search, sound

plump burly, buxom, chubby, full, obese, podgy, portly, rotund, round, stout, tubby

plunder 1. *v.* despoil, loot, pillage, raid, ransack, ravage, rifle, rob, sack, spoil, steal, strip **2.** *n.* booty, loot, pillage, prize, spoils

plunge 1. *v.* cast, descend, dip, dive, douse, drop, fall, immerse, jump, pitch, sink, submerge, swoop, throw, tumble **2.** *n.* descent, dive, drop, fall, jump, swoop

plus 1. *prep.* added to, and, with **2.** *adj.* added, additional, extra, positive

ply carry on, exercise, follow, practise, pursue, work at

poach infringe, intrude, plunder, rob, trespass

pocket 1. *n.* bag, hollow, pouch, receptacle, sack **2.** *adj.* abridged, compact, concise, little, portable, small

podium dais, platform, rostrum, stage

poem lyric, ode, rhyme, song, sonnet, verse

poet bard, lyricist, versifier

poetic elegiac, lyrical, metrical

poetry rhyme, rhyming, verse

poignancy 1. emotion, feeling, pathos, sadness, sentiment, tenderness **2.** bitterness, intensity, keenness, piquancy, pungency, sharpness

poignant 1. agonizing, bitter, distressing, intense, moving, painful, sad, touching, upsetting **2.** acute, biting, caustic, keen, piercing, pointed, sarcastic, severe

point *n.* **1.** dot, mark, period, stop **2.** location, place, position, site, spot, stage, station **3.** apex, end, nib, prong, spike, spur, summit, tip, top **4.** bill, cape, headland, promontory **5.** condition, degree, extent, position, stage **6.** instant, juncture, moment, time **7.** aim, design, end, goal, intent, intention, motive, object, purpose, reason, use **8.** burden, core, drift, essence, gist, heart, import, matter, question, subject, text, theme **9.** aspect, attribute, characteristic, peculiarity **10.** score, unit **11. beside the point** immaterial, incidental, irrelevant, unimportant **12. to the point** applicable, apt, brief, fitting, germane, pertinent, pointed, relevant, terse ~*v.* **13.** bespeak, denote, designate, direct, indicate, show

point-blank 1. *adj.* abrupt, blunt, direct, explicit, express, plain **2.** *adv.* bluntly, brusquely, frankly, openly, plainly, straight

pointer 1. guide, hand, needle **2.** advice, caution, hint, tip, warning

pointless aimless, futile, inane, senseless, silly, stupid, useless, vague, vain, worthless

point out identify, indicate, mention, remind, reveal, show, specify

poise 1. *n.* aplomb, calmness, composure, dignity, elegance, grace, presence, serenity **2.** *v.* balance, float, hang, hold, hover, position, support, suspend

poised 1. calm, collected, composed, dignified, graceful, self-confident, serene, urbane **2.** prepared, ready, waiting

poison *n.* **1.** bane, toxin, venom **2.** bane, blight, contamination, corruption, malignancy, miasma, virus ~*v.* **3.** contaminate, envenom, infect, kill, murder, pollute

poisonous 1. deadly, fatal, lethal, mortal, virulent **2.** baleful, corruptive, evil, malicious, pernicious

poke *v.* **1.** butt, dig, elbow, hit, jab, nudge, prod, punch, push, shove, stab, stick, thrust **2. poke fun at** chaff, jeer, make a mock of, make fun of, mock, rib (*Inf.*), ridicule, send up (*Brit. inf.*) ~*n.* **3.** butt, dig, hit, jab, nudge, prod, punch, thrust

pole bar, mast, post, rod, shaft, spar, staff, standard, stick

police 1. *n.* constabulary **2.** *v.* control, guard, patrol, protect, regulate, watch

policeman bobby, constable

policy action, approach, code, course, custom, plan, practice, programme, rule, scheme, theory

polish *v.* **1.** brighten, buff, burnish, clean, rub, shine, smooth, wax **2.** enhance, refine ~*n.* **3.** brightness, finish, glaze, gloss, lustre, sheen **4.** varnish, wax **5.** elegance, finesse, grace, refinement

polished 1. bright, gleaming, glossy, shining, slippery, smooth **2.** *Fig.* accomplished, civilized, cultivated, polite, refined, urbane, well-bred **3.** adept, expert, fine, masterly, skilful

polite affable, civil, courteous, gracious, mannerly, obliging, respectful, well-mannered

politic 1. artful, astute, canny, crafty, cunning, intriguing, scheming, shrewd, sly, subtle, unscrupulous **2.** discreet, expedient, judicious, prudent, sensible, wise

politician legislator, statesman

politics civics, government, statesmanship

poll *n.* 1. figures, vote, voting 2. ballot, canvass, census, count, sampling, survey

pollute 1. befoul, contaminate, dirty, foul, infect, mar, poison, soil, spoil, stain, taint 2. besmirch, corrupt, debase, defile, desecrate, profane, sully

pomp 1. ceremony, flourish, grandeur, pageantry, splendour, state 2. display, ostentation, show

pompous 1. arrogant, grandiose, imperious, ostentatious, portentous, pretentious, showy 2. boastful, bombastic, inflated, turgid

ponder brood, cogitate, consider, deliberate, meditate, muse, reflect, ruminate, study, think, weigh

pool[1] 1. lake, mere, pond, splash, tarn 2. swimming bath

pool[2] *n.* 1. combine, consortium, group, syndicate, team, trust 2. bank, funds, jackpot, kitty, pot, stakes ~*v.* 3. combine, league, merge, share

poor 1. destitute, impoverished, indigent, needy, penniless, penurious 2. deficient, inadequate, incomplete, insufficient, meagre, miserable, niggardly, pitiable, reduced, scanty, slight, sparse 3. faulty, feeble, inferior, low-grade, mediocre, shabby, shoddy, sorry, valueless, weak, worthless 4. bad, bare, barren, depleted, exhausted, fruitless, infertile, sterile, unfruitful, unproductive 5. hapless, luckless, miserable, pathetic, pitiable, unfortunate, unlucky, wretched 6. humble, insignificant, lowly, mean, modest, paltry, plain, trivial

poorly badly, crudely, inadequately, incompetently, insufficiently, meanly, unsatisfactorily

pop *v.* 1. bang, burst, crack, explode, go off, report, snap 2. insert, push, put, shove, slip, stick, thrust, tuck ~*n.* 3. bang, burst, crack, explosion, noise, report

populace crowd, masses, mob, multitude, people, rabble, throng

popular 1. accepted, approved, famous, fashionable, favourite, in, in demand, in favour, liked 2. common, conventional, current, general, prevailing, public, standard, stock, universal

popularity acceptance, acclaim, approval, celebrity, esteem, fame, favour, recognition, regard, renown, repute, vogue

popularly commonly, customarily, generally, ordinarily, regularly, usually, widely

populate colonize, occupy, settle

population community, inhabitants, natives, people, residents, society

pore *v.* brood, dwell on, examine, peruse, ponder, read, study

port anchorage, harbour, haven

portable compact, convenient, handy, light, manageable, movable

portend augur, betoken, bode, foreshadow, foretell, herald, indicate, omen, predict, presage, promise, threaten

portent augury, harbinger, omen, presage, presentiment, prognostication, sign, threat, warning

porter[1] bearer, carrier

porter[2] caretaker, doorman, gatekeeper

portion 1. bit, fragment, morsel, part, piece, scrap, section, segment 2. allocation, allotment, lot, measure, parcel, quantity, quota, ration, share 3. helping, piece 4. fate, fortune, lot, luck

portrait image, likeness, painting, photograph, picture

portray 1. depict, draw, figure, illustrate, paint, picture, render, represent, sketch 2. describe

pose *v.* 1. arrange, model, position, sit 2. *Often with* **as** feign, impersonate, sham 3. affect, posture 4. advance, put, set, state, submit ~*n.* 5. attitude, bearing, position, posture, stance 6. act, air, façade, front, posturing, pretence, role

poser enigma, problem, puzzle, question, riddle

position *n.* 1. area, bearings, location, place, point, post, reference, site, situation, spot, station 2. arrangement, attitude, pose, posture, stance 3. angle, attitude, belief, opinion, outlook, slant, stance, standpoint, view 4. circumstances, condition, pass, plight, situation, state 5. caste, class, importance, place, prestige, rank, reputation, standing, station, stature, status 6. capacity, duty, function, job, occupation, office, place, post, role, situation ~*v.* 7. arrange, array, dispose, fix, locate, place, put, set, settle, stand

positive 1. absolute, actual, affirmative, categorical, certain, clear-cut, decisive, definite, direct, explicit, express, firm, real 2. assured, certain, confident, convinced, sure 3. assertive, cocksure, decided, emphatic, firm, forceful, resolute 4. beneficial, constructive, efficacious, forward-looking, helpful, practical, productive, progressive, useful 5. complete, consummate, perfect, rank

positively absolutely, certainly, definitely, emphatically, firmly, surely

possess 1. enjoy, have, hold, own 2. acquire, control, dominate, hold, occupy, seize

possessed bewitched, crazed, cursed, demented, obsessed

possession 1. control, custody, hold, occupation, ownership, title 2. *Plural* assets, belongings, chattels, estate, property

possibility 1. likelihood, potentiality, workableness 2. chance, hazard, hope, liability, odds, prospect, risk

possible 1. conceivable, credible, hypothetical, imaginable, likely, potential 2. feasible, viable, workable 3. hopeful, likely, potential, probable, promising

possibly perhaps

post[1] 1. *n.* column, newel, pale, picket, pillar, pole, shaft, stake, stock, support, upright 2. *v.* advertise, affix, announce, display, proclaim, promulgate, publicize, publish

post[2] 1. *n.* appointment, employment, job, office, place, position, situation 2. *v.* assign, establish, locate, place, put, situate, station

post[3] 1. *n.* collection, delivery, mail 2. *v.* dispatch, mail, send, transmit

poster advertisement, bill, notice, placard, sticker

posterity 1. children, descendants, family, heirs, issue, offspring 2. future

postpone adjourn, defer, delay, shelve, suspend, table

postscript addition, afterthought, supplement

postulate advance, assume, predicate, propose, suppose

posture 1. *n.* attitude, bearing, carriage, disposition, set, stance 2. *v.* affect

potent forceful, mighty, powerful, strong, vigorous

potential 1. *adj.* dormant, future, hidden, inherent, latent, likely, possible, promising 2. *n.* ability, aptitude, capacity, power, the makings, wherewithal

potter dabble, fritter, tinker

pouch bag, pocket, purse, sack

pounce 1. *v.* ambush, attack, drop, jump, snatch, spring, strike, swoop 2. *n.* assault, attack, bound, jump, leap, spring, swoop

pound 1. batter, beat, strike, thrash, thump 2. bruise, crush, powder, pulverize

pour 1. decant, spill, splash 2. course, emit, flow, gush, run, rush, spout, stream 3. teem

pout lower, mope, sulk

poverty 1. beggary, distress, hardship, insolvency, necessity, need, penury, privation, want 2. dearth, deficiency, lack, paucity, scarcity, shortage 3. bareness, deficiency, infertility, sterility, unfruitfulness

powder *n.* 1. dust, pounce, talc ~*v.* 2. crush, granulate, grind, pestle, pound, pulverize 3. cover, dredge, dust, scatter, sprinkle, strew

power 1. ability, capacity, competence, faculty, potential 2. brawn, energy, force, intensity, might, muscle, strength, vigour, weight 3. authority, command, control, dominance, dominion, influence, mastery, rule, sovereignty, sway 4. authorization, licence, prerogative, privilege, right, warrant

powerful 1. energetic, mighty, potent, robust, stalwart, strapping, strong, sturdy, vigorous 2. authoritative, commanding, dominant, influential, prevailing, supreme 3. cogent, compelling, convincing, effective, forceful, impressive, persuasive, telling, weighty

powerless 1. disabled, feeble, frail, helpless, impotent, incapable, infirm, paralysed, prostrate, weak 2. dependent, ineffective, subject, tied, unarmed, vulnerable

practicability feasibility, possibility, use

practicable attainable, doable, feasible, possible, workable

practical 1. applied, empirical, factual, pragmatic, realistic, utilitarian 2. businesslike, down-to-earth, hard-headed, mundane 3. proficient, qualified, seasoned, skilled, trained, veteran

practically 1. almost, basically, essentially, fundamentally, nearly, virtually, well-nigh 2. clearly, matter-of-factly, rationally, realistically, sensibly

practice 1. custom, habit, method, routine, rule, system, usage, way, wont 2. drill, exercise, rehearsal, repetition, study, training, work-out 3. business, career, profession, vocation, work

practise 1. drill, exercise, polish, prepare, rehearse, repeat, study, train 2. apply, do, follow, observe, perform 3. carry on, engage in, ply, pursue, undertake

pragmatic efficient, practical, realistic, sensible, utilitarian

praise *n.* 1. acclaim, accolade, applause, approval, commendation, compliment, congratulation, eulogy, kudos, panegyric, plaudit, tribute 2. devotion, glory, homage, thanks, worship ~*v.* 3. acclaim, admire, applaud, approve, cheer, congratulate, eulogize, extol, honour, laud 4. bless, exalt, glorify, worship

pray ask, beg, beseech, crave, entreat, implore, importune, invoke, petition, plead, request, sue, supplicate, urge

prayer 1. devotion, litany, orison, supplication 2. appeal, entreaty, petition, plea, request, suit

preach 1. address, evangelize, exhort, orate 2. admonish, advocate, exhort, harangue, lecture, moralize, sermonize, urge

preacher evangelist, minister, missionary, parson

preamble foreword, introduction, preface, prelude

precarious dangerous, doubtful, hazardous, insecure, perilous, risky, tricky, uncertain, unsafe, unsure

precaution 1. insurance, protection, provision, safeguard 2. care, caution, forethought, providence, prudence, wariness

precede antedate, head, herald, introduce, lead, preface, usher

precedent *n.* authority, criterion, example, instance, model, pattern, standard

precept 1. canon, command, decree, direction, instruction, law, mandate, order, principle, rule, statute 2. guideline, maxim, motto, principle, rule, saying

precinct 1. confine, enclosure, limit 2. area, district, quarter, section

precious 1. beloved, cherished, darling, dear, favourite, idolized, loved, prized, treasured, valued 2. costly, dear, exquisite, fine, priceless, prized, rare, valuable

precipice bluff, brink, cliff, crag, height

precipitate *v.* 1. advance, dispatch, expedite, further, hasten, hurry, press, quicken ~*adj.* 2. breakneck, headlong, plunging, rapid, rushing, swift, violent 3. abrupt, brief, quick, sudden, unexpected

precise accurate, clear-cut, correct, definite, exact, express, fixed, literal, particular, specific, strict

precisely accurately, correctly, exactly, just so, strictly
precision accuracy, care, exactitude, nicety, particularity, rigour
preclude check, debar, exclude, inhibit, obviate, prevent, prohibit, restrain, stop
precocious advanced, ahead, bright, developed, forward, quick, smart
precursor forerunner, herald, messenger, usher, vanguard
predatory hunting, rapacious
predecessor antecedent, forerunner
predetermined agreed, fixed, prearranged
predicament corner, dilemma, emergency, mess, pinch, quandary, situation
predict augur, divine, forecast, foretell, portend, prophesy
predictable certain, expected, foreseeable, reliable
prediction augury, forecast, prophecy
predisposed amenable, inclined, ready, willing
predominant chief, leading, main, prevailing, principal, ruling, superior, supreme
pre-eminence distinction, prestige, renown, superiority, transcendence
pre-eminent chief, distinguished, excellent, matchless, peerless, renowned, superior, supreme, transcendent, unrivalled, unsurpassed
preface **1.** *n.* foreword, introduction, preamble, preliminary, prelude, prologue **2.** *v.* begin, introduce, launch, open, precede, prefix
prefer choose, desire, elect, fancy, favour, pick, select, wish
preferable best, better, choice, chosen, worthier
preferably rather, sooner
preference **1.** choice, desire, favourite, option, partiality, pick, selection **2.** advantage, favouritism, precedence, priority
preferment advancement, dignity, elevation, promotion, rise
prejudge presume, presuppose
prejudice *n.* **1.** bias, partiality, prejudgment **2.** chauvinism, intolerance, racism, sexism, unfairness **3.** detriment, harm, hurt, impairment, loss, mischief ~*v.* **4.** bias, colour, distort, influence, poison, prepossess, slant, sway, warp **5.** damage, harm, hinder, hurt, impair, injure, mar, spoil, undermine
prejudicial damaging, harmful, hurtful, inimical, injurious
preliminary **1.** *adj.* first, initial, introductory, opening, pilot, preparatory, prior, qualifying, test, trial **2.** *n.* beginning, groundwork, initiation, introduction, opening, preamble, preface, prelims, prelude, start
prelude beginning, introduction, overture, preamble, preface, prologue, start
premature **1.** early, immature, incomplete, raw, unripe, unseasonable, untimely **2.** *Fig.* hasty, ill-considered, impulsive
premeditated calculated, considered, deliberate, intentional, planned
premier *n.* **1.** chancellor, prime minister ~*adj.* **2.** arch, chief, first, foremost, head, highest, leading, main, primary, prime, principal, top **3.** earliest, first, initial, original
premiere debut, opening
premise, premiss argument, assertion, ground, hypothesis, postulate
premises building, place, property, site
premium **1.** bonus, boon, bounty, fee, perquisite, prize, recompense, reward **2.** appreciation, regard, stock, store, value
premonition feeling, foreboding, hunch, idea, intuition, omen, portent, presentiment, sign, suspicion
preoccupation absorption, daydreaming, musing, oblivion, reverie
preoccupied absorbed, distrait, engrossed, heedless, immersed, intent, oblivious, rapt, unaware
preparation **1.** groundwork, preparing **2.** anticipation, foresight, precaution, provision, readiness, safeguard **3.** compound, concoction, medicine, mixture **4.** homework, study
preparatory introductory, opening, preliminary
prepare **1.** adapt, adjust, arrange, coach, dispose, form, groom, plan, practise, prime, train, warm up **2.** brace, fortify, gird, ready, steel, strengthen **3.** assemble, concoct, construct, contrive, fashion, make, produce
prepared **1.** ready, set **2.** able, disposed, inclined, minded, willing
preposterous absurd, bizarre, crazy, excessive, extreme, foolish, impossible, insane, monstrous, outrageous, ridiculous, senseless, shocking, unthinkable
prerequisite **1.** *adj.* essential, indispensable, mandatory, necessary, required, vital **2.** *n.* condition, necessity, qualification, requirement
prerogative authority, choice, claim, due, liberty, privilege, right
prescribe appoint, assign, decree, define, dictate, direct, lay down, ordain, require, rule, set, specify, stipulate
prescription drug, medicine, mixture, remedy
presence **1.** company, existence, occupancy, residence **2.** closeness, nearness, propinquity, proximity, vicinity **3.** air, appearance, aspect, aura, bearing, demeanour, ease, personality, poise, self-assurance
present[1] *adj.* **1.** existing, immediate, instant **2.** accounted for, available, here, nearby, ready, there ~*n.* **3.** today **4. at present** now, nowadays **5. for the present** provisionally, temporarily
present[2] *v.* **1.** introduce **2.** demonstrate, display, exhibit, give, mount, put on, show, stage **3.** advance, declare, expound, extend, offer, pose, proffer, relate, state, submit, suggest, tender ~*n.* **4.** boon, bounty, donation, favour, gift, grant, gratuity, largess, offering
presentation **1.** award, bestowal, conferral, donation, investiture, offering **2.** arrangement, delivery, staging, submission **3.** display, exhibition, performance, production, show
presently by and by, shortly, soon
preservation protection, safekeeping, safety, salvation, security, storage, support
preserve **1.** *v.* care for, defend, guard, keep, protect, safeguard, save, secure, shelter **2.** *n.* area, domain, field, realm, sphere
preside administer, chair, conduct, control, direct, govern, head, lead, manage, run
press *v.* **1.** condense, crush, jam, mash, push, reduce, squeeze, stuff **2.** finish, flatten, iron, mangle, smooth **3.** clasp, crush, enfold, hug, squeeze **4.** compel, constrain, demand, enforce, enjoin, force **5.** beg, entreat, exhort, implore, importune, petition, plead, sue, urge **6.** cluster, crowd, flock, gather, hasten, herd, hurry, mill, push, rush, seethe, surge, swarm, throng ~*n.* **7. the press** journalism, newspapers, the papers
pressure **1.** crushing, force, squeezing, weight **2.** compulsion, constraint, force, influence, power, sway
prestige authority, credit, distinction, esteem, fame, honour, importance, influence, renown, reputation, status
presume believe, conjecture, infer, suppose, surmise, think
presumption audacity, boldness, effrontery, insolence, temerity
presuppose accept, assume, consider, imply, postulate, presume
pretence **1.** acting, charade, deceit, deception, falsehood, feigning, invention, sham, simulation, trickery **2.** affectation, artifice, display, façade, show, veneer
pretend **1.** affect, allege, assume, fake, falsify, feign, impersonate, profess, sham, simulate **2.** act, imagine, play, suppose
pretender aspirant, claimant, claimer
pretension **1.** aspiration, assumption, claim, demand, pretence, profession **2.** affectation, airs, conceit, hypocrisy, show, snobbery, vanity
pretentious affected, conceited, exaggerated, extravagant, grandiose, high-flown, hollow, inflated, mannered, ostentatious, showy, snobbish
pretext cloak, cover, device, excuse, guise, mask, ploy, pretence, ruse, semblance, show, veil
pretty **1.** *adj.* attractive, beautiful, charming, cute, fair, good-looking, graceful, lovely **2.** *adv.* moderately, quite, rather, reasonably, somewhat
prevail **1.** overcome, overrule, succeed, triumph, win **2.** abound, obtain, predominate **3.** *Often with* **on** *or* **upon** convince, dispose, incline, influence, persuade, prompt, sway, talk into, win over
prevailing common, current, customary, fashionable, general, ordinary, popular, prevalent, set, usual, widespread
prevaricate cavil, deceive, dodge, equivocate, evade, hedge, lie, palter, quibble, shift, shuffle
prevent avert, avoid, balk, bar, block, check, forestall, frustrate, hamper, hinder, impede, inhibit, obstruct, obviate, preclude, restrain, stop, thwart
prevention **1.** avoidance, deterrence, elimination, precaution, safeguard, thwarting **2.** bar, check, deterrence, hindrance, impediment, interruption, obstacle, obstruction, stoppage
preventive, preventative **1.** *adj.* hampering, hindering, impeding, obstructive **2.** *n.* block, hindrance, impediment, obstacle, obstruction
previous earlier, former, past, preceding, prior
previously before, earlier, formerly, once, then
prey **1.** game, kill, quarry **2.** dupe, target, victim
price *n.* **1.** amount, assessment, bill, charge, cost, estimate, expense, fee, figure, outlay, payment, rate, valuation, worth **2.** consequences, cost, penalty, sacrifice, toll ~*v.* **3.** assess, cost, estimate, evaluate, rate, value
priceless cherished, costly, dear, expensive, precious, rare, rich, treasured
prick *v.* **1.** bore, jab, lance, pierce, pink, punch, stab **2.** bite, itch, prickle, smart, sting, tingle ~*n.* **3.** cut, gash, hole, pinhole, puncture, wound
prickly **1.** barbed, bristly, spiny, thorny **2.** scratchy, sharp, smarting, stinging, tingling **3.** bad-tempered, edgy, fractious, grumpy, irritable, peevish, pettish, petulant, snappish, tetchy, touchy, waspish **4.** complicated, difficult, thorny, ticklish, tricky
pride *n.* **1.** dignity, honour **2.** arrogance, conceit, egotism, hauteur, loftiness, pretension, self-importance, snobbery, vanity **3.** boast, gem, jewel, prize, treasure **4.** choice, cream, elite, glory ~*v.* **5.** boast, brag, crow, exult, plume, preen
priest clergyman, cleric, curate, divine, father, minister, vicar
prig pedant, prude, puritan
prim demure, fastidious, formal, fussy, particular, precise, proper, strait-laced
primarily basically, chiefly, essentially, fundamentally, generally, mainly, mostly
primary **1.** best, capital, cardinal, chief, first, greatest, highest, leading, main, prime, principal, top **2.** basic, essential, fundamental, radical
prime *adj.* **1.** best, choice, first-class, first-rate, highest, quality, select, selected, superior, top **2.** basic, earliest, underlying **3.** chief, leading, main, pre-eminent, principal, ruling, senior ~*n.* **4.** bloom, flower, height, peak, zenith ~*v.* **5.** coach, fit, groom, prepare, train **6.** brief, inform, notify, tell
primitive **1.** earliest, original, primary, primeval, primordial, pristine **2.** barbarian, crude, rough, rude, simple, uncivilized, unrefined
prince lord, monarch, ruler, sovereign
princely bounteous, generous, gracious, lavish, liberal, rich
principal *adj.* **1.** cardinal, chief, dominant, first, foremost, highest, key, leading, main, para-

mount, pre-eminent, prime, strongest ~*n.* **2.** chief, director, head, leader, master, ruler **3.** dean, director, headmaster, headmistress, master, rector **4.** assets, capital, money

principally chiefly, especially, mainly, mostly, predominantly, primarily

principle **1.** axiom, canon, criterion, doctrine, dogma, ethic, formula, law, maxim, precept, proposition, rule, standard, truth **2.** belief, code, ethic, morality, opinion **3.** integrity, morals, probity, rectitude, scruples

print *v.* **1.** engrave, issue, mark, publish, stamp ~*n.* **2.** book, magazine, newspaper, periodical, publication, typescript **3.** copy, engraving, photograph, picture

priority precedence, preference, rank, seniority, superiority, supremacy

prison confinement, dungeon, gaol, jail

prisoner **1.** convict, jailbird **2.** captive, hostage, internee

privacy isolation, retirement, retreat, seclusion, solitude

private **1.** confidential, inside, secret, unofficial **2.** exclusive, intimate, own, personal, special **3.** concealed, isolated, retired, secluded, secret, separate, solitary, withdrawn

privilege birthright, claim, concession, due, entitlement, freedom, immunity, liberty, right

prize[1] *n.* **1.** award, honour, reward, trophy **2.** purse, stakes, winnings **3.** aim, ambition, conquest, desire, gain, goal, hope **4.** booty, capture, loot, pickings, pillage, plunder, trophy ~*adj.* **5.** best, champion, outstanding, top

prize[2] *v.* cherish, esteem, treasure, value

probability expectation, likelihood, odds, prospect

probable apparent, credible, feasible, likely, ostensible, plausible, presumable, reasonable

probably doubtless, likely, maybe, perhaps, possibly

probe *v.* **1.** examine, explore, go into, investigate, query, scrutinize, search, sift, sound, test, verify **2.** explore, feel around, poke, prod ~*n.* **3.** detection, examination, exploration, inquest, inquiry, investigation, study

problem *n.* **1.** difficulty, dispute, doubt, predicament, quandary, trouble **2.** conundrum, enigma, poser, puzzle, question, riddle ~*adj.* **3.** delinquent, difficult, intractable, unruly

procedure action, conduct, course, custom, form, method, performance, policy, practice, process, routine, scheme, step, strategy, system

proceed **1.** advance, continue, go on, press on, progress **2.** arise, come, derive, emanate, ensue, flow, follow, issue, result, spring, stem

proceeding **1.** act, action, deed, measure, move, step, undertaking, venture **2.** *Plural* account, affairs, annals, archives, dealings, doings, matters, minutes, records, report

proceeds earnings, gain, income, profit, receipts, returns, takings, yield

process *n.* **1.** action, course, manner, means, measure, method, mode, operation, performance, practice, system, transaction **2.** advance, course, development, evolution, formation, growth, movement, progress, stage, step ~*v.* **3.** fulfil, handle **4.** alter, convert, prepare, refine, transform, treat

procession column, cortege, file, march, parade, train

proclaim announce, circulate, declare, herald, indicate, profess, promulgate, publish

proclamation declaration, decree, edict, notice, pronouncement, publication

procrastinate adjourn, dally, defer, delay, postpone, prolong, protract, put off, retard, stall, temporize

procure acquire, buy, earn, effect, find, gain, get, obtain, pick up, purchase, secure, win

prod *v.* **1.** dig, drive, elbow, jab, nudge, poke, prick, push, shove **2.** goad, impel, move, prompt, rouse, spur, stimulate, urge ~*n.* **3.** boost, dig, elbow, jab, nudge, poke, push, shove **4.** goad, spur, stick **5.** boost, cue, prompt, reminder, signal, stimulus

prodigal **1.** *adj.* excessive, extravagant, improvident, profligate, reckless, spendthrift, wanton, wasteful **2.** *n.* profligate, spendthrift, wastrel

prodigious **1.** enormous, huge, immense, massive, stupendous, tremendous, vast **2.** abnormal, astounding, fabulous, impressive, marvellous, miraculous, remarkable, startling, striking, wonderful

prodigy **1.** genius, mastermind, talent **2.** marvel, miracle, phenomenon, wonder

produce *v.* **1.** compose, construct, create, develop, invent, make, originate, turn out **2.** bear, beget, breed, deliver, furnish, give, render, supply, yield **3.** cause, effect, generate, provoke, set off **4.** advance, demonstrate, exhibit, offer, present, show **5.** direct, do, exhibit, mount, present, show, stage **6.** *Geometry* extend, lengthen, protract ~*n.* **7.** crop, greengrocery, harvest, product, yield

producer **1.** director, impresario **2.** farmer, grower, maker

product **1.** artefact, creation, goods, invention, merchandise, work **2.** consequence, effect, fruit, issue, legacy, offshoot, outcome, result, returns, spin-off, upshot, yield

production **1.** construction, creation, fabrication, manufacture, origination, preparation, producing **2.** direction, management, presentation, staging

productive creative, dynamic, fecund, fertile, fruitful, generative, inventive, plentiful, prolific, rich, teeming, vigorous

productivity output, production, work rate, yield

profane *adj.* **1.** godless, heathen, impious, irreverent, pagan, sinful, ungodly, wicked **2.** lay, secular, temporal, unholy, worldly **3.** abusive, coarse, crude, filthy, foul, obscene, vulgar ~*v.* **4.** abuse, contaminate, debase, defile, desecrate, misuse, pervert, pollute, vitiate

profanity blasphemy, curse, execration, impiety, malediction, obscenity, sacrilege, swearword

profess admit, affirm, announce, assert, aver, avow, certify, confess, confirm, declare, maintain, own, proclaim, state, vouch

professed **1.** avowed, confirmed, declared **2.** alleged, apparent

profession **1.** business, calling, career, employment, line, occupation, office, position, sphere **2.** assertion, avowal, claim, declaration, statement, testimony, vow

professional **1.** *adj.* adept, competent, efficient, expert, masterly, polished, practised, proficient, qualified, skilled, trained **2.** *n.* adept, expert, master, virtuoso

professor don, fellow

proficiency ability, aptitude, competence, expertise, facility, knack, skill, talent

proficient able, adept, apt, capable, clever, competent, expert, gifted, masterly, qualified, skilful, talented, trained

profile *n.* **1.** drawing, figure, form, outline, portrait, shape, silhouette, sketch **2.** biography, sketch **3.** analysis, chart, diagram, examination, graph, review, study, survey, table

profit *n.* **1.** *Often plural* earnings, emoluments, gain, proceeds, receipts, return, revenue, surplus, takings, winnings, yield **2.** advantage, avail, benefit, gain, good, interest, use, value ~*v.* **3.** aid, avail, benefit, better, contribute, gain, help, improve, promote, serve **4.** exploit, use **5.** clear, earn, gain, make money

profitable **1.** commercial, cost-effective, fruitful, paying, rewarding, worthwhile **2.** beneficial, fruitful, productive, rewarding, serviceable, useful, valuable, worthwhile

profligate *adj.* **1.** debauched, degenerate, depraved, dissipated, dissolute, immoral, licentious, loose, shameless, vicious, wicked, wild **2.** extravagant, immoderate, reckless, spendthrift, wasteful ~*n.* **3.** degenerate, libertine, rake, reprobate, roué

profound **1.** abstruse, deep, discerning, erudite, learned, serious, skilled, subtle, thoughtful, weighty, wise **2.** abysmal, cavernous, deep, fathomless, yawning **3.** extreme, great, heartfelt, intense, keen, sincere

profuse **1.** ample, copious, overflowing, plentiful, prolific, teeming **2.** excessive, exuberant, generous, lavish, liberal, prodigal

profusion bounty, excess, extravagance, glut, multitude, plethora, quantity, riot, surplus, wealth

progeny children, descendants, family, issue, offspring, race, seed, stock, young

programme *n.* **1.** curriculum, line-up, list, listing, plan, schedule, syllabus **2.** broadcast, performance, production, show **3.** design, plan, procedure, project, scheme ~*v.* **4.** arrange, bill, book, design, engage, formulate, list, plan, schedule

progress *n.* **1.** advance, course, movement, passage, way **2.** advance, breakthrough, development, gain, growth, headway, improvement, increase ~*v.* **3.** advance, continue, move on, proceed, travel **4.** advance, blossom, develop, gain, grow, improve, increase

progressive **1.** advancing, continuing, growing, increasing, intensifying, ongoing **2.** avant-garde, dynamic, enlightened, liberal, modern, radical, reformist

prohibit **1.** ban, debar, forbid, outlaw, veto **2.** constrain, hamper, hinder, impede, obstruct, preclude, prevent, stop

prohibition **1.** constraint, exclusion, obstruction, prevention, restriction **2.** ban, bar, embargo, injunction, interdict, proscription, veto

prohibitive **1.** forbidding, repressive, restraining, restrictive, suppressive **2.** *Esp. of prices* excessive, exorbitant, extortionate

project *n.* **1.** activity, design, enterprise, job, plan, programme, proposal, scheme, task, venture, work ~*v.* **2.** contemplate, contrive, design, devise, draft, frame, outline, plan, propose, purpose, scheme **3.** cast, discharge, fling, hurl, launch, propel, shoot, throw, transmit **4.** extend, jut, overhang, protrude

projectile bullet, missile, rocket, shell

proletariat commoners, labouring classes, plebs, the common people, the masses, wage-earners, working class

prolific bountiful, copious, fertile, fruitful, luxuriant, productive, profuse, rank, rich, teeming

prologue foreword, introduction, preamble, preface, prelude

prolong continue, delay, extend, lengthen, perpetuate, protract, spin out, stretch

promenade *n.* **1.** esplanade, parade, walkway **2.** airing, saunter, stroll, turn, walk ~*v.* **3.** saunter, stroll, walk

prominence **1.** cliff, crag, crest, height, mound, pinnacle, rise, spur **2.** bulge, jutting, swelling **3.** conspicuousness, precedence, salience, weight **4.** celebrity, distinction, eminence, fame, greatness, importance, name, prestige, rank, reputation

prominent **1.** bulging, standing out **2.** conspicuous, eye-catching, noticeable, obtrusive, obvious, remarkable, striking **3.** celebrated, chief, distinguished, eminent, famous, foremost, important, leading, main, renowned, respected, top, well-known

promiscuous **1.** debauched, dissipated, dissolute, fast, immoral, lax, loose, wanton, wild **2.** careless, casual, heedless, irresponsible, random, uncritical, unselective

promise *v.* **1.** assure, contract, engage, guarantee, pledge, plight, stipulate, swear, undertake, vouch, vow, warrant **2.** augur, bespeak, betoken, bid fair, denote, indicate, suggest ~*n.* **3.** assurance, bond, commitment, compact, covenant, engagement, guarantee, oath, pledge, undertaking, vow, word **4.** ability, capacity, flair, potential, talent

promising 1. bright, encouraging, favourable, hopeful, likely, propitious, reassuring, rosy **2.** able, gifted, likely, rising, talented

promote 1. aid, assist, back, boost, develop, encourage, forward, foster, help, stimulate, support **2.** dignify, elevate, exalt, honour, prefer, raise, upgrade **3.** advocate, champion, endorse, espouse, popularize, recommend, sponsor, support, urge **4.** advertise, publicize, push, sell

promotion 1. advancement, elevation, exaltation, honour, preferment, rise **2.** advancement, backing, cultivation, encouragement, furtherance, progress, support **3.** advertising, propaganda, publicity

prompt *adj.* **1.** early, instant, punctual, quick, rapid, speedy, swift, timely, unhesitating **2.** alert, brisk, eager, expeditious, quick, ready, smart, willing *~adv.* **3.** *Inf.* exactly, punctually, sharp *~v.* **4.** cause, impel, incite, induce, inspire, instigate, motivate, move, provoke, spur, stimulate, urge **5.** assist, cue, prod, remind **6.** cause, elicit, occasion, provoke *~n.* **7.** cue, help, hint, jog, jolt, prod, reminder, spur, stimulus

promptly directly, immediately, punctually, quickly, speedily, swiftly, unhesitatingly

promptness alertness, briskness, eagerness, haste, punctuality, quickness, readiness, speed, willingness

promulgate advertise, broadcast, circulate, declare, decree, issue, notify, proclaim, promote, publish, spread

prone 1. flat, horizontal, prostrate, recumbent, supine **2.** apt, bent, disposed, given, inclined, liable, likely, predisposed, subject, susceptible, tending

pronounce 1. accent, articulate, say, sound, speak, stress, utter, vocalize, voice **2.** announce, declare, decree, deliver, proclaim

pronouncement declaration, decree, dictum, edict, judgment, proclamation, statement

pronunciation accent, articulation, diction, elocution, inflection, intonation, speech, stress

proof *n.* **1.** attestation, confirmation, demonstration, evidence, substantiation, testimony, verification **2.** *Printing* galley, pull, slip *~adj.* **3.** impenetrable, impervious, repellent, resistant, strong, tight, treated

prop *v.* **1.** bolster, brace, buttress, maintain, shore, stay, support, sustain, truss, uphold **2.** lean, rest, set, stand *~n.* **3.** brace, buttress, stay, support

propaganda advertising, information, newspeak, promotion, publicity

propagate 1. beget, breed, engender, generate, increase, multiply, procreate, produce, reproduce **2.** broadcast, circulate, disseminate, promote, promulgate, publicize, spread

propel drive, force, impel, launch, push, send, shoot, shove, start, thrust

propensity aptness, bent, bias, inclination, leaning, penchant, proclivity, tendency, weakness

proper 1. apt, becoming, befitting, fit, fitting, legitimate, right, suitable, suited **2.** decent, decorous, genteel, mannerly, polite, refined, respectable, seemly **3.** accepted, accurate, conventional, correct, established, exact, formal, orthodox, precise, right

property 1. assets, belongings, building(s), capital, chattels, effects, estate, goods, holdings, house(s), means, possessions, resources, riches, wealth **2.** estate, freehold, holding, land, title **3.** ability, attribute, feature, hallmark, idiosyncrasy, mark, peculiarity, quality, trait, virtue

prophecy forecast, prediction, prognosis, soothsaying

prophesy divine, forecast, foresee, foretell, forewarn, predict, presage

prophet clairvoyant, diviner, forecaster, oracle, seer, sibyl

prophetic oracular, predictive, prescient, prognostic

propitious bright, encouraging, favourable, fortunate, happy, lucky, opportune, rosy, timely

proportion 1. ratio **2.** agreement, balance, congruity, harmony, symmetry **3.** amount, division, fraction, measure, part, percentage, quota, segment, share **4.** *Plural* breadth, bulk, capacity, dimensions, expanse, extent, range, scope, size, volume

proportional, proportionate balanced, compatible, consistent, corresponding, equitable, even, in proportion, just

proposal bid, design, motion, offer, overture, plan, programme, project, scheme, suggestion, tender

propose 1. advance, present, proffer, propound, submit, suggest, tender **2.** introduce, invite, name, nominate, present, recommend **3.** aim, design, intend, mean, plan, purpose, scheme **4.** offer marriage, pay suit

proposition motion, plan, project, scheme, suggestion

proprietor, proprietress landlady, landlord, landowner, owner, titleholder

propriety 1. aptness, correctness, fitness, rightness, seemliness **2.** courtesy, decorum, etiquette, politeness, seemliness

prosaic boring, dry, dull, everyday, flat, humdrum, matter-of-fact, mundane, ordinary, pedestrian, routine, stale, tame, trite

proscribe 1. ban, censure, condemn, damn, doom, embargo, forbid, interdict, prohibit, reject **2.** banish, deport, exclude, exile, expatriate, expel, ostracize, outlaw

prosecute 1. *Law* arraign, indict, litigate, sue, summon, try **2.** carry on, conduct, direct, discharge, manage, perform, practise

prospect *n.* **1.** anticipation, calculation, expectation, future, hope, odds, opening, outlook, plan, promise, proposal, thought **2.** landscape, outlook, panorama, perspective, scene, sight, spectacle, view, vision, vista **3.** *Sometimes plural* chance, likelihood, possibility *~v.* **4.** explore, search, seek, survey

prospective anticipated, awaited, coming, destined, eventual, expected, future, imminent, intended, likely, looked-for, possible, potential

prospectus catalogue, list, outline, plan, programme, scheme, syllabus, synopsis

prosper advance, bloom, flourish, flower, progress, succeed, thrive

prosperity affluence, ease, fortune, luxury, plenty, prosperousness, riches, success, wealth, well-being

prosperous 1. blooming, booming, fortunate, lucky, prospering, successful, thriving **2.** affluent, opulent, rich, wealthy, well-off

prostitute 1. *n.* call girl, courtesan, harlot, trollop, whore **2.** *v.* cheapen, debase, degrade, demean, devalue, pervert, profane

prostrate *adj.* **1.** abject, flat, prone **2.** dejected, depressed, desolate, exhausted, inconsolable, overcome, spent, worn out **3.** defenceless, disarmed, helpless, paralysed, powerless, reduced *~v.* **4.** *Of oneself* abase, cringe, grovel, kneel, kowtow, submit **5.** crush, depress, disarm, overthrow, paralyse, reduce, ruin

protagonist hero, heroine, lead, principal

protect cover, defend, foster, guard, harbour, keep, safeguard, save, screen, secure, shelter, shield, support

protection 1. care, charge, custody, defence, safeguard, safety, security **2.** armour, barrier, bulwark, cover, guard, refuge, screen, shelter, shield

protective defensive, fatherly, maternal, motherly, paternal, possessive, vigilant, warm, watchful

protector bodyguard, champion, counsel, defender, guardian, patron

protégé, protégée charge, student, ward

protest 1. *n.* complaint, dissent, objection, outcry, remonstrance **2.** *v.* complain, demonstrate, demur, disagree, disapprove, object, oppose

protester agitator, demonstrator, rebel

protocol 1. conventions, customs, decorum, etiquette, manners, propriety **2.** agreement, concordat, contract, convention, covenant, pact, treaty

prototype example, first, model, original, pattern, precedent, standard, type

proud 1. content, glad, gratified, pleased, satisfied, well-pleased **2.** arrogant, boastful, conceited, disdainful, haughty, imperious, lordly, overbearing, self-satisfied, snobbish, supercilious, vain

prove 1. authenticate, confirm, demonstrate, determine, establish, justify, show, substantiate, verify **2.** analyse, assay, check, examine, experiment, test, try **3.** end up, result, turn out

proverb adage, dictum, maxim, saw, saying

proverbial axiomatic, conventional, current, famed, famous, legendary, notorious, traditional, typical, well-known

provide 1. cater, equip, furnish, outfit, stock up, supply **2.** add, afford, bring, give, impart, lend, present, produce, render, serve, yield **3.** *With* **for** *or* **against** anticipate, forearm, plan ahead, plan for, prepare for **4.** *With* **for** keep, maintain, support, sustain, take care of

providence 1. destiny, fate, fortune **2.** care, caution, discretion, foresight, prudence

provident careful, cautious, discreet, far-seeing, forearmed, frugal, prudent, shrewd, thrifty, vigilant, well-prepared, wise

providing, provided *conj.* as long as, given, in case, subject to

province 1. colony, department, district, division, region, section, tract, zone **2.** *Fig.* area, business, capacity, charge, concern, duty, field, function, line, orbit, part, post, responsibility, role, sphere

provision 1. catering, equipping, furnishing, providing, supplying **2.** arrangement, plan, precaution, preparation **3.** *Fig.* agreement, clause, condition, demand, requirement, stipulation, term

provisional conditional, contingent, interim, limited, qualified, temporary, tentative

provisions comestibles, eatables, fare, food, foodstuff, rations, stores, supplies, victuals

proviso clause, condition, qualification, requirement, rider, stipulation

provocation 1. cause, grounds, incitement, motivation, reason, stimulus **2.** affront, annoyance, challenge, dare, grievance, insult, offence, taunt

provocative annoying, goading, insulting, offensive, provoking, stimulating

provoke 1. anger, annoy, chafe, enrage, exasperate, gall, incense, infuriate, insult, irk, irritate, madden, offend, pique, rile, vex **2.** call forth, cause, draw forth, elicit, evoke, excite, fire, incite, inspire, kindle, move, occasion, produce, promote, prompt, rouse, stimulate, stir

prowess accomplishment, adeptness, aptitude, expertise, genius, mastery, skill, talent

proximity closeness, nearness, vicinity

proxy agent, delegate, deputy, factor, representative, substitute

prudence 1. care, caution, common sense, discretion, judgment, vigilance, wariness, wisdom **2.** foresight, planning, precaution, preparedness, providence, saving, thrift

prudent 1. careful, cautious, discerning, discreet, judicious, politic, sensible, shrewd, vigilant, wary, wise **2.** canny, careful, economical, far-sighted, provident, sparing, thrifty

prune clip, cut, dock, reduce, shape, shorten, snip, trim

pry interfere, intrude, meddle, peep, peer, poke

psalm chant, hymn

pseudo *adj.* artificial, bogus,

fake, false, imitation, mock, pretended, sham, spurious
pseudonym alias, assumed name, incognito, pen name
psyche anima, individuality, mind, personality, self, soul, spirit, subconscious, true being
psychiatrist analyst, psychoanalyst, psychologist
psychic extrasensory, mystic, occult, supernatural, telepathic
psychological 1. cerebral, intellectual, mental 2. emotional, imaginary, irrational, subconscious
psychology 1. behaviourism 2. *Inf.* attitude, way of thinking
psychopath lunatic, madman, maniac
pub *or* **public house** bar, inn, tavern
puberty adolescence, teenage, teens
public *adj.* 1. civic, common, general, national, popular, social, state, universal, widespread 2. accessible, communal, open, unrestricted 3. acknowledged, exposed, known, notorious, obvious, open, overt, patent, plain 4. important, prominent, respected, well-known ~*n.* 5. citizens, community, electorate, everyone, nation, people, populace, society, voters 6. audience, buyers, clientele, followers, patrons, supporters 7. **in public** openly
publication brochure, handbill, issue, leaflet, magazine, newspaper, pamphlet, periodical
publicity attention, boost, press, promotion
publicize advertise, broadcast, make known, play up, promote, puff, push, spotlight
publish 1. issue, print, produce, put out 2. advertise, announce, broadcast, circulate, declare, disclose, divulge, impart, leak, proclaim, promulgate, reveal, spread
puerile babyish, childish, foolish, immature, inane, juvenile, naive, petty, silly, trivial, weak
puff *n.* 1. blast, breath, draught, gust, whiff 2. smoke 3. commendation, good word, sales talk ~*v.* 4. blow, breathe, exhale, gasp, gulp, pant, wheeze 5. drag (*Sl.*), draw, inhale, pull at *or* on, smoke, suck 6. *Usually with* **up** bloat, dilate, distend, expand, inflate, swell
pugilist boxer, fighter
pugnacious aggressive, bellicose, belligerent, choleric, combative, hot-tempered, irascible, irritable, petulant, quarrelsome
pull *v.* 1. drag, draw, haul, jerk, tow, trail, tug, yank 2. cull, extract, gather, pick, pluck, remove, uproot, weed 3. dislocate, rend, rip, sprain, strain, stretch, tear, wrench 4. *Inf.* attract, draw, entice, lure, magnetize 5. **pull strings** influence ~*n.* 6. jerk, tug, twitch, yank 7. attraction, effort, exertion, force, influence, lure, magnetism, power 8. influence, muscle, weight
pull down destroy, raze, remove
pull out depart, evacuate, leave, quit, retreat, withdraw
pull through rally, recover, survive
pull up 1. brake, halt, stop 2. admonish, reprimand, reprove
pulp *n.* 1. flesh, soft part 2. mash, mush, paste ~*v.* 3. crush, mash, squash ~*adj.* 4. cheap, lurid, trashy
pulse 1. *n.* beat, beating, rhythm, stroke, throb, vibration 2. *v.* beat, throb, tick, vibrate
pump *v.* 1. drive, force, inject, pour, push, send, supply 2. interrogate, probe, quiz
pun double entendre, quip, witticism
punch[1] *v.* 1. box, hit, slam, smash, strike ~*n.* 2. blow, hit, knock, thump 3. *Inf.* bite, drive, forcefulness, impact, point, verve, vigour
punch[2] *v.* bore, cut, drill, pierce, pink, prick, puncture, stamp
punctilious careful, ceremonious, exact, finicky, formal, fussy, nice, proper, scrupulous
punctual early, exact, precise, prompt, strict, timely
punctuality promptitude, promptness, readiness, regularity
punctuate 1. break, interrupt, pepper, sprinkle 2. emphasize, mark, stress, underline
puncture *n.* 1. break, cut, damage, hole, leak, nick, opening, slit 2. flat, flat tyre ~*v.* 3. bore, cut, nick, penetrate, perforate, pierce, prick, rupture 4. deflate, go down, go flat
pungent 1. acid, acrid, bitter, hot, peppery, piquant, seasoned, sharp, sour, spicy, strong, tart 2. acute, barbed, biting, caustic, cutting, incisive, keen, mordant, piercing, poignant, pointed, sarcastic, scathing, sharp, stinging
punish 1. beat, castigate, chasten, chastise, correct, discipline, flog, penalize, scourge, sentence, whip 2. abuse, batter, harm, hurt, injure, manhandle, misuse, oppress
punishable blameworthy, criminal, culpable, indictable
punishment 1. chastening, chastisement, correction, discipline, penalty, penance, retribution, sanction 2. *Inf.* abuse, beating, manhandling, pain, victimization
punt 1. *v.* back, bet, gamble, lay, stake, wager 2. *n.* bet, gamble, stake, wager
punter backer, better, gambler
puny diminutive, dwarfish, feeble, frail, little, sickly, stunted, tiny, underfed, weak, weakly
pupil beginner, disciple, learner, novice, scholar, schoolboy, schoolgirl, student
puppet 1. doll, marionette 2. *Fig.* creature, dupe, instrument, mouthpiece, pawn, stooge, tool
purchase *v.* 1. acquire, buy, come by, gain, get, invest in, obtain, pay for, pick up, procure, secure 2. achieve, attain, earn, gain, realize, win ~*n.* 3. asset, buy, gain, investment, possession, property
pure 1. authentic, clear, flawless, genuine, natural, neat, perfect, real, simple, straight, true, unalloyed, unmixed 2. clean, germ-free, immaculate, sanitary, spotless, sterile, sterilized, unadulterated, uncontaminated, unpolluted, untainted, wholesome 3. blameless, chaste, honest, innocent, maidenly, modest, true, virgin, virtuous
purely absolutely, completely, entirely, exclusively, just, merely, only, simply, solely, wholly
purge *v.* 1. dismiss, eject, eradicate, expel, exterminate, kill, liquidate, oust, remove 2. absolve, cleanse, clear, exonerate, expiate, forgive, pardon, purify, wash ~*n.* 3. cleanup, crushing, ejection, elimination, eradication, liquidation, removal, suppression, witch hunt
purify 1. clarify, clean, cleanse, disinfect, filter, fumigate, refine, wash 2. absolve, cleanse, exonerate, lustrate, redeem, sanctify, shrive
purist formalist, pedant, stickler
puritan 1. *n.* fanatic, moralist, prude, rigorist, zealot 2. *adj.* ascetic, austere, intolerant, narrow-minded, prudish, severe, strait-laced, strict
purpose *n.* 1. aim, design, idea, intention, object, point, reason 2. aim, ambition, design, desire, end, goal, hope, intention, object, plan, project, scheme, target, view, wish 3. determination, firmness, persistence, resolution, resolve, tenacity, will 4. **on purpose** deliberately, designedly, intentionally, knowingly ~*v.* 5. aim, aspire, contemplate, decide, design, determine, intend, mean, meditate, plan, propose, resolve
purposely consciously, deliberately, expressly, intentionally, knowingly, wilfully, with intent
purse 1. pouch, wallet 2. exchequer, funds, means, money, resources, treasury, wealth 3. award, gift, present, prize, reward
pursue 1. accompany, attend, chase, dog, follow, harass, harry, haunt, hound, hunt, hunt down, plague, run after, shadow, stalk, tail, track 2. desire, purpose, seek, strive for, try for, work towards 3. adhere to, carry on, continue, cultivate, maintain, persist in, proceed 4. court
pursuit 1. chase, hunt, inquiry, quest, search, seeking, trail, trailing 2. activity, hobby, interest, line, occupation, pastime, pleasure
push *v.* 1. depress, drive, press, propel, ram, shove, thrust 2. elbow, jostle, move, shoulder, shove, squeeze, thrust 3. encourage, expedite, hurry, impel, incite, persuade, press, spur, urge 4. advertise, boost, promote, publicize ~*n.* 5. butt, jolt, nudge, poke, prod, shove, thrust 6. *Inf.* ambition, determination, drive, dynamism, energy, enterprise, initiative, vigour 7. *Inf.* advance, assault, attack, charge, effort, offensive, thrust
pushing 1. ambitious, determined, driving, go-ahead, purposeful, resourceful 2. bold, brash, impertinent, intrusive, self-assertive
put 1. bring, deposit, establish, fix, lay, place, position, rest, set, settle, situate 2. assign, constrain, employ, force, induce, make, oblige, require, set 3. advance, forward, offer, posit, present, propose, submit, tender 4. cast, fling, heave, hurl, lob, pitch, throw, toss
put across *or* **over** convey, explain, spell out
put aside *or* **by** deposit, lay by, save, stockpile, store
put away 1. put back, replace, tidy away 2. deposit, keep, lay in, put by, save, set aside
put down 1. enter, inscribe, log, record, transcribe 2. crush, quash, quell, repress, silence, stamp out, suppress 3. *With* **to** ascribe, attribute, impute 4. destroy 5. condemn, crush, deflate, dismiss, disparage, humiliate, mortify, reject, shame, slight, snub
put forward advance, introduce, move, nominate, present, press, propose, recommend, submit, suggest
put off 1. defer, delay, postpone, reschedule 2. abash, confuse, discomfit, disconcert, dismay, distress, nonplus, perturb, unsettle 3. discourage, dishearten, dissuade
put on 1. do, mount, present, produce, show, stage 2. add, gain, increase by
put out 1. anger, annoy, confound, disturb, harass, irk, irritate, nettle, perturb, provoke, vex 2. blow out, extinguish, quench, smother 3. bother, discomfit, discommode, discompose, disconcert, disturb, embarrass, incommode, inconvenience, trouble, upset
put through achieve, bring off, conclude, do, effect, execute, manage
put up 1. build, construct, erect, fabricate, raise 2. accommodate, board, entertain, house, lodge 3. float, nominate, offer, present, propose, recommend, submit 4. advance, give, invest, pay, pledge, provide, supply 5. **put up with** abide, bear, brook, endure, stomach, suffer, swallow, take, tolerate
puzzle *v.* 1. baffle, bewilder, confound, confuse, mystify, perplex, stump 2. brood, muse, ponder, study, think hard, wonder 3. *Usually with* **out** crack, decipher, resolve, see, solve, unravel ~*n.* 4. conundrum, enigma, mystery, paradox, poser, problem, question, riddle 5. bafflement, confusion, difficulty, dilemma, perplexity, uncertainty
puzzling abstruse, baffling, bewildering, enigmatic, hard, incomprehensible, involved, knotty, mystifying, perplexing

Q

quack *n.* charlatan, fake, fraud, humbug, impostor, mountebank, pretender
quagmire 1. bog, fen, marsh, mire, quicksand, slough, swamp 2. difficulty, entanglement, impasse, pass, pinch, plight, predicament, quandary
quail blanch, blench, cower, cringe, droop, faint, falter, flinch, quake, recoil, shake, shrink
quaint bizarre, curious, droll, eccentric, fanciful, odd, old-fashioned, peculiar, queer, singular, strange, unusual, whimsical
quake move, quiver, rock,

shake, shiver, shudder, throb, totter, tremble, vibrate, waver

qualification 1. ability, aptitude, capability, capacity, eligibility, fitness, skill, suitability 2. allowance, caveat, condition, exception, limitation, modification, requirement, reservation, stipulation

qualified 1. able, adept, capable, certificated, competent, efficient, equipped, experienced, expert, fit, practised, proficient, skilful, talented, trained 2. bounded, conditional, confined, equivocal, guarded, limited, modified, provisional, reserved, restricted

qualify 1. certify, commission, condition, empower, endow, equip, fit, ground, permit, prepare, ready, sanction, train 2. abate, adapt, assuage, diminish, ease, lessen, limit, moderate, reduce, regulate, restrain, restrict, soften, temper, vary

quality 1. aspect, attribute, condition, feature, mark, property, trait 2. description, essence, kind, make, nature, sort 3. calibre, distinction, excellence, grade, merit, position, rank, standing, status, superiority, value, worth

quandary difficulty, dilemma, doubt, impasse, perplexity, plight, puzzle, strait, uncertainty

quantity allotment, amount, lot, number, part, sum, total

quarrel 1. *n.* affray, argument, brawl, breach, controversy, disagreement, discord, dispute, dissension, feud, fight, row, squabble, strife, tiff, tumult, vendetta 2. *v.* argue, bicker, brawl, clash, differ, disagree, dispute, fight, row, wrangle

quarrelsome argumentative, combative, cross, disputatious, fractious, irascible, irritable, peevish, petulant, querulous

quarry aim, game, goal, objective, prey, prize, victim

quarter *n.* 1. area, district, locality, neighbourhood, part, place, point, position, province, region, side, spot, station, territory 2. favour, forgiveness, leniency, mercy, pity ~*v.* 3. accommodate, billet, board, house, install, lodge, place, post, station

quarters abode, barracks, billet, chambers, domicile, dwelling, lodging, post, residence, rooms, shelter, station

quash annul, cancel, invalidate, nullify, overrule, overthrow, rescind, reverse, revoke

quaver *v.* flicker, flutter, quake, shake, shudder, thrill, tremble, trill, vibrate, waver

queen consort, monarch, ruler, sovereign

queer *adj.* 1. abnormal, curious, droll, extraordinary, funny, odd, peculiar, remarkable, singular, strange, uncanny, uncommon, unnatural, weird 2. doubtful, dubious, irregular, mysterious, suspicious 3. crazy, eccentric, irrational, mad, odd, touched ~*v.* 4. botch, endanger, harm, impair, imperil, injure, mar, ruin, spoil

quench check, crush, douse, end, extinguish, put out, smother, stifle, suppress

querulous captious, carping, complaining, critical, cross, dissatisfied, fretful, grumbling, irascible, irritable, peevish, petulant, plaintive, sour, testy, touchy

query *v.* 1. ask, enquire, question 2. challenge, disbelieve, dispute, distrust, doubt, mistrust, suspect ~*n.* 3. demand, doubt, hesitation, inquiry, objection, problem, question, suspicion

question *v.* 1. ask, cross-examine, enquire, examine, interrogate, interview, probe, quiz 2. challenge, disbelieve, dispute, doubt, mistrust, oppose, query, suspect ~*n.* 3. inquiry, investigation 4. argument, contention, controversy, debate, difficulty, dispute, doubt, misgiving, problem, query 5. issue, motion, point, proposal, proposition, subject, theme, topic

questionable controversial, debatable, doubtful, equivocal, moot, problematical, suspect, uncertain, unreliable

queue chain, file, line, order, sequence, series, string, train

quibble 1. *v.* carp, cavil, evade, pretend, shift 2. *n.* cavil, complaint, criticism, evasion, nicety, objection, pretence, quirk, shift, subterfuge, subtlety

quick 1. active, brief, brisk, express, fast, fleet, hasty, headlong, hurried, prompt, rapid, speedy, swift 2. agile, alert, animated, energetic, flying, keen, lively, nimble, spirited, spry, vivacious 3. able, acute, adept, adroit, apt, astute, bright, clever, deft, discerning, intelligent, perceptive, quick-witted, receptive, sharp, shrewd, skilful, smart

quicken 1. accelerate, expedite, hasten, hurry, impel, speed 2. arouse, excite, incite, inspire, revive, stimulate

quickly abruptly, briskly, fast, hastily, hurriedly, promptly, rapidly, soon, speedily, swiftly

quiet *adj.* 1. dumb, hushed, inaudible, low, peaceful, silent, soft, soundless 2. calm, contented, gentle, mild, pacific, peaceful, placid, restful, serene, smooth, tranquil 3. private, retired, secluded, secret 4. modest, plain, restrained, simple, sober, subdued, unobtrusive 5. docile, even-tempered, gentle, meek, mild, reserved, retiring, sedate, shy ~*n.* 6. calmness, ease, peace, repose, rest, serenity, silence, tranquillity

quieten allay, appease, blunt, calm, compose, deaden, dull, hush, lull, muffle, mute, quell, quiet, silence, soothe, stifle, still, stop, subdue

quietly 1. inaudibly, mutely, noiselessly, privately, secretly, silently, softly 2. calmly, contentedly, meekly, mildly, patiently, placidly, serenely 3. coyly, humbly, unobtrusively, unpretentiously

quietness calm, hush, peace, repose, rest, serenity, silence, stillness, tranquillity

quip *n.* gibe, jest, joke, pleasantry, repartee, retort, witticism

quit 1. abandon, decamp, depart, desert, exit, go, leave, resign, retire, surrender, withdraw 2. cease, discontinue, drop, end, halt, stop, suspend

quite 1. completely, entirely, fully, largely, totally, wholly 2. fairly, rather, somewhat

quiver *v.* oscillate, palpitate, pulsate, shiver, shudder, tremble, vibrate

quiz 1. *n.* questioning, test 2. *v.* ask, examine, investigate, question

quota allowance, assignment, part, portion, ration, share, slice

quotation 1. cutting, excerpt, extract, passage, reference 2. *Commerce* charge, cost, estimate, figure, price, rate, tender

quote attest, cite, detail, instance, name, proclaim, recall, recite, recollect, refer to, repeat, retell

R

rabble crowd, herd, horde, mob, swarm, throng

rabid berserk, crazed, frantic, furious, mad, raging, violent, wild

race[1] 1. *n.* chase, contest, dash, pursuit, rivalry 2. *v.* career, compete, contest, dart, dash, fly, gallop, hurry, run, speed, tear

race[2] blood, breed, clan, family, folk, house, issue, kin, kindred, line, nation, offspring, people, progeny, stock, tribe, type

rack *n.* 1. frame, framework, stand, structure 2. agony, anguish, misery, pain, pang, persecution, suffering, torment, torture ~*v.* 3. afflict, agonize, crucify, harass, harrow, oppress, pain, torment, torture

racket 1. clamour, din, fuss, noise, outcry, row, shouting, tumult, uproar 2. fraud, scheme

racy animated, buoyant, energetic, entertaining, exciting, heady, lively, sparkling, spirited

radiance 1. brightness, brilliance, glare, gleam, glitter, glow, light, lustre, shine 2. delight, gaiety, happiness, joy, pleasure, rapture, warmth

radiant bright, brilliant, gleaming, glittering, glorious, glowing, luminous, resplendent, shining

radiate 1. diffuse, emit, gleam, pour, scatter, send out, shed, shine, spread 2. diverge, issue

radical *adj.* 1. basic, deep-seated, essential, innate, native, natural, profound 2. complete, entire, excessive, extreme, extremist, fanatical, severe, sweeping, thorough, violent ~*n.* 3. extremist, fanatic, militant

rage 1. *n.* anger, frenzy, fury, ire, madness, obsession, rampage, violence, wrath 2. *v.* chafe, fret, fume, rave, seethe, storm

ragged mean, poor, rent, shabby, threadbare, torn, unkempt, worn-out

raid 1. *n.* attack, foray, incursion, inroad, invasion, sally, seizure, sortie 2. *v.* assault, attack, foray, invade, pillage, plunder, rifle, sack

raider attacker, forager (*Military*), invader, marauder, plunderer, reiver (*Dialect*), robber, thief

railing balustrade, barrier, fence, paling, rails

rain *n.* 1. deluge, downpour, drizzle, fall, showers 2. deluge, flood, hail, shower, spate, stream, torrent ~*v.* 3. drizzle, fall, pour, shower, teem

raise 1. build, elevate, erect, exalt, heave, hoist, lift, promote, rear, uplift 2. advance, aggravate, amplify, boost, enhance, enlarge, heighten, increase, inflate, intensify, magnify, strengthen 3. advance, elevate, exalt, prefer, promote, upgrade 4. cause, create, engender, occasion, originate, produce, provoke, start 5. advance, broach, introduce, moot, suggest 6. collect, form, gather, get, levy, mass, muster, obtain, rally, recruit 7. breed, cultivate, develop, grow, nurture, produce, propagate, rear

rake[1] *v.* 1. collect, gather, remove 2. harrow, hoe, scour, scrape, scratch

rake[2] *n.* lecher, libertine, playboy, profligate, roué

rally *v.* 1. reassemble, re-form, regroup, reorganize, unite ~*n.* 2. reunion, stand ~*v.* 3. assemble, collect, convene, gather, marshal, mobilize, muster, organize, round up, summon, unite ~*n.* 4. convention, convocation, gathering, meeting, muster ~*v.* 5. improve, pick up, recover, recuperate, revive ~*n.* 6. improvement, recovery, renewal, revival

ram butt, crash, dash, drive, force, hit, impact, smash, strike

ramble *v.* 1. drift, range, roam, rove, saunter, straggle, stray, stroll, walk, wander 2. chatter, digress, maunder, wander ~*n.* 3. excursion, hike, saunter, stroll, tour, trip, walk

rambler hiker, rover, walker, wanderer, wayfarer

ramification 1. branch, division, extension, offshoot 2. complication, consequence, development, result, sequel, upshot

rampage 1. *v.* rage, storm 2. *n.* fury, rage, storm, tempest, tumult, uproar, violence

rampant aggressive, flagrant, outrageous, raging, riotous, unbridled, wanton, wild

rampart bastion, bulwark, defence, fence, fort, guard, security, wall

ramshackle crumbling, decrepit, derelict, flimsy, rickety, shaky, unsafe, unsteady

random accidental, aimless, casual, chance, fortuitous, haphazard, hit or miss, incidental, spot

range *n.* 1. area, bounds, distance, extent, field, latitude, limits, orbit, province, radius, reach, scope, span, sphere, sweep ~*v.* 2. align, arrange, array, dispose, line up, order 3. cruise, explore, ramble, roam, rove, stray, stroll, sweep, wander

rank[1] *n.* 1. caste, class, degree, dignity, division, grade, level, order, position, quality, sort, station, status, type 2. column, file, group, line, range, row, series, tier ~*v.* 3. align, arrange, array, class, classify, grade, locate, marshal, order, range, sort

rank[2] 1. dense, lush, productive, profuse, vigorous 2. bad, fetid, foul, fusty, musty, off, putrid, rancid

rankle anger, annoy, chafe, gall, irk

ransack 1. explore, rake, scour, search 2. despoil, gut, loot, pillage, plunder, raid, ravage, rifle, sack, strip

ransom *n.* 1. liberation, redemption, release, rescue 2. money, payment, payoff, price ~*v.* 3. deliver, liberate, redeem, release, rescue

rant bluster, cry, declaim, rave, roar, shout, yell

rape *n.* 1. outrage, violation 2. despoilment, pillage, rapine, sack 3. abuse, desecration, maltreatment, violation ~*v.* 4. outrage, ravish, violate 5. despoil, loot, pillage, plunder, sack

rapid brisk, express, fast, fleet, flying, hasty, hurried, prompt, quick, swift

rapidly briskly, fast, hastily, promptly, quickly, speedily, swiftly

rapt absorbed, engrossed, enthralled, gripped, held, intent, spellbound

rapture bliss, delight, ecstasy, exaltation, happiness, joy, spell, transport

rapturous blissful, delighted, exalted, happy, joyful, transported

rare 1. few, infrequent, scarce, singular, sparse, strange, uncommon, unusual 2. choice, extreme, fine, great, peerless, superb

rarely hardly, little, seldom

rarity 1. curio, find, gem, pearl, treasure 2. infrequency, shortage

rascal blackguard, devil, disgrace, imp, miscreant, rake, reprobate, rogue, scamp, scoundrel, villain, wastrel, wretch

rash[1] brash, careless, foolhardy, hasty, headlong, heedless, hotheaded, ill-advised, impetuous, imprudent, impulsive, incautious, reckless

rash[2] 1. eruption, outbreak 2. flood, outbreak, plague, series, spate, wave

rate *n.* 1. degree, proportion, ratio, scale, standard 2. charge, cost, dues, duty, fee, figure, hire, price, tariff, tax 3. measure, pace, speed, tempo, time 4. class, degree, grade, quality, rank, status, value, worth 5. **at any rate** anyhow, anyway, nevertheless ~*v.* 6. appraise, assess, class, consider, count, estimate, evaluate, grade, measure, rank, reckon, regard, value, weigh

rather 1. a bit, a little, fairly, moderately, quite, relatively, slightly, somewhat, to some degree, to some extent 2. noticeably, significantly, very 3. instead, preferably, sooner

ratify affirm, approve, bind, confirm, corroborate, endorse, establish, sanction, sign, uphold

rating class, degree, estimate, grade, order, placing, position, rank, rate, status

ratio fraction, percentage, proportion, rate, relation

ration *n.* 1. allotment, allowance, dole, helping, measure, part, portion, provision, quota, share 2. *Plural* food, provisions, stores, supplies ~*v.* 3. *With* **out** allocate, allot, deal, distribute, dole, give out, issue, mete 4. budget, conserve, control, limit, restrict, save

rational enlightened, intelligent, logical, lucid, realistic, reasonable, sane, sensible, sound, wise

rationalize 1. excuse, justify, vindicate 2. elucidate, resolve

rattle *v.* 1. bang, clatter 2. bounce, jar, jolt, shake, vibrate 3. disconcert, frighten, scare, shake, upset

raucous grating, harsh, hoarse, husky, loud, noisy, rasping, rough, strident

ravage demolish, despoil, destroy, devastate, loot, pillage, plunder, ransack, ruin, sack, spoil

rave fume, go mad, rage, rant, roar, splutter, storm, thunder

ravenous famished, starved

ravine canyon, defile, gorge, gully, pass

raving crazed, delirious, frantic, frenzied, furious, hysterical, insane, irrational, mad, rabid, raging, wild

raw 1. fresh, natural, uncooked, undressed, unprepared 2. basic, coarse, crude, green, natural, organic, rough, unprocessed, unrefined, unripe 3. chafed, grazed, open, skinned, sore, tender 4. callow, green, immature, inexperienced, new 5. biting, bitter, bleak, chill, cold, damp, harsh

ray 1. bar, beam, flash, gleam, shaft 2. flicker, glimmer, hint, spark, trace

raze demolish, destroy, flatten, level, remove, ruin

reach *v.* 1. attain, make 2. contact, extend to, grasp, stretch to, touch 3. arrive at, attain, drop, fall, move, rise, sink ~*n.* 4. ambit, capacity, command, compass, distance, extension, extent, grasp, influence, jurisdiction, mastery, power, range, scope, spread, stretch, sweep

react 1. answer, reply, respond 2. act, behave, function, operate, proceed, work

reaction 1. answer, feedback, reply, response 2. recoil 3. conservatism, the right

reactionary 1. *adj.* blimpish, conservative 2. *n.* die-hard, obscurantist, rightist

read 1. look at, peruse, pore over, scan, study 2. announce, declaim, deliver, recite, speak, utter 3. comprehend, construe, decipher, discover, interpret, see, understand 4. display, indicate, record, register, show

readily 1. eagerly, freely, gladly, promptly, quickly, willingly 2. easily, effortlessly, quickly, smoothly, speedily, unhesitatingly

readiness 1. fitness, maturity, 2. aptness, eagerness, inclination, keenness, willingness 3. adroitness, dexterity, ease, facility, promptness

reading 1. inspection, perusal, review, scrutiny, study 2. lecture, lesson, recital, rendering, sermon 3. grasp, impression, interpretation, treatment, version 4. education, erudition, knowledge, learning, scholarship

ready 1. arranged, completed, fit, organized, prepared, primed, ripe, set 2. agreeable, apt, disposed, eager, glad, happy, inclined, keen, prone, willing 3. acute, adroit, alert, apt, astute, bright, clever, deft, expert, handy, perceptive, prompt, quick, rapid, sharp, skilful, smart 4. accessible, available, convenient, handy, near, present

real absolute, actual, authentic, certain, factual, genuine, honest, intrinsic, positive, right, rightful, sincere, true, unfeigned, valid, veritable

realistic 1. common-sense, level-headed, matter-of-fact, practical, real, sensible, sober 2. authentic, faithful, genuine, lifelike, natural, true, truthful

reality actuality, fact, realism, truth, validity, verity

realization 1. awareness, cognizance, conception, grasp, imagination, perception, recognition, understanding 2. completion, fulfilment

realize 1. appreciate, comprehend, conceive, grasp, imagine, recognize, understand 2. accomplish, bring off, complete, consummate, do, effect, fulfil, perform 3. acquire, clear, earn, gain, get, make, net, obtain, produce

really actually, categorically, certainly, genuinely, indeed, positively, surely, truly

reap acquire, collect, cut, derive, gain, garner, gather, get, harvest, win

rear[1] 1. *n.* back, end, rearguard, stern, tail, tail end 2. *adj.* back, following, hindmost, last

rear[2] *v.* 1. breed, cultivate, educate, foster, grow, nurse, nurture, raise, train 2. build, construct, erect, fabricate

reason *n.* 1. brains, intellect, judgment, logic, mentality, mind, sanity, sense(s), soundness, understanding 2. aim, basis, cause, design, end, goal, grounds, impetus, incentive, inducement, intention, motive, object, occasion, purpose, target, warrant 3. bounds, limits, moderation, propriety, sense, wisdom ~*v.* 4. conclude, deduce, infer, make out, ratiocinate, resolve, solve, think, work out

reasonable 1. arguable, believable, credible, intelligent, logical, plausible, practical, sane, sensible, sober, sound, tenable, wise 2. average, equitable, fair, fit, honest, inexpensive, just, moderate, modest, proper, right, tolerable

reasoning 1. analysis, logic, thinking, thought 2. argument, case, exposition, hypothesis, interpretation, proof

reassure comfort, encourage, hearten, inspirit, restore confidence to

rebel *v.* 1. mutiny, resist, revolt 2. defy, disobey, dissent 3. flinch, recoil, show repugnance, shrink, shy away ~*n.* 4. insurgent, revolutionary, revolutionist, secessionist 5. apostate, dissenter, heretic, schismatic ~*adj.* 6. insurgent, rebellious

rebellion 1. mutiny, resistance, revolt, revolution, rising, uprising 2. defiance, dissent, heresy, schism

rebellious 1. defiant, disloyal, disobedient, disorderly, insurgent, mutinous, rebel, revolutionary, unruly 2. difficult, refractory, resistant

rebound *v.* 1. bounce, recoil, return 2. backfire, boomerang, misfire, recoil ~*n.* 3. bounce, kickback, return, ricochet

rebuff 1. *v.* cold-shoulder, cut, decline, deny, discourage, refuse, reject, repulse, resist, slight, snub, spurn 2. *n.* check, defeat, denial, discouragement, opposition, refusal, rejection, repulse, slight, snub

rebuke 1. *v.* admonish, blame, castigate, censure, chide, lecture, reprehend, reproach, reprove, scold, upbraid 2. *n.* blame, censure, lecture, reprimand, reproach, reproof

recall *v.* 1. evoke, recollect, remember, 2. annul, cancel, countermand, repeal, retract, revoke, withdraw ~*n.* 3. cancellation, repeal, retraction, withdrawal 4. memory, remembrance

recant deny, disclaim, disown, recall, repudiate, retract, revoke, withdraw

recapitulate outline, recount, repeat, restate, review, summarize

recede 1. abate, ebb, fall back, regress, retire, retreat, return, subside, withdraw 2. decline, dwindle, fade, lessen, shrink, sink, wane

receipt 1. stub, voucher 2. acceptance, delivery, receiving, reception

receive 1. accept, acquire, collect, derive, get, obtain, pick up, take 2. apprehend, gather, hear 3. bear, encounter, experience, suffer, sustain, undergo 4. accommodate, admit, entertain, greet, meet, take in, welcome

recent current, fresh, late, latter, modern, new, novel, young

receptacle container, holder

reception 1. admission, receipt 2. acknowledgment, greeting, reaction, response, treatment, welcome 3. function, levee, party, soirée

receptive alert, bright, perceptive, responsive, sensitive

recess 1. alcove, bay, corner, hollow, niche, nook, oriel 2. break, closure, holiday, interval, respite, rest, vacation

recession decline, depression, slump

recipe 1. ingredients, instructions 2. formula, method, prescription, procedure, process, technique

reciprocate barter, exchange, reply, requite, respond, return, swap, trade

recital account, narrative, performance, reading, rehearsal, rendering, statement, story, tale, telling

recitation lecture, passage, piece, reading, recital

recite declaim, deliver, describe, detail, itemize, narrate, perform, recount, repeat, speak, tell

reckless careless, hasty, headlong, heedless, imprudent, indiscreet, mindless, precipitate, rash, thoughtless, wild

reckon 1. add up, compute, count, figure, number, tally, total 2. account, appraise, consider, count, deem, esteem, gauge, hold, judge, rate, regard 3. assume, believe, imagine, suppose, surmise, think

reckoning 1. addition, calculation, count, estimate, working 2. bill, charge, due, score

reclaim recapture, recover, redeem, reform, regain, reinstate

recline lean, loll, lounge, repose, rest, sprawl

recluse anchoress, anchorite, ascetic, hermit, monk, solitary

recognition 1. discovery, recall, remembrance 2. acceptance, admission, allowance, appreciation, avowal, confession, notice, perception, respect

recognize 1. identify, know, notice, place, recall, recollect, remember, spot 2. accept, admit, allow, avow, concede, confess, grant, own, perceive, realize, respect, see, understand

recoil *v.* 1. jerk back, kick, react, rebound, spring back 2. draw back, falter, quail, shrink 3. backfire, misfire, rebound ~*n.* 4. backlash, kick, reaction, rebound, repercussion

recollect place, recall, remember, summon up

recollection impression, memory, recall, reminiscence

recommend advance, advise, advocate, counsel, enjoin, exhort, propose, put forward, suggest, urge

recommendation 1. advice, counsel, proposal 2. advocacy, approval, blessing, endorsement, praise, reference, sanction, testimonial

reconcile 1. accept, resign, submit, yield 2. appease, conciliate, propitiate, reunite 3. adjust, compose, harmonize, rectify, resolve, settle, square

reconciliation conciliation, reunion, understanding

recondite arcane, concealed, dark, deep, difficult, hidden, mysterious, obscure, occult, profound, secret

reconnaissance exploration, observation, patrol, scan, survey

reconnoitre explore, inspect, investigate, observe, patrol, scan, scout, spy out, survey

reconsider reassess, rethink, review, revise

reconstruct 1. rebuild, recreate, re-establish, regenerate, remodel, renovate, reorganize, restore 2. build up, deduce

record *n.* 1. account, chronicle, diary, entry, file, journal, log, memoir, minute, register, report 2. evidence, testimony, trace, witness 3. background, career, history, performance 4. album, disc, recording, release, single 5. **off the record** confidential, private, unofficial ~*v.* 6. document, enrol, enter, inscribe, log, minute, note, register, report, transcribe

recorder archivist, chronicler, clerk, diarist, historian, scorer, scribe

recording disc, record, tape, video

recount depict, detail, enumerate, narrate, portray, recite, rehearse, relate, repeat, report, tell

recover 1. recapture, reclaim, redeem, regain, repair, repossess, restore, retrieve 2. convalesce, get better, get well, heal, improve, mend, rally, recuperate, revive

recovery 1. healing, improvement, mending, rally, revival 2. betterment, improvement, rally, restoration, revival, upturn

recreation amusement, diversion, enjoyment, exercise, fun, hobby, pastime, play, pleasure, relaxation, relief, sport

recruit *v.* 1. draft, enlist, enrol, impress, levy, mobilize, muster, raise 2. engage, procure 3. augment, refresh, reinforce, renew, restore, strengthen, supply ~*n.* 4. apprentice, beginner, convert, helper, initiate, learner, novice, trainee

rectify adjust, amend, correct, emend, fix, improve, mend, redress, reform, remedy, repair, right, square

rectitude decency, goodness, honesty, honour, integrity, justice, morality, principle, probity, uprightness, virtue

recuperate convalesce, improve, mend, recover

recur come again, happen again, persist, reappear, repeat, return, revert

recurrent continued, frequent, habitual, periodic

red 1. cardinal, carmine, cherry, coral, crimson, rose, ruby, scarlet, vermilion, wine 2. bay, chestnut, flaming, foxy, reddish, sandy, titian 3. blushing, florid, flushed, rubicund 4. bloodstained, bloody, gory, sanguine

redeem 1. reclaim, recover, regain, repossess, repurchase, retrieve, win back 2. change, exchange 3. acquit, carry out, discharge, fulfil, keep, meet, perform, satisfy 4. deliver, emancipate, free, liberate, ransom

redress 1. make amends 2. adjust, amend, balance, correct, ease, mend, relieve, remedy, repair

reduce 1. abate, abridge, curtail, decrease, dilute, diminish, impair, lessen, lower, moderate, shorten, truncate, weaken 2. bring, conquer, drive, force, master, overpower, subdue, vanquish 3. cheapen, cut, discount, lower, slash 4. break, degrade, downgrade, humble

redundant 1. excessive, superfluous, supernumerary, surplus, unwanted 2. diffuse, padded, prolix, verbose, wordy

reek 1. *v.* smell, stink 2. *n.* odour, smell, stench, stink

reel 1. lurch, pitch, rock, roll, stagger, sway 2. revolve, spin, swim, swirl, twirl, whirl

refer 1. advert, allude, cite, hint, invoke, mention 2. direct, guide, point, recommend, send 3. apply, consult, go, turn to 4. apply, belong, be relevant to, concern, pertain, relate

referee 1. *n.* arbiter, arbitrator, judge, umpire 2. *v.* adjudicate, arbitrate, judge, umpire

reference 1. allusion, mention, note, quotation, remark 2. bearing, concern, connection, consideration, regard, relation, respect 3. character, recommendation, testimonial

referendum plebiscite, public vote

refine 1. clarify, cleanse, distil, filter, process, purify, rarefy 2. civilize, cultivate, elevate, hone, improve, perfect, polish, temper

refined 1. civilized, courtly, cultivated, elegant, gracious, ladylike, polished, polite, urbane 2. delicate, discerning, exact, fastidious, fine, nice, precise, punctilious, sensitive, sublime, subtle

refinement 1. cleansing, filtering 2. fine point, nicety, nuance, subtlety 3. civility, courtesy, courtliness, cultivation, culture, discrimination, finish, gentility, graciousness, polish

reflect 1. echo, mirror, reproduce, return, throw back 2. cogitate, consider, meditate, muse, ponder, ruminate, think, wonder

reflection 1. echo, image 2. cogitation, consideration, idea, meditation, musing, observation, opinion, pondering, study, thinking, view

reform 1. *v.* amend, correct, emend, improve, mend, rebuild, reclaim, regenerate, remodel, renovate, repair, restore 2. *n.* amendment, betterment, improvement, rehabilitation

refrain *v.* abstain, avoid, cease, desist, forbear, renounce, stop

refresh 1. brace, cheer, cool, enliven, freshen, reinvigorate, revitalize, revive, revivify, stimulate 2. prompt, renew, stimulate

refreshing bracing, cooling, fresh, invigorating, new, novel, original, stimulating

refreshment 1. enlivenment, freshening, renewal, repair, revival, stimulation 2. *Plural* drinks, snacks, titbits

refuge asylum, harbour, haven, hide-out, resort, retreat, shelter

refugee émigré, escapee, exile, fugitive, runaway

refund 1. *v.* pay back, reimburse, repay, restore, return 2. *n.* repayment, return

refusal 1. denial, rebuff, rejection, repudiation 2. choice, consideration, option

refuse *v.* decline, deny, reject, repel, repudiate, withhold

regain recapture, recoup, recover, repossess, retake, retrieve

regard *v.* 1. behold, eye, mark, notice, observe, remark, view, watch 2. adjudge, believe, consider, deem, esteem, hold, imagine, rate, see, suppose, think, treat, value, view 3. attend, heed, listen to, mind, note, respect ~*n.* 4. attention, heed, mind, notice 5. affection, care, concern, deference, esteem, honour, love, note, repute, respect, store, sympathy, thought

regardless 1. *adj.* heedless, inconsiderate, indifferent, neglectful, rash, reckless, remiss, unmindful 2. *adv.* anyway, nevertheless, nonetheless

regime government, leadership, management, reign, rule, system

region area, country, district, expanse, land, locality, part, place, quarter, section, sector, territory, tract, zone

regional district, local, parochial, provincial, sectional, zonal

register *n.* 1. archives, catalogue, chronicle, diary, file, ledger, list, log, record, roll, roster, schedule ~*v.* 2. catalogue, chronicle, enlist, enrol, enter, inscribe, list, note, record, take down 3. betray, display, exhibit, express, indicate, manifest, mark, read, record, reflect, reveal, say, show

regret 1. *v.* bemoan, bewail, deplore, grieve, lament, miss, mourn, repent, rue 2. *n.* bitterness, compunction, contrition, disappointment, penitence, remorse, repentance, ruefulness, sorrow

regrettable disappointing, distressing, lamentable, pitiable, sad, shameful, unfortunate

regular 1. common, customary, daily, everyday, habitual, normal, ordinary, routine, typical, usual 2. consistent, constant, even, fixed, ordered, periodic, set, stated, steady, systematic, uniform 3. balanced, even, flat, level, smooth, straight, symmetrical, uniform

regulate adjust, arrange, balance, conduct, control, direct, fit, govern, guide, handle, manage, monitor, order, rule, run, settle, supervise, tune

regulation *n.* 1. adjustment, control, direction, government, management, supervision 2. decree, dictate, direction, edict, law, order, precept, procedure, requirement, rule, statute

rehearsal drill, practice, preparation, reading

rehearse act, drill, practise, prepare, ready, recite, repeat, run through, study, train, try out

reign 1. *n.* command, control, dominion, empire, influence, monarchy, power, rule, sway 2. *v.* administer, command, govern, influence, rule

rein *n.* brake, bridle, check, control, curb, harness, hold, restraint

reinforce bolster, emphasize, fortify, harden, increase, prop, stiffen, strengthen, stress, support, toughen, underline

reinforcement 1. enlargement, fortification, increase, strengthening, supplement 2. brace, buttress, prop, shore, stay, support 3. *Plural* reserves, support

reinstate recall, rehabilitate, replace, restore, return

reject 1. *v.* decline, deny, despise, discard, jettison, rebuff, refuse, renounce, repel, scrap, spurn, throw away *or* out, turn down, veto 2. *n.* castoff, discard, failure, second

rejection dismissal, exclusion, rebuff, refusal, repudiation, veto

rejoice celebrate, delight, exult, glory, joy, revel, triumph

rejoicing celebration, elation, exultation, gladness, happiness, joy, jubilation, merrymaking, revelry, triumph

relapse *v.* 1. degenerate, fail, lapse, regress, revert, weaken 2. deteriorate, fade, fail, sicken, sink, weaken, worsen ~*n.* 3. lapse, regression, retrogression, reversion 4. deterioration, weakening, worsening

relate 1. describe, detail, narrate, present, recite, rehearse, report, tell 2. associate, connect, coordinate, couple, join, link 3. apply, concern, pertain, refer

related 1. affiliated, akin, associated, connected, interconnected, joint, linked **2.** akin, kin, kindred

relation 1. affinity, kindred, kinship **2.** kin, kinsman, relative **3.** bearing, bond, comparison, connection, link, pertinence, reference, regard, similarity

relations 1. affairs, connections, contact, interaction, intercourse, liaison, meetings, rapport, terms **2.** clan, family, kin, kindred, tribe

relationship affair, bond, conjunction, connection, exchange, kinship, liaison, link, proportion, similarity, tie-up

relative *adj.* **1.** allied, connected, contingent, dependent, reciprocal, related, respective **2.** applicable, apposite, appropriate, appurtenant, apropos, germane, pertinent, relevant ~*n.* **3.** kinsman

relatively comparatively, rather, somewhat

relax 1. abate, ease, ebb, lessen, let up, loosen, lower, moderate, reduce, relieve, slacken, weaken **2.** calm, laze, soften, unwind

relaxation enjoyment, fun, leisure, pleasure, recreation, refreshment, rest

relay *n.* **1.** relief, shift, turn **2.** dispatch, message, transmission ~*v.* **3.** broadcast, carry, hand on, pass on, send, spread, transmit

release *v.* **1.** deliver, discharge, drop, extricate, free, liberate, loose, set free, unchain, undo, unfasten, unfetter, unloose, untie **2.** absolve, excuse, exempt, exonerate **3.** circulate, distribute, issue, launch, present, publish, put out, unveil ~*n.* **4.** acquittal, delivery, discharge, freedom, liberty, relief

relent be merciful, capitulate, forbear, melt, soften, unbend, yield

relentless cruel, fierce, grim, hard, harsh, pitiless, remorseless

relevant admissible, apposite, appropriate, apt, fitting, material, pertinent, proper, related, significant, suited

reliable dependable, faithful, honest, predictable, regular, responsible, safe, sound, stable, sure, true

relic fragment, keepsake, memento, remnant, scrap, token, trace, vestige

relief 1. balm, comfort, cure, deliverance, ease, mitigation, release, remedy, solace **2.** aid, assistance, help, succour, support **3.** break, diversion, remission, respite, rest

relieve 1. alleviate, appease, assuage, calm, comfort, console, cure, dull, ease, mitigate, mollify, relax, soften, solace, soothe **2.** aid, assist, help, succour, support, sustain **3.** stand in for, substitute for

religious devotional, devout, faithful, godly, holy, pious, pure, reverent, righteous, sacred, spiritual

relish *v.* **1.** delight in, enjoy, fancy, like, prefer, savour, taste ~*n.* **2.** appreciation, enjoyment, fancy, fondness, gusto, liking, love, partiality, penchant, stomach, taste, zest **3.** condiment, sauce, seasoning **4.** flavour, savour, smack, spice, tang, taste, trace

reluctance aversion, dislike, distaste, hesitancy, loathing, repugnance

reluctant disinclined, grudging, hesitant, loath, slow, unwilling

rely bank, bet, count, depend, lean, reckon, trust

remain abide, cling, continue, delay, dwell, endure, last, linger, persist, prevail, rest, stand, stay, survive, tarry, wait

remainder balance, excess, leavings, residue, residuum, rest, surplus, trace

remaining left, lingering, outstanding, persisting, surviving, unfinished

remains balance, crumbs, debris, dregs, fragments, leavings, leftovers, oddments, pieces, relics, remnants, residue, rest, scraps, traces, vestiges

remark *v.* **1.** comment, declare, mention, observe, pass comment, reflect, say, state **2.** espy, heed, mark, note, notice, observe, perceive, regard, see ~*n.* **3.** comment, declaration, reflection, statement, thought, utterance, word

remarkable distinguished, extraordinary, famous, impressive, notable, outstanding, phenomenal, pre-eminent, rare, signal, singular, strange, striking, surprising, uncommon, unusual, wonderful

remedy 1. *n.* cure, medicine, nostrum, panacea, relief, treatment **2.** *v.* alleviate, assuage, control, cure, ease, heal, help, relieve, restore, soothe, treat

remember call up, commemorate, recall, recognize, recollect, reminisce, retain

remind call up, prompt

reminiscence anecdote, memoir, recall, review

reminiscent remindful, similar, suggestive

remiss careless, dilatory, forgetful, heedless, inattentive, lax, negligent, slack, tardy, thoughtless, unmindful

remission 1. absolution, amnesty, discharge, excuse, exemption, exoneration, forgiveness, pardon, release, reprieve **2.** alleviation, lull, moderation, reduction, relaxation, respite, suspension

remit *v.* **1.** dispatch, forward, mail, post, send, transmit **2.** cancel, desist, forbear, halt, repeal, rescind, stop ~*n.* **3.** brief, guidelines, instructions, orders

remittance allowance, fee, payment

remnant balance, bit, end, fragment, leftovers, piece, remainder, remains, residue, rest, scrap, shred, vestige

remorse anguish, compassion, compunction, contrition, grief, guilt, pity, regret, shame

remorseless 1. inexorable, relentless **2.** callous, cruel, hard, harsh, inhumane, merciless, pitiless

remote 1. distant, far, inaccessible, isolated, secluded **2.** alien, foreign, irrelevant, outside, removed **3.** abstracted, aloof, cold, detached, distant, removed, reserved, standoffish, withdrawn

removal 1. dislodgment, dismissal, dispossession, ejection, elimination, eradication, expulsion, extraction, stripping, subtraction, taking off, uprooting, withdrawal **2.** departure, move, relocation, transfer

remove 1. abolish, delete, depose, detach, discharge, dismiss, displace, doff, efface, eject, eliminate, erase, expel, extract, move, oust, purge, relegate, shed, transfer, transport, unseat, withdraw **2.** depart, move away, quit, relocate, shift, transfer, vacate

remuneration earnings, emolument, fee, income, payment, profit, reparation, retainer, return, reward, salary, stipend, wages

remunerative lucrative, paying, profitable, rich, worthwhile

renaissance, renascence reappearance, reawakening, rebirth, renewal, restoration, revival

render 1. deliver, furnish, give, pay, present, provide, show, submit, supply, tender, turn over, yield **2.** display, evince, exhibit, manifest, show **3.** exchange, give, return, swap, trade **4.** leave, make **5.** act, depict, do, give, interpret, perform, play, portray, present, represent **6.** construe, explain, interpret, put, reproduce, restate, transcribe, translate **7.** repay, restore, return

renew continue, extend, mend, modernize, overhaul, reaffirm, recreate, refit, refurbish, rejuvenate, renovate, reopen, repair, repeat, replace, restock, restore, resume, transform

renounce abjure, abstain from, cast off, decline, deny, discard, disown, forgo, forsake, forswear, quit, recant, reject, relinquish, repudiate, resign, spurn, waive

renovate modernize, overhaul, recondition, refit, reform, renew, repair, restore

renowned celebrated, distinguished, eminent, esteemed, famous, notable, noted, well-known

rent[1] **1.** *n.* fee, hire, lease, payment, rental, tariff **2.** *v.* charter, hire, lease, let

rent[2] gash, hole, opening, rip, slash, slit, split, tear

repair 1. *v.* fix, heal, mend, patch, patch up, recover, rectify, redress, renew, renovate, restore **2.** *n.* darn, mend, overhaul, patch

reparation atonement, damages, redress, repair, restitution, satisfaction

repartee badinage, banter, sally, wit, wordplay

repay 1. compensate, refund, reimburse, requite, restore, square **2.** avenge, reciprocate, retaliate, revenge

repeal 1. *v.* abolish, annul, cancel, invalidate, nullify, recall, reverse, revoke, withdraw **2.** *n.* annulment, invalidation, rescindment, withdrawal

repeat 1. *v.* echo, iterate, quote, recite, rehearse, reiterate, relate, renew, replay, reproduce, restate, retell **2.** *n.* duplicate, echo, reiteration, repetition, replay, reproduction, reshowing

repeatedly frequently, many times, often

repel 1. check, confront, decline, fight, oppose, parry, rebuff, refuse, reject, repulse, resist **2.** disgust, nauseate, offend, revolt, sicken

repent atone, deplore, regret, relent, rue, sorrow

repentant ashamed, chastened, contrite, rueful, sorry

repercussion backlash, consequence, echo, rebound, recoil, result

repetition echo, recital, recurrence, rehearsal, reiteration, relation, renewal, repeat, replication, restatement, return, tautology

replace follow, oust, re-establish, reinstate, restore, substitute, succeed, supersede, supplant, supply

replacement double, proxy, substitute, successor, surrogate, understudy

replenish fill, furnish, provide, refill, reload, replace, restore, supply, top up

replica carbon copy, copy, duplicate, facsimile, imitation, model, reproduction

reply 1. *v.* answer, counter, echo, react, reciprocate, rejoin, respond, retaliate, retort, return **2.** *n.* answer, counter, echo, reaction, rejoinder, response, retort, return

report *n.* **1.** account, announcement, article, declaration, description, detail, dispatch, message, news, note, paper, piece, statement, story, tale, tidings, word, write-up **2.** gossip, hearsay, rumour, talk **3.** bang, blast, boom, crack, crash, detonation, discharge, explosion, noise, sound ~*v.* **4.** air, broadcast, circulate, cover, declare, describe, detail, document, inform of, mention, narrate, note, pass on, proclaim, publish, recite, record, recount, relate, relay, state, tell **5.** appear, arrive, come, turn up

reporter correspondent, journalist, newspaperman, pressman, writer

repose 1. ease, peace, quietness, relaxation, respite, rest, sleep, slumber, stillness, tranquillity **2.** calmness, composure, dignity, poise, serenity, tranquillity

reprehensible bad, culpable, delinquent, disgraceful, errant, ignoble, remiss, shameful, unworthy

represent 1. act for, be, betoken, express, mean, serve as, speak for, stand for, symbolize **2.** embody, epitomize, exemplify, personify, symbolize, typify **3.** denote, depict, describe, evoke, outline, picture, portray, render, reproduce, show, sketch **4.** act, enact, exhibit, perform, produce, put on, show, stage

representation 1. account, description, illustration, image, likeness, model, picture, portrait, portrayal, relation, sketch **2.** *Often plural* argument, exposition, remonstrance, statement

representative *n.* **1.** agent, rep, salesman, traveller **2.** embodiment, exemplar, type **3.** agent, councillor, delegate, deputy, member, proxy ~*adj.* **4.** archetypal, characteristic, illus-

trative, symbolic, typical 5. chosen, delegated, elected, elective
repress chasten, check, control, crush, curb, inhibit, master, muffle, overcome, overpower, quash, quell, restrain, silence, smother, stifle, subdue, suppress, swallow
repression constraint, control, despotism, domination, restraint, subjugation, suppression, tyranny
reprieve 1. *v.* abate, allay, alleviate, mitigate, palliate, relieve, respite 2. *n.* amnesty, deferment, pardon, postponement, remission, suspension
reprimand 1. *n.* blame, censure, rebuke, reprehension, reproach, reproof, row 2. *v.* blame, censure, check, chide, rebuke, reproach, scold, upbraid
reproach 1. *v.* blame, censure, chide, condemn, criticize, discredit, find fault with, rebuke reprimand, reprove, scold, upbraid 2. *n.* abuse, blemish, censure, contempt, disgrace, disrepute, scorn, shame, slight, slur, stain, stigma
reproduce 1. copy, echo, imitate, match, mirror, print, recreate, repeat 2. breed, multiply, proliferate, propagate, spawn
reproduction 1. generation, increase, multiplication 2. copy, duplicate, facsimile, imitation, picture, print, replica
reproof blame, censure, condemnation, criticism, rebuke, reprimand, scolding
repudiate deny, desert, discard, disclaim, disown, forsake, reject, renounce, rescind
repulsive abominable, disagreeable, distasteful, foul, hateful, hideous, objectionable, odious, revolting, sickening, ugly, vile
reputable creditable, excellent, good, honourable, legitimate, reliable, respectable, trustworthy, upright, worthy
reputation credit, esteem, fame, honour, name, opinion, stature
reputed alleged, believed, considered, deemed, estimated, held, reckoned, regarded, said, supposed
reputedly allegedly, apparently, ostensibly, seemingly, supposedly
request 1. *v.* ask (for), beg, beseech, demand, desire, entreat, petition, pray, seek, solicit 2. *n.* appeal, asking, begging, call, demand, desire, petition, prayer, suit
require 1. crave, desire, lack, miss, need, want, wish 2. ask, beg, bid, command, compel, constrain, demand, direct, enjoin, exact, insist upon, oblige, order
requirement demand, essential, lack, must, need, precondition, stipulation, want
requisite called for, essential, indispensable, necessary, needed, needful, obligatory, vital
requisition *n.* 1. call, demand, request, summons 2. commandeering, occupation, seizure, takeover ~*v.* 3. demand, request 4. appropriate, commandeer, occupy, seize
rescue 1. *v.* deliver, free, get out, liberate, recover, redeem, release, salvage, save 2. *n.* deliverance, liberation, recovery, release, relief, salvage, saving
research 1. *n.* examination, exploration, probe, study 2. *v.* analyse, examine, experiment, explore, investigate, probe, scrutinize, study
resemblance comparison, correspondence, facsimile, image, kinship, likeness, semblance
resemble duplicate, echo, look like, remind one of, take after
resent begrudge, dislike, grudge, take exception to
resentful angry, bitter, incensed, indignant, irate, jealous, piqued
resentment anger, bitterness, displeasure, fury, grudge, hurt, ire, malice, pique, rage, umbrage, wrath
reservation 1. condition, doubt, scepticism, scruple, stipulation 2. enclave, homeland, preserve, sanctuary, territory, tract
reserve *v.* 1. hoard, hold, husband, keep, preserve, put by, retain, save, stockpile, store, withhold 2. book, engage, prearrange, retain, secure 3. defer, delay, keep back, postpone, put off, withhold ~*n.* 4. backlog, cache, capital, fund, hoard, reservoir, savings, stock, store, supply 5. park, preserve, reservation, sanctuary, tract 6. coolness, formality, restraint, reticence, shyness, silence ~*adj.* 7. auxiliary, extra, spare, substitute
reserved 1. booked, engaged, held, kept, retained, taken 2. cautious, cold, cool, demure, modest, restrained, reticent, secretive, shy, silent
reservoir basin, lake, pond, tank
reside abide, dwell, inhabit, live, lodge, remain, settle, sojourn, stay
residence 1. domicile, dwelling, habitation, home, house, lodging, place, quarters 2. hall, manor, mansion, palace, seat, villa
resident citizen, inhabitant, local, lodger, occupant, tenant
resign abandon, abdicate, cede, forgo, forsake, hand over, leave, quit, relinquish, renounce, surrender, turn over, vacate, yield
resignation 1. abdication, departure, notice, retirement, surrender 2. acquiescence, compliance, endurance, fortitude, passivity, patience, submission, sufferance
resigned compliant, long-suffering, patient, stoical, subdued
resist battle, check, combat, confront, curb, defy, dispute, hinder, oppose, refuse, repel, thwart, weather, withstand
resistance battle, contention, defiance, fight, hindrance, impediment, obstruction, opposition, refusal, struggle
resolute bold, constant, determined, dogged, firm, fixed, obstinate, relentless, set, staunch, steadfast, stubborn, unbending, undaunted, unflinching, unshakable
resolution 1. boldness, courage, dedication, determination, doggedness, earnestness, firmness, fortitude, purpose, resolve, sincerity, steadfastness, tenacity, willpower 2. aim, decision, declaration, intent, intention, judgment, motion, purpose, resolve, verdict
resolve *v.* 1. agree, conclude, decide, determine, fix, intend, purpose, settle, undertake 2. answer, fathom, work out 3. analyse, break down, clear, disintegrate ~*n.* 4. decision, design, project, purpose, resolution 5. boldness, courage, firmness
resort *v.* 1. employ, exercise, look to, turn to, use, utilize 2. frequent, go, haunt, head for, repair, visit ~*n.* 3. haunt, refuge, retreat, spot, tourist centre
resound echo, re-echo, resonate, reverberate, ring
resource 1. ability, capability, cleverness, ingenuity, initiative, talent 2. hoard, reserve, source, stockpile, supply 3. course, device, expedient, means, resort
resourceful able, bright, capable, clever, creative, ingenious, inventive, quick-witted, sharp, talented
resources assets, capital, funds, holdings, money, property, reserves, riches, supplies, wealth
respect *n.* 1. admiration, consideration, deference, esteem, honour, recognition, regard, veneration 2. aspect, detail, feature, matter, particular, point, sense, way 3. bearing, connection, reference, regard, relation ~*v.* 4. admire, adore, appreciate, defer to, esteem, honour, look up to, recognize, regard, value, venerate 5. abide by, adhere to, attend, follow, heed, honour, notice, obey, observe, regard
respectable 1. decent, decorous, dignified, estimable, good, honest, proper, upright, venerable, worthy 2. ample, appreciable, decent, fair, goodly, presentable, reasonable, sizable, substantial, tolerable
respective individual, own, particular, personal, relevant, several, specific
respite break, cessation, halt, interval, lull, pause, recess, relaxation, relief, rest
respond answer, counter, react, reciprocate, rejoin, reply, retort, return
response answer, feedback, reaction, rejoinder, reply, retort, return, riposte
responsibility 1. accountability, answerability, care, charge, duty, liability, obligation, onus, trust 2. authority, importance, power 3. blame, burden, fault, guilt
responsible 1. in charge, in control 2. accountable, answerable, bound, chargeable, duty-bound, liable, subject 3. executive, high, important 4. at fault, culpable, guilty, to blame
rest[1] *n.* 1. calm, doze, leisure, nap, relaxation, relief, repose, siesta, sleep, slumber, stillness, tranquillity 2. break, cessation, halt, holiday, interlude, intermission, interval, lull, pause, stop, time off, vacation 3. base, holder, prop, shelf, stand, support, trestle ~*v.* 4. doze, nap, relax, sit down, sleep, slumber 5. lay, lean, lie, prop, recline, repose, sit, stand
rest[2] balance, excess, others, remainder, remnants, residue, rump, surplus
restful calm, calming, pacific, peaceful, placid, quiet, relaxed, serene, sleepy, tranquil
restive agitated, edgy, fidgety, fretful, impatient, jumpy, nervous, uneasy, unquiet, unruly
restless 1. active, bustling, hurried, irresolute, nomadic, roving, transient, turbulent, unsettled, unstable, unsteady, wandering 2. agitated, disturbed, edgy, fidgety, fitful, fretful, jumpy, nervous, restive, sleepless, troubled, uneasy, unquiet
restoration 1. recovery, refreshment, rehabilitation, renewal, renovation, repair, revival 2. recovery, replacement, restitution, return
restore 1. fix, mend, recover, refurbish, renew, renovate, repair, retouch, touch up 2. build up, refresh, revitalize, revive, strengthen 3. give back, hand back, recover, reinstate, replace, return, send back
restrain bridle, check, confine, contain, control, curb, curtail, debar, govern, hamper, hinder, hold, hold back, inhibit, keep, limit, prevent, repress, restrict, subdue, suppress
restrained 1. calm, controlled, mild, moderate, muted, reticent, soft, steady 2. discreet, quiet, subdued, tasteful, unobtrusive
restraint 1. compulsion, constraint, control, curtailment, grip, hindrance, hold, inhibition, moderation, self-control, self-discipline, suppression 2. arrest, captivity, chains, confinement, detention, imprisonment 3. ban, bridle, check, curb, embargo, interdict, limit, limitation, rein
restrict bound, confine, contain, hamper, handicap, hem in, impede, inhibit, limit, regulate, restrain
restriction check, condition, containment, control, handicap, inhibition, limitation, regulation, restraint, rule
result 1. *n.* consequence, decision, development, effect, end, event, fruit, issue, outcome, product, reaction, sequel, upshot 2. *v.* appear, arise, derive, develop, emanate, ensue, flow, follow, happen, issue, spring, stem, turn out
resume begin again, carry on, continue, go on, proceed, reopen, restart
resumption continuation, re-establishment, renewal, reopening, restart, resurgence
resurrect bring back, reintroduce, renew, revive
resurrection reappearance, rebirth, renaissance, renewal, restoration, resurgence, resuscitation, return, revival
resuscitate renew, rescue, restore, resurrect, revive, save
retain 1. absorb, contain, grasp, grip, hold, hold back, keep, maintain, preserve, reserve, restrain, save 2. memorize, recall, recollect, remember 3. employ, engage, hire, pay, reserve
retainer 1. attendant, domestic, flunky, footman, lackey, servant, supporter, valet, vassal 2. advance, deposit, fee
retaliate give tit for tat, make

reprisal, reciprocate, strike back, take revenge
retaliation counterblow, reciprocation, repayment, reprisal, retribution, revenge, vengeance
reticence reserve, restraint, silence
reticent mum, quiet, reserved, secretive, silent
retire 1. give up work, stop working 2. depart, exit, go away, leave, remove, withdraw 3. go to bed, go to sleep
retirement obscurity, privacy, retreat, seclusion, solitude, withdrawal
retiring coy, demure, diffident, humble, meek, modest, quiet, reserved, reticent, shy, timid, timorous, unassertive, unassuming
retract 1. pull back, sheathe 2. cancel, deny, disavow, disclaim, disown, recall, recant, repeal, repudiate, reverse, revoke, take back, unsay, withdraw
retreat *v.* 1. depart, draw back, ebb, fall back, go back, leave, pull back, recede, recoil, retire, shrink, turn tail, withdraw ~*n.* 2. ebb, flight, retirement, withdrawal 3. den, haunt, haven, refuge, resort, retirement, sanctuary, seclusion
retribution compensation, justice, reckoning, redress, repayment, reprisal, requital, retaliation, revenge, reward, satisfaction, vengeance
retrieve recall, recapture, recoup, recover, redeem, regain, repair, rescue, restore, salvage, save, win back
retrospect hindsight, review, survey
return *v.* 1. come back, go back, reappear, rebound, recur, repair, retreat, revert, turn back 2. convey, give back, put back, re-establish, reinstate, remit, render, replace, restore, send, take back, transmit 3. give back, pay back, refund, reimburse, repay, requite 4. bring in, earn, make, net, repay, yield 5. choose, elect, pick, vote in ~*n.* 6. homecoming, rebound, recoil, recurrence, retreat, reversion 7. reinstatement, replacement, restoration 8. advantage, benefit, gain, income, interest, proceeds, profit, revenue, takings, yield 9. recompense, reimbursement, reparation, repayment, requital, retaliation, reward 10. account, form, list, report, statement, summary 11. answer, rejoinder, reply, response, retort
reveal 1. betray, broadcast, disclose, divulge, give away, give out, impart, leak, let on, let out, let slip, proclaim, publish, tell 2. bare, display, exhibit, manifest, open, show, uncover, unearth, unmask, unveil
revel *v.* 1. *With* **in** delight, gloat, indulge, joy, lap up, luxuriate, rejoice, relish, savour, wallow 2. carouse, celebrate ~*n.* 3. *Often plural* carousal, celebration, debauch, festivity, gala, jollification, party, spree
revelation disclosure, discovery, display, exhibition, exposition, giveaway, leak, news, publication, telling
reveller carouser, partygoer
revelry celebration, debauch, festivity, fun, jollification, party, spree
revenge 1. *n.* reprisal, retaliation, retribution, satisfaction 2. *v.* avenge, repay, requite, retaliate
revenue gain, income, proceeds, profits, receipts, returns, rewards, yield
reverberate echo, rebound, recoil, re-echo, resound, ring, vibrate
revere adore, defer to, exalt, honour, respect, reverence, venerate, worship
reverence admiration, adoration, awe, deference, devotion, homage, honour, respect, worship
reverent adoring, awed, deferential, devout, humble, loving, meek, pious, respectful, solemn
reverse *v.* 1. invert, transpose, turn back, turn over, turn round, turn upside down, upend 2. alter, annul, cancel, change, countermand, invalidate, overrule, overturn, quash, repeal, rescind, retract, revoke, undo, upset 3. back, go backwards, move backwards, retreat ~*n.* 4. contrary, converse, inverse, opposite 5. adversity, affliction, blow, check, defeat, failure, hardship, mishap, repulse, reversal, setback, trial ~*adj.* 6. backward, contrary, inverted, opposite
review *v.* 1. reassess, reconsider, re-examine, rethink, revise, think over 2. recall, recollect, remember, summon up 3. assess, criticize, examine, inspect, judge, study, weigh ~*n.* 4. examination, report, scrutiny, study, survey 5. commentary, criticism, critique, evaluation, judgment, notice, study 6. journal, magazine, periodical 7. fresh look, reassessment, reconsideration, re-examination, rethink, revision 8. *Military* display, inspection, march past, parade, procession
reviewer commentator, critic, essayist, judge
revise alter, amend, change, correct, edit, emend, review, rework, rewrite, update
revision 1. amendment, change, correction, emendation, modification, review, rewriting 2. homework, rereading, studying
revival reawakening, rebirth, recrudescence, renaissance, renewal, restoration, resurgence, resuscitation
revive awaken, bring round, cheer, comfort, invigorate, quicken, rally, reanimate, recover, refresh, rekindle, renew, renovate, restore, resuscitate, rouse
revoke abrogate, annul, call back, cancel, countermand, disclaim, invalidate, negate, nullify, quash, recall, recant, renounce, repeal, repudiate, rescind, retract, reverse, withdraw
revolt *n.* 1. insurgency, insurrection, rebellion, revolution, rising, uprising ~*v.* 2. defect, mutiny, rebel, resist, rise 3. disgust, nauseate, offend, repel, sicken
revolting abhorrent, disgusting, foul, horrible, nasty, nauseating, obnoxious, obscene, offensive, repugnant, repulsive, shocking, sickening
revolution 1. coup, insurgency, mutiny, rebellion, revolt, rising, uprising 2. innovation, reformation, shift, transformation, upheaval 3. circle, circuit, cycle, gyration, lap, orbit, rotation, round, spin, turn, wheel, whirl
revolutionary *n.* 1. insurgent, mutineer, rebel, revolutionist ~*adj.* 2. extremist, insurgent, radical, rebel, subversive 3. different, drastic, experimental, fundamental, innovative, new, novel, progressive, radical
revolve circle, gyrate, orbit, rotate, spin, turn, twist, wheel, whirl
revulsion abhorrence, abomination, aversion, disgust, distaste, loathing, repugnance
reward *n.* 1. benefit, bonus, bounty, gain, honour, merit, payment, premium, prize, profit, return, wages 2. desert, punishment, retribution ~*v.* 3. honour, pay, recompense, repay
rewarding edifying, enriching, fulfilling, gainful, gratifying, pleasing, productive, profitable, satisfying, valuable
rhetoric 1. eloquence, oratory 2. bombast, hyperbole, rant, verbosity, wordiness
rhetorical bombastic, flamboyant, flashy, florid, pretentious, showy, verbose
rhyme 1. *n.* ode, poem, poetry, song, verse 2. *v.* harmonize, sound like
rhythm accent, beat, cadence, flow, lilt, metre, movement, pattern, pulse, swing, tempo, time
ribald bawdy, blue, broad, coarse, earthy, filthy, gross, indecent, licentious, naughty, obscene, racy, rude, scurrilous, vulgar
rich 1. affluent, moneyed, opulent, prosperous, wealthy, well-off 2. full, productive, well-stocked, well-supplied 3. abounding, abundant, ample, copious, exuberant, fertile, fruitful, full, lush, luxurious, plentiful, productive, prolific 4. costly, elaborate, elegant, expensive, exquisite, fine, gorgeous, lavish, palatial, precious, priceless, splendid, superb, valuable 5. creamy, delicious, juicy, luscious, savoury, spicy, succulent, sweet, tasty
riches affluence, assets, fortune, gold, money, plenty, property, resources, substance, treasure, wealth
rid 1. clear, deliver, disburden, disencumber, free, make free, purge, relieve, unburden 2. **get rid of** dump, eject, eliminate, expel, jettison, remove, unload
riddle brain-teaser (*Inf.*), conundrum, enigma, mystery, poser, problem, puzzle
ride *v.* 1. control, handle, manage, sit on 2. float, go, journey, move, progress, sit, travel ~*n.* 3. drive, jaunt, journey, lift, outing, trip
ridicule 1. *n.* banter, chaff, derision, gibe, irony, jeer, laughter, mockery, raillery, sarcasm, satire 2. *v.* banter, caricature, chaff, deride, humiliate, jeer, lampoon, mock, parody, pooh-pooh, satirize, scoff, sneer, taunt
ridiculous absurd, comical, derisory, farcical, foolish, funny, incredible, laughable, outrageous, risible, silly, stupid
rift 1. breach, break, chink, cleft, crack, crevice, fault, fissure, flaw, gap, space, split 2. breach, disagreement, division, quarrel, schism, separation, split
rig *v.* 1. equip, fit out, furnish, provision, supply, turn out 2. arrange, engineer, fake, falsify, gerrymander, juggle, manipulate ~*n.* 3. apparatus, equipment, fittings, fixtures, gear, machinery, outfit, tackle
right *adj.* 1. equitable, ethical, fair, good, honest, just, lawful, moral, proper, true, virtuous 2. accurate, admissible, authentic, correct, exact, factual, genuine, precise, sound, true, unerring, valid 3. appropriate, becoming, convenient, deserved, desirable, done, due, favourable, fit, ideal, proper, propitious, seemly, suitable 4. lucid, normal, rational, reasonable, sane, sound, well 5. conservative, reactionary 6. absolute, complete, real, thorough, utter ~*adv.* 7. accurately, correctly, exactly, factually, genuinely, precisely, truly 8. appropriately, aptly, fittingly, properly, satisfactorily, suitably 9. directly, promptly, quickly, straight 10. exactly, precisely, squarely 11. absolutely, completely, entirely, perfectly, quite, thoroughly, totally, utterly, wholly 12. ethically, fairly, honestly, justly, morally, properly 13. favourably, fortunately, well ~*n.* 14. business, claim, due, freedom, interest, liberty, licence, permission, power, prerogative, privilege, title 15. equity, good, goodness, honour, integrity, justice, lawfulness, legality, morality, propriety, reason, truth, virtue 16. **by rights** equitably, justly, properly ~*v.* 17. correct, fix, rectify, redress, repair, settle, sort out
rigid austere, exact, fixed, harsh, inflexible, rigorous, set, severe, stern, stiff, strict, unalterable, uncompromising
rigorous 1. challenging, demanding, exacting, firm, hard, harsh, inflexible, severe, stern, strict, tough 2. bad, bleak, extreme, harsh, inclement, severe
rigour austerity, hardship, inflexibility, ordeal, sternness, suffering, trial
rim border, brim, brink, edge, lip, margin, verge
ring[1] *n.* 1. band, circle, circuit, halo, hoop, loop, round 2. arena, circus, enclosure, rink 3. association, band, cartel, clique, combine, coterie, gang, group, mob, syndicate ~*v.* 4. encircle, enclose, gird, girdle, hem in, surround
ring[2] *v.* 1. chime, clang, peal, reverberate, sound, toll 2. call, phone, telephone ~*n.* 3. chime, knell, peal 4. call, phone call
riot *n.* 1. anarchy, confusion, disorder, fray, lawlessness, quarrel, row, strife, tumult, turbulence, turmoil, uproar 2. carousal, excess, festivity, frolic, revelry, romp 3. display, flourish, show, splash 4. **run riot** a. go wild, rampage b. grow profuse-

ly, luxuriate ~*v.* **5.** carouse, cut loose, frolic, revel, romp

riotous 1. disorderly, lawless, rampageous, rebellious, refractory, rowdy, unruly, violent **2.** loud, noisy, unrestrained, wild

ripe 1. mature, mellow, ready, seasoned **2.** favourable, ideal, opportune, right, suitable, timely

ripen burgeon, develop, mature, prepare, season

rise *v.* **1.** get up, stand up, surface **2.** ascend, climb, enlarge, go up, grow, improve, increase, intensify, lift, mount, soar, swell, wax **3.** advance, progress, prosper **4.** appear, crop up, emanate, emerge, eventuate, flow, happen, issue, occur, originate, spring **5.** mutiny, rebel, resist, revolt **6.** ascend, climb, get steeper, go uphill, mount, slope upwards ~*n.* **7.** advance, climb, improvement, increase, upsurge, upturn **8.** advancement, climb, progress, promotion **9.** ascent, incline, upward slope **10.** increment, pay increase

risk 1. *n.* chance, danger, gamble, hazard, jeopardy, peril, speculation, uncertainty, venture **2.** *v.* chance, dare, endanger, gamble, hazard, imperil, jeopardize, venture

rite act, ceremonial, custom, form, liturgy, mystery, observance, practice, procedure, sacrament, service, solemnity, usage

rival 1. *n.* adversary, challenger, competitor, contender, contestant, opponent **2.** *adj.* competing, conflicting, opposed **3.** *v.* come up to, compare with, compete, contend, equal, match, oppose, vie with

rivalry antagonism, competition, conflict, contention, contest, duel, opposition

road avenue, course, highway, lane, motorway, path, pathway, roadway, route, street, thoroughfare, track, way

roam prowl, ramble, range, rove, stray, stroll, travel, walk, wander

roar *v.* **1.** bawl, bay, bellow, clamour, crash, cry, howl, rumble, shout, yell **2.** guffaw, hoot ~*n.* **3.** bellow, clamour, crash, cry, howl, outcry, rumble, shout, thunder, yell

rob burgle, cheat, defraud, despoil, dispossess, gyp (*Sl.*), hold up, loot, pillage, plunder, raid, ransack, rifle, sack, strip, swindle

robber bandit, brigand, burglar, cheat, fraud, highwayman, pirate, plunderer, raider, stealer, thief

robbery burglary, fraud, holdup, larceny, pillage, plunder, raid, rapine, stealing, swindle, theft

robe 1. *n.* costume, gown, habit **2.** *v.* attire, clothe, drape, dress, garb

robust 1. athletic, brawny, fit, hale, hardy, healthy, hearty, lusty, muscular, powerful, rude, rugged, sinewy, sound, staunch, stout, strong, sturdy, tough, vigorous, well **2.** coarse, earthy, indecorous, raw, rough, rude, unsubtle

rock[1] **1.** boulder, stone **2.** anchor, bulwark, mainstay, protection, support

rock[2] **1.** lurch, pitch, reel, roll, sway, swing, toss **2.** astonish, astound, daze, jar, shake, shock, stagger, stun, surprise

rocky 1. craggy, rough, rugged, stony **2.** firm, flinty, hard, rugged, solid, steady, tough

rod bar, baton, birch, cane, mace, pole, sceptre, shaft, staff, stick, wand

rogue charlatan, cheat, fraud, rascal, reprobate, scamp, scoundrel, swindler, villain

role 1. character, part, portrayal, representation **2.** capacity, duty, function, job, part, position, post, task

roll *v.* **1.** elapse, flow, go round, gyrate, pass, pivot, reel, revolve, rock, rotate, run, spin, swivel, trundle, turn, twirl, wheel, whirl **2.** bind, coil, curl, enfold, entwine, envelop, furl, swathe, twist, wind, wrap **3.** flatten, level, press, smooth, spread **4.** boom, drum, echo, reverberate, roar, rumble, thunder **5.** billow, lurch, reel, rock, sway, swing, toss, tumble, wallow, welter **6.** lumber, lurch, reel, stagger, sway ~*n.* **7.** cycle, reel, revolution, rotation, run, spin, turn, twirl, wheel, whirl **8.** annals, catalogue, census, chronicle, directory, index, inventory, list, record, register, schedule, scroll, table **9.** boom, growl, grumble, resonance, reverberation, roar, rumble, thunder

romance 1. affair, amour, attachment, intrigue, liaison, passion, relationship **2.** charm, colour, excitement, fascination, glamour, mystery, sentiment **3.** fantasy, fiction, idyll, legend, melodrama, novel, story, tale

romantic *adj.* **1.** amorous, fond, loving, passionate, sentimental, tender **2.** colourful, exciting, exotic, fascinating, glamorous, mysterious, nostalgic, picturesque **3.** dreamy, high-flown, idealistic, quixotic, utopian, visionary, whimsical ~*n.* **4.** dreamer, idealist, sentimentalist, visionary

room 1. area, capacity, compass, expanse, extent, leeway, margin, play, range, scope, space, territory, volume **2.** apartment, chamber, office **3.** chance, occasion, scope

root *n.* **1.** rhizome, stem, tuber **2.** base, bottom, cause, core, crux, derivation, foundation, fundamental, germ, heart, nucleus, occasion, origin, seat, seed, source **3.** *Plural* birthplace, cradle, family, heritage, home, origins **4. root and branch** completely, entirely, finally, radically, thoroughly, totally, utterly, wholly ~*v.* **5.** anchor, embed, entrench, establish, fasten, fix, ground, implant, moor, set, stick

rope 1. *n.* cable, cord, hawser, line, strand **2.** *v.* bind, fasten, hitch, lash, lasso, moor, pinion, tether, tie

rope in engage, enlist, inveigle, involve, persuade

roster agenda, catalogue, list, register, roll, rota, scroll, table

rosy 1. pink, red **2.** blooming, blushing, fresh, glowing, reddish, roseate, rubicund, ruddy **3.** auspicious, bright, cheerful, encouraging, favourable, hopeful, optimistic, promising, sunny

rot *v.* **1.** corrupt, crumble, decay, decompose, deteriorate, go bad, moulder, perish, putrefy, spoil, taint **2.** decline, deteriorate, waste away ~*n.* **3.** blight, canker, corruption, decay, mould, putrefaction

rotate 1. go round, gyrate, pivot, reel, revolve, spin, swivel, turn, wheel **2.** alternate, interchange, switch

rotation 1. orbit, reel, revolution, spin, spinning, turn, turning, wheel **2.** cycle, sequence, succession, switching

rotten 1. bad, corrupt, crumbling, decayed, decomposed, festering, fetid, foul, mouldy, perished, putrid, rank, sour, stinking, tainted, unsound **2.** corrupt, deceitful, degenerate, dishonest, disloyal, faithless, immoral, perfidious, treacherous, venal, vicious **3.** bad, deplorable, disappointing, regrettable, unfortunate, unlucky

rotter bad lot, blackguard, swine

rotund 1. globular, round, spherical **2.** chubby, corpulent, fat, heavy, plump, podgy, portly, stout, tubby

rough *adj.* **1.** broken, bumpy, craggy, irregular, jagged, rocky, stony, uneven **2.** bristly, bushy, coarse, disordered, tangled, uncut, unshorn **3.** boisterous, choppy, squally, stormy, turbulent, wild **4.** bearish, bluff, blunt, brusque, churlish, coarse, curt, discourteous, ill-bred, ill-mannered, impolite, loutish, rude, uncivil, uncouth, uncultured, unmannerly, unrefined **5.** cruel, curt, drastic, extreme, hard, harsh, nasty, rowdy, severe, sharp, tough, unjust, unpleasant, violent **6.** grating, gruff, harsh, husky, jarring, rasping, raucous **7.** arduous, hard, rugged, spartan, tough, unpleasant, unrefined **8.** basic, crude, cursory, hasty, imperfect, incomplete, quick, raw, rudimentary, shapeless, sketchy, unpolished **9.** estimated, foggy, general, hazy, imprecise, inexact, sketchy, vague ~*n.* **10.** bully boy, ruffian, thug, tough

round *adj.* **1.** circular, curved, cylindrical, disc-shaped, globular, rotund, rounded, spherical **2.** ample, fleshy, full, full-fleshed, plump, rotund **3.** full, mellifluous, orotund, resonant, rich, rotund ~*n.* **4.** ball, band, circle, disc, globe, orb, ring, sphere **5.** bout, cycle, sequence, series, session, succession **6.** division, lap, level, period, session, stage, turn **7.** ambit, beat, circuit, compass, course, routine, schedule, series, tour, turn **8.** bullet, discharge, shell, shot ~*v.* **9.** bypass, circle, encircle, flank, go round, skirt, turn

roundabout *adj.* circuitous, devious, discursive, evasive, indirect, oblique, tortuous

round off cap, close, complete, conclude, crown, finish off, settle

round up collect, drive, gather, group, herd, marshal, muster, rally

rouse 1. awaken, call, rise, wake, wake up **2.** agitate, anger, animate, disturb, excite, incite, inflame, instigate, move, provoke, startle, stimulate, stir, whip up

rout 1. *n.* beating, debacle, defeat, drubbing, headlong flight, overthrow, ruin, shambles, thrashing **2.** *v.* beat, chase, conquer, crush, defeat, destroy, dispel, overpower, overthrow, scatter, thrash

route beat, circuit, course, direction, itinerary, journey, passage, path, road, round, run, way

routine *n.* **1.** custom, formula, groove, method, order, pattern, practice, programme, usage, way ~*adj.* **2.** customary, everyday, familiar, habitual, normal, ordinary, standard, typical, usual, workaday **3.** boring, dull, humdrum, predictable, tedious, tiresome

row[1] bank, column, file, line, queue, range, rank, sequence, series, string, tier

row[2] **1.** *n.* brawl, dispute, disturbance, fray, fuss, noise, quarrel, racket, rumpus, squabble, tiff, trouble, tumult, uproar **2.** *v.* argue, brawl, dispute, fight, wrangle

rowdy disorderly, loud, noisy, rough, unruly, uproarious, wild

royal 1. imperial, kingly, princely, queenly, regal, sovereign **2.** august, grand, impressive, majestic, splendid, stately, superb, superior

rub *v.* **1.** caress, chafe, clean, fray, grate, massage, polish, scour, scrape, shine, smooth, stroke, wipe **2.** apply, put, smear, spread ~*n.* **3.** caress, massage, polish, shine, stroke, wipe

rubbish 1. debris, dregs, dross, garbage, junk, litter, lumber, offal, refuse, scrap, trash, waste **2.** bunkum, drivel, gibberish, nonsense, piffle (*Inf.*), rot, tommyrot, twaddle

rub out cancel, delete, efface, erase, expunge, obliterate, remove, wipe out

rude 1. abrupt, abusive, blunt, brusque, cheeky, churlish, curt, discourteous, ill-mannered, impertinent, impolite, impudent, insolent, insulting, offhand, short, unmannerly **2.** boorish, brutish, coarse, crude, graceless, gross, illiterate, loutish, low, oafish, obscene, rough, savage, uncivilised, uncouth, uncultured, vulgar **3.** artless, crude, inartistic, inelegant, makeshift, primitive, raw, rough, simple **4.** abrupt, harsh, sharp, startling, sudden, unpleasant, violent

rudimentary basic, early, fundamental, immature, initial, primitive, vestigial

rudiments basics, beginnings, elements, essentials, first principles, foundation, fundamentals

ruffian brute, bully, hooligan, miscreant, rascal, rogue, rowdy, scoundrel, thug, tough, villain, wretch

ruffle 1. derange, disarrange, discompose, disorder, rumple, tousle, wrinkle **2.** agitate, annoy, confuse, disquiet, disturb, fluster, harass, irritate, nettle, perturb, put out, stir, torment, trouble, unsettle, upset, vex, worry

rugged 1. broken, bumpy, craggy, difficult, jagged, ragged, rocky, rough, stark, uneven **2.** furrowed, lined, rough-hewn, weathered, worn, wrinkled

ruin **1.** *n.* bankruptcy, breakdown, collapse, crash, damage, decay, defeat, destruction, devastation, disrepair, dissolution, downfall, failure, fall, havoc, overthrow, wreckage **2.** *v.* bankrupt, break, bring down, crush, defeat, demolish, destroy, devastate, impoverish, lay waste, overthrow, overturn, overwhelm, pauperize, raze, shatter, smash, wreck

rule *n.* **1.** axiom, canon, decree, direction, guideline, law, maxim, order, ordinance, precept, principle, regulation, standard **2.** ascendancy, authority, command, control, direction, domination, empire, government, influence, leadership, mastery, power, regime, reign, supremacy, sway **3.** condition, convention, custom, form, habit, practice, procedure, routine, wont **4.** course, formula, method, policy, procedure, way ~*v.* **5.** administer, command, control, direct, dominate, govern, guide, hold sway, lead, manage, preside over, regulate, reign **6.** decide, decree, determine, establish, find, judge, lay down, pronounce, resolve, settle

ruler **1.** commander, controller, emperor, empress, governor, king, leader, lord, monarch, potentate, prince, princess, queen, sovereign **2.** measure, rule, straight edge, yardstick

ruling *n.* **1.** adjudication, decision, decree, finding, judgment, pronouncement, resolution, verdict ~*adj.* **2.** commanding, controlling, dominant, governing, leading, reigning, upper **3.** chief, current, dominant, main, predominant, pre-eminent, prevailing, principal, regnant, supreme

rumour buzz, canard, gossip, hearsay, news, report, story, talk, tidings, whisper, word

run *v.* **1.** bolt, career, dart, dash, gallop, hare (*Brit. inf.*), hasten, hie, hotfoot, hurry, jog, race, rush, scamper, scramble, scud, scurry, speed, sprint **2.** abscond, bolt, decamp, depart, escape, flee **3.** go, operate, ply **4.** function, go, operate, perform, tick, work **5.** administer, carry on, conduct, control, coordinate, direct, head, lead, manage, operate, oversee, own, regulate, supervise **6.** continue, extend, go, last, lie, proceed, range, reach, stretch **7.** discharge, flow, go, gush, leak, spill, spout, stream **8.** dissolve, fuse, go soft, liquefy, melt **9.** ladder, tear, unravel **10.** be current, circulate, climb, creep, go round, spread, trail **11.** display, feature, print, publish **12.** challenge, compete, contend, stand, take part **13.** bootleg, ship, smuggle, sneak, traffic ~*n.* **14.** dash, gallop, jog, race, rush, sprint, spurt **15.** drive, excursion, jaunt, journey, lift, outing, ride, round **16.** course, cycle, passage, period, round, season, sequence, series, spell, stretch, string **17.** ladder, rip, snag, tear **18.** coop, enclosure, pen **19. in the long run** eventually, ultimately **20. on the run a.** at liberty, escaping, fugitive, in flight, on the loose **b.** defeated, fleeing, in flight, in retreat, retreating

run across encounter, meet, run into

runaway *n.* **1.** deserter, escapee, fugitive, refugee, truant ~*adj.* **2.** fleeing, fugitive, loose, wild **3.** easily won, easy, effortless

run away abscond, bolt, clear out, decamp, escape, flee, take flight, take off

run-down **1.** below par, debilitated, drained, enervated, exhausted, unhealthy, weak, weary, worn-out **2.** broken-down, decrepit, dilapidated, dingy, ramshackle, seedy, shabby, worn-out

run down **1.** curtail, cut, cut back, decrease, drop, reduce, trim **2.** exhaust, tire, weaken **3.** belittle, criticize adversely, decry, defame, disparage, revile **4.** hit, knock down, run over, strike

run into **1.** collide with, hit, ram, strike **2.** be beset by, bump into, chance upon, come across, come upon, encounter, meet

running *adj.* **1.** constant, continuous, incessant, perpetual, together, unbroken, uninterrupted **2.** flowing, moving, streaming ~*n.* **3.** charge, conduct, control, direction, leadership, management, organization, regulation, supervision **4.** operation, performance, working **5.** competition, contention, contest

run-of-the-mill average, common, fair, mediocre, middling, ordinary, passable, tolerable, undistinguished

run out cease, close, dry up, end, expire, fail, finish, terminate

run over **1.** hit, knock over, run down, strike **2.** brim over, overflow, spill **3.** check, rehearse, reiterate, review, survey

rupture *n.* **1.** breach, break, burst, cleavage, cleft, crack, rent, split, tear **2.** break, contention, disruption, feud, hostility, quarrel, rift, schism, split ~*v.* **3.** break, burst, cleave, crack, fracture, rend, separate, sever, split, tear **4.** break off, disrupt, divide, split

rural agricultural, country, pastoral, rustic, sylvan

ruse artifice, blind, device, dodge, hoax, imposture, ploy, sham, stratagem, subterfuge, trick, wile

rush **1.** *v.* bolt, career, dart, dash, fly, hasten, hurry, press, push, quicken, race, run, scramble, scurry, shoot, speed, sprint, tear **2.** *n.* charge, dash, expedition, haste, hurry, race, scramble, speed, surge, swiftness, urgency

rust *n.* **1.** corrosion, oxidation **2.** blight, mildew, mould, must, rot ~*v.* **3.** corrode, oxidize

rustic *adj.* **1.** country, pastoral, rural, sylvan **2.** artless, homespun, plain, simple, unaffected, unpolished, unrefined **3.** awkward, boorish, churlish, clownish, coarse, crude, loutish, rough, uncouth ~*n.* **4.** boor, bumpkin, clod, countryman, peasant, yokel

rustle **1.** *v.* crackle, whisper **2.** *n.* crackle, rustling, whisper

rut **1.** furrow, gouge, groove, indentation, score, track, wheelmark **2.** dead end, groove, habit, pattern, routine, system

ruthless brutal, callous, cruel, ferocious, fierce, hard, harsh, heartless, inexorable, inhuman, merciless, pitiless, relentless, savage, severe, stern, unmerciful

S

sabotage **1.** *v.* damage, destroy, disable, disrupt, subvert, undermine, vandalize, wreck **2.** *n.* damage, destruction, disruption, subversion, treachery, treason, wrecking

sack[1] *v.* discharge, dismiss

sack[2] *v.* demolish, despoil, destroy, devastate, loot, maraud, pillage, plunder, raid, ravage, rifle, rob, ruin, spoil, strip

sacred **1.** blessed, divine, hallowed, holy, revered, sanctified, venerable **2.** inviolable, protected, sacrosanct, secure **3.** holy, religious, solemn

sacrifice **1.** *v.* give up, immolate, lose, offer, surrender **2.** *n.* destruction, loss, oblation, renunciation, surrender

sacrilege blasphemy, heresy, impiety, irreverence, mockery, profanation, violation

sad **1.** blue, depressed, disconsolate, dismal, doleful, down, gloomy, glum, grieved, lugubrious, melancholy, mournful, pensive, sombre, unhappy, wistful, woebegone **2.** calamitous, dark, dismal, grievous, moving, pathetic, pitiable, pitiful, poignant, sorry, tearful, tragic **3.** bad, dismal, lamentable, miserable, regrettable, serious, shabby, sorry, unfortunate, unhappy, wretched

sadden cast down, dash, deject, depress, distress, grieve

saddle *v.* burden, charge, encumber, load

sadistic barbarous, brutal, cruel, ruthless, vicious

sadness bleakness, depression, gloominess, grief, melancholy, misery, mournfulness, poignancy, sorrow, unhappiness

safe *adj.* **1.** guarded, intact, protected, secure, undamaged, unharmed, unhurt **2.** harmless, pure, tame, wholesome **3.** cautious, conservative, dependable, discreet, prudent, realistic, reliable, sure, trustworthy ~*n.* **4.** coffer, repository, safe-deposit box, strongbox, vault

safeguard **1.** *v.* defend, preserve, protect, screen, shield **2.** *n.* aegis, armour, bulwark, convoy, defence, escort, security, shield, surety

safety assurance, cover, immunity, protection, refuge, sanctuary, security, shelter

sage **1.** *adj.* acute, canny, discerning, learned, politic, prudent, sensible, wise **2.** *n.* authority, elder, expert, master, philosopher, savant, wise man

sail *v.* **1.** embark, set sail **2.** captain, cruise, navigate, pilot, skipper, steer, voyage **3.** drift, float, fly, glide, scud, shoot, skim, skirr, soar, sweep, wing **4.** *Inf. With* **in** *or* **into** assault, attack, begin, fall upon

sailor marine, mariner, navigator, salt, sea dog, seafarer, seaman

saintly beatific, blessed, devout, god-fearing, godly, holy, pious, righteous, virtuous, worthy

sake account, behalf, consideration, gain, good, interest, profit, regard, respect, welfare

salary earnings, emolument, income, pay, remuneration, stipend

sale **1.** deal, disposal, transaction **2.** demand, market, outlet, purchasers **3. for sale** available, in stock, obtainable, on offer

sally *v.* erupt, go forth, issue, rush, set out, surge

salt **1.** *n.* flavour, relish, savour, seasoning, taste **2.** *adj.* brackish, briny, saline, salted, salty

salutation address, greeting, salute, welcome

salute *v.* **1.** acknowledge, address, greet, hail, kiss, welcome **2.** acknowledge, honour, recognize ~*n.* **3.** address, greeting, kiss, obeisance, recognition, salutation, tribute

salvage *v.* glean, recover, redeem, rescue, restore, retrieve, save

salvation deliverance, escape, preservation, redemption, rescue, saving

same *adj.* **1.** aforementioned, aforesaid **2.** corresponding, duplicate, equal, identical, twin

sample **1.** *n.* example, illustration, instance, model, pattern, sign **2.** *v.* experience, inspect, taste, test, try **3.** *adj.* pilot, representative, specimen, test, trial

sanctimonious canting, false, hypocritical, pious, self-satisfied, smug, unctuous

sanction *n.* **1.** approval, authority, backing, confirmation, countenance, endorsement, ratification, support **2.** *Often plural* ban, boycott, embargo, penalty ~*v.* **3.** allow, approve, authorize, back, endorse, permit, support

sanctuary **1.** altar, church, shrine, temple **2.** asylum, haven, protection, refuge, retreat, shelter

sane **1.** lucid, mentally sound, normal, rational **2.** balanced, judicious, level-headed, moderate, reasonable, sensible, sober, sound

sanguine assured, buoyant, cheerful, confident, hopeful, lively, optimistic, spirited

sanitary clean, germ-free, healthy, hygienic, wholesome

sanity **1.** normality, rationality, reason, stability **2.** good sense, level-headedness, rationality, sense

sap[1] *n.* **1.** essence, lifeblood, vital fluid **2.** *Inf.* fool, idiot, noddy, simpleton

sap[2] *v.* bleed, drain, erode, exhaust, rob, undermine, weaken, wear down

sarcasm bitterness, contempt, cynicism, derision, irony, mockery, satire

sarcastic biting, caustic, cutting, cynical, derisive, disparaging, ironical, mocking, mordant, sardonic, satirical, sharp, taunting

sardonic bitter, cynical, derisive, dry, ironical, jeering, malicious, mocking, mordant, sarcastic, wry

satanic black, devilish, diabolic, evil, fiendish, hellish, inhuman, malevolent, malignant, wicked

satellite *n.* 1. moon, sputnik 2. *Fig.* attendant, follower, hanger-on, lackey, minion, parasite, retainer, vassal *~adj.* 3. *Fig.* dependent, puppet, tributary

satiate 1. cloy, glut, gorge, jade, nauseate, overfill, stuff 2. sate, slake, surfeit

satire burlesque, irony, lampoon, parody, raillery, ridicule, sarcasm

satirical, satiric biting, bitter, burlesque, caustic, cutting, cynical, incisive, ironical, mocking, mordant, pungent

satisfaction 1. comfort, content, contentment, ease, enjoyment, happiness, pleasure, pride, repletion, well-being 2. assuaging, fulfilment, gratification, resolution, settlement 3. amends, compensation, damages, justice, redress, reparation, restitution, settlement, vindication

satisfactory acceptable, adequate, all right, average, competent, fair, passable, sufficient, suitable

satisfied at ease, complacent, content, convinced, happy, pacified, positive, smug, sure

satisfy 1. appease, assuage, content, fill, gratify, indulge, mollify, pacify, please, quench, sate, slake, surfeit 2. answer, do, fulfil, meet, qualify, serve, suffice 3. assure, convince, persuade, quiet, reassure 4. answer, discharge, fulfil, meet, settle 5. atone, indemnify

saturate drench, imbue, soak, souse, steep, suffuse, waterlog

sauce impertinence, impudence, insolence, rudeness

saucy disrespectful, flippant, forward, impertinent, impudent, insolent, pert, rude

saunter 1. *v.* amble, dally, linger, meander, ramble, roam, rove, stroll, tarry, wander 2. *n.* airing, amble, constitutional, promenade, ramble, stroll, turn, walk

savage *adj.* 1. rough, rugged, untamed, wild 2. barbarous, beastly, bloody, brutal, brutish, cruel, devilish, ferocious, fierce, harsh, murderous, pitiless, ruthless, vicious 3. primitive, rude, unspoilt *~n.* 4. aboriginal, barbarian, heathen, native, primitive 5. bear, boor 6. beast, brute, fiend, monster *~v.* 7. attack, lacerate, mangle, maul

savagery brutality, cruelty, ferocity, fierceness, inhumanity, viciousness

save 1. deliver, free, liberate, recover, redeem, rescue, salvage, set free 2. collect, economize, gather, hoard, hold, husband, keep, lay by, put by, reserve, retrench, salt away, set aside, store, treasure up 3. conserve, guard, keep safe, look after, preserve, protect, screen, shield

saving 1. *adj.* qualifying, redeeming 2. *n.* bargain, discount, economy, reduction

saviour defender, deliverer, guardian, liberator, preserver, protector, rescuer, salvation

savour *n.* 1. flavour, piquancy, relish, smack, smell, tang, taste 2. distinctive quality, flavour, interest, salt, spice, zest *~v.* 3. appreciate, enjoy, like, luxuriate in, partake, relish

savoury 1. agreeable, dainty, delectable, delicious, good, luscious, palatable, piquant, rich, spicy, tasty 2. decent, edifying, honest, reputable, respectable, wholesome

saw adage, aphorism, axiom, byword, dictum, maxim, proverb, saying

say *v.* 1. add, affirm, announce, assert, declare, maintain, mention, pronounce, remark, speak, state, utter, voice 2. answer, disclose, divulge, reply, respond, reveal, tell 3. allege, claim, noise abroad, put about, report, rumour, suggest 4. deliver, do, orate, perform, read, recite, rehearse, render, repeat 5. assume, conjecture, estimate, guess, imagine, judge, presume, suppose, surmise 6. communicate, convey, express, imply *~n.* 7. authority, influence, power, sway, weight

saying adage, aphorism, axiom, byword, dictum, maxim, proverb, saw

scale *n.* 1. gradation, graduation, hierarchy, ladder, progression, ranking, register, sequence, series, spectrum, spread, steps 2. proportion, ratio 3. degree, extent, range, reach, scope, way *~v.* 4. ascend, climb, escalade, mount, surmount

scamp devil, imp, monkey, rascal, rogue, wretch

scamper dart, dash, fly, hasten, hurry, romp, run, scoot, sprint

scan check, examine, glance over, investigate, run over, scour, scrutinize, search, skim, survey, sweep

scandal 1. crime, disgrace, embarrassment, offence, sin, wrongdoing 2. defamation, discredit, disgrace, ignominy, infamy, offence, reproach, shame 3. abuse, aspersion, backbiting, dirt, gossip, rumours, slander, talk, tattle

scandalous 1. atrocious, disgraceful, disreputable, infamous, monstrous, odious, outrageous, shameful, shocking, unseemly 2. defamatory, gossiping, libellous, scurrilous, untrue

scant bare, deficient, inadequate, insufficient, limited, little, minimal

scanty bare, deficient, inadequate, meagre, narrow, poor, restricted, short, skimpy, slender, sparing, thin

scar 1. *n.* blemish, injury, mark 2. *v.* brand, damage, disfigure, mark

scarce deficient, few, infrequent, insufficient, rare, uncommon, unusual, wanting

scarcely 1. barely, hardly 2. definitely not, hardly

scarcity dearth, deficiency, insufficiency, lack, paucity, rareness, shortage, want

scare 1. *v.* alarm, dismay, frighten, intimidate, panic, shock, startle, terrify 2. *n.* alarm, alert, fright, panic, shock, start, terror

scathing biting, caustic, critical, cutting, harsh, mordant, sarcastic, scornful, trenchant

scatter 1. diffuse, disseminate, fling, litter, shower, sow, spread, sprinkle, strew 2. disband, dispel, disperse, dissipate

scattering few, handful, scatter, smatter, smattering, sprinkling

scenario outline, résumé, rundown, scheme, sketch, summary, synopsis

scene 1. display, pageant, picture, show, sight, spectacle, tableau 2. area, locality, place, position, setting, site, spot 3. backdrop, location, set, setting 4. act, division, episode, incident, part, stage 5. commotion, exhibition, fuss, performance, row, tantrum, to-do, upset 6. landscape, panorama, prospect, view, vista

scenery 1. landscape, surroundings, terrain, view, vista 2. *Theatre* backdrop, décor, flats, set, setting, stage set

scent *n.* 1. aroma, bouquet, fragrance, odour, perfume, smell 2. spoor, track, trail *~v.* 3. detect, discern, nose out, recognize, sense, smell, sniff

sceptic agnostic, cynic, disbeliever, doubter

sceptical cynical, doubtful, dubious, hesitating, incredulous, quizzical, scoffing

schedule 1. *n.* agenda, calendar, catalogue, inventory, list, plan, programme, timetable 2. *v.* appoint, arrange, be due, book, organize, plan, programme, time

scheme *n.* 1. contrivance, design, device, plan, programme, project, proposal, strategy, system, tactics, theory 2. arrangement, blueprint, chart, diagram, disposition, draft, layout, outline, pattern, schedule, system 3. conspiracy, intrigue, manoeuvre, plot, ploy, ruse, shift, stratagem, subterfuge *~v.* 4. contrive, design, devise, frame, imagine, plan, project 5. collude, conspire, intrigue, machinate, manoeuvre, plot

scholar 1. academic, intellectual, savant 2. disciple, learner, pupil, schoolboy, schoolgirl, student

scholarship 1. accomplishments, attainments, book-learning, education, erudition, knowledge, learning, lore 2. bursary, exhibition, fellowship

school *n.* 1. academy, college, department, discipline, faculty, institution, seminary 2. adherents, circle, class, clique, denomination, devotees, disciples, faction, followers, group, pupils, sect, set 3. creed, faith, outlook, persuasion *~v.* 4. coach, discipline, drill, educate, indoctrinate, instruct, prepare, prime, train, tutor, verse

schooling 1. education, formal education, teaching, tuition 2. coaching, drill, grounding, guidance, instruction, preparation, training

science 1. discipline 2. art, skill, technique

scientific accurate, controlled, exact, mathematical, precise, systematic

scoff belittle, deride, despise, flout, gibe, jeer, mock, pooh-pooh, revile, ridicule, scorn, sneer, taunt, twit

scold 1. *v.* berate, blame, castigate, censure, chide, lecture, nag, rate, rebuke, reprimand, reproach, reprove, vituperate 2. *n.* nag, shrew, termagant

scolding lecture, piece of one's mind (*Inf.*), rebuke, row

scoop *n.* 1. dipper, ladle, spoon 2. exclusive, exposé, revelation, sensation *~v.* 3. bail, dig, dip, empty, excavate, gouge, hollow, ladle, scrape, shovel

scope area, capacity, compass, extent, freedom, latitude, liberty, opportunity, orbit, outlook, purview, range, reach, room, space, span, sphere

scorch blacken, blister, burn, char, parch, roast, sear, shrivel, singe, wither

score *n.* 1. grade, mark, outcome, points, record, result, total 2. account, basis, cause, ground, grounds, reason 3. grievance, grudge, injury, injustice, wrong 4. account, amount due, bill, charge, debt, tally, total *~v.* 5. achieve, amass, gain, make, win 6. count, keep count, record, register, tally 7. cut, deface, gouge, graze, indent, mar, mark, nick, notch, scrape, scratch, slash 8. *With* **out** *or* **through** cancel, cross out, delete, obliterate, strike out 9. *Music* adapt, arrange, orchestrate, set 10. triumph

scorn 1. *n.* contempt, derision, disdain, disparagement, mockery, sarcasm, slight, sneer 2. *v.* be above, contemn, deride, disdain, flout, reject, scoff at, slight, spurn

scornful contemptuous, defiant, derisive, disdainful, haughty, insolent, insulting, mocking, sarcastic, sardonic, scathing, slighting, sneering

scoundrel blackguard, cheat, good-for-nothing, heel (*Sl.*), incorrigible, miscreant, rascal, reprobate, rogue, scamp, vagabond, villain, wretch

scour[1] abrade, buff, clean, flush, polish, purge, scrub, wash

scour[2] beat, comb, hunt, rake, ransack, search

scourge *n.* 1. affliction, bane, curse, infliction, misfortune, pest, plague, punishment, terror, torment, visitation 2. cat, lash, strap, switch, thong, whip *~v.* 3. beat, belt, cane, chastise, flog, horsewhip, lash, leather, punish, thrash, trounce, whale, whip

scout *v.* 1. investigate, observe, probe, reconnoitre, spy, survey, watch *~n.* 2. escort, lookout, outrider, precursor, reconnoitrer, vanguard 3. recruiter

scowl 1. *v.* frown, glower, lower 2. *n.* black look, frown, glower

scramble *v.* 1. climb, crawl, push, struggle, swarm 2. contend, hasten, jostle, push, run, rush, strive, vie *~n.* 3. climb, trek 4. commotion, competition, confusion, hassle (*Inf.*), hustle, melee, muddle, race, rush, struggle, tussle

scrap[1] *n.* 1. atom, bit, bite, crumb, fragment, grain, morsel, mouthful, part, particle, piece, portion, snatch, snippet, trace 2. junk, off cuts, waste 3. *Plural* bits, leavings, leftovers, remains, scrapings *~v.* 4. abandon, demolish, discard, drop, jettison, shed, write off

scrap[2] battle, brawl, dispute, fight, quarrel, row, tiff, wrangle

scrape *v.* **1.** bark, graze, rub, scratch, scuff, skin **2.** grate, grind, rasp, scratch, squeak **3.** clean, erase, file, remove, rub, scour **4.** pinch, save, scrimp, skimp, stint

scratch *v.* **1.** claw, cut, damage, etch, grate, graze, incise, mark, rub, score, scrape **2.** annul, cancel, delete, eliminate, erase, withdraw *~n.* **3.** blemish, gash, graze, laceration, mark, scrape *~adj.* **4.** haphazard, impromptu, improvised, rough

scream *v.* **1.** bawl, cry, screech, shriek, shrill, squeal, yell **2.** clash, jar, shriek *~n.* **3.** howl, outcry, screech, shriek, wail, yell, yelp

screen *v.* **1.** cloak, conceal, cover, hide, mask, shade, shroud, veil **2.** defend, guard, protect, shelter, shield **3.** evaluate, examine, filter, gauge, grade, process, scan, sieve, sift, sort, vet **4.** present, put on, show *~n.* **5.** awning, canopy, cloak, concealment, cover, guard, hedge, mantle, shade, shelter, shield, shroud **6.** mesh, net, partition, room divider

screw *v.* **1.** tighten, turn, twist **2.** coerce, constrain, force, pressurize, squeeze

scribe clerk, copyist, secretary, writer

script **1.** handwriting, letters, longhand, writing **2.** book, copy, dialogue, libretto, lines, text, words

scrounge beg, cadge, sponge

scrounger cadger, parasite, sponger

scrub *v.* **1.** clean, cleanse, rub, scour **2.** *Inf.* abolish, call off, cancel, delete, drop, forget about, give up

scruffy disreputable, frowzy, mangy, ragged, run-down, seedy, shabby, slovenly, sluttish, squalid, tattered, untidy

scrupulous careful, exact, fastidious, honourable, meticulous, minute, nice, precise, principled, punctilious, rigorous, strict, upright

scrutinize dissect, examine, explore, inspect, investigate, peruse, probe, scan, search, sift, study

scrutiny analysis, examination, exploration, inquiry, inspection, investigation, perusal, search, sifting

scuffle **1.** *v.* clash, contend, fight, grapple, jostle, struggle, tussle **2.** *n.* brawl, commotion, disturbance, fight, fray, tussle

sculpture *v.* carve, chisel, cut, form, hew, model, mould, sculpt, shape

scum **1.** dross, film, froth **2.** rabble, riffraff

scurrilous abusive, coarse, foul, gross, indecent, infamous, low, obscene, ribald, scandalous, slanderous, vulgar

sea *n.* **1.** main, ocean, the deep, the waves **2.** expanse, mass, multitude, plethora, profusion, sheet **3. at sea** adrift, astray, baffled, bewildered, confused, lost, mystified, puzzled, upset *~adj.* **4.** aquatic, briny, marine, ocean, salt, saltwater

seal *v.* **1.** close, enclose, fasten, plug, secure, shut, stop, stopper, waterproof **2.** assure, attest, confirm, establish, ratify, stamp, validate **3.** clinch, conclude, consummate, finalize, settle **4.** *With* **off** isolate, quarantine, segregate *~n.* **5.** assurance, imprimatur, insignia, notification, stamp

search *v.* **1.** check, comb, examine, explore, ferret, inquire, inspect, investigate, look, probe, pry, ransack, rummage through, scour, scrutinize, seek, sift *~n.* **2.** examination, exploration, hunt, inquiry, inspection, investigation, pursuit, quest, rummage, scrutiny **3. in search of** hunting for, in need of, in pursuit of, looking for, making enquiries concerning, on the lookout for, on the track of, seeking

season *n.* **1.** division, interval, juncture, occasion, opportunity, period, spell, term, time *~v.* **2.** colour, enliven, flavour, lace, pep up, salt, spice **3.** accustom, discipline, harden, mature, prepare, toughen, train

seasoned experienced, hardened, mature, old, practised, veteran

seat *n.* **1.** bench, chair, pew, settle, stall, stool **2.** capital, centre, cradle, heart, hub, place, site, situation, source, station **3.** base, bed, bottom, cause, footing, foundation, ground **4.** abode, ancestral hall, house, mansion, residence **5.** chair, constituency, membership, place *~v.* **6.** accommodate, cater for, contain, hold, sit, take **7.** fix, install, locate, place, set, settle, sit

secluded cloistered, cut off, isolated, lonely, private, reclusive, remote, retired, sheltered, solitary

second[1] *adj.* **1.** following, next, subsequent, succeeding **2.** additional, alternative, extra, further, other **3.** inferior, lesser, lower, subordinate, supporting **4.** double, duplicate, reproduction, twin *~n.* **5.** backer, helper, supporter *~v.* **6.** aid, approve, assist, back, endorse, forward, further, help, promote, support

second[2] *n.* flash, instant, minute, moment, trice, twinkling

secondary **1.** derived, indirect, resultant **2.** contingent, inferior, lesser, lower, minor, subordinate, unimportant **3.** alternate, backup, extra, relief, reserve, subsidiary, supporting

second-hand **1.** *adj.* nearly new, used **2.** *adv.* indirectly

second-rate cheap, commonplace, inferior, mediocre, poor, rubbishy, shoddy, substandard

secrecy **1.** concealment, mystery, privacy, retirement, seclusion, silence, solitude **2.** furtiveness, secretiveness, stealth

secret *adj.* **1.** backstairs, close, concealed, covered, disguised, furtive, hidden, reticent, underground, undisclosed, unknown, unseen **2.** abstruse, arcane, clandestine, classified, cryptic, mysterious, occult, recondite **3.** hidden, private, retired, secluded, unknown **4.** close, deep, discreet, reticent, secretive, sly, stealthy, underhand *~n.* **5.** code, confidence, enigma, formula, key, mystery, recipe

secretive close, cryptic, deep, enigmatic, reserved, reticent, withdrawn

secretly confidentially, furtively, privately, quietly, stealthily, surreptitiously, unobserved

sectarian bigoted, doctrinaire, exclusive, factional, hidebound, insular, limited, parochial, partisan, rigid

section component, division, fraction, instalment, part, passage, piece, portion, sample, segment, slice

sector area, district, division, part, quarter, region, subdivision, zone

secular civil, earthly, laic, lay, profane, state, temporal, worldly

secure *adj.* **1.** immune, protected, safe, sheltered, unassailable, unharmed **2.** dependable, fast, fastened, firm, fixed, immovable, stable, steady, tight **3.** assured, certain, easy, reassured, sure **4.** absolute, conclusive, definite, reliable, solid, steadfast, well-founded *~v.* **5.** acquire, gain, get, obtain, procure **6.** attach, batten down, bolt, chain, fasten, fix, lash, lock, lock up, moor, padlock, rivet, tie up

security **1.** asylum, care, cover, custody, preservation, refuge, retreat, safety **2.** defence, protection, surveillance **3.** assurance, certainty, confidence, conviction, positiveness, reliance, sureness **4.** collateral, gage, guarantee, hostage, insurance, pawn, pledge, surety

sedate calm, collected, composed, cool, deliberate, dignified, earnest, grave, placid, proper, quiet, seemly, serene, serious, sober, solemn, staid, tranquil

sedative **1.** *adj.* anodyne, calming, relaxing, soothing **2.** *n.* anodyne, narcotic, opiate, tranquillizer

sedition agitation, subversion, treason

seduce **1.** betray, corrupt, deflower, deprave, dishonour **2.** allure, attract, beguile, deceive, decoy, ensnare, entice, lure, mislead, tempt

seductive alluring, attractive, bewitching, enticing, inviting, irresistible, provocative, ravishing, specious, tempting

see *v.* **1.** behold, descry, discern, distinguish, espy, glimpse, heed, identify, look, mark, note, notice, observe, perceive, recognize, regard, sight, spot, view, witness **2.** appreciate, fathom, feel, follow, get, grasp, know, realize, understand **3.** ascertain, determine, discover, find out, investigate, learn **4.** ensure, guarantee, mind, take care **5.** consider, decide, deliberate, judge, reflect **6.** confer with, consult, encounter, interview, meet, receive, run into, speak to, visit **7.** accompany, attend, escort, lead, show, usher, walk **8.** anticipate, divine, envisage, foretell, imagine, picture, visualize

seed **1.** egg, embryo, germ, grain, kernel, ovum **2.** beginning, germ, inkling, nucleus, source, start, suspicion

seedy decaying, dilapidated, faded, grubby, mangy, old, rundown, shabby, sleazy, slovenly, squalid, unkempt, worn

seeing *conj.* as, inasmuch as, since

seek **1.** follow, hunt, inquire, pursue, search for **2.** aim, aspire to, attempt, endeavour, essay, strive, try **3.** ask, beg, entreat, inquire, invite, petition, request, solicit

seem appear, assume, look, pretend

seemly becoming, befitting, decent, decorous, fit, fitting, nice, proper, suitable, suited

see over inspect, look round, tour

seesaw *v.* alternate, fluctuate, oscillate, pitch, swing, teeter

seethe **1.** boil, bubble, churn, ferment, fizz, foam, froth **2.** fume, rage, simmer, storm **3.** be alive with, swarm, teem

see through **1.** fathom, penetrate **2. see (something** *or* **someone) through** help out, keep at, persist, see out, support

see to arrange, attend to, do, look after, manage, organize

segregate discriminate against, dissociate, isolate, separate, set apart

seize **1.** clutch, fasten, grab, grasp, grip, lay hands on, snatch, take **2.** catch, get, grasp **3.** abduct, annex, arrest, capture, commandeer, confiscate, impound

seizure **1.** arrest, capture, commandeering, grabbing, taking **2.** attack, convulsion, fit, paroxysm, spasm

seldom infrequently, not often, occasionally, rarely

select **1.** *v.* choose, pick, prefer, sort out **2.** *adj.* choice, excellent, first-rate, hand-picked, picked, preferable, prime, rare, selected, special, superior

selection **1.** choice, choosing, option, pick, preference **2.** assortment, choice, collection, line-up, medley, range, variety

selective careful, discerning, discriminating, particular

self-centred egotistic, narcissistic, selfish, self-seeking

self-confidence aplomb, nerve, poise, self-assurance

self-confident assured, fearless, poised, secure

self-conscious affected, awkward, bashful, diffident, embarrassed, ill at ease, insecure, nervous, sheepish

self-control restraint, willpower

self-evident clear, incontrovertible, obvious, undeniable

self-government autonomy, home rule, independence, sovereignty

self-important arrogant, conceited, overbearing, strutting, swaggering

self-indulgence excess, extravagance, intemperance, sensualism

selfish egoistic, egotistical, greedy, mean, mercenary, narrow, self-seeking, ungenerous

self-possessed collected, confident, cool, poised, self-assured, unruffled

self-respect dignity, morale, pride, self-esteem

self-righteous complacent, pi-

ous, priggish, sanctimonious, self-satisfied, smug, superior
self-sacrifice altruism, generosity, self-denial, selflessness
self-satisfaction complacency, contentment, pride, smugness
self-satisfied complacent, smug, well-pleased
sell 1. barter, exchange, trade 2. deal in, handle, market, peddle, retail, stock, trade in, traffic in, vend
seller agent, dealer, merchant, rep, retailer, salesman, shopkeeper, tradesman, vendor
sell out 1. dispose of, get rid of, sell up 2. betray, fail, give away, play false, rat on
send 1. consign, convey, direct, dispatch, forward, remit, transmit 2. cast, deliver, fire, fling, hurl, let fly, propel, shoot
send for call for, order, request, summon
sendoff departure, farewell, leave-taking, start, valediction
senile decrepit, doting, failing, imbecile
senior *adj.* elder, higher ranking, older, superior
seniority eldership, precedence, priority, rank, superiority
sensation 1. consciousness, feeling, impression, perception, sense, tingle 2. agitation, commotion, excitement, furore, scandal, stir, surprise, thrill
sensational amazing, astounding, dramatic, electrifying, exciting, lurid, melodramatic, revealing, shocking, spectacular, staggering, startling, thrilling
sense *n.* 1. faculty, feeling, sensation 2. atmosphere, aura, awareness, consciousness, feel, impression, perception, premonition, presentiment 3. definition, drift, gist, implication, import, interpretation, meaning, message, nuance, purport, significance, substance 4. *Sometimes plural* brains (*Inf.*), cleverness, discernment, discrimination, intelligence, judgment, mother wit, quickness, reason, sagacity, tact, understanding, wisdom ~*v.* 5. appreciate, discern, divine, feel, grasp, notice, observe, perceive, pick up, realize, suspect, understand
senseless 1. absurd, crazy, fatuous, foolish, halfwitted, idiotic, illogical, inane, incongruous, inconsistent, irrational, ludicrous, mad, mindless, nonsensical, pointless, ridiculous, silly, simple, stupid, unreasonable, unwise 2. cold, insensate, numb, out, stunned, unconscious
sensible canny, discreet, down-to-earth, far-sighted, intelligent, judicious, practical, prudent, rational, realistic, sage, sane, shrewd, sober, sound, wise
sensitive 1. acute, delicate, fine, keen, perceptive, precise, reactive, responsive, susceptible 2. delicate, irritable, temperamental, tender, touchy
sensual 1. animal, bodily, carnal, fleshly, luxurious, physical, voluptuous 2. erotic, lascivious, lecherous, lewd, lustful, sexual, unchaste
sensuous epicurean, gratifying, hedonistic, lush, rich, sybaritic
sentence 1. *n.* condemnation, decision, decree, doom, judgment, order, ruling, verdict 2. *v.* condemn, doom, penalize
sentiment 1. emotion, sensibility, tenderness 2. *Often plural* attitude, belief, feeling, idea, judgment, opinion, persuasion, view, way of thinking 3. emotionalism, romanticism
sentimental dewy-eyed, emotional, impressionable, maudlin, nostalgic, overemotional, pathetic, romantic, simpering, soft-hearted, tearful, tender, touching
sentimentality bathos, nostalgia, romanticism, tenderness
separate *v.* 1. come away, detach, disconnect, disjoin, divide, remove, sever, split, sunder, uncouple 2. isolate, segregate, single out, sort out 3. bifurcate, break up, disunite, diverge, divorce, estrange, part, split up ~*adj.* 4. detached, disconnected, discrete, disjointed, divided, divorced, isolated 5. alone, apart, distinct, independent, individual, particular, single, solitary
separately alone, apart, independently, individually, personally, severally, singly
separation 1. break, disconnection, dissociation, disunion, division, gap, segregation, severance 2. break-up, divorce, farewell, parting, rift, split
sepulchre burial place, grave, tomb
sequel conclusion, continuation, development, end, follow-up, issue, outcome, result, upshot
sequence arrangement, chain, course, cycle, order, procession, progression, series, succession
seraphic angelic, beatific, blissful, celestial, divine, heavenly, holy, pure
serene 1. calm, composed, peaceful, placid, tranquil, undisturbed, unruffled, untroubled 2. clear, cloudless, fair
series chain, course, line, order, progression, run, sequence, set, string, succession, train
serious 1. grave, pensive, sedate, sober, solemn, stern, thoughtful, unsmiling 2. deliberate, determined, earnest, genuine, honest, in earnest, resolute, sincere 3. crucial, deep, difficult, fateful, grim, important, momentous, pressing, significant, urgent, weighty, worrying 4. acute, alarming, critical, dangerous, grave, severe
seriously 1. earnestly, gravely, sincerely, solemnly, thoughtfully 2. acutely, badly, critically, dangerously, distressingly, gravely, grievously, severely, sorely
sermon 1. address, homily 2. harangue, lecture
servant attendant, domestic, help, helper, maid, retainer, slave, vassal
serve 1. aid, assist, help, minister to, oblige, succour, wait on, work for 2. act, attend, complete, discharge, do, fulfil, observe, officiate, pass, perform 3. answer, be acceptable, be adequate, content, do, function as, satisfy, suffice, suit 4. arrange, deal, deliver, dish up, distribute, handle, present, provide, set out, supply
service *n.* 1. advantage, assistance, avail, benefit, help, supply, usefulness, utility 2. check, maintenance, overhaul 3. business, duty, employ, labour, office, work 4. ceremony, function, observance, rite, worship ~*v.* 5. check, fine tune, go over, maintain, overhaul, recondition, repair, tune (up)
session assembly, conference, discussion, hearing, meeting, period, sitting, term
set[1] *v.* 1. aim, apply, direct, fasten, fix, lay, locate, lodge, mount, park, place, plant, put, rest, seat, situate, station, stick, turn 2. allocate, appoint, arrange, assign, conclude, decide, determine, establish, fix, name, ordain, regulate, resolve, schedule, settle, specify 3. arrange, lay, make ready, prepare, spread 4. adjust, rectify, regulate, synchronize 5. cake, congeal, crystallize, harden, solidify, stiffen, thicken 6. allot, decree, impose, ordain, prescribe, specify 7. decline, dip, disappear, go down, sink, subside, vanish ~*n.* 8. attitude, bearing, carriage, fit, hang, position, posture, turn 9. scene, scenery, setting ~*adj.* 10. agreed, appointed, arranged, customary, decided, definite, firm, fixed, prescribed, regular, scheduled, settled, usual 11. entrenched, firm, hard and fast, hardened, hidebound, immovable, inflexible, rigid, strict, stubborn
set[2] *n.* 1. band, circle, class, clique, company, coterie, crowd, faction, gang, group, sect 2. assortment, batch, collection, compendium, kit, outfit, series
set about 1. attack, begin 2. assail, assault, attack, belabour
setback blow, check, defeat, disappointment, hitch, hold-up, misfortune, rebuff, reverse, upset
set off 1. depart, embark, leave, start out 2. detonate, explode, ignite, light, touch off
set on assail, assault, attack, fly at, go for, incite, spur on, urge
set out 1. arrange, array, describe, detail, display, dispose, exhibit, explain, lay out, present, set forth 2. begin, embark, start out
setting backdrop, background, context, location, perspective, scene, scenery, site, surroundings
settle 1. adjust, dispose, order, regulate, straighten out, work out 2. choose, clear up, complete, conclude, decide, dispose of, reconcile, resolve 3. calm, compose, lull, pacify, quell, quiet, quieten, reassure, relax, relieve, sedate, soothe 4. alight, descend, land, light 5. dwell, inhabit, live, move to, reside 6. colonize, found, people, pioneer, plant, populate 7. clear, discharge, pay, quit 8. decline, fall, sink, subside
settlement 1. agreement, arrangement, conclusion, confirmation, disposition, resolution 2. clearance, clearing, defrayal, discharge, payment 3. colony, community, encampment, hamlet, outpost, peopling
settler colonist, immigrant, pioneer, planter
set up 1. arrange, begin, compose, establish, found, initiate, institute, organize, prearrange, prepare 2. back, build up, establish, finance, promote, strengthen, subsidize 3. assemble, build, construct, elevate, erect, raise
set upon ambush, assail, assault, attack, beat up, turn on
several *adj.* different, disparate, distinct, diverse, individual, many, particular, respective, single, some, sundry, various
severe 1. austere, cruel, hard, harsh, oppressive, pitiless, relentless, rigid, strict, unrelenting 2. cold, dour, flinty, forbidding, grave, grim, serious, sober, stern, strait-laced, unsmiling 3. acute, bitter, critical, dangerous, extreme, fierce, inclement, intense, violent 4. ascetic, austere, chaste, classic, forbidding, plain, restrained, simple, unadorned, unfussy 5. arduous, demanding, difficult, exacting, fierce, hard, rigorous, stringent, taxing, tough
severely 1. harshly, sternly, strictly 2. acutely, badly, critically, dangerously, extremely, hard, sorely
sex 1. gender 2. *Inf.* coition, coitus, copulation, (sexual) intercourse, intimacy, lovemaking 3. desire, libido, reproduction
shabby 1. dilapidated, faded, frayed, mean, neglected, poor, ragged, run-down, seedy, tattered, tatty, threadbare, worn-out 2. cheap, contemptible, despicable, dirty, dishonourable, ignoble, low, mean, shameful, shoddy, unworthy
shade *n.* 1. dimness, dusk, gloom, obscurity, screen, shadow 2. **put into the shade** eclipse, outclass, outshine, overshadow 3. blind, canopy, cover, covering, curtain, screen, shield, veil 4. colour, hue, stain, tinge, tint, tone 5. ghost, phantom, shadow, spectre, spirit ~*v.* 6. cloud, conceal, cover, darken, dim, hide, mute, obscure, protect, screen, shadow, shield, veil
shadow *n.* 1. cover, darkness, dimness, dusk, gloaming, gloom, protection, shade, shelter 2. hint, suggestion, suspicion, trace 3. ghost, image, phantom, remnant, spectre, vestige 4. blight, cloud, gloom, sadness ~*v.* 5. darken, overhang, screen, shade, shield 6. dog, follow, stalk, trail
shadowy 1. dark, dim, dusky, gloomy, indistinct, murky, obscure, shaded 2. dim, dreamlike, faint, ghostly, illusory, imaginary, intangible, nebulous, obscure, phantom, spectral, undefined, unreal, unsubstantial, vague
shady 1. cool, dim, leafy, shaded 2. *Inf.* crooked, disreputable, dubious, shifty, slippery, suspect
shaft 1. handle, pole, rod, shank, stem 2. beam, gleam, ray, streak 3. barb, cut, dart, gibe, sting, thrust
shake *v.* 1. bump, jar, quake, rock, shiver, shudder, sway, totter, tremble, vibrate, waver 2. brandish, flourish, wave 3. discompose, distress, disturb, frighten, intimidate, move, shock, unnerve, upset ~*n.* 4.

agitation, convulsion, disturbance, jerk, quaking, shiver, shock, shudder, trembling, tremor, vibration

shake off elude, leave behind, lose, throw off

shaky 1. faltering, insecure, precarious, quivery, rickety, trembling, unstable, unsteady, weak 2. dubious, suspect, uncertain

shallow empty, flimsy, foolish, frivolous, idle, ignorant, puerile, simple, slight, superficial, surface, trivial, unintelligent

sham 1. *n.* feint, forgery, fraud, hoax, humbug, imitation, impostor, pretence 2. *adj.* artificial, bogus, counterfeit, false, feigned, imitation, mock, pretended, simulated, spurious, synthetic 3. *v.* affect, assume, fake, feign, imitate, pretend, put on, simulate

shame *n.* 1. blot, derision, disgrace, disrepute, infamy, obloquy, odium, reproach, scandal, smear 2. abashment, chagrin, compunction, humiliation, ignominy ~*v.* 3. abash, confound, disconcert, embarrass, humble, reproach, ridicule 4. blot, debase, defile, degrade, dishonour, smear, stain

shameful 1. base, degrading, disgraceful, ignominious, indecent, low, mean, scandalous, unbecoming, wicked 2. degrading, humiliating, shaming

shameless audacious, brash, brazen, corrupt, depraved, dissolute, flagrant, hardened, immodest, improper, impudent, indecent, insolent, profligate, unabashed, unprincipled, wanton

shape *n.* 1. build, configuration, contours, cut, figure, form, lines, make, outline, profile, silhouette 2. frame, model, mould, pattern 3. aspect, form, guise, likeness, semblance 4. condition, fettle, health, kilter, state, trim ~*v.* 5. create, fashion, form, make, model, mould, produce 6. adapt, define, develop, devise, frame, guide, plan, prepare, regulate

share 1. *v.* assign, distribute, divide, partake, participate, receive, split 2. *n.* allotment, allowance, contribution, division, due, lot, part, portion, quota, ration

sharp *adj.* 1. acute, jagged, keen, pointed, serrated, spiky 2. abrupt, distinct, extreme, marked, sudden 3. alert, apt, astute, bright, clever, knowing, observant, perceptive, quick, ready, subtle 4. acute, distressing, fierce, intense, painful, piercing, severe, sore, stabbing, violent 5. clear, clear-cut, crisp, distinct, well-defined 6. bitter, caustic, cutting, harsh, hurtful, sardonic, scathing, severe, trenchant, vitriolic 7. acerbic, acid, acrid, burning, hot, piquant, pungent, sour, tart, vinegary ~*adv.* 8. exactly, on time, precisely, promptly, punctually

sharpen edge, grind, strop, whet

shatter 1. break, burst, crack, crush, demolish, explode, pulverize, shiver, smash, split 2. blast, blight, demolish, destroy, disable, exhaust, impair, overturn, ruin, torpedo, wreck 3. crush, devastate

sheer 1. abrupt, precipitous, steep 2. arrant, complete, downright, pure, rank, total, unalloyed, unqualified, utter

sheet 1. coat, film, folio, layer, leaf, overlay, pane, panel, piece, plate, slab, surface, veneer 2. area, blanket, covering, expanse, stretch, sweep

shell *n.* 1. case, husk, pod ~*v.* 2. husk 3. attack, blitz, bomb, bombard, strike ~*n.* 4. frame, framework, hull, structure

shelter 1. *v.* cover, defend, guard, harbour, hide, protect, safeguard, shield 2. *n.* asylum, cover, defence, guard, haven, protection, refuge, retreat, safety, sanctuary, screen, security, umbrella

sheltered cloistered, ensconced, isolated, protected, quiet, retired, screened, withdrawn

shelve defer, freeze, mothball, pigeonhole, postpone

shield *n.* 1. buckler 2. aegis, bulwark, cover, defence, guard, protection, safeguard, screen, shelter ~*v.* 3. cover, defend, guard, protect, safeguard, screen, shelter

shift *v.* 1. alter, budge, change, displace, move, relocate, remove, reposition, swerve, switch, transfer, transpose, vary, veer ~*n.* 2. alteration, change, fluctuation, move, removal, shifting, switch, transfer, veering 3. artifice, craft, device, dodge, equivocation, evasion, expedient, move, resource, ruse, stratagem, trick, wile

shimmer dance, gleam, glisten, twinkle

shine *v.* 1. beam, flash, glare, gleam, glisten, glitter, glow, radiate, sparkle, twinkle 2. be conspicuous, excel, stand out, star ~*n.* 3. brightness, glare, gleam, light, radiance, shimmer, sparkle

shining 1. beaming, bright, brilliant, gleaming, glistening, radiant, resplendent, shimmering, sparkling 2. *Fig.* brilliant, celebrated, conspicuous, distinguished, eminent, glorious, leading, splendid

shirk avoid, dodge, evade, shun, sidestep

shock 1. *v.* agitate, astound, disgust, disquiet, horrify, jar, jolt, nauseate, numb, offend, outrage, revolt, shake, sicken, stagger, stun, stupefy, unsettle 2. *n.* blow, bombshell, breakdown, collapse, distress, disturbance, stupor, trauma, upset

shocking appalling, atrocious, detestable, disgraceful, disquieting, dreadful, foul, frightful, ghastly, hideous, horrible, monstrous, odious, offensive, outrageous, revolting, scandalous, sickening, unspeakable

shoddy inferior, poor, second-rate, slipshod, tawdry, trashy

shoemaker bootmaker, cobbler

shoot[1] *v.* 1. bag, hit, kill, open fire, pick off 2. discharge, emit, fire, fling, hurl, launch, project, propel 3. bolt, charge, dart, dash, flash, fly, hurtle, race, rush, speed, spring, streak, tear, whisk

shoot[2] 1. *n.* branch, bud, slip, sprig, sprout, twig 2. *v.* bud, germinate, sprout

shore beach, coast, sands, seashore, waterside

short *adj.* 1. brief, compressed, concise, curtailed, laconic, pithy, succinct, summary, terse 2. dumpy, little, low, petite, small, squat 3. brief, fleeting, momentary 4. *Often with* **of** deficient, lacking, limited, meagre, poor, scant, scanty, scarce, slender, slim, tight, wanting ~*adv.* 5. abruptly, by surprise, suddenly, unaware 6. **fall short** disappoint, fail 7. **in short** briefly, in essence

shortage dearth, deficit, failure, lack, paucity, poverty, scarcity, want

shortcoming defect, failing, fault, flaw, frailty, imperfection, weakness

shorten abbreviate, curtail, cut, decrease, diminish, dock, lessen, reduce, trim, turn up

shot *n.* 1. discharge, lob, pot shot, throw 2. ball, bullet, lead, pellet, projectile, slug 3. marksman, shooter 4. *Inf.* attempt, chance, effort, endeavour, essay, go, guess, opportunity, stab, surmise, try, turn 5. **have a shot** *Inf.* attempt, tackle, try 6. **like a shot** eagerly, immediately, quickly, unhesitatingly

shoulder *n.* 1. **give (someone) the cold shoulder** ignore, rebuff, shun, snub 2. **rub shoulders with** *Inf.* associate with, consort with, hobnob with, mix with 3. **shoulder to shoulder** as one, jointly, together, united 4. **straight from the shoulder** candidly, directly, frankly, outright, plainly, straight ~*v.* 5. accept, assume, bear, be responsible for, carry, take on 6. elbow, jostle, press, push, shove, thrust

shout 1. *n.* bellow, call, cry, roar, scream, yell 2. *v.* bawl, bay, bellow, call (out), cry (out), roar, scream, yell

shove *v.* crowd, drive, elbow, impel, jostle, press, propel, push, thrust

show *v.* 1. appear, disclose, display, divulge, evidence, exhibit, indicate, manifest, present, register, reveal 2. assert, clarify, demonstrate, explain, instruct, present, prove, teach 3. attend, conduct, escort, guide, lead ~*n.* 4. array, demonstration, display, exhibition, fair, pageant, parade, sight, spectacle, view 5. affectation, air, appearance, display, illusion, likeness, ostentation, parade, pose, pretence, pretext, profession

showdown clash, climax, crisis

shower 1. *n.* barrage, deluge, rain, stream, torrent, volley 2. *v.* deluge, heap, lavish, load, pour, rain, spray, sprinkle

showman entertainer, impresario, performer, publicist

show off 1. advertise, display, exhibit, flaunt, parade, spread out 2. boast, brag, swagger

show up 1. expose, lay bare, pinpoint, reveal, unmask 2. appear, stand out 3. *Inf.* embarrass, let down, mortify, shame 4. *Inf.* appear, arrive, come, turn up

shrewd acute, artful, astute, canny, clever, crafty, cunning, discerning, far-seeing, intelligent, keen, knowing, perceptive, perspicacious, sharp, sly, smart, wily

shrewdness acumen, discernment, grasp, judgment, perspicacity, sagacity, sharpness, smartness

shrill acute, high, penetrating, piercing, piping, screeching, sharp

shrink 1. contract, decrease, diminish, dwindle, lessen, narrow, shorten, shrivel, wither, wrinkle 2. cower, cringe, draw back, flinch, hang back, quail, recoil, retire, wince, withdraw

shrivel 1. burn, parch, scorch, sear 2. desiccate, dwindle, shrink, wilt, wither, wizen, wrinkle

shudder 1. *v.* convulse, quake, quiver, shake, shiver, tremble 2. *n.* quiver, spasm, tremor

shuffle 1. drag, scrape, shamble 2. confuse, disarrange, disorder, intermix, mix, rearrange, shift

shun avoid, elude, eschew, evade

shut bar, close, draw to, fasten, push to, seal, secure, slam

shut down cease, close, discontinue, halt, stop

shut out bar, debar, exclude, keep out, lock out

shut up 1. box in, cage, confine, coop up, immure, imprison, incarcerate, intern, keep in 2. *Inf.* gag, hush, muzzle, silence

shy bashful, cautious, chary, coy, diffident, hesitant, modest, nervous, reserved, reticent, retiring, shrinking, suspicious, timid, wary

sick 1. ill, nauseated, qualmish, queasy 2. ailing, diseased, feeble, indisposed, unwell, weak 3. *Inf.* black, ghoulish, macabre, morbid, sadistic

sicken 1. disgust, nauseate, repel, revolt 2. contract, fall ill, take sick

sickly 1. ailing, bloodless, delicate, faint, feeble, infirm, languid, peaky, pining, unhealthy, wan, weak 2. cloying, mawkish, nauseating

sickness 1. nausea, vomiting 2. affliction, ailment, bug (*Inf.*), complaint, disease, disorder, illness, indisposition, infirmity, malady

side *n.* 1. border, boundary, division, edge, limit, margin, part, perimeter, rim, sector, verge 2. aspect, face, facet, flank, hand, part, surface, view 3. angle, light, opinion, position, slant, stand, standpoint, viewpoint 4. camp, cause, faction, party, sect, team 5. *Brit. sl.* airs, arrogance, insolence, pretentiousness ~*adj.* 6. lateral 7. ancillary, incidental, indirect, lesser, marginal, minor, secondary, subsidiary

sidetrack deflect, distract, divert

sideways 1. *adv.* edgeways, laterally 2. *adj.* oblique, slanted

siesta catnap, doze, nap, rest, sleep

sift 1. filter, part, riddle, separate, sieve 2. analyse, examine, fathom, investigate, probe, screen, scrutinize

sigh *v.* breathe, complain, grieve, lament, moan, sorrow

sight *n.* 1. eye, eyes, seeing,

vision **2.** appearance, ken, perception, view, viewing **3.** display, exhibition, pageant, scene, show, spectacle, vista **4.** **catch sight of** descry, espy, glimpse, recognize, spot, view ~*v.* **5.** behold, discern, distinguish, make out, observe, perceive, see, spot

sign *n.* **1.** clue, evidence, gesture, hint, indication, mark, note, proof, signal, suggestion, symptom, token, trace, vestige **2.** board, notice, placard, warning **3.** badge, cipher, device, emblem, ensign, figure, logo, mark, symbol **4.** augury, auspice, foreboding, omen, portent, warning ~*v.* **5.** autograph, endorse, initial, inscribe, subscribe **6.** beckon, gesticulate, gesture, indicate, signal, use sign language, wave

signal **1.** *n.* beacon, cue, gesture, indication, indicator, mark, sign, token **2.** *v.* beckon, gesticulate, gesture, indicate, motion, nod, sign, wave

significance **1.** force, import, meaning, message, point, purport, sense **2.** consequence, importance, matter, moment, relevance, weight

significant **1.** eloquent, expressive, indicative, knowing, meaning, suggestive **2.** critical, important, material, momentous, noteworthy, serious, vital, weighty

signify betoken, connote, convey, denote, evidence, exhibit, express, imply, indicate, intimate, matter, mean, portend, proclaim, represent, show, stand for, suggest, symbolize

silence *n.* **1.** calm, hush, lull, peace, quiet, stillness **2.** dumbness, muteness, reticence, taciturnity ~*v.* **3.** cut off, cut short, deaden, extinguish, gag, muffle, quell, quieten, stifle, still, subdue, suppress

silent **1.** hushed, muted, quiet, soundless, still **2.** dumb, mum, mute, speechless, taciturn, tongue-tied, voiceless, wordless **3.** implicit, implied, tacit, understood, unspoken

silently dumbly, mutely, noiselessly, quietly, soundlessly, speechlessly

silhouette **1.** *n.* form, outline, profile, shape **2.** *v.* etch, outline, stand out

silky silken, sleek, smooth, velvety

silly **1.** absurd, asinine, brainless, childish, fatuous, foolhardy, foolish, frivolous, giddy, idiotic, immature, inane, irresponsible, meaningless, pointless, puerile, ridiculous, stupid **2.** benumbed, dazed, stunned, stupefied

similar alike, comparable, in agreement, resembling, uniform

similarity affinity, agreement, analogy, closeness, correspondence, likeness, relation, resemblance

similarly correspondingly, likewise

simple **1.** clear, easy, intelligible, lucid, plain, uncomplicated, understandable, uninvolved **2.** classic, clean, natural, plain, unfussy **3.** elementary, pure, single, uncombined, unmixed **4.** artless, childlike, frank, guileless, innocent, naive, natural, sincere, unsophisticated **5.** bald, basic, direct, frank, honest, naked, plain, sincere, stark **6.** homely, humble, lowly, modest, rustic **7.** brainless, dense, feeble, foolish, moronic, obtuse, shallow, silly, slow, stupid, thick

simpleton blockhead, dolt, dunce, fool, idiot, moron

simplicity **1.** clarity, clearness, ease **2.** modesty, naturalness, plainness, purity, restraint **3.** artlessness, candour, directness, innocence, naivety, openness

simplify abridge, disentangle, facilitate, streamline

simply **1.** clearly, directly, easily, modestly, naturally, plainly, unaffectedly, unpretentiously, without any elaboration **2.** just, merely, only, purely, solely

sin **1.** *n.* crime, error, evil, guilt, iniquity, misdeed, offence, trespass, unrighteousness, wickedness, wrong **2.** *v.* err, fall, lapse, offend, transgress

sincere artless, candid, earnest, frank, genuine, guileless, heartfelt, honest, natural, open, real, serious, true, unaffected

sincerely earnestly, genuinely, honestly, really, seriously, truly

sincerity candour, frankness, genuineness, good faith, honesty, probity, seriousness, truth

sinful bad, corrupt, criminal, erring, guilty, immoral, iniquitous, ungodly, unholy, unrighteous, wicked

sing carol, chant, chirp, croon, pipe, trill, warble, yodel

singer chorister, crooner, minstrel, songster, vocalist

single **1.** distinct, individual, lone, one, only, separate, sole, solitary, unique **2.** free, unattached, unmarried, unwed **3.** exclusive, individual, separate, unblended, undivided, unmixed, unshared

single-minded dedicated, determined, dogged, fixed, steadfast, stubborn, tireless

singular **1.** eminent, exceptional, noteworthy, outstanding, prodigious, rare, remarkable, uncommon, unique, unparalleled **2.** curious, eccentric, odd, out-of-the-way, peculiar, puzzling, queer, strange, unusual **3.** individual, separate, single, sole

sinister dire, disquieting, evil, malignant, menacing, ominous, threatening

sink *v.* **1.** decline, descend, dip, disappear, droop, drop, drown, ebb, engulf, fall, founder, lower, merge, plunge, sag, slope, submerge, subside **2.** abate, collapse, drop, fall, lapse, slip, subside **3.** decay, decline, depreciate, die, diminish, dwindle, fade, fail, flag, lessen, weaken, worsen **4.** bore, dig, drill, drive, excavate, lay **5.** defeat, destroy, finish, overwhelm, ruin **6.** stoop, succumb

sip **1.** *v.* sample, sup, taste **2.** *n.* drop, swallow, taste, thimbleful

siren charmer, Circe, seductress, temptress, witch

sit **1.** perch, rest, settle **2.** assemble, convene, deliberate, meet, officiate, preside

site **1.** *n.* ground, location, place, plot, position, spot **2.** *v.* install, locate, place, position, set, situate

sitting *n.* consultation, hearing, meeting, period, session

situation **1.** location, place, position, seat, setting, site, spot **2.** case, circumstances, condition, plight, state **3.** rank, sphere, station, status **4.** employment, job, office, place, position, post

size amount, bulk, dimensions, extent, immensity, mass, proportions, range, vastness, volume

skeleton *Fig.* bones, draft, framework, outline, sketch

sketch **1.** *v.* delineate, depict, draft, draw, outline, paint, plot, portray, represent, rough out **2.** *n.* delineation, design, draft, drawing, outline, plan

sketchy bitty, crude, cursory, inadequate, incomplete, outline, perfunctory, rough, scrappy, skimpy, slight, superficial, vague

skilful able, adept, adroit, apt, clever, experienced, expert, handy, masterly, practised, professional, proficient, quick, ready, skilled, trained

skill ability, adroitness, aptitude, art, cleverness, competence, dexterity, expertise, facility, finesse, handiness, ingenuity, knack, readiness, talent, technique

skilled able, experienced, expert, masterly, practised, professional, proficient, skilful, trained

skin *n.* **1.** hide, pelt **2.** casing, coating, crust, film, husk, outside, peel, rind **3.** **get under one's skin** annoy, irk, irritate, nettle ~*v.* **4.** bark, flay, graze, peel, scrape

skinny emaciated, lean, thin, undernourished

skip *v.* **1.** bob, caper, dance, flit, frisk, gambol, hop, prance, trip **2.** eschew

skirmish **1.** *n.* affair, battle, brush, clash, combat, conflict, contest, encounter, engagement, fracas, incident, spat, tussle **2.** *v.* clash, collide

skirt *v.* border, edge, flank

slab chunk, lump, piece, portion, slice, wedge

slack *adj.* **1.** baggy, easy, flexible, lax, limp, loose, relaxed **2.** easy-going, idle, inactive, inattentive, lax, lazy, neglectful, negligent, permissive, remiss, tardy **3.** dull, inactive, quiet, slow, slow-moving, sluggish ~*n.* **4.** excess, leeway, play, room ~*v.* **5.** dodge, flag, idle, neglect, relax, shirk

slacken (off) abate, decrease, diminish, drop off, lessen, loosen, moderate, reduce, relax, release

slacker dodger, idler, loafer, passenger, shirker

slam bang, crash, dash, fling, hurl, smash, throw, thump

slander **1.** *n.* calumny, libel, misrepresentation, scandal, smear **2.** *v.* calumniate, decry, defame, detract, disparage, libel, malign, muckrake, slur, smear, traduce, vilify

slant *v.* **1.** bend, bevel, cant, incline, lean, list, shelve, slope, tilt ~*n.* **2.** camber, gradient, incline, pitch, rake, ramp, slope, tilt ~*v.* **3.** angle, bias, colour, distort, twist, weight ~*n.* **4.** angle, bias, emphasis, leaning, one-sidedness, prejudice, viewpoint

slanting angled, aslant, bent, canted, diagonal, inclined, oblique, sideways, sloping, tilted, tilting

slap **1.** *n.* bang, blow, cuff, smack, spank, whack **2.** *v.* bang, clap, cuff, hit, spank, strike, whack

slapdash careless, clumsy, hasty, hurried, messy, perfunctory, slipshod, slovenly, untidy

slash **1.** *v.* cut, gash, hack, lacerate, rend, rip, score, slit **2.** *n.* cut, gash, incision, laceration, rent, rip, slit

slate *v.* berate, blame, censure, criticize, scold, slang

slaughter **1.** *n.* bloodshed, butchery, carnage, extermination, killing, massacre, murder, slaying **2.** *v.* butcher, destroy, kill, liquidate, massacre, murder, slay

slave **1.** *n.* drudge, serf, servant, skivvy, vassal, villein **2.** *v.* drudge, slog, toil

slavery bondage, captivity, serfdom, servitude, thrall

slavish abject, base, cringing, despicable, fawning, low, mean, menial, obsequious, servile

slay assassinate, butcher, destroy, dispatch, eliminate, exterminate, kill, massacre, murder, slaughter

sleek glossy, lustrous, shiny, smooth, well-fed, well-groomed

sleep **1.** *v.* catnap, doze, drowse, slumber, snore **2.** *n.* dormancy, doze, nap, repose, rest, siesta, slumber(s)

sleepless restless, wakeful

sleepy **1.** drowsy, dull, heavy, inactive, lethargic, sluggish, torpid **2.** dull, hypnotic, inactive, slow, somnolent

slender **1.** lean, narrow, slight, slim, willowy **2.** inadequate, insufficient, little, meagre, scanty, small, spare **3.** faint, feeble, flimsy, fragile, poor, remote, slight, slim, tenuous, thin, weak

slice **1.** *n.* cut, helping, piece, portion, segment, share, sliver, wedge **2.** *v.* carve, cut, divide, sever

slick **1.** glib, plausible, polished, smooth, specious **2.** adroit, deft, dextrous, polished, sharp, skilful

slide *v.* coast, glide, skim, slip, slither, veer

slight *adj.* **1.** feeble, insignificant, meagre, minor, modest, paltry, scanty, small, superficial, trivial, unimportant, weak **2.** delicate, feeble, fragile, lightly-built, slim, small, spare ~*v.* **3.** affront, disdain, disparage, ignore, insult, neglect, scorn, snub ~*n.* **4.** affront, contempt, discourtesy, disdain, disrespect, insult, neglect, rebuff, snub

slightly a little, somewhat

slim *adj.* **1.** lean, narrow, slender, slight, sylphlike, thin, trim **2.** faint, poor, remote, slender, slight ~*v.* **3.** diet, reduce

slimy **1.** clammy, glutinous, miry, muddy, viscous **2.** creeping, obsequious, oily, servile, sycophantic, unctuous

slip *v.* **1.** glide, skate, slide, slither **2.** fall, skid **3.** conceal, creep, hide, sneak, steal **4.** *Sometimes* *with* **up** blunder, err, miscalculate, mistake **5. let slip** disclose, divulge, leak, reveal *~n.* **6.** blunder, error, failure, fault, indiscretion, mistake, omission, oversight **7. give (someone) the slip** dodge, elude, evade, lose (someone), outwit

slippery 1. glassy, greasy, icy, perilous, smooth, unsafe, unsteady **2.** crafty, cunning, devious, dishonest, evasive, false, tricky, two-faced, unpredictable, unreliable

slipshod careless, loose, slapdash, slovenly, untidy

slit 1. *v.* cut (open), gash, knife, lance, pierce, rip, slash **2.** *n.* cut, gash, incision, opening, rent, split, tear

slogan catchword, jingle, motto

slope 1. *v.* drop away, fall, incline, lean, pitch, rise, slant, tilt **2.** *n.* descent, gradient, incline, ramp, rise, scarp, slant, tilt

sloppy 1. sludgy, slushy, splashy, watery, wet **2.** *Inf.* careless, clumsy, inattentive, messy, slipshod, slovenly, unkempt, untidy, weak

slot 1. aperture, channel, groove, hole, slit **2.** *Inf.* opening, place, position, space, time, vacancy

sloth idleness, inactivity, inertia, laziness, slackness, sluggishness, torpor

slovenly careless, disorderly, loose, negligent, slack, slapdash, slipshod, untidy

slow 1. dawdling, deliberate, easy, laggard, lazy, leaden, leisurely, measured, ponderous, sluggish, unhurried **2.** backward, behind, delayed, dilatory, late, long-delayed, tardy **3.** gradual, lingering, prolonged, protracted **4.** boring, conservative, dead, dull, inactive, quiet, slack, sleepy, stagnant, tame, tedious, uninteresting **5.** bovine, dense, dim, dull, dull-witted, obtuse, retarded, stupid, thick, unresponsive

slowly gradually, leisurely, ploddingly, steadily, unhurriedly

sluggish dull, heavy, inactive, indolent, inert, lethargic, lifeless, listless, slothful, slow, torpid

slumber doze, nap, repose, sleep

slump 1. *v.* collapse, crash, deteriorate, fall, fall off, plunge, sink, slip **2.** *n.* collapse, crash, decline, depression, downturn, failure, fall, low, recession, reverse, trough

slur *n.* affront, aspersion, blot, discredit, disgrace, innuendo, insinuation, insult, reproach, smear, stain, stigma

sly 1. *adj.* artful, astute, clever, crafty, cunning, devious, furtive, guileful, scheming, secret, shifty, stealthy, subtle, underhand, wily **2.** *n.* **on the sly** covertly, privately, secretly, surreptitiously, underhandedly, under the counter (*Inf.*)

small 1. diminutive, immature, little, mini, miniature, minute, petite, puny, slight, tiny, undersized, wee, young **2.** insignificant, lesser, minor, negligible, paltry, petty, trifling, trivial **3.** inadequate, insufficient, limited, meagre, scanty **4.** humble, modest, unpretentious **5.** base, grudging, illiberal, mean, narrow, petty, selfish

small-minded bigoted, envious, grudging, hidebound, intolerant, mean, petty, rigid, ungenerous

smart[1] *adj.* **1.** acute, adept, agile, apt, astute, bright, brisk, canny, clever, ingenious, intelligent, keen, nimble, quick, ready, sharp, shrewd **2.** chic, elegant, fine, modish, neat, snappy, spruce, stylish, trim **3.** effective, impertinent, pointed, ready, saucy, witty

smart[2] *v.* burn, hurt, pain, sting, throb, tingle

smash *v.* **1.** break, collide, crash, crush, demolish, pulverize, shatter, shiver *~n.* **2.** accident, collision, crash *~v.* **3.** defeat, destroy, lay waste, overthrow, ruin, wreck *~n.* **4.** collapse, defeat, disaster, downfall, failure, ruin

smear *v.* **1.** bedaub, bedim, blur, coat, cover, daub, dirty, patch, plaster, smudge, soil, spread over, stain, sully *~n.* **2.** blot, blotch, daub, smudge, splotch, streak *~v.* **3.** asperse, blacken, sully, tarnish, traduce, vilify *~n.* **4.** calumny, libel, slander, vilification

smell *n.* **1.** aroma, bouquet, fragrance, odour, perfume, scent, whiff *~v.* **2.** nose, scent, sniff **3.** reek, stink

smooth *adj.* **1.** even, flat, flush, horizontal, level, plain, plane **2.** glossy, polished, shiny, silky, sleek, soft, velvety **3.** calm, equable, glassy, peaceful, serene, tranquil, undisturbed, unruffled **4.** agreeable, bland, mellow, mild, pleasant, soothing **5.** facile, glib, persuasive, silky, slick, suave, unctuous, urbane **6.** easy, effortless, flowing, fluent, regular, rhythmic, steady, uniform, well-ordered *~v.* **7.** flatten, iron, level, plane, polish, press **8.** allay, appease, assuage, calm, ease, facilitate, mitigate, mollify, palliate, soften

smoothness 1. evenness, regularity, unbrokenness **2.** silkiness, sleekness, softness **3.** calmness, placidity, serenity, stillness **4.** glibness, oiliness, suavity, urbanity **5.** ease, efficiency, felicity, finish, flow, fluency, polish, rhythm, slickness

smother 1. choke, snuff, stifle, strangle, suffocate **2.** conceal, hide, muffle, repress, stifle, suppress

smoulder *Fig.* be resentful, boil, burn, fester, fume, rage, seethe, simmer

smug complacent, conceited, priggish, superior

smuggler bootlegger, gentleman, runner, wrecker

snack bite, break, light meal, nibble, refreshment(s), titbit

snag catch, difficulty, disadvantage, drawback, hitch, inconvenience, obstacle, problem, stumbling block

snap *v.* **1.** break, crack, separate **2.** bite, catch, grip, nip, seize, snatch **3.** bark, flare out, flash, growl, lash out at, retort, snarl **4.** click, crackle, pop *~adj.* **5.** abrupt, immediate, instant, sudden

snap up grab, grasp, seize

snare 1. *v.* catch, entrap, net, seize, trap, wire **2.** *n.* catch, gin net, noose, pitfall

snarl *v.* complain, growl, grumble, mumble, murmur

snatch 1. *v.* clutch, gain, grab, grasp, grip, pluck, pull, rescue, seize, take, win, wrench, wrest **2.** *n.* bit, fragment, part, piece, smattering, snippet, spell

sneak *v.* **1.** cower, lurk, pad, sidle, skulk, slink, slip, smuggle, spirit, steal **2.** *Inf.* inform on, tell tales *~n.* **3.** informer, telltale

sneaking 1. hidden, private, secret, unconfessed, unexpressed, unvoiced **2.** nagging, persistent, uncomfortable, worrying

sneer 1. *v.* deride, disdain, gibe, jeer, laugh, mock, ridicule, scoff, scorn, sniff at, snigger **2.** *n.* derision, disdain, gibe, jeer, mockery, ridicule, scorn, snigger

sniff *v.* breathe, inhale, smell, snuff, snuffle

snigger giggle, laugh, sneer, titter

snip *v.* **1.** clip, crop, cut, nick, notch, shave, trim *~n.* **2.** bit, clipping, fragment, piece, scrap, shred **3.** *Inf.* bargain, giveaway

snobbery airs, condescension, pretension, pride

snobbish arrogant, condescending, patronizing, pretentious, superior

snooze 1. *v.* catnap, doze, nap **2.** *n.* catnap, doze, nap, siesta

snub 1. *v.* cold-shoulder, humble, humiliate, mortify, rebuff, shame, slight **2.** *n.* affront, insult

snug comfortable, cosy, homely, intimate, sheltered, warm

soak bathe, damp, drench, immerse, infuse, moisten, penetrate, permeate, saturate, steep, wet

soaking drenched, dripping, saturated, soaked, sodden, sopping, streaming, waterlogged, wringing wet

sob *v.* boohoo, cry, howl, snivel, weep

sober 1. abstemious, abstinent, moderate, temperate **2.** calm, cold, composed, cool, dispassionate, grave, lucid, peaceful, practical, rational, realistic, reasonable, sedate, serene, serious, solemn, sound, staid, steady, unexcited, unruffled **3.** dark, drab, plain, quiet, severe, sombre, subdued

sociable affable, approachable, companionable, convivial, cordial, familiar, friendly, genial, gregarious, outgoing, social, warm

social 1. *adj.* collective, common, communal, community, general, group, organized, public **2.** *n.* gathering, get-together (*Inf.*)

society 1. civilization, culture, mankind, people, the community, the public **2.** companionship, company, fellowship, friendship **3.** association, circle, club, fellowship, fraternity, group, guild, institute, league, sisterhood, union **4.** beau monde, elite, gentry, high society, upper classes

soft 1. cushioned, elastic, gelatinous, pulpy, spongy, squashy, swampy, yielding **2.** bendable, elastic, flexible, plastic, pliable, supple **3.** downy, feathery, fleecy, flowing, fluid, rounded, silky, smooth, velvety **4.** balmy, bland, caressing, delicate, diffuse, dim, dulcet, faint, gentle, light, low, mellow, mild, murmured, muted, pale, pastel, pleasing, quiet, restful, shaded, subdued, sweet, temperate, twilight, whispered **5.** compassionate, gentle, kind, pitying, sensitive, sentimental, sympathetic, tender **6.** effeminate, flabby, flaccid, limp, pampered, podgy, weak

soften abate, allay, appease, calm, cushion, ease, lessen, lighten, lower, melt, mitigate, moderate, mollify, muffle, palliate, quell, relax, soothe, still, subdue, temper

soil[1] *n.* clay, dirt, dust, earth, ground, loam

soil[2] *v.* befoul, begrime, defile, dirty, foul, muddy, pollute, smear, spatter, spot, stain, sully, tarnish

solace 1. *n.* comfort, consolation, relief **2.** *v.* allay, alleviate, comfort, console, mitigate, soften, soothe

soldier fighter, man-at-arms, redcoat, serviceman, trooper, warrior

sole alone, individual, one, single, singular, solitary

solecism blunder, gaffe, gaucherie, impropriety, lapse, mistake

solely alone, completely, entirely, exclusively, merely, only, singly

solemn 1. earnest, glum, grave, portentous, sedate, serious, sober, staid, thoughtful **2.** august, ceremonial, dignified, formal, grand, grave, imposing, impressive, momentous, stately

solicit ask, beg, canvass, crave, entreat, implore, importune, petition, pray, seek, supplicate

solicitous anxious, attentive, careful, caring, eager, troubled, uneasy, worried, zealous

solid *adj.* **1.** compact, concrete, dense, firm, hard, massed, stable, strong, sturdy, unshakable **2.** genuine, good, pure, real, reliable, sound **3.** constant, decent, dependable, reliable, sensible, serious, sober, trusty, upright, worthy

solidarity accord, camaraderie, cohesion, concordance, harmony, soundness, stability, team spirit, unanimity, unity

solidify cake, coagulate, cohere, congeal, harden, jell, set

solitary 1. desolate, hidden, lonely, remote, retired, secluded, unvisited **2.** alone, lone, single, sole **3.** cloistered, companionless, friendless, lonely, lonesome, reclusive, unsociable, unsocial

solitude isolation, loneliness, privacy, retirement, seclusion

solution 1. answer, elucidation, explanation, key, resolution, result, solving, unfolding **2.** blend, compound, mix, mixture, solvent dissolution, liquefaction, melting

solve answer, clear up, crack, decipher, disentangle, elucidate, explain, expound, interpret, resolve, unfold

sombre dark, dim, dismal, doleful, drab, dull, dusky, gloomy, grave, joyless, mournful, obscure, sad, sepulchral, shadowy, shady, sober

somebody *n.* celebrity, dignitary, household name, luminary, name, notable, personage, star, superstar

sometimes at times, occasionally

somnolent dozy, drowsy, half-awake, sleepy, soporific, torpid

song air, anthem, ballad, carol, chant, chorus, ditty, hymn, lay, lyric, melody, number, psalm, shanty, strain, tune

soon before long, in the near future, shortly

soothe allay, alleviate, appease, assuage, calm, compose, ease, hush, lull, mitigate, mollify, pacify, quiet, relieve, settle, soften, still, tranquillize

sophisticated **1.** cosmopolitan, cultivated, cultured, refined, seasoned, urbane, worldly **2.** advanced, complex, complicated, delicate, elaborate, intricate, refined, subtle

soporific **1.** *adj.* sedative, sleepy, somnolent, tranquillizing **2.** *n.* anaesthetic, hypnotic, opiate, tranquillizer

sorcerer enchanter, magician, sorceress, warlock, witch, wizard

sordid **1.** dirty, filthy, foul, mean, seedy, slovenly, squalid, unclean, wretched **2.** base, debauched, degenerate, low, shabby, shameful, vicious, vile **3.** avaricious, corrupt, covetous, grasping, miserly, niggardly, selfish, venal

sore **1.** angry, burning, inflamed, irritated, painful, raw, sensitive, smarting, tender **2.** annoying, severe, sharp, troublesome **3.** acute, critical, desperate, dire, extreme, pressing, urgent **4.** afflicted, angry, hurt, irked, irritated, pained, resentful, stung, upset, vexed

sorrow **1.** *n.* anguish, distress, grief, heartache, misery, mourning, regret, sadness, unhappiness, woe **2.** *v.* agonize, bemoan, bewail, grieve, lament, moan, mourn, weep

sorrowful dejected, depressed, distressing, grievous, lamentable, lugubrious, melancholy, miserable, mournful, painful, piteous, rueful, sad, sorry, tearful, unhappy, woebegone, woeful, wretched

sorry **1.** contrite, penitent, regretful, remorseful, repentant, shamefaced **2.** disconsolate, distressed, grieved, mournful, sad, sorrowful, unhappy **3.** moved, pitying, sympathetic **4.** abject, base, deplorable, dismal, distressing, mean, miserable, paltry, pathetic, piteous, pitiable, pitiful, poor, sad, shabby, vile, wretched

sort **1.** *n.* brand, breed, category, character, class, denomination, description, family, genus, group, ilk, kind, make, nature, order, quality, race, species, stamp, style, type, variety **2.** *v.* arrange, assort, catalogue, categorize, choose, class, classify, divide, file, grade, group, order, rank, select, separate, systematize

sort out **1.** organize, resolve, tidy up **2.** pick out, segregate, select, separate, sift

soul **1.** essence, intellect, life, mind, psyche, reason, spirit **2.** being, body, creature, individual, man, mortal, person, woman **3.** essence, personification, quintessence, type

sound[1] *n.* **1.** din, noise, report, reverberation, tone, voice **2.** drift, idea, impression, look, tenor **3.** earshot, hearing, range ~*v.* **4.** echo, resound, reverberate **5.** appear, look, seem **6.** announce, articulate, declare, enunciate, express, pronounce, signal, utter

sound[2] *adj.* **1.** complete, entire, firm, fit, hale, healthy, intact, perfect, robust, solid, sturdy, substantial, unhurt, uninjured, vigorous, whole **2.** correct, fair, just, logical, orthodox, proper, prudent, rational, reasonable, reliable, responsible, right, sensible, true, trustworthy, valid, well-founded, wise **3.** established, orthodox, proven, recognized, reliable, reputable, safe, secure, solid, solvent, stable, tried-and-true

sound[3] *v.* fathom, plumb, probe

sour **1.** acetic, acid, bitter, pungent, sharp, tart **2.** acrid, churlish, crabbed, cynical, disagreeable, discontented, embittered, grudging, ill-natured, jaundiced, peevish, tart, ungenerous, waspish

source **1.** author, begetter, beginning, cause, derivation, origin, rise, spring, wellspring **2.** authority, informant

souse drench, dunk, immerse, marinate (*Cookery*), pickle, soak, steep

souvenir keepsake, memento, relic, reminder

sovereign *n.* **1.** chief, emperor, empress, king, monarch, potentate, prince, queen, ruler, shah, tsar ~*adj.* **2.** absolute, chief, dominant, imperial, kingly, predominant, principal, regal, royal, ruling, supreme **3.** effectual, efficacious, efficient, excellent

sow broadcast, disseminate, implant, lodge, plant, scatter, seed

space **1.** capacity, expanse, extent, leeway, margin, play, room, scope, volume **2.** blank, distance, gap, interval, omission **3.** duration, interval, period, span, time, while

spacious ample, broad, comfortable, commodious, expansive, extensive, huge, large, roomy, sizable, vast

span *n.* **1.** amount, distance, extent, length, reach, spread, stretch **2.** duration, period, spell, term ~*v.* **3.** bridge, cover, cross, link, traverse, vault

spank *v.* cuff, slap, smack

spar *v.* argue, bicker, dispute, skirmish, squabble, wrangle, wrestle

spare *adj.* **1.** additional, emergency, extra, free, leftover, odd, over, superfluous, surplus, unoccupied, unused, unwanted **2.** gaunt, lank, lean, meagre, slender, slight, slim, wiry **3.** economical, frugal, meagre, modest, scanty, sparing ~*v.* **4.** afford, allow, bestow, dispense with, give, grant, part with, relinquish **5.** be merciful to, have mercy on, leave, pardon, refrain from, release, relieve from, save from

sparing careful, chary, economical, frugal, prudent, saving, thrifty

spark **1.** flare, flash, flicker, gleam, glint, spit **2.** atom, hint, jot, scrap, trace, vestige

sparkle *v.* **1.** beam, dance, flash, gleam, glint, glisten, glitter, glow, shimmer, shine, spark, twinkle, wink **2.** bubble, fizz, fizzle ~*n.* **3.** brilliance, dazzle, flash, flicker, gleam, glint, radiance, spark, twinkle **4.** dash, élan, gaiety, life, spirit, vitality

spartan abstemious, ascetic, austere, bleak, disciplined, extreme, frugal, plain, rigorous, severe, stern, strict

spasm **1.** contraction, convulsion, paroxysm, twitch **2.** access, burst, eruption, fit, frenzy, outburst, seizure

speak **1.** articulate, converse, discourse, express, pronounce, say, state, talk, tell, utter, voice **2.** address, argue, declaim, descant, discourse, harangue, lecture, plead, speechify

speaker lecturer, orator, public speaker, spokesman

special **1.** distinguished, especial, exceptional, extraordinary, festive, gala, important, memorable, significant, uncommon, unique, unusual **2.** appropriate, certain, distinctive, individual, particular, peculiar, precise **3.** chief, main, major, particular, primary

species breed, category, class, description, group, kind, sort, type, variety

specific **1.** definite, exact, explicit, express, limited, particular, precise, unequivocal **2.** characteristic, especial, peculiar, special

specify cite, define, designate, detail, enumerate, indicate, mention, name, particularize

specimen copy, example, exemplification, exhibit, individual, instance, model, pattern, proof, sample, type

speckled dappled, dotted, flecked, mottled, spotted, sprinkled

spectacle **1.** display, event, pageant, parade, performance, show, sight **2.** curiosity, laughing stock, marvel, scene, sight, wonder

spectacular daring, dazzling, dramatic, grand, impressive, magnificent, marked, remarkable, splendid, staggering, striking

spectator beholder, bystander, eyewitness, looker-on, observer, onlooker, viewer, watcher, witness

speculate **1.** conjecture, consider, meditate, muse, scheme, suppose, surmise, theorize, wonder **2.** gamble, hazard, risk

speech **1.** communication, conversation, dialogue, discussion, intercourse, talk **2.** address, discourse, harangue, homily, lecture, oration

speechless **1.** dumb, inarticulate, mum, mute, silent, wordless **2.** *Fig.* aghast, amazed, astounded, dazed, shocked

speed *n.* **1.** celerity, expedition, fleetness, haste, hurry, pace, quickness, rapidity, rush, swiftness, velocity ~*v.* **2.** career, dispatch, expedite, flash, gallop, hasten, hurry, quicken, race, rush, sprint, tear, urge, zoom **3.** advance, aid, assist, boost, expedite, facilitate, further, help, impel, promote

speedy expeditious, express, fast, fleet, hasty, headlong, hurried, immediate, nimble, precipitate, prompt, quick, rapid, summary, swift, winged

spell[1] *n.* bout, course, interval, period, season, stint, stretch, term, time, turn

spell[2] *n.* charm, incantation, sorcery, witchery

spelling orthography

spell out **1.** clarify, elucidate, specify **2.** discern, make out, puzzle out

spend **1.** disburse, expend **2.** consume, deplete, dispense, drain, empty, exhaust, run through, squander, use up, waste **3.** fill, occupy, pass, while away

spent **1.** burnt out, debilitated, drained, exhausted, prostrate, tired out, weakened, weary, worn out **2.** consumed, expended, finished, gone, used up

sphere **1.** ball, circle, globe, orb **2.** capacity, compass, domain, field, function, pale, province, range, rank, realm, scope, station, territory

spherical globe-shaped, rotund, round

spice **1.** relish, savour, seasoning **2.** colour, excitement, gusto, pep, piquancy, tang, zest

spike **1.** *n.* barb, point, prong, spine **2.** *v.* impale, spear, spit, stick

spill discharge, disgorge, overflow, overturn, scatter, shed, slop over, spill *or* run over, throw off, upset

spin *v.* **1.** pirouette, reel, revolve, rotate, turn, twirl, twist, wheel, whirl **2.** grow dizzy, reel, swim, whirl ~*n.* **3.** gyration, revolution, roll, twist, whirl

spin out amplify, delay, drag out, draw out, extend, lengthen, prolong

spiral **1.** *adj.* circular, coiled, corkscrew, scrolled, winding **2.** *n.* coil, corkscrew, helix, screw, whorl

spirit *n.* **1.** air, breath, life, soul, vital spark **2.** attitude, character, complexion, disposition, essence, humour, outlook, quality, temper, temperament **3.** ardour, backbone, courage, energy, enterprise, enthusiasm, fire, force, grit, life, liveliness, mettle, resolution, sparkle, vigour, warmth, zest **4.** resolution, resolve, will, willpower **5.** atmosphere, feeling, gist, humour, tenor, tone **6.** essence, intent, intention, meaning, purport, purpose, sense, substance **7.** *Plural* feelings, humour, mood, morale **8.** apparition, ghost, phantom, spectre, sprite, vision ~*v.* **9.** *With* **away** *or* **off** abduct, abstract, carry, convey, purloin, remove, seize, steal, whisk

spiritual devotional, divine, ghostly, holy, pure, religious, sacred

spit **1.** *v.* eject, expectorate, hiss, splutter, throw out **2.** *n.* dribble, drool, saliva, slaver, spittle

spite **1.** animosity, gall, grudge, hate, hatred, malice, pique, rancour, spitefulness, spleen, venom **2. in spite of** despite, notwithstanding, regardless of

spiteful barbed, cruel, ill-natured, malevolent, malicious, venomous, vindictive

splash *v.* **1.** shower, slop, spatter, spray, spread, sprinkle, squirt, strew, wet **2.** bathe, dabble, plunge, wade, wallow **3.** batter, break, buffet, dash, smack, strike, surge, wash **4.** broadcast, flaunt, headline, plaster, publicize, tout, trumpet ~*n.* **5.** burst, dash, patch, spattering, splodge, touch **6.** *Inf.* display, effect, impact, sensation, splurge, stir

splendid 1. admirable, brilliant, glorious, grand, heroic, illustrious, magnificent, outstanding, rare, renowned, sterling, sublime, superb, supreme **2.** costly, dazzling, gorgeous, impressive, lavish, luxurious, magnificent, ornate, resplendent, rich, sumptuous, superb **3.** excellent, fine, glorious, great (*Inf.*), marvellous, wonderful **4.** beaming, bright, brilliant, glittering, glowing, lustrous, radiant, refulgent

splendour brightness, brilliance, dazzle, display, glory, grandeur, lustre, magnificence, majesty, pomp, radiance, renown, resplendence, richness, show, solemnity, spectacle, sumptuousness

splinter 1. *n.* chip, flake, fragment, needle, shaving **2.** *v.* disintegrate, fracture, shatter, shiver, split

split *v.* **1.** branch, break, burst, cleave, crack, disband, disunite, diverge, fork, gape, open, part, rend, rip, separate, slash, slit, snap, splinter **2.** allocate, allot, apportion, distribute, divide, halve, parcel out, partition, share out, slice up ~*n.* **3.** breach, crack, damage, division, fissure, gap, rent, rip, slash, slit, tear **4.** breach, break, break-up, difference, discord, dissension, disunion, division, estrangement, partition, rift, rupture, schism ~*adj.* **5.** broken, cleft, cracked, divided, dual, ruptured, twofold

split up break up, disband, divorce, part, separate

spoil 1. blemish, damage, deface, destroy, disfigure, harm, impair, injure, mar, mess up, ruin, upset, wreck **2.** coddle, cosset, indulge, mollycoddle, overindulge, pamper **3.** addle, curdle, decay, go bad, mildew, putrefy, rot, turn

spoken expressed, oral, phonetic, put into words, said, told, unwritten, uttered, verbal, viva voce, voiced

spongy absorbent, cushioned, cushiony, elastic, light, porous, springy

sponsor 1. *n.* backer, godparent, patron, promoter **2.** *v.* back, finance, fund, guarantee, patronize, promote, subsidize

spontaneous free, impulsive, instinctive, natural, unforced, unprompted, voluntary, willing

sporadic intermittent, irregular, isolated, occasional, random, scattered, spasmodic

sport *n.* **1.** amusement, diversion, exercise, game, pastime, play, recreation **2.** badinage, banter, frolic, fun, jest, joking, merriment, mirth, teasing **3.** buffoon, butt, derision, game, mockery, plaything, ridicule ~*v.* **4.** *Inf.* display, exhibit, wear

spot *n.* **1.** blemish, blot, blotch, daub, flaw, mark, pimple, smudge, speck, stain, taint **2.** location, place, point, position, scene, site **3.** *Inf.* difficulty, mess, plight, predicament, quandary, trouble ~*v.* **4.** detect, discern, espy, identify, observe, recognize, see, sight **5.** besmirch, blot, dirty, dot, fleck, mark, soil, spatter, speckle, splodge, stain, sully, taint, tarnish

spotted dappled, dotted, flecked, mottled, pied, specked

spouse consort, helpmate, husband, mate, partner, wife

spout *v.* discharge, emit, erupt, gush, jet, shoot, spray, spurt, squirt, stream, surge

sprawl *v.* flop, loll, lounge, ramble, slouch, slump, spread, straggle, trail

spray[1] *v.* **1.** diffuse, scatter, shower, sprinkle ~*n.* **2.** drizzle **3.** aerosol, atomizer, sprinkler

spray[2] *n.* bough, branch, corsage, shoot, sprig

spread *v.* **1.** bloat, broaden, dilate, expand, extend, open, sprawl, stretch, swell, unfold, unfurl, unroll, widen **2.** multiply, mushroom, proliferate ~*n.* **3.** advance, development, diffusion, dispersion, escalation, expansion, increase, transmission **4.** compass, extent, period, reach, span, stretch, sweep, term

spree bacchanalia, bender (*Inf.*), binge (*Inf.*), carouse, debauch, fling, jag (*Sl.*), junketing, orgy, revel

sprightly active, agile, airy, alert, blithe, brisk, cheerful, gay, jaunty, joyous, lively, nimble, perky, playful, spirited, spry

spring *v.* **1.** bounce, bound, hop, jump, leap, rebound, recoil, vault **2.** *Often with* **from** arise, come, derive, descend, emanate, emerge, grow, issue, originate, proceed, start, stem **3.** *With* **up** appear, develop, mushroom, shoot up ~*n.* **4.** bound, buck, hop, jump, leap, vault **5.** buoyancy, elasticity, flexibility, recoil, resilience **6.** beginning, cause, origin, root, source, well

sprinkle dredge, dust, pepper, powder, scatter, shower, spray, strew

sprout *v.* bud, develop, grow, push, shoot, spring

spruce dainty, dapper, elegant, neat, smart, trim, well-groomed

spry active, agile, alert, brisk, nimble, quick, ready, sprightly, supple

spur *v.* **1.** animate, drive, goad, impel, incite, press, prick, prod, prompt, stimulate, urge ~*n.* **2.** goad, prick **3.** impetus, impulse, incentive, incitement, inducement, motive, stimulus

spurious artificial, bogus, deceitful, fake, false, forged, imitation, mock, pretended, sham, specious, unauthentic

spurn despise, disdain, rebuff, reject, repulse, scorn, slight, snub

spurt *v.* burst, erupt, gush, jet, shoot, spew, squirt, surge

spy 1. *n.* mole, undercover agent **2.** *v.* descry, espy, glimpse, notice, observe, spot

squabble 1. *v.* argue, bicker, brawl, clash, dispute, fight, quarrel, row, wrangle **2.** *n.* argument, disagreement, dispute, fight, row, tiff

squad band, company, crew, force, gang, group, team, troop

squalid decayed, dirty, fetid, filthy, foul, low, nasty, repulsive, seedy, sleazy, slovenly, slummy, sordid, unclean

squalor decay, filth, foulness, meanness, squalidness, wretchedness

squander consume, dissipate, expend, fritter away, lavish, misspend, misuse, scatter, spend, waste

square *Fig. adj.* **1.** aboveboard, decent, ethical, fair, genuine, honest, just, straight, upright **2.** *Inf.* bourgeois, conservative, conventional, old-fashioned, stuffy ~*n.* **3.** *Inf.* antediluvian, conservative, die-hard, traditionalist

squash *v.* **1.** compress, crush, distort, flatten, mash, pound, press, pulp, smash **2.** annihilate, crush, humiliate, quash, quell, silence, suppress

squeak *v.* peep, pipe, shrill, squeal, whine, yelp

squeal 1. *n.* scream, screech, shriek, wail, yell, yelp, yowl **2.** *v.* scream, screech, shout, shriek, shrill, wail, yelp

squeamish 1. delicate, fastidious, particular, prudish, scrupulous, strait-laced **2.** queasy, queer, sick

squeeze *v.* **1.** clutch, compress, crush, grip, nip, pinch, press, squash, wring **2.** cram, crowd, force, jam, jostle, pack, press, ram, stuff, thrust, wedge **3.** clasp, cuddle, embrace, enfold, hug **4.** extort, milk, oppress, pressurize, wrest ~*n.* **5.** clasp, embrace, handclasp, hold, hug **6.** congestion, crowd, crush, jam, press, squash

stab *v.* **1.** cut, gore, injure, jab, knife, pierce, spear, stick, thrust, transfix, wound ~*n.* **2.** gash, incision, jab, puncture, rent, thrust, wound **3.** ache, pang, prick, twinge **4. make a stab at** attempt, endeavour, essay, try

stability constancy, firmness, solidity, steadfastness, steadiness, strength

stable abiding, constant, durable, enduring, established, fast, firm, fixed, invariable, lasting, permanent, reliable, secure, sound, steadfast, steady, strong, sturdy, sure, well-founded

stack 1. *n.* heap, hoard, load, mass, mound, mountain, pile **2.** *v.* amass, assemble, bank up, heap up, load, pile

staff *n.* **1.** employees, officers, organization, personnel, teachers, team, workers, work force **2.** cane, pole, prop, rod, stave, wand

stage division, lap, leg, length, level, period, phase, point, step

stagger 1. falter, hesitate, lurch, reel, sway, vacillate, waver, wobble **2.** amaze, astonish, astound, confound, nonplus, overwhelm, shake, shock, stun, stupefy, surprise **3.** alternate, overlap, step, zigzag

stagnant brackish, quiet, sluggish, stale, standing, still

stagnate decay, decline, fester, idle, languish, rot, rust

staid calm, composed, grave, quiet, sedate, serious, sober, steady

stain *v.* **1.** blemish, blot, colour, dirty, discolour, dye, mark, soil, spot, tarnish, tinge **2.** blacken, corrupt, defile, deprave, disgrace, sully, taint ~*n.* **3.** blemish, blot, dye, spot, tint **4.** blemish, disgrace, dishonour, infamy, reproach, shame, slur, stigma

stake *n.* **1.** ante, bet, chance, hazard, peril, pledge, risk, venture, wager **2.** claim, concern, interest, investment, involvement, share ~*v.* **3.** bet, chance, gamble, hazard, imperil, pledge, put on, risk, venture, wager

stale decayed, dry, faded, fetid, flat, fusty, hard, insipid, musty, old, sour, tasteless

stalk *v.* follow, haunt, hunt, pursue, shadow, track

stalwart athletic, brawny, dependable, lusty, manly, muscular, redoubtable, robust, rugged, sinewy, staunch, stout, strong, sturdy, valiant, vigorous

stamina energy, force, power, resilience, resistance, strength, vigour

stammer *v.* falter, hesitate, pause, splutter, stumble, stutter

stamp *v.* **1.** beat, crush, trample **2.** engrave, fix, impress, imprint, inscribe, mark, mould, print ~*n.* **3.** brand, cast, earmark, hallmark, imprint, mark, mould, signature **4.** breed, cast, character, cut, description, fashion, form, kind, sort, type

stampede *n.* charge, flight, rout, rush

stamp out crush, destroy, eliminate, eradicate, extinguish, extirpate, quell, quench, scotch, suppress

stance 1. bearing, carriage, deportment, posture **2.** attitude, position, stand, standpoint, viewpoint

stand *v.* **1.** be upright, erect, mount, place, position, put, rank, rise, set **2.** belong, be valid, continue, exist, halt, hold, obtain, pause, prevail, remain, rest, stay, stop **3.** abide, allow, bear, brook, countenance, endure, experience, handle, stomach, suffer, support, sustain, take, tolerate, undergo, weather, withstand ~*n.* **4.** halt, rest, stay, stop **5.** attitude, determination, opinion, position, stance

standard 1. *n.* average, canon, criterion, example, grade, guide, measure, model, norm, pattern, principle, requirement, rule, sample, specification, type **2.** *adj.* accepted, average, basic, customary, normal, orthodox, prevailing, regular, set, staple, stock, typical, usual

standardize assimilate, institutionalize, mass-produce, regiment

standing *n.* condition, credit, eminence, estimation, footing, position, rank, reputation, repute, station, status

stand out bulk, large, project

standpoint angle, position, post, stance, station

stand up for champion, defend, support, uphold

star 1. *n.* celebrity, idol, lead, luminary, name 2. *adj.* brilliant, celebrated, leading, major, principal, prominent, well-known

stare *v.* gape, gawk, gaze, look, watch

start *v.* 1. appear, arise, begin, commence, depart, issue, leave, originate, set off, set out 2. activate, initiate, instigate, open, originate, turn on 3. begin, create, establish, father, found, inaugurate, initiate, institute, introduce, launch, pioneer, set up 4. blench, flinch, jerk, jump, recoil, shy, twitch ~*n.* 5. beginning, birth, dawn, foundation, inception, initiation, onset, opening, outset 6. advantage, edge, lead 7. jar, jump, spasm, twitch

startle agitate, alarm, amaze, frighten, scare, shock, surprise

starving famished, hungry, ravenous, starved

state[1] *v.* 1. affirm, articulate, assert, aver, declare, explain, expound, express, present, propound, put, report, say, specify, voice ~*n.* 2. case, category, circumstances, condition, mode, pass, plight, position, shape, situation 3. attitude, frame of mind, humour, mood, spirits 4. ceremony, dignity, display, glory, grandeur, majesty, pomp, splendour, style

state[2] *n.* commonwealth, country, federation, government, kingdom, land, nation, republic, territory

stately august, dignified, elegant, grand, imperial, lofty, majestic, measured, noble, pompous, regal, royal, solemn

statement account, communiqué, declaration, explanation, proclamation, recital, relation, report

static changeless, constant, fixed, immobile, inert, motionless, stagnant, stationary, still, unmoving, unvarying

station *n.* 1. base, depot, headquarters, location, place, position, post, seat, situation 2. appointment, business, calling, employment, grade, occupation, position, post, rank, situation, sphere, standing, status ~*v.* 3. assign, establish, fix, garrison, install, locate, post, set

stationary fixed, inert, moored, motionless, parked, standing, static, stock-still

status condition, consequence, degree, distinction, eminence, grade, position, prestige, rank, standing

stay *v.* 1. abide, continue, delay, halt, hover, linger, loiter, pause, remain, reside, settle, stand, stop, tarry, wait 2. adjourn, defer, discontinue, hold over, prorogue, put off, suspend ~*n.* 3. holiday, sojourn, stop, stopover, visit

steadfast constant, dedicated, dependable, faithful, fast, firm, fixed, intent, loyal, persevering, reliable, resolute, stable, staunch, steady, unswerving, unwavering

steady *adj.* 1. firm, fixed, safe, stable, substantial, uniform 2. balanced, calm, dependable, equable, imperturbable, level-headed, reliable, sensible, serene, settled, sober, staid, steadfast 3. ceaseless, confirmed, consistent, constant, continuous, even, faithful, habitual, incessant, nonstop, persistent, regular, rhythmic, unbroken, uninterrupted, unvarying ~*v.* 4. balance, brace, secure, stabilize, support

steal 1. appropriate, embezzle, filch, misappropriate, pilfer, plagiarize, poach, purloin, shoplift, take, thieve 2. creep, flit, insinuate oneself, slink, slip, sneak, tiptoe

stealth secrecy, slyness, surreptitiousness, unobtrusiveness

stealthy clandestine, furtive, secret, secretive, sly, sneaking, surreptitious

steep *adj.* 1. abrupt, headlong, precipitous, sheer 2. *Inf.* exorbitant, extortionate, extreme, high, unreasonable

steer 1. conduct, control, direct, govern, guide, pilot 2. **steer clear of** avoid, circumvent, eschew, evade, shun

stem[1] *n.* axis, branch, shoot, stalk, stock, trunk

stem[2] *v.* check, contain, curb, dam, oppose, stop, withstand

step *n.* 1. footfall, footprint, footstep, gait, impression, pace, print, stride, trace, track, walk 2. act, action, deed, expedient, means, measure, move 3. **take steps** act, intervene, prepare 4. advance, move, phase, point, process, stage 5. degree, level, rank, remove 6. **in step** coinciding, conforming, in line 7. **out of step** erratic, incongruous ~*v.* 8. move, pace, tread, walk

stereotype 1. *n.* formula, mould, pattern 2. *v.* categorize, dub, standardize, typecast

sterile 1. bare, barren, dry, empty, fruitless, unfruitful, unproductive, unprofitable 2. aseptic, disinfected, germ-free, sterilized

stern austere, bitter, cruel, flinty, forbidding, frowning, grim, hard, harsh, inflexible, relentless, rigid, serious, severe, strict, unyielding

stick[1] *v.* 1. adhere, affix, attach, bind, bond, cement, cleave, cling, fasten, fix, fuse, glue, hold, hold on, join, paste, weld 2. dig, gore, insert, jab, penetrate, pierce, pin, poke, prod, puncture, spear, stab, thrust, transfix 3. *With* **out, up** *etc.* bulge, extend, jut, obtrude, poke, project, protrude, show 4. catch, clog, jam, lodge, snag, stop 5. linger, persist, remain, stay 6. **stick up for** *Inf.* champion, defend, support, uphold

stick[2] baton, birch, cane, pole, rod, staff, stake, switch, twig, wand

sticky 1. adhesive, clinging, gluey, glutinous, gummy, syrupy, tacky, tenacious, viscous 2. *Inf.* awkward, delicate, difficult, embarrassing, nasty, painful, thorny, tricky, unpleasant

stiff 1. firm, hard, inelastic, inflexible, rigid, solid, taut, tense, tight, unbending, unyielding 2. artificial, austere, chilly, cold, constrained, forced, formal, laboured, mannered, pompous, priggish, prim, standoffish, uneasy, wooden 3. awkward, clumsy, crude, graceless, inelegant, jerky, ungainly, ungraceful, unsupple

stiffen brace, congeal, harden, jell, reinforce, set, solidify, starch, tauten, tense, thicken

stifle 1. choke, smother, strangle, suffocate 2. check, curb, extinguish, hush, muffle, prevent, repress, restrain, silence, smother, stop, suppress

still 1. *adj.* calm, hushed, inert, motionless, peaceful, placid, quiet, restful, serene, silent, smooth, stationary, tranquil, undisturbed 2. *v.* allay, alleviate, appease, calm, hush, lull, pacify, quieten, settle, silence, smooth, soothe, subdue, tranquillize 3. *conj.* but, however, nevertheless, notwithstanding, yet

stimulant excitant, restorative, reviver, tonic

stimulate animate, arouse, encourage, fan, fire, goad, impel, incite, instigate, prompt, provoke, quicken, rouse, spur, urge

stimulus encouragement, goad, incentive, inducement, provocation, spur

sting burn, hurt, pain, smart, tingle, wound

stint period, quota, share, shift, spell, stretch, term, time, tour, turn

stipulate agree, contract, covenant, engage, guarantee, lay down, pledge, postulate, promise, require, settle, specify

stipulation agreement, clause, condition, contract, engagement, provision, qualification, requirement, restriction, settlement, specification, term

stir *v.* 1. agitate, beat, disturb, flutter, mix, move, quiver, rustle, shake, tremble 2. *Often with* **up** arouse, awaken, excite, incite, inflame, prompt, provoke, quicken, raise, spur, stimulate, urge 3. bestir, be up and about (*Inf.*), budge, hasten, mill about, move ~*n.* 4. activity, ado, agitation, bustle, commotion, disorder, excitement, ferment, flurry, fuss, movement, to-do, tumult, uproar

stirring dramatic, emotive, exciting, heady, impassioned, inspiring, lively, moving, rousing, spirited, stimulating, thrilling

stock *n.* 1. array, assets, choice, commodities, fund, goods, hoard, inventory, range, reserve, selection, stockpile, store, supply, variety, wares 2. *Animals* beasts, cattle, flocks, herds, horses, livestock, sheep 3. *Money* capital, funds, investment, property 4. **take stock** appraise, estimate, weigh up ~*adj.* 5. banal, basic, conventional, customary, formal, ordinary, overused, regular, routine, set, standard, staple, traditional, trite, usual, worn-out ~*v.* 6. deal in, handle, keep, sell, supply, trade in 7. *With* **up** amass, buy up, gather, hoard, replenish, save, supply

stoicism acceptance, calmness, dispassion, fatalism, fortitude, impassivity, indifference, patience, resignation, stolidity

stolid apathetic, doltish, dull, heavy, obtuse, slow, stupid, unemotional, wooden

stomach *n.* 1. belly, pot, tummy (*Inf.*) 2. appetite, desire, inclination, mind, relish, taste ~*v.* 3. abide, bear, endure, suffer, swallow, take, tolerate

stony *Fig.* blank, callous, chilly, expressionless, frigid, hard, heartless, hostile, icy, indifferent, merciless, pitiless, unforgiving, unresponsive

stoop *v.* bend, bow, crouch, descend, duck, hunch, incline, kneel, lean, squat

stop *v.* 1. cease, conclude, cut short, desist, discontinue, draw up, end, finish, halt, leave off, pause, put an end to, quit, refrain, run down, shut down, stall, terminate 2. arrest, bar, block, break, check, close, frustrate, hinder, hold back, impede, intercept, interrupt, obstruct, plug, prevent, repress, restrain, seal, silence, staunch, stem, suspend 3. lodge, put up, rest, sojourn, stay, tarry ~*n.* 4. cessation, conclusion, end, finish, halt, standstill 5. break, rest, sojourn, stay, visit 6. bar, block, break, check, control, hindrance, impediment, plug 7. depot, destination, halt, stage, station, termination, terminus

stoppage arrest, close, closure, cutoff, deduction, halt, hindrance, shutdown, standstill, stopping

store *v.* 1. deposit, garner, hoard, husband, keep, put aside, put by, put in storage, reserve, salt away, save, stockpile ~*n.* 2. accumulation, cache, fund, hoard, lot, mine, plenty, plethora, provision, quantity, reserve, stock, supply, wealth 3. emporium, market, mart, outlet, shop, supermarket 4. depository, repository, storeroom, warehouse

storm *n.* 1. blast, blizzard, cyclone, gale, gust, hurricane, squall, tempest, tornado, whirlwind 2. *Fig.* agitation, anger, clamour, commotion, disturbance, furore, outburst, outcry, passion, roar, row, rumpus, stir, strife, tumult, turmoil, violence ~*v.* 3. assail, assault, beset, charge, rush ~*n.* 4. assault, attack, blitz, blitzkrieg, offensive, onset, onslaught, rush ~*v.* 5. bluster, complain, fume, rage, rant, rave, scold, thunder 6. flounce, fly, rush, stalk, stamp

stormy blustery, boisterous, dirty, foul, gusty, raging, rough, squally, turbulent, wild, windy

story 1. account, anecdote, history, legend, narrative, novel, recital, record, relation, romance, tale, version, yarn 2. article, feature, news, news item, report, scoop

stout 1. big, bulky, burly, fat, fleshy, heavy, overweight, plump, portly, rotund, substantial, tubby 2. able-bodied, athletic, brawny, hardy, hulking, lusty, robust, stalwart, strapping, strong, sturdy, tough, vigorous 3. bold, brave, courageous, fearless, gallant, manly, plucky, resolute, valiant

straggle drift, lag, loiter, ramble, range, roam, rove, stray, wander

straight *adj.* 1. direct, near, short 2. aligned, erect, even, horizontal, level, plumb, right, smooth, square, true, upright, vertical 3. above board, accurate, authentic, decent, equitable, fair, honest, honourable, just, reliable, respectable, trustworthy, upright **4.** arranged, in order, neat, orderly, organized, put to rights, shipshape, sorted out, tidy **5.** consecutive, continuous, nonstop, running, solid, successive, sustained, through **6.** neat, pure, unadulterated, undiluted, unmixed ~*adv.* **7.** at once, directly, immediately, instantly

straightaway at once, directly, immediately, instantly, now, right away

straightforward 1. candid, direct, forthright, genuine, guileless, honest, open, sincere, truthful **2.** clear-cut, easy, elementary, routine, simple, uncomplicated

strain[1] *v.* **1.** distend, extend, stretch, tauten, tighten **2.** drive, exert, fatigue, injure, overtax, overwork, pull, sprain, tax, tear, tire, twist, weaken, wrench **3.** endeavour, labour, strive, struggle **4.** filter, percolate, purify, riddle, screen, seep, separate, sieve, sift ~*n.* **5.** effort, exertion, force, injury, pull, sprain, struggle, tautness, tension, wrench **6.** anxiety, burden, pressure, stress, tension

strain[2] *n.* ancestry, blood, descent, extraction, family, race, stock

strained artificial, awkward, difficult, embarrassed, false, forced, laboured, put on, stiff, tense, uneasy, unnatural

strait-laced moralistic, narrow, prim, proper, prudish, puritanical, strict

straits *n. Sometimes singular* **1.** crisis, difficulty, dilemma, distress, emergency, extremity, hardship, mess, pass, plight, predicament **2.** channel, narrows, sound

strand *n.* fibre, filament, length, lock, rope, string, thread, tress, twist

stranded aground, ashore, beached, grounded, marooned, wrecked

strange 1. abnormal, bizarre, curious, eccentric, exceptional, extraordinary, fantastic, funny, marvellous, mystifying, odd, peculiar, queer, rare, remarkable, singular, uncanny, unheard of, weird, wonderful **2.** alien, exotic, foreign, new, novel, remote, unfamiliar, unknown, untried

stranger alien, foreigner, guest, incomer, newcomer, outlander, visitor

strangle 1. asphyxiate, choke, smother, suffocate, throttle **2.** inhibit, repress, stifle, suppress

strap 1. *n.* belt, leash, thong, tie **2.** *v.* bind, buckle, fasten, lash, secure, tie

stratagem artifice, device, dodge, feint, intrigue, plan, plot, ploy, ruse, scheme, trick

strategy approach, grand design, plan, policy, procedure, programme

stray *v.* **1.** deviate, digess, diverge, ramble **2.** drift, err, meander, range, roam, rove, straggle, wander ~*adj.* **3.** abandoned, homeless, lost, roaming, vagrant

streak *n.* **1.** band, layer, line, slash, strip, stripe, stroke, vein **2.** dash, element, strain, touch, trace, vein ~*v.* **3.** dart, flash, fly, hurtle, speed, sprint, sweep, tear, whistle, zoom

stream 1. *n.* beck, brook, burn, course, current, drift, flow, rill, river, run, rush, surge, tide, torrent, tributary **2.** *v.* cascade, course, emit, flood, flow, glide, gush, issue, pour, run, shed, spill, spout

street avenue, lane, road, roadway, row, terrace

strength 1. backbone, brawn, courage, firmness, fortitude, health, might, muscle, robustness, sinew, stamina, stoutness, sturdiness, toughness **2.** effectiveness, efficacy, energy, force, intensity, potency, power, resolution, spirit, vehemence, vigour **3.** advantage, anchor, asset, mainstay, security

strengthen 1. brace up, consolidate, encourage, fortify, harden, hearten, invigorate, nerve, nourish, restore, stiffen, toughen **2.** bolster, brace, build up, buttress, confirm, enhance, establish, harden, heighten, increase, intensify, justify, reinforce, steel, support

strenuous 1. arduous, demanding, hard, laborious, taxing, toilsome, tough, unrelaxing, uphill **2.** active, bold, determined, eager, earnest, energetic, persistent, resolute, spirited, strong, tireless, zealous

stress *n.* **1.** emphasis, force, importance, significance, urgency, weight **2.** anxiety, burden, pressure, strain, tension, trauma, worry **3.** accent, accentuation, beat, emphasis ~*v.* **4.** accentuate, dwell on, emphasize, harp on, point up, repeat, rub in, underline

stretch *v.* **1.** cover, extend, put forth, reach, spread, unfold, unroll **2.** distend, draw out, elongate, expand, inflate, lengthen, pull, rack, strain, swell, tighten ~*n.* **3.** area, distance, expanse, extent, spread, sweep, tract

strict 1. austere, authoritarian, firm, harsh, rigid, rigorous, severe, stern, stringent **2.** accurate, close, exact, faithful, meticulous, particular, precise, religious, scrupulous, true **3.** absolute, total, utter

strife battle, clash, combat, conflict, contention, contest, discord, friction, quarrel, rivalry, row, struggle, warfare

strike *v.* **1.** beat, box, buffet, chastise, cuff, hammer, hit, knock, punish, slap, smack, smite, thump **2.** bump into, clash, dash, hit, run into, touch **3.** drive, force, hit, impel, thrust **4.** affect, come to, hit, impress, occur to, reach, seem **5.** affect, assail, assault, attack, devastate, hit, invade, set upon, smite **6.** achieve, arrange, arrive at, attain, effect, reach **7.** down tools, mutiny, revolt, walk out

striking conspicuous, dazzling, extraordinary, forcible, impressive, memorable, noticeable, outstanding

string *n.* **1.** cord, fibre, twine **2.** chain, file, line, procession, row, sequence, series, strand, succession

strip[1] *v.* **1.** bare, denude, deprive, despoil, divest, empty, gut, loot, peel, pillage, plunder, ransack, rob, sack, skin, spoil **2.** disrobe, unclothe, undress

strip[2] *n.* band, belt, bit, fillet, piece, ribbon, shred, slip, tongue

striped banded, barred, striated, stripy

strive attempt, compete, contend, endeavour, fight, labour, strain, struggle, toil, try, try hard

stroke *n.* **1.** achievement, blow, feat, flourish, hit, knock, move, pat, rap, thump **2.** apoplexy, attack, collapse, fit, seizure, shock ~*v.* **3.** caress, fondle, pat, pet, rub

stroll 1. *v.* amble, ramble, saunter, wander **2.** *n.* airing, constitutional, excursion, promenade, ramble, turn, walk

strong 1. athletic, brawny, burly, capable, hale, hardy, healthy, muscular, powerful, robust, sound, stalwart, stout, strapping, sturdy, tough, virile **2.** brave, courageous, determined, forceful, high-powered, plucky, resilient, resolute, steadfast, stouthearted, tenacious, tough, unyielding **3.** acute, dedicated, deep, eager, fervent, fierce, firm, intense, keen, severe, staunch, vehement, violent, zealous **4.** clear, compelling, convincing, distinct, effective, formidable, great, marked, persuasive, potent, redoubtable, sound, telling, unmistakable, urgent, weighty, well-founded **5.** drastic, extreme, forceful, severe **6.** durable, hard-wearing, heavy-duty, reinforced, sturdy, substantial, well-built **7.** acrid, biting, concentrated, heady, highly-flavoured, highly-seasoned, hot, pungent, pure, sharp, spicy, undiluted

stronghold bastion, bulwark, castle, citadel, fort, fortress, keep

structure *n.* **1.** arrangement, conformation, design, fabric, form, formation, make, make-up, organization **2.** building, construction, edifice, erection, pile ~*v.* **3.** arrange, assemble, build up, design, organize, shape

struggle *v.* **1.** exert oneself, labour, strain, strive, toil, work ~*n.* **2.** effort, exertion, labour, pains, scramble, toil, work ~*v.* **3.** battle, compete, contend, fight, grapple, scuffle, wrestle ~*n.* **4.** battle, brush, clash, combat, conflict, contest, encounter, skirmish, strife, tussle

stubborn cross-grained, dogged, dour, fixed, headstrong, inflexible, intractable, obdurate, obstinate, persistent, pig-headed, recalcitrant, self-willed, tenacious, unbending, unshakable, unyielding, wilful

stuck 1. cemented, fast, fastened, firm, fixed, glued, joined **2.** *Inf.* baffled, beaten, nonplussed, stumped

student apprentice, disciple, learner, observer, pupil, scholar, undergraduate

studied conscious, deliberate, intentional, planned, premeditated, wilful

studious academic, assiduous, attentive, bookish, careful, diligent, eager, earnest, meditative, reflective, scholarly, serious, thoughtful

study *v.* **1.** cogitate, consider, contemplate, examine, learn, meditate, ponder, pore over, read, read up **2.** analyse, deliberate, examine, investigate, peruse, research, scrutinize, survey ~*n.* **3.** application, learning, lessons, reading, research, school work, thought **4.** analysis, attention, contemplation, inquiry, investigation, review, scrutiny, survey

stuff *v.* **1.** cram, crowd, fill, force, jam, load, pack, pad, push, ram, shove, squeeze, stow, wedge **2.** gorge, guzzle, overindulge, sate ~*n.* **3.** belongings, effects, equipment, gear, impedimenta, junk, kit, luggage, objects, tackle, things, trappings **4.** cloth, fabric, material, raw material, textile **5.** essence, matter, pith, staple, substance

stuffy 1. airless, close, frowsty, heavy, muggy, oppressive, stale, stifling, sultry, unventilated **2.** deadly, dreary, dull, fusty, pompous, priggish, prim, staid, stilted, stodgy

stumble 1. fall, falter, flounder, hesitate, lurch, reel, slip, stagger, trip **2.** *With* **on** *or* **upon** discover, encounter, find, turn up

stump *v.* baffle, bewilder, confound, confuse, foil, mystify, outwit, perplex, puzzle, stop

stun *Fig.* astonish, astound, bewilder, confound, confuse, knock out, overcome, overpower, shock, stagger, stupefy

stunning beautiful, brilliant, dazzling, gorgeous, impressive, lovely, marvellous, sensational, spectacular, striking, wonderful

stunt *n.* act, deed, exploit, feat, feature, trick

stupefy amaze, astound, bewilder, daze, numb, shock, stagger, stun

stupendous amazing, astounding, breathtaking, colossal, enormous, gigantic, huge, marvellous, overwhelming, phenomenal, prodigious, staggering, superb, surprising, vast, wonderful

stupid 1. brainless, deficient, dense, dim, dull, foolish, gullible, half-witted, moronic, naive, obtuse, simple, simple-minded, slow, slow-witted, sluggish, stolid, thick, unintelligent, witless **2.** futile, idiotic, inane, indiscreet, laughable, ludicrous, mindless, pointless, puerile, rash, senseless, unintelligent **3.** dazed, groggy, insensate, semiconscious, senseless, stunned, stupefied

stupidity 1. brainlessness, denseness, dimness, dullness, imbecility, obtuseness, puerility, simplicity, slowness, thickness **2.** absurdity, fatuity, folly, idiocy, inanity, ineptitude, lunacy, madness, silliness

sturdy athletic, brawny, determined, durable, firm, flourishing, hardy, hearty, muscular, powerful, resolute, robust, secure, solid, staunch, steadfast, substantial, vigorous, well-built, well-made

style *n.* **1.** cut, design, form, hand, manner **2.** fashion, mode, rage, trend, vogue **3.** approach, custom, manner, method, mode, way **4.** chic, dash, elegance, flair, grace, panache, polish, refinement, smartness, sophistication, taste, urbanity **5.** affluence, comfort, ease, elegance, grandeur, luxury **6.** appearance, category, genre, kind, pattern, sort, spirit, strain, tenor, tone, type, variety *~v.* **7.** adapt, arrange, cut, design, dress, fashion, shape, tailor **8.** address, call, denominate, designate, dub, entitle, label, name, term

stylish chic, dapper, fashionable, modish, polished, smart, urbane, voguish

subconscious *adj.* hidden, inner, intuitive, latent, repressed, subliminal

subdue 1. break, conquer, control, crush, defeat, discipline, humble, master, overcome, overpower, overrun, quell, tame, trample, vanquish **2.** check, control, mellow, moderate, repress, soften, suppress, tone down

subject *n.* **1.** affair, business, issue, matter, object, point, question, substance, theme, topic **2.** case, client, participant, patient, victim **3.** citizen, dependant, liegeman, national, vassal *~adj.* **4.** disposed, exposed, liable, open, prone, susceptible, vulnerable **5.** conditional, contingent, dependent **6.** answerable, bound by, captive, dependent, inferior, obedient, satellite, subordinate *~v.* **7.** expose, lay open, submit, treat

subjective biased, emotional, intuitive, personal, prejudiced

sublime elevated, eminent, exalted, glorious, grand, great, high, imposing, lofty, magnificent, majestic, noble

submerge deluge, dip, drown, duck, engulf, flood, immerse, overflow, overwhelm, plunge, sink, swamp

submission 1. assent, capitulation, surrender, yielding **2.** compliance, deference, docility, meekness, obedience, passivity, resignation **3.** argument, contention, proposal **4.** entry, presentation, tendering

submit 1. accede, bend, bow, capitulate, comply, defer, endure, give in, stoop, succumb, surrender, tolerate, yield **2.** commit, hand in, present, proffer, refer, table, tender

subordinate *adj.* **1.** dependent, inferior, junior, lesser, lower, minor, secondary, subject **2.** ancillary, auxiliary, subsidiary, supplementary *~n.* **3.** aide, assistant, attendant, inferior, junior, second, underling

subscribe contribute, donate, give, offer, pledge, promise

subscription donation, dues, gift, membership fee, offering

subsequent after, ensuing, following, later, succeeding, successive

subsequently afterwards, consequently, later

subside abate, decrease, diminish, dwindle, ease, ebb, lessen, melt away, moderate, peter out, quieten, recede, slacken, wane

subsidiary aiding, ancillary, assistant, auxiliary, helpful, lesser, minor, secondary, subordinate, supplementary, useful

subsidize finance, fund, promote, sponsor, support, underwrite

subsidy aid, allowance, assistance, contribution, grant, help, support

subsist be, continue, endure, exist, last, live, remain, survive

subsistence existence, food, keep, living, maintenance, provision, rations, support, survival, sustenance, upkeep

substance 1. body, fabric, material, stuff, texture **2.** burden, essence, gist, import, matter, meaning, pith, significance, subject, theme **3.** actuality, concreteness, entity, force, reality **4.** affluence, assets, estate, means, property, resources, wealth

substantial ample, big, generous, goodly, important, large, significant, sizable, worthwhile

substantiate authenticate, confirm, establish, prove, support, verify

substitute 1. *v.* change, exchange, interchange, replace, switch **2.** *n.* agent, deputy, equivalent, expedient, locum, makeshift, proxy, relief, replacement, representative, reserve, stand-by, stopgap, sub, supply **3.** *adj.* acting, additional, alternative, proxy, replacement, reserve, second, surrogate, temporary

subterfuge artifice, deception, dodge, evasion, excuse, ploy, pretence, quibble, ruse, shift, stall, stratagem, trick

subtle 1. deep, delicate, ingenious, nice, profound, refined, sophisticated **2.** delicate, faint, implied, indirect, slight **3.** artful, astute, crafty, cunning, designing, devious, intriguing, keen, shrewd, sly, wily

subtlety 1. acumen, cleverness, delicacy, intricacy, nicety, refinement, sagacity, skill, sophistication **2.** astuteness, craftiness, cunning, guile, wiliness

subtract deduct, detract, diminish, remove, take from, take off

suburbs environs, neighbourhood, outskirts, precincts, residential areas, suburbia

subversive destructive, overthrowing, riotous, seditious, underground

succeed 1. flourish, make good, prosper, thrive, triumph, work **2.** come next, ensue, follow, result, supervene

succeeding ensuing, following, next, subsequent, successive

success 1. ascendancy, fame, fortune, happiness, luck, prosperity, triumph **2.** celebrity, market leader, sensation, somebody, star, winner

successful acknowledged, booming, favourable, flourishing, fortunate, fruitful, lucky, lucrative, paying, profitable, prosperous, rewarding, thriving, top, unbeaten, victorious, wealthy

successfully favourably, victoriously, well

succession 1. chain, course, cycle, flow, order, progression, run, sequence, series, train **2.** accession, assumption, elevation, inheritance, taking over

successive consecutive, following, sequent

succinct brief, compact, concise, condensed, laconic, pithy, summary, terse

succour 1. *v.* aid, assist, comfort, encourage, foster, help, nurse, relieve, render assistance to, support **2.** *n.* aid, assistance, comfort, help, relief, support

succulent juicy, luscious, lush, rich

succumb capitulate, die, fall, submit, surrender, yield

sudden abrupt, hasty, hurried, quick, rapid, rash, swift, unexpected

suddenly abruptly, unexpectedly, without warning

sue 1. charge, indict, prosecute, summon **2.** appeal for, beg, beseech, entreat, petition, plead, solicit

suffer 1. ache, agonize, grieve, hurt **2.** bear, endure, experience, feel, support, sustain, tolerate, undergo **3.** deteriorate, fall off

suffering *n.* agony, anguish, discomfort, distress, hardship, misery, ordeal, pain, torment

suffice answer, content, do, satisfy, serve

sufficient adequate, competent, enough

suggest 1. advise, move, propose, recommend **2.** connote, evoke **3.** hint, imply, indicate, insinuate, intimate

suggestion 1. motion, plan, proposal, proposition **2.** breath, hint, indication, intimation, trace, whisper

suit *v.* **1.** agree, answer, become, befit, conform to, do, gratify, harmonize, match, please, satisfy, tally **2.** accommodate, adapt, adjust, fashion, fit, modify, proportion, tailor *~n.* **3.** *Law* action, case, cause, lawsuit, proceeding, prosecution, trial **4.** clothing, costume, dress, ensemble, habit, outfit **5. follow suit** copy, emulate

suitability aptness, fitness, rightness, timeliness

suitable applicable, apposite, appropriate, apt, becoming, befitting, convenient, due, fit, fitting, opportune, pertinent, proper, relevant, right, satisfactory

suite 1. apartment, rooms, series, set **2.** attendants, entourage, escort, followers, retainers, retinue, train

sulk brood, look sullen, pout

sulky aloof, churlish, cross, ill-humoured, moody, morose, perverse, petulant, querulous, resentful, sullen, vexed

sullen brooding, cheerless, cross, dismal, dull, gloomy, heavy, moody, morose, obstinate, silent, sombre, sour, surly, unsociable

sultry close, hot, humid, oppressive, sticky, stifling, stuffy

sum aggregate, amount, quantity, score, tally, total, whole

summarily arbitrarily, immediately, promptly, speedily, swiftly

summarize abridge, condense, encapsulate, epitomize, outline, précis, review, sum up

summary abridgment, abstract, digest, epitome, extract, outline, précis, résumé, review, rundown, synopsis

summit acme, apex, crown, head, height, peak, pinnacle, top, zenith

summon arouse, bid, call, cite, convene, convoke, invite, rally, rouse

sumptuous costly, dear, gorgeous, grand, lavish, luxurious, opulent, rich, splendid, superb

sum up 1. close, conclude, recapitulate, review, summarize **2.** estimate

sundry assorted, different, miscellaneous, several, some, varied, various

sunken 1. drawn, haggard, hollow **2.** buried, depressed, lower, recessed, submerged

sunny 1. bright, brilliant, clear, fine, radiant, summery, sunlit, unclouded **2.** *Fig.* beaming, blithe, buoyant, cheerful, genial, happy, joyful, pleasant

sunrise cockcrow, dawn, daybreak, daylight

sunset dusk, eventide, gloaming, nightfall, sundown

superb admirable, choice, excellent, exquisite, fine, first-rate, gorgeous, grand, magnificent, marvellous, splendid, superior, unrivalled

supercilious arrogant, contemptuous, disdainful, haughty, imperious, insolent, lofty, lordly, overbearing, patronizing, proud, scornful

superficial 1. exterior, external, on the surface, peripheral, shallow, skin-deep, slight, surface **2.** casual, cursory, desultory, hasty, hurried, perfunctory, sketchy, slapdash

superficially apparently, externally, ostensibly

superfluous excess, extra, left over, needless, redundant, remaining, residuary, spare, supererogatory, supernumerary, surplus, uncalled-for, unnecessary, unrequired

superhuman 1. heroic, prodigious, stupendous, valiant **2.** divine, paranormal, supernatural

superintend administer, control, direct, inspect, manage, overlook, oversee, run, supervise

superintendent chief, controller, director, governor, inspector, manager, overseer, supervisor

superior *adj.* **1.** better, grander, greater, higher, paramount, preferred, surpassing, unrivalled **2.** choice, de luxe, distinguished, excellent, exceptional, exclusive, fine, first-class, first-rate, good **3.** airy, condescending, disdainful, haughty, lofty, lordly, patronizing, pretentious, snobbish *~n.* **4.** boss (*Inf.*), chief, director, manager, principal, senior, supervisor

superiority advantage, ascendancy, excellence, lead, preponderance, supremacy

superlative *adj.* excellent, greatest, highest, matchless, outstanding, peerless, supreme, surpassing, transcendent, unparalleled, unrivalled, unsurpassed

supernatural dark, ghostly, hidden, miraculous, mysterious, mystic, occult, paranormal, phantom, psychic, spectral, supranatural, uncanny, unearthly

supervise administer, conduct, control, direct, handle, inspect, look after, manage, oversee, run, superintend

supervision administration, care, charge, control, direction, guidance, management, oversight

supervisor administrator, chief, foreman, manager, overseer, steward

supplant displace, oust, remove, replace, undermine, unseat

supple bending, elastic, flexible, limber, lithe, plastic, pliable, pliant

supplement 1. *n.* addition, codicil, extra, insert, postscript, pull-out, sequel 2. *v.* add, augment, complement, extend, fill out, reinforce, top up

supplementary additional, ancillary, auxiliary, extra, secondary

suppliant 1. *adj.* begging, craving, entreating, imploring, importunate 2. *n.* applicant, petitioner, suitor, supplicant

supply *v.* 1. afford, contribute, endow, fill, furnish, give, grant, outfit, produce, provide, replenish, satisfy, stock, store, yield ~*n.* 2. cache, fund, hoard, quantity, reserve, reservoir, source, stock, store 3. *Usually plural* equipment, food, foodstuff, materials, necessities, provisions, rations, stores

support *v.* 1. bear, brace, buttress, carry, hold, prop, reinforce, sustain, underpin, uphold 2. buoy up, cherish, finance, foster, fund, keep, maintain, nourish, provide for, strengthen, sustain, underwrite 3. aid, assist, back, champion, defend, forward, help, promote, second, side with, uphold 4. bear, brook, countenance, endure, stomach, submit, suffer, tolerate, undergo ~*n.* 5. back, brace, foundation, lining, pillar, post, prop, shore, stay, underpinning 6. aid, approval, assistance, backing, blessing, comfort, encouragement, friendship, help, loyalty, patronage, protection, relief, succour, sustenance 7. keep, subsistence, sustenance, upkeep 8. backbone, backer, comforter, mainstay, prop, second, stay, supporter

supporter adherent, advocate, champion, fan, follower, friend, helper, patron, sponsor, wellwisher

suppose 1. assume, conjecture, expect, imagine, infer, judge, opine, presume, surmise, granted, think 2. believe, conceive, conclude, conjecture, consider, fancy, imagine, pretend

supposition conjecture, doubt, guess, hypothesis, idea, presumption, speculation, surmise, theory

suppress 1. beat down, check, conquer, crush, extinguish, overpower, overthrow, quash, quell, quench, stop, subdue, trample on 2. censor, conceal, contain, curb, muffle, muzzle, repress, restrain, silence, smother, stifle, withhold

supremacy ascendancy, dominance, lordship, mastery, predominance, primacy, sovereignty, sway

supreme cardinal, chief, crowning, extreme, final, first, foremost, greatest, head, highest, leading, matchless, paramount, peerless, pre-eminent, prevailing, prime, principal, sovereign, superlative, surpassing, top, ultimate, utmost

sure 1. assured, certain, clear, confident, convinced, decided, definite, persuaded, positive, satisfied 2. accurate, dependable, effective, foolproof, honest, indisputable, infallible, precise, reliable, trustworthy, trusty, undeniable, undoubted, unerring, unfailing 3. assured, bound, guaranteed, inescapable, inevitable, irrevocable

surely certainly, definitely, doubtlessly, inevitably, undoubtedly, unquestionably

surface 1. *n.* covering, exterior, face, outside, plane, side, skin, top, veneer 2. *v.* appear, come to light, come up, crop up (*Inf.*), emerge, materialize, rise, transpire

surfeit 1. *n.* excess, glut, plethora, superfluity 2. *v.* cram, fill, glut, gorge, overfeed, stuff

surge billow, eddy, gush, heave, rise, roll, rush, swell, swirl, tower, undulate, well forth

surly churlish, crabbed, cross, crusty, gruff, morose, perverse, sulky, sullen, testy, uncivil, ungracious

surmise 1. *v.* conclude, conjecture, consider, deduce, fancy, guess, imagine, infer, opine, presume, speculate, suppose, suspect 2. *n.* conclusion, conjecture, deduction, guess, idea, inference, notion, speculation, supposition, suspicion

surmount conquer, exceed, master, overcome, pass, surpass, vanquish

surpass beat, best, eclipse, exceed, excel, outdo, outshine, outstrip, override, transcend

surplus 1. *n.* balance, excess, remainder, residue, surfeit 2. *adj.* excess, extra, odd, remaining, spare, superfluous, unused

surprise *v.* 1. amaze, astonish, astound, bewilder, confuse, disconcert, stagger, stun 2. discover, spring upon, startle ~*n.* 3. amazement, astonishment, incredulity, wonder 4. bombshell, jolt, revelation, shock

surprised amazed, disconcerted, incredulous, speechless, startled, thunderstruck

surprising amazing, astounding, extraordinary, incredible, remarkable, staggering, unexpected, unusual, wonderful

surrender *v.* 1. abandon, cede, concede, forego, part with, relinquish, renounce, resign, waive, yield 2. capitulate, give in, give way, quit, submit, succumb, yield ~*n.* 3. capitulation, delivery, renunciation, resignation, submission

surreptitious covert, fraudulent, furtive, secret, sly, stealthy, underhand, veiled

surround encircle, enclose, encompass, envelop, environ, girdle, ring

surroundings background, environs, location, milieu, setting

surveillance care, control, direction, inspection, scrutiny, supervision, vigilance, watch

survey *v.* 1. contemplate, examine, inspect, observe, research, review, scan, scrutinize, study, view 2. appraise, assess, estimate, measure, plan, plot, prospect, size up, triangulate ~*n.* 3. examination, inquiry, inspection, overview, perusal, random sample, review, scrutiny, study

survive be extant, endure, exist, last, live, live on, outlast, outlive, remain alive, subsist

suspect *v.* 1. distrust, doubt, mistrust 2. believe, conclude, conjecture, consider, fancy, feel, guess, speculate, suppose, surmise ~*adj.* 3. doubtful, dubious, questionable

suspend 1. attach, dangle, hang, swing 2. arrest, cease, cut short, debar, defer, delay, discontinue, interrupt, postpone, put off, shelve, stay, withhold

suspense anxiety, apprehension, doubt, expectation, indecision, insecurity, irresolution, tension, uncertainty, wavering

suspicion 1. distrust, doubt, jealousy, misgiving, mistrust, qualm, scepticism, wariness 2. conjecture, guess, hunch, idea, impression, notion, supposition, surmise 3. glimmer, hint, shade, shadow, *soupçon*, strain, streak, suggestion, tinge, touch, trace

suspicious 1. doubtful, jealous, sceptical, unbelieving, wary 2. doubtful, dubious, funny, irregular, queer, questionable

sustain 1. bear, carry, support, uphold 2. bear, endure, experience, feel, suffer, withstand 3. aid, assist, comfort, foster, help, keep alive, nourish, nurture, relieve 4. approve, confirm, continue, maintain, prolong, protract, ratify 5. endorse, uphold, validate, verify

sustenance 1. comestibles, eatables, food, nourishment, rations, refreshments, victuals 2. livelihood, subsistence, support

swagger 1. *v.* bluster, boast, brag, bully, hector, parade, prance, strut 2. *n.* arrogance, bluster, display, pomposity, show

swallow absorb, consume, devour, drink, eat, gulp, ingest, swill, wash down

swamp 1. *n.* bog, fen, marsh, mire, morass, quagmire, slough 2. *v.* capsize, drench, engulf, flood, inundate, overwhelm, sink, submerge, upset, waterlog

swap, swop *v.* bandy, barter, exchange, interchange, switch, trade, traffic

swarm *n.* 1. army, bevy, crowd, drove, flock, herd, horde, host, mass, multitude, myriad, shoal, throng ~*v.* 2. crowd, flock, mass, stream, throng 3. *With* **with** abound, bristle, crawl, teem

swarthy black, brown, dark, dusky

swashbuckling bold, dashing, gallant, spirited, swaggering

sway *v.* 1. bend, incline, lean, lurch, oscillate, rock, roll, swing, wave 2. affect, control, direct, dominate, govern, guide, induce, influence, persuade ~*n.* 3. ascendency, authority, command, control, influence, jurisdiction, power, predominance, rule, sovereignty

swear 1. affirm, assert, attest, avow, declare, depose, promise, testify, vow, warrant 2. blaspheme, curse, imprecate

sweat *n.* 1. perspiration 2. *Inf.* agitation, anxiety, distress, panic, strain, worry 3. *Inf.* chore, drudgery, effort, labour ~*v.* 4. glow, perspire 5. *Inf.* agonize, chafe, fret, suffer, torture oneself, worry

sweep *v.* 1. brush, clean, clear, remove 2. career, fly, glance, glide, hurtle, pass, sail, scud, skim, tear, zoom ~*n.* 3. arc, bend, curve, move, stroke, swing 4. compass, extent, range, scope, stretch

sweet *adj.* 1. cloying, honeyed, luscious, melting, sweetened 2. affectionate, agreeable, amiable, appealing, beautiful, charming, engaging, fair, gentle, kind, lovable, tender, unselfish, winning 3. beloved, darling, dear, dearest, pet, precious 4. aromatic, balmy, clean, fragrant, fresh, new, pure, wholesome 5. *Usually plural* confectionery

sweeten 1. honey, sugar 2. alleviate, appease, pacify, soothe

sweetheart admirer, beau, beloved, boyfriend, darling, dear, girlfriend, love, lover, suitor

swell *v.* 1. balloon, belly, billow, bloat, bulge, dilate, distend, enlarge, expand, extend, fatten, grow, increase, protrude, rise, tumefy, well up 2. add to, aggravate, augment, enhance, heighten, intensify, mount, surge ~*n.* 3. billow, rise, surge, wave

swelling *n.* bruise, bulge, bump, dilation, enlargement, inflammation, lump, protuberance

swerve *v.* bend, deflect, deviate, diverge, incline, shift, stray, swing, turn, turn aside, veer, wander, wind

swift abrupt, express, fast, fleet, flying, hurried, nimble, prompt, quick, rapid, ready, short, speedy, sudden, winged

swindle 1. *v.* cheat, deceive, defraud, dupe, fleece, overcharge, trick 2. *n.* deceit, deception, fraud, knavery, racket, roguery, trickery

swindler charlatan, cheat, fraud, impostor, mountebank, rascal, rogue, shark, trickster

swing *v.* 1. dangle, hang, suspend 2. fluctuate, oscillate, rock, sway, vary, veer, vibrate, wave ~*n.* 3. fluctuation, stroke, sway, vibration

swirl *v.* churn, eddy, spin, surge, twist

switch 1. *v.* change, deflect, deviate, divert, exchange, shift, substitute, trade 2. *n.* alteration, change, exchange, reversal, shift, substitution

swollen bloated, distended, enlarged, inflamed, tumid

swoop 1. *v.* descend, dive, pounce, rush, stoop, sweep 2. *n.* drop, lunge, pounce, rush

sword 1. blade 2. **cross swords** argue, dispute, fight, spar, wrangle

syllabus course of study, curriculum

symbol badge, emblem, figure, image, representation, sign, token, type

symmetrical balanced, proportional, regular

symmetry agreement, balance, evenness, harmony, order, proportion

sympathetic 1. caring, compassionate, concerned, condoling, feeling, interested, kind, kindly, pitying, responsive, supportive, tender, warm 2. agreeable, appreciative, compatible, congenial, friendly, responsive

sympathize 1. commiserate, condole, feel for, pity 2. agree, understand

sympathizer partisan, supporter, well-wisher

sympathy 1. compassion, pity, tenderness, understanding 2. affinity, agreement, congeniality, harmony, rapport, union, warmth

symptom expression, indication, mark, note, sign, token, warning

synthesis 1. amalgamation, combination, integration, welding 2. amalgam, blend, combination, composite, compound, fusion, union

synthetic artificial, fake, man-made, mock

system 1. arrangement, classification, coordination, organization, scheme, structure 2. method, practice, procedure, routine, technique, theory, usage 3. method, orderliness, regularity

systematic efficient, methodical, orderly, organized, precise

T

table *n.* 1. bench, board, counter, slab, stand 2. board, diet, fare, food 3. agenda, chart, diagram, graph, index, list, plan, record, register, roll, schedule ~*v.* 4. enter, move, propose, put forward, submit, suggest

taboo 1. *adj.* banned, forbidden, outlawed, prohibited, proscribed, unmentionable, unthinkable 2. *n.* anathema, ban, prohibition, proscription, restriction

tacit implicit, implied, inferred, silent, understood, unspoken, unstated

taciturn aloof, cold, distant, dumb, mute, quiet, reserved, reticent, silent, unforthcoming

tack *n.* 1. nail, pin, staple 2. approach, bearing, course, direction, heading, line, method, path, tactic, way ~*v.* 3. affix, attach, fasten, fix, nail, pin, staple 4. baste, stitch

tackle *n.* 1. apparatus, equipment, gear, outfit, rigging, tools, trappings 2. block, challenge, stop ~*v.* 3. attempt, begin, embark upon, engage in, essay, undertake 4. block, bring down, grab, grasp, halt, seize, stop, throw

tact address, delicacy, diplomacy, discretion, judgment, perception, skill

tactful careful, considerate, delicate, diplomatic, discreet, judicious, polite, sensitive, subtle, thoughtful

tactic 1. approach, course, device, line, means, method, move, ploy, policy, scheme, trick, way 2. *Plural* campaign, plans, strategy

tactical artful, clever, cunning, politic, shrewd, skilful, smart

tactless careless, clumsy, gauche, harsh, impolite, inconsiderate, indiscreet, insensitive, maladroit, rough, rude, sharp, thoughtless, unfeeling, unkind

tail *n.* 1. conclusion, end, extremity, train 2. file, line, queue ~*v.* 3. *Inf.* follow, shadow, stalk, track, trail

tail off *or* **away** decrease, drop, dwindle, fade, fall away, wane

tailor 1. *n.* clothier, dressmaker, outfitter, seamstress 2. *v.* adapt, adjust, alter, convert, cut, fashion, fit, modify, mould, shape, style, suit

taint 1. *v.* contaminate, corrupt, dirty, foul, infect, pollute, spoil 2. *n.* blemish, blot, defect, disgrace, dishonour, fault, flaw, shame, smear, spot, stain, stigma

take 1. abduct, acquire, arrest, capture, catch, clutch, entrap, get, grasp, grip, have, obtain, receive, secure, seize, win 2. abstract, appropriate, filch, pocket, purloin, steal 3. book, buy, engage, hire, lease, pay for, pick, purchase, rent, reserve, select 4. abide, bear, brave, brook, endure, pocket, stand, stomach, suffer, swallow, tolerate, undergo, withstand 5. consume, drink, eat, imbibe, ingest, inhale, swallow 6. accept, adopt, assume, undertake 7. assume, believe, consider, deem, hold, perceive, presume, receive, regard, understand 8. bear, bring, carry, cart, convey, ferry, fetch, haul, transport 9. accompany, bring, conduct, convoy, escort, guide, lead, usher 10. deduct, eliminate, remove, subtract 11. accept, contain, hold

take back disclaim, recant, renounce, retract, withdraw

take down 1. minute, note, record, transcribe 2. deflate, humble, humiliate, mortify

take in 1. absorb, assimilate, comprehend, digest, grasp, understand 2. comprise, contain, cover, embrace, encompass, include 3. admit, let in, receive 4. cheat, deceive, dupe, fool, hoodwink, mislead, swindle, trick

takeoff 1. departure, launch, liftoff 2. *Inf.* caricature, imitation, lampoon, mocking, parody, satire, travesty

take off 1. discard, doff, drop, peel off, remove, strip off 2. take to the air 3. *Inf.* beat it (*Sl.*), decamp, depart, disappear, go, hit the road (*Sl.*), leave, set out, split (*Sl.*), strike out 4. *Inf.* caricature, imitate, lampoon, mimic, mock, parody, satirize

take on 1. employ, engage, enlist, enrol, hire, retain 2. accept, tackle, undertake 3. face, fight, oppose, vie with

take up 1. adopt, assume, engage in, start 2. continue, go on, pick up, proceed, restart, resume 3. absorb, consume, cover, fill, occupy

taking 1. *adj.* attractive, charming, compelling, delightful, enchanting, intriguing, pleasing, winning 2. *n. Plural* earnings, gain, gate, income, proceeds, profits, receipts, returns, yield

tale 1. account, anecdote, fable, fiction, legend, novel, relation, report, romance, saga, story 2. fabrication, falsehood, fib, lie, rigmarole, rumour, untruth

talent ability, aptitude, bent, capacity, endowment, faculty, flair, genius, gift

talented able, artistic, brilliant, gifted, well-endowed

talk *v.* 1. chat, chatter, converse, gossip, natter, prate, say, speak, utter 2. confer, have a confab (*Inf.*), hold discussions, negotiate, parley 3. crack, inform ~*n.* 4. address, discourse, harangue, lecture, oration, sermon, speech 5. chat, chatter, chitchat, conversation, gossip, hearsay, natter, rumour 6. colloquy, conclave, conference, consultation, dialogue, discussion, meeting, parley, seminar, symposium 7. argot, dialect, jargon, language, slang, speech, words

talking-to criticism, lecture, rebuke, reprimand, reproach, reproof, row, scolding

tall 1. big, giant, high, lanky, lofty, soaring 2. *Inf.* demanding, difficult, hard

tally *v.* 1. accord, agree, coincide, concur, conform, fit, match, square, suit 2. compute, mark, reckon, record, register, total ~*n.* 3. count, mark, reckoning, record, score, total

tame *adj.* 1. broken, cultivated, disciplined, docile, gentle, obedient 2. compliant, docile, meek, subdued, unresisting 3. bland, boring, dull, flat, insipid, prosaic, tedious ~*v.* 4. break in, domesticate, pacify, train 5. break the spirit of, conquer, curb, discipline, enslave, humble, master, repress, subjugate, suppress

tamper 1. alter, interfere, intrude, meddle, muck about (*Brit. sl.*), poke one's nose into (*Inf.*), tinker 2. bribe, corrupt, fix, influence, manipulate, rig

tangible actual, concrete, definite, evident, manifest, material, objective, perceptible, physical, positive, real, solid, substantial, touchable

tangle *n.* 1. coil, confusion, knot, mass, mat, mesh, snarl, twist, web 2. complication, imbroglio, labyrinth, maze, mess, mix-up ~*v.* 3. coil, confuse, jam, kink, knot, mat, mesh, snarl, twist

tangled 1. jumbled, knotted, scrambled, snarled, tousled, twisted 2. complex, complicated, confused, knotty, messy

tantalize baffle, balk, entice, frustrate, provoke, taunt, tease, thwart, torment, torture

tantamount equal, equivalent, synonymous

tantrum fit, ill humour, outburst, storm, temper

tap[1] 1. *v.* beat, drum, knock, pat, rap, strike, touch 2. *n.* beat, knock, light blow, pat, rap, touch

tap[2] *n.* 1. spigot, spout, stopcock, valve 2. bung, plug, stopper ~*v.* 3. bleed, broach, drain, open, pierce, unplug 4. draw on, exploit, milk, mine, use, utilize

tape *n.* 1. band, ribbon, strip ~*v.* 2. bind, seal, secure 3. record, video

taper come to a point, narrow, thin

target 1. aim, bull's-eye, end, goal, intention, mark, object, objective 2. butt, quarry, scapegoat, victim

tariff 1. duty, excise, impost, levy, rate, tax, toll 2. charges, menu, schedule

tarnish befoul, blacken, blemish, blot, darken, dim, dull, rust, soil, spot, stain, sully, taint

tart[1] 1. pastry, pie 2. harlot, loose woman, prostitute, slut, strumpet, trollop, whore

tart[2] 1. acid, bitter, pungent, sharp, sour, tangy 2. astringent, biting, caustic, crusty, harsh, nasty, sharp, short, snappish, testy

task *n.* assignment, charge, chore, duty, employment, enterprise, exercise, job, labour, mission, toil, work

taste *n.* 1. flavour, relish, savour, smack, tang 2. bit, bite, dash, drop, morsel, mouthful, nip, sample, sip, swallow, titbit, touch 3. appetite, bent, desire, fancy, inclination, leaning, liking, palate, penchant, preference, relish 4. appreciation, cultivation, culture, discernment, discrimination, elegance, grace, judgment, perception, polish, refinement, style ~*v.* 5. differentiate, discern, distinguish, perceive 6. assay, nibble, relish, sample, savour, sip, test, try 7. experience, feel, know, undergo

tasteful artistic, beautiful, charming, cultivated, delicate, elegant, exquisite, fastidious, graceful, handsome, harmonious, polished, refined, restrained, smart, stylish

tasteless 1. bland, boring, dull, flat, insipid, mild, stale, tame, thin, uninteresting, vapid, weak 2. cheap, coarse, crass, crude, flashy, garish, gaudy, graceless, gross, improper, indelicate, inelegant, low, rude, tawdry, uncouth, vulgar

tasty appetizing, delectable, delicious, flavourful, luscious, palatable, sapid, savoury

taunt 1. *v.* deride, flout, gibe, insult, jeer, mock, revile, ridicule, tease, torment, upbraid 2. *n.* barb, censure, cut, derision, dig, gibe, insult, jeer, reproach, ridicule, sarcasm

taut flexed, rigid, strained, stretched, tense, tight

tawdry cheap, flashy, gaudy, meretricious, raffish, showy, tasteless, tinsel, vulgar

tax *n.* 1. assessment, charge, customs, duty, excise, impost, levy, rate, tariff, tithe, toll, tribute 2. burden, demand, drain, load, pressure, strain, weight ~*v.* 3. assess, charge, demand, exact, impose, rate 4. burden, drain, enervate, exhaust, load, overburden, push, sap, strain, stretch, task, try, weaken, weary 5. accuse, arraign, blame, charge, impeach, impugn, incriminate

taxing burdensome, demanding, exacting, heavy, onerous, tiring, tough, trying, wearing

teach advise, coach, direct, drill, educate, enlighten, guide, impart, implant, inculcate, inform, instil, instruct, school, show, train, tutor

teacher coach, don, educator, guide, instructor, lecturer, master, mentor, mistress, pedagogue, professor, schoolmaster, schoolmistress, trainer, tutor

team 1. *n.* band, body, bunch, company, crew, gang, group, set, side, squad, troupe 2. *v. Often with* **up** cooperate, couple,

join, link, unite, work together, yoke
tear *v.* 1. claw, divide, mangle, rend, rip, rive, run, scratch, sever, shred, split, sunder 2. bolt, career, charge, dart, dash, fly, gallop, hurry, race, run, rush, shoot, speed, sprint 3. grab, pluck, pull, rip, seize, snatch ~*n.* 4. hole, mutilation, rent, rip, run, rupture, scratch, split
tearful crying, sobbing, weeping, whimpering
tears distress, lamentation, mourning, pain, regret, sadness, sobbing, sorrow, wailing, weeping, woe
tease annoy, badger, bait, bedevil, chaff, gibe, goad, mock, needle, pester, provoke, rag, ridicule, taunt, torment, vex
technique 1. course, fashion, means, method, mode, procedure, style, system, way 2. address, art, artistry, craft, execution, facility, knack, proficiency, skill, touch
tedious banal, boring, drab, dreary, dull, irksome, laborious, lifeless, monotonous, prosaic, soporific, tiring, unexciting, uninteresting, vapid, wearisome
tedium banality, boredom, drabness, dreariness, dullness, monotony, routine, tediousness
teem abound, bear, brim, bristle, overflow, swarm
teeming alive, brimful, bursting, crawling, fruitful, full, numerous, overflowing, packed, replete, swarming, thick
telegraph *n.* 1. teleprinter, telex 2. cable, radiogram, telegram ~*v.* 3. cable, send, telex, transmit
telepathy mind-reading, sixth sense
telephone 1. *n.* handset, line, phone 2. *v.* call, call up, dial, phone, ring (*Brit.*)
telescope *n.* 1. glass, spyglass ~*v.* 2. crush, squash 3. compress, condense, curtail, cut, shorten, shrink, trim, truncate
tell 1. announce, communicate, confess, disclose, divulge, express, impart, inform, mention, notify, proclaim, reveal, say, speak, state, utter 2. bid, call upon, command, direct, enjoin, instruct, order, require, summon 3. depict, describe, narrate, portray, recount, rehearse, relate, report 4. discover, see, understand 5. discern, distinguish, identify 6. carry weight, register, weigh 7. calculate, compute, count, enumerate, number, reckon, tally
temper *n.* 1. attitude, disposition, humour, mind, mood, nature, vein 2. fury, passion, rage, tantrum 3. anger, annoyance, heat, irritability, passion, peevishness, petulance, surliness 4. calm, calmness, composure, equanimity, moderation, tranquillity ~*v.* 5. abate, admix, allay, assuage, calm, lessen, moderate, restrain, soften, soothe
temperament bent, character, complexion, constitution, humour, make-up, mettle, nature, outlook, personality, quality, soul, spirit
temperamental 1. capricious, emotional, erratic, excitable, fiery, impatient, irritable, moody, passionate, sensitive, touchy, volatile 2. erratic, inconsistent, unreliable
temperance 1. forbearance, moderation, restraint, self-control, self-restraint 2. abstinence, prohibition, sobriety, teetotalism
temperate 1. agreeable, balmy, calm, cool, fair, gentle, mild, pleasant, soft 2. calm, dispassionate, equable, mild, moderate, reasonable, sensible, stable 3. abstemious, abstinent, continent, moderate, sober
temple church, sanctuary, shrine
temporarily briefly, fleetingly, momentarily, pro tem
temporary brief, ephemeral, fleeting, impermanent, interim, momentary, passing, provisional, transient
tempt 1. allure, attract, coax, decoy, draw, entice, inveigle, invite, lure, seduce, woo 2. bait, dare, provoke, risk, test, try
temptation allurement, appeal, attraction, bait, blandishments, coaxing, decoy, draw, inducement, invitation, lure, pull, seduction, snare, tantalization
tempting alluring, attractive, enticing, inviting, seductive, tantalizing
tenacious 1. clinging, fast, firm, forceful, iron, strong, tight 2. retentive, unforgetful 3. adamant, determined, dogged, firm, inflexible, obstinate, persistent, resolute, staunch, stubborn, sure, unyielding
tenacity 1. firmness, force, power, strength 2. firm grasp, retention 3. application, determination, diligence, doggedness, firmness, intransigence, obstinacy, persistence, resolution, resolve, stubbornness
tenancy holding, lease, occupancy, possession, residence
tenant holder, inhabitant, leaseholder, lessee, occupier, resident
tend[1] gravitate, incline, lean, trend
tend[2] attend, control, cultivate, feed, guard, handle, keep, maintain, manage, nurse, protect, wait on, watch, watch over
tendency bent, inclination, leaning, partiality, penchant, predilection, predisposition, propensity
tender[1] 1. delicate, feeble, fragile, frail, soft, weak 2. green, immature, new, raw, sensitive, unripe, vulnerable, young 3. affectionate, amorous, benevolent, caring, compassionate, fond, gentle, humane, kind, loving, merciful, pitiful, sympathetic, warm 4. difficult, risky, sensitive, ticklish, touchy, tricky 5. aching, acute, bruised, inflamed, irritated, painful, raw, sensitive, smarting, sore
tender[2] 1. *v.* extend, give, offer, present, proffer, propose, submit, suggest, volunteer 2. *n.* bid, estimate, offer, proffer, proposal
tenderness 1. feebleness, fragility, softness, weakness 2. callowness, greenness, immaturity, newness, youth 3. affection, attachment, care, compassion, fondness, gentleness, liking, love, mercy, pity, sympathy 4. ache, bruising, irritation, pain, rawness, smart
tense 1. rigid, strained, stretched, taut, tight 2. edgy, fidgety, jumpy, keyed up, nervous, restless, strained, wrought up 3. exciting, moving, stressful, worrying
tension 1. pressure, stiffness, stress, tautness, tightness 2. anxiety, hostility, pressure, strain, stress, unease
tentative 1. experimental, indefinite, provisional, speculative, unsettled 2. cautious, diffident, doubtful, faltering, hesitant, timid, uncertain, unsure
tepid 1. lukewarm, warmish 2. apathetic, cool, indifferent, lukewarm
term *n.* 1. denomination, designation, expression, name, phrase, title, word 2. period, season, space, span, spell, time 3. course, session 4. bound, close, conclusion, confine, culmination, end, finish, limit, terminus ~*v.* 5. call, denominate, designate, dub, entitle, label, name, style
terminate cease, close, complete, conclude, cut off, discontinue, end, expire, finish, issue, lapse, result, run out, stop, wind up
termination cessation, close, conclusion, discontinuation, effect, end, ending, expiry, finale, finish, issue, result
terminology argot, cant, jargon, language, phraseology, terms, vocabulary
terminus 1. close, end, extremity, goal, limit, target, termination 2. depot, garage, station
terms 1. language, phraseology, terminology 2. conditions, particulars, provisions, qualifications, specifications, stipulations 3. charges, fee, payment, price, rates
terrible 1. bad, dangerous, extreme, serious, severe 2. awful, bad, dire, dreadful, frightful, hideous, loathsome, odious, offensive, poor, repulsive, revolting, unpleasant, vile 3. awful, dreadful, fearful, frightful, gruesome, harrowing, horrible, horrifying, monstrous, shocking
terrific 1. awful, dreadful, enormous, extreme, fearful, fierce, great, harsh, huge, intense, severe, tremendous 2. amazing, breathtaking, excellent, fine, marvellous, outstanding, superb, wonderful
terrified alarmed, appalled, awed, dismayed, horrified, intimidated, petrified, scared, shocked, terror-stricken
terrify alarm, appal, awe, dismay, frighten, horrify, intimidate, petrify, scare, shock, terrorize
territory area, country, district, land, province, region, state, tract, zone
terror alarm, anxiety, awe, dismay, dread, fear, fright, horror, intimidation, panic, shock
terrorize 1. browbeat, bully, intimidate, menace, oppress, threaten 2. alarm, awe, dismay, frighten, horrify, intimidate, petrify, scare, shock, terrify
terse 1. brief, clipped, compact, concise, crisp, incisive, laconic, neat, pithy, short, succinct, summary 2. abrupt, brusque, curt, short, snappy
test 1. *v.* analyse, assess, check, experiment, investigate, prove, try, verify 2. *n.* analysis, assessment, attempt, catechism, check, evaluation, examination, investigation, ordeal, proof, trial
testify affirm, assert, attest, witness, certify, corroborate, declare, evince, show, state, swear, vouch, witness
testimonial certificate, commendation, endorsement, reference, tribute
testimony affidavit, attestation, avowal, corroboration, deposition, evidence, profession, statement, submission, witness
text 1. body, matter 2. wording, words 3. argument, matter, motif, subject, theme, topic
texture character, consistency, fabric, feel, grain, make, quality, structure, surface, tissue, weave
thanks appreciation, credit, gratefulness, gratitude, recognition, thanksgiving
thaw defrost, melt, soften, warm
theatrical affected, artificial, ceremonious, dramatic, exaggerated, histrionic, mannered, overdone, pompous, showy, stagy, stilted, unreal
theft fraud, larceny, pilfering, robbery, stealing, swindling
theme 1. argument, idea, keynote, matter, subject, text, thesis, topic 2. motif 3. composition, dissertation, essay, exercise, paper
theoretical abstract, academic, ideal, impractical, pure, speculative
theorize conjecture, formulate, guess, project, speculate, suppose
theory 1. assumption, guess, hypothesis, speculation, surmise, thesis 2. philosophy, plan, proposal
therapeutic corrective, curative, good, healing, remedial, salutary, sanative
therefore accordingly, consequently, ergo, so, then, thus, whence
thick 1. broad, deep, fat, solid, wide 2. close, clotted, compact, crowded, deep, dense, heavy, opaque 3. bristling, bursting, chock-a-block, chock-full, covered, crawling, frequent, full, numerous, packed, replete, swarming, teeming 4. brainless, dense, dull, obtuse, slow, stupid, thickheaded 5. dense, heavy, soupy 6. distorted, guttural, hoarse, husky, inarticulate, indistinct, throaty 7. broad, decided, distinct, marked, pronounced, rich, strong 8. close, devoted, familiar, friendly, inseparable, intimate
thicken cake, clot, condense, congeal, deepen, gel, jell, set
thief bandit, burglar, cheat, embezzler, housebreaker, pickpocket, plunderer, robber, shoplifter, stealer, swindler
thieve cheat, embezzle, filch, misappropriate, peculate, pilfer, plunder, poach, purloin, rob, steal, swindle
thin *adj.* 1. fine, narrow, threadlike 2. delicate, filmy, fine, flimsy, gossamer, sheer, unsubstantial 3. bony, lank, lanky, lean, light, meagre, skinny, slender, slight, slim, spare 4. deficient,

meagre, scanty, scarce, scattered, skimpy, sparse, wispy **5.** diluted, runny, watery, weak **6.** feeble, flimsy, inadequate, lame, poor, scant, scanty, shallow, slight, superficial, weak

thing **1.** affair, article, body, concept, entity, fact, matter, object, part, portion, substance **2.** act, deed, event, feat, incident, occurrence, proceeding **3.** apparatus, contrivance, device, gadget, implement, instrument, machine, means, mechanism, tool **4.** aspect, detail, facet, factor, feature, item, particular, point, statement, thought **5.** *Plural* baggage, belongings, clothes, effects, equipment, goods, luggage, possessions, stuff

think **1.** believe, conceive, conclude, consider, deem, esteem, estimate, hold, imagine, judge, reckon, regard, suppose, surmise **2.** brood, cerebrate, cogitate, consider, deliberate, meditate, muse, ponder, reason, reflect, revolve **3.** recall, recollect, remember **4.** anticipate, envisage, expect, foresee, imagine, plan for, presume, suppose **5. think better of** reconsider, repent **6. think much of** admire, esteem, respect, value

thinking *adj.* contemplative, cultured, intelligent, philosophical, rational, reasoning, reflective, thoughtful

think over consider, contemplate, ponder, weigh up

third-rate bad, indifferent, inferior, mediocre, poor, shoddy

thirst *n.* **1.** drought, dryness, thirstiness **2.** appetite, craving, longing, passion, yearning

thirsty arid, dry, parched

thorny **1.** bristly, pointed, prickly, sharp, spinous **2.** awkward, difficult, hard, irksome, ticklish, tough, trying, worrying

thorough *or* **thoroughgoing** **1.** assiduous, careful, complete, conscientious, efficient, exhaustive, full, intensive, painstaking, scrupulous, sweeping **2.** absolute, arrant, complete, downright, entire, perfect, pure, sheer, total, unqualified, utter

thoroughly **1.** carefully, completely, efficiently, exhaustively, fully, painstakingly, scrupulously, sweepingly, throughout **2.** absolutely, entirely, completely, downright, entirely, perfectly, quite, totally, to the full, utterly

though allowing, even if, granted, notwithstanding, while

thought **1.** cogitation, consideration, contemplation, deliberation, introspection, meditation, musing, reflection, regard **2.** assessment, belief, concept, conclusion, conviction, idea, judgment, opinion, thinking, view **3.** attention, heed, regard, scrutiny, study **4.** aim, design, idea, intention, notion, object, plan, purpose **5.** dream, expectation, hope, prospect **6.** anxiety, care, compassion, concern, kindness, regard, sympathy

thoughtful **1.** attentive, caring, considerate, helpful, kind, kindly, solicitous, unselfish **2.** contemplative, deliberative, meditative, musing, pensive, rapt, reflective, ruminative, serious, studious, wistful

thoughtless **1.** impolite, insensitive, rude, selfish, tactless, uncaring, unkind **2.** careless, foolish, heedless, inattentive, mindless, neglectful, rash, reckless, remiss, silly, stupid, unthinking

thrash **1.** beat, belt, birch, cane, drub, flog, horse-whip, leather, punish, scourge, spank, whip **2.** beat, clobber (*Brit. sl.*), crush, defeat, drub, maul, overwhelm, rout, trounce

thrash out debate, discuss, resolve, settle

thread **1.** *n.* cotton, fibre, line, strand, string, yarn **2.** *v.* ease, inch, loop, pass, string, wind

threat **1.** menace, warning **2.** foreboding, omen, portent, presage

threaten **1.** endanger, jeopardize **2.** forebode, foreshadow, impend, portend, presage, warn **3.** browbeat, bully, cow, intimidate, menace

threshold **1.** door, doorway, entrance, sill **2.** beginning, brink, dawn, opening, outset, start, verge

thrift carefulness, economy, parsimony, prudence, saving

thrill *n.* **1.** adventure, glow, pleasure, sensation, tingle, titillation **2.** flutter, quiver, shudder, throb, tremble, tremor, vibration ~*v.* **3.** arouse, electrify, excite, flush, glow, move, stimulate, stir, tingle **4.** flutter, quake, quiver, shake, shudder, throb, tremble, vibrate

thrilling **1.** exciting, gripping, rousing, sensational, stimulating, stirring **2.** quaking, shaking, shivering, shuddering, trembling, vibrating

thrive advance, bloom, boom, develop, flourish, grow, increase, prosper, succeed, wax

throb **1.** *v.* beat, pound, pulsate, thump, vibrate **2.** *n.* beat, pounding, pulse, thump, thumping, vibration

throng **1.** *n.* crowd, crush, horde, host, jam, mass, mob, multitude, pack, press, swarm **2.** *v.* bunch, converge, cram, crowd, fill, flock, hem in, herd, jam, pack, press, troop

throttle *v.* **1.** choke, strangle **2.** control, inhibit, silence, stifle, suppress

through *prep.* **1.** between, by, past **2.** because of, by means of, by way of, using, via **3.** during, in, in the middle of, throughout ~*adj.* **4.** completed, done, ended, finished

throughout everywhere, the whole time

throw **1.** *v.* cast, heave, hurl, launch, pitch, project, propel, put, send, shy, sling, toss **2.** *n.* cast, fling, heave, pitch, put, shy, sling, toss

throw away **1.** discard, jettison, reject, scrap **2.** lose, squander, waste

throw off **1.** abandon, discard, drop, shake off **2.** elude, evade, lose, outdistance, outrun, shake off **3.** confuse, disconcert, disturb, unsettle, upset

throw out **1.** discard, dismiss, eject, evict, expel, jettison, reject, scrap **2.** confuse, disconcert, disturb, unsettle, upset

thrust *v.* **1.** drive, force, impel, jam, plunge, poke, press, prod, propel, push, ram, shove, urge **2.** jab, lunge, pierce, stab, stick ~*n.* **3.** drive, lunge, poke, prod, push, shove, stab **4.** impetus, momentum

thud *n./v.* clump, crash, knock, smack, thump

thug assassin, bandit, gangster, hooligan, killer, murderer, robber, ruffian, tough

thumb *n.* **1.** pollex **2. thumbs down** disapproval, negation, refusal, rejection **3. thumbs up** acceptance, affirmation, approval, encouragement

thump **1.** *n.* bang, blow, crash, knock, rap, smack, thud, whack **2.** *v.* bang, batter, beat, crash, hit, knock, pound, rap, smack, strike, thrash, throb, thud

thunder **1.** *n.* boom, crash, detonation, explosion, pealing, rumble, rumbling **2.** *v.* blast, boom, clap, crack, crash, peal, resound, reverberate, roar, rumble

thunderstruck aghast, amazed, astonished, astounded, nonplussed, petrified, shocked, staggered

thus **1.** like this, so **2.** accordingly, consequently, ergo, hence, then, therefore

tick[1] *n.* **1.** clack, click, tap **2.** dash, mark, stroke ~*v.* **3.** clack, click, tap **4.** choose, indicate, mark, select

tick[2] account, credit

ticket **1.** card, coupon, pass, slip, token, voucher **2.** card, label, marker, slip, sticker, tab, tag

ticklish critical, delicate, risky, sensitive, thorny, touchy, tricky, unsteady

tick off **1.** check off, mark off **2.** censure, chide, lecture, reprimand, scold, upbraid

tide course, current, ebb, flow

tidings advice, greetings, message, news, report, word

tidy **1.** *adj.* clean, methodical, neat, ordered, shipshape, spruce, trim, well-ordered **2.** *v.* clean, groom, neaten, order, order, straighten

tie *v.* **1.** attach, bind, connect, fasten, join, lash, link, moor, rope, secure, tether, unite **2.** bind, confine, hamper, hinder, hold, limit, restrain **3.** be even, draw, equal, match ~*n.* **4.** band, bond, cord, fastening, fetter, joint, knot, link, rope, string **5.** affiliation, bond, commitment, duty, kinship, liaison, obligation, relationship **6.** dead heat, deadlock, draw, stalemate **7.** *Brit.* fixture, game, match

tier bank, file, layer, level, line, order, rank, row, series

tight **1.** close, compact, constricted, cramped, fast, firm, fixed, narrow, rigid, secure, snug, stiff, stretched, taut, tense **2.** impervious, proof, sealed, sound **3.** close, grasping, mean, miserly, sparing, stingy **4.** close, even, near, well-matched **5.** drunk, intoxicated, tipsy

tighten close, cramp, fasten, fix, narrow, screw, secure, stretch, tense

till[1] cultivate, dig, plough, work

till[2] cash box, cash register

tilt *v.* **1.** cant, lean, list, slant, slope, tip **2.** attack, clash, contend, duel, encounter, fight, joust, spar ~*n.* **3.** angle, cant, incline, list, pitch, slant, slope

timber beams, boards, forest, logs, planks, trees, wood

time *n.* **1.** age, date, epoch, era, generation, hour, interval, period, season, space, span, spell, stretch, term **2.** allotted span, day, duration, life, season **3.** heyday, hour, peak **4.** *Mus.* beat, measure, metre, rhythm, tempo **5. all the time** always, continuously, ever **6. at one time** formerly, hitherto, once, previously **7. at times** now and then, occasionally, sometimes **8. behind the times** dated, old-fashioned, square **9. for the time being** for now, meantime, meanwhile **10. in good time** early, on time **11. in time a.** early, on schedule, on time **b.** eventually, one day, someday, ultimately **12. time and again** frequently, often, repeatedly ~*v.* **13.** clock, control, count, judge, measure, regulate, schedule, set

timely convenient, judicious, opportune, prompt, punctual, seasonable, suitable

timetable calendar, curriculum, diary, list, programme, schedule

timid afraid, bashful, cowardly, coy, diffident, fearful, irresolute, modest, nervous, retiring, shy

tinge *n.* **1.** cast, colour, dye, shade, stain, wash **2.** bit, dash, drop, pinch, smack, sprinkling, touch, trace ~*v.* **3.** colour, dye, imbue, shade, stain, suffuse

tinker *v.* dabble, meddle, play, potter, toy

tint *n.* **1.** cast, colour, hue, shade, tone **2.** dye, rinse, stain, wash ~*v.* **3.** colour, dye, rinse, stain **4.** affect, colour, influence

tiny diminutive, insignificant, little, minute, negligible, petite, slight, small, trifling, wee

tip[1] apex, cap, crown, end, head, peak, point, top

tip[2] *v.* **1.** cant, capsize, incline, lean, list, slant, spill, upset **2.** dump, empty, pour out, unload ~*n.* **3.** refuse heap, rubbish heap

tip[3] *n.* **1.** gift **2.** *Also* **tip-off** clue, forecast, hint, pointer, suggestion, warning, word ~*v.* **3.** remunerate, reward **4.** *Also* **tip off** advise, caution, suggest

tire **1.** drain, droop, exhaust, fail, flag, jade, sink, weary **2.** annoy, bore, harass, irk, irritate, weary

tired drained, drowsy, exhausted, fatigued, sleepy, spent, weary, worn out

tireless determined, energetic, industrious, resolute, vigorous

tiresome dull, exasperating, flat, irksome, laborious, tedious, trying, vexatious, wearing, wearisome

tiring arduous, exacting, fatiguing, strenuous, tough, wearing

titillate arouse, excite, interest, provoke, stimulate, tantalize, tease, thrill, tickle, turn on (*Sl.*)

title *n.* **1.** caption, heading, label, legend, name, style **2.** designation, epithet, name, nickname, pseudonym, sobriquet, term **3.** championship, crown, laurels **4.** claim, entitlement, ownership, privilege, right ~*v.* **5.** call, designate, label, name, style, term

toady **1.** *n.* hanger-on, jackal, lackey, parasite, sycophant, yes man **2.** *v.* crawl, creep, cringe, flatter, grovel

toast *n.* **1.** drink, health, pledge, salute, tribute **2.** darling, favourite, heroine *~v.* **3.** drink to

together 1. closely, in concert, in unison, jointly, mutually **2.** concurrently, en masse, in unison, simultaneously **3.** consecutively, continuously, on end, successively

toil 1. *n.* drudgery, effort, exertion, hard work, industry, labour, pains, slog, sweat, travail **2.** *v.* drudge, grub, labour, slave, slog, strive, struggle, work

toilet 1. bathroom, closet, convenience, latrine, lavatory, loo, outhouse, privy, urinal, washroom, W.C. **2.** ablutions, bathing, dressing, grooming, toilette

token *n.* **1.** badge, clue, earnest, evidence, index, mark, note, proof, sign, symbol, warning **2.** keepsake, memento, remembrance, reminder, souvenir *~adj.* **3.** hollow, nominal, superficial, symbolic

tolerable 1. acceptable, bearable, endurable, supportable **2.** acceptable, adequate, average, fair, indifferent, mediocre, middling, ordinary, unexceptional

tolerance 1. charity, magnanimity, patience, sufferance, sympathy **2.** endurance, fortitude, hardness, resilience, resistance, stamina, toughness **3.** fluctuation, play, swing, variation

tolerant 1. charitable, fair, forbearing, liberal, open-minded, patient, unbigoted, unprejudiced **2.** indulgent, lax, lenient, permissive, soft

tolerate abide, accept, admit, allow, bear, brook, condone, endure, permit, pocket, receive, sanction, stand, stomach, suffer, swallow, take, undergo, wink at

toleration condonation, endurance, indulgence, sufferance

toll[1] *v.* **1.** chime, clang, knell, peal, ring, sound, strike **2.** call, signal, warn *~n.* **3.** chime, clang, knell, peal, ring

toll[2] **1.** charge, customs, demand, duty, fee, impost, levy, payment, rate, tariff, tax, tribute **2.** cost, damage, inroad, loss, penalty

tomb crypt, grave, sepulchre, vault

tombstone gravestone, marker, memorial, monument

tone *n.* **1.** accent, emphasis, force, modulation, pitch, strength, stress, timbre, volume **2.** air, approach, aspect, attitude, character, drift, effect, feel, frame, grain, manner, mood, note, quality, spirit, style, temper, vein **3.** cast, colour, hue, shade, tinge, tint *~v.* **4.** blend, go well with, harmonize, match, suit

tongue 1. dialect, idiom, language, speech, talk, vernacular **2.** speech, utterance, voice

tonic boost, cordial, fillip, refresher, stimulant

too 1. also, as well, besides, further, likewise, moreover, to boot **2.** excessively, extremely, unduly

tool *n.* **1.** appliance, contrivance, device, gadget, implement, instrument, machine, utensil **2.** agent, means, medium, vehicle **3.** cat's-paw, creature, hireling, jackal, minion, pawn, puppet

top *n.* **1.** apex, crest, crown, head, height, meridian, peak, pinnacle, summit, vertex, zenith **2.** cap, cork, cover, lid **3.** head, lead **4. over the top** excessive, immoderate, inordinate *~adj.* **5.** best, chief, crowning, dominant, elite, finest, first, greatest, head, highest, lead, prime, principal, ruling, sovereign, superior, topmost, upper *~v.* **6.** be first, command, head, lead, rule **7.** beat, best, better, outdo, surpass, transcend

topic issue, matter, point, subject, text, theme, thesis

topical current, popular

topmost foremost, highest, leading, loftiest, supreme, top, upper, uppermost

topsy-turvy chaotic, confused, disorderly, inside-out, jumbled, messy, untidy

torment *v.* **1.** afflict, agonize, distress, harrow, pain, rack, torture **2.** annoy, bedevil, bother, harass, persecute, pester, provoke, trouble *~n.* **3.** agony, anguish, distress, hell, misery, pain, suffering, torture **4.** affliction, bother, nuisance, persecution, pest, plague, scourge, trouble, vexation, worry

tornado cyclone, gale, squall, storm, tempest, typhoon, whirlwind

torrent cascade, deluge, flood, flow, gush, rush, spate, stream, tide

tortuous bent, crooked, curved, indirect, sinuous, twisted, twisting, winding

torture 1. *v.* afflict, agonize, distress, lacerate, martyr, pain, persecute, torment **2.** *n.* affliction, agony, anguish, distress, hell, martyrdom, misery, pain, persecution, suffering, torment

toss *v.* **1.** cast, fling, hurl, launch, pitch, project, propel, shy, sling, throw **2.** agitate, disturb, jolt, rock, roll, shake, thrash, tumble *~n.* **3.** cast, fling, pitch, shy, throw

total 1. *n.* all, amount, entirety, mass, sum, whole **2.** *adj.* all-out, complete, consummate, downright, entire, full, gross, integral, outright, perfect, sheer, thorough, unqualified, utter, whole **3.** *v.* add up, amount to, reach, reckon

touch *n.* **1.** feel, feeling **2.** blow, brush, caress, contact, hit, pat, push, stroke, tap **3.** bit, dash, detail, drop, hint, jot, pinch, smack, smattering, speck, spot, taste, trace, whiff **4.** approach, manner, method, style, way **5.** ability, adroitness, art, artistry, deftness, facility, flair, knack, mastery, skill, virtuosity *~v.* **6.** brush, caress, contact, feel, finger, fondle, graze, handle, hit, pat, push, strike, stroke, tap **7.** abut, adjoin, border, brush, contact, converge, graze, meet **8.** affect, disturb, impress, influence, inspire, mark, melt, move, soften, stir, strike, upset **9.** come near, compare with, equal, match, rival

touching affecting, melting, moving, piteous, pitiful, poignant, sad, stirring, tender

tough *adj.* **1.** durable, firm, hard, leathery, resistant, rigid, rugged, solid, stiff, strong, sturdy **2.** brawny, fit, hardy, resilient, seasoned, stalwart, stout, strong, sturdy, vigorous **3.** rough, ruffianly, ruthless, vicious, violent **4.** callous, firm, merciless, obstinate, resolute, severe, stern, strict, unbending **5.** difficult, hard, irksome, knotty, strenuous, thorny, troublesome, uphill **6.** hard luck, regrettable *~n.* **7.** brute, hooligan, rowdy, ruffian, thug

tour *n.* **1.** excursion, journey, outing, progress, trip **2.** circuit, course, round *~v.* **3.** explore, holiday in, journey, sightsee, visit

tourist holiday-maker, sightseer, traveller, tripper, voyager

tournament contest, event, match, meeting, series

tow *v.* drag, haul, lug, pull, trail, tug

towards 1. for, to **2.** about, concerning, for, regarding **3.** almost, nearing, nearly

tower *n.* **1.** belfry, column, pillar, skyscraper, steeple, turret **2.** castle, citadel, fort, keep, refuge, stronghold *~v.* **3.** ascend, dominate, exceed, loom, mount, overlook, rear, rise, soar, top

toy 1. *n.* doll, game, plaything **2.** *v.* flirt, play, sport, trifle, wanton

trace *n.* **1.** evidence, mark, record, relic, remnant, sign, survival, token **2.** bit, dash, drop, hint, shadow, suggestion, touch, trifle, whiff *~v.* **3.** detect, determine, discover, find, follow, pursue, seek, shadow, stalk, track, trail, unearth **4.** chart, copy, draw, map, outline, record, show, sketch

track *n.* **1.** footmark, footprint, footstep, mark, path, scent, slot, trace, trail, wake **2.** course, flight path, line, path, pathway, road, track, way **3.** line, rail, rails **4. keep track of** follow, watch **5. lose track of** lose, misplace *~v.* **6.** chase, dog, follow, pursue, shadow, stalk, trace, trail

tracks 1. impressions, imprints, wheelmarks **2. make tracks** depart, disappear, leave

tract area, district, estate, extent, lot, plot, quarter, region, stretch, zone

trade *n.* **1.** barter, business, commerce, dealing, exchange, traffic, truck **2.** business, calling, craft, job, line, occupation, profession, pursuit, skill **3.** deal, exchange, swap **4.** clientele, custom, market, patrons, public *~v.* **5.** bargain, barter, deal, exchange, peddle, traffic, transact, truck **6.** barter, exchange, swap, switch

tradesman 1. dealer, merchant, seller, shopkeeper, vendor **2.** craftsman, workman

tradition custom, customs, folklore, habit, institution, ritual, usage

traditional accustomed, ancestral, conventional, customary, established, fixed, folk, historic, old, oral, unwritten, usual

traffic *n.* **1.** freight, movement, passengers, transport, vehicles **2.** barter, business, commerce, dealing, doings, exchange, relations, trade, truck *~v.* **3.** bargain, barter, deal, exchange, market, peddle, trade, truck

tragedy adversity, affliction, calamity, disaster, misfortune

tragic appalling, awful, catastrophic, deadly, dire, disastrous, doleful, dreadful, fatal, grievous, ill-fated, ill-starred, miserable, pathetic, ruinous, sad, shocking, sorrowful, unfortunate, woeful, wretched

trail *v.* **1.** drag, draw, haul, pull, stream, tow **2.** chase, follow, hunt, pursue, shadow, stalk, trace, track **3.** dawdle, follow, lag, linger, loiter, straggle *~n.* **4.** footsteps, mark, path, scent, spoor, trace, track, wake **5.** beaten track, footpath, path, road, route, track, way

train *v.* **1.** coach, drill, educate, guide, instruct, prepare, rear, school, teach, tutor **2.** aim, direct, focus, level, point *~n.* **3.** chain, course, order, series, set, string **4.** caravan, column, convoy, file, procession **5.** appendage, tail, trail **6.** court, entourage, followers, retinue, staff, suite

trainer coach

training 1. discipline, education, guidance, instruction, tuition, upbringing **2.** exercise, practice, preparation

trait attribute, feature, mannerism, quality, quirk

traitor betrayer, deceiver, deserter, informer, quisling, rebel, renegade, turncoat

trajectory course, flight, flight path, line, path, route, track

tramp *v.* **1.** hike, march, range, roam, rove, slog, trek, walk **2.** march, plod, stamp, toil, trudge **3.** crush, stamp, trample, tread *~n.* **4.** vagabond, vagrant **5.** hike, march, ramble, slog, trek

trample 1. crush, squash, stamp, tread **2.** hurt, infringe, violate

trance daze, dream, muse, rapture, reverie, spell, stupor

tranquil calm, composed, cool, pacific, peaceful, placid, quiet, restful, sedate, serene, still

tranquillizer bromide, opiate, sedative

transact accomplish, conduct, discharge, do, enact, handle, manage, perform, prosecute, settle

transaction action, affair, bargain, business, coup, deal, event, matter, occurrence, proceeding, undertaking

transcribe 1. engross, note, reproduce, rewrite, transfer **2.** interpret, render, translate **3.** record, tape

transcript copy, duplicate, manuscript, note, record, reproduction, version

transfer 1. *v.* carry, change, convey, displace, move, remove, shift, translate, transport, turn over **2.** *n.* change, handover, move, removal, shift, transposition

transform alter, change, make over, reconstruct, remodel, renew, translate

transformation change, conversion, revolution

transgress break, defy, disobey, encroach, err, exceed, infringe, lapse, misbehave, offend, overstep, sin, violate

transgressor criminal, culprit, felon, miscreant, offender, sinner, villain, wrongdoer

transient brief, fleeting, flying, fugitive, momentary, passing, short, temporary

transit *n.* 1. carriage, crossing, motion, passage, shipment, travel 2. change, shift, transition 3. **in transit** en route ~*v.* 4. cross, journey, move, pass, travel

transition change, conversion, flux, passage, passing, shift, transit, upheaval

transitional changing, fluid, passing, unsettled

transitory brief, ephemeral, fleeting, flying, fugacious, momentary, passing, short, temporary, transient

translate 1. convert, decode, render, transcribe 2. elucidate, explain, simplify 3. alter, change, convert, transform, turn 4. carry, convey, move, remove, send, transfer, transport

translation 1. decoding, gloss, paraphrase, rendering, version 2. paraphrase, simplification 3. alteration, change 4. conveyance, move, removal

transmission 1. carriage, conveyance, sending, shipment, spread, transfer, transport 2. broadcasting, relaying, sending, showing 3. broadcast, programme

transmit 1. bear, carry, convey, diffuse, dispatch, forward, impart, remit, send, spread, transport 2. broadcast, radio, relay, send

transparency 1. clarity, limpidity, pellucidity, pellucidness, sheerness, translucency 2. photograph, slide

transparent 1. clear, diaphanous, filmy, limpid, lucent, lucid, translucent 2. apparent, distinct, easy, evident, explicit, manifest, obvious, patent, plain, recognizable, visible 3. candid, direct, forthright, frank, open, straight, straightforward

transpire 1. *Inf.* arise, befall, chance, happen, occur, turn up 2. come out

transport *v.* 1. bear, bring, carry, convey, fetch, haul, move, remove, run, ship, take, transfer 2. banish, deport, exile 3. captivate, delight, electrify, enchant, enrapture, move, ravish ~*n.* 4. conveyance, vehicle 5. carriage, conveyance, removal, shipment, shipping 6. enchantment, euphoria, heaven, rapture 7. bliss, delight, ecstasy, ravishment

transpose alter, change, exchange, move, relocate, reorder, shift, substitute, swap (*Inf.*), switch, transfer

trap *n.* 1. ambush, net, noose, pitfall, snare, springe 2. ambush, artifice, device, ruse ~*v.* 3. catch, corner, enmesh, ensnare, snare, take 4. ambush, beguile, deceive, dupe, inveigle, trick

trappings adornments, dress, equipment, finery, fittings, fixtures, gear, livery, panoply

trash 1. balderdash, drivel, foolish talk, hogwash, inanity, nonsense, rot, rubbish, tripe (*Inf.*), trumpery, twaddle 2. dregs, dross, garbage, junk, litter, offscourings, refuse, rubbish

trashy cheap, flimsy, meretricious, tawdry, tinsel, worthless

travel cross, go, journey, move, proceed, progress, ramble, roam, rove, tour, traverse, voyage, walk, wander

traveller explorer, gypsy, hiker, migrant, nomad, passenger, tourist, tripper, voyager, wanderer, wayfarer

travelling *adj.* itinerant, migrant, mobile, restless, roaming, roving, unsettled, wandering

traverse bridge, cover, cross, negotiate, pass over, ply, range, roam, span, wander

travesty 1. *n.* caricature, lampoon, mockery, parody, sham 2. *v.* burlesque, caricature, deride, distort, mock, parody, ridicule, sham

treacherous 1. deceitful, disloyal, faithless, false, perfidious, treasonable, unfaithful, unreliable, untrue 2. dangerous, hazardous, icy, perilous, risky, slippery, tricky, unsafe, unstable

treachery betrayal, disloyalty, duplicity, infidelity, perfidy, treason

tread *v.* 1. hike, march, pace, plod, stamp, step, stride, tramp, walk 2. squash, trample 3. bear down, crush, oppress, quell, repress, subdue, subjugate, suppress ~*n.* 4. footstep, gait, pace, step, stride, walk

treason disloyalty, mutiny, perfidy, sedition, treachery

treasure *n.* 1. cash, fortune, funds, gold, jewels, money, riches, valuables, wealth 2. darling, gem, jewel, paragon, pearl, precious, prize ~*v.* 3. adore, cherish, esteem, idolize, love, prize, revere, value, venerate, worship

treasury 1. bank, cache, hoard, store, vault 2. assets, capital, coffers, exchequer, finances, funds, money, resources, revenues

treat *n.* 1. banquet, entertainment, feast, gift, party 2. delight, enjoyment, fun, joy, pleasure, satisfaction, surprise, thrill ~*v.* 3. consider, deal with, handle, manage, regard, use 4. attend to, care for, doctor, nurse 5. buy for, feast, give, lay on, pay for, provide, regale 6. be concerned with, contain, discuss, go into, touch upon

treatise dissertation, essay, monograph, pamphlet, paper, study, thesis, tract, work, writing

treatment 1. care, cure, healing, medicine, remedy, surgery 2. conduct, dealing, handling, manipulation, reception, usage

treaty agreement, alliance, bond, compact, concordat, contract, convention, covenant, entente, pact

trek 1. *n.* hike, journey, march, slog, tramp 2. *v.* footslog, hike, journey, march, plod, range, roam, rove, slog, tramp

tremble 1. *v.* quake, quiver, rock, shake, shiver, shudder, teeter, totter, vibrate 2. *n.* quake, quiver, shake, shiver, shudder, tremor, vibration

tremendous 1. awesome, awful, colossal, dreadful, enormous, fearful, frightful, great, huge, immense, monstrous, stupendous, towering, vast 2. amazing, excellent, exceptional, great, incredible, marvellous, wonderful

trench channel, cut, ditch, drain, furrow, gutter, pit, trough

trenchant acerbic, acid, acute, biting, caustic, cutting, incisive, keen, mordant, pungent, severe, sharp, tart

trend 1. bias, course, current, drift, flow, leaning, tendency 2. craze, fashion, look, mode, rage, style, thing, vogue

trespass 1. *v.* encroach, infringe, intrude, poach 2. *n.* encroachment, infringement, poaching

trial *n.* 1. audition, check, examination, experience, experiment, probation, proof, test, testing 2. contest, hearing, litigation, tribunal 3. attempt, effort, endeavour, go, stab, try, venture 4. adversity, affliction, burden, grief, hardship, load, misery, ordeal, pain, suffering, tribulation, trouble, woe 5. bane, bother, irritation, nuisance, pest, vexation ~*adj.* 6. experimental, pilot, probationary, provisional

tribe blood, clan, class, division, family, house, people, race, seed, stock

tribulation adversity, affliction, blow, burden, care, curse, distress, grief, misery, misfortune, ordeal, pain, sorrow, suffering, trial, trouble, vexation, woe, worry

tribunal bar, bench, court, hearing, trial

tribute 1. acknowledgment, applause, compliment, esteem, gift, honour, praise, recognition, respect 2. charge, customs, duty, excise, homage, impost, offering, payment, ransom, subsidy, tax, toll

trick *n.* 1. artifice, deceit, deception, device, dodge, feint, fraud, gimmick, hoax, imposture, ploy, ruse, stratagem, swindle, trap, wile 2. antic, caper, device, feat, frolic, gambol, jape, joke, juggle, prank, stunt 3. art, command, craft, device, expertise, gift, knack, secret, skill, technique ~*v.* 4. cheat, deceive, delude, dupe, fool, hoax, mislead, trap

trickle 1. *v.* crawl, creep, drip, drop, exude, ooze, run, seep, stream 2. *n.* dribble, drip, seepage

tricky complicated, delicate, difficult, risky, ticklish

trifle *n.* 1. gewgaw, nothing, plaything, toy, triviality 2. bit, dash, drop, jot, little, pinch, spot, touch, trace ~*v.* 3. amuse oneself, coquet, dally, dawdle, flirt, idle, palter, play, toy, wanton, waste

trigger *v.* activate, cause, elicit, generate, produce, prompt, start

trim *adj.* 1. compact, dapper, neat, nice, orderly, smart, spruce, tidy, well turned-out 2. fit, shapely, sleek, slender, slim, streamlined, willowy ~*v.* 3. barber, clip, crop, curtail, cut, dock, lop, pare, prune, shave, shear, tidy 4. adorn, array, bedeck, decorate, dress, embellish, embroider, garnish, ornament 5. adjust, arrange, balance, distribute, order, prepare, settle

trimming 1. adornment, braid, decoration, edging, embellishment, frill, fringe, piping 2. *Plural* accessories, extras, frills, garnish, ornaments, trappings

trinity threesome, trilogy, trio, triple, triumvirate

trinket bagatelle, ornament, toy, trifle

trio threesome, trinity, triplet, triptych, triumvirate, triune

trip *n.* 1. errand, excursion, expedition, foray, jaunt, journey, outing, ramble, run, tour, travel, voyage 2. blunder, error, fall, indiscretion ~*v.* 3. blunder, err, fall, lapse, miscalculate, misstep, slip, stumble, tumble 4. catch out, confuse, disconcert, trap, unsettle

tripe claptrap, drivel, garbage, inanity, nonsense, rot, rubbish, trash, twaddle

triple 1. *adj.* threefold, three-way 2. *n.* threesome, trinity, trio

tripper journeyer, sightseer, tourist

trite banal, commonplace, dull, hack, ordinary, pedestrian, routine, stale, stock, tired, worn

triumph *n.* 1. elation, joy, pride, rejoicing 2. accomplishment, achievement, attainment, conquest, coup, feat, mastery, success, victory ~*v.* 3. celebrate, exult, gloat, glory, rejoice, revel

triumphant celebratory, conquering, dominant, elated, exultant, glorious, proud, rejoicing, successful, victorious

trivial commonplace, everyday, frivolous, incidental, inconsequential, inconsiderable, insignificant, little, meaningless, minor, negligible, paltry, petty, puny, slight, small, trifling, trite, unimportant, valueless, worthless

troop *n.* 1. band, body, company, contingent, crowd, drove, flock, gang, gathering, group, herd, horde, multitude, squad, swarm, team, unit 2. *Plural* armed forces, army, men, military, soldiers ~*v.* 3. crowd, flock, march, parade, stream, swarm

trophy award, booty, cup, laurels, prize, souvenir, spoils

tropical hot, humid, lush, steamy, stifling, sultry, torrid

trot 1. *v.* canter, jog, lope, run, scamper 2. *n.* brisk pace, canter, jog, lope

trouble *n.* 1. annoyance, anxiety, disquiet, distress, grief, irritation, misfortune, pain, sorrow, suffering, torment, vexation, woe, worry 2. discontent, discord, disorder, disturbance, row, strife, tumult, unrest 3. ailment, complaint, defect, disease, disorder, failure, illness, upset 4. bother, concern, danger, difficulty, dilemma, mess, nuisance, pest, problem 5. attention, bother, care, effort, exertion, inconvenience, labour, pains, struggle, thought, work ~*v.* 6. afflict, annoy, bother, disconcert, disquiet, distress, disturb, fret, grieve, harass, pain, perplex, perturb, pester, plague, sadden, torment, upset, vex, worry 7. bother, burden, disturb, incommode, inconvenience, put out 8. make an effort, take pains

troublesome 1. annoying, bothersome, difficult, harassing, hard, irritating, oppressive, taxing, tiresome, upsetting, wearisome 2. disorderly, insubordinate, recalcitrant, rowdy, turbulent, uncooperative, undisciplined, unruly, violent

trounce beat, crush, drub, overwhelm, rout, thrash

truancy absence, malingering

truant absentee, delinquent, deserter, malingerer, shirker

truce armistice, break, ceasefire, cessation, interval, lull, peace, respite, rest, stay, treaty

truck 1. commodities, goods, merchandise, stock, stuff, wares 2. barter, business, commerce, dealings, exchange, relations, trade, traffic

truculent aggressive, bellicose, combative, contentious, cross, defiant, fierce, hostile, obstreperous, pugnacious, sullen, violent

trudge 1. *v.* hike, lumber, march, plod, slog, stump, tramp, trek 2. *n.* footslog, haul, hike, march, slog, tramp, trek

true *adj.* 1. accurate, actual, authentic, bona fide, correct, exact, factual, genuine, natural, precise, pure, real, right, valid, veracious, veritable 2. confirmed, constant, dedicated, devoted, dutiful, faithful, fast, firm, honest, loyal, pure, sincere, staunch, steady, trusty, upright 3. accurate, correct, exact, perfect, precise, proper, unerring *~adv.* 4. honestly, rightly, veraciously 5. accurately, correctly, perfectly, precisely, properly

truly 1. accurately, correctly, factually, precisely, really, rightly 2. constantly, devotedly, loyally, sincerely, with dedication, with devotion 3. exceptionally, greatly, indeed, really, very

trumpet *n.* 1. bugle, horn 2. bay, bellow, call, cry, roar 3. **blow one's own trumpet** boast, brag, crow, vaunt *~v.* 4. advertise, announce, broadcast, extol, proclaim, publish, sound loudly

truncate clip, crop, curtail, cut, lop, pare, prune, shorten, trim

trunk 1. bole, stalk, stem, stock 2. body, torso 3. proboscis, snout 4. bin, box, case, chest, coffer, crate, locker

trust *n.* 1. belief, certainty, confidence, credit, faith, hope, reliance 2. duty, obligation, responsibility 3. care, charge, custody, guard, protection, trusteeship *~v.* 4. assume, believe, expect, hope, presume, suppose, surmise 5. believe, rely upon, swear by 6. assign, command, commit, confide, consign, delegate, entrust, give

trustworthy dependable, honest, honourable, mature, reliable, responsible, righteous, sensible, steadfast, true, truthful, upright

truth 1. accuracy, exactness, fact, genuineness, legitimacy, precision, reality, veracity 2. candour, dedication, devotion, dutifulness, faith, fidelity, honesty, integrity, loyalty, uprightness 3. axiom, fact, law, maxim, reality, truism

truthful accurate, candid, correct, exact, faithful, honest, literal, precise, realistic, reliable, sincere, veritable

try *v.* 1. aim, attempt, endeavour, essay, seek, strive, struggle, undertake 2. appraise, evaluate, examine, inspect, prove, sample, taste, test 3. afflict, annoy, irk, irritate, pain, strain, tax, tire, trouble, upset, vex, weary 4. adjudge, adjudicate, examine, hear *~n.* 5. attempt, effort, endeavour, essay, go, stab

try out check out, evaluate, inspect, sample, taste, test

tuck *v.* 1. fold, gather, insert, push *~n.* 2. fold, gather, pinch, pleat 3. food, victuals

tuck in 1. enfold, fold under, make snug, swaddle, wrap up 2. eat heartily, get stuck in (*Sl.*)

tug 1. *v.* drag, draw, haul, heave, jerk, lug, pull, tow, wrench, yank 2. *n.* drag, haul, heave, jerk, pull, tow, yank

tuition education, instruction, lessons, schooling, teaching, training

tumble 1. *v.* drop, fall, flop, pitch, plummet, roll, stumble, topple, toss, trip up 2. *n.* collapse, drop, fall, flop, plunge, roll, spill, stumble, toss, trip

tumult ado, agitation, bedlam, brawl, commotion, din, disorder, excitement, fracas, outbreak, quarrel, racket, riot, row, stir, strife, turmoil, unrest, uproar

tune *n.* 1. air, melody, motif, song, strain, theme 2. concert, concord, euphony, harmony, pitch, unison *~v.* 3. adapt, adjust, attune, pitch, regulate

tunnel 1. *n.* burrow, channel, hole, passage, shaft, subway 2. *v.* burrow, dig, excavate, mine, undermine

turbulence agitation, commotion, confusion, disorder, roughness, storm, turmoil, unrest

turbulent 1. agitated, boiling, choppy, disordered, foaming, furious, raging, rough, unsettled, unstable 2. boisterous, lawless, obstreperous, riotous, rowdy, tumultuous, undisciplined, unruly, violent, wild

turf 1. clod, divot, grass, green, sod, sward 2. **the turf** racing, the flat

turmoil agitation, bedlam, bustle, chaos, confusion, disorder, flurry, noise, row, stir, strife, trouble, tumult, uproar, violence

turn *v.* 1. circle, gyrate, pivot, revolve, roll, rotate, spin, swivel, twirl, twist, wheel, whirl 2. go back, move, return, reverse, shift, switch, veer, wheel 3. arc, come round, corner, negotiate, pass 4. adapt, alter, become, change, convert, divert, fashion, fit, form, mould, mutate, remodel, shape, transfigure, transform 5. curdle, go sour, spoil, taint 6. appeal, apply, approach, go, look, resort 7. nauseate, sicken, upset 8. apostatize, change sides, defect, desert, influence, persuade, prejudice, retract 9. construct, deliver, execute, fashion, frame, make, mould, perform, shape, write 10. **turn tail** bolt, flee, run away *~n.* 11. bend, change, circle, curve, cycle, gyration, pivot, reversal, spin, swing, twist, whirl 12. bias, direction, drift, heading, tendency, trend 13. bend, curve, departure, deviation, shift 14. chance, fling, go, opportunity, period, round, shift, spell, stint, time, try 15. aptitude, bent, bias, flair, gift, leaning, propensity, talent 16. act, action, deed, favour, gesture, service 17. bend, distortion, twist, warp 18. **by turns** alternately, reciprocally

turning point change, crisis, crossroads, crux

turn off 1. branch off, depart from, deviate, leave, quit 2. cut out, kill, put out, shut down, stop, switch off, turn out, unplug

turn on 1. activate, ignite, start 2. balance, depend, hang, hinge, pivot, rest 3. assail, assault, attack

turn out 1. turn off, unplug 2. fabricate, finish, make, manufacture, process, produce, put out 3. banish, cashier, discharge, dismiss, evict, expel, oust, throw out, unseat 4. become, develop, emerge, evolve, happen, result, work out 5. attire, clothe, dress, fit, outfit, rig out

turn up 1. appear, arrive, attend, come 2. appear, disclose, discover, expose, find, pop up, reveal, transpire, unearth

tussle 1. *v.* battle, brawl, contend, fight, grapple, scuffle, struggle, vie, wrestle 2. *n.* battle, bout, brawl, competition, conflict, contest, fight, fracas, fray, scuffle, struggle

tutor 1. *n.* coach, governor, guardian, guide, instructor, lecturer, master, mentor, schoolmaster, teacher 2. *v.* coach, direct, edify, educate, guide, instruct, lecture, school, teach, train

twilight *n.* 1. dusk, evening, half-light, sundown, sunset 2. decline, ebb *~adj.* 3. darkening, dim, evening

twin 1. *n.* counterpart, double, fellow, likeness, match, mate 2. *adj.* double, dual, duplicate, identical, matching, paired, twofold

twine *n.* 1. cord, string, yarn 2. coil, twist 3. knot, snarl, tangle *~v.* 4. braid, interlace, knit, plait, splice, twist, weave 5. bend, coil, curl, encircle, loop, meander, spiral, surround, twist, wind, wrap

twinkling 1. blink, flash, flicker, gleam, glimmer, shimmer, sparkle, twinkle, wink 2. flash, instant, moment, second, tick (*Inf.*), trice

twirl 1. *v.* gyrate, revolve, rotate, spin, turn, twist, wheel, whirl, wind 2. *n.* gyration, revolution, rotation, spin, turn, twist, wheel, whirl

twist *v.* 1. coil, curl, entwine, screw, spin, swivel, weave, wind, wrap, wreathe, wring 2. contort, distort 3. rick, sprain, turn, wrench 4. alter, change, misquote, warp *~n.* 5. coil, curl, spin, swivel, twine, wind 6. braid, coil, curl, plug, quid, roll 7. change, slant, surprise, turn, variation 8. arc, bend, convolution, curve, meander, turn, zigzag 9. defect, distortion, flaw, imperfection, kink, warp 10. jerk, pull, sprain, turn, wrench 11. bent, crotchet, fault, foible, oddity, quirk, trait 12. confusion, entanglement, kink, knot, mess, mix-up, snarl, tangle

twit ass, clown, fool, halfwit, idiot, nitwit, simpleton

twitch 1. *v.* blink, jerk, pluck, pull, snatch, tug, yank 2. *n.* blink, flutter, jerk, jump, pull, spasm, tic, twinge

tycoon baron, capitalist, financier, industrialist, magnate, mogul, potentate

type 1. category, class, form, group, ilk, kind, order, sort, species, strain, variety 2. case, face, fount, print, printing 3. essence, example, exemplar, model, original, pattern, personification, standard

typhoon cyclone, squall, storm

typical average, characteristic, classic, essential, indicative, model, normal, orthodox, representative, standard, stock, usual

typify embody, epitomize, exemplify, illustrate, personify, symbolize

tyrannical arbitrary, autocratic, cruel, despotic, dictatorial, domineering, high-handed, imperious, inhuman, oppressive, overbearing, overweening, severe, unjust, unreasonable

tyranny authoritarianism, autocracy, coercion, cruelty, despotism, dictatorship, imperiousness, oppression, unreasonableness

tyrant autocrat, despot, dictator, oppressor, slave-driver

tyro apprentice, beginner, initiate, learner, novice, novitiate, pupil, student, trainee

U

ubiquitous ever-present, everywhere, pervasive

ugly 1. hard-featured, misshapen, plain, unattractive, unprepossessing, unsightly 2. disagreeable, distasteful, frightful, hideous, horrid, monstrous, repugnant, repulsive, shocking, unpleasant, vile 3. dangerous, menacing, ominous, sinister 4. angry, dark, evil, malevolent, nasty, spiteful, sullen, surly

ulterior concealed, covert, hidden, secret, selfish, unexpressed

ultimate 1. decisive, end, eventual, extreme, final, furthest, last 2. extreme, greatest, highest, paramount, superlative, supreme, topmost, utmost

umbrage anger, displeasure, grudge, huff, offence, pique, resentment

umpire 1. *n.* arbiter, arbitrator, judge, moderator, referee 2. *v.* adjudicate, judge, referee

unabashed blatant, bold, brazen, unconcerned, undismayed

unable impotent, incapable, ineffectual, powerless, unfit, unfitted, unqualified

unabridged complete, full-length, unshortened, whole

unacceptable displeasing, distasteful, inadmissible, objectionable, offensive, unpleasant

unaccompanied a cappella (*Music*), alone, lone, solo, unescorted

unaccustomed *With* **to** green, inexperienced, unused to

unaffected artless, genuine, honest, naive, natural, plain, simple, sincere

unalterable fixed, immutable, permanent

unanimous agreed, common,

concerted, harmonious, like-minded, of one mind, united
unanimously nem. con., unitedly, without exception
unanswerable absolute, conclusive, incontestable
unanswered disputed, open, undecided, unresolved
unapproachable 1. aloof, chilly, cool, distant, frigid, remote, reserved, unfriendly, withdrawn 2. inaccessible, out of reach, remote
unarmed defenceless, exposed, helpless, open, weak
unassailable impregnable, invincible, secure
unassuming diffident, humble, modest, quiet, reserved, retiring, simple
unattached 1. free, independent 2. available
unattended 1. abandoned, unguarded 2. alone, unaccompanied
unauthorized illegal, unlawful
unavailing bootless, fruitless, futile, idle, ineffective, pointless, unsuccessful, useless, vain
unavoidable certain, fated, inevitable, necessary
unaware heedless, ignorant, unconscious, uninformed, unsuspecting
unawares 1. by surprise, off guard, suddenly, unexpectedly 2. accidentally, inadvertently, unwittingly
unbalanced 1. irregular, shaky, uneven, wobbly 2. crazy, demented, deranged, eccentric, insane, irrational, lunatic, mad, unsound
unbearable insufferable, intolerable, unacceptable
unbeatable invincible, unconquerable, unstoppable
unbeaten triumphant, undefeated, victorious
unbecoming 1. ill-suited, unattractive, unbefitting, unsuitable 2. discreditable, improper, offensive, tasteless
unbelievable astonishing, impossible, improbable, incredible, preposterous, staggering, unthinkable
unbending 1. aloof, distant, inflexible, rigid, stiff 2. firm, intractable, resolute, severe, strict, stubborn, tough, uncompromising
unbiased disinterested, equitable, fair, impartial, just, neutral, objective
unbind free, loosen, release, unfasten, unloose, untie
unblemished flawless, immaculate, perfect, pure, spotless, untarnished
unborn 1. awaited, embryonic, expected 2. coming, future, hereafter
unbreakable durable, indestructible, lasting, rugged, solid, strong
unbridled excessive, licentious, riotous, unchecked, unrestrained, unruly, violent, wanton
unbroken complete, entire, intact, solid, total, whole
unburden 1. discharge, empty, lighten, relieve, unload 2. confess, confide, disclose, reveal
uncalled-for gratuitous, needless, undeserved, unnecessary, unwarranted
uncanny 1. eerie, mysterious, queer, strange, supernatural, unnatural, weird 2. astounding, exceptional, extraordinary, incredible, inspired, miraculous, remarkable, singular, unusual
unceasing constant, continual, endless, incessant, nonstop, perpetual
uncertain 1. doubtful, indefinite, indistinct, questionable, risky, speculative 2. dubious, hazy, irresolute, unclear, unconfirmed, undecided, unsettled, unsure, vague
uncertainty ambiguity, confusion, doubt, hesitancy, indecision, perplexity, quandary, scepticism, unpredictability
unchangeable constant, fixed, immutable, invariable, permanent, stable, steadfast, strong, unalterable
uncivil bad-mannered, discourteous, impolite, rude, surly, uncouth
uncivilized 1. barbarian, primitive, savage, wild 2. churlish, coarse, gross, philistine, uneducated, vulgar
unclean corrupt, defiled, dirty, evil, filthy, foul, impure, polluted, soiled, stained
uncomfortable 1. awkward, cramped, hard, painful, rough 2. awkward, confused, disquieted, distressed, disturbed, troubled, uneasy
uncommon 1. curious, novel, odd, peculiar, queer, rare, scarce, strange, unusual 2. distinctive, extraordinary, inimitable, notable, outstanding, rare, remarkable, special
uncommonly 1. hardly ever, infrequently, occasionally, rarely, seldom 2. extremely, particularly, unusually, very
uncommunicative close, curt, reserved, reticent, retiring, secretive, short, shy, silent, taciturn
uncompromising firm, inexorable, inflexible, intransigent, strict, stubborn, unbending
unconcerned aloof, cool, detached, dispassionate, distant, unmoved
unconditional absolute, complete, entire, full, outright, positive, unlimited, unreserved
uncongenial antipathetic, incompatible, uninviting, unsuited, unsympathetic
unconnected 1. detached, divided, separate 2. illogical, incoherent, irrelevant, meaningless, unrelated
unconscious 1. insensible, numb, out, senseless, stunned 2. heedless, ignorant, oblivious, unaware, unknowing 3. accidental, unintentional, unwitting 4. inherent, innate, reflex, repressed
uncontrollable frantic, furious, mad, strong, unruly, violent, wild
uncontrolled furious, rampant, riotous, unbridled, unchecked, undisciplined, unrestrained
unconventional bizarre, bohemian, eccentric, individual, informal, odd, offbeat, unorthodox, unusual
uncouth awkward, boorish, clownish, clumsy, coarse, crude, graceless, gross, loutish, rough, rude, uncultivated, vulgar
uncover 1. bare, open, show, strip, unwrap 2. disclose, make known, reveal, unearth, unmask
uncritical indiscriminate, unselective, unthinking
undecided 1. dithering, hesitant, irresolute, torn, uncertain, uncommitted, unsure 2. indefinite, moot, open, pending, tentative, unsettled, vague
undefined 1. formless, indefinite, shadowy, vague 2. imprecise, inexact, unclear, unspecified
undeniable certain, clear, evident, indisputable, manifest, obvious, patent, proven, sound, sure
under *prep.* 1. below, beneath, underneath 2. governed by, secondary to, subject to, subservient to 3. comprised in, included in *~adv.* 4. below, beneath, down, lower
underclothes lingerie, undergarments, underwear, undies
undercover concealed, confidential, covert, hidden, intelligence, private, secret, spy
undercurrent 1. rip, riptide, undertow 2. aura, drift, feeling, flavour, hint, murmur, sense, suggestion, tendency, tinge, trend, undertone
underestimate belittle, hold cheap, minimize, miscalculate, underrate, undervalue
undergo bear, endure, experience, stand, suffer, sustain, withstand
underground *adj.* 1. buried, covered, subterranean 2. clandestine, concealed, covert, hidden, secret *~n.* 3. **the underground** the metro, the subway, the tube
undergrowth bracken, briars, brush, scrub, underwood
underhand crafty, deceitful, devious, dishonest, fraudulent, furtive, secret, sly, sneaky, stealthy, treacherous, unscrupulous
underline 1. mark, underscore 2. accentuate, emphasize, highlight, stress
underlying 1. concealed, hidden, lurking, veiled 2. basic, elementary, intrinsic, primary, prime
undermine 1. erode, excavate, mine, tunnel 2. disable, impair, sabotage, sap, subvert, threaten, weaken
underprivileged deprived, destitute, impoverished, needy, poor
underrate belittle, discount, underestimate, undervalue
undersized dwarfish, miniature, pygmy, small, squat, stunted, tiny
understand 1. appreciate, apprehend, comprehend, conceive, discern, fathom, follow, get, grasp, know, make out, penetrate, perceive, realize, recognize, see, take in 2. assume, believe, conclude, gather, hear, learn, presume, suppose, think 3. accept, appreciate
understanding *n.* 1. appreciation, awareness, discernment, grasp, insight, judgment, knowledge, perception, sense 2. belief, conclusion, idea, judgment, notion, opinion, view 3. accord, agreement, pact *~adj.* 4. compassionate, considerate, discerning, forgiving, kind, patient, perceptive, responsive, sensitive, tolerant
understood 1. implicit, implied, inferred, tacit, unspoken, unstated 2. accepted, assumed
understudy *n.* double, replacement, reserve, sub, substitute
undertake 1. agree, bargain, contract, covenant, engage, guarantee, pledge, promise, stipulate 2. attempt, begin, commence, endeavour, tackle, try
undertaking 1. affair, attempt, business, effort, enterprise, game, operation, project, task, venture 2. assurance, pledge, promise, word, vow, word
undertone 1. murmur, whisper 2. feeling, flavour, hint, tinge, touch, trace
underwater submarine, sunken
under way afoot, begun, started
underwear lingerie, underclothes, undies
underworld 1. criminals, gangsters 2. Hades, hell, the inferno
underwrite 1. back, finance, fund, guarantee, insure, sponsor, subsidize 2. endorse, initial, sign, subscribe 3. agree to, approve, consent, sanction
undesirable disliked, distasteful, dreaded, offensive, unacceptable, unattractive, unsavoury, unsuitable
undeveloped immature, latent, potential
undignified inappropriate, indecorous, inelegant, unbecoming, unrefined, unsuitable
undisciplined erratic, obstreperous, uncontrolled, unreliable, unsteady, wayward, wild, wilful
undisguised complete, evident, genuine, obvious, open, overt, patent, transparent, utter
undisputed accepted, certain, conclusive, indisputable, recognized, sure, unchallenged, undeniable
undistinguished everyday, indifferent, mediocre, ordinary, pedestrian, prosaic, unexceptional, unimpressive, unremarkable
undisturbed 1. quiet, untouched 2. calm, collected, composed, even, placid, serene, tranquil, unperturbed, untroubled
undivided complete, concentrated, entire, exclusive, full, solid, thorough, united, whole
undo 1. disentangle, loose, open, unbutton, unfasten, untie, unwrap 2. annul, cancel, neutralize, nullify, offset, reverse 3. defeat, destroy, impoverish, mar, overturn, quash, ruin, shatter, undermine, upset, wreck
undoing 1. collapse, defeat, disgrace, downfall, overthrow, overturn, reversal, ruin, shame 2. blight, curse, misfortune, trial, trouble
undone left, neglected, omitted, unfinished, unfulfilled, unperformed
undoubted certain, definite, evident, obvious, sure
undoubtedly assuredly, certainly, definitely, surely
undress 1. *v.* disrobe, shed, strip 2. *n.* disarray, dishabille, nudity

undue excessive, extreme, improper, needless, overmuch, undeserved, unseemly
unduly excessively, overmuch, unnecessarily, unreasonably
unearth 1. dig up, dredge up, excavate, exhume 2. discover, expose, find, reveal, uncover
unearthly 1. eerie, ghostly, haunted, phantom, spectral, strange, uncanny, weird 2. ethereal, heavenly, sublime, supernatural 3. absurd, ridiculous, strange
uneasiness agitation, alarm, anxiety, disquiet, doubt, misgiving, qualms, suspicion, worry
uneasy 1. agitated, anxious, disturbed, edgy, impatient, nervous, perturbed, restive, restless, troubled, upset, worried 2. awkward, insecure, precarious, shaky, strained, tense, uncomfortable
uneconomic loss-making, unprofitable
uneducated 1. ignorant, illiterate, unread, untaught 2. lowbrow, uncultivated
unemotional cold, cool, impassive, listless, reserved, unexcitable, unresponsive
unemployed idle, jobless, laid off, redundant, workless
unending ceaseless, continual, endless, eternal, interminable, perpetual, unceasing
unenthusiastic apathetic, bored, neutral, unresponsive
unenviable thankless, uncomfortable, undesirable, unpleasant
unequalled incomparable, matchless, nonpareil, paramount, peerless, supreme, unrivalled
unethical dishonest, disreputable, illegal, immoral, improper, unprincipled, unprofessional, unscrupulous, wrong
uneven 1. bumpy, rough 2. broken, changeable, fitful, fluctuating, irregular, jerky, patchy, variable 3. lopsided, odd, unbalanced 4. disparate, unequal, unfair
uneventful boring, dull, humdrum, monotonous, ordinary, quiet, routine, tedious, uninteresting, unvaried
unexpected abrupt, astonishing, chance, fortuitous, startling, sudden, surprising, unforeseen, unpredictable
unfailing 1. bottomless, boundless, ceaseless, continuous, endless, persistent, unflagging, unlimited 2. certain, constant, faithful, loyal, reliable, staunch, sure, true
unfair 1. biased, bigoted, one-sided, partial, partisan, prejudiced, unjust 2. dishonest, unethical, unscrupulous, unsporting, wrongful
unfaithful 1. deceitful, disloyal, false, perfidious, recreant (*Archaic*), traitorous, treacherous, treasonable, untrustworthy 2. adulterous, faithless, fickle, inconstant
unfamiliar alien, curious, different, new, novel, uncommon, unknown, unusual
unfashionable antiquated, dated, obsolete, old hat, passé, unpopular
unfasten detach, let go, loosen, open, separate, undo, untie
unfavourable 1. adverse, bad, hostile, low, negative, poor, unfortunate, unfriendly, unsuited 2. inauspicious, threatening, unlucky, unpropitious, untimely, untoward
unfinished 1. incomplete, lacking, uncompleted, undone, unfulfilled, wanting 2. bare, crude, natural, raw, rough, sketchy
unfit 1. inadequate, incapable, no good, not equal to, not up to, unprepared, unqualified, untrained, useless 2. inadequate, ineffective, unsuitable, unsuited, useless 3. decrepit, feeble, flabby, unhealthy
unflattering 1. blunt, candid, critical, honest 2. plain, unattractive, unbecoming
unfold 1. disentangle, expand, flatten, open, straighten, undo, unfurl, unravel, unroll, unwrap 2. *Fig.* clarify, describe, disclose, divulge, explain, illustrate, present, reveal, show, uncover
unforeseen abrupt, accidental, startling, sudden, surprise, unexpected
unforgettable exceptional, impressive, memorable, notable
unforgivable deplorable, disgraceful, inexcusable, shameful, unpardonable
unfortunate 1. adverse, disastrous, ill-starred, ruinous, unfavourable, untoward 2. cursed, doomed, hapless, luckless, poor, unhappy, unlucky, unsuccessful, wretched 3. ill-advised, infelicitous, lamentable, regrettable, unbecoming, unsuitable
unfounded baseless, false, idle, spurious, unproven, vain
unfrequented godforsaken, isolated, lone, remote, sequestered, solitary, unvisited
unfriendly 1. aloof, chilly, cold, distant, hostile, inhospitable, quarrelsome, sour, surly, unsociable 2. alien, hostile, inhospitable, inimical, unfavourable
ungainly awkward, clumsy, gawky, inelegant, lumbering, slouching, uncouth
ungodly corrupt, depraved, godless, immoral, impious, irreligious, profane, sinful, vile, wicked
ungovernable rebellious, unruly, wild
ungracious churlish, discourteous, impolite, rude, uncivil
ungrateful heedless, selfish, unappreciative
unguarded 1. careless, foolhardy, heedless, impolitic, imprudent, rash, thoughtless, unthinking, unwary 2. defenceless, undefended, unprotected, vulnerable
unhappy 1. blue, dejected, depressed, dispirited, down, downcast, gloomy, miserable, mournful, sad, sorrowful 2. cursed, hapless, ill-fated, ill-omened, luckless, wretched 3. awkward, clumsy, gauche, inept, malapropos, tactless, unsuitable
unharmed intact, safe, sound, undamaged, unhurt, unscathed, untouched, whole
unhealthy 1. ailing, delicate, feeble, frail, infirm, invalid, sick, unwell, weak 2. detrimental, harmful, insanitary, noisome, unwholesome
unheard-of 1. obscure, unfamiliar, unknown, unsung 2. inconceivable, new, novel, singular, unexampled, unique, unprecedented, unusual 3. offensive, outlandish, outrageous, shocking
unhesitating 1. resolute, unfaltering, unquestioning, unreserved, wholehearted 2. immediate, instant, prompt, ready
unholy base, corrupt, dishonest, evil, immoral, profane, sinful, ungodly, vile, wicked
unhurried calm, easy, leisurely, sedate, slow
unidentified mysterious, nameless, unfamiliar, unnamed, unrecognized
uniform *n.* 1. costume, dress, garb, habit, livery, outfit, regalia, suit *~adj.* 2. consistent, constant, even, regular, smooth, unchanging 3. alike, equal, like, same, similar
unimaginable fantastic, impossible, incredible, unbelievable
unimaginative barren, dry, dull, hackneyed, lifeless, ordinary, pedestrian, prosaic, routine, tame, unromantic, usual
unimportant insignificant, irrelevant, minor, nugatory, paltry, petty, slight, trifling, trivial, worthless
uninhabited barren, desert, desolate, empty, unpopulated, vacant, waste
uninspired dull, ordinary, prosaic, stale, stock, uninspiring
unintelligent brainless, dense, dull, foolish, obtuse, slow, stupid, thick
unintelligible inarticulate, incoherent, indistinct, jumbled, meaningless, muddled
unintentional accidental, casual, inadvertent, unconscious, unintended
uninterested apathetic, blasé, bored, distant, incurious, indifferent, listless, unconcerned
uninteresting boring, drab, dreary, dry, dull, flat, monotonous, tedious, uneventful, unexciting, wearisome
uninterrupted constant, continuous, nonstop, peaceful, steady, sustained, unbroken
union 1. amalgamation, blend, combination, conjunction, fusion, junction, mixture, uniting 2. alliance, association, coalition, confederacy, federation, league 3. accord, agreement, concord, harmony, unison, unity
unique 1. lone, only, single, solitary 2. incomparable, inimitable, matchless, peerless, unequalled, unmatched, unrivalled
unison accord, accordance, agreement, concert, concord, harmony
unit 1. assembly, detachment, entity, group, section, whole 2. component, constituent, element, item, member, module, part, portion, section, segment
unite 1. amalgamate, blend, combine, consolidate, couple, fuse, join, link, marry, merge, unify, wed 2. ally, band, close ranks, cooperate, league, pool
united 1. affiliated, allied, banded together, collective, combined, concerted, leagued, pooled, unified 2. agreed, one, unanimous
unity 1. entity, integrity, singleness, undividedness, union, wholeness 2. accord, agreement, concord, consensus, harmony, peace, solidarity
universal common, entire, general, total, unlimited, whole, widespread, worldwide
universally always, everywhere, invariably, uniformly
universe cosmos, creation, nature
unjust biased, one-sided, partial, partisan, prejudiced, undeserved, unfair, wrong, wrongful
unkind cruel, harsh, inhuman, insensitive, malicious, mean, nasty, spiteful, thoughtless, uncharitable, unfeeling, unfriendly, unsympathetic
unknown 1. alien, concealed, dark, hidden, mysterious, new, secret, strange, unrevealed, untold 2. anonymous, nameless, uncharted, undiscovered, unidentified, unnamed 3. humble, obscure, unfamiliar
unlawful banned, criminal, forbidden, illegal, illicit, outlawed, prohibited
unlike different, dissimilar, distinct, diverse, ill-matched, incompatible, opposite, unequal, unrelated
unlikely 1. doubtful, faint, improbable, remote, slight 2. incredible, questionable, unconvincing
unlimited 1. boundless, countless, endless, extensive, great, immense, infinite, limitless, unbounded, vast 2. absolute, complete, full, total, unfettered, unqualified, unrestricted
unload discharge, dump, empty, relieve, unpack
unloved forsaken, loveless, neglected, rejected, spurned, unpopular, unwanted
unlucky 1. cursed, hapless, luckless, miserable, unfortunate, unhappy, wretched 2. doomed, ill-fated, inauspicious, ominous, untimely
unmarried bachelor, maiden, single, unwed, virgin
unmask bare, disclose, discover, expose, reveal, uncover, unveil
unmentionable disgraceful, forbidden, indecent, scandalous, shameful, shocking, taboo, unspeakable
unmerciful brutal, cruel, hard, implacable, merciless, pitiless, remorseless, ruthless, unsparing
unmistakable certain, clear, decided, distinct, evident, indisputable, manifest, obvious, plain, positive, sure, unequivocal
unmitigated 1. grim, harsh, intense, persistent, unbroken, undiminished, unrelieved 2. absolute, arrant, complete, downright, outright, perfect, rank, sheer, thorough, utter
unmoved 1. fast, firm, steady, unchanged, untouched 2. cold, impassive, indifferent, unimpressed, unresponsive, untouched 3. determined, firm, resolute, resolved, steadfast, unwavering
unnatural 1. abnormal, anomalous, irregular, odd, perverse, perverted, unusual 2. extraordinary, freakish, queer, strange, unaccountable, uncanny 3. af-

fected, artificial, assumed, contrived, false, feigned, forced, insincere, laboured, stagy, stiff, stilted, strained, studied, theatrical

unnecessary expendable, inessential, needless, redundant, superfluous, unrequired, useless

unnerve confound, demoralize, disarm, discourage, dishearten, dismay, fluster, frighten, intimidate, shake, upset

unobtrusive inconspicuous, meek, modest, quiet, restrained, retiring, subdued, unostentatious, unpretentious

unoccupied empty, uninhabited, vacant

unofficial informal, personal, private, unauthorized, unconfirmed, wildcat

unorthodox abnormal, irregular, unusual, unwonted

unpaid 1. due, outstanding, overdue, owing, payable, unsettled 2. honorary, voluntary

unpalatable bitter, displeasing, distasteful, offensive, repugnant, unpleasant, unsavoury

unpardonable deplorable, disgraceful, outrageous, scandalous, unforgivable

unperturbed calm, composed, cool, placid, poised, tranquil, unruffled, untroubled, unworried

unpleasant bad, disagreeable, displeasing, distasteful, nasty, repulsive, unattractive

unpopular disliked, rejected, shunned, unattractive, undesirable, unwelcome

unprecedented abnormal, extraordinary, freakish, new, novel, original, remarkable, singular, unheard-of

unpredictable chance, doubtful, erratic, fickle, inconstant, random, unforeseeable, unreliable, unstable, variable

unprejudiced balanced, fair, impartial, just, objective, openminded

unpremeditated extempore, impromptu, impulsive, offhand, spontaneous, unprepared

unprepared 1. ill-considered, incomplete, unfinished, unplanned 2. surprised, unaware, unready, unsuspecting 3. ad-lib, improvised, spontaneous

unpretentious homely, honest, humble, modest, plain, simple, straightforward, unostentatious

unprincipled amoral, crooked, deceitful, dishonest, immoral, tricky, underhand, unethical

unproductive 1. fruitless, futile, idle, otiose, unrewarding, useless, vain, worthless 2. barren, dry, fruitless, sterile, unprolific

unprofessional 1. improper, lax, negligent, unethical, unseemly, unworthy 2. amateurish, inefficient, untrained

unprotected defenceless, helpless, open, unarmed, undefended, vulnerable

unqualified 1. ill-equipped, incapable, incompetent, ineligible, unfit, unprepared 2. downright, outright, unreserved 3. absolute, complete, downright, total, utter

unquestionable absolute, certain, clear, conclusive, definite, faultless, incontestable, manifest, patent, perfect, sure, unequivocal, unmistakable

unravel disentangle, free, separate, undo, unwind

unreal 1. dreamlike, fabulous, fanciful, illusory, imaginary, storybook, visionary 2. immaterial, insubstantial, intangible, nebulous 3. artificial, fake, false, insincere, mock, pretended, seeming, sham

unrealistic impracticable, improbable, quixotic, romantic, theoretical, unworkable

unreasonable 1. excessive, extortionate, immoderate, undue, unfair, unjust, unwarranted 2. arbitrary, biased, blinkered, erratic, headstrong, inconsistent, opinionated, quirky

unrelated 1. different, unconnected, unlike 2. extraneous, inapplicable, inappropriate, irrelevant, unassociated, unconnected

unreliable 1. irresponsible, treacherous, unstable, untrustworthy 2. deceptive, delusive, fallible, false, implausible, inaccurate, uncertain, unconvincing, unsound

unreserved 1. extrovert, forthright, frank, free, open, outgoing, outspoken, unrestrained 2. absolute, complete, entire, full, total, unlimited, wholehearted

unresolved doubtful, moot, pending, problematical, unanswered, undecided, unsettled, unsolved, vague

unrest 1. agitation, discontent, discord, dissension, protest, rebellion, sedition, strife, tumult 2. agitation, anxiety, distress, restlessness, worry

unrestrained abandoned, free, inordinate, intemperate, natural, unbounded, unchecked, uncontrolled, uninhibited

unrestricted 1. absolute, free, open, unbounded, unlimited, unregulated 2. clear, open, public

unrivalled beyond compare, incomparable, matchless, peerless, supreme, unmatched, unparalleled, unsurpassed, without equal

unruly disobedient, fractious, lawless, mutinous, rebellious, riotous, rowdy, turbulent, wayward, wild, wilful

unsafe dangerous, insecure, perilous, risky, threatening, uncertain, unreliable, unsound

unsatisfactory deficient, displeasing, inadequate, insufficient, mediocre, poor, unacceptable, unsuitable, weak

unsavoury 1. distasteful, nasty, obnoxious, offensive, repellent, repulsive, revolting, unpleasant 2. nauseating, unappetizing

unscrupulous corrupt, dishonest, immoral, improper, knavish, roguish unethical, unprincipled

unseemly disreputable, improper, indecorous, indelicate, unbecoming, undignified

unseen concealed, hidden, invisible, lurking, obscure, undetected, unnoticed

unselfish altruistic, devoted, generous, kind, liberal, noble, selfless

unsettle agitate, bother, confuse, disconcert, disturb, fluster, perturb, ruffle, trouble, unbalance, upset

unsettled 1. disorderly, shaky, unstable, unsteady 2. changing, inconstant, uncertain, variable 3. agitated, anxious, confused, disturbed, flustered, restive, restless, shaken, tense, unnerved 4. doubtful, moot, open, undecided, undetermined, unresolved 5. due, outstanding, owing, payable, pending

unsightly disagreeable, hideous, horrid, repulsive, ugly, unattractive

unskilled inexperienced, unprofessional, unqualified

unsociable chilly, cold, distant, hostile, retiring, unfriendly, unneighbourly, withdrawn

unsolicited free-will, gratuitous, unforced, uninvited, unsought, unwelcome, voluntary

unsophisticated 1. artless, childlike, inexperienced, ingenuous, natural, unaffected 2. plain, simple, uncomplicated, unrefined, unspecialized

unsound 1. ailing, defective, delicate, diseased, frail, ill, unhealthy, unstable, unwell, weak 2. defective, fallacious, false, flawed, illogical, shaky, specious, weak

unspeakable 1. inconceivable, inexpressible, unbelievable, unimaginable, wonderful 2. abominable, appalling, awful, bad, dreadful, evil, execrable, frightful, heinous, horrible, monstrous, shocking

unspoiled, unspoilt 1. intact, perfect, preserved, undamaged, untouched 2. artless, innocent, natural, unstudied, wholesome

unspoken implicit, implied, not spelt out, tacit, undeclared, understood, unexpressed, unspoken, unstated

unsteady 1. infirm, insecure, reeling, shaky, treacherous, unsafe 2. changeable, erratic, flighty, fluctuating, inconstant, irregular, unsettled, volatile, wavering

unsuccessful 1. bootless, failed, fruitless, futile, unavailing, useless, vain 2. balked, defeated, foiled, hapless, losing, luckless, unlucky

unsuitable improper, inapt, ineligible, unacceptable, unbecoming, unfitting, unseemly, unsuited

unsure 1. unassured, unconfident 2. distrustful, doubtful, hesitant, mistrustful, sceptical, suspicious

unsuspecting credulous, gullible, trustful, trusting, unwarned, unwary

unsympathetic callous, cold, cruel, hard, harsh, heartless, indifferent, soulless, unconcerned, unkind, unmoved

untangle disentangle, explain, extricate, solve, unravel

unthinkable 1. absurd, impossible, unlikely, unreasonable 2. implausible, inconceivable, incredible, unimaginable

untidy chaotic, cluttered, disorderly, littered, messy, rumpled, slipshod, slovenly, unkempt

untie free, loosen, release, unbind, undo, unfasten, unknot, unlace

untimely awkward, early, inappropriate, inauspicious, inconvenient, inopportune, premature, unfortunate, unsuitable

untiring constant, dedicated, devoted, dogged, patient, persistent, staunch, unremitting, unwearied

untouched 1. intact, undamaged, unharmed, unhurt 2. dry-eyed, indifferent, unaffected, unconcerned, unimpressed, unmoved, unstirred

untoward 1. annoying, disastrous, inconvenient, irritating, troublesome, unfortunate 2. adverse, contrary, inopportune, unfavourable, unlucky, untimely 3. improper, unbecoming, unfitting, unseemly, unsuitable

untrained amateur, green, inexperienced, raw, uneducated, unqualified, unskilled, untaught

untroubled calm, composed, cool, peaceful, placid, serene, steady, tranquil, unflustered, unperturbed, unruffled, unworried

untrue 1. deceptive, dishonest, erroneous, false, inaccurate, incorrect, lying, spurious, wrong 2. deceitful, disloyal, faithless, false, inconstant, treacherous, unfaithful, untrustworthy 3. deviant, distorted, inaccurate, off

untrustworthy deceitful, devious, dishonest, disloyal, false, fickle, slippery, treacherous, tricky, unfaithful, unreliable, untrue, untrusty

untruth deceit, falsehood, fib, fiction, lie, story, tale, trick

untruthful deceitful, deceptive, dishonest, false, lying, mendacious

unusual bizarre, curious, different, extraordinary, odd, queer, rare, remarkable, singular, strange, surprising, uncommon, unexpected, unfamiliar

unveil bare, disclose, divulge, expose, lay open, reveal, uncover

unwanted outcast, rejected, undesired, uninvited, unneeded, unsolicited, unwelcome, useless

unwary careless, hasty, heedless, imprudent, indiscreet, rash, reckless

unwavering consistent, determined, resolute, staunch, steadfast, steady, unshakable, unshaken

unwelcome 1. excluded, rejected, unacceptable, undesirable, unpopular, unwanted 2. disagreeable, displeasing, distasteful, thankless, unpleasant

unwell ailing, ill, sick, sickly, unhealthy

unwholesome 1. harmful, poisonous, tainted, unhealthy, unnourishing 2. bad, corrupting, degrading, demoralizing, evil, immoral, wicked

unwieldy 1. awkward, cumbersome, inconvenient, unmanageable 2. bulky, clumsy, hefty, massive, ponderous

unwilling averse, disinclined, grudging, indisposed, loath, opposed, reluctant, resistant, unenthusiastic

unwind 1. slacken, uncoil, undo, unreel, unroll, untwine, untwist 2. relax, take it easy

unwise foolhardy, ill-advised, ill-judged, improvident, imprudent, inadvisable, indiscreet, irresponsible, rash, reckless, senseless, silly, stupid

unwitting 1. ignorant, innocent, unaware, unknowing, unsuspecting 2. accidental, chance, involuntary, unintended, unmeant, unplanned

unworldly 1. metaphysical, religious, spiritual 2. green, idealistic, innocent, naive, raw, trusting 3. ethereal, unearthly

unworthy 1. base, contemptible, degrading, discreditable, disgraceful, dishonourable, disreputable, ignoble, shameful 2. undeserving

unwritten 1. oral, vocal 2. accepted, customary, tacit, understood

unyielding adamant, firm, hardline, inexorable, inflexible, obdurate, obstinate, relentless, resolute, rigid, steadfast, stubborn, tough, uncompromising

upbringing breeding, care, cultivation, education, tending, training

upgrade advance, better, elevate, enhance, improve, promote, raise

upheaval disorder, disruption, eruption, revolution, turmoil

uphill *adj.* 1. ascending, climbing, mounting, rising 2. arduous, difficult, exhausting, gruelling, hard, laborious, strenuous, taxing, tough

uphold advocate, aid, back, champion, defend, encourage, endorse, justify, maintain, promote, support, sustain

upkeep 1. keep, maintenance, repair, running, subsistence 2. expenditure, outlay, overheads

uplift *v.* 1. elevate, hoist, lift up, raise 2. advance, better, civilize, cultivate, edify, improve, inspire, raise, refine, upgrade ~*n.* 3. edification, enhancement, enlightenment, enrichment, improvement, refinement

upper 1. high, higher, loftier, top, topmost 2. elevated, eminent, greater, important, superior

upper hand advantage, ascendancy, dominion, edge, mastery, supremacy, sway

uppermost 1. highest, loftiest, top, topmost 2. chief, dominant, greatest, leading, main, principal, supreme

upright 1. erect, straight, vertical 2. conscientious, ethical, faithful, good, honest, just, principled, righteous, true, virtuous

uproar brawl, clamour, commotion, confusion, din, furore, mayhem, noise, outcry, racket, riot, turbulence, turmoil

upset *v.* 1. capsize, overturn, spill 2. change, disorder, disturb, spoil 3. agitate, bother, discompose, disconcert, dismay, distress, disturb, fluster, grieve, ruffle, trouble 4. conquer, defeat, overcome, triumph over ~*n.* 5. defeat, reverse, surprise 6. complaint, disorder, illness, malady, sickness 7. agitation, bother, discomposure, disquiet, distress, disturbance, shock, trouble, worry ~*adj.* 8. capsized, overturned, spilled, toppled, tumbled 9. disordered, disturbed, gippy (*Sl.*), ill, queasy, sick 10. agitated, bothered, confused, dismayed, distressed, disturbed, frantic, grieved, hurt, ruffled, troubled, worried 11. chaotic, confused, disordered, muddled 12. beaten, conquered, defeated, overcome, overthrown

upshot culmination, end, end result, event, finale, issue, outcome, result

upside down 1. inverted, overturned, upturned 2. confused, disordered, muddled, topsy-turvy

upstart arriviste, nobody

up-to-date current, fashionable, in, modern, newest, stylish

urban city, civic, metropolitan, municipal, town

urbane civil, civilized, courteous, cultured, debonair, elegant, polished, refined, smooth, suave

urchin brat, gamin, ragamuffin, waif

urge *v.* 1. beg, beseech, entreat, exhort, implore, plead, press, solicit 2. advise, advocate, champion, counsel, recommend, support 3. compel, drive, encourage, force, goad, hasten, impel, incite, induce, instigate, press, propel, push, spur, stimulate ~*n.* 4. desire, drive, fancy, impulse, itch, longing, wish, yearning

urgency extremity, gravity, hurry, importance, importunity, necessity, need, pressure, stress

urgent 1. compelling, critical, crucial, immediate, imperative, important, instant, pressing 2. clamorous, earnest, importunate, insistent, intense, persuasive

usable available, current, functional, practical, serviceable, utilizable, valid, working

usage 1. control, employment, management, operation, running, treatment 2. convention, custom, form, habit, method, mode, practice, procedure, regime, routine, rule, tradition

use *v.* 1. apply, employ, exercise, operate, ply, practise, utilize, wield, work 2. exploit, handle, manipulate, treat 3. consume, exhaust, expend, run through, spend, waste ~*n.* 4. application, employment, exercise, handling, operation, practice, service, usage 5. advantage, application, avail, benefit, good, help, point, profit, service, value, worth 6. custom, habit, practice, way, wont

used cast-off, second-hand, shopsoiled, worn

useful advantageous, effective, fruitful, helpful, practical, profitable, salutary, valuable, worthwhile

useless 1. disadvantageous, fruitless, futile, hopeless, idle, ineffective, pointless, profitless, unavailing, unproductive, unworkable, vain, valueless, worthless 2. *Inf.* hopeless, ineffectual, inept, stupid, weak

use up absorb, consume, devour, drain, exhaust, finish, waste

usher 1. *n.* attendant, doorkeeper, escort, guide 2. *v.* conduct, direct, escort, guide, lead, pilot, steer

usual common, constant, customary, everyday, expected, familiar, fixed, general, habitual, normal, ordinary, regular, routine, standard, stock, typical

usually commonly, generally, habitually, mainly, mostly, normally, ordinarily, regularly, routinely

utility avail, benefit, convenience, efficacy, fitness, point, practicality, profit, service

utmost *adj.* 1. chief, extreme, greatest, highest, maximum, paramount, pre-eminent, supreme 2. extreme, farthest, final, last ~*n.* 3. best, greatest, hardest, highest

utter[1] *v.* 1. articulate, express, pronounce, say, speak, voice 2. declare, divulge, proclaim, promulgate, publish, reveal, state

utter[2] *adj.* absolute, complete, downright, entire, perfect, sheer, stark, total, unqualified

utterly absolutely, entirely, extremely, fully, perfectly, thoroughly, totally

V

vacancy 1. job, opportunity, position, post, room, situation 2. abstraction, inanity, inattentiveness

vacant 1. available, empty, free, idle, unemployed, unfilled, untenanted, void 2. abstracted, blank, dreamy, idle, inane

vacuum emptiness, gap, space, void

vague dim, doubtful, hazy, ill-defined, imprecise, indefinite, indistinct, lax, loose, obscure, shadowy, uncertain, unclear, unknown, unspecified, woolly

vain 1. arrogant, egotistical, overweening, proud, swaggering, vainglorious 2. abortive, empty, fruitless, futile, hollow, idle, pointless, senseless, unimportant, unproductive, unprofitable, useless, worthless 3. **in vain** bootless, ineffectual(ly), unsuccessfully, wasted

valiant bold, brave, doughty, heroic, plucky, stouthearted, worthy

valid authentic, bona fide, genuine, lawful, legal, legitimate, official

valley coomb, cwm (*Welsh*), dale, dell, depression, dingle, glen, hollow, strath (*Scot.*), vale

valuable *adj.* 1. costly, dear, precious 2. cherished, esteemed, helpful, important, prized, serviceable, treasured, useful, valued, worthy

value *n.* 1. cost, rate 2. advantage, benefit, desirability, help, importance, merit, profit, use, worth 3. *Plural* ethics, standards, principles ~*v.* 4. account, assess, estimate, price, rate, survey 5. cherish, esteem, prize, regard highly, respect, treasure

vanguard forefront, front rank, leaders, spearhead, trendsetters, van

vanish disappear, evaporate, exit, fade

vanity 1. airs, arrogance, conceit, egotism, ostentation, pride, vainglory 2. emptiness, frivolity, futility, inanity, triviality, unreality

vapour breath, fog, fumes, haze, mist, smoke, steam

variable changeable, fickle, fitful, inconstant, mercurial, shifting, unstable, unsteady

variance difference, disagreement, discord, discrepancy, dissension, divergence, inconsistency, strife, variation

variation alteration, change, departure, deviation, difference, diversity, innovation, novelty

varied assorted, different, miscellaneous, mixed, motley, sundry, various

variety 1. change, difference, diversity, variation 2. array, assortment, collection, medley, mixture, range 3. brand, breed, category, class, kind, make, order, sort, species, strain, type

various assorted, different, disparate, distinct, diverse, many, miscellaneous, several, sundry

varnish *v.* adorn, decorate, gild, glaze, gloss, polish

vary alter, change, depart, diverge, diversify, fluctuate, modify, reorder, transform

vast boundless, enormous, extensive, great, huge, immense, limitless, massive, monstrous, prodigious, sweeping, tremendous, unbounded, unlimited

vault[1] *v.* bound, clear, hurdle, jump, leap, spring

vault[2] *n.* 1. arch, ceiling, roof, span 2. cellar, crypt 3. depository, strongroom ~*v.* 4. arch, bend, bow, curve, span

veer be deflected, change, change course, change direction, sheer, shift, swerve, tack, turn

vegetate idle, languish, moulder, stagnate

vehemence eagerness, emphasis, energy, enthusiasm, fervour, fire, force, forcefulness, heat, intensity, keenness, passion, vigour, warmth, zeal

vehement ardent, eager, earnest, emphatic, fervent, fierce, forceful, forcible, impetuous, intense, passionate, strong, violent

veil 1. *v.* cloak, conceal, cover, dim, disguise, hide, mantle, mask, obscure, screen, shield 2. *n.* blind, cloak, cover, curtain, disguise, film, mask, screen, shade, shroud

vein 1. course, current, seam, streak, stripe 2. dash, hint, strain, streak, thread, trait 3. bent, faculty, humour, mode, mood, note, style, temper, tenor, tone, turn

vendetta feud, quarrel

veneer *n. Fig.* appearance, façade, front, gloss, guise, pretence

venerable august, esteemed, grave, honoured, sage, sedate, wise

venerate adore, esteem, honour, respect, worship

vengeance avenging, reprisal, retaliation, retribution

venom 1. bane, poison, toxin 2. acrimony, bitterness, grudge, hate, malice, rancour, spite, spleen, virulence

vent 1. *n.* aperture, duct, hole, outlet, split 2. *v.* air, discharge, emit, empty, express, release, utter, voice

ventilate *Fig.* air, broadcast, debate, discuss, examine, scrutinize, sift

venture *v.* 1. chance, hazard, imperil, risk, speculate, stake, wager 2. advance, dare, hazard, presume, volunteer ~*n.* 3. chance, endeavour, enterprise, fling, gamble, hazard, project, risk

verbal literal, oral, spoken

verbatim exactly, precisely, word for word

verdict conclusion, decision, finding, judgment, opinion, sentence

verge 1. *n.* border, brim, brink, edge, extreme, limit, lip, margin, roadside, threshold 2. *v.* approach, border

verification authentication, confirmation, proof

verify attest, authenticate, check, confirm, prove, support, validate

vernacular 1. *adj.* common, informal, local, native, popular, vulgar 2. *n.* argot, cant, dialect, idiom, parlance, patois, speech

versatile adaptable, flexible, functional, handy, protean, resourceful, variable

versed accomplished, competent, experienced, familiar, practised, proficient, qualified, seasoned, skilled

version account, exercise, portrayal, reading, rendering, side, translation

vertical erect, on end, upright

vertigo dizziness, giddiness

verve animation, dash, élan, energy, force, gusto, life, liveliness, sparkle, spirit, vigour, vitality, zeal

very absolutely, acutely, decidedly, deeply, eminently, exceedingly, extremely, greatly, highly, noticeably, particularly, really, remarkably, truly, unusually, wonderfully

vessel 1. boat, craft, ship 2. container, pot, receptacle, utensil

vest *v. With* **in** *or* **with** authorize, upon, bestow, confer, consign, empower, endow, entrust, furnish, lodge, place, settle

vet *v.* appraise, check, examine, investigate, look over, pass under review, review, scan, scrutinize

veteran 1. *n.* master, trouper 2. *adj.* adept, expert, old, proficient, seasoned

veto 1. *v.* ban, forbid, negative, prohibit, reject, rule out, turn down 2. *n.* ban, embargo, interdict, prohibition

vex afflict, agitate, annoy, bother, displease, distress, disturb, exasperate, harass, irritate, molest, offend, perplex, pester, plague, provoke, put out, rile, tease, torment, trouble, upset, worry

vexed afflicted, agitated, annoyed, bothered, confused, displeased, distressed, disturbed, exasperated, fed up, harassed, perplexed, provoked, riled, ruffled, tormented, troubled, upset, worried

vibrant 1. oscillating, pulsating, quivering, trembling 2. alive, animated, colourful, dynamic, sensitive, sparkling, spirited, vivacious, vivid

vibrate fluctuate, pulsate, quiver, shake, shiver, sway, swing, throb, tremble

vibration oscillation, pulse, quiver, resonance, shaking, throb, trembling, tremor

vice corruption, depravity, evil, evildoing, immorality, iniquity, sin, wickedness

vicious 1. abandoned, atrocious, bad, corrupt, cruel, dangerous, degraded, depraved, fiendish, foul, immoral, monstrous, savage, sinful, vile, violent, wicked, worthless, wrong 2. cruel, malicious, mean, slanderous, spiteful, vindictive

victim 1. casualty, fatality, martyr, sacrifice, scapegoat, sufferer 2. dupe

victimize 1. persecute, pick on 2. cheat, deceive, defraud, dupe, exploit, fool, swindle

victor champion, conqueror, first, winner

victorious champion, first, successful, triumphant, winning

victory conquest, laurels, mastery, success, superiority, triumph, win

view *n.* 1. aspect, outlook, panorama, picture, prospect, scene, vista 2. sight, vision 3. *Sometimes plural* attitude, belief, feeling, impression, notion, opinion, sentiment, thought ~*v.* 4. behold, examine, explore, eye, inspect, look at, observe, regard, scan, survey, watch, witness 5. consider, deem, judge, regard, think about

viewer observer, onlooker, spectator, watcher

viewpoint angle, perspective, view, position, slant, stance, standpoint, vantage point

vigilant alert, attentive, careful, cautious, sleepless, unsleeping, wakeful, watchful

vigorous active, brisk, effective, energetic, flourishing, forceful, hale, hardy, healthy, intense, lively, lusty, powerful, robust, sound, spirited, strong, virile, vital

vigour activity, animation, dash, dynamism, energy, force, gusto, health, liveliness, might, power, soundness, spirit, strength, verve, virility, vitality

vile 1. bad, base, coarse, contemptible, corrupt, debased, degenerate, degrading, depraved, disgraceful, evil, ignoble, impure, loathsome, low, mean, miserable, perverted, shocking, sinful, ugly, vicious, vulgar, wicked, worthless, wretched 2. disgusting, foul, horrid, loathsome, nasty, repellent, repugnant, repulsive, sickening

villain blackguard, criminal, miscreant, profligate, reprobate, rogue, scoundrel, wretch

villainous bad, base, criminal, cruel, debased, evil, fiendish, hateful, infamous, mean, ruffianly, sinful, thievish, vicious, vile, wicked

vindicate absolve, acquit, clear, defend, exculpate, excuse, exonerate, justify, rehabilitate

vindication apology, defence, excuse, justification, plea, support

vindictive malicious, malignant, rancorous, resentful, revengeful, spiteful, vengeful

vintage 1. *n.* crop, era, harvest, origin, year 2. *adj.* best, choice, mature, prime, rare, ripe, select, superior

violate 1. break, disobey, disregard, infract, infringe, transgress 2. abuse, assault, debauch, defile, desecrate, dishonour, invade, outrage, pollute

violence 1. bloodshed, brutality, cruelty, ferocity, fighting, force, frenzy, fury, passion, savagery, wildness 2. power, raging, storminess, tumult, wildness

violent 1. berserk, brutal, cruel, fiery, forcible, furious, headstrong, impetuous, passionate, powerful, raging, riotous, rough, savage, strong, ungovernable, vehement, vicious, wild 2. devastating, powerful, raging, ruinous, strong, tempestuous, turbulent, wild

virgin 1. *n.* girl, vestal 2. *adj.* chaste, fresh, immaculate, maidenly, modest, new, pure, undefiled, untouched, unused, vestal

virtual essential, implicit, implied, indirect

virtually as good as, effectually, in effect, nearly, practically

virtue 1. excellence, goodness, incorruptibility, integrity, justice, morality, probity, rectitude, uprightness, worth 2. advantage, asset, attribute, credit, merit, strength 3. chastity, honour, innocence, purity, virginity

virtuoso 1. *n.* artist, genius, maestro, master 2. *adj.* brilliant, dazzling, masterly

virtuous 1. blameless, excellent, exemplary, good, honest, incorruptible, moral, pure, righteous, upright, worthy 2. celibate, chaste, innocent, pure, spotless, virginal

virulent 1. deadly, infective, lethal, poisonous, septic 2. bitter, hostile, malevolent, malicious, resentful, vicious, vindictive

visible apparent, clear, detectable, discernible, distinguishable, evident, manifest, noticeable, observable, obvious, perceivable, plain, unconcealed

vision 1. eyes, eyesight, perception, seeing, sight, view 2. discernment, foresight, imagination, insight, intuition 3. concept, daydream, dream, fantasy, idea, image 4. apparition, delusion, ghost, illusion, mirage, revelation, spectre, wraith

visionary 1. *adj.* idealistic, romantic 2. *n.* dreamer, idealist, mystic, prophet, seer

visit *v.* 1. inspect, stay with 2. afflict, assail, attack, befall, haunt, smite ~*n.* 3. call, sojourn, stay, stop

visitation 1. examination, inspection, visit 2. bane, blight, calamity, disaster, ordeal, trial

visitor caller, company, guest, visitant

visual 1. optic, optical 2. discernible, observable, perceptible, visible

visualize envisage, imagine, picture

vital 1. basic, cardinal, essential, indispensable, requisite 2. critical, crucial, decisive, important, key, significant, urgent 3. animated, dynamic, energetic, forceful, lively, spirited, vivacious, zestful 4. alive, lifegiving, live, living

vitality animation, energy, life, liveliness, sparkle, stamina, strength, vigour, vivacity

vivacious cheerful, ebullient, frolicsome, gay, jolly, lighthearted, lively, merry, spirited, sprightly, vital

vivid 1. bright, brilliant, clear, glowing, intense, rich 2. distinct, graphic, lifelike, memorable, powerful, sharp, stirring, strong, telling

vocabulary dictionary, glossary, language, lexicon, wordbook, words

vocal *adj.* 1. articulate, oral, said, spoken, uttered, voiced 2. blunt, clamorous, eloquent, expressive, forthright, frank, noisy, outspoken, strident

vocation business, calling, career, employment, job, mission, office, post, profession, pursuit, role, trade

vociferous clamant, loud, noisy, shouting, strident, vehement

vogue 1. craze, custom, fashion, mode, style, trend, way 2. acceptance, currency, favour, popularity, prevalence, usage, use

voice *n.* 1. language, sound, tone, utterance, words 2. decision, expression, part, say, view, vote, will, wish 3. instrument, medium, mouthpiece, organ, spokesman, vehicle ~*v.* 4. air, articulate, assert, declare, divulge, enunciate, express, utter

void *adj.* 1. bare, clear, drained, empty, free, unfilled, unoccupied, vacant 2. *With* **of** destitute, devoid, lacking, without 3. dead, invalid, useless, vain, worthless ~*n.* 4. blank, emptiness, gap, lack, opening, space, vacuum, want ~*v.* 5. discharge, drain, eject, emit, empty, evacuate

volatile airy, changeable, erratic, explosive, fickle, flighty, gay, giddy, inconstant, lively, mercurial, sprightly, unsettled, unstable, unsteady, up and down (*Inf.*), variable

volley *n.* barrage, blast, burst, discharge, explosion, hail, salvo, shower

volume 1. aggregate, amount, body, bulk, capacity, mass, quantity, total 2. book, publication, tome, treatise

voluntarily freely, willingly

voluntary free, gratuitous, honorary, intentional, optional, spontaneous, unforced, unpaid, willing

volunteer *v.* advance, offer, present, proffer, propose, suggest, tender

vomit *v.* be sick, disgorge, eject, emit, heave, regurgitate, retch

voracious avid, devouring, gluttonous, greedy, hungry, omnivorous, ravenous, uncontrolled

vote 1. *n.* ballot, franchise, plebiscite, poll, referendum, suffrage 2. *v.* ballot, elect, opt, return

vouch *Usually with* **for** affirm, answer for, assert, back, certify, confirm, guarantee, support, uphold

vow 1. *v.* affirm, dedicate, devote, pledge, promise, swear 2. *n.* oath, pledge, promise

voyage *n.* crossing, cruise, journey, passage, travels, trip

vulgar 1. boorish, coarse, common, crude, dirty, flashy, gaudy, gross, ill-bred, impolite, improper, indecent, indelicate, low, nasty, naughty, ribald, rude, suggestive, tasteless, tawdry, unmannerly, unrefined 2. general, native, ordinary, unrefined

vulgarity bad taste, coarseness, crudeness, grossness, in-

delicacy, ribaldry, rudeness, tawdriness
vulnerable assailable, defenceless, exposed, sensitive, susceptible, tender, weak, wide open

W

wade 1. ford, paddle, splash 2. *With* **in** *or* **into** assail, attack, go for, set about, tackle
waft *v.* bear, carry, convey, drift, float, ride, transport
wag 1. *v.* bob, flutter, nod, quiver, rock, shake, stir, wave 2. *n.* bob, flutter, nod, oscillation, quiver, shake, toss, wave
wage *n. Also* **wages** allowance, compensation, earnings, emolument, fee, hire, pay, payment, remuneration, reward, stipend
wager 1. *n.* bet, gamble, pledge, stake 2. *v.* bet, chance, gamble, hazard, lay, pledge, punt, risk, stake
waif foundling, orphan, stray
wail 1. *v.* bemoan, cry, deplore, grieve, howl, lament, weep 2. *n.* complaint, cry, grief, howl, lament, moan, weeping
wait 1. *v.* abide, dally, delay, hang fire, hold back, linger, pause, remain, rest, stay, tarry 2. *n.* delay, halt, interval, pause, rest, stay
waiter, waitress attendant, server, steward, stewardess
wait on *or* **upon** attend, minister to, serve, tend
waive abandon, defer, forgo, give up, postpone, put off, relinquish, remit, renounce, resign, surrender
wake[1] *v.* 1. arise, bestir, get up, rouse, stir 2. activate, animate, arouse, awaken, enliven, excite, fire, galvanize, kindle, provoke, quicken, stimulate, stir up
wake[2] backwash, path, track, trail, train, wash, waves
wakeful 1. insomniac, restless, sleepless 2. alert, alive, attentive, heedful, observant, unsleeping, vigilant, wary, watchful
waken activate, arouse, enliven, fire, galvanize, get up, kindle, quicken, rouse, stimulate, stir
walk *v.* 1. advance, go, hike, move, pace, promenade, saunter, step, stride, stroll, tramp, trek, trudge 2. accompany, convoy, escort, take ~*n.* 3. hike, march, promenade, ramble, saunter, stroll, tramp, trek, trudge, turn 4. carriage, gait, pace, step, stride 5. alley, avenue, footpath, lane, path, pathway, pavement, promenade, sidewalk, trail 6. area, arena, calling, career, course, field, line, sphere, trade
walker hiker, pedestrian, rambler
walkout protest, stoppage, strike
wall 1. divider, enclosure, panel, partition, screen 2. barricade, embankment, fortification, parapet, rampart 3. barrier, block, fence, hedge, impediment, obstacle 4. **go to the wall** be ruined, collapse, fail, fall
wallet case, holder, notecase, pouch, purse
wallow 1. lie, splash around, tumble, welter 2. flounder, lurch, stagger, stumble, wade 3. bask, delight, glory, luxuriate, relish, revel
wan anaemic, ashen, colourless, ghastly, livid, pale, pallid, pasty, sickly
wand baton, rod, sprig, stick, twig
wander *v.* 1. cruise, drift, meander, peregrinate, ramble, range, roam, rove, straggle, stray, stroll 2. depart, digress, diverge, err, lapse, veer 3. babble, ramble, rave ~*n.* 4. cruise, excursion, meander, ramble
wanderer drifter, gypsy, itinerant, nomad, rambler, ranger, rover, stroller, traveller, vagabond, voyager
wandering drifting, itinerant, nomadic, rambling, rootless, roving, strolling, travelling, vagabond, vagrant
wane 1. *v.* abate, decline, decrease, dim, drop, dwindle, ebb, fade, fail, lessen, sink, subside, weaken, wind down, wither 2. *n.* **on the wane** declining, dropping, dwindling, ebbing, fading, subsiding, weakening, withering
want *v.* 1. covet, crave, desire, need, require, wish, yearn for 2. be short of, be without, call for, demand, lack, miss, need, require ~*n.* 3. appetite, craving, demand, desire, fancy, hankering, hunger, longing, need, thirst, wish 4. absence, dearth, default, deficiency, famine, lack, scarcity, shortage 5. destitution, need, penury, poverty
wanting 1. absent, incomplete, lacking, less, missing, short, shy 2. defective, faulty, imperfect, patchy, poor, sketchy, substandard, unsound
wanton *adj.* 1. abandoned, dissolute, fast, immoral, lewd, libertine, licentious, loose, shameless, unchaste 2. cruel, evil, gratuitous, malicious, motiveless, needless, senseless, spiteful, unjustified, unprovoked, vicious, wicked, wilful ~*n.* 3. Casanova, debauchee, harlot, lecher, libertine, profligate, prostitute, rake, slut, trollop, whore ~*v.* 4. debauch, dissipate, revel, riot, whore 5. misspend, squander, waste
war 1. *n.* battle, bloodshed, combat, conflict, contest, enmity, fighting, hostilities, strife, struggle, warfare 2. *v.* battle, clash, combat, contend, contest, fight, struggle
ward 1. area, district, division, precinct, quarter, zone 2. charge, minor, protégé, pupil 3. care, charge, custody, keeping, protection
warden administrator, caretaker, curator, guardian, janitor, keeper, ranger, steward, warder, watchman
warder, wardress custodian, gaoler, guard, jailer, keeper, prison officer
ward off avert, avoid, block, deflect, forestall, parry, repel, thwart
wardrobe 1. closet, clothes cupboard 2. apparel, attire, clothes, outfit
warehouse depository, depot, stockroom, store, storehouse
wares commodities, goods, merchandise, produce, stock, stuff
warfare arms, battle, blows, combat, conflict, contest, discord, fighting, hostilities, strategy, strife, struggle, war
warily carefully, cautiously, gingerly, guardedly, suspiciously, vigilantly, watchfully
warlike aggressive, belligerent, combative, hawkish, hostile, jingoistic, martial, militaristic, pugnacious, warmongering
warm *adj.* 1. balmy, heated, pleasant, sunny 2. affable, affectionate, amiable, amorous, cheerful, cordial, friendly, genial, happy, hearty, kindly, loving, pleasant, tender 3. ardent, earnest, effusive, emotional, enthusiastic, fervent, glowing, heated, keen, lively, passionate, spirited, vigorous, violent 4. irritable, passionate, quick, sensitive, short 5. heat, melt, thaw 6. animate, awaken, excite, interest, rouse, stimulate, stir
warmonger belligerent, hawk, militarist
warmth 1. heat, warmness 2. animation, ardour, eagerness, enthusiasm, excitement, fervour, fire, heat, intensity, passion, spirit, vigour, violence, zeal, zest 3. affability, affection, cordiality, happiness, heartiness, kindliness, love, tenderness
warn admonish, advise, alert, caution, forewarn, inform, notify, summon, tip off
warning *n.* admonition, advice, alarm, alert, caution, hint, notice, notification, omen, premonition, sign, signal, threat, tip, token
warrant *n.* 1. assurance, authority, authorization, commission, guarantee, licence, permission, permit, pledge, sanction, security ~*v.* 2. affirm, assure, attest, avouch, certify, declare, guarantee, pledge, underwrite, uphold 3. approve, authorize, commission, demand, empower, entitle, excuse, justify, license, permit, require, sanction
warrior combatant, fighter, soldier
wary alert, attentive, careful, cautious, chary, distrustful, guarded, heedful, prudent, suspicious, vigilant, watchful
wash *v.* 1. bath, bathe, clean, cleanse, launder, moisten, rinse, scrub, shower, wet 2. *With* **away** carry off, erode, move, sweep away, wash off 3. *Inf.* be convincing, hold water 4. **wash one's hands of** abandon ~*n.* 5. ablution, bath, cleaning, rinse, scrub, shampoo, shower, washing 6. flow, roll, surge, sweep, swell, wave
washout disappointment, disaster, failure, fiasco, mess
waste *v.* 1. dissipate, lavish, misuse, squander 2. consume, corrode, crumble, decay, decline, disable, drain, dwindle, exhaust, fade, gnaw, perish, sink, undermine, wane, wither 3. despoil, destroy, pillage, rape, ravage, raze, ruin, sack, spoil ~*n.* 4. extravagance, loss, misapplication, misuse, prodigality, squandering, wastefulness 5. desolation, destruction, devastation, havoc, ravage, ruin 6. debris, dregs, dross, garbage, leavings, litter, offal, refuse, rubbish, scrap, trash 7. desert, solitude, void, wilderness ~*adj.* 8. superfluous, unused, worthless 9. bare, barren, desolate, dismal, dreary, empty, unproductive, wild
wasteful extravagant, lavish, prodigal, ruinous, spendthrift, thriftless, uneconomical
watch *v.* 1. contemplate, eye, look, mark, note, observe, regard, see, stare at, view 2. attend, be watchful, look out, take heed, wait 3. guard, keep, look after, mind, protect, tend ~*n.* 4. chronometer, clock, timepiece 5. eye, heed, lookout, notice, surveillance, vigil, vigilance
watchdog 1. guard dog 2. custodian, inspector, monitor, protector, scrutineer
watcher lookout, observer, onlooker, spectator, spy, viewer, witness
watchful alert, attentive, guarded, heedful, observant, suspicious, vigilant, wary, wide awake
watchman caretaker, custodian, guard, security man
watch over defend, guard, preserve, protect, shelter, shield, stand guard over
water *n.* 1. aqua, H_2O ~*v.* 2. dampen, drench, flood, hose, irrigate, moisten, soak, souse, spray, sprinkle 3. adulterate, dilute, thin, weaken
waterfall cascade, cataract, chute, fall
watertight 1. sound, waterproof 2. airtight, firm, flawless, foolproof, impregnable, sound, unassailable
watery 1. damp, fluid, humid, liquid, marshy, moist, soggy, squelchy, wet 2. adulterated, diluted, insipid, runny, tasteless, thin, washy, weak
wave *v.* 1. brandish, flourish, flutter, oscillate, quiver, ripple, shake, stir, sway, swing, undulate, wag, wield 2. beckon, direct, gesture, indicate, sign, signal ~*n.* 3. billow, breaker, ridge, ripple, roller, sea surf, swell 4. current, drift, flood, movement, outbreak, rash, rush, stream, surge, sweep, tendency, trend, upsurge
waver 1. dither, falter, hesitate, seesaw, vacillate 2. flicker, fluctuate, quiver, reel, shake, sway, undulate, vary, wave, weave, wobble
wax *v.* develop, dilate, enlarge, expand, grow, increase, magnify, mount, rise, swell
way 1. approach, fashion, manner, means, method, mode, plan, practice, procedure, process, scheme, system, technique 2. access, avenue, channel, course, direction, lane, path, road, route, street, track, trail 3. elbowroom, opening, room, space 4. distance, journey, length, stretch, trail 5. advance, approach, journey, march, passage, progress 6. characteristic, conduct, custom, habit, manner, nature, personality, practice, style, trait, usage, wont 7. aspect, detail, feature, particular, point, respect, sense 8. **by the way** incidentally, in passing 9. **give way** a. break down, cave in, collapse, crack, crumple, fall, give, subside b. accede, acknowledge

defeat, acquiesce, concede, withdraw, yield **10. under way** afoot, begun, going, moving, started

wayfarer globetrotter, itinerant, nomad, rover, traveller, voyager, walker, wanderer

wayward capricious, contrary, cross-grained, disobedient, erratic, fickle, flighty, headstrong, incorrigible, mulish, obdurate, obstinate, perverse, rebellious, self-willed, stubborn, ungovernable, unpredictable, unruly, wilful

weak 1. anaemic, debilitated, decrepit, delicate, effete, exhausted, faint, feeble, fragile, frail, infirm, puny, shaky, sickly, spent, tender, unsteady, wasted **2.** cowardly, impotent, indecisive, ineffectual, infirm, irresolute, powerless, soft, spineless **3.** distant, dull, faint, low, muffled, poor, quiet, slight, small, soft **4.** deficient, faulty, inadequate, lacking, poor, wanting **5.** feeble, flimsy, hollow, inconclusive, invalid, lame, pathetic, shallow, slight, unsatisfactory **6.** defenceless, exposed, helpless, unprotected, unsafe, untenable, vulnerable, wide open **7.** diluted, insipid, runny, tasteless, thin, watery

weaken 1. abate, depress, diminish, droop, dwindle, enervate, fade, fail, flag, impair, invalidate, lessen, lower, moderate, reduce, sap, temper, tire, undermine, wane **2.** cut, debase, dilute, thin

weakness 1. faintness, feebleness, frailty, impotence, infirmity, powerlessness, vulnerability **2.** blemish, defect, deficiency, failing, fault, flaw, imperfection, lack, shortcoming **3.** fondness, inclination, liking, passion, penchant, proneness, soft spot

wealth 1. affluence, assets, capital, cash, estate, fortune, funds, goods, means, money, opulence, possessions, property, resources, riches, substance **2.** abundance, bounty, fullness, plenty, profusion, richness, store

wealthy affluent, comfortable, moneyed, opulent, prosperous, rich, well-off

wear *v.* **1.** bear, carry, clothe oneself, don, have on, put on, sport **2.** display, exhibit, fly, show **3.** abrade, consume, corrode, deteriorate, erode, fray, grind, impair, rub, use, wash away, waste **4.** bear up, endure, hold up, last, stand up **5.** annoy, drain, harass, irk, pester, tax, vex, weaken, weary *~n.* **6.** employment, mileage (*Inf.*), service, use, utility **7.** apparel, attire, clothes, costume, dress, garments, gear, habit, outfit **8.** abrasion, attrition, damage, depreciation, erosion, friction, use

weariness drowsiness, exhaustion, fatigue, lassitude, lethargy, prostration, tiredness

wearisome annoying, boring, bothersome, burdensome, dull, exhausting, fatiguing, irksome, oppressive, prosaic, tedious, troublesome, trying, wearing

wear off abate, decrease, diminish, dwindle, ebb, fade, subside, wane, weaken

wear out 1. consume, deteriorate, erode, fray, impair **2.** enervate, exhaust, fatigue, sap, tire, weary

weary *adj.* **1.** dead beat (*Inf.*), drained, drowsy, exhausted, fatigued, flagging, jaded, sleepy, spent, tired, wearied, worn out **2.** arduous, irksome, laborious, taxing, wearing *~v.* **3.** burden, drain, droop, enervate, fade, fail, fatigue, sap, tax, tire, wear out **4.** annoy, become bored, bore, exasperate, irk, jade, plague, sicken, vex

weather *n.* **1.** climate, conditions **2. under the weather** ailing, ill, indisposed, off-colour, sick *~v.* **3.** expose, harden, season, toughen **4.** brave, endure, overcome, pull through, resist, stand, suffer, surmount, survive, withstand

weave 1. blend, braid, entwine, fuse, intermingle, intertwine, introduce, knit, merge, plait, twist, unite **2.** build, construct, contrive, create, fabricate, make, spin **3.** wind, zigzag

web 1. cobweb **2.** lattice, mesh, net, network, screen, tangle, toils, weave

wed espouse, join, make one, marry, unite

wedding marriage, nuptials, wedlock

wedge 1. *n.* block, chock, chunk, lump **2.** *v.* block, cram, force, jam, lodge, pack, split, squeeze, stuff, thrust

weep bemoan, bewail, complain, cry, lament, moan, mourn, snivel, sob, ululate, whimper

weigh 1. consider, contemplate, evaluate, examine, ponder, study **2.** count, cut any ice (*Inf.*), have influence, impress, matter, tell **3.** burden, oppress, prey

weight *n.* **1.** burden, gravity, heaviness, load, mass, pressure, tonnage **2.** ballast, load, mass **3.** burden, load, millstone, pressure, strain **4.** onus, preponderance **5.** authority, consequence, consideration, emphasis, impact, importance, influence, moment, power, substance, value *~v.* **6.** ballast, charge, freight, load **7.** burden, encumber, handicap, impede, oppress, overburden **8.** bias, load, unbalance

weighty 1. burdensome, dense, heavy, massive, ponderous **2.** considerable, critical, crucial, forcible, grave, important, momentous, serious, significant, solemn, substantial **3.** crushing, demanding, difficult, exacting, onerous, oppressive, taxing, worrying

weird bizarre, eerie, freakish, ghostly, grotesque, mysterious, odd, queer, strange, uncanny, unearthly, unnatural

welcome *adj.* **1.** acceptable, agreeable, delightful, desirable, gratifying, pleasant, pleasing, pleasurable, refreshing, wanted **2.** free, invited *~n.* **3.** acceptance, greeting, hospitality, reception, salutation *~v.* **4.** embrace, greet, hail, meet, receive

welfare advantage, benefit, good, happiness, health, interest, profit, prosperity, success, wellbeing

well[1] *adv.* **1.** agreeably, capitally, happily, nicely, pleasantly, satisfactorily, smoothly, splendidly, successfully **2.** ably, adeptly, adequately, admirably, correctly, effectively, efficiently, expertly, proficiently, properly, skilfully **3.** accurately, attentively, carefully, closely **4.** comfortably, flourishingly, prosperously **5.** correctly, easily, fairly, fittingly, justly, properly, readily, rightly, suitably **6.** closely, completely, deeply, fully, intimately, personally, profoundly, thoroughly **7.** approvingly, favourably, glowingly, graciously, highly, kindly, warmly **8.** abundantly, amply, completely, considerably, fully, greatly, heartily, highly, substantially, sufficiently, thoroughly, very much *~adj.* **9.** able-bodied, fit, hale, healthy, hearty, robust, sound, strong

well[2] *n.* **1.** pool, source, spring **2.** bore, hole, pit, shaft *~v.* **3.** flow, gush, jet, ooze, pour, rise, run, seep, spout, spring, spurt, stream, surge, trickle

well-balanced graceful, harmonious, proportional

well-known celebrated, famous, illustrious, notable, noted, popular, renowned

well-off comfortable, flourishing, fortunate, lucky, successful, thriving

wet *adj.* **1.** damp, dank, dripping, humid, moist, saturated, soaking, sodden, soggy, sopping, waterlogged **2.** clammy, dank, drizzling, humid, misty, pouring, raining, rainy, showery, teeming *~n.* **3.** dampness, humidity, liquid, moisture *~v.* **4.** damp, dip, douse, drench, irrigate, moisten, saturate, soak, splash, spray, sprinkle, steep

wharf dock, jetty, pier, quay

wheedle cajole, charm, coax, court, draw, entice, flatter, persuade

wheel 1. *n.* circle, pivot, revolution, roll, rotation, spin, turn, twirl, whirl **2.** *v.* circle, orbit, revolve, roll, rotate, spin, swing, swivel, turn, twirl, whirl

wheeze *v.* **1.** cough, gasp, hiss, rasp, whistle *~n.* **2.** cough, gasp, hiss, rasp, whistle **3.** *Brit. sl.* idea, plan, ploy, ruse, scheme, stunt, trick

whereabouts location, position, site, situation

whet edge, file, grind, hone, sharpen, strop

whiff 1. *n.* aroma, blast, breath, draught, gust, hint, odour, puff, scent, smell, sniff **2.** *v.* breathe, inhale, puff, smell, smoke, sniff, waft

whim caprice, conceit, craze, fancy, humour, impulse, notion, quirk, urge, vagary

whimper 1. *v.* cry, moan, snivel, sob, weep **2.** *n.* moan, snivel, sob, whine

whine *n.* **1.** cry, moan, sob, wail **2.** complaint, grouse, grumble, moan *~v.* **3.** carp, complain, cry, grouse, grumble, moan, sob, wail

whip *v.* **1.** beat, cane, castigate, flog, lash, punish, scourge, spank, strap, switch, thrash **2.** exhibit, flash, jerk, produce, pull, remove, seize, show, snatch, whisk **3.** beat, whisk *~n.* **4.** birch, cane, crop, horsewhip, lash, rawhide, scourge, switch, thong

whirl *v.* **1.** circle, pirouette, pivot, reel, revolve, roll, rotate, spin, swirl, turn, twirl, twist, wheel **2.** reel, spin *~n.* **3.** circle, pirouette, reel, revolution, roll, rotation, spin, swirl, turn, twist, wheel **4.** confusion, daze, dither, flurry, giddiness, spin

whirlwind 1. *n.* tornado, waterspout **2.** *adj.* hasty, headlong, lightning, quick, rapid, rash, short, speedy, swift

whisper *v.* **1.** breathe, murmur **2.** gossip, hint, insinuate, intimate, murmur **3.** hiss, murmur, rustle, sigh *~n.* **4.** low voice, murmur, undertone **5.** hiss, murmur, rustle, sigh, sighing **6.** breath, fraction, hint, shadow, suggestion, suspicion, tinge, trace, whiff **7.** gossip, innuendo, insinuation, report, rumour

white 1. ashen, bloodless, grey, pale, pasty, wan **2.** grey, grizzled, hoary, silver, snowy **3.** clean, immaculate, innocent, pure, spotless, stainless, unsullied

whiten blanch, bleach, blench, fade, pale

whitewash 1. *n.* concealment, cover-up, deception, extenuation **2.** *v.* conceal, extenuate, suppress

whole *adj.* **1.** complete, entire, full, integral, total, uncut **2.** faultless, flawless, good, intact, mint, perfect, sound, unbroken, unimpaired, uninjured, unscathed, untouched **3.** able-bodied, better, cured, fit, hale, healed, healthy, recovered, robust, sound, strong, well *~n.* **4.** aggregate, all, everything, lot, sum total, total **5.** ensemble, entirety, entity, fullness, piece, totality, unit, unity

wholehearted committed, dedicated, determined, devoted, earnest, enthusiastic, genuine, real, sincere, true, unreserved, unstinting, warm, zealous

wholesale 1. *adj.* broad, extensive, far-reaching, indiscriminate, mass, sweeping **2.** *adv.* comprehensively, extensively

wicked 1. abandoned, amoral, atrocious, bad, corrupt, debased, dissolute, evil, fiendish, flagitious, foul, guilty, heinous, immoral, iniquitous, irreligious, nefarious, scandalous, shameful, sinful, unrighteous, vicious, vile, villainous, worthless **2.** arch, impish, mischievous, naughty, rascally, roguish **3.** bothersome, difficult, distressing, galling, offensive, troublesome, trying, unpleasant

wide *adj.* **1.** ample, broad, comprehensive, encyclopedic, expanded, expansive, general, immense, inclusive, large, sweeping, vast **2.** away, distant, off, remote **3.** dilated, distended, expanded, outspread, outstretched **4.** ample, baggy, commodious, full, loose, roomy, spacious *~adv.* **5.** completely, fully **6.** astray, nowhere near, off course, out

widen broaden, dilate, enlarge, expand, extend, spread, stretch

widespread broad, common, extensive, general, popular, prevalent, rife, sweeping, universal, wholesale

width breadth, compass, diameter, extent, girth, range, reach, scope, span

wield 1. brandish, employ, flourish, handle, manage, manipulate, ply, swing, use 2. apply, command, control, exercise, exert, have, hold, maintain, manage, possess, utilize

wife bride, helpmate, mate, partner, spouse

wild *adj.* 1. ferocious, fierce, savage, untamed 2. free, native, natural 3. desert, desolate, empty, trackless, uncivilized, uncultivated, unpopulated 4. barbaric, brutish, ferocious, fierce, primitive, rude, savage, uncivilized 5. boisterous, chaotic, disorderly, lawless, noisy, riotous, rough, turbulent, undisciplined, unrestrained, unruly, uproarious, violent, wayward 6. berserk, crazy, delirious, demented, excited, frantic, frenzied, hysterical, irrational, mad, maniacal, rabid, raving

wilderness desert, jungle, waste

wile artfulness, artifice, cheating, craft, craftiness, cunning, fraud, guile, slyness, trickery

wilful 1. determined, dogged, headstrong, inflexible, obstinate, persistent, perverse, self-willed, stubborn, unyielding 2. conscious, deliberate, intentional, purposeful, voluntary, willed

will *n.* 1. choice, decision, discretion, option 2. declaration, testament 3. choice, decision, decree, desire, fancy, mind, pleasure, wish 4. aim, determination, intention, purpose, resolution, resolve 5. attitude, disposition, feeling ~*v.* 6. bid, cause, command, decree, determine, direct, effect, ordain, order, resolve 7. choose, desire, elect, opt, prefer, see fit, want, wish 8. bequeath, confer, give, leave, pass on, transfer

willing agreeable, amenable, consenting, content, desirous, disposed, eager, enthusiastic, favourable, game, happy, inclined, pleased, prepared, ready

willingly cheerfully, eagerly, freely, gladly, happily, readily, voluntarily

willingness agreement, consent, desire, enthusiasm, favour, good will, inclination, volition, will, wish

willpower determination, drive, grit, resolution, resolve, self-control

win *v.* 1. be victorious, come first, conquer, overcome, prevail, succeed, triumph 2. accomplish, achieve, acquire, attain, catch, collect, earn, gain, get, net, obtain, procure, receive, secure ~*n.* 3. *Inf.* conquest, success, triumph, victory

wind[1] *n.* 1. air, blast, breath, breeze, draught, gust, zephyr 2. bluster, empty talk, humbug, talk 3. breath, puff, respiration 4. **in the wind** approaching, coming, imminent, impending, near

wind[2] *v.* 1. coil, curl, furl, loop, reel, roll, spiral, twine, twist, wreathe 2. bend, curve, deviate, meander, ramble, turn, twist, zigzag ~*n.* 3. bend, curve, meander, turn, twist, zigzag

windfall bonanza, find, godsend

winding 1. *n.* bend, convolution, curve, meander, turn, twist, undulation 2. *adj.* anfractuous, bending, circuitous, convoluted, crooked, curving, flexuous, indirect, meandering, roundabout, serpentine, sinuous, spiral, tortuous, turning, twisting

wind up close, conclude, end, finalize, finish, liquidate, settle, terminate

windy blustery, breezy, gusty, squally, stormy, wild, windswept

wing *n.* 1. pennon 2. arm, branch, circle, clique, coterie, faction, group, section, set, side 3. annexe, extension ~*v.* 4. fly, glide, soar 5. fleet, fly, hasten, hurry, race, speed, zoom 6. clip, hit, nick, wound

wink *v.* 1. bat, blink, flutter 2. flash, gleam, sparkle, twinkle ~*n.* 3. blink, flutter 4. flash, gleam, glimmering, sparkle, twinkle 5. instant, moment, second, split second

winner champion, conqueror, first, master, victor

winning alluring, amiable, bewitching, captivating, charming, delightful, disarming, endearing, engaging, fetching, lovely, pleasing, sweet, taking

winnow comb, divide, fan, part, screen, select, separate, sift

wintry 1. chilly, cold, harsh, icy, snowy 2. bleak, cheerless, cold, desolate, dismal

wipe *v.* 1. brush, clean, dry, dust, mop, rub, sponge, swab 2. erase, remove ~*n.* 3. brush, lick, rub, swab

wipe out annihilate, destroy, eradicate, erase, massacre, obliterate

wisdom astuteness, discernment, enlightenment, erudition, foresight, insight, intelligence, judgment, knowledge, learning, prudence, reason, sagacity, sapience, sense

wise aware, clever, discerning, enlightened, erudite, informed, intelligent, judicious, knowing, perceptive, politic, prudent, rational, reasonable, sage, sapient, sensible, shrewd, sound, well-advised, well-informed

wisecrack barb, jest, jibe, joke, quip, smart remark, witticism

wish *v.* 1. aspire, covet, crave, desiderate, desire, hanker, hope, hunger, long, need, thirst, want, yearn 2. bid 3. ask, bid, command, desire, direct, instruct, order, require ~*n.* 4. aspiration, desire, hankering, hope, hunger, liking, longing, thirst, urge, want, whim, will, yearning

wistful contemplative, dreaming, forlorn, longing, meditative, melancholy, mournful, musing, pensive, reflective, sad, yearning

wit 1. badinage, banter, fun, humour, levity, pleasantry, raillery, repartee 2. comedian, humorist, joker, wag 3. acumen, brains, cleverness, comprehension, discernment, ingenuity, insight, intellect, judgment, mind, perception, reason, sense, understanding, wisdom

witch enchantress, magician, occultist, sorceress

witchcraft enchantment, incantation, magic, sorcery, spell, wizardry

withdraw 1. extract, remove 2. disavow, disclaim, recall, recant, rescind, retract, revoke, take back, unsay 3. oneself, back out, depart, disengage, drop out, go, leave, pull back, pull out, retire, retreat, secede

withdrawal 1. extraction, removal 2. disavowal, disclaimer, recall, repudiation, retraction, revocation 3. departure, exit, exodus, retirement, retreat, secession

withdrawn aloof, detached, distant, introverted, quiet, reserved, retiring, shy, silent, taciturn

wither 1. blast, blight, decay, decline, disintegrate, droop, dry, fade, languish, perish, shrink, wane, waste, wilt 2. abash, blast, mortify, shame, snub

withering 1. blasting, devastating, hurtful, scornful, snubbing 2. deadly, destructive, killing

withhold check, conceal, deduct, hide, hold back, keep, keep back, refuse, repress, reserve, resist, restrain, retain, suppress

witness *n.* 1. beholder, observer, onlooker, spectator, viewer, watcher 2. deponent, testifier 3. **bear witness a.** depose, testify **b.** betoken, confirm, corroborate, demostrate, evince, prove, show, vouch for ~*v.* 4. attend, be present at, mark, note, notice, observe, perceive, see, view, watch 5. attest, bear out, confirm

wits acumen, astuteness, faculties, ingenuity, intelligence, judgment, reason, sense, understanding

witty amusing, brilliant, clever, droll, epigrammatic, facetious, fanciful, funny, gay, humorous, ingenious, jocular, lively, original, piquant, sparkling, waggish, whimsical

wizard 1. conjurer, enchanter, magician, necromancer, sorcerer, witch 2. adept, expert, genius, maestro, master, prodigy, star, virtuoso

wizened dried up, gnarled, lined, shrivelled, shrunken, withered, wrinkled

woe adversity, affliction, agony, anguish, burden, curse, depression, disaster, distress, gloom, grief, hardship, melancholy, misery, pain, sadness, sorrow, suffering, trial, tribulation, trouble, wretchedness

woman 1. female, girl, lady, lass, lassie, maid, maiden, miss, she 2. chambermaid, domestic, handmaiden, housekeeper

wonder *n.* 1. admiration, astonishment, awe, bewilderment, curiosity, fascination, surprise 2. curiosity, marvel, miracle, portent, prodigy, rarity, sight, spectacle ~*v.* 3. ask oneself, conjecture, inquire, meditate, ponder, puzzle, query, question, speculate, think 4. boggle, gape, gawk, marvel, stare

wonderful 1. amazing, astounding, extraordinary, marvellous, miraculous, odd, peculiar, remarkable, staggering, startling, strange, surprising 2. admirable, brilliant, excellent, magnificent, outstanding, sensational, stupendous, superb, terrific, tremendous

woo chase, court, pursue

wooden 1. timber 2. awkward, clumsy, gauche, gawky, graceless, inelegant, rigid, stiff 3. blank, colourless, deadpan, dull, emotionless, lifeless, vacant 4. dense, dim, dull, obtuse, slow, stupid, thick, witless 5. dull, muffled

wool fleece, hair, yarn

woolly *adj.* 1. fleecy, woollen 2. blurred, clouded, confused, foggy, fuzzy, hazy, ill-defined, indefinite, indistinct, muddled, nebulous, unclear, vague

word *n.* 1. chat, colloquy, consultation, discussion 2. comment, declaration, expression, remark, utterance 3. expression, name, term 4. account, advice, bulletin, dispatch, information, intelligence, message, news, notice, report, tidings 5. command, order, signal 6. affirmation, assertion, assurance, guarantee, oath, parole, pledge, promise, solemn oath, undertaking, vow 7. bidding, command, commandment, decree, edict, mandate, order 8. countersign, slogan ~*v.* 9. couch, express, phrase, put, say, state, utter

words 1. lyrics, text 2. argument, bickering, disagreement, dispute, quarrel, row, squabble

wordy diffuse, discursive, garrulous, long-winded, loquacious, prolix, rambling, verbose, windy

work *n.* 1. drudgery, effort, exertion, industry, labour, slog, sweat, toil 2. business, calling, craft, duty, employment, job, line, occupation, office, profession, pursuit, trade 3. assignment, chore, commission, duty, job, stint, task, undertaking 4. achievement, composition, creation, handiwork, opus, performance, piece, production 5. art, craft, skill, workmanship 6. **out of work** idle, jobless, unemployed ~*v.* 7. drudge, labour, slave, sweat, toil 8. be employed, have a job 9. act, control, direct, drive, handle, manage, manipulate, move, operate, ply, use, wield 10. function, go, operate, perform, run 11. cultivate, dig, farm, till 12. *Often with* **up** arouse, excite, move, prompt, provoke, rouse, stir

worker artisan, craftsman, employee, hand, labourer, tradesman

working *n.* 1. action, manner, method, operation, running 2. *Plural* diggings, excavations, mine, pit, quarry, shaft ~*adj.* 3. active, employed, labouring 4. functioning, going, operative, running 5. effective, practical, useful, viable

workman artisan, craftsman, employee, hand, labourer, mechanic, tradesman

work out 1. accomplish, achieve, attain, win 2. calculate, clear up, figure out, find out, resolve, solve 3. arrange, construct, contrive, develop, devise, elaborate, evolve, form, plan 4. flourish, prosper, succeed 5. amount to, come to, reach

works 1. factory, mill, plant, shop 2. canon, output, productions, writings 3. actions, acts, deeds, doings 4. action, machinery, mechanism, movement, parts

workshop atelier, factory, mill, plant, shop, studio

work up agitate, animate, arouse, excite, generate, incite, inflame, move, rouse, spur

world 1. earth, globe 2. everybody, everyone, humanity, man, mankind, men 3. cosmos, creation, existence, life, nature, universe 4. planet, star 5. area, domain, environment, field, kingdom, province, realm, sphere, system 6. age, days, epoch, era, period, times 7. **on top of the world** ecstatic, elated, exultant, happy 8. **out of this world** *Inf.* incredible, indescribable, marvellous, superb, unbelievable, wonderful

worldly 1. carnal, earthly, fleshly, lay, mundane, physical, profane, secular, temporal, terrestrial 2. avaricious, covetous, grasping, greedy, materialistic, selfish 3. blasé, experienced, knowing, politic, sophisticated, urbane

worldwide general, global, international, ubiquitous, universal

worn 1. frayed, ragged, shabby, shiny, tattered, tatty, threadbare 2. careworn, drawn, haggard, lined, pinched 3. exhausted, fatigued, jaded, spent, tired, wearied, weary

worried afraid, anxious, bothered, concerned, distraught, distressed, fearful, frightened, nervous, overwrought, perturbed, tense, tormented, troubled, uneasy, upset

worry 1. *v.* agonize, annoy, bother, brood, disquiet, distress, disturb, fret, harass, harry, importune, irritate, perturb, pester, plague, tantalize, tease, torment, trouble, unsettle, upset, vex 2. *n.* annoyance, care, irritation, pest, plague, problem, torment, trial, trouble, vexation

worsen aggravate, decline, degenerate, deteriorate, exacerbate, get worse, go downhill (*Inf.*), go from bad to worse, sink

worship 1. *v.* adore, adulate, deify, exalt, glorify, honour, laud, love, praise, respect, revere, venerate 2. *n.* adoration, devotion, exaltation, glorification, glory, homage, honour, love, praise, regard, respect, reverence

worst *v.* beat, best, conquer, crush, defeat, master, overcome, overpower, overthrow, subdue, subjugate, vanquish

worth 1. aid, assistance, avail, benefit, credit, estimation, excellence, goodness, help, importance, merit, quality, usefulness, value, virtue 2. cost, price, rate, value

worthless 1. futile, ineffectual, insignificant, meaningless, paltry, pointless, poor, rubbishy, trashy, trifling, trivial, unavailing, unimportant, unusable, useless 2. abandoned, base, depraved, despicable, ignoble, useless, vile

worthwhile beneficial, constructive, gainful, good, helpful, productive, profitable, useful, valuable

worthy 1. *adj.* admirable, commendable, creditable, decent, deserving, estimable, excellent, good, honest, laudable, meritorious, reliable, reputable, respectable, righteous, upright, valuable 2. *n.* dignitary, luminary, notable

wound *n.* 1. cut, gash, harm, hurt, injury, lesion, slash 2. anguish, distress, grief, heartbreak, injury, insult, offence, pain, pang, shock, slight, torment, torture ~*v.* 3. cut, damage, gash, harm, hit, hurt, injure, irritate, lacerate, pierce, slash, wing 4. annoy, distress, grieve, hurt, offend, pain, shock, sting

wrangle 1. *v.* argue, bicker, brawl, contend, disagree, dispute, quarrel, row, scrap 2. *n.* brawl, clash, contest, dispute, quarrel, row, squabble, tiff

wrap *v.* absorb, bind, cloak, cover, encase, enclose, enfold, envelop, fold, muffle, pack, package, sheathe, shroud, surround, swathe, wind

wrapper case, cover, envelope, jacket, paper, sheath, sleeve

wrath anger, displeasure, fury, indignation, ire, passion, rage, temper

wreath band, chaplet, coronet, crown, festoon, garland, loop, ring

wreathe adorn, coil, crown, enfold, entwine, festoon, intertwine, surround, twine, twist, wind, wrap

wreck *v.* 1. break, demolish, destroy, devastate, mar, ravage, ruin, shatter, smash, spoil 2. founder, shipwreck, strand ~*n.* 3. derelict, hulk

wreckage debris, fragments, hulk, pieces, remains, rubble, ruin, wrack

wrench *v.* 1. force, jerk, pull, rip, tear, tug, twist, wrest, wring, yank 2. distort, rick, sprain, strain ~*n.* 3. jerk, pull, rip, tug, twist, yank 4. sprain, strain, twist 5. ache, blow, pain, pang, shock, upheaval

wrestle battle, combat, contend, fight, grapple, strive, struggle

wretch 1. outcast, profligate, rascal, rogue, ruffian, scoundrel, vagabond, villain 2. poor thing, unfortunate

wretched 1. abject, cheerless, comfortless, dejected, deplorable, depressed, distressed, downcast, forlorn, gloomy, hapless, hopeless, miserable, pitiful, poor, sorry, unhappy, woebegone, woeful 2. calamitous, deplorable, inferior, miserable, paltry, pathetic, poor, sorry

wriggle *v.* 1. squirm, turn, twist, wag, writhe 2. crawl, slink, snake, worm, zigzag 3. crawl, dodge, sneak, worm ~*n.* 4. jerk, squirm, turn, twist, wag

wring 1. coerce, extort, extract, force, screw, squeeze, twist, wrench, wrest 2. distress, hurt, lacerate, pain, pierce, rack, rend, stab, tear at, wound

wrinkle 1. *n.* crease, crow's-foot, crumple, fold, furrow, gather, line, pucker, rumple 2. *v.* crease, crumple, fold, furrow, gather, line, ruck

writ decree, document, summons

write compose, copy, create, draft, inscribe, pen, record, scribble, tell, transcribe

write off 1. cancel, disregard 2. *Inf.* crash, destroy, smash up, wreck

writer author, columnist, essayist, hack, novelist, penman, scribbler, scribe

writhe contort, distort, jerk, squirm, struggle, thrash, thresh, toss, twist, wiggle, wriggle

writing 1. calligraphy, hand, handwriting, print, scrawl, scribble, script 2. book, composition, document, letter, opus, publication, work

wrong *adj.* 1. erroneous, fallacious, false, faulty, inaccurate, incorrect, mistaken, out, unsound, untrue 2. bad, criminal, crooked, dishonest, evil, illegal, illicit, immoral, sinful, unfair, unjust, unlawful, wicked, wrongful 3. funny, improper, inapt, incorrect, not done, unacceptable, undesirable, unfitting, unhappy, unseemly, unsuitable 4. amiss, askew, awry, defective, faulty 5. inside, inverse, opposite, reverse ~*adv.* 6. amiss, askew, astray, awry, badly, erroneously, inaccurately, incorrectly, mistakenly, wrongly 7. **go wrong** a. fail, miscarry, misfire b. err, go astray c. break down, fail, misfire d. err, lapse, sin ~*n.* 8. abuse, crime, error, grievance, infraction, infringement, injury, injustice, misdeed, offence, sin, sinfulness, transgression, trespass, wickedness ~*v.* 9. abuse, cheat, discredit, harm, hurt, ill-use, injure, malign, maltreat, mistreat, oppress

wrongdoer criminal, culprit, evildoer, lawbreaker, miscreant, offender, sinner, transgressor

wrongful blameworthy, criminal, dishonest, dishonourable, evil, felonious, illegal, illegitimate, illicit, immoral, improper, reprehensible, unethical, unfair, unjust, unlawful, wicked

wry 1. askew, aslant, crooked, deformed, distorted, twisted, uneven, warped 2. droll, dry, ironic, mocking, sardonic

Y

yank *v./n.* hitch, jerk, pull, snatch, tug, wrench

yardstick criterion, gauge, measure, standard

yarn *n.* 1. fibre, thread 2. *Inf.* anecdote, cock-and-bull story (*Inf.*), fable, story, tale, tall story

yawning cavernous, chasmal, gaping, vast, wide, wide-open

yearly annual, annually, every year, once a year, per annum

yearn ache, covet, crave, desire, hanker, have a yen for (*Inf.*), hunger, itch, languish, long, lust, pant, pine

yell 1. *v.* bawl, holler (*Inf.*), howl, scream, shout, shriek, squeal 2. *n.* cry, howl, scream, screech, shriek

yes man bootlicker (*Inf.*), bosses' lackey, company man, crawler (*Sl.*), creature, minion, sycophant, timeserver, toady

yet 1. so far, thus far 2. however, still 3. as well, besides, further, moreover, still, to boot 4. already, now, right now, so soon

yield *v.* 1. afford, bear, earn, furnish, generate, give, net, pay, produce, provide, return, supply ~*n.* 2. crop, earnings, harvest, output, produce, profit, return, takings ~*v.* 3. bow, capitulate, cede, give way, part with, relinquish, resign, submit, succumb, surrender 4. accede, agree, allow, bow, comply, concede, consent, grant, permit

yielding 1. accommodating, acquiescent, biddable, compliant, docile, easy, flexible, obedient, pliant, submissive, tractable 2. elastic, pliable, quaggy, resilient, soft, spongy, springy, supple, unresisting

yoke *n.* 1. bond, chain, coupling, link, tie 2. bondage, burden, enslavement, oppression, service, servitude, slavery, thraldom ~*v.* 3. bracket, connect, couple, harness, hitch, join, link, tie, unite

yokel boor, countryman, peasant, rustic

young *adj.* 1. adolescent, green, growing, immature, infant, junior, little, youthful 2. early, new, newish, recent

youngster boy, cub, girl, juvenile, lad, lass, teenager, urchin

youth 1. boyhood, girlhood, immaturity 2. adolescent, boy, kid (*Inf.*), lad, stripling, teenager, youngster

youthful 1. boyish, childish, immature, juvenile, puerile, young 2. active, fresh, spry, vigorous

Z

zeal ardour, devotion, enthusiasm, fervency, fervour, fire, gusto, keenness, militancy, passion, spirit, verve, warmth, zest

zealot bigot, enthusiast, extremist, fanatic, maniac, militant

zealous afire, ardent, burning, devoted, eager, earnest, enthusiastic, fanatical, fervent, fervid, impassioned, keen, militant, passionate, rabid, spirited

zenith apex, climax, height, high point, meridian, peak, pinnacle, summit, top, vertex

zero naught, nil, nothing, nought

zest 1. appetite, delectation, enjoyment, gusto, keenness, relish, zeal, zing (*Inf.*) 2. charm, flavour, interest, kick (*Inf.*), piquancy, pungency, relish, savour, smack, spice, tang, taste

zip 1. *n. Fig.* brio, drive, energy, get-up-and-go (*Inf.*), go (*Inf.*), gusto, life, liveliness, oomph (*Inf.*), pep, pizazz (*Sl.*), punch (*Inf.*), sparkle, spirit, verve, vigour, vim (*Sl.*), vitality, zest, zing (*Inf.*) 2. *v.* dash, flash, fly, hurry, rush, shoot, speed, tear, whiz (*Inf.*), zoom

zone area, belt, district, region, section, sector, sphere